SO-EKW-899

Handbook of
Borderline Disorders

Handbook of Borderline Disorders

edited by

Daniel Silver, M.D.
Michael Rosenbluth, M.D.

International Universities Press, Inc.
Madison   Connecticut

Library of Congress Cataloging-in-Publication Data

Handbook of borderline disorders / edited by Daniel Silver, Michael Rosenbluth.
    p.   cm.
  Includes bibliographical references and index.
  ISBN 0-8236-2290-8
  1. Borderline personality disorder. I. Silver, Daniel.
II. Rosenbluth, Michael.
  [DNLM: 1. Borderline Personality Disorder—therapy. WM 190 H236]
RC569.5.B67H36 1992
616.85'852—dc20
DNLM/DLC
for Library of Congress   91-20814
                                                  CIP

Manufactured in the United States of America

For Ruth, Abby, Mark and Carolyn

For Ronni, Sarah and Daniel, and my parents Sam and Annette

Contents

Contributors

Gerald Adler, M.D.
Training and Supervising Analyst, Boston Psychoanalytic Society and Institute; Director of Medical Education in Psychiatry, Massachusetts General Hospital; Lecturer on Psychiatry, Harvard Medical School.

Hagop S. Akiskal, M.D.
Professor of Psychiatry, University of Tennessee, Memphis, TN; Director of Section of Affective Disorders Program, University of Tennessee, Memphis.

Victoria Alexander, B.A.
Editorial Director, Massachusetts Mental Health Center, Boston, MA; Editor of the Program in Psychiatry and the Law, Boston, MA.

George Atwood, Ph.D.
Professor of Psychology, Rutgers University; Core Faculty, Institute for Psychoanalytic Study of Subjectivity, New York.

Bernard Brandchaft, M.D.
Training and Supervising Analyst, Los Angeles Psychoanalytic Institute; Assistant Clinical Professor of Psychiatry, UCLA School of Medicine.

Rex Collins, Ph.D.
Clinical Psychologist, Private Practice in Toronto, Canada.

Rex W. Cowdry, M.D.
Chief Executive Officer, National Institute of Mental Health; Neuropsychiatric Research Hospital, Washington, DC; Associate Clinical Professor, Georgetown Medical School, Washington, DC.

Douglas Frayn, M.D.
Director, Toronto Institute of Psychoanalysis; Associate Professor of Psychiatry, University of Toronto.

Ruth Gallop, Ph.D.
Assistant Professor, Faculty of Nursing and Department of Psychiatry, University of Toronto; Ontario Career Scientist.

Paul E. Garfinkel, M.D.
Director and Psychiatrist-in-Chief, Clarke Institute of Psychiatry; Professor and Chairman, Department of Psychiatry, University of Toronto.

Edward J. Glassman, Ph.D.
Clinical Psychologist, North York General Hospital, Toronto, Ontario.

John G. Gunderson, M.D.
Director of Psychotherapy and Psychosocial Research, McLean Hospital, Belmont, MA.

Thomas G. Gutheil, M.D.
Associate Professor of Psychiatry, Harvard Medical School, Boston, MA; Co-Director of the Program in Psychiatry and the Law, Boston, MA.

Paul C. Horton, M.D.
Private Practitioner, Meriden, CT; Consultant to Child Guidance Clinic for Central Connecticut.

Marshall Korenblum, M.D.
Consultant, Division of Adolescent Psychiatry, Sunnybrook Medical Centre, Toronto, Canada.

Stanley P. Kutcher, M.D.
Co-Head, Division of Adolescent Psychiatry, Sunnybrook Medical Centre, Toronto, Canada; Associate Professor of Psychiatry, University of Toronto.

Molyn Leszcz, M.D.
Assistant Professor of Psychiatry, University of Toronto; Head, Group Therapy Service, Mount Sinai Hospital and Baycrest Centre for Geriatric Care, Toronto, Canada.

Joshua Levy, Ph.D.
Private Practice; Training Analyst, Toronto Institute of Psycho-
analysis; Associate Professor of Psychiatry, University of
Toronto.

Marsha M. Linehan, Ph.D.
University of Washington, Seattle, WA.

Christopher G. Lovett, Ph.D.
Candidate, Boston Psychoanalytic Institute; Department of Psychiatry, Harvard Medical School, Cambridge Hospital.

John T. Maltsberger, M.D.
Faculty, Boston Psychoanalytic Institute; Department of Psychiatry, Harvard Medical School, McLean Hospital.

Thomas H. McGlashan, M.D.
Director, Yale Psychiatric Institute; Professor of Psychiatry,
Yale University School of Medicine.

Robert Michels, M.D.
Barklie McKee Henry Professor and Chairman, Department of
Psychiatry, Cornell University Medical College; Psychiatrist-
in-Chief, The New York Hospital.

Klaus Minde, M.D.
Director, Department of Psychiatry, The Montreal Children's
Hospital, Montreal, Canada; Professor of Child Psychiatry
and Pediatrics, McGill University, Montreal.

Edgar P. Nace, M.D.
Chief of Service for Substance Abuse Programs, Director of
Health Professionals Program, Timberlawn Psychiatric
Hospital, Dallas, TX; Associate Professor of Clinical Psychi-
atry, The University of Texas, Southwestern Medical
School, Dallas, TX.

Michael Rosenbluth, M.D.
Psychiatrist-in-Chief, Toronto East General Hospital, Toronto,
Canada; Assistant Professor of Psychiatry, University of To-
ronto.

Joel Sadavoy, M.D.
Associate Professor, University of Toronto; Head, Department
of Psychiatry, Baycrest Centre for Geriatric Care, Toronto,
Canada.

Edward R. Shapiro, M.D.
Associate Clinical Professor of Psychiatry, Harvard Medical
School; Medical Director, The Austen Riggs Center, Stock-
bridge, MA.

Daniel Silver, M.D.
Associate Professor of Psychiatry, University of Toronto; Head,
Ambulatory Services, Department of Psychiatry, Mount Si-
nai Hospital, Toronto, Canada.

Robert Stolorow, Ph.D.
Training and Supervising Analyst, Institute of Contemporary
Psychoanalysis, Los Angeles; Core Faculty, Institute for Psy-
choanalytic Study of Subjectivity, New York.

Michael H. Stone, M.D.
Professor of Clinical Psychiatry, Columbia College of Physicians
and Surgeons.

Alex Tarnopolsky, M.D.
Consultant Psychotherapist, The Maudsley Hospital, London,
England; Psychoanalyst, Private Practice.

Introduction

Psychiatry has long concerned itself with the difficult to treat patient. Who this patient is has changed as our knowledge has increased, and as limitations in the capacity to treat certain groups have been accepted. Clinically, the borderline patient has emerged as one of the most difficult patients to treat.

Conceptually, the borderline is of interest because some of the central controversies in psychiatry are reflected in this patient population. Not only are broader conflicts between biological and psychodynamic approaches demonstrated but also between drive, object relations, and self psychology theories of personality development. Thus, the study of the borderline patient is an opportunity to study the critical questions of contemporary psychiatry.

In this book we hope to outline some of the controversies surrounding the care of the borderline patient. Scholarship in this area has a long and proud history. Beginning with Stern, continuing with Deutsch, Schmideberg, Knight, Grinker, Masterson, Giovacchini, Modell, Rosenfeld, and Searles (amongst others), and as reflected in the ongoing contributions of Kernberg, a strong clinical foundation for the contemporary study of the borderline patient has been laid. This handbook seeks to present the most contemporary views, questions, and methods which add to this foundation. The relatively homogeneous perspective of the first generation of workers with its psychoanalytic emphasis has been enriched by a spirit of research and empiricism, and the creation of new models of treatment going beyond the psychodynamic. Even within the psychodynamic framework, there has been considerable debate about different conceptualizations and their implications in the treatment of the borderline patient.

It is the richness and diversity of the second generation of workers that this book hopes to capture. Part I describes basic issues regarding the diagnosis, natural history, and validity of the borderline concept. Stone distinguishes between traits and symptoms and challenges our view of borderline personality disorder (BPD) as solely an Axis II disorder. He calls for the separation of the symptom and syndromal aspects of what is now termed borderline, from the purely personality aspects, to enhance diagnostic precision and promote a more rational approach to treatment. In particular he calls for the Axis II BPD diagnosis to be moved to Axis I as borderline syndrome to distinguish the symptomatic from the trait aspects. In so doing, Stone not only points out important diagnostic and treatment issues, but sets the tone for this volume where the contributors have sought to preserve the best of our clinical and conceptual heritage while at the same time challenging us to reconsider our most basic assumptions.

Current clinical work and research into BPD has been enriched by the field of follow-up studies. Tarnopolsky reviews the considerable literature on BPD validity, reliability, follow-up studies, relationship to other disorders, family studies, and pharmacotherapy. His careful conclusion is that the concept of borderline personality disorder is a valid one and has achieved the significance of other current psychiatric disorders. McGlashan summarizes and integrates his findings on the long-term course of BPD and views borderline as a heterogeneous disorder with a high rate of comorbidity and a wide outcome variance. He describes the relatively good outcome of borderline patients, linking better outcome with higher intelligence, lower affective lability, less chronicity, an ability to experience pleasure, to tolerate psychological pain, and to contain aggression in relationships.

Although each chapter in this book contains different controversial statements, Part II on concepts and controversies highlights several critical areas in the borderline field. Minde and Frayn emphasize how infant observation heightens our awareness of the importance of relationships in personality formation, and how inappropriate environmental responses can create deficits which result in defensive and negative behaviors. They remain cautious by calling for the identification of more specific factors which distinguish the backgrounds of borderline children, and more specific research regarding what facilitates the child's development of an adequate sense of self. The authors emphasize both the continuities and discontinuities between infant observation and the borderline adult patient.

Michels emphasizes that the borderline patient has provided the profession with an opportunity to examine the role of theory in patient care and observe how treatment failure inspires new theory to develop. Michels suggests that the increasing emphasis on preoedipal issues has caused a shift from focusing on insight, verbal communication, and genetic reconstruction more appropriate for oedipal level psychopathology, to treatments aimed at providing the psychological nutrients that the individual was unable to experience in the original course of development. Michels views the most valuable contribution of the borderline patient as enriching the dialogue regarding the theory of therapy and in so doing enriching the treatment of all patients.

The shift in emphasis from oedipal to preoedipal, and from insight to therapeutic process, is taken further by Brandchaft, Stolorow, and Atwood. In their emphasis on the difficulty therapists have in comprehending the archaic intersubjective contexts in which borderline pathology arises, they state that the concept of borderline personality organization (BPO) may be largely, if not entirely, an iatrogenic myth. The authors see the theoretical emphasis on pathognomonic pathological defenses as theory centered on the therapist's part, and a missed opportunity to use fully what has actually transpired between patient and therapist. They dramatically draw our attention to the opportunity the therapist has to use failures in the therapeutic relationship to reconstruct and correct earlier developmental frustrations.

An equally serious criticism of the concept is presented by Akiskal. He disputes the validity of the borderline diagnosis, suggesting that the term represents a nonspecific cluster of unstable personality disturbances activated by a variety of non-classical psychiatric disorders, mostly in the affective realm. He sees the borderline diagnosis as reflecting, in part, the clinician's countertransference to disorganizing affective storms created by these patients.

Thus both chapters, though devastating in their criticism of the borderline concept, encourage us to examine our most basic assumptions about the borderline patient. In this way they represent the questioning spirit that has been behind the burgeoning interest in this disorder.

A chapter on the British point of view is included in this collection because of the editors' view that British authors have laid the foundation for so much of the basic theoretical principles and controversies that have been important from a psychodynamic point of view. The British school represents a paradigm of the movement away from drive theory to object relations or relationship–structure theory and are the precursors to the Kernberg/Kohut conceptual debates. Tarnopolsky also overviews technical implications of the differing conceptual frameworks he describes.

Part III reflects the wide range of therapeutic issues and treatment modalities which are currently part of our clinical repertoire. Silver and Rosenbluth's contributions on the assessment of the borderline patient and the inpatient treatment of this population reflect primarily their own combined "hands on" experience in treating these patients both as inpatients, outpatients, and in private practice. They address many basic issues, frequently taken for granted or overlooked, which the authors feel should be clinically useful for therapists at all levels of experience. Collins and Glassman overview the psychological assessment of borderline patients. They emphasize how structured interviews, self-report measures, and Rorschach testing contribute to diagnosis, treatment planning, and research in this area.

Gerald Adler's chapter represents his latest views and theoretical understanding of an important concept he introduced a decade ago. He continues to expand his thoughts on the differences and similarities between a therapeutic alliance and a self–object bond. His additional contributions on projective identification, ambiguity, and the therapeutic alliance will clarify many puzzling issues facing the clinician in his day-to-day work with borderline patients.

Paul Horton expands his seminal contribution of conceptualizing solacing agents as important factors in the borderline personality disorders in his chapter on "A Borderline Treatment Dilemma: To Solace or Not To Solace." He examines a pivotal developmental and therapeutic problem in the borderline patient's difficulty in finding solace and examines its role in emotional development. In his discussion of some of the therapeutic hurdles for borderline patients, Horton focuses on their attachment to inappropriate solacers; use of paradoxical solacers; addictive substances as solacing agents; and the reliance on anger for solace. Finally, he addresses the therapist's attitude about solace and the dilemma of whether "to solace or not to solace."

John Gunderson addresses a dimension of psychotherapy with borderline patients rarely described or even alluded to in the literature. In reviewing individual case histories, Gunderson describes the ongoing process of psychotherapy. He provides important milestones during the therapeutic process which offer some guidelines for the clinician's monitoring of the therapeutic process. He also introduces the "bucket brigade" concept which should encourage rather than discourage therapists doing a "piece of work" with these patients who often go from one therapist to another.

Psychotherapeutic stalemates are a common occurrence in treating borderline patients. Joshua Levy, in his chapter, addresses the emotional strain that therapeutic stalemates produce in the therapist and reviews the literature on the subject, which has, for the most part, remained disjointed and piecemeal. Levy uses detailed material from a case study to outline specific dynamics in therapist–patient interactions that could produce stalemates and suggests a particular kind of consultative process to facilitate its resolution. He also discusses the characteristics of the therapeutic stalemate, the dynamics of this problem, and various strategies of resolving stalemates.

Maltsberger and Lovett's chapter on suicide is a continuation and elaboration of many of the issues that the senior author of the chapter has been engaged in for many years. Here Drs. Maltsberger and Lovett introduce a number of new ideas which will help the clinician to identify times of special danger; to distinguish characterologic depression from melancholic depressive symptoms (although both may occur concomitantly—which the authors label "double depression"), and summarize many of their central ideas by reviewing Victor Tausk's clinical history and suicide.

Gutheil and Alexander outline the main areas of medicolegal vulnerability for therapists treating borderline patients. They emphasize the particular dynamics involved, the need for promoting a strong therapeutic alliance, and being mindful of countertransference issues. Their chapter is a useful reminder and elaboration of how critical medicolegal, ethical, and countertransference dimensions can overlap.

Marsha Linehan's chapter, "Behavior Therapy, Dialectics, and the Treatment of Borderline Personality Disorders," is perhaps the most important new addition to what behavioral–cognitive approaches have offered to date. Her treatment strategies emphasize different aspects of treatment than those usually addressed by psychoanalytic and biological approaches. Her chapter describes a biosocial theory of borderline personality disorders and a treatment approach she has developed over the past decade. It suggests a novel and refreshing approach to the dilemmas that occur in working with borderline patients.

Group therapy has become an important modality of treatment for borderline patients. Molyn Leszcz's chapter reflects his wide experience in treating these patients both individually and in group therapy. His clear discussions of the group composition, orientation, concurrent group and individual therapy, and the assessment process for group therapy, should prove very helpful to all therapists, regardless of their treatment orientation. Special emphasis is paid to the group as a holding environment, enabling the acquisition of empathy, and providing opportunities for internalization.

Dr. Shapiro provides a clear exposition of the concept of projective identification, delineating its various components particularly as demonstrated through family dynamics. He addresses and clarifies through family therapy vignettes the concepts of holding environment, empathy failures, and regression, while reviewing and expanding his own concept of pathological certainty as a mode of communication.

Dr. Cowdry's chapter on diagnostic and treatment implications of the psychobiology and psychopharmacology aspects of the borderline personality disorder highlights these important issues. He also points out that the future direction of investigations will be in "understanding the complex interactions between biological predispositions and experience in shaping the borderline's affective life, mechanisms of defense, motivation, and cognitive states."

Part IV on particular populations highlights several subgroups within the borderline spectrum that have received increasing clinical and research attention. While the editors of this volume believe these are not the only subgroups in the heterogeneous borderline diagnosis, this grouping underlines several basic points. Consideration of the borderline patient in adolescence and senescence reminds us of the longitudinal perspective that must be brought to the consideration of all borderline patients. The chapters by Kutcher and Korenblum, and Sadavoy draw particular attention to the clinical and conceptual issues in these age groups. Furthermore, the difference in perspective between the two chapters reflects the vitality and richness of the borderline patient and the borderline field. Kutcher and Korenblum write largely from outside a traditional dynamic perspective, bringing a questioning scientific attitude to bear. Sadavoy, writing largely from within a dynamic perspective, is equally thought-provoking and challenging.

Furthermore, in emphasizing how the elderly borderline patient moves away from impulsive action-oriented defenses with age, Sadavoy underlines the conceptual centrality of impulsivity. This provides an important link with the chapters on the eating disorders and the alcoholic borderline patient. Garfinkel and Gallop address the relationship between eating disorders and personality disorders. In so doing, they stimulate more general questions about our definition and concept of borderline. The authors note that a narrow definition of borderline classifies bulimic anorexics, but not restricting anorexics as having a considerable relationship with BPD. Yet, when a wider definition is used, both are seen as related to BPD. This difference highlights the crucial role of impulsivity in making a borderline personality diagnosis. Their chapter raises the issue of whether it is useful, or for that matter, of any consequence to say that bulimic anorexics are borderline while restricting anorexics have severe character pathology but are not borderline. Or is it more important that the interest in BPD causes us to be more aware of character pathology in general and causes the clinician to pay more attention to Axis II considerations with regard to the assessment and treatment process?

The study of the alcoholic borderline patient is another expression of the relationship conceptually and clinically between impulsivity and borderline personality disorder. Nace's chapter also reminds us of the crucial importance of determining the presence of Axis II comorbidity and the reciprocal influences of Axis I and Axis II disorder for treatment planning.

Finally, the epilogue provides an opportunity to "hear" several of the contributors respond to a wide range of clinical and theoretical questions. This discussion took place at a meeting on borderline personality disorder held October 15th, 1988, in Toronto, Canada.

It is hoped that this book's overview of the considerable intellectual and clinical activity in the field of borderline disorders will engage the reader and encourage a consideration of the multiple perspectives necessary for the care of the borderline patient. An approach that includes constitutional, biological, developmental, and longitudinal perspectives invites the clinician to use a multifaceted model that includes, where necessary, combinations of several different modalities of treatment. Even for those patients requiring an exclusively psychodynamic approach, the current controversies in the field invite the clinician to carefully choose a model that fits both the patient and the clinician. The contemporary study of the borderline with its considerable diversity frees the clinician from a Procrustean bed approach to the care of the borderline patient.

This consideration of the borderline field also invites some reflection on the development of knowledge in psychiatry. Psychiatry is not a science; rather, it uses science to reach a goal—optimal patient care. Clinical observation generates clinical hypotheses, then research attempts to prove or disprove these hypotheses. There are two opposing dangers: one is to become too dogmatic about our clinical hypotheses and fail to recognize the need to confirm them. The corresponding and equal danger is to become too preoccupied with science. While we continue to categorize, define, and research in order to develop our knowledge, we must resist the tendency to lose sight of the borderline patient's actual clinical and human needs. Otherwise, we may find and define borderline personality disorder but lose the person.

In conclusion we hope this book by its breadth and diversity encourages the reader in his or her own work with borderline patients. From a scientific perspective many critical questions remain to be answered. From a clinical perspective the diversity of possible approaches allows the clinician to maximize his or her own diagnostic and therapeutic acumen. The borderline patient demands that we as clinicians continue to develop and extend our technical skills and conceptual frameworks. Perhaps the greatest legacy of working with borderline patients is the increased skill, sensitivity, intuition, and capacity we bring to the care of less disturbed patients as a result of our endeavors with borderlines.

From a human perspective, working with borderline patients demands that we be able to experience, contain, confront, and respond to the most basic affects in an immediate and authentic fashion. The borderline patient's struggle to achieve intimacy, to comfort and be comforted, and to develop a stable and meaningful identity is similar to our own, just experienced and expressed in a more intense and disturbing manner. For this reason, our work with these patients permits us to confront the most basic issues of human experience and emerge richer for so doing.

PART 1

Diagnosis, Classification, and Outcome

1.

The Borderline Patient: Diagnostic Concepts and Differential Diagnosis

Michael H. Stone, M.D.

DIAGNOSTIC CONCEPTS

The diagnosis of the "borderline" in psychiatry constitutes a particularly intriguing topic; this, for at least two reasons: to begin with, alone among the thirteen personality disorders of Axis II in *The Diagnostic and Statistical Manual of Mental Disorders* (DSM-III-R) (American Psychiatric Association, 1987), including the two provisional entries, *borderline* is the one adjective that denotatively tells the clinician nothing as to what the term might signify. The other dozen descriptors are all signature words that typify what the personality type of which they are the label is all about. Adjectives like *dependent, sadistic,* and *narcissistic* make clear at the outset what will be the chief characteristics of the personality disorders for which they are the labels. *Borderline*, in contrast, lacks face meaning.

The second reason why the borderline diagnosis is so intriguing is because borderline personality disorder (BPD) as defined in DSM-III is in the strict sense of the word not a personality disorder; schizotypal personality disorder (STP) also shares this peculiarity. As for *borderline*, this idiosyncratic usage evolved within a certain historical context, which I have sketched briefly below. Meantime, the prevailing custom of classifying borderline and schizotypal with the personality disorders bears reexamination.

Just as borderline needs to be differentiated from its diagnostic near-neighbors (a topic addressed later in this chapter) the term *personality* needs to be defined in such a way as to allow it to overlap at all with other terms that are conceptually contiguous. Etymologically, the word *personality* comes from the Latin *per + sonare*: literally, "to sound through." The origin of the word is interesting. The actors of the Roman (and before them, of the Greek) stage, lacking electronic amplifiers and acoustically designed enclosed theaters, had to project their voices so as to be heard in the furthest seats of an outdoor amphitheater. To accomplish this they wore masks behind whose mouth-openings small megaphones were placed. Their voices would then *sound through* (per + sonare) these devices and achieve the necessary amplification. *Personality* refers then to the habitual features of interaction that give each human being his individual and distinctive stamp. Personality represents the amalgam of one's characteristic traits, as these become manifest in one's transactions with other people. In this connection Theodore Millon (1988) has recently made a most useful distinction in analogizing personality with the body's immune system. Psychologically speaking, personality is our first line of defense. If, for example, one confronts a personnel manager at a job interview or introduces oneself at a social gathering, one will display one's characteristic exuberance or diffidence or wariness or braggadocio or whatever; in a word, personality. The emergence of panic in these settings or of ideas of reference would mean that the first line of defense was breached. Symptoms take over where personality left off. Axis I is in effect the catalog of those symptoms, the collective failure of personality, comparable to the list of infectious diseases that set in when the immune mechanisms have been overwhelmed.

The DSM-III definitions of BPD and of what used to be called borderline schizophrenia (now, schizotypal personality disorder) are based on items only half of which, even after a generous bending of semantic rules, belong to the concept of personality. In lay language we are apt to describe borderline patients as unreasonable, moody, fickle, demanding, clingy, cranky, and hostile. These are all *personality* adjectives. They translate into unstable relationships, inordinate anger, and affective instability. The latter can progress to anxiety, as mentioned in DSM-III: this is already a symptom. Inability to tolerate being alone or frantic efforts to avoid abandonment, suicidal acts, bingeing, and substance abuse (as examples of impulsivity) are likewise symptoms. In a similar way, the nine items of the revised definition of schizotypal contain only three personality traits: aloofness, eccentricity, and suspiciousness, whereas all the descriptors of schizoid—a true personality disorder—are indeed personality traits.

Because of their mixed (symptom/trait) nature, borderline and schizotypal as currently defined do not fit neatly into either Axis I or Axis II.

The patients we consider borderline do, of course, exhibit personality disorders of one sort or another as prominent features of their overall condition. But in the early stages, at least, when borderline patients first seek our help, severe and disabling symptoms usually dominate the clinical picture. These symptoms often coalesce into such Axis I entities as anorexia/bulimia, major affective disorder, or agoraphobia. In the current generation of first-admission borderline patients, substance abuse is a common accompaniment.

The DSM-III/DSM-III-R definitions are actually derived in equal parts from Kernberg's criteria (1967), and from those elaborated by Gunderson and Singer in 1975. Both use the word *personality* in their formulation. Yet Kernberg's definition covers more than personality and relates actually to a level of *mental* organization, situated between a higher and a lower level of mental organization; that is, neurotic and psychotic.

The Kernberg definition is broad, covering a whole band of the population roughly between the first and second standard deviation to the left of center—of the gaussian curve of mental health. This is a heterogeneous realm etiologically and nosologically, taking in, besides those with BPD as defined by DSM-III or Gunderson, also many eating disorder patients, alcoholics, sociopaths, and others.

Each diagnostic approach has a number of advantages and disadvantages. The DSM-III definition, though it has a foot in both boats with respect to Axes I and II, is simpler to use than the more inferential approach of Kernberg and admits of more easily achieved interrater reliability. We then, however, confront an objection along a quite different line of discourse; namely, that the DSM description is excessively polythetic. There are ninety-three ways of being borderline in DSM-III or DSM-III-R. This contributes to a certain disjointedness in what is written and spoken about borderline patients. One effect of this is the following: in the minds of clinicians more familiar with the psychoanalytic literature, their impressions tend to crystallize around the guidelines suggested by Kernberg. They seek evidence of identity disturbance before they would feel comfortable applying the borderline label. But DSM-III allows twenty-nine ways of circumventing what for Kernberg is this essential ingredient—and still coming up with a valid diagnosis of "BPD." This creates problems for the psychoanalytic community and hinders communication across schools of thought. Stephen Hurt (Hurt, Clarkin, Widiger, Eyer, Sullivan, Stone, and Frances, 1988) has recently analyzed the array of positive DSM-III items found in nearly five hundred patients accorded this personality diagnosis, including the 206 BPD borderlines of my follow-up study (Stone, 1990), and twenty-six outpatients in Dr. Allen Frances' study. Hurt felt he could tease out three major clusters within the DSM-III description: one related to affective features, another to impulsivity, and a third to identity disorder. The two largest subgroups in the whole BPD domain were the affective + impulsive and the affective + identity disordered. The most important items were impulsivity, unstable relations, affective instability, and identity disturbance. Any three of these four would serve quite well as a detector of a BPD "case." Anger was a common feature also (79%). Self-damaging traits were noted in two-thirds of the patients and were usually found in conjunction with impulsivity. The importance of impulsivity that emerges from this naturalistic and atheoretic study squares well with the observation of Perry and Klerman (1978) that impulsivity was the one attribute mentioned in all the then popular definitions of borderline that formed the basis of their comparative study.

If we concentrate on keeping genuine personality traits separate from symptoms (and from nonsymptomatic peculiarities of mental life like identity disturbance), we can see from Hurt's analysis of the data that the *personality* aliquot of BPD is fundamentally composed of impulsivity and affective traits like moodiness or irritability. And even impulsivity, as it progresses toward an extreme, breaks down into Axis I-like symptoms, such as alcohol abuse or bingeing.

Another point with regard to the excessively polythetic nature of the DSM-III definition of BPD is this: a patient could exhibit the necessary five items, but might not manifest impulsivity, identity disturbance, or affective instability. Such patients, though they would be identified as BPD by DSM-III, would not qualify as borderline according to Gunderson, Kernberg, or any other accepted definition in common use. Patients of this sort would be in effect stepchildren of the manual, unrelated to all previous literature and tradition regarding borderline cases.

One way around the inconveniences of so potentially diverse a polythetic definition is a more restrictive definition, especially one that captures most of what has come to be regarded as the essence of the disorder in question. Though it does not avoid the problems related to mixing personality traits with symptoms, the Gunderson definition has the great advantages of being (1) a much more restrictive, hence a purer definition, and (2) also nearer to the essence of this elusive "borderline," as we refine it in the alembic of Hurt's computer. The Gunderson definition is also polythetic, but because patients must score a 1 or a 2 on at least four or five main clusters (concerning work, socialization, impulsivity, psychotic episodes, and interpersonal relationships), there are only half a dozen varieties of *borderline personality disorder* in his system. This means that the least similar Gunderson borderlines are still very similar (3 items out of 5 in common), whereas the least similar DSM-III borderlines have only two features in common and might be clinically very different (2 items out of 8 in common). A useful byproduct of the tighter Gunderson definition is the greater likelihood that persons diagnosed as BPD according to his criteria will manifest

the impulsivity and affective features (moodiness, inappropriate anger) that Hurt has distilled out as the main ingredients
of the borderline patient.

Because symptoms (e.g., brief psychotic reactions), personality traits, and complex attributes that overlap symptoms and
traits (suicide gestures: a symptom representing the extreme of
manipulativeness) are comingled within the Gunderson definition, the latter constitutes, strictly speaking, a *syndrome*. The
DSM-III definition also has the quality of a syndrome, though
less unambiguously defined.

Taking these remarks into consideration, what can we say
regarding the utility of the borderline concept? In what direction should we go in our efforts the better to define and refine
the concept in the immediate future?

There does exist a large group of patients—not psychotic
except transitorily, but difficult to treat—that deserve to be
singled out for special attention as examples of the syndrome
thus far best defined by Gunderson but adumbrated also in the
DSM-III definition of borderline personality disorder.

In many cases, especially in the patients who first begin to
show the features of this condition or who require residential
care, one can discern through the thicket of flamboyant symptomatology a true personality disorder that is at the same time
distinctive. This personality disorder does not stand in the same
neat etiological relationship either to the symptom-laden syndrome we call BPD or to manic-depressive illness (MDP)—as
does schizoid personality to either schizotypal personality or to
their parent condition, schizophrenia. The latter are as three
bands along a spectrum, labeled "schizotype" by Meehl (1972)
that relates to genetic predisposition to introversion and eccentricity. There are cases one could claim were dilute versions of
manic-depressive psychosis (i.e., "borderline" with respect to
MDP) but their proportion in samples of "borderline" (BPD)
patients will vary from a small fraction to 10 or 20 or 30 or
more percent. Much of the controversy concerning the relationship, or lack of it, between BPD and MDP dissolves when we
take into account the characteristics of samples from different
parts of the world and from ambulatory versus residential settings. Though many patients with the borderline syndrome

have the personality characteristics I will outline shortly, etiologically they constitute a diverse group. In my long-term follow-up study of borderlines (Stone, 1990), some 10 percent
went on, within ten or fifteen years after release from the hospital, to develop full-blown MDP, some unipolar, some bipolar.
Others came by their symptoms and their personality disorder
through a different pathway.

Recently I have expressed the view (Stone, 1988b) that the
red thread running through what we currently subsume under
the heading of BPD is irritability; specifically, a special sort
of nervous system irritability, heterogeneous in etiology, that
conduces to impulsive, often chaotic behavior. Wilhelm Reich
(1925) was not far off the mark when he described similar
patients under the heading *triebhafte* or "impulse-ridden" character. Some label of this sort would be much more appropriate
as a signature word for the prototypic personality disorder such
patients manifest to greater or lesser degree. What are some of
the traits that would go to make up this quintessential impulse-
ridden, hitherto "borderline," patient. I have enumerated some
twenty-six traits in Table 1.2 that capture, from the standpoint
of true personality traits, the qualities singled out by Kernberg,
Gunderson, and the DSM-III committee on Axis II as important in their various conceptions of borderline personality.

Table 1.1 presents the diagnostic items derived from the
descriptions of BPD or borderline personality organization offered by Gunderson, the DSM-III, and Kernberg. Because of
their overlap, the nineteen items within these three systems can
be condensed to thirteen. Assigning each item a number from
one to thirteen, I then constructed Table 1.2 which contains
some twenty-six personality traits frequently noted in patients
diagnosed as "borderline" according to one or more of the
above-mentioned systems. Opposite these traits, wherever possible, I placed one or more numbers from Table 1.1, by way of
showing the correspondence between many of the diagnostic
items— even those that constitute symptoms—and true personality traits.

Several of the traits listed in Table 1.2 are nearly synonymous, but emphasize different aspects of some central attribute.
Fickle, flighty, inconstant, and desultory, for example, are

TABLE 1.1
Diagnostic Items Within
Three Systems for Defining "Borderline"

A. *From DSM-III-R*
    1   Identity Disturbance
    2   Labile Affect
    3   Disturbed Interpersonal Relationships
    4   Inordinate Anger
    5   Self-Damaging Acts
    6   Impulsivity
    7   Emptiness/Boredom
    8   Frantic Efforts to Avoid Abandonment

B. *From Gunderson and Singer*
    9   Lowered Work Achievement
    6   Impulsivity; viz,
    5   Manipulative Suicide Gestures
    10   Good Socialization
    11   Brief Psychotic Episodes
    3, 2, 4   Disturbed Interpersonal Relationships with Ten-
                    dency to Become Depressed or Angry in Situation
                    of Loss or Rejection

C. *From Kernberg*
    1   Identity Disturbance
    12   Adequate Reality Testing
    6   Impulsivity
    13   Lowered Anxiety Tolerance
    9   Poor Sublimatory Channeling

shades of meaning related to impulsivity. "Fickle" is used of sexual object choice and is rarely applied to males, who, if they are fickle, are called "inconstant." "Desultory" refers to leaping from one interest to another. This trait is not synonymous with, though related to "flighty," which emphasizes the inability to persevere with one interest.

There are a number of other personality traits commonly noted in borderline patients that are less easily captured in conventional language. The *as-if* quality described by Helene Deutsch (1942) is an example. She coined this term to represent

TABLE 1.2
Personality Traits Common to Borderline Patients
and Their Relationship to the Diagnostic Items of Table 1.1

Alternatingly awed (adoring) or contemptuous 3
Chaotic 6
Childish 3, 5, 6
Clingy 8
Cranky 4
Demanding 3, 8
Desultory 6, 9
Extreme(s), going to 2, 5, 6
Fickle 1, 6
Flighty 3, 6
Fragile 11, 13
Hostile 4
Importunate 3, 8
Inconstant 3, 6
Irritable 4
Manipulative 3, 5, 8
Mercurial 2
Moody 2
Possessive 3, 8
Reckless 6
Restless 9
Seductive 8
Shallow 1, 9
Unpredictable 2, 6
Unreasonable 4, 3, 8
Vehement 4
Volatile 2, 4

---

the tendency certain patients exhibited in taking on the values
and attitudes of persons who have become important to them,
so that the latter will find them more appealing. Terms like
plastic or *insincere*, though in the same realm of discourse, would
not be adequate substitutes for "as-if." In everyday parlance
pejorative expressions like "flaky" are sometimes used in referring to a combination of attributes some borderline persons
manifest, such as vagueness, impracticality, and, in conversation, overpersonalized or tangential responses. These peculiarities may reflect the identity disturbance common to borderline
persons, or else a degree of cognitive slippage.

The above-mentioned list of personality traits is not exhaustive but can serve as an initial approach toward the cataloging and more methodical assessment of traits most characteristic of persons now subsumed under the borderline rubric. It remains to be determined which traits are the most frequent, and which the best in discriminating from other personality disorders. The item, "hypersensitivity to criticism," to take but one example, is currently a part of DSM-III's schizotypal personality disorder (STP). Yet many BPD patients take criticism and certain neutral comments in an intensely personal way. Such an item would probably be a poor discriminator between BPD and STP, whereas impulsivity might be a fairly reliable discriminator.

Ideally, we would want a label for the prototypic patient that readily identified the personality subtype in question. "Narcissistic," "avoidant," "self-defeating," for example, serve well in this capacity. *Borderline* began as a term designating clinical states in between neurosis and psychosis ("borderline" with respect to psychosis) and later was employed as a term for dilute or incipient schizophrenia. When the term became decoupled from psychosis or schizophrenia beginning in the 1950s (Knight, 1953a; O. F. Kernberg, 1967; Grinker, Werble, and Drye, 1968; Gunderson and Singer, 1975), it became a kind of linguistic minister without portfolio, defined in terms unrelated to more serious conditions already in the nomenclature. It would be useful at this time to find a more descriptive adjective for the hallmark personality traits of BPD; that is, for the true personality component of this condition. Though impulsivity may be the key attribute, the terms *impulsive* or *impulse-ridden* overlap too much with *antisocial* and convey too little about the rapidly fluctuating moods of the typical borderline patient. Spitzer, Endicott, and Gibbon (1979) used the term *unstable* in referring to what is now BPD but which he originally called "*unstable* borderline," as opposed to "*schizotypal* borderline." Earlier in the century patients whose clinical picture was considered borderline with respect to manic-depressive illness were called "cycloid." Since only a certain proportion of borderline (BPD) patients fall into this category, *cycloid* would be an inap propriate label because of its surplus meaning as attenuated MDP (Fish, 1964). In the nineteenth century, when more attention was paid to temperament than is now customary, the phrases depressive–irritable (melancholico–choleric) or hypomanic–irritable (sanguineo–choleric) were often applied to patients we currently call borderline (Griesinger, 1871). Again, these terms carry a bias toward affective illness, and would be less suitable for patients who have developed the borderline syndrome more because of parental abusiveness than out of genetic predisposition to manic-depressive illness. At least for now, the term *unstable* (hence, "unstable personality disorder") may be the most bias-free, appropriate, and denotatively meaningful adjective. I would recommend, then, the substitution in Axis II of unstable personality disorder (UPD) in the place of BPD. The defining traits of this UPD should be chosen from among the traits outlined above in Table 1.2. One could go a step further and refine Table 1.2, taking note of the fact that the twenty-six true personality traits listed there could be compartmentalized further into about eight main categories: (1) *Impulsive* (childish, desultory, going to extremes, chaotic, fickle, flighty, inconstant, reckless, restless, unpredictable); (2) *Irritable* (cranky, hostile, irritable); (3) *Moody* (mercurial, moody, volatile); (4) *Manipulative* (demanding, importunate, manipulative, possessive, seductive); (5) *Extreme* (adoring/contemptuous, childish, unreasonable, vehement); (6) *Dependent* (clingy); (7) *Vulnerable* (fragile); and (8) *Interpersonally Lacking in Depth* (shallow). One might, for heuristic purposes, begin by requiring (1) and (2) plus any three of the remaining six categories, as necessary to the diagnosis of UPD.

As for the syndromal and largely symptomatic aspects of BPD, I would favor a restructuring in our official nomenclature in line with Gunderson's model because of its more restrictive and therefore more sharply boundaried definition. The syndrome might better be included within Axis I.

Separation of the symptom/syndromal aspects of what we are now calling borderline from the purely personality aspects might, at all events, enhance diagnostic precision and promote a more rational approach to treatment.

DIFFERENTIAL DIAGNOSIS

Schizophrenia

Before the present generation, the term *borderline* was often used, in a rather imprecise and off-hand manner, as a synonym for incipient or dilute schizophrenia, in much the same way psychiatrists during World War I used the label "preschizophrenic." The tighter definitions constructed over the past fifteen years have rendered *borderline* and *schizophrenia* quite dissimilar terms. Discrimination between the two can now be made reliably. Follow-up studies have provided considerable evidence that BPD as currently defined almost never evolves into schizophrenia. Conceivably a patient presenting in an emergency ward with an acute schizophreniform picture, especially if caused or aggravated by drug abuse, could prove diagnostically challenging: is one confronted with a borderline patient having an acute and brief psychotic (e.g., paranoid) episode; a patient abusing mescaline, barbiturates, or amphetamines who in other respects is not borderline; or an "acute" schizophrenic whose course will turn out to be chronic, that of an eventually clear-cut schizophrenia? Usually, continued observation over a matter of days will provide answers to these questions.

Schizotypal Personality (STP)

The distinction between BPD and STP is fairly clear conceptually. In actual practice, however, many BPD patients show an admixture of STP traits, sometimes enough to trigger the additional diagnosis of schizotypal personality. A patient with an equal balance of attributes that would render him a "mixed" borderline case (in the older nosology), or a BPD case with STP comorbidity, could just as well be viewed as an STP case with BPD comorbidity. Here we get hoisted on the petard of our own categorical distinctions. The number of such overlap cases, however, is not great. Less than a dozen of the 206 BPD patients in my follow-up study satisfied enough criteria simultaneously to qualify as cases of BPD × STP. Borderline patients are often given to magical thinking and are sometimes referential under emotional stress. They tend to overpersonalize certain comments made by others with no or only minor critical intent. These qualities are manifestations of the "cognitive slippage" borderlines may exhibit when anxious, but the majority of borderlines do not show the more typical signs of STP such as odd speech or aloofness.

Manic-Depressive Illness

Depending on the series—which in turn depends on factors including the locale and the predominant subculture—a moderate to large proportion of BPD patients will show concomitant major affective disorder. The latter may go on over the next ten years or so to evolve along classically manic-depressive lines. Some patients when seen by a consultant already manifest BPD and one form or another of MDP so as to end up with two diagnoses, either one of which may be awarded pride of place—in accordance usually with the major area of interest of the interviewer. Commonly, the BPD × MDP combination arises where the MDP component is of the bipolar II type. This conjunction of abnormalities is common in my practice and in several of the hospitals where I have worked. Oldham (1988) has found that 70 percent of patients hospitalized with BPD have some form of mood disorder at the same time (though not necessarily bipolar II). Nevertheless, BPD without concomitant mood disorder also occurs. I have also worked briefly in hospital units, such as the one at the Belmont Hospital in Brisbane, Australia, where the BPD patients had all experienced severe trauma and abuse in their formative years; almost none had either the clinical stigmata or a family history of affective illness.

Patients with bipolar II disorder often resemble borderline patients, owing to their impulsivity, unstable relations, moodiness, and tendency toward boredom and uneasiness when alone. They are usually very people oriented and sensation seeking, often overspend, overindulge in alcoholic beverages, and overreact angrily when frustrated. The "hysteroid dys-phoric" patients described by D. Klein and M. Liebowitz often show BPD with bipolar II "comorbidity."

Another way in which MDP, especially the bipolar variants, may be confused with (or overlap with) BPD is in the area of identity disturbance. Some patients with bipolar illness are rapid cyclers and change state, including attitude toward oth-ers, their general disposition, frequently and abruptly. One may see a Jekyll and Hyde phenomenon, where a person is pleasant much of the time and suddenly irritable, even cruel or demonic, for days at a time. Others experience such persons as "two different people." The Jekyll and Hyde person may be equally bewildered as to who he really is—and in this way manifests an identity disorder. If other signs of BPD are also present, one might say that the underlying illness has, as a kind of side effect, engendered a borderline personality disorder as well—one that waxes and wanes in intensity, along with the affective cycle.

Late Luteal Phase Dysphoria (Premenstrual Tension)

Closely related to the phenomenon just mentioned is that of severe premenstrual syndrome (PMS). A small percent of women (perhaps 4%) develop extreme irritability and depres-sion just before or within the first few days of their menstrual period. *Paramenstrual*, meaning around-the-time-of, rather than premenstrual is the better term for this reason. This per-centage is much elevated in affectively ill and in borderline women, especially in borderline women with distinct affective comorbidity. I have worked with anorectic borderline women who have told me they purposely drove themselves toward an-orexia in order to extinguish their periods—as a way of control-ling their otherwise overwhelming PMS which they became aware of during adolescence. I do not, in citing this example, mean to imply that anorexia is a drastic self-cure for PMS, but in isolated instances there is a connection. Severe PMS may, at all events, be accompanied by a sudden change in personality in the direction of irritability, hostility, dysphoria, even suicidality. Again, such women appear different even to themselves, as well as to those around them. This may create an identity disorder and also may resemble or in some cases constitute a borderline picture, given the tendency to exhibit some of the other BPD qualities also (affect lability, relational instability, inordinate anger, etc.).

Whether one considers a case an example of PMS alone or of BPD × PMS would depend upon the lasting versus intermittent nature of the BPD traits. If the latter disappear completely until the next cycle, one should only diagnose PMS.

Major Affective Disorder

Major affective disorder (MAD), especially serious depressive episodes with vegetative signs occurring in younger persons, may be a harbinger of MDP still in an incipient stage. More often the MAD may be one of a few isolated instances, without subsequent evolution into uni- or bipolar illness. Either way, the condition may coexist with BPD. Whether and how often the genetic liability to manic depression leads to BPD as one of its phenotypes is a vexing question. In some instances I believe this sequence occurs, in which event MAD and BPD with their partly overlapping attributes are, in effect, two sides of the same coin. Certain family pedigrees offer impressive evidence of this connection. In other cases, MAD is unrelated to BPD, occurs without the signs of BPD and, as Clarkin, Widiger, Frances, Hurt, and Gilmore (1983) have pointed out, may occur alongside other personality disorders. Inordinate anger and impulsivity are not intrinsic to the concept of MAD, whereas they are to the concept of BPD, and thus may serve as discriminating features.

Cyclothymia

"*Cyclothymic* temperament" Kraepelin (1921) defined as the conjunction of the depressive and hypomanic temperaments. He considered cyclothymic the rarest of the four types (the fourth being the "irritable") found in association with MDP (either in the patients themselves or in some of their close relatives). A similar term, *cycloid*, was used about forty to fifty years ago to describe certain cases in the penumbra of MDP: "borderline" cases of MDP. DSM-III-R mentions cyclothymia as an entity to consider in the differential diagnosis of BPD. Here again we are in a region where affective disorders and BPD overlap or are even two expressions of the same underlying constitutional factors. The following vignette is illustrative.

An executive in a large corporation, a man in his early forties, displays cyclothymia in an unmistakable manner. He is extremely extroverted, hail fellow well met, often giddy and euphoric, less often tearful and sad—the latter mood coming over him when in difficult circumstances. But his personality insures that he is often in difficult circumstances, since he is impulsive, drives and drinks recklessly, is engaged to an extremely volatile and pathologically jealous woman—to whom he promises eternal fidelity, only to have, after their arguments, one-night stands with a "pick-up."

He spends foolishly on baubles either to please his fiancée or one of the women of his brief dalliances—the existence of which he invariably telegraphs to his fiancée via telltale objects left about his apartment. Her discovery of these objects leads to destructive scenes where each has come close to mutilating the other. During their numerous and transitory break-ups he becomes irascible, his anger magnified by alcohol, and will saunter into bars frequented by members of an organized crime family, there to hurl ethnic slurs at some of the beefier customers. He emerges battered and bleeding from the encounters that predictably ensue. Strictly speaking, the bruises are not self-inflicted and therefore not part of the BPD definition. If, however, one reasons that such behavior is just a self-damaging act in thin disguise, then this becomes his fifth BPD "item" (besides unstable relations, impulsivity, anger, and avoidance of being alone).

Whether this is best viewed as BPD "comorbidity" in a cyclothymic or as simply the cyclothymic brand of BPD seems a casuistical question. One should also keep in mind that milder forms of cyclothymia also exist—where one sees the mercurial mood swings without the irascibility and impulsivity of this patient.

Dysthymia

Depressive neurosis has been renamed dysthymia, and contains elements in common with the depressive temperament as adumbrated in Kraepelin's monograph. Many BPD patients exhibit dysthymia; only a few dysthymics present with the BPD picture as well. Again, the irritability, impulsivity, and instability are lacking in uncomplicated dysthymia. The discrimination in the latter case from BPD is usually not difficult. There may be more difficulty in dealing with the more broadly defined "borderline personality organization," (BPO as outlined by Kernberg). In BPO one need only find identity disturbance in the presence of adequate reality testing capacity. This quality is more widespread in the population than BPD. About 12 percent of the 299 BPO cases in my long-term follow-up study were dysthymics—who did *not* meet DSM-III criteria for BPD. In my experience, the relative absence of irritable–impulsive qualities in the dysthymics was associated with better long-term outcome (Stone, 1990). None suicided and the average follow-up Global Assessment Scale (GAS) was higher than in any other subgroup of the hospitalized patients I later traced.

Irritable Temperament

The traits of Kraepelin's irritable temperament include irascibility, abusiveness, dogmatism, pathological jealousy, impracticality, and mild paranoid trends. This innate tendency gives rise to a deformation of the personality, discernible throughout life. The chronic nature of this disorder would serve to distinguish it from intermittent explosive disorder (DSM-III-R, 312.34) where generalized impulsiveness or aggressiveness is not present between episodes. The latter condition, which resembles BPD in several ways, is sometimes on an organic basis, as in the "episodic dyscontrol" syndrome described (chiefly in adolescent males) by Andrulonis (Andrulonis, Glueck, Stroebel, Vogel, Shapiro, and Aldridge, 1981). Extreme forms of irritability may be found in what Wilhelm Reich (1925) described under the heading of "impulse-ridden character." Patients with impulse-ridden character are usually also alcoholic, antisocial, abusive, irascible, impetuous, reckless, and mercurial. Some are self-destructive episodically, as well as destructive toward others. The majority of such persons would satisfy BPD criteria. Many are poorly educated, work sporadically at menial jobs, drift from one community to another, abandon their mates, and so on. Their antisociality distinguishes them from the less chaotic and more treatment-amenable borderline patients that analysts (e.g., Volkan, Chessik, Kohut, Kernberg, Abend, Bryce Boyer) have in mind when they discuss their therapeutic efforts on behalf of "borderline" patients.

Not all irritable temperament lies in the penumbra of MDP. Organic factors and early corporal abuse play the major etiologic roles in some cases—especially the "impulse-ridden" cases just mentioned. John Frosch (1977) also described "impulsive" personalities—which he discussed as similar to but in some ways distinct from borderline cases.

Posttraumatic Stress Disorder

Though DSM-III-R alludes in its description of posttraumatic stress disorder (PTSD) to distressing events "outside the range of usual human experience," many people suffer from less intense forms of the syndrome—response to childhood physical abuse or sexual abuse by caretakers; at times by persons external to the family. Incest, especially father–daughter and if accompanied by hostility or cruelty, can induce the clinical picture we now recognize as the incest profile. This may include nightmares, flashbacks, impulsive behavior, psychogenic amnesia, anger outbursts, sleep disturbances, exaggerated startle response, and other of the signs and symptoms also associated with PTSD. Extreme abuse can, in my opinion, and in the opinion of others who have also examined this realm of psychopathology, give rise to BPD quite in the absence of risk genes for MDP (Herman, 1981; Goodwin, 1982; van der Kolk, 1987). In some samples, hospitalized ones in particular, a large percentage of BPD patients have the kind of traumatic history and the symptomatology that makes a compelling case for the coexistence (or if not, the causative influence) of PTSD or a *forme fruste* of this syndrome. Originally, of course, PTSD was invoked to refer to certain cases of war-trauma victims.

Temporal Lobe Epilepsy

Partial complex seizures has tended to replace temporal lobe epilepsy as a term designating the constellation of strange automatisms and sensory experiences, along with hyperirritable personality changes, that may be set in motion by abnormal temporal lobe foci. Sometimes the clinical picture can resemble if not "pure" BPD, at least a kind of "mixed" unstable/schizotypal borderline with eccentricities of thought as well as impulse and inappropriate behavior. Anger and irascibility may be accompaniments. The diagnosis often exists within a disputed territory, some clinicians convinced of the underlying organic factor even when the electroencephalograph (EEG) is negative, others convinced the diagnosis is one of desperation, invoked (like "minimal brain damage") when the clinician simply doesn't know and takes refuge in an unfalsifiable position. Some cases of BPD with episodic dyscontrol appear to stem from this temporal lobe abnormality. One patient I saw in consultation several years ago was a man of thirty who had been ill and on disability throughout most of his twenties with BPD *plus* macropsia–micropsia and other strange illusory experiences, especially when under stress. He gave up driving when he once had the terrifying sensation while on the highway that the steering wheel was melting in his hands. Some consultants considered him schizoaffective, though he never had delusions and always seemed too intact to support that diagnosis. He is still ill, was recently hospitalized, and remains diagnostically puzzling, since his EEG, even with sleep record and nasopharyngeal leads, was "equivocal." He had been severely abused as a child by his father and older brothers.

At all events, some BPD patients with strange behavior, fugue states, or illusions may be comorbid for TLE, just as there are (many more) TLE patients with unusual personalities—yet who don't meet criteria for BPD.

Schizoaffective Psychosis

Borderline personality disorder patients who typify Grinker's Type I case—the "border with psychosis"—may resemble schizoaffectives and vice versa. The longest "brief psychotic episode" still compatible with BPD (by Gunderson's criteria) may be difficult to distinguish from the ordinarily longer but still transitory delusional states of some schizoaffective patients. The latter are sometimes considered instances of what Ming Tsuang, Dempsey, and Rauscher (1976) call "Atypical Psychosis," where there are usually clear-cut precipitants and fairly intact premorbid personality. In this generation a number of patients with schizoaffective illness, of the predominantly affective type particularly, are stabilized via neuroleptic and other medications—such that they become very similar to the more fragile, self-mutilative, and impulsive BPD patients. Mixed BPD × STP patients often seem like dilute versions of schizoaffective illness, because of their combined cognitive and mood-dysregulatory symptoms.

Severe cases of childhood sexual or physical abuse can present with a schizoaffective picture initially (a posttraumatic psychosis, in effect), which may, with treatment, improve to the level of BPD, and thus represent a combination PTSD/BPD condition.

Alcoholism

Alcohol, probably because of its central nervous system (CNS) serotonin antagonism, acts as a disinhibitor and intensifies the anger, impulsivity, and explosiveness or violence-proneness of BPD patients, who as a group abuse alcohol more often than is the case in the general population. Many of the suicides, murders, and arsons committed by the borderlines in the "PI-500" (i.e., New York State Psychiatric Institute Long-Term Follow-up of 550 Patients) had been precipitated by alcohol abuse. But, as Gunderson has underlined, the two conditions should be kept separate diagnostically and it is not common for alcohol by itself to induce the clinical picture of BPD. Even so, the diagnostician's awareness of the other stigmata of alcohol excess and of a patient's alcohol history should suffice to make the distinction.

In the PI-500 there was one curious exception to this rule, where a "schizoaffective" (at other times, "borderline") condition seemed to have originated primarily because of alcoholism. But the connection between alcohol abuse and the disorder in question was never made during any of the man's five hospitalizations at PI. The doctors never inquired about an alcohol history, in part because the man was a devout Orthodox Jew, whom they supposed would be unlikely, in that era, to abuse alcohol. But he had become a professional athlete and took to drinking excessively to keep up with his teammates. Even small amounts of alcohol produced a clinical picture, in him, of paranoid thinking, delusory preoccupations about the Mafia, alternate crying and giddiness, and suicide gestures, which led to the diagnoses mentioned above. He never volunteered the information about his drinking during the seven years he was known to the hospital, because he had not as yet become aware of the connection. Later on he finally did, joined Alcoholics Anonymous (AA) and has been abstinent, and clinically well, for the past sixteen years.

Other Personality Disorders

While the prototype BPD is reasonably distinct enough to give it construct validity and to discriminate it from other personality disorders, in patients one will encounter at the hospital or in practice, admixtures with other personality features are the rule rather than the exception (Oldham, 1988). Patients with BPD are likely to show traits of the other types in the DSM-III "Dramatic" cluster; namely, histrionic, antisocial, and narcissistic. In some segments of the psychoanalytic literature the terms *borderline* and *narcissistic* were often used together as near synonyms. Kohut (1971) used the terms to designate regions of a spectrum, the "borderlines" being in effect the narcissistic patients one couldn't successfully analyze, the narcissistic patients being the borderlines one could. Since these distinctions rest upon knowledge of the course and outcome they are not diagnostic terms in the true sense, when used in this fashion. This aside, patients with nearly equal mixtures of narcissistic traits (as outlined in DSM-III) and BPD traits or of antisocial or histrionic and BPD traits, present a confusing picture from the standpoint of category-based diagnosis. Therapists who work with prisoners may note self-destructive/self-mutilative tendencies in some of their clients. They often refer to this under the heading of "borderline personality." In fashioning an appropriate therapy, however, the emphasis should be on the antisociality, since that will be the factor governing long-term outcome.

Histrionic patients with marked manipulativeness, demandingness, primitive emotionality, hostility, and stormy interpersonal relationships are to that extent also borderline. These patients were called hysteroid by Easser and Lesser (1965), infantile personalities (a subtype of borderline personality organization) by Kernberg (1967), and hysteroid dysphorics by Donald Klein (Klein and Davis, 1969).

From the standpoint of conditional probability, we know something about the likelihood given BPD, of also being antisocial, or histrionic or narcissistic. As to the reverse, given any of those three, what is the likelihood of concomitant BPD? I would estimate the percentage would be highest among the antisocials, next highest (but already much lower) among the histrionic persons, and lowest among those with NPD. Because the presence of BPD, especially in hospitalized cases, is so often accompanied by other personality disorder diagnoses, there would be a great advantage to the adoption of a *dimensional* approach to assessment of personality disorders, as advocated by Mezzich (1988), Oldham (1988), and others.

Identity Disorder

DSM-III-R lists identity disorder (ID) in the note on differential diagnosis vis-à-vis BPD. Identity disturbance ("identity diffusion") is an essential element in Kernberg's psychostructural definition of BPO and a commonly (but not universally) diagnosed item in BPD patients. But ID as a separate entity consists of uncertainty about several areas of identity (including long-term goals, career choice, sexual orientation, etc.) along with some impairment in social or occupational function (perhaps sufficient to be noteworthy in relation to Gunderson's BPD item concerning work). Such elements as anger, impulsivity, or self-damaging acts are not present. The condition should be readily distinguishable from BPD, though not always so readily from BPO.

A rarer form of identity disorder, reminiscent of BPO, was mentioned by Akiskal (1981), in describing a young black woman who was born with albinism, in relation to which she developed considerable identity confusion in the area of her cultural–racial affiliations.

CONCLUSION

As a summary to the above material I have prepared a figure outlining the interrelationships among the diagnostic entities reviewed here. Figure 1.1 shows schizophrenia and schizoaffective psychosis as "near neighbors," whereas the other conditions can either be more readily confused with BPD, can coexist with BPD, or, on occasion, represent variants of BPD simply viewed from a different vantage point.

This figure emphasizes the relationships between BPD and other disorders, as currently described. The new designation of "unstable personality" which I have sketched above, would

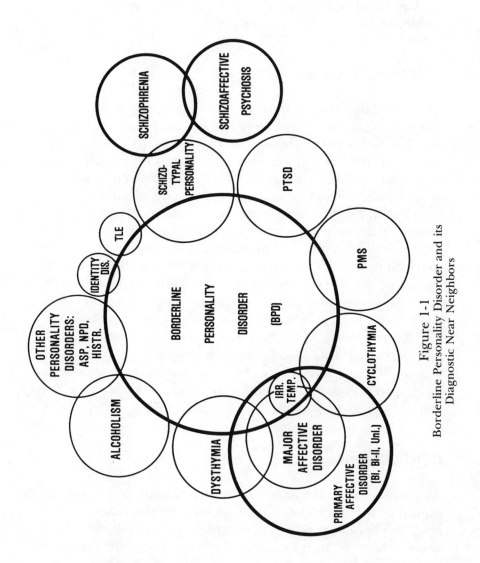

Figure 1-1
Borderline Personality Disorder and its
Diagnostic Near Neighbors

emphasize the importance of separating the symptom–syndromal aspect of what is currently called "borderline," from the
purely personality aspects. This would enhance diagnostic precision and promote a more rational approach to treatment.

Many patients whom we are currently diagnosing as BPD
by DSM-III-R standards, especially those from whom hospitalization is part of their life course, would be designated as unstable personality (UPD). This would be applicable to the "infantile" subtype described by Kernberg (1967) as an important
variant of borderline personality organization.

Some patients within the borderline syndrome have either
a mixture of "unstable" and schizotypal features; some have
relatively few unstable features, presenting instead mainly with
narcissistic paranoid, self-defeating, or other traits. All these
complexities and varieties would be fairly easy to address in the
multidimensional diagnostic model embodied in the newest and
forthcoming revisions of DSM-III. In the schema I am proposing, what had been "borderline personality disorder" in Axis II
would be moved to Axis I as "borderline syndrome," its definition reworked along the lines of Gunderson's BPD. Many patients with this borderline syndrome, it could be footnoted, also
exhibit UPD as defined in Axis II. This would be especially true
of younger patients with the syndrome. Not all patients with
UPD show the borderline syndrome, especially as they improve
with treatment or with age (Stone, 1990). Some patients with
the borderline syndrome might show the traits of narcissistic,
histrionic, antisocial, or self-defeating personality disorder
more strikingly than the traits of UPD.

2.

The Validity of the Borderline Personality Disorder

Alex Tarnopolsky, M.D., F.R.C.Psych.

Research reviews of the validity of the borderline personality disorder (BPD) (Dahl, 1985b; Kroll and Ogata, 1987; Links, 1987) have varied from critical to sympathetic, and the concept itself evokes controversies that are fundamental to psychiatry. Do we treat "illness," or some type of variability from the norm? What is the norm from which a personality departs to become "disordered"? The numerous ways that personality disorder can present is in contrast to the precise entities advocated by Kraepelin. Moreover, the field of personality disorders is constantly changing as nearly every new research article proposes corrections to the diagnostic criteria employed.

In the midst of such changing times, a discussion of validity is essential. "Validity" may be defined as the evidence that a criterion, expressed in a research instrument, identifies what it is supposed to do. However, concepts have a penumbra of meanings. What type of validity are we aiming at in psychiatry? How is the modern concept of BPD regarded in the light of contemporary scientific standards?

Acknowledgment. I am grateful to the B. Rosenstadt Foundation of the University of Toronto for their support which allowed me to write this chapter.

29

In medicine, illnesses are ultimately validated by the demonstration of specific etiologies, but in psychiatry the researcher has to marshal information from several areas in order to construct a convincing argument for or against the status of the disorder in question. The areas to examine are listed by Robins and Guze (1970). Traditional clinical description includes both the consistency and unity of the symptomatology; and extends into assessing the distinctiveness of the disorder in question from other disorders, and persistence of its uniqueness over time. This is enhanced by studying the family distribution and possible laboratory evidence. Data from therapeutic studies are worth including because the data may suggest pathogenic chains that can then be researched with other means. Liebowitz (1979) concluded that "available data do not weigh conclusively for or against the borderline status as an independent entity" (p. 23). With the appearance of systematic diagnostic criteria, that is, the diagnostic interview for borderlines (DIB) (Gunderson, Kolb, and Austin, 1981) and *The Diagnostic and Statistical Manual of Mental Disorders* (DSM-III) (American Psychiatric Association, 1980, DIB), and considerable new research, a new assessment of the concept was presented by Tarnopolsky and Berelowitz (1987). Their conclusion was that "the scale has tipped in favour of the diagnostic status of borderline personality" (p. 732).

RELIABILITY

The existence of defined criteria and standardized interviewing has solved the preliminary but crucial problem of reliability; that is, agreement between observers as to the presence or absence of the disorder, and of its individual traits and symptoms. Even with different methods, satisfactory kappa coefficients above 0.7 and 0.8 were repeatedly obtained for both inpatients and outpatients (Tarnopolsky and Berelowitz, 1987). More recent assessments have supported this finding. Widiger, Trull, Hurt, Clarkin, and Frances (1987), using lay interviewers essentially indifferent to the concept and classification of personality disorders, reported k = 0.75 among relatively severe BPD inpatients.

Reliability studies have also specified that certain items can be collected more readily than others. There is some consensus that impulsivity (including self-destructive behavior), particular conflicts in interpersonal relationships, and social adaptation, brief psychotic episodes, and extreme anger, are borderline symptoms that can be reliably assessed. "Identity disturbance," one of Kernberg's original diagnostic triad (1967), is clinically relevant in spite of its low reliability and relatively moderate support in empirical research (Widiger, Frances, Warner, and Bluhm, 1986; McGlashan, 1987a).

The conclusion I draw from the reliability studies on BPD and its individual items is that sufficient agreement has been reached to justify proceeding to more substantive issues. Reliability is a prerequisite of research. Lower reliabilities than those reported for borderlines are common in research of traditional psychiatric disorders. Furthermore, it has been argued that in general "reliability of psychiatric systems is actually no better and no worse than diagnosis in other medical fields" (Kraemer, Pruyn, Gibbons, Greenhouse, Grochocinski, Waternaux, and Kupfer, 1987, p. 1101); that excessive purism may impair rather than benefit psychiatric research; and that, rather than generate new diagnostic systems, there should be more investment "in testing the validity of existing systems to disclose what, with current systems, is valuable and what should be discarded and replaced" (Kraemer et al., 1987, p. 1101). This seems to be the direction that research on BPD has taken.

A CORE BORDERLINE SYMPTOMATOLOGY?

The existence of two important and not completely coincident criteria, DIB and DSM-III, triggered a number of studies where both sets were applied to the same patients and/or their clinical histories (summarized in Tarnopolsky and Berelowitz [1987]). For example, 252 admissions were examined in detail by Kroll, Sines, Martin, Lari, Pyle, and Zander (1981), and Barrash, Kroll, Carey, and Sines (1983). The DIB identified a larger number of cases than DSM-III. There were some false positives and some false negatives, mostly cases that met the DIB criteria and not those of DSM-III. The most common diagnosis for these discordant cases was nonborderline personality disorder. Cluster analysis improved the agreement and yielded a high sensitivity (0.83) and specificity (0.89) for the DIB against the DSM-III criteria. This agreement is very satisfactory considering a possible source of disparity: DIB is a research tool whereas the DSM-III data were obtained in clinical interviews.

The study of individual symptoms refines the construct by specifying criteria for their inclusion or exclusion from the diagnostic set (Widiger et al., 1986), and by singling out the most frequent, the most characteristic, and the most discriminatory items of BPD when compared with other diagnoses. In recent research, sensitivity and specificity (the proportions of cases and controls correctly identified by an item or an instrument) have been supplemented with predictive value, an epidemiological statistic (Vecchio, 1966) that describes the probability of an item (present or absent) identifying a case.

Data from Frances, Clarkin, Gilmore, Hurt, and Brown (1984) showed that the most frequent features of borderline personality derived from the DIB were social adaptation, affects, and interpersonal relationships; and from the DSM-III set, impulsivity, affective instability, inappropriate anger, interpersonal relationships, emptiness–boredom. The items which discriminated BPD from other personality disorders were impulsivity–action patterns, brief psychosis (DIB), and emptiness–boredom, intolerance of being alone, impulsivity–unpredictability, and conflicts in interpersonal relationships (DSM-III). Although brief psychosis and social adaptation have no equivalence in the DSM-III, many other items of one system include items of the other. More recently, McGlashan (1987a) compared BPD to schizotypal personalities and found that for BPD the core symptom criteria were unstable relationships, impulsivity, and self-damaging acts. Other symptoms at medium level of support were identity disturbance, affective instability, and emptiness–boredom. Although the most discriminating symptoms may differ according to which control group they are discriminating against, the coincidence of core symptoms across different studies strengthens the descriptive validity of borderline personality disorders, and provides the requisites for a unitary description.

The objection has been raised that "borderline personality" was strictly a psychoanalytic construct or a North American phenomenon. However, researchers who have identified DSM-III or DIB cases elsewhere are now numerous. As British psychiatrists are known for their dislike of this category, it is valuable to note the work by Kroll, Carey, Sines, and Roth (1982), who identified cases in Britain. In addition, a survey was done of British psychiatrists who were asked to compare a borderline patient with another equally severe nonborderline personality disorder. Their responses are in broad agreement with the core symptomatology described above. The two most frequent items were a pattern of unstable interpersonal relationships and impulsiveness, and unpredictability in potentially self-damaging areas, both DSM-III items. The most discriminating item, however, was brief, stress-related, psychotic episodes or regressions (a DIB item) (Tarnopolsky and Berelowitz, 1984).

Further support is provided by the consistency of the diagnostic set in different conditions. For example, do the criteria cluster by statistical means beyond the possible bias imposed by a questionnaire or a rater? The answer is reasonably affirmative in a variety of circumstances (Spitzer, Endicott, and Gibbon, 1979; Barrash et al., 1983; Gunderson, Siever, and Spauldin, 1983; Livesley and Jackson, 1986; Widiger et al., 1986).

Finally, some changes were introduced in the revision of DSM-III (Widiger, Frances, Spitzer, and Williams, 1988) and reports on the relation between the old and revised borderline criteria are appearing (Morey, 1988a).

A VARIANT OF SCHIZOPHRENIA?

To gain credibility as a diagnosis, the borderline concept had to prove its separateness from schizophrenia because initially it was viewed as bordering on this psychosis.

Even before the appearance of the DIB, Gunderson, Carpenter, and Strauss (1975), assessing inpatients from the International Pilot Study of Schizophrenia, found that the "borderline" cases had significantly fewer psychotic symptoms than the schizophrenic group, with no evidence of thought disorder. Instead, derealization, a frenetic and stormy life-style, unusual and occult experiences, marked interpersonal difficulties, and suicide threats were common. Their psychotic symptoms are not typically schizophrenic (Chopra and Beatson, 1986). Other studies of inpatients early in the 1980s, applying DIB or DSM-III criteria, rarely found schizophrenic cases among borderline-defined samples at intake (Kroll et al., 1981; Pope, Jonas, Hudson, Cohen, and Gunderson, 1983) or at follow-up (Pope et al. [1983]; Barasch, Frances, Hurt, Clarkin, and Cohen [1985]; reviewed in Tarnopolsky and Berelowitz [1987]). In a five-year follow-up, Carpenter and Gunderson (1977) reversed some of the conclusions of an earlier shorter study (Gunderson et al., 1975). They found all the schizophrenic patients retained their diagnoses, and only one borderline (N = 24) was relabeled schizophrenic in spite of persistent diagnostic uncertainty among the group. Later, the separation of borderline (unstable) from schizotypal personalities clarified the issue. McGlashan (1983a) showed that after discharge 44 to 50 percent of BPD retained their diagnosis, 16 to 24 percent of BPD received a diagnosis of schizophrenia, but 55 percent of schizotypals (STP) changed into schizophrenia.

All this work was done with inpatient samples. At the same time, one could observe an intriguing disappearance of papers addressing the differences between BPD and less severe forms of schizophrenia, particularly among outpatients. The issue was never satisfactorily studied nor clearly resolved (Sheehy, Goldsmith, and Charles [1980]; Koenigsberg, Kernberg, and Schomer [1983]; reviewed in Tarnopolsky and Berelowitz [1987]). This disinterest probably related to the growing concern regarding the distinction between borderline and schizotypal personalities, and to the consistent evidence from follow-up studies.

FOLLOW-UP STUDIES

Initially, there were few projects which included follow-up data based on systematically diagnosed samples (Pope et al., 1983; Barasch et al., 1985; Akiskal, Chen, Davis, Puzantan, Kashgarian, and Bolinger, 1985a). The early studies had small samples, short observation periods and were not purposely designed for follow-up. More recently, new studies have become available (Paris, 1988). They are relatively large and extend over long periods (about 15 years), but some methodological difficulties remain. A common concern has been to distinguish the natural course of BPD from treatment effects. Nonetheless, these follow-up studies are relevant because BPD outcome is shown to be quite different from schizophrenia outcome (Plakun, Burkhardt, and Muller, 1985; McGlashan, 1986a; Stone, Stone, and Hurt, 1987a). In contrast to the established chronicity, marginal social functioning, and poor outcome of most schizophrenics, borderline patients tended to improve over time, being at their best about ten to twenty years after discharge (McGlashan, 1986a). Compared with schizophrenics, they were relatively more autonomous, productively employed, more frequently married or with children, in spite of having persistent symptoms and repeated brief, crisis-oriented hospitalizations. Stone et al. (1987a) noted a lower rate of suicide than in schizophrenics. McGlashan and Heinssen (1988) have recently shown that diagnosis itself (of BPD, schizophrenia, etc.) is the most powerful predictor of the type of discharge, the circumstances of discharge, and postdischarge events. They found that 51 percent of schizophrenics were transferred from a psychoanalytically oriented hospital to other facilities, while 40 percent of borderlines discharged themselves and 46 percent were discharged with medical accord. These results support the predictive validity of a diagnosis of borderline personality disorder.

FAMILY STUDIES

The argument about the affiliation of BPD to schizophrenia developed in the context of the debate on the distinctiveness of borderline personalities from schizotypal personalities. This demarcation (Spitzer et al., 1979) was a most useful conceptual approach, which not only clarified a muddled field but also had a direct impact on family and genetic studies. The schizotypal personality criteria were obtained from a sample of "borderline schizophrenics or B-3 cases" of the seminal Danish Adoption Study (Kety, Rosenthal, Wender, and Schulsinger, 1968). B-3 cases were mainly relatives of schizophrenic index cases, and therefore supported a genetic line between the two. Kendler, Gruenberg, and Strauss (1981b) confirmed that schizotypal personality was more frequent among the biological relatives of chronic schizophrenics than among relatives of controls, or relatives of index B-3 cases. Gunderson et al. (1983) further showed that the most common diagnosis in the B-3 index cases was borderline personality (9 out of 10), and that their B-3 relatives had borderline rather than schizotypal features. These two studies therefore allow for two genetic propositions: (1) the mentally ill biological relatives of chronic schizophrenics are schizotypal and not borderline, and (2) the mentally ill relatives of borderline personalities are, in the main, themselves borderline. These findings were supported using other populations (Baron, Gruen, Asnis, and Lord, 1985). In addition, Loranger, Oldham, and Tunis (1982) found that borderline personality was ten times more common in the treated relatives of borderline patients than in the relatives of schizophrenic patients. A substantive twins study by Torgersen (1984) showed that monozygotic twins of schizotypal patients have schizotypal disorders (33%) and not borderline disorders (0%).

Despite some methodological criticisms (Tarnopolsky and Berelowitz, 1987), the evidence nonetheless gives weight to the hypothesis that borderline personality is genetically distinct from schizophrenia and from schizotypal personality. This is particularly interesting because borderline and schizotypal dimensions coexist in many subjects. A recent study by Links, Steiner, and Huxley (1988a) found no schizophrenic patients among relatives of borderlines.

OTHER STUDIES

Some investigators found differences in physiological measures between BPD and subjects with schizotypal personality or schizophrenia (Schubert, Saccuzzo, and Braff, 1985; Chapin, Wightman, Lycaki, Josef, and Rosenbaum, 1987). Kutcher, Blackwood, St. Clair, Gaskell, and Muir (1987), however, reported a detailed analysis of electroencephalograph (EEG) responses to auditory stimulation among several carefully described groups. Electrophysiological responses distinguished BPD from other personality disorders and from affective disorders, but were shared by schizotypals and were present among schizophrenics. (It is interesting to note that borderlines may benefit from low dose neuroleptics.) Kutcher et al. argue that although borderline and schizotypals share an electrophysiological response, their different symptomatologies and course may result from complex familial, interpersonal, and social influences.

The literature on psychological testing is critically reviewed elsewhere in this book by Collins and Glassman (chapter 10).

In conclusion, the independence of borderline personality from schizophrenia is supported by the differences in their symptoms, evolution, outcome after treatment, and family aggregation. Further contributory data from psychophysiological studies and psychological tests are not definitive.

REALLY A SUBAFFECTIVE DISORDER?

The coincidence of affective illness with borderline personality is much greater than statistically expected (Gunderson and Elliot, 1985; Perry, 1985). This relationship is also more complicated than the previously postulated inclusion of borderline personality under schizophrenia. Gunderson and Elliot (1985) have listed four hypotheses to explain the issue. The first two are that one disorder can be reduced to the other; that is, drug taking or promiscuity to relieve feelings of emptiness, dysphoria, or depression; or depression resulting from impulsivity and unsatisfactory relationships; the third is that both disorders coexist independently in the same subjects; and the last is that affective symptoms or character traits arise from an interaction of influences peculiar to each individual.

Depressive syndromes are very common, very different from each other, and are attributable to a variety of causes. However, the literature has predominantly dealt with the proposition that borderline personalities are expressions of an endogenously based depression. Kroll and Ogata (1987) referred to the assumptions and prejudices that abound in this area of research.

Description

Evidence about the possibility of distinguishing between BPD and a variety of affective states at the symptomatic level was initially equivocal. Some studies (Gunderson and Kolb, 1978; Sheehy et al., 1980; Soloff and Ulrich, 1981; Barrash et al., 1983) have found clear differences between the two groups. The items characteristic of each disorder were different (e.g., impulsivity vs. affective state), and the attendant emotions were different, in that borderline "depression" was characterized by boredom and emptiness. Borderline personalities also felt easily disappointed and let down, wanted to hurt themselves, and were well aware of their rage. These symptomatic differences were confirmed by McGlashan (1987b) who also found that borderlines broke down younger and had fewer premorbid instrumental skills than unipolars. By contrast, other studies of BPD inpatients (Pope et al., 1983) and outpatients (Akiskal et al., 1985a) have found a proportion as high as 50 percent of major and minor affective illnesses and DIB-positive patients. Akiskal argued that these cases were not "mixed with" but "similar to" depressives, and rearranged the symptom–trait list of borderline personality to give priority to features of mood, "turning" BPD into a spectrumlike subaffective disorder.

This issue cannot be fully resolved with single cross-sectional descriptive studies where the distinction between long-term personality traits and episodic affective symptoms is obscured; nor in a single center, because sample variations influence the intake of patients to individual institutions. There was little unanimity of description of the type of depression involved (Tarnopolsky and Berelowitz, 1987). Some of these objections were dealt with by new research. Soloff, George, Nathan, and Schulz (1987) selected patients that were both borderline and depressed, and assessed them for a variety of affective disorder criteria. The degree of comorbidity was naturally high, but no combination was outstanding. The predominance of a single affective diagnosis would have been an important objection to the validity of BPD because it would point to a common etiology, or at least an affiliation, of the borderline group as a whole. Rather than a single type, Soloff et al. found that multiple affective diagnoses were possible for many borderline patients, and that the syndrome was not well described with the current cross-sectional instruments.

Responding to the issue of comorbidity, Fyer, Frances, Sullivan, Hurt, and Clarkin (1988) followed the basic epidemiological caution of examining the prevalence rates for psychiatric disorders in the hospitals from which borderline samples were drawn. Their data showed that comorbidity was generally heterogeneous. More important, there were no significant differences between the rate of affective disorders across borderline versus other personality disorders; nor across BPD versus other psychiatric diagnoses. Examining the literature, they found that the reported rates of depression among BPDs were comparable to the rates in the general clientele of the same hospitals. There was "no special association between BPD and affective disorder" (p. 350).

Follow-Up

Follow-up studies can show whether borderline patients eventually develop an affective disorder of which the borderline features were only a prodrome. Surprisingly, the analysis of such data did not always distinguish between "pure" and "mixed" cases. Pope et al. (1983) found that of the mixed (borderline and affective) cases, 74 percent had possible–probable affective illness at follow-up, while the corresponding figure for the "pure" borderline was only 23 percent. Data from Akiskal et al. (1985a) show 20 percent of melancholic episodes among initially "pure" borderlines. In both studies the vast majority of BPD did not turn into depressives. McGlashan (1987b) showed that only 11 percent changed from BPD to affective disorders over the years; 6 percent were either bipolar or unipolar.

The possibility exists that BPD may develop affective disorders more frequently than other personality disorders, but this is not the case. Barasch et al. (1985) found that major depressions were equally prevalent among other personality disorders after three years. Gunderson and Elliot (1985) noted that no studies had been undertaken to find out whether affective illness resolved into a borderline state. McGlashan (1987b) reported that one-third of unipolar depression became BPD at follow-up (one-third retained an affective diagnosis and one-third had other diagnoses). In cross-sectional studies, many affectively disordered patients present abnormal personalities (Friedman, Aronoff, Clarkin, Corn, and Hurt, 1983; Zimmerman, Pfohl, Cosyell, Stangl, and Corenthal, 1988), but these are not exclusively or predominantly borderline (Shea, Glass, Pilkonis, Watkins, and Dogherty, 1987; Pilkonis and Frank, 1988).

Comparison of outcome is not clear. One sample showed worse scores at four to seven years (Pope et al., 1983). Another sample showed similar scores to affective cases at fifteen years (McGlashan, 1983a). However, as was repeatedly pointed out, there is no reason to assume that different diagnoses should not have similar long-term social functioning. Moreover, unipolars do not change over the decades in the same manner as BPD, but social functioning, employment, and relationships scores of both groups tend to be similar in long-term follow-up (McGlashan, 1984a, 1986a).

Pharmacotherapy

The response of disorders to medication may delineate them pharmacologically and suggest the existence of specific pathogenic pathways. However, few controlled studies exist. Early pharmacotherapy studies illustrate, more than anything else, the conviction of the writers as to which of the major psychoses borderlines should be affiliated with. The finding that treatment with antidepressants improves the interpersonal, impulsive, and other traits of nondepressed borderline personalities would have provided strong support for an underlying biological imbalance common to affective and borderline disorders. Such evidence does not exist. There are two relevant double-blind, placebo-controlled trials with criteria-defined patients. Soloff, George, Nathan, Schulz, Ulrich, and Perel (1986a) compared haloperidol, amitriptyline, and placebo in a sample (N = 61). While haloperidol was effective, antidepressant medication did not improve BPD even if there was an affective dimension included. (Major depressive diagnoses had been excluded or were analyzed apart.) The other trial (Cowdry and Gardner, 1988) showed the beneficial effects of a monoamine oxidase inhibitor (MAOI) on BPD patients who presented atypical affective disorders, and of an anticonvulsant on behavioral control. The implication is that other pathways and brain locations may be required for an explanation of typical borderline symptoms.

Lucas, Gardner, Wolkowitz, and Cowdry (1987) reported unexpected, unpleasant reactions of BPD to methylphenidate (Ritalin), different from the ameliorating effect shown by depressives. It is not known if these patients rated positively for schizotypal symptoms, a distinction borne out by Schulz, Cornelius, Schulz, and Soloff (1988) who used amphetamines to test whether this dopamine agonist would trigger psychosis in borderlines. Patients with both schizotypal and borderline features were rated as worse on thought disturbance and activation, and they also subjectively felt worse. The "pure" borderline group felt subjectively better but had no change in specifically rated

symptoms. The authors argue that the first findings help affili-
ate schizotypals to schizophrenia, and that "pure schizotypals"
should be studied next. In their view, the second set of findings
support the association of borderlines with affective disorders,
but the improvement may have been restricted to some change
of mood. Depressions were not excluded and it is not clear how
borderlines fared in this respect.

Family Studies

Soloff and Millward (1983b) support the genetic link between
BPD and affective illness, as they found more borderline than
depressed probands had relatives with mood swings. This result, however, refers to a mixed group of nineteen borderlines,
nine schizotypals, and twenty cases who met both criteria. Further analysis revealed that the "depression" was actually more
prevalent among relatives of schizotypals than borderlines.
Links et al. (1988a) found alcoholism and recurrent unipolar
depressions were the most frequent diagnoses among relatives
of borderlines. In this sample, the vast majority of the patients
presented a concomitant depressive diagnosis. The homogeneity of the sample and precise description of the affective syndrome seem to be crucial methodological precautions. Pope et
al. (1983) and Andrulonis and Vogel (1984) simply separated
"pure" borderlines from those who also had an affective illness,
and found that the prevalence of depression was raised only in
the relatives of the second, mixed, group. Torgersen (1984)
reached the same conclusion: "All the co-twins with an affective
disorder were co-twins of schizotypal and borderline patients
with a concurrent affective disorder as well" (p. 550). A preliminary communication by Zanarini and Gunderson (1988) reported that borderline patients were significantly more likely to
have a family history of BPD than either antisocial or dysthymic
controls; they are also significantly more likely than antisocial
controls to have a first-degree relative with major depression
or dysthymic disorder.

Biological Markers

In order to establish validity, the same rigor in defining the purity of samples and controls that was necessary in pharmacological and genetic studies is demanded from investigations on biological markers. Much of the work done with the Dexamethasone Suppression Test (DST) is questionable because the cases studied had both syndromes concurrently or because adequate controls were not available (Carroll, Greden, Feinberg, Lohr, James, Steiner, Haskett, Albala, De Vigne, and Tarika, 1981; Silk, Lohr, Cornell, Hasel, Saakvitne, Buttenheim, and Zis, 1985). That borderlines were not depressed at the time of the study is insufficient, as the DST may remain high for six months after recovery from an endogenous depression (Peselow, Baxter, Fiebe, and Barouche, 1987). Steiner, Links, and Korzekwa (1988) recently reviewed the dozen studies available. In some small or preliminary samples where cases were divided between "pure" and "comorbid" with depressive disorders, it was clear that DST nonsuppressors were frequent among the "depressive" group and almost or completely absent among "pure" BPD (Krishnan, Davidson, Rayasam, and Shope, 1984).

Affiliation to the affective area would be evident if never-depressed (or not predominantly depressed) borderlines shared substantial biological responses with depressive patients, in particular with those varieties where biological factors are assumed to be prevalent (major, bipolar). An example for such data is Kontaxakis, Markianos, Vaslamatzis, Markidis, Kanellos, and Stefanis (1987). Borderline personality disorder patients were all male, free of psychotropic or hormonal treatment, had no atypical baselines, and were free of Axis I diagnoses. Controls had major depression or schizophrenia. No mention is made of the authors' reliability using the DIB; other diagnoses were informal but followed DSM-III criteria. Borderline personality disorders had significantly lower Hamilton Depression Scale scores but nonetheless shared with the major depressions an elevated response to DST: half of each group were nonsuppressors. Borderline personality disorders also shared with schizophrenics a reduced response to thyroid releasing hormone (TRH). It would have been interesting to know how many of the depressives had "melancholic" features. Pursuing a different area of investigation, Coid, Allolio, and Rees (1984) found a higher level of plasma metenkephalin among self-mutilators who met DSM-III borderline criteria than in normal controls. Metenkephalin is a neuropeptide that blocks the perception of pain. Another line of study describes the sleep architecture of borderlines. Akiskal, Yerevanian, Davis, King, and Lemmi (1985b) described a REM sleep pattern in borderlines similar to that found in depressives. There were differences, however, between those borderlines who had an affective diagnosis at any time in the past and those who had not. Other studies arguing for the intrinsic relationship have considered borderline patients that scored as highly as the major depressives in the Hamilton Scale, or had numerous diagnoses in the major depressive area (Reynolds, Soloff, Kupfer, Taska, Restifo, Coble, and McNamara, 1985).

Overview of the Relationship to Affective Disorders

This subject may be summarized as follows:
1. Characteristic symptoms of borderline personality are different from those of major affective disorders (impulsivity, chaotic relationships vs. melancholia).
2. There is an association between BPD and a variety of affective syndromes: some writers believe that no adequate description of the syndromes has ever been provided, although others find no difficulty in classifying them among known categories. No single category seems to be prominent across the board.
3. The epidemiological safeguard of comparing the rate of Axis I disorders in borderline versus general hospital samples has been demonstrated. One study showed that the rate of affective disorders among borderlines did not differ from the rate in the hospital populations from which the borderline samples were drawn. It is not known if the comorbidity is the result of self-selection of patients for treatment. A community study or a study of untreated borderline relatives of borderline patients may shed light on this.

4. At follow-up, about 10 to 20 percent of BPDs present with concomitant severe depressive disorders; or their diagnoses have changed into a depressive disorder. Conversely, one-third of unipolars are rediagnosed BPD on long-term follow-up.

5. In cross-sectional studies and in follow-up, other personality disorders are found to be equally at risk for depressions. This finding argues against a specific unity between borderline and affective disorders. BPD does not seem to be a "special case."

6. In family distribution and genetic studies, an excess of affective disorders was found among the relatives of the "mixed" (borderline plus affective) probands, but not among the relatives of "pure" borderlines. In other studies, the most frequent diagnosis among the latter is borderline personality itself.

7. The literature on biological markers is ambiguous. Dexamethasone Suppression Test nonsuppressors are frequent among severely depressed BPD, but this is not sufficient as only one paper shows DST abnormal responses among nondepressed BPD. Sleep EEG may be a more useful predictor of endogenous depression among borderlines than DST (Silk, Lohr, Shipley, Eiser, and Feinberg, 1988).

8. Borderline personality disorder per se is not responsive to tricyclic antidepressants (BPD plus major affective disorders are less responsive than affective disorders alone). Borderline personality disorder plus atypical depression has been successfully treated with MAOI. Experiments with drugs (e.g., Lucas et al., 1987), have not shown affectivelike responses.

9. The affiliation between BPD and affective disorders may have explanations other than biological ones. For example, comorbidity with affective disorders is less frequent when the borderline patient also presents antisocial features, perhaps due to externalized aggression (Perry, 1985).

My conclusion is that the hypothesis that borderline personality as a whole should be subsumed under affective disorders is not supported by the literature. The nature of the relationship has not been elucidated, but different writers (Kroll and Ogata, 1987; Soloff et al., 1987) have proposed that the apparent kinship may refer not to the group in toto, but to parts of it. There may be several subgroups, like BPD, who are relatively free of depressive symptomatology; BPD who present major depressions; BPD who suffer from "neurotic" depressions; and those who show BPD years after presenting a unipolar depression.

Obviously, different explanations would apply to each subgroup: the "neurotic" depressive subgroup is understandable as a consequence of the appalling problems and symptoms that plague the life of borderline patients; the group of BPDs plus major affective disorders contains the possible biological argument for unity. However, other subgroups were proposed on the basis of organic antecedents, cognitive style, and individual psychodynamics, and as we move into the next section to consider other reasons for heterogeneity or unity, it may be asked if we are contemplating the true complexity of psychiatric pathogenesis or a dissolution of the concept of BPD itself.

A NONSPECIFIC EXPRESSION OF SEVERITY?

Early in the decade, several studies failed to discriminate between inpatients with DIB borderline and nonborderline personality disorders (Kolb and Gunderson, 1980; Kroll et al., 1981, 1982). On the other hand, cases could be distinguished in at least three outpatient samples (Perry and Klerman, 1980; Sheehy et al., 1980; Koenigsberg et al., 1983). All these could be used to argue that when personality disorders are severe, they look or become "borderline."

However, Barrash et al. (1983), using cluster techniques, reanalyzed Kroll's inpatient samples, and distinguished between borderline and other personality disorders, indicating that rater or instrument bias could not be discounted in the existing papers. Also, it became apparent that the overlap between personality disorders was circumscribed. For instance, Pope et al. (1983) found that DSM-III BPD overlapped with histrionic personality disorder in women, and with antisocial behavior in men. It could be argued that: (1) these assessments ignored the multidimensional presentation of personality disorders; borderline features might also have been common among other, not examined, pathological personalities; (2) standardized interviews applying set criteria for all disorders were necessary; and (3) the analysis of some data was too broad; mean group scores may simply refer to differences in severity, not to substantive differences in the composition of the syndrome, and analysis of individual items was necessary.

First, I will reiterate the evidence for the existence of core characteristic features of BPD. New research has confirmed these findings. Nunberg, Hurt, Feldman, and Suh (1988) compared BPD patients with normal hospital staff who were adequately screened. The six most discriminative criteria were: impulsivity, interpersonal relationships, identity disturbance, chronic emptiness–boredom–loneliness, acting out, and affective disturbance. McGlashan (1988a) reported on the symptoms that distinguished BPD from schizotypal personality in various conditions. For BPD these were affective instability, unstable relationships, and impulsivity; for STP, odd communication, and suspiciousness–paranoia.

Instruments addressing the whole spectrum of Axis II diagnoses became available. Stangl, Pfohl, Zimmerman, Bowers, and Corenthal (1985) applied their own interview to a sample of 131 inpatients, of which 50 percent received Axis II diagnoses. There was satisfactory overall agreement ($k = >0.7$) for the presence of any personality disorder and for the presence of three individual types: borderline, histrionic, and dependent. Half of the personality disorder cases merited more than one designation, the most frequent combination being borderline plus histrionic. Thus, support was furnished for previous observations of a similar combination. Using only routinely collected data, Kass, Skodol, Charles, Spitzer, and Williams (1985) studied the intercorrelations between personality diagnoses. The majority of cases met criteria for more than one disorder, and the highest intercorrelations did not involve borderlines. The associations were circumscribed rather than random; the latter would have been expected if demonstrable borderline features were a nonspecific dimension of severity.

Research reported so far was conducted within a categorical framework. However, the analysis of results progressively imposed a dimensional model as used in clinical practice. The relationship between borderline and other personality disorders, reviewed elsewhere (Tarnopolsky and Berelowitz, 1987), may be summarized as follows: (1) an adequate number of individual diagnostic items of BPD can be reliably assessed; (2) they cluster in stable sets, confirmed statistically; (3) varieties do exist, defined by the severity or the completeness of the sets; (4) personality disorders may present in relatively pure forms or in combinations; (5) some combinations are more frequent than others (borderlines tend to associate with schizotypal [George and Soloff, 1986]) and with "dramatic" varieties); and (6) as other personality disorders equally meet criteria for more than one disorder, borderlines are not a special case.

Recent research further specifies these relationships. Some studies examined whether individual symptoms correlated as expected, that is, positively with the rest of the borderline set and minimally with other disorders' sets; other studies examined whether the global categories (borderline, antisocial, narcissistic, etc.) overlap with each other (Livesley and Jackson, 1986; Morey, 1988b; Pfohl, Coryell, Zimmerman, and Stangl, 1986; Widiger et al., 1986, 1987).

FOLLOW-UP

All borderline studies available are of treated cases. I have already noted McGlashan's (1986a) description of a typical hill-shaped course with a dome ten to twenty years after discharge, for borderline patients who had had intense residential psychoanalytic treatment. The Global Adaptation Scale score was similar to that found by Stone et al. (1987a). It is characteristic that improvement in social functioning occurs in spite of some persistent symptomatology. Recent work has identified predictors of discharge status and the effect of gender on long-term outcome (Bardenstein and McGlashan, 1988; Heinssen and McGlashan, 1988; McGlashan and Heinssen, 1988).

The question of BPD stability over time was addressed by several writers. It was shown that the original diagnosis was largely unchanged over short periods (2 years), medium periods (4–7 years), or long periods (average 15 years). The reported percentages of unchanged cases range from 44 percent or 50 percent to 60 to 90 percent for different diagnostic criteria (Pope et al., 1983; McGlashan, 1983a, 1986a; Barasch et al., 1985; Mitton and Links, 1988). The study by Barasch et al. is very illustrative. They compared borderline and other personality disorders at intake and after three years and found that most BPD and others retained their diagnoses. However, having started from the same level of severity, they exhibited a similar improvement over time. This data does not support the view that "borderline" was a diagnosis related to clinical worsening, although the numbers probably do not allow more refined cross-tabulations.

Developmental Issues

The search for specific etiologic factors leads to examining early personal and familial events suggested by psychoanalysis.

Bradley (1979) reviewed the charts of a small sample of borderline youngsters seen by herself in clinical consultations. She found that the borderline cases had experienced significantly more separations from mother before age five than two other groups, nonborderline psychiatric cases and delinquent nonpsychiatric controls. Bradley argued that these findings were consistent with Mahler's and Bowlby's views of a disruption in the early mother–infant relationship, resulting in character pathology.

Links, Steiner, Offord, and Eppel (1988b) interviewed a sample of borderline inpatients, and divided them into two groups, those with a confirmed DIB disorder and those with only borderline traits. The patients were questioned about their childhood upbringing, and a number of significant differences emerged. Confirmed borderlines, as compared with milder cases, exhibited higher frequency of separations longer than three months (age not specified), placements in foster homes, and a history of physical or sexual abuse. The predominant reason for the disruption of the original home was also different: separation or divorce versus death of spouse, in severe and milder cases respectively.

The next step, examining nonborderline controls, was provided by several preliminary communications. However, the control groups were not exclusively "Other Personality Disorders." Paris, Nowlis, and Brown (1988) found that borderlines had had significantly more separations and losses than major depressive controls. Herman, Perry, and van der Kolk (1988) investigated childhood trauma with in-depth interviews conducted by researchers blind to the clinical diagnoses. Abuse histories were more common among definite BPD, less frequent among subjects with borderline traits, and least common in the cases with other diagnoses (schizotypal, antisocial, bipolar II). Histories of trauma before age six were found almost exclusively in borderline subjects. Ogata, Silk, Goodrich, and Lohr (1988) reported that borderlines had a significantly higher rate of sexual abuse than manic depressives; and abuse was related to higher frequency of psychoticlike symptoms. Stone (1988c) showed that 19 percent of female borderlines but only 5 percent of female schizophrenics had an incest history; in general, borderlines of either sex had been more frequently abused by their parents than schizophrenic patients.

Using detailed charts, Gunderson, Kerr, and Englund (1980) reviewed the history of intact families that had a borderline offspring and compared them with families with schizophrenic or neurotic children. A high score of physical abuse was one of the features differentiating borderline from schizophrenic families, but the findings mainly describe a pattern of tight marital bonds that resulted in lack of attention and support, or neglect of the children.

Extending the study of psychoanalytic hypotheses with ordinary research techniques, Morris, Gunderson, and Zanarini (1986) examined whether transitional object use distinguishes BPD from other personality disorders, schizophrenia, and from normal controls. They found that borderlines are high transitional object users; other personality disorders are low users; and schizophrenics and normals are roughly in the middle.

Horton, Louy, and Cappolillo (1974) had reported the absence of transitional relatedness in an antisocial group. The transitional object concept is relatively complex and extends beyond the possession of a pet; these papers necessarily address what is most public and verifiable of it.

Perry and Cooper (1986) studied the characteristic defenses and conflicts of borderline versus antisocial and bipolar patients. By scoring videotaped interviews with moderate reliabilities, their statistical analysis suggested independent profiles for each group.

Thus the papers reviewed in this section support the validity of distinguishing BPD from controls and other personality disorders by discussing the characteristic, or at least more frequent, separations, traumata, styles of attachments, defenses, and conflicts. They also demonstrate the feasibility of studying objectively some psychoanalytic hypotheses, and the value of the to and fro between the two methods, although many problems are still to be solved. (See Gunderson [1986], for a discussion of this interface in borderline research.)

In summary, the validity of borderline personality is strengthened by the studies reviewed, which also support a multidimensional approach to personality disorders. Characteristic symptomatology, internal cohesion of the criteria, and a degree of distinctiveness from other personality disorders were reported. The diagnosis is relatively stable over time, and family studies show that BPD is the most frequent, or a predominant diagnosis, among the relatives of "pure" borderline probands.

The idea that demonstrating borderline features is a nonspecific dimension of severity is not supported by results obtained with the empirical/categorical type of research just reviewed. If the symptoms of BPD were a pathway common to other disorders, akin to the deterioration state of chronic schizophrenics but present among personality disorders, some of the following should have obtained: (1) it should have been clinically more apparent; (2) it should not start as early in life as BPD does, but should appear frequently when the original condition worsens; (3) change of diagnosis from other personality disorders to borderline should be more frequent, while, as we have seen, stability is common; (4) double diagnoses should be the rule in many grave cases (i.e., the original plus the "severe" borderline component); and (5) single diagnosis should be more common among outpatients or less disabled cases than among inpatients. Finally, we should not forget the data on outcome, which suggests that many borderlines get better, and seem to have a distinctive pattern of improvement without completely losing their typical symptomatology.

CONCLUSION

What do we need in terms of validity? A circumspect judgment of the firmness of a concept when it is subjected to repeated testing, or a permanent imprimatur of respectability, granted by an imaginary court? The literature has led me to conclude that the concept of borderline personality disorder has achieved, in many ways, the significance of other current psychiatric diagnoses. By this I mean that it provides a reasonable working description, assessed with acceptable objective criteria, allowing systematic investigation of its contents and of its limits, and is even useful in guiding clinical decisions (Tarnopolsky and Berelowitz, 1987). Further research and clinical experience may strain the concept to its limits or batter it to extinction, and then it will be modified or replaced; or it may show that it is robust enough to sustain further waves of investigations.

3.

The Longitudinal Profile of Borderline Personality Disorder: Contributions from the Chestnut Lodge Follow-Up Study

Thomas H. McGlashan, M.D.

INTRODUCTION

Contemporary nosology has helped to elevate "Borderline" from a pejorative disorder to a personality disorder. The articulation of *The Diagnostic and Statistical Manual of Mental Disorders* (DSM-III) operational diagnostic criteria almost a decade ago catalyzed a wealth of empirical research (American Psychiatric Association, 1980). This has clarified some questions, and raised many more. For example, it appears that borderline personality disorder (BPD) is a valid diagnostic entity with a relatively distinct clinical presentation, family pedigree, and long-term natural history. On the other hand, BPD also appears to be quite heterogeneous, with a high rate of comorbidity and a wide outcome variance. One of the more remarkable realizations to emerge from all this investigative activity has been the extent of our ignorance about the natural history of this disorder. Little to no data exist about what happens to men and women with BPD over time. Does the disorder persist? Is it expressed

53

differently in men versus women? Can it be considered a personality disorder (i.e., chronic, lifelong, and pervasive)? What questions have we answered? What do we have yet to discern?

This chapter attempts to summarize and integrate (for the first time) our findings about the long-term course of patients with operationally defined BPD (DSM-III or DSM-III-R [1987]) from the Chestnut Lodge follow-up study. The chapter is organized in three sections. First is a summary of our findings about the long-term course and outcome of BPD patients, including their longitudinal profiles across diagnosis (BPD versus other major Axis I diagnostic groups), and their profiles within diagnosis (male versus female BPD patients, prototypic courses, the effects of time). Second is a compilation of the BPD prognostic factors that we have identified to date and a prognostic scale that we offer for testing. Third is an integration of our findings concerning the comorbidity (diagnostic overlap) of BPD with Axis I disorders and other personality disorders. Finally, we offer some tentative speculations about the implications of these data for the nature of BPD.

THE LONG-TERM COURSE AND OUTCOME OF BPD

Our longitudinal study of BPD was part of a larger, comprehensive investigation of patients treated at Chestnut Lodge, a private psychiatric hospital located in Rockville, Maryland, that specializes in the long-term residential treatment of severely ill and treatment resistant patients, most of whom are either schizophrenic (S), affectively disordered, or borderline. The follow-up study's design and methodology has been elaborated in detail elsewhere (McGlashan, 1984a,b). Briefly, the study was retrospective and incorporated six elements to ensure methodologic rigor: operationally defined diagnostic criteria, adequate demographic/predictor characterization of samples, outcome measured multidimensionally, independent of follow-up data collection from the baseline diagnostic and demographic/predictor data collection, reliability testing of all measures, and bias testing of missing subject subsamples.

Included in the follow-up study were all patients discharged from the hospital between 1950 and 1975 and a smaller cohort of nondischarged inpatients from a comparable period. Selected were those without organic brain syndrome who were between sixteen and fifty-five years of age on admission and who were treated at Chestnut Lodge for a minimum of ninety days. Two realms of data were of interest: outcome and baseline diagnostic–demographic, the evaluations of which were conducted independently.

Outcome data were collected, following informed consent, an average of fifteen years after discharge (range, 2 to 32 years) via interviews with the subjects and/or significant others. The majority of interviews were by telephone and averaged two hours in length.

For baseline diagnostic/demographic assessment, the voluminous index hospitalization medical records were transposed onto a 25-page document called the Chart Abstract, from which each patient was rated on many demographic/predictor and sign and symptom variables. Using these abstracted clinical data, all patients were scored according to current diagnostic systems. The diagnosis of schizophrenia (S), bipolar affective disorder (BI), and unipolar affective disorder (UNI) was given to any subject satisfying DSM-III criteria. The diagnosis of borderline was given to any patient meeting either the DSM-III criteria for BPD or the Gunderson and Kolb (Gunderson and Kolb, 1978) criteria for borderline.

Outcome of BPD Patients Compared to Patients with Major Axis I Psychopathology

Over the years, more information about long-term outcome has been collected for S and UNI than for any other major mental illness. Accordingly, in order to place BPD outcome within a larger and well-informed perspective, we first compared our BPD patients to patients from the follow-up study with S and UNI (McGlashan, 1986a).

Figure 3.1 schematically summarizes the frequency distribution of the global functioning scores for each of these three

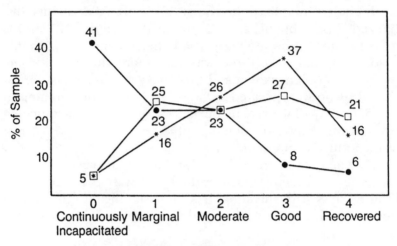

Clinical Global Functioning Score
FIGURE 3.1
Borderline Personality Disorder and Comparison Groups
Frequencies of Global Functioning Since Discharge

groups. The meaning of each scale point can be approximated as follows. A score of 0 or "chronic" meant that, on the average, the patient spent three-quarters of the follow-up period institutionalized and was virtually unemployed, socially isolated, and symptomatic the entire time. A patient scoring 1 or "marginal" was likely to spend about one-quarter of the follow-up period in sheltered settings, work about one-fifth of the time, experience some role-specific social contacts, and cope with symptomatic expressions of illness for about three-quarters of the period. A patient scoring 2 or "moderate" spent a small amount of follow-up time in structured settings, worked more than half of the time, had friends but saw them infrequently, and experienced some time free of symptoms. A patient scoring 3 or "good" was seldom rehospitalized and never for lengthy periods, was employed and socially active most of the time, and remained symptom free for the majority of the follow-up period. A patient scoring 4 or "recovered" was similar to "good" on these dimensions only better. Furthermore, such patients were usually capable of stable intimacy and/or generativity in relationships.

Figure 3.1 highlights the differences between the diagnostic groups, especially S on the one hand and UNI and BPD on the other. Taking a global score of 2 or more as representing a reasonable outcome, only one-third of the S patients reached such a state compared with about three-fourths of the UNI patients and about four-fifths of the BPD patients. More UNI patients were chronically compromised in comparison with BPD patients, but more also reached a state of complete recovery. A plurality of BPD patients rated a good outcome, but lingering problems, mostly of a characterologic nature, prevented them from achieving recovery more frequently.

Focusing on the BPD cohort, the following clinical profile emerged. Consistent with other studies of clinical populations, the majority of our BPD patients were single and female. Onset of disorder was usually in late adolescence with illness escalating through the twenties. Onset was seldom precipitated by specific stress but appeared more in the nature of a pattern change in response to altered developmental demands. Prior to first psychiatric contact, BPD patients were likely to be at least moderately impaired in all adaptive spheres: social, sexual, and instrumental. First treatment contact occurred in the third decade, as with S patients but not as with UNI patients. Like most patients referred to Chestnut Lodge, the BPD cohort was chronically ill and had experienced many prior treatment exposures without remarkable success. For the BPD patients, however, this was more likely to be in the form of outpatient psychosocial treatment as opposed to inpatient and somatic treatments, which were more usual for the patients with psychosis. Also, in keeping with their classification as having Axis II personality disorders, our BPD patients were less ill at their index (Chestnut Lodge) admission in the nature and degree of productive symptomatology.

Although treated residentially without time limitations, the BPD patients at Chestnut Lodge did not tend to become institutionalized. Their inpatient time was the shortest of the diagnostic groups and they were among the least likely to require transfer to other institutions. They were also far less passive and compliant (traits characteristic of the "institutionalized patient") as evidenced by a high rate of signing out of the hospital against medical advice.

At follow-up, the BPD patients were doing well in their basic living situations. Most lived autonomously, many with intimate partners, and some with children. They were similar to the UNI patients in this arena and strikingly divergent from the S patients.

The hospitalizations required by some of the BPD patients after Chestnut Lodge were frequently brief and crisis oriented. Although medication was not used extensively after discharge, psychosocial outpatient treatments (usually individual or group psychotherapy) was very common, with nearly half of the patients requesting or requiring further therapeutic support.

Instrumentally, BPD patients proved quite productive in terms of both amount and quality of work and they generally had accumulated good work records. In fact, many appeared to work diligently despite an otherwise dismal existence. Also, BPD patients scored a mean of 2.9 on the Hollingshead scale of occupational level (Hollingshead, 1952) at follow-up, indicating jobs equivalent to administrative managers, small-business owners, minor professionals, and so on. This may simply reflect good baseline socioeconomic status, but the BPD patients were able to make productive use of such resources.

One of the cornerstones of BPD psychopathology rests in the area of relationships, which tend to be stormy, conflict-ridden, and labile in intensity. Therefore, their outcome in the social sphere was of particular interest. At follow-up, the Chestnut Lodge BPD patients proved to be moderately active socially. Here, however, the distribution of scores was bimodal. One group was functioning well and had managed to create and maintain meaningful relationships with stability over time. They further clustered roughly into three subgroups: good social but no intimate relations; partial intimate but no generative relations; and intact intimate and generative relations. The other bimodal cluster of patients, however, essentially dealt with this problematic area by studious avoidance of relationships. They appeared to be people who had concluded that their emotional equilibrium required abstinence in object relations.

Overall, these patients' characteristic labile relationships appeared with time to resolve in one or the other direction; that is, either steadily social or regularly distant.

Symptomatically, most BPD patients demonstrated distinct evidence of persisting psychopathology. They often managed to compartmentalize and effectively prevent their symptoms from intruding on their instrumental capacities, but they were less successful in sequestering conflicts from the social sphere. The nature of their continuing psychopathology was consistent with the signs and symptoms leading to the initial diagnosis. Depressive signs and symptoms were very common, as was substance abuse.

In summary, we found our patients with BPD doing quite well on the whole. The findings were at variance with a few previous follow-up reports of adult borderline patients studied prior to the advent of DSM-III operational diagnostic criteria (Hoch, Cattell, Strahl, and Pennes, 1962; Grinker, Werble, and Drye, 1968; Werble, 1970; Gunderson, Carpenter, and Strauss, 1975; Carpenter and Gunderson, 1977; Carpenter, Gunderson, and Strauss, 1977) and one prior follow-up report which used these criteria but which assessed the patients over a shorter follow-up period of four to seven years (Pope, Jonas, Hudson, Cohen, and Gunderson, 1983). Three long-term follow-up studies (10–22 years) of DSM-III-diagnosed BPD patients were conducted contemporaneously with ours (Plakun, Burkhardt, and Muller, 1986; Paris, Brown, and Nowlis, 1987; Stone, 1987; Stone, Hurt, and Stone, 1987b). These findings basically replicated ours and strongly suggested that the thrust toward long-term improvement noted in our BPD patients was not a spurious finding unique to Chestnut Lodge's population.

Profiles of Outcome Within the BPD Sample by Gender and Follow-up Length

We were also interested in whether outcome varied with time after discharge. Previous analyses demonstrated this not to be the case for our S and UNI cohorts (McGlashan, 1984b). That is, outcome scores for S and UNI patients interviewed shortly

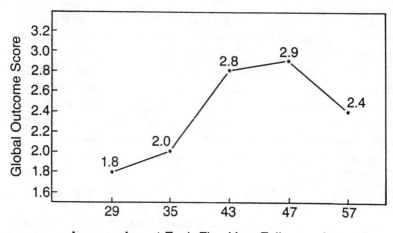

Average Age at Each Five-Year Follow-up Interval
FIGURE 3.2
Borderline Personality Disorder
Global Outcome by Follow-Up Age and Interval

after discharge were basically equivalent to scores for S and UNI patients followed up many years after discharge. In contrast, the outcome scores for the BPD patients varied significantly with time postdischarge. As illustrated in Figure 3.2, their global outcome profile traced an inverted U with the apogee occurring in the second postdischarge decade when the average subject was in his or her forties (McGlashan, 1986a).

We also found, upon closer scrutiny, that male and female BPD patients differed in several aspects of their clinical profiles. This, plus the variability in functioning over time, prompted an investigation into the long-term natural history of BPD by gender (Bardenstein and McGlashan, 1988). We divided the follow-up period into three time intervals: zero to nine years, ten to nineteen years, and twenty or more years postdischarge, and compared our male and female BPD patients across follow-up interval and across gender.

Our principal findings were as follows. At baseline (Chestnut Lodge admission), more female BPD patients were married and they related better heterosexually than the males. Their manifest illness presented with more depressive symptoms and self-destructive behaviors. The male BPD patients, on the other hand, were more antisocial and uncooperative (AMA discharges). Over the follow-up intervals, the female BPD patients remained married more frequently, but the male BPD patients proved to be consistently more active socially. Both male and female BPD patients advanced occupationally, symptomatically, and globally with time. The female BPD cohort in the third follow-up interval (20 or more years) fell off in their symptomatic and global functioning, but this sample was small (N = 9) and likely biased by cohort effects (e.g., their *baseline* functioning on several of these domains was significantly inferior to start with). Their representativeness, therefore, remains in question. Finally, when outcome was good, no gender differences emerged. When outcome was bad, however, the poor outcome female patients were more self-damaging at baseline *and* follow-up and the poor outcome male patients were more antisocial at baseline and prone to alcohol abuse at follow-up.

Case Illustrations

The following two BPD cases, one female patient with a moderate outcome and one male patient with a good outcome, both from the third follow-up interval, illustrate some of the above patterns.

Ms. Y.

Ms. Y. was a thirty-five-year-old, married female admitted to Chestnut Lodge at a time when the BPD diagnosis was uncommon. She was given a diagnosis then of chronic paranoid state, but upon review of her record, she easily achieved the borderline category by DSM-III criteria.

When Ms. Y. was sixteen, her father died, after which she periodically starved herself, became anxious, and had difficulty concentrating. While active socially, she was described as unpredictably snobbish with her friends. Shortly after graduating from college she met her future husband. Her mother moved in with them after they were married.

Ms. Y. was embarrassed by and avoided sexual intercourse as much as possible. At age twenty-eight, after three years of unhappy marriage, Ms. Y. felt irritable, depressed, inadequate, and inferior. She criticized her husband constantly, and was finally hospitalized for marked lability of mood. During her stay, she discovered she was pregnant.

After discharge, Ms. Y.'s relationship with her husband deteriorated. She began experiencing homosexual feelings along with periods of depression and hostility. She developed frequent, violent temper outbursts, often directed toward her mother or toward her young son whom she whipped and fantasized destroying. After the delivery of her second child, a daughter, Ms. Y. behaved suicidally, developed somatic complaints, and neglected her appearance. At age thirty-five she was admitted to a psychiatric hospital and transferred to Chestnut Lodge where she was described as labile in mood, critical, overweight, and somatically preoccupied. Staff found her manipulative and splitting.

After many years of inpatient and day patient treatment, Ms. Y. was discharged from Chestnut Lodge with medical advice. During her stay, she had separated from her husband and her mother had died. Upon leaving the hospital, Ms. Y. passed a civil service examination and worked full time supporting herself completely thereafter. She became a placement specialist for the unemployed and received awards for her work. Over the years Ms. Y. had two prolonged sexual affairs, one with a married man and the other with a man ten years her junior. She did not feel close to her daughter and avoided her son whom she suspected was gay.

At follow-up Ms. Y. lived alone in an apartment, socialized rarely, and had to struggle just to attend church on Sunday mornings. She had one or two casual friends whom she visited monthly and on holidays. Ms. Y. was never rehospitalized, but she had engaged continuously in intensive psychotherapy with four successive therapists. She also took medication for depression and somatic complaints. She experienced suicidal ideation and made several mild, "passive" attempts. She had mild difficulty with drinking and overeating. She had severe phobias about crossing bridges, riding elevators, and other outside activities to the extent that she was often unable to attend psychotherapy. She felt resigned to being the victim of a bad life. She received a global functioning score of 2 or moderate.

Mr. Z.

Mr. Z., a twenty-one-year-old, single male, was admitted to Chestnut Lodge with a clinical diagnosis of schizophrenic reaction, other and unspecified. Onset of difficulties occurred when he was in college, marked by falling grades, anxiety, and difficulty concentrating. Mr. Z. was socially isolated and he alienated peers with his rudeness and arrogant intellectualizing. After being evicted from the dormitory suite, he lived alone. He never dated nor participated in school activities.

Mr. Z. began outpatient psychotherapy, but after the first of three suicide attempts at age nineteen, he had to be hospitalized. Eight hospitalizations followed, in between which he became more and more anxious and nonfunctional. At index hospitalization, Mr. Z. was described as unrealistically demanding, rejecting, and unable to tolerate criticism or change. He was often depressed, suicidal, and complained of loneliness. Socially, he was initially cold, superficial, and suspicious. Mr. Z. was also prone to anxiety attacks and was intensely disturbed by therapy.

After thirty months of treatment, Mr. Z. was discharged from Chestnut Lodge while absent without leave (AWOL). Thereafter, he traveled for six months, allegedly to find jobs, but found none. He returned to the Rockville area to visit staff and patients at Chestnut Lodge. After tutoring math at a local university for two years, he returned home and entered college full time. He engaged in heavy marijuana smoking and was arrested in a drug raid after three semesters of college. He was convicted but not jailed. Mr. Z. left school and worked odd jobs while living at home. He eventually resumed his education and received a bachelor's degree in physics and math. Mr. Z. subsequently worked for several electronics firms, started an unsuccessful consulting firm, and finally accepted a high-paying job with a computer company.

At follow-up, Mr. Z. was single and living alone. He dated occasionally, but not seriously. He saw people regularly but his relationships were superficial. Mr. Z. visited his parents monthly. No problems with drug or alcohol abuse were present. Mr. Z. complained of slight depression most of the time, but he was never rehospitalized. He had received no psychiatric treatment since his discharge from Chestnut Lodge. He received a global functioning score of 3 or good.

Prototypic Longitudinal Profile: The Female Borderline Patient

Based on our sample analyses and prototypic cases (such as those above), the natural history of our residentially treated female borderline patient can be described as follows (Bardenstein and McGlashan, 1988). Her premorbid and morbid functioning are characterized by multiple symptoms, especially depression and unstable marital/heterosexual relationships. In the first phase postdischarge, there is a continuation of these symptoms, often exacerbated by the loss of hospital structure and support. More severe symptomatic episodes seem to be episodic, occasionally warranting further, briefer hospitalizations.

The BPD female, at least from this era, seeks stability and need satisfaction in intimate relationships. She seems capable of being productive so long as she has an intact and stable relationship. As she begins to develop occupationally in the second decade postdischarge, hospitalization and/or outpatient treatment becomes less necessary. Her symptoms diminish in severity but can still be episodically severe. Prescription drugs for somatic complaints replace self-medication with alcohol or with illicit drugs.

With advancing age, the BPD woman may become more symptomatic again, especially if she loses her stable relationships through divorce or death. While her instrumental competence continues to develop, her interpersonal contacts dwindle. Outpatient treatment and work are the predominant sources of stability, continuity, structure, and social contact.

The need for involvement in unstable heterosexual relationships is present in most cases and appears to play an important role in her adjustment. In contrast to the outcome of the schizophrenic woman in the follow-up study, where marriage is associated with better socialization and occupational functioning (McGlashan and Bardenstein, 1990), marriage for the borderline woman more often than not provides an arena for the enactment of psychopathology. Even when married, the borderline woman frequently remains socially isolated, with superficial and infrequent contact with friends. Her regressive neediness and dependency precludes an ability to nurture or care for others, and she frequently has estranged relationships with her children.

Prototypic Longitudinal Profile: The Male Borderline Patient

Our residentially treated male BPD patient's postdischarge profile differed from that of our BPD female in both pattern and detail. He usually leaves the institution against medical advice (AMA). His initial period after discharge is characterized by continuing typical symptoms and trouble with the law. The borderline male maintains little contact with mental health professionals or institutions. He works at various jobs somewhat nomadically. He remains single, lives alone, and socializes frequently but superficially. Major antisocial symptoms appear to diminish in intensity, but not the sense of isolation or lack of direction seen premorbidly.

The second phase after hospitalization includes locking into an occupational identity and achieving a stable income and sense of competency. Mild depression may continue, but the sense of isolation is ameliorated by structured interpersonal contacts through work. The borderline man clearly relies more on institutional than on intimate interpersonal relationships for gratification and structure.

In the third phase after hospitalization, the borderline man consolidates and improves upon his career and enjoys the greater activity that ensues. He tolerates and even seeks longer relationships and may consider marriage. He develops further support systems through other institutional affiliations such as religious membership or Alcoholics Anonymous (AA). In this way, he can covertly gratify anaclitic needs while remaining comfortably distant from intimacy.

Comment on the Profiles

Since we lacked a normal control sample, we could not address the degree to which our findings reflected "normal" aging trends. Nevertheless, the gender-specific interactions of BPD pathology with time parallels observations of the normal population from this historical time period (1950–1975); specifically, men rely more on work for satisfaction while women rely more on the affective aspects of relationships (Cleary and Mechanic, 1983). The influence of such cultural parameters may have been critical given the era in which our sample lived. Around the middle of this century, women had less opportunity and/or encouragement to live independently and to develop careers. There was social pressure to get married and to be supported by a man. This may account for much of the borderline woman's more limited and vulnerable interpersonal adjustment.

Methodologic artifact may limit inferences drawn from the study. We did not track changes across time in the same individual, nor did we use the same rating scales as repeated measures. The natural history profiles are composites of individuals in different follow-up intervals rather than narratives of the same individual across follow-up intervals. As such, many of our results may stem from sample biasing, especially cohort effects. Furthermore, our male borderline patients may have been skewed toward better functioning because their more violent, alcoholic, antisocial, and criminal counterparts were incarcerated rather than hospitalized. While the borderline men and women did not differ in severity of illness at admission, the possibility that the most seriously disturbed borderline men were screened out at admission qualifies our findings.

BPD PROGNOSTIC FACTORS

While the nosologic validity of BPD seems more assured, it remains a very heterogeneous entity. Patients labeled borderline have variable clinical presentations, functional incapacities, and longitudinal outcomes. This variability in disorder prognosis limits the utility of the borderline concept for treatment planning. Efforts to reduce this heterogeneity via the identification of key prognostic dimensions could greatly enhance the clinical relevance of BPD. The following section summarizes our efforts in these directions using the follow-up study BPD sample.

BPD Predictors of Outcome

Predictors aim at providing some notion about subsequent course. They may be factors predisposing to illness (etiologic), factors affecting the course of illness (environmental and treatment), or factors otherwise correlated with various outcomes (prognostic). From the follow-up study, our baseline assessments of each patient included ratings of multiple ($N = 153$) potential clinical predictors. This universe of predictors could be divided roughly into four classes: (1) background variables (e.g., demography, family characteristics, pregnancy, birth, and perinatal complications, central nervous system [CNS] compromise); (2) premorbid variables (e.g., social, sexual, and instrumental functioning during infancy, childhood, and adolescence and/or early adulthood); (3) manifest illness variables (e.g., onset of illness, manifest signs and symptoms, and diagnosis); (4) course of illness variables (e.g., length and pattern of illness, and response to treatment).

Using a variety of multivariate analytic techniques, these variables were tested as predictors (McGlashan, 1985). Three variables emerged most frequently and consistently as predictors of global outcome: IQ, affective instability, and length of previous hospitalizations. Higher IQ was associated with better global outcome. The mean IQ for the poor global outcome group was 112 and for the good global outcome group was 120. The relationship between superior intellectual endowment and better outcome held no surprise, although such a relationship was not found for our sample of schizophrenic patients. Affective instability involves marked shifts from normal mood to depression, irritability, or anxiety over brief periods of time (hours, rarely more than a few days). It was present in 53 percent of the poor outcome subjects compared to only 16 percent of the good outcome patients. Length of previous hospitalizations was the third strong predictor of global outcome. Prior to index admission, the poor outcome group averaged ten months in other institutions whereas the good outcome group averaged exactly one-half that amount of time. Established illness or chronicity, therefore, emerged as a strong predictor. This is consistent with similar findings from studies with schizophrenic populations (McGlashan, 1986b).

Several more variables emerged as predictive when multi-dimensional outcome was considered (hospitalization, work functioning, social functioning, intimate relations, symptomatology, and global functioning). Among the characteristics associated with better outcome were the following.

1. Male gender. Male BPD patients did better in general although, as noted above, this may represent sampling artifact deriving from differential hospital admission policies for male versus female BPD patients.

2. Less family history of substance abuse. Although this variable included any and all forms of chemical abuse, alcohol was the identified substance in the vast majority of cases. Substance abuse was the only personality disorder criterion that could be rated reliably from the family history records, making it the only variable reflecting character pathology in the family.

3. Better premorbid heterosexual functioning. Superior outcomes were associated with "better" premorbid heterosexual

functioning, that is, regular (not promiscuous) dating, marriage, or living with a sexual partner for an extended time.

4. Absence of magical thinking. Under the dimension of psychopathology, magical thinking (superstitiousness, clairvoyance, telepathy, sixth sense, "others can feel my feelings") emerged as important. It constitutes one of the DSM-III symptom criteria for STP. Its presence in patients with BPD, therefore, suggests concomitant schizotypal traits. Since follow-up demonstrated an overall poorer outcome in patients with STP compared to patients with BPD (McGlashan, 1986c), it was not surprising that the presence of a criterion symptom for STP carried negative prognostic valence.

5. Presence of felt affect. These variables relating to affective symptoms in the manifest illness proved predictive: dysphoria and elation were predictive of good outcome and inadequate affect was predictive of poor outcome. Dysphoria was defined as chronic feelings of dysphoria and anhedonia, emptiness or loneliness (i.e., clearly distressing subjective affects). Elation meant essentially the opposite, that is, the presence of euphoria or pleasurable affects. Both may have been related to good outcome insofar as they reflected the presence of an intact capacity for hedonic experience, discrimination, and motivation. This was further suggested by the association of poorer outcomes with inadequate affect, which may have represented the absence of hedonic capacity. That is, inadequate affect was defined in this study as an emotional life that was rigid, dull, and minimally reactive to stimulations of any strength. This triad of predictive symptoms suggests that the ability to experience pleasure and to tolerate psychological pain (unpleasure) may be as important to health and strength in patients with BPD as it is in patients with S (McGlashan, 1984b).

6. Control of aggression (absence of devaluation, manipulation, and hostility) in relationships. Devaluation, manipulation, and hostility refers to the nature of the patient's object relations. The variable derives from the Gunderson and Kolb (1978) criteria for BPD and is defined as follows: the patient has recurrent problems with devaluation (discredits or ignores other's strengths and personal significance); or manipulation (uses covert ways to control and gain support from others);

or hostility (repeatedly and knowingly hurts others) in close relationships. In essence, the dimension rates the borderline patient's ability to contain ambivalence in attachments or to control aggression in significant relationships. The more this could be done, the better the outcome and vice versa.

7. Minimal evidence of chronicity. The final two strong predictors related to illness course. Greater length of index hospitalization and transfer to another institution rather than discharge from Chestnut Lodge were both associated with poorer outcomes. Again, this held no surprise and these findings basically extended the earlier discussed (similar) predictive value of length of previous hospitalization.

BPD Prognostic Scale

In another study aiming to maximize the clinical utility of these predictors (McGlashan, 1988b), we used many of the above variables to create a "prognostic scale" for our BPD female patients (we could not construct a similar scale for the male patients because their outcome possessed too little variance). We collected a total of six variables which could be dichotomized as present/absent (or 1/0: a score of 1 meaning good prognosis, and a score of 0 meaning poor prognosis). This gave us a scale with scores ranging from 0 to 6. The scale is outlined in Table 3.1. The ability of this scale to predict global outcome is detailed in Table 3.2, a "contingency table" which cross-tabulates the patients' prognostic scale scores and global outcome scores. The italic numbers represent the "conditional probabilities" of different global outcomes given various prognostic scale scores. For example, a prognostic score between 0 and 2 was associated with a 67 percent chance of a poor (0, 1) global outcome, whereas a prognostic score of 5 or 6 was associated with a 91 percent chance of a good (3, 4) global outcome.

Because the population of patients used for this contingency table was the same population from which the scale was derived, the scale itself remains to be tested and validated with independent samples. At this point it represents but a first approximation.

TABLE 3.1
Prognostic Scale for Borderline Personality Disorder
Noncomorbid Inpatient Females
(N = 46)

1. Quality of social relations within 1 year prior to admission

   Score 1 if at least one or more moderately close relationships.
   Score 0 if at most one or more rather superficial relationships.

2. Affective instability: Marked shifts from normal mood to depression, irritability, or anxiety, usually lasting a few hours and only rarely more than a few days, with a return to normal mood.

   Score 1 if absent.
   Score 0 if present.

3. Splitting: Past treatment relations ever involved staff splitting, forming "special" relationships, or evoking noteworthy countertransference problems by a therapist.

   Score 1 if absent.
   Score 0 if present.

4. Devaluation: Devaluation, manipulation, and hostility recur in close relationships.

   Score 1 if absent.
   Score 0 if present.

5. Magical thinking: Examples are superstitiousness, clairvoyance, telepathy, "sixth sense," "others can feel my feelings."

   Score 1 if absent.
   Score 0 if present.

6. Depressed thinking: Diminished ability to think or concentrate such as slowed thinking or indecisiveness not associated with marked loosening of associations or incoherence.

   Score 1 if absent.
   Score 0 if present.

TABLE 3.2
Conditional Probability of Global Outcome
Noncomorbid Inpatient Borderline Personality Disordered Females
(N = 46)

		Poor 0, 1	Moderate 2	Good 3, 4	
	0–2	6	2	1	9
		.67	.22	.11	20%
Prognostic Scale Score	3, 4	5	12	8	25
		.20	.48	.32	54%
	5, 6	0	1	11	12
		.00	.09	.91	26%
		11 24%	15 33%	20 44%	46 100%

To our knowledge, our findings represent the only systematic empirical prognostic data thus far generated for BPD. Other more anecdoted reports do exist, however. Stone (1988a), for example, found good outcome among the BPD patients with high artistic talent, exceptional attractiveness (females), and high IQ. He found below average outcomes among patients with a history of rape (female) and/or parental brutality. He also found poor outcome among BPD patients with comorbid antisocial and schizotypal personality disorders. This leads us into the issue of disorder comorbidity, to which we now turn.

BPD COMORBIDITY

Comorbidity refers to the coexistence of more than one psychiatric disorder in the same patient. Many BPD patients, for example, also suffer from depression, substance abuse, agoraphobia, schizotypal personality disorder (STP), and so on. Such diagnostic overlap can have a profound effect upon the clinical presentation, morbidity, treatment responsiveness, and natural history of patients with BPD. Our investigations included co-morbidity of BPD with both Axis I and Axis II disorders. Our finding at each interface will be integrated.

BPD Comorbidity with Psychotic and Mood Disorders

From the beginning, the concept of comorbidity was implicit in the term *borderline* which suggested an entity hovering between (at least) two syndromes (McGlashan, 1983a). Its first use, for example, was to describe patients who were "borderline psychotic," that is, not overly clinically psychotic, but suffering from a similar but milder, preclinical, genetically linked, or variant form of psychosis. Historically, borderline was initially understood this way as "borderline schizophrenia." This implicated the syndrome as a variant of S and placed it within the realm of the schizophrenic group of disorders.

Later, a second use of the term emerged to describe a cohort of personality organization behaviors that, although ranging in domain of severity between neurosis and psychosis, nevertheless represented a syndrome unto itself. This use flourished within psychoanalytic milieux and led to efforts to define and delineate borderline as a unique psychopathologic entity without close affiliation with other psychosyndromes. This divergence of meanings led, in part, to the DSM-III subdivision of borderline into schizotypal personality disorder (STP) and borderline personality disorder (BPD).

The Chestnut Lodge follow-up study offered the first longitudinal data supporting the DSM-III division. Information was available about the long-term clinical profiles of four key diagnostic groups: BPD, STP, S, and UNI. Analyses of diagnostic overlap at index admission, diagnostic change over the follow-up period, and comparative long-term functional outcome between our borderline and psychotic samples supported the hypothesis that STP was a variant of S and suggested an affiliation of BPD with affective disorder (McGlashan, 1983a). Our findings concerning the comorbidity of BPD with S and STP on the one hand, and of BPD with UNI on the other are summarized below.

BPD with the Schizophrenic Spectrum (S and STP)

To study the border between BPD and the schizophrenic spectrum, we tracked the long-term course of six nonoverlapping samples, three of which were "pure," BPD, STP, and S, and three of which were mixed or comorbid, BPD/STP, BPD/STP/ S, and STP/S (McGlashan, 1986c). Their sum global outcome scores are illustrated in Figure 3.3. The sum global represents the added scores of four outcome dimensions: further hospitalization, symptomatology, work functioning, and social functioning during the entire follow-up period. The scores could range from 0 (poor) to 16 (good). On this and other outcome measures (not shown in the figure), the S cohort was clearly the worst and the BPD cohort was clearly the best. The STP/S sample scored closer to S, and the BPD/STP sample scored closer to BPD. The BPD/STP/S group was the best of the three Axis I comparison groups but worse than Axis II. The STP group, on the other hand, was the worst of the three Axis II comparison groups, but better than Axis I.

Borderline personality disorder and STP frequently overlapped diagnostically. From the perspective of long-term outcome, however, the comorbid BPD/STP syndrome "behaved" much more like BPD than STP. This was particularly apparent in the social sphere. At follow-up, the STP patients were loners like the S patients, but more capable than the latter of forming some viable, albeit detached relationships. Generally, among the Axis II groups, the BPD cohort could make friends, good friends, and lovers; the STP cohort could make none of these; and the BPD/STP cohort could make friends and good friends, but not lovers. Thus, there seemed to exist an interpersonal "object seeking" factor associated with BPD that appeared to be relatively powerful because, as the BPD/STP/S cohort showed, it persisted despite the S process and contributed to a better social outcome in patients with the latter affliction.

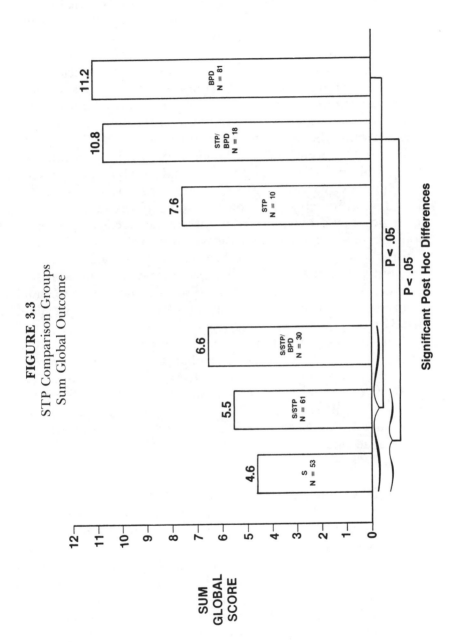

FIGURE 3.3
STP Comparison Groups
Sum Global Outcome

This BPD object seeking factor may help to explain our unexpected finding among the three Axis I S comparison groups. The pure S group had superior premorbid functioning compared with the BPD/STP/S and STP/S cohorts, yet emerged inferior to them on most outcome dimensions (especially in comparison with the BPD/STP/S cohort). That is, the worst Axis I outcomes were in the S patients without comorbid borderline disorders and with decent premorbid functioning, whereas, paradoxically, the best Axis I outcomes were in the S patients with "double disorders" and poorer premobid functioning. This result may suggest that S associated with STP and BPD is somehow less virulent, or that rigidly structured personality disorders with their stereotypic reaction patterns and defensive strategies may prove more resistant to S personality deterioration. Finally, this result may derive from differential positive natural history or treatment effects on the personality disorder part but not on the S part of these comorbid syndromes. If so, then cohorts of S with personality disorders have more to gain from time and/or treatment, a differential advantage that ultimately emerges over the long term.

In summary, the long-term clinical profile of comorbid BPD and STP ranges in between that of more compromised STP and less compromised BPD. Overall, however, it is closer to the latter disorder. A similar shift in a healthier direction occurs when BPD is "added" to S. This finding calls into question our a priori assumptions that two disorders are invariably worse than one.

BPD with the Affective Spectrum (UNI)

Our BPD and S cohorts defined clearly different longitudinal profiles (McGlashan, 1986a), thus strongly implying they are different psychopathologic entities. The similarity in outcomes between our BPD and UNI cohorts, on the other hand, imply an affiliation. This similarity does not, however, demonstrate such a relationship. Guze (1975) observed that considerable differences in course and outcome strongly call into question any assumption of similarity between syndromes. It does not follow, however, that strong similarities in course and outcome negate an assumption of differences between syndromes. It remains plausible that BPD and UNI are different entities that happen to generate similar long-term outcomes.

We looked closer at the borderline/affective disorder interface by tracking and comparing the longitudinal profiles of three follow-up study patient groups defined largely by DSM-III: "pure" UNI, "pure" BPD, and a comorbid BPD/UNI cohort (McGlashan, 1987a).

Psychopathologically, although some UNI patients presented with psychotic symptoms (hallucinations and delusions), BPD/UNI patients never did, thus supporting the shibboleth that character pathology substitutes for or protects against psychotic symptom formation. Age of onset occurred in the late teens for BPD and in the late twenties for UNI. Borderline personality disorder comorbidity accelerated onset among patients with UNI, and UNI comorbidity delayed onset among patients with BPD, resulting in an age of onset for BPD/UNI midway between the two noncomorbid syndromes.

At outcome, the three cohorts were strikingly similar; only three variables (among approximately three dozen) discriminated them, and all at marginal levels of significance. They were (1) alcohol abuse (best to worse pattern: UNI, BPD/UNI, BPD); (2) follow-up psychiatric treatment of any kind (lower to higher percent in treatment: UNI, BPD, BPD/UNI); and (3) suicide rate (BPD = 2%, UNI = 8%, BPD/UNI = 16%).

Results of follow-up diagnostic stability and change found that of the baseline "pure" BPD cohort, 72 percent retained a BPD diagnosis at follow-up and 6 percent changed to affective disorder (BI or UNI). The BPD/UNI cohort follow-up diagnoses, as expected, were divided between affective disorder (30%) and BPD (45%). Unexpectedly, "pure" UNI cohort was far less diagnostically stable; only 32 percent retained a follow-up diagnosis of affective disorder whereas 36 percent changed diagnosis to BPD.

In summary, comorbid BPD/UNI, in comparison with UNI, developed earlier, seldom presented with psychotic symptoms, and resulted in more suicide, substance abuse, and psychiatric treatment use over the long-term course. Comorbid

BPD/UNI, in comparison to BPD, developed later and resulted in more suicide and psychiatric treatment use over the long term. Longitudinal diagnostic assessment found BPD to be stable, UNI to be unstable, and BPD/UNI to reflect its constituent comorbidity.

These data are offered with several caveats. Overall, our comparison cohorts registered very comparable long-term functional outcomes, a similarity strongly suggesting that affiliation between UNI and BPD cannot be ruled out. Our findings regarding diagnostic stability and change, however, contest the assertion that BPD is a variant of UNI. The high rate of diagnostic change from UNI to BPD, and the paucity of long-term functional outcome differences, may reflect sampling effects; that is, our UNI comparison cohort may not have been free of character pathology and/or our BPD comparison cohort may not have been free of affective pathology. The lack of differences at outcome also suggests that time somehow homogenizes the psychopathologic distinctions between UNI and BPD.

What do comorbid effects have to say about the relationship between UNI and BPD? Overall, findings to date suggest that the answers are likely to be more complex than anticipated; sometimes the syndromes are alike and sometimes they are different. The following speculations are suggested by the data. Borderline personality disorder and UNI are alike in that symptom formation for both is driven by affective disregulation. The differences, however, reside in the manner by which this disregulation becomes manifest. In UNI it finds expression in disorders of affect intensity and baseline level. In BPD it finds expression in disorders of affect quality and baseline stability. The classical view elaborates upon these distinctions. Symptom formation in affective disorder is regarded as more autoplastic in nature, involving "internal" alterations of experienced affect and cognition. Such changes are often episodic, field independent, and consciously regarded as personally alien or dystonic. Symptom formation in BPD, on the other hand, is considered more alloplastic, involving externally directed alterations in impulse control and action patterns. Such changes are usually habitual, field dependent, and consciously regarded as willed and personally syntonic.

Studies of comorbidity, however, challenge these distinctions by documenting a remarkable degree of symptom substitution between these disorders over time. In our study this was seen indirectly in their similar long-term outcomes and directly in a high frequency of diagnostic change from baseline to follow-up. This change occurred in both directions, from BPD to UNI and from UNI to BPD. The latter was especially common and surprising because, to our knowledge, diagnostic instability in the UNI syndrome has not been studied and/or reported.

These findings suggest that we are dealing with highly fluid and heterogeneous entities among which we must also include the more "classical" affection disorders. Our follow-up diagnostic data, in fact, question the validity of UNI as a distinct, homogeneous syndrome. In recent times, many forms of psychopathology, in addition to BPD, have been labeled as "variants" of affective disorder, including schizoaffective disorder, anorexia nervosa, and bulimia. Our findings suggest that such overlap may be common because the DSM-III affective disorders represent a heterogeneous collection of disorders defined broadly and nonspecifically enough to encompass wide, and often differing, realms of psychopathology.

Comment on the Axis I Interface

Overall, we feel our data suggest that STP "borders" with S and that BPD "borders" with AD, but the details of these links, for the most part, remain to be elucidated. We also suggest that the nature of the two borders are different structurally as well as phenomenologically. For example, in a nosologic exercise with our follow-up study cohorts (McGlashan, 1987b), we determined that the most characteristic or core DSM-III symptoms of STP were odd communication, suspiciousness/paranoid ideation, and social isolation. We also found that transient psychosis, brief paranoid experiences, and/or regressions in treatment discriminated for STP but against BPD, and therefore fit better as STP criteria. To us as clinicians all of these phenomenologies "feel" familiar as milder variants of S, and we have no difficulty placing STP within the schizophrenic spectrum.

The border between BPD and affective disorder, on the other hand, seems much different. The most characteristic DSM-III symptoms of BPD from our study were unstable relationships, impulsivity, and self-damaging acts, while the least discriminating symptoms were inappropriate anger and intolerance of aloneness. These are primarily problems with behavior, not with mood. How then are these signs and symptoms related to affective disorder? To us as clinicians, the differences between BPD and affective disorder do not feel like one of degree as do the differences between STP and S. The differences seem to be more in kind. Perhaps the link between BPD and affective disorder, as suggested above, is a core of affective disregulation. Their differences, however, come from alternate pathophysiologic expressions of this driving core. Perhaps BPD will prove to consist of patients with other personality disorders like histrionic, narcissistic, or antisocial personality disorder who *also* have an affective disorder. We do not know, but the data thus far do suggest a link between BPD and affective disorder that deserves further study.

BPD Comorbidity with Other Personality Disorders

It is known that BPD has high rates of comorbidity with other personality disorders, especially those from DSM-III's cluster B (the dramatic cluster). This raises the question as to whether any of them are really different. Again, long-term course and outcome information can address this question, with differences in profiles suggesting that the syndromes are indeed different diagnostic entities.

Using our follow-up study BPD cohort, we were able to conduct such a preliminary test of the long-term predictive validity of the most current (DSM-III-R) definitions of BPD, narcissistic personality disorder (NPD), and antisocial personality disorder (APD) (McGlashan and Heinssen, 1989). That is, many of our BPD patients also displayed traits meeting some of the DSM-III-R criteria for NPD and APD and we were able to constitute three cohorts to study: "pure" BPD, BPD with narcissistic features (N/BPD), and BPD with antisocial features

(A/BPD). Narcissistic/BPD and A/BPD differed from non-comorbid BPD in several important ways. Antisocial patients (BPD patients with antisocial traits) were younger at onset, less likely to harm themselves, and more likely to direct their aggressions outward. They were also more compromised instrumentally at index admission. Narcissistic patients (BPD patients with narcissistic traits) had the oldest age at onset (23 years) and age at index admission. Interpersonally, both N/BPD and A/BPD patients appeared less stable than members of the non-comorbid BPD group, who were already compromised significantly in this realm.

Despite these differences in baseline symptom profile, our three subgroups were roughly equivalent across almost all long-term course and outcome dimensions. This merger of clinical profiles over an average of fifteen years was particularly striking for our A/BPD patients who were the most compromised initially.

These results suggest that BPD, APD, and NPD have more in common than they have differences. In fact, our findings validate Kernberg's (1976) notion of borderline personality organization which includes borderline, narcissistic and antisocial personalities. Our findings also validate DSM-III-R's aggregation of BPD, APD, and NPD into a larger cluster of personality disorders (cluster B) that share common features like dramatic presentation, impulsive acting out, and unpredictability. Cluster B also includes histrionic personality disorder (HPD), but we did not have a significantly large N of BPD patients with histrionic features to construct an H/BPD subgroup for use in our analyses.

Comment on the Nature of BPD Among the Personality Disorders

The above study restated the important finding that patients with BPD, on the whole, got better with time, and it extended this finding to patients with narcissistic and antisocial features. Such results challenge the assertion in DSM-III-R that the Axis II personality disorders are pervasive, inflexible, and enduring.

In fact, we feel our data support more dynamic models of personality disorder, at least for BPD and the other Cluster B personality disorders.

For example, as speculated elsewhere (McGlashan and Heinssen, 1989), BPD may be viewed, in part, as a state of delayed developmental maturation rather than as an enduring trait or chronic defect. As such, BPD may relent as development progresses over time (or begins anew after a period of stagnation).

Our data also suggest an interpersonal model for BPD and the other cluster B personality disorders. In this model, social factors are important in determining the vicissitudes of personal social styles. For example, the cluster B syndromes, par excellence, are disorders of interpersonal interaction. Such patients typically act out in ways that elicit social opprobrium and recrimination, and their dystonic styles may eventually yield to the relentless negative feedback they elicit. We speculate that the three DSM-III-R personality disorder clusters (A, B, and C) are quite distinct on the interpersonal dimension. The odd and eccentric cluster A patients are generally unrelated and in their quiet withdrawal do not generate antipathy. Cluster B patients want from others but use them and are unconcerned about the wants of others. The anxious and fearful cluster C patients also want from others but they remain sensitive to and comply with others' wants, often out of object fear. Patients from clusters A and C generate little conflict with society, although for different reasons. From the interpersonal model perspective of personality disorder, these two clusters are likely to have more stable and chronic long-term clinical profiles than patients from the B cluster. Ironically, patients with BPD (along with APD, NPD, and possibly HPD) may get better with age because they are the most *overtly* maladaptive of the personality disorders. They may also get better with age because they represent developmentally immature patterns of coping that can change, albeit sluggishly.

CONCLUSIONS

Borderline patients who met current criteria for BPD and who were sick enough to require residential treatment did well overall. They advanced with time, like our affectively disordered patients, but unlike our schizophrenic patients. It remains impossible to tell if this is a result of treatment, social pressures, maturational factors, or natural history of the disorder. Probably it involves some combination of all of these.

Not surprisingly, we found female BPD patients more prone to depressive, self-destructive psychopathology and male BPD patients more antisocial. Unexpectedly, however, time (and perhaps *the* times) appeared to be more generous with the borderline men, who proved more capable of avoiding intimacy and of channeling their aggressions instrumentally.

Diagnostically, BPD appears to be a valid but heterogeneous entity. Efforts to enhance the predictive power of our clinical assessments should consider a wide range of phenomena, many of which are easy to assess and amenable to scaling. Better outcomes in BPD patients appeared to be linked with higher intelligence, lower affective lability, and less chronicity. Other positive prognostic characteristics of note were an ability to experience pleasure, to tolerate psychological pain, and to contain aggression in relationships.

Our patients who met the DSM-III criteria for BPD were not "borderline schizophrenic" patients; the latter resided in our schizotypal follow-up cohort. If our BPD patients bordered at all, it was with affective disorders, although the nature of this interface was far from clear and deserves further study.

The clinical profiles of the more antisocial and narcissistic subgroups of our BPD sample did not differ significantly in long-term course and outcome from the "pure" borderline group, suggesting that a broad definition of borderline like Kernberg's may be valid. Our results call into question the distinctions between many of the DSM-III and DSM-III-R personality disorders, especially those in the B cluster. At another level, our findings that all of these BPD types improve with time challenge the assumption that Axis II personality disorders consist of pervasive, rigid, and chronically etched trait reactivities. We feel our data suggest that several models of personality disorder may be valid, and that dynamic, developmental, and interpersonal perspectives may contribute greatly in our future efforts to understand this perplexing and pleomorphic disorder.

PART II

CONCEPTS AND CONTROVERSIES

4.

The Contribution of Infant Studies to Understanding Borderline Personality Disorders

**Klaus Minde, M.D., F.R.C.P.(C), and
Douglas Frayn, M.D., F.R.C.P.(C)**

INTRODUCTION

Since the earliest awareness of the importance childhood experiences and retrospective fantasies may have for subsequent development of adult psychopathology, it has been assumed that observations of the infant during his actual development would render these mysteries understandable and therefore later manifestations of difficulties more amenable to treatment. This has not happened and thus the theoretical emphasis of psychoanalysis on childhood oedipal conflicts with its paternal phallocentric viewpoint has given way to the study of the infant within the caretaker–infant unit. The Freudian concepts of libidinal structural conflicts have been replaced by interest in defects of attachment, separation, or autonomy, initially described by Bowlby (1969, 1973) and Mahler and her group (Mahler, Pine, and Bergman, 1975). As a consequence, contemporary theoretical understanding of borderline disorders now

87

tends toward the assumption that these individuals have experienced early developmental arrests which have caused the disturbances in identity, self-esteem, and regulation described by Winnicott (1965a) and Kohut (1977).

The borderline patient, who was virtually ignored twenty years ago, is now studied because he presents with major social and intrapsychic difficulties. Yet, unlike the psychotic patient who may show a similar symptomatology, he is often accessible to verbal intervention and a degree of psychic self-reflection which allows interpersonal therapeutic exploration. Furthermore, our more precise diagnostic criteria now identify many individuals as borderline disorders who, in the past, would have been diagnosed as emotionally unstable, hysterical, and psychopathic characters or ambulatory and pseudoneurotic schizophrenics.

What has brought about the confusing pattern of transient thought disorders, primitive transferences, and disturbances in self-esteem and affect regulation that we see in adult borderline patients? Are they prepsychotic children grown up or are they individuals with chronic unresolved neurotic behaviors who finally cannot cope with increasing reality forces and/or decreasing external supports?

Psychoanalysis is the only science where the word *genetic* is in fact used to describe "ontogenetic" events. This reflects an attitude, albeit possibly unjustifiable, which stresses that events which happen to the infant during his early years provide the major factors which hamper him from developing into a happy, healthy, well-functioning child and adult. Ethology would suggest that this is a leap of faith not supported by observations of other species where behavior characteristics are firmly inborn so that, for example, strains of mice bred for aggression can be produced almost irrespective of any environmental manipulation during their development. However, most psychotherapists would not be in practice if they shared the belief that "nature" is overriding "nurture" in the final developmental outcome.

The development of infant psychiatry as a distinct subspecialty of child psychiatry has brought about an increased awareness of the need for developmental thinking in the study of psychopathology in both children and adults (Minde, 1987). Of course, children have long been seen as organisms whose changing needs can only be understood within the context of their physical, emotional, and cognitive development. Furthermore, traditional psychoanalysis has always been firmly based on epigenetic principles inherent in specific structural or psychosexual theories (A. Freud, 1965). Thus, here again, the developmental process of the individual's urges and the defenses or gratifications associated with them, has been essential in theoretical thinking and clinical work.

What then has been learned? We submit that a major change in our understanding of infant development has been the realization, first enunciated by Daniel Stern (1985a), that the life of an infant can be understood from an observational and clinical perspective. Thus an infant can be observed, using the finely tuned methods of the developmental psychologist. However, to relate observed behavior to subjective experience requires inferential leaps. In order to define the infant's intrapsychic experiences, therefore, we require clinical insights which traditionally come from patient reports. These have in the past mainly been obtained from adults and have provided the basic principles of traditional psychoanalytic developmental theory. Stern's concept of the "observed" and the "clinical" infant (Stern, 1985a) has led to the development of a methodology which allows us to use the clinical infant to enhance our understanding of the observed infant. This also means that observations of young infants can now help us to develop general theories which explain how the clinical infant can build his subjective life and how later disorders may be linked to early experiences.

In the present chapter we shall try to make use of this new thinking regarding infant development and attempt to relate some data derived from it to the understanding of borderline personality disorders.

RECENT CHANGES IN THE UNDERSTANDING OF CHILD DEVELOPMENT

In the present section we shall argue that four fundamental changes have taken place in our understanding of normal and abnormal behaviors in children and adults which have helped us link the "observed" and "clinical" individual. These are:

1. our new knowledge about the continuities and discontinuities of behaviors during the life span;
2. the relevance internal representations of caretakers have for the psychological development of their children;
3. the redefinition of psychiatric problems as relationship disorders; and
4. our new understanding of the beginning development of the self.

Continuities and Discontinuities

Recent studies of infants and their families have taught us that people cannot be divided into those who are normal and those who are disordered. Beginning with the work of Emde and his colleagues (Emde, Gaensbauer, and Harmon, 1976), we have learned that infants undergo well-demarcated biologically determined cognitive and emotional reorganizations and behavioral transformations at specific ages (McCall, 1981). This means that at predictable times in an infant's life there will occur a significant reorganization of his or her behavior. For example, at six weeks of age an infant will suddenly show a social smile (i.e., respond to a familiar figure by smiling). This greatly increases the infant's contribution to the social interactions with his or her environment and consequently can bring about a very significant change in the perception others have of him or her. An infant who smiles readily may be viewed as good natured or friendly and may be treated quite differently by his caretakers than a baby who smiles little and cries a great deal.

While the appearance of the social smile seems to highlight the "hatching" of the baby from an inwardly focused organism to a true social being, scientists have identified two further early life periods during which biologically programmed behavioral reorganizations take place. At nine to twelve months infants suddenly utilize their fine motor skills to advance significant adaptive and social behaviors. In particular, they now look for a toy behind a screen, telling us that they remember what happened before, and also imitate scribbling on paper and specific social rituals like waving bye-bye. This demonstrates not only that the infant has now understood cause and effect and has thus gained the ability to "make things happen," but also shows that consequences are now sought through imitation of fine motor and social behaviors rather than through mere manipulation of an object.

The final developmental reorganization occurs from eighteen months onward and is characterized by the increasing predominance of verbal communication (McCall, 1981). The more skillful use of language is associated with the ability to recognize oneself in the mirror (Amsterdam, 1972) and in photographs and films (Lewis and Brooks-Gunn, 1979). This, in turn, allows children to form their gender identity (Galenson and Roiphe, 1974) and has an immense effect on the type of relationships children form with those around them. It also influences the discovery and consolidation of their own "selves."

It cannot be emphasized enough that these apparently biologically programmed behavioral changes have powerful effects on the infant's social environment, as an infant can appear to behave completely differently after each transformation. At the same time, these biological changes reflect opportunities when old and new developmental tasks can be reworked. These phenomena can create the appearance of behavioral discontinuities since a previously "abnormal" youngster can suddenly be transformed into a "normal" and apparently well-adjusted child.

While such behavioral shifts are especially striking in childhood, there is ample evidence that all of us encounter important transitions throughout our lives. Some of these transitions are fairly universal (e.g., the choice of a career, marriage, becoming a parent, retirement), while others are more individual (e.g., losing a parent before age 5). However, as Rutter points out in a very recent article (Rutter, 1989), the outcome of such important transitions is substantially determined by an individual's past behavior and experience. Thus, chain effects are common, and through our increased ability to analyze each of the links in the chain, we are beginning to determine how they interconnect.

One way to analyze these connections is to see life transitions both as products of past processes and instigators of future ones. For example, Brown, Harris, and Bifulco (1986) documented that aberrant separations women experienced in early childhood were frequently associated with poor parental care and that many of these children would later on experience premarital pregnancy, marriage to an undependable husband, and depression. However, the fact that illegitimate children and depression were uncommon in women who had experienced an aberrant separation from their families which was not associated with poor parental care, shows that each link in this chain was contingent on how the previous life transition was negotiated.

One final note on this topic. As previously pointed out, behavioral transformations can bring about significant changes in parent–child interactions. Since transformations early in life are triggered primarily by maturational processes, the infant's actual behavioral changes cannot be readily predicted. However, modifications in the parent–infant relationship resulting from these transformations usually reflect both the infant's new behavioral repertoire and the individual caretaker's interpretation of these new behaviors or intentions of the infant. Traditional psychoanalytic thinking, while based on the "clinical infant," (i.e., the infant reconstructed in the psychoanalysis of adults) suggests that we adults interpret the actions of an infant in ways which were molded by our own internal structures or representations, and that they reflect the sum total of the personal compromise between our drives and defenses operating at this particular time. Psychoanalytic theory has therefore been helpful in establishing constructs which can help in exploring behaviors retroactively. However, it has done little to validate these constructs empirically. Changes here have come from the works of those interested in attachment behavior and the concept of "internal representations."

Internal Representations

Recently, researchers exploring the development of attachment behavior have found new ways to conceptualize the formation of some specific internal representations which make it possible to study them empirically. In addition, through their studies, they also provide illustrations of how the dialogue between the clinical and observed infant can illuminate the infant's subjective experiences. Using the example of the developing attachment relationship between an infant and its caretakers, we know that parents must meet the infant's changing need for security for him to develop a positive internal representation of the world and those who inhabit it. This security may be achieved initially by a caretaker's physical holding of a young infant. By four to six months, however, the "holding" may be done on the knee or across space through the eyes or the voice (Brazelton, Koslowski, and Main, 1974). By ten to twelve months, just looking or the sharing of affect may be sufficient to convey to the child a sense of security. Therefore, the process of developing a secure attachment begins with a caregiver who is responsive to an infant's signals, and continues through a more reciprocal relationship in which the infant is an increasingly active participant. This means that the behavioral transformations of the infant, while superficially suggesting a discontinuous type of developmental sequence, in fact provide a cohesive system within which the baby and his caretakers negotiate the regulation of his overall behavior. It also suggests that it is actual interpersonal events which make up the matrix from which we develop our future internal representations.

Ainsworth and her group (Ainsworth, Blehar, Waters, and Wall, 1978) were able to empirically demonstrate this process through their attachment paradigm. Thus, mothers who early on had responded sensitively to the signals of their infants had children who, at twelve months, seemed securely attached. These children used the caretaker as a base for exploration, could be readily comforted after a short separation, and were eager to explore their environment when their mothers were around. This in turn paved the way for the emergence of an autonomous inner organization (Sroufe and Fleeson, 1988) and finally the construction of particular internal representations, also called *internal working models*. This term was initially used by Bowlby (1973) who stated that "in the working model of the world that anyone builds, a key feature is the infant's notion of who his attachment figures are . . . and how they may be expected to respond" (p. 203).

This means that a working model is the assembly of many specific types of interactions (e.g., sensitive or insensitive maternal responses) into a larger representation of a person's repertoire associated with certain conditions. Working models can gradually change as new experiences are added or old ones are reorganized (Main, Kaplan, and Cassidy, 1985). Nevertheless, there is a good deal of evidence which speaks for the stability of these early working models. Individuals tend to select partners or form relationships that perpetuate existing working models, even though this may happen unconsciously (Sroufe and Fleeson, 1986). Children and adults alike also tend to elicit input confirming their preexisting models and ignore countervailing information. This tends to make these working models self-stabilizing and resistant to change.

Psychopathology as Disorders of Relationships

Another important change is the recognition by infant psychiatrists that the development and maintenance of social relationships are the primary source which feeds the developmental process. In fact, Sameroff and Emde in their preface to a recently published book (Sameroff and Emde, 1989) state that "the individual based nosology for adult psychopathology cannot easily be extended downwards to early childhood" (p. vii). They therefore created an assessment scheme which was based on the developmental model for relationships and examined, among other things, the adaptational functions early relationships provide for the child, and the connection between early and later relationships.

While the shift from a disease-oriented nomenclature and treatment scheme to the description of the process between the child and his or her world is not new to psychoanalysts, it contradicts the emphasis DSM-III has placed on the patient's specific symptoms when describing a disorder. Unlike the traditional psychoanalysts, however, the authors who subscribe to the present developmental model have assembled empirical data in support of their theory. For example, Zeanah and his colleagues (Zeanah, Benoit, and Barton, 1988) have developed an interview schedule which assesses the parents' internal representations of their infants. Interestingly, according to Zeanah and his colleagues, parents from early on differ not only in the content of describing their infants but also in certain qualitative features of these representations, demonstrated by differences in the richness of their perceptions, their openness to change (e.g., the flexibility of their representation to accommodate new information about the infant), their intensity of involvement, as well as the coherence of their narrative descriptions.

The importance of this work is underscored by studies which have shown that infants as young as three months have already learned to deal with the degree of sensitivity they can expect from their mothers (Tronick, Ricks, and Cohn, 1982). In Tronick's work, mothers were asked to create certain perturbations, such as suddenly emptying their face of all expression. Their infants usually responded by looking puzzled and then making specific sounds as if to get mother to "be normal again." If this did not work, they finally looked away. Tronick and his colleagues report that some infants will look away and therefore appear to give up quickly, while others try much longer to get their mother's attention back. It is of interest that those babies who readily turned away from their mothers at age three months, nine months later were usually described to be insecurely attached. Direct observations of their mothers also revealed them to be less sensitive to these children's signals. This could explain both the children's behavior at three and twelve months and reflect less optimal qualitative features in their parents' internal representations. It also documents the process by which specific internal representations of caretakers may cause relationship disorders in the caretaker–child dyad which in turn can create aberrant internal representations or working models in the infants.

The Development of the Self

There has always been agreement among those interested in the dynamics of development that the relationship between an infant and others around him is of crucial importance for the process of normal development. One important difference between most present-day clinicians and those in the past, however, is the degree to which the early reality of an infant is understood to be of a subjective nature and thus determined in large part by psychobiological contributions thought to exist outside objective life events. Freud (1965) as well as Klein (1952) suggest that early relationships are primarily the result of the ontogeny of fantasy life which unfurls in the same order, no matter what the child's beginnings. Sullivan (1953) and others subscribing to the object relationships school of development (e.g., Fairbairn, 1954; Guntrip, 1971) have believed that social relativeness exists from birth onward. Bowlby (1969), in addition, maintained that real rather than fantasy life experiences are the key to understanding future developmental pathways. More recently, a number of psychoanalysts have also developed a coherent therapeutic theory (Kohut, 1977; Stechler and Kaplan, 1980) that places the self as a structure at the center of their psychology. Previous investigators had considered the experiences of the self and other as secondary to traditional libidinal or ego development. Even Margaret Mahler, whose developmental theory has focused on the experience of self and other, sees the subjective experiences of an infant to be derived from the ego and the id (Mahler et al., 1975).

These long-established developmental principles have recently been challenged by Daniel Stern who in an extraordinary book presents a working hypothesis of development which makes the sense of the self a major developmental organizing principle (Stern, 1985a). Stern's thesis is, among others, based on the assertion that the infant has subjective experiences all along and that these experiences are the factual working parts which make the sense of self a reality.

It is obviously not possible to do justice to Stern's innovative thoughts within the constraints of a brief chapter. For this reason we will concentrate on the early developmental period which Stern sees as most relevant for the understanding of the borderline patient, and touch only briefly on other aspects of his understanding of the development of the self.

Stern claims that the traditional phases of development such as orality or symbiosis have little clinical relevance since they are represented by behaviors which may have different meanings. For example, the capacity to walk and wander away from the mother at one's own initiative is used as the decisive event of autonomy by Mahler and Furer (1968), while Freud claims bowel control to be the key point in this process. In contrast, Spitz (1957) feels it is the ability to say "no" to the mother which makes the child independent. As the reader will recognize, these cited examples for the establishment of autonomy occur at ages ranging from twelve to twenty-four months. This is puzzling, especially since we are all aware that a baby can assert her independence at four months by looking away equally well as when she runs away at sixteen months. Thus there are good indications that the basic clinical issues of autonomy are not phase specific but present at all times in situations of social engagement. That means that traditional clinical developmental achievements may not be yoked to specific sequential "sensitive" life phases but that development can be understood better by looking at current adaptive tasks and how they are negotiated by infant and caregivers. It is for these reasons that Stern claims that the sense of self is a very central construct which functions as an organizing principle of development; that is, provides the infant with experiences which give an overall structure to his development.

Stern subdivides the building of this sense of self into three phases. He feels that from the second month onward, the infant has a physical self which is experienced as "a willful, physical entity with a unique affective life and history that belong to it" (Stern, 1985a, p. 26). Stern calls this the core sense of self and feels that this structure is based on four types of experiences available to the infant:

1. Self-agency. This means that an infant has a sense of volition over self-generated actions, such as the movement of an arm.

2. Self-coherence. This suggests that an infant at this age has some sense of being a nonfragmented whole with specific boundaries.
3. Self-affectivity. The infant experiences inner qualities of feeling.
4. Self-history. The infant has a sense of enduring, a sense that one can change while remaining the same.

Stern asserts that caretakers usually assist infants to experience these feelings or states through games or repetitive actions. For example, early forms of pat-a-cake, where mothers make their hands and the hands of their infants do the same, can further self-coherence or self-affectivity as these games often lead to a predictable escalation of smiles or laughter.

Sometime between the seventh and ninth months following the second behavioral reorganization, infants discover that there are other people out there and that they as infants can share subjective experiences with them. This sense of sharing requires the infant to have a notion that two people can have different minds (as otherwise they could not share), but also have a shared framework of meanings (i.e., both can experience similar and mutually comprehensible emotion). Stern calls this the intersubjective self and states that the child now also experiences a new type of empathy which senses the bridging of two minds. Empirically, this new intersubjective self is documented by:

1. The infant's shared attention. This means that the baby will now look at the box or a cup when mother points at it and therefore make the jump from the end of the finger to the object.
2. The infant's documented intentions. For example, the child will now reach out for a cookie or make special noises in order to get one, being sure that mother or father will understand what each special noise signifies;
3. The child's use of social referencing. This phenomenon, identified by Emde, Kligman, Reich, and Wade (1978) and Campos and Stenberg (1981), describes the behavior pattern typical for twelve-month-old children who are of two minds

about something. The prototypic situation used by these researchers has been an experiment where children are lured to cross an apparent visual cliff by a toy and a smiling mother. When they reach the apparent drop-off, the children most often stop and look at their mothers for secondary appraisal. If mothers encourage the child at that point, the cliff will be crossed. If a mother frowns, the baby usually turns around and crawls away.

Stern sees the shift from regulating behaviorally overt self experiences to the sharing of subjective experiences with another person and the influencing of these experiences as the principal developmental achievement of this stage. However, in order to develop a smoothly organized system of intersubjective relatedness, the caregivers must be able to be sensitive and share the infant's subjective experience. This phenomenon Stern calls attunement (Stern, 1985a), and he accords it a very major role in the development of the intersubjective self. Thus attunement does not simply reflect a mother's awareness of her baby's physical needs, but it permits the parent to "convey to the infant what is shareable, that is, which subjective experiences are within and which are beyond the pale of mutual consideration and acceptance" (p. 208). In fact, the parents, through their responsivity, act as a template to shape and create corresponding inner experiences in the child. This also means that through attunement parental private fears and fantasies can be reflected in the child.

Attunement can be measured empirically (Beebe and Sloate, 1982; Stern, 1985b) but should not be confused with imitation, which renders form while attunement renders the feeling. Examples of the latter phenomenon are a mother who joins her infant banging a soft toy by falling into his rhythm and saying "taaa-bam, taaa-bam," making the second syllable synchronous with the banging of the child. It follows that parents who show attunement to their children can use the same or a different modality from that employed by the infant. In our example, mother used her voice to bring out the affect displayed by the child in his banging.

There is one final characteristic which differentiates attunement from other child-oriented activities, and that is the unconscious or near automatic way in which parents practice it. Thus one frequently observes parents participating in their children's play in the way described above without having any idea that they do so (Papousek and Papousek, 1981).

As infants from three weeks onward are able to understand transmodal affects (e.g., they appreciate mother's vocal sounds as an affective validation of their own arm movements), parents can use a wide array of activities to show their children that they understand how they feel (Bower, 1976; Meltzoff and Moore, 1977, 1983).

A word of caution must be added here. Attunement should not be confused with the concept of "mirroring" as used by Kohut (1977). Mirroring implies that the mother helps the infant to validate something (e.g., a feeling or internal state) of which the infant is only dimly aware before, while attunement goes beyond participating in the child's inner world but suggests broadening the infant's sense of being in the world.

How similar is attunement to empathy? Stern suggests that the two are very different concepts. Empathy involves the mediation of cognitive processes. This includes an initial resonance of feeling states, a transient role identification, and then an empathic response. Attunement, on the other hand, takes the experience of emotional resonance and expresses it in another form (banging to vocalizing) without adding an empathic response.

Anna and Paul Ornstein, who have had a long-standing interest in the effects of various parenting styles, have identified a group of children who have not received "phase appropriate environmental responses" (Ornstein and Ornstein, 1985). As feelings are increasingly differentiated within the self object matrix, inappropriate environmental responses can create deficits which later on are "filled in" with defensive and negativistic behaviors. Thus the Ornsteins believe that such experiences are structure building, much as Stern describes the formation of an intersubjective self to be an important regulating influence of a child's overall development.

These authors also reinterpret some of the important concepts developed by Mahler and her group. They take particular exception to the process Mahler and her colleagues call the "separation–individuation phase of development" (Mahler et al., 1975). As is well known, Mahler observed and labeled various specific behaviors in infants from seven to twenty-four months. For example, she called the preference seven- to ten-month-old infants show for looking at rather than touching their mothers or their wish to explore mother's face, as "differentiating behaviors." From ten to fifteen months, babies appear to practice endlessly the physical separation from their caretakers by joyously running away from them. This Mahler called the "practicing phase," which after eighteen months is followed by a period she calls "rapprochement." This period is characterized by a decrease in the overall confrontational behaviors between toddlers and their caregivers. Mahler feels this is due to the fact that toddlers now realize the tasks they have mastered (e.g., their increased fine motor control or ability to verbalize) and accept their limitations much more gracefully.

The reader will have noticed already that many of the infant behaviors Mahler sees as the infant's attempts to separate or establish a separate identity will be interpreted by Stern and the Ornsteins as an infant's new way of being close and connected with those around him. Thus while Mahler sees the developmental process as going from a near fusion or symbiosis to autonomy and independence, Stern understands development as a process in which the infant develops an increasingly more differentiated self or sense of self. This then allows him to discover a new way to be with others as the concept of the self can only be experienced through the dyadics of the subjective experience of self and others.

The third and last aspect of self-development occurs during the second year of life when language emerges and the infant develops the sense of a verbal self. Language obviously makes part of the child's experience more shareable with others and can create new mutual experiences of meanings. Among other things, this leads to symbolic play and affective meanings of words can now be negotiated between a child and her parents. Thus being "a good girl" may have one meaning in

Joanie's home but quite another one in Mary's family. However, with the development of language we also see a potential trans- formation of at least some experiences of core and intersubjec- tive relatedness as words can change their nonverbal impact and their associated conglomerate of feelings or sensations. In fact, in a very general way one could state that language is a far better vehicle in describing "observed" phenomena than in transmitting accounts of internal states. Also, language describ- ing life-as-lived (e.g., breakfast at my house) often depicts gen- eralized episodes (e.g., what happens usually at breakfast in my house) but does not do so well in describing a specific breakfast six months ago during which mother suddenly got sick, because the cited specific instance usually has no particular name. Thus the sense of a verbal self first makes possible the division be- tween conscious and unconscious thoughts and affects, or ver- bal versus nonverbal material. Language also gives children the tools to distort and change reality and potentially provides the soil for later neurotic constructs.

THE DIAGNOSIS OF BORDERLINE PERSONALITY DISORDERS

What relevance do the above issues and ideas have for the understanding of borderline disorders? We submit that these disorders have a symptomatology which suggests a disturbance of very basic interpersonal functions. The definition used in DSM-III-R states that individuals with borderline disorders show significant instability in their overall interpersonal behav- ior, mood, and self-image. This overlaps with many of the crite- ria developed by Gunderson (1984) although he provides a more dynamic description of this condition. For example, Gunderson claims that the basic symptom in borderline individ- uals is the patient's overall devaluation of the strengths of im- portant others. This devaluation, according to Gunderson, is associated and possibly caused by a powerful fear of abandon- ment and can document itself in various defensive behavior patterns. Examples are a compulsive sociality or drug and alco- hol abuse. In these cases the patient allegedly uses drugs or a false sociability as means to gain an overall cohesiveness of his or her sense of self. Gunderson has developed a scale and diagnostic interview for his criteria for borderline patients and reports satisfactory reliability (Gunderson, Kolb, and Austin, 1981).

It is of interest that in the one study that has attempted to examine the evaluation of attachment relationships cited by Gunderson, Bradley (1979) found that in a small number of borderline children (N = 14), early separation experiences had occurred more commonly (64%) in the borderline children than in a group of matched delinquent youngsters. This suggests that the disorder, at least on one level, has to do with the abnormal development of the sense of self, defined as a subjective reality which tells us "how we experience ourselves in relation to others" (Stern, 1985a, p. 6).

Other empirical studies also suggest that this sense of self is a major integrating factor in the overall developmental process of each human being. As we have seen in our previous discussion of behavioral transformations, the sense of self will also undergo changes within the developmental process. For example, an infant's cognitive ability to see himself as an independent human being, newly acquired around age nine months, will obviously change this infant's subjective reality. Equally important, however, is the facilitating role of the primary caregivers, as their interpretation of the infant will also change following his behavioral transformation and thus validate the infant's new sense of self.

Disorders in the sense of self could theoretically be expected in individuals whose environment lacks specific facilitative characteristics or who suffer from conditions which may compromise the normal evolution of cognitive structures. The previously cited study by Bradley (1979) provides some support of the dysfunctional nature of some families of borderline children. Bemporad, Smith, Hanson, and Cicchetti (1982) also reported that, in twenty-two out of twenty-four cases their group had examined, borderline children showed both evidence of organic impairment (e.g., hyperactivity, severe learning problems, or motor clumsiness) as well as bizarre and often abusive

mothers. While the authors give few details about these difficulties, they mention that some of these mothers fed their children LSD during their preschool years or behaved in a highly
intrusive manner (e.g., wiped their bottoms after toileting up
to age 8).

Psychoanalytic writers also point to the disturbance of early
relationships in these individuals. For example, Mahler (1972a)
states that borderline patients are fixated at the rapprochement
stage of their development (i.e., from 16 to 25 months). Masterson and Rinsley (1975) agree with Mahler but specify her
speculation by adding that the child's individuation constitutes
a threat to mother's need to cling to the infant and causes her
to withdraw her "libidinal availability." Kernberg (1968, 1977a)
also agrees with the developmental period during which the
disturbance begins, but places more emphasis on constitutional
factors such as oral aggression.

The preceding data indicate an association between parental psychopathology, possible biological vulnerabilities, and
later disorders. However, the described constellation of risk
factors is quite general and applies to many forms of problem
behavior in children and adults. It is therefore necessary to
identify more specific factors in the early caretaking environment of borderline patients. For example, it would be important to know more about the facilitative characteristics which
assist children in developing a sense of self and what evidence
there is that borderline patients indeed lack specific key experiences.

CLINICAL MANIFESTATIONS AND STRATEGIES WITH BORDERLINE PERSONALITIES

As discussed in the previous section, developments in recent
psychoanalytic thought suggest that borderline conditions are
associated with early developmental defects or arrests rather
than the structural oedipal conflicts seen in neurotic disorders.
These disorders also do not present with specific symptoms.
Rather, patients may have variable symptomatic complaints
with rapidly fluctuating levels of ego functioning and unstable

or unrewarding interpersonal relationships. Their primitive transference relationships vary from seeming unrelatedness to intense symbiotic dependencies. There may also be a blurring of psychic boundaries so that patients experience their wished-for ideals or feared deficiencies through their subjective experience of the therapist. At times these primitive transferences are only expressed as somatic or physiological reactions, truly an archaic return of the repressed, as this implies a return to the times where there were no words or coherent affective integration. The therapist therefore finds him- or herself often cast in strangely different transference roles than he or she is accustomed to. Instead of being the longed for but incestuously unavailable father or nurturing mother he or she may be a corpse, a supernatural force, or an inanimate container for unwanted affects and fantasy. He may also be seen as part of the patient or even an anatomical part object rather than a separate entity.

As a possible result of these unusual behaviors, perplexing countertransference reactions can occur when the therapist begins to feel unwanted and useless, similar to the patient's original feelings of being misunderstood, unappreciated, and basically unwanted. These feelings on the therapist's part should be used to better understand this unique intersubjective situation and lead to a more meaningful empathy with the patient's traumatic and disillusioning past (Frayn, 1987).

However, this understanding is often made difficult as these patients do not wish to remember nor do they want to freely associate. They do not experience a cathartic thrill at being able to say what comes to mind nor do they experience relief of object hunger by the mere presence of the listening therapist. Patients with restricted fantasy expect the therapist to do the fantasizing for them. Some of the others paradoxically may flood the therapy with reams of fantasy material, including multiple elaborate dreams, early traumatic remembrances, and unrestrained transference suggestions. Yet they do not integrate these fantasies nor do they experience their associated affects; this the therapist is left to do. In summary, these patients show behaviors which avoid attachments and leave the therapist often unwittingly assuming the role of the patient's observing and experiencing ego.

If one could say that there is a typical transference manifestation of these patients it is that of an unrelatedness to the therapist. This can be expressed by the meaningless chatter or story-telling as well as the more obvious ignoring or avoidance of the therapist and his interventions. This is not an expression of wish but the defensive counterimpulse against making contact. Grinker (1977) states "these patients do not develop a transference, which corresponds to their inability to attain or maintain affectionate relationships. Therapists are things to be used" (p. 163). Meaningfully relating to the therapist is equated with being controlled, smothered, or invaded with the subsequent fears of loss of psychic and body integrity. Fears of disintegration, abandonment, and maternal retribution and/or engulfment predominate. These fears are manifested within the transference as a mistrust of closeness, a painful emptiness in the presence of the transference object, that being the therapist within the analytic situation.

BORDERLINE PERSONALITY AND CONTEMPORARY INFANT RESEARCH: WHAT ARE THE CONNECTIONS?

In this chapter we have evaluated some recent work which has provided us with new ways of looking at the process of development in early childhood. In particular, we have examined the connection, proposed in the recent literature, between attachment patterns and internal cognitive structures in infants between eight and twenty-four months. This has led us to the assumption, supported by Gunderson and Kernberg and others, that borderline disorders are a reflection of character pathology which is rooted in specific failures of the caretakers' sensitivity during the last part of the first and the second year of life.

To what degree does the concept and clarification of the subjective self as understood by Stern, however, help us in delineating more specific etiological factors in borderline disorders? In our opinion, there are two issues which need to be considered to answer this question. The first one is related to the clinical reality we encounter when working with individuals who show serious deficits in self-cohesion that manifest as borderline disorders. Patients with this disorder indeed often show symptoms and concerns which invite the speculation that they experienced failures in attunement or maternal empathy. Understanding our patients from this angle can help us devise and provide more appropriate forms of treatment (Kohut, 1971, 1984; Klein, 1975; Johansen, 1979). It also allows us to feel less threatened by the anger and the despair so often encountered in the work with these individuals (Masterson, 1976).

The second issue we need to stress, however, are the lessons epidemiological studies have taught us about the pathways from childhood to adult life (Rutter, 1989). The most persuasive data here show a rather complex mix of continuities and discontinuities all through the life span (Minde, 1987). The reasons and mechanisms which account for these varied outcomes are not yet clear, although some basic principles have been established. For example, we have long known that man is a social animal, and because social interaction occurs in relation to a person's interactions with other people, and key experiences such as marriage, child bearing, and retirement occur later in life, one would expect social and psychological change to take place all through a person's life span (Erikson, 1963; Hinde, 1987). On the other hand, we have evidence which suggests that the timing of an event may be important. For example, we know that specific events such as prenatal androgens or brain damage have different long-term effects at different ages (Mayer-Bahlberg, Ehrhardt, and Feldman, 1986; Goodman, 1987) as they impact upon a more or less sensitive central nervous system (CNS). Taking the example of the borderline patient, some clinicians may claim that nonempathic caretaking techniques compromise the development of a cohesive self and this leads invariably to faulty development. Such a view would still have to explain why the development of a cohesive self would not also be affected by a failure at the level of core relatedness or of verbal relatedness which occur before and after the period when intersubjective relatedness develops.

Furthermore, we need data which indicate the degree to which the negotiations of later normal life transitions (e.g., leaving school, starting work, etc.) are affected by these early experiences and, possibly in conjunction with other factors, either perpetuate or modify their effect on the internal working models of an individual. What the work of infant psychiatrists helps us discover, however, are the processes and mechanisms which are involved in the direct or indirect chains of the developmental process. For example, if we were to show that a cohesive self is a major factor in the building of self-esteem, and connect this to the present-day understanding that high self-esteem and a positive social orientation are the main markers of later adaptive psychosocial outcome (Masten and Garmezy, 1985), we would have made a major contribution to the understanding of behavioral linkages over time. As methodologies are now available to study these developmental processes, empathic clinical understanding of individuals showing the behaviors described as borderline disorder is an important first step in the elucidation of the varied pathways leading to this incapacitating condition.

5.

The Borderline Patient: Shifts in Theoretical Emphasis and Implications for Treatment

Robert Michels, M.D.

INTRODUCTION: THEORIES AND PSYCHIATRIC TREATMENT

The optimal strategy for constructing a treatment plan for a psychiatric patient requires scientific knowledge about the treatment; that is, studies that evaluate its effects and side effects, its benefits and costs, comparing it to other treatments and to no treatment, and providing the basis for a systematic and rational strategy for helping the patient. Unfortunately, we do not often have that kind of knowledge in psychiatry. In fact, we do not often have it in any area of medicine. Modern medicine, and modern psychiatry, have come to recognize the scientific study of the efficacy of treatment as a goal, but they also recognize that we must care for and treat patients before that kind of knowledge is available.

When we do not have systematic scientific knowledge we fall back on our second most reliable source of guidance, clinical experience: the beliefs of experienced professionals regarding the indications and contraindications for treatment. We teach our students by sharing our clinical experience, but the wiser and more senior members of the profession, those who have accumulated the clinical experience, know that their beliefs are subject to error for a number of reasons. Their data cannot be analyzed systematically and may be contaminated by bias. There are no control groups. Doctors treat patients who get better and then tend to believe that their treatment had something to do with the patient's improvement or, conversely, they treat patients who get worse and then discontinue the treatment, without considering the possibility that the patient might have become even worse without the treatment. There are serious sampling biases; the more famous the clinician, the more likely that cases referred to him are preselected in accord with his interests and, consequently, the more he is tempted to believe that his theory fits the world rather than recognizing that he has trained his referring sources to fit his theory.

When we turn our attention to the study of the treatment of borderline patients, there are special methodologic problems in addition to these general ones. These patients tend to be extremely "therapeuphilic," repeatedly seeking out a treatment only to discard it and replace it with another one. It is extremely difficult to maintain an untreated control group or one that receives a stable alternative treatment, and any control group that seems to have those characteristics may be unrepresentative of borderline patients as a whole.

If we do not yet have systematic scientific data, and our clinical experience is largely chaotic, contradictory, or untrustworthy, we turn to our third and least reliable source of guidance for clinical practice—our theories. Theories help in the absence of either data or clinical experience. Indeed, we must first have theories in order to collect useful data. They organize our perceptions and classify the fragments of knowledge that we have collected, allowing us to interpolate or extrapolate from them. Without theories, we function in a chaotic or random way; we do not know what strategy to pursue, what hypothesis to test, what question to ask. Therefore, it is important that we generate new theories, study them, use them, and (particularly difficult for psychiatrists), feel free to discard them when we find better ones.

Theories also have an additional, special function in psychodynamic psychotherapy. They not only guide our thinking about clinical problems, but they also generate interpretations, the primary tools of the dynamic psychotherapist. Therapists meet patients, establish relationships with them, listen to them, and say things to them. One of the major concerns of the therapist is deciding what to say. It should be empathic, honest, sensitive, and interesting. It is relatively easy to be one or the other of these four, but it is often difficult to be all four at once. Our best theories offer valuable guidelines for constructing interventions that meet these criteria, especially interventions that are interesting. They do this by generating metaphors that link the experience of the clinical process to a theory of human psychology. Therefore, our theories about borderline patients serve two important functions: they offer strategies for conceptualizing treatment planning in the absence of scientific data or coherent clinical experience, and they generate valuable metaphors for those of us who do psychotherapy with these patients and who want help in deciding what to say to them. Both of these functions are helpful for psychiatrists working with borderline patients.

Some would think of a psychotherapist using a theory as equivalent to a traveler using a map while exploring a wilderness. Certainly it is easy to think of the world of borderline personality as a wilderness. Others, more cynical, suggest that if theories are maps, most of them have been drawn by cartographers who know little about the terrain and whose maps reveal more about their imagination than about the wilderness. Perhaps so, but there is an interesting possibility that a map may be valuable even if wrong. When embarking on a difficult journey, a map can be comforting and reassuring, suggesting a place to start. If we are open-minded and willing to modify and reconstruct the map as the journey progresses, it offers a strategy for collecting and organizing new observations and learning from the journey as we continue on it. Theories understood in this way motivate psychotherapists to persevere in difficult, distressing, painful, and sometimes boring situations and to stay with the patient to the end of the journey. It may be that any theory that supports the therapist for the course of the therapy is a good enough theory, because staying with the patient is more important than the elegance of our conceptual understanding. We do not have the data necessary to answer that question, but it is possible to study it, and it is worth thinking about.

THE BORDERLINE CONCEPT

Historically, the concept of borderline personality was initially developed to explain an unexpected and distressing observation. Some patients who were thought to be good candidates for exploratory psychodynamic psychotherapy—young, intelligent, verbal, motivated, psychologically minded, capable of powerful transference relationships, with good reality testing—did poorly as the treatment progressed. They became angry, sullen, resentful, destructive, impulsive, had regressive episodes and transference crises, even transference psychoses. They had intense emotional experiences in the treatment situation, but seemed unable to observe themselves or to use the experience as a substrate for psychological exploration. The therapist's initial enthusiasm changed to concern that he had made an error in selection and the treatment might be doing more harm than good.

The concept of borderline personality begins with the attempt to understand how these patients were different from other patients. One obvious hypothesis was that something was wrong with the conduct of the treatment or with the theory that guided it, but clearly a preferred hypothesis was that there was some hidden defect in the patient that had not been recognized. When data contradict theory, the careful student always begins by scrutinizing the data before reassessing the theory.

One consequence of these negative therapeutic experiences was that psychotherapists attempted to develop criteria that would screen candidates for intensive psychotherapy. They hoped to identify in advance patients who would respond poorly to the treatment. These criteria were the beginning of our current diagnostic descriptions of borderline personality disorder (BPD). The therapists also evaluated psychodiagnostic procedures for detecting characteristics that, although hidden from casual clinical observation, might predict negative responses. For example, they observed that some borderline patients performed well with structured diagnostic assessments, but had unusual difficulty when the structure was removed, a predictor of disorganized response to the unstructured aspects of the therapeutic setting. However, even if these screening devices were effective, deciding not to prescribe dynamic psychotherapy, although it may be preferable to prescribing it inappropriately, is not a satisfying strategy for a psychiatrist trying to help a borderline patient.

Treatment failures also stimulated interest in new theories that might not only explain the failures, but also suggest modifications in the treatment that would improve the results and enhance our clinical ability. Two types of theoretical developments ensued. The first involved theories of psychology and psychopathology—the dynamics and genetics of patients with this particular syndrome as compared to those with other conditions treated by psychotherapists. The second involved our theory of treatment itself, how it works, what are its components, and which of these might be contributing to the negative effect and might be modified so that the positive impact of other aspects of the treatment could predominate. In effect, we reassessed both our understanding of the patients and our strategy for working with them.

THEORIES OF CLINICAL PROCESS

The earlier formulations of the theory of clinical process had emphasized the central role of insight, of making the unconscious conscious. Borderline patients often seemed quite insightful, motivated to explore at least some of their unconscious fantasies, and gifted at expressing them. However, the failure of this to lead to much benefit called attention to the importance of factors other than insight, particularly to the transference and the therapeutic relationship that forms the matrix of the therapeutic process. If earlier theories focused on the impact of the insight that was provided to the patient by the therapy, the later theories shifted to the significance of the therapeutic process through which that insight was communicated. It may be suggested that a modern theory of psychodynamic psychotherapy would see the attempt of finding insight as a kind of occupational therapy activity in which what's really therapeutic is not the insight that is gained but rather the collaborative process of searching between patient and therapist; and that it was this collaborative process and its impact on the patient that served as the agent of change in psychodynamic psychotherapy. There was also renewed attention directed to the regression that is part of any psychoanalytic psychotherapy and to a variety of strategies for limiting the pathogenic impact of that regression. Patients who benefit from the treatment are able to tolerate the regression and find that its facilitation of emotional growth is more than worth its discomfort. However, for patients who lack the adaptive capacity to cope with the regressive aspects of the treatment and may slip into secondarily autonomous pathologic states as a result, the treatment should be modified in order to decrease that risk, even if its goals must be limited in order to do so.

Attempts to limit the potentially regressogenic features of psychoanalytic psychotherapy and improve the risk:benefit ratio for borderline patients led to modifications of the typical arrangements for psychotherapy. These included the shift from the couch to vis-à-vis sessions, reducing the frequency of sessions, and emphasizing the actual, genuine, authentic emotional presence of the therapist (often suppressed because of a misunderstanding of the psychoanalytic concept of "technical neutrality"). Controlled environments, including hospital settings, were used to limit impulsive behavior and dangerous acting out. The integrative difficulties of these patients, together with their tendency to use splitting or disavowal, required an active pursuit of split-off mental contents. It was not possible to wait for the spontaneous emergence of such material because, in the experience of most therapists, such waiting would mean that important aspects of the patient's inner experience would never emerge into the therapeutic dialogue.

DYNAMIC AND GENETIC THEORIES

In addition to these reconsiderations of the theory of the therapeutic process, there have been theoretical reconceptualizations of the dynamic and genetic characteristics of these patients. These have emphasized prestructural, preoedipal, dyadic psychodynamics rather than the structural, oedipally centered, triadic dynamics that characterize the traditional formulations of neurotic psychopathology. Separation and individuation are more prominent than lust and jealous rivalry. A corollary to this shift is that genetic reconstructions seem less plausible since the psychopathology is thought to be related to a developmental epoch in which experiences are not encoded symbolically; that is, to the first few years of life. The shift to earlier developmental themes also supports the shift in clinical theory away from verbal symbolic communication and insight toward viewing the treatment as a potential source of the psychological nurturance that the patient had been unable to experience in the original course of development. The therapeutic experience is conceptualized as a new opportunity to traverse a developmental phase that had not been negotiated successfully the first time. That is quite different from the traditional view of treatment as the setting in which the patient becomes aware of latent or repressed conflicts and brings them to consciousness in order to seek more adaptive resolutions. The new model also encourages strategies that attempt to identify and modify psychological characteristics that interfered with the patient's capacity to experience good enough parenting and to develop the psychic structures that result from the internalization of early parent–child relationships. The psychological characteristics that have received the greatest attention as the sources of such interference are excessive endowments of aggression and impairments in integrative capacities, particularly the capacity to construct integrated representations of primary objects. In other words, these patients are viewed as having excessive hostile rage and/or defects in their capacity to form cohesive, integrated representations that can sustain them after separation from their primary objects.

Of course, these reformulations not only lead to conjecture regarding the internal barriers to these essential developmental experiences, but also suggest consideration of interpersonal models of developmental pathogenesis. These models assume actually defective or unempathic parenting rather than, as in traditional psychoanalytic thinking, a disturbance in the patient's subjective experience of the parent–child relationship, without specifying whether that experience is a reflection or a distortion of the actual relationship. For example, some followers of the contemporary school of self psychology tend to assume that patients' reports of having experienced unempathic parenting reflect defects in parental empathy.

One therapeutic strategy that follows directly from interpersonal schemes of pathogenesis is intervention directed at the cause of the disorder, that is, the family. This tends to be particularly appealing in working with younger patients who are still enmeshed in their families of origin, especially if family pathology can be identified. Of course, the approach assumes that the contemporary family pathology is actively maintaining or supporting the patient's psychopathology rather than merely providing a plausible historical explanation for why that pathology developed.

A second therapeutic strategy that can be developed from an interpersonal model of pathogenesis leads to an individual psychotherapy that, on the surface, seems quite similar to traditional dynamic psychotherapies. However, the goal of the treatment is no longer to diminish internal barriers in order to allow the undisturbed experience of object relations, or even to repair the psychological defects that have developed secondary to impaired experiences, but rather to provide a good object for a new and positive relationship that can supplant and replace prior defective objects and pathological relationships.

The different views of pathogenesis and of treatment, implicit in these alternatives, reflect one of the fundamental themes in the widely discussed views of Otto Kernberg and the late Heinz Kohut. Of course, it is important to recognize that Drs. Kohut and Kernberg are not using the same definition and are talking about different groups of individuals when they use the term *borderline*. However, their theories have been influential with those who treat these patients and especially with those who develop conceptual strategies for thinking about them. Kohut's typical formulation emphasized the pathological consequences of defects in parenting, particularly in the parent's capacity to resonate and empathize with the child's experience. An empathic therapist offered the patient a second chance of a developmental step that had gone awry the first time because the child had been deprived of the essential psychological substrate for development, an empathic other.

Kernberg's typical formulation emphasizes the impact of the child's destructive rage, along with his defective capacity for tolerating tension and integrating discrepant (and specifically dysphoric) experiences. The psychopathology stems from the effect of these on the optimal internalization of primary relationships and the structure formation that should result.

For Kernberg, Kohut's approach denies the patient's primitive rage, fails to integrate the disavowed aspects of experience, and at times even suggests that these disavowed aspects of experience are inappropriate or unacceptable. Kernberg could further argue that Kohut accepts the psychic reality of a fantasy of parental empathic failure as though it were a veridical account of actual parental failures. In many ways this reflects what happened ninety years ago, when Freud first accepted the psychic reality of his patients' accounts of parental trauma or seduction as though they were accurate descriptions of childhood events. Today we recognize that while sometimes this is so, often it is not.

In contrast, for Kohut's followers, Kernberg's approach repeats the pathogenic parental failure of empathy by challenging the child's experience and disclaiming responsibility for it, arguing that the child's view of the parent is a distortion by the child rather than recognizing it as at least one possible version of the truth, although one that might be enriched by supplementing it with others. They go on to argue that, by interpreting the enraged response to parental empathic failure as evidence of a primary defect in the emotional regulation of the child, Kernberg attacks and blames the patient rather than supporting the resumption of an arrested developmental process.

THE DEFINITION RECONSIDERED

The development of diagnostic criteria that were originally intended to identify patients not suitable for psychoanalytic psychotherapy, the beginning of the borderline concept, led at first to the more precise characterization of these patients and then to the recognition of their similarity to certain other clinical populations (e.g., "pseudoneurotic schizophrenia"). The history of the syndrome is virtually unique in that it began not with the more common recognition of a cluster of signs and symptoms and then with the development of concepts of etiology, pathogenesis, and treatment, but rather with the identification of a series of unexpected treatment failures and then with attempts to identify the phenomena that would predict such failure. However, in time some investigators began to think of borderline patients not as those who got worse when they should have gotten better, but rather as those who were diagnostically confusing and had been categorized incorrectly. Others viewed them as persons who had a milder, *forme fruste* version of a more serious psychiatric disorder or perhaps a genetic, constitutional, or developmental vulnerability to such a disorder. Schizophrenia was the first candidate (e.g., "ambulatory schizophrenia") and later affective disease or even organic brain disease. Studies demonstrated the increased prevalence of various psychopathologies in the families of borderline patients and also the increased prevalence of borderlinelike psychopathology in the families of patients with major disorders.

One therapeutic strategy that stemmed from this new notion of the syndrome was the attempt to explore treatments that had been found successful with the major disorders upon which "borderline" was thought to border. The use of antipsychotic drugs with some borderline patients, particularly those with schizotypal features; of antidepressant drugs with patients thought to border on the affective syndromes; of lithium with cyclothymic or affectively unstable patients thought to have subclinical bipolar disorder; of anticonvulsants with patients who have episodic rage or impulsivity, particularly those with abnormal electroencephalographs (EEGs); and of stimulants with patients who have a history of attention deficit disorder and "soft" neurologic signs are all examples of attempts to develop treatment strategies based on the concept of a borderline syndrome that borders on another disorder that we know how to treat.

THEORIES AND THE PSYCHOTHERAPY OF BORDERLINE PATIENTS

Theories provide comfort to psychotherapists, suggest interpretations, and in general play the role of internal supervisors. Each of the several psychodynamic formulations of borderline psychopathology has inspired an interpretive strategy; however, the original observations regarding the negative effects of psychoanalytic psychotherapy have led to skepticism regarding the general value of interpretations in work with these patients. There is general agreement that the current realities of the patient's life and the immediate manifestations of transference responses in the therapeutic process and in current relationships are the more appropriate domain for psychotherapeutic effort with these patients than attempts at genetic reconstruction or the uncovering of unconscious dynamic constellations not immediately related to contemporary life issues. Of course, some would say that this is true of all patients in psychotherapy, it is only that these patients need more, and therefore respond more negatively when they do not get it.

In spite of this caveat, there have been important attempts to develop interpretive strategies based on separation–individuation dynamics, particularly the rapprochement phase, concepts of transitional phenomena, good enough mothering, holding environments, and internal object relations. To a cynic, these tell us more about the profession than about the patients. However, one theme emerges that is interesting. Work with more traditional neurotic patients has been most enriched by theories that dissect the mind into components and offer models for telling patients that, although they think that they are integrated, they really have internal divisions and conflicts. In contrast, in work with borderline patients, the theories that have been most helpful, such as object relations and self psychology theories, have exactly the opposite message. They emphasize the inherently cohesive and integrated quality of mental life, even if it is experienced subjectively as chaotic or fragmented. We tell neurotic patients, "You are not aware of it, but you really are of two minds, not one, conflicted within yourself as to what you want and who you are." We tell borderline patients, "You feel that you are one person at one time and another at another, inconstant, fragmented, without a stable center, but this is the result of a defensive attempt to avoid what you would experience if you were aware of each of these themes as only one aspect of a single self." Thus the focus of therapy has shifted from a theory of psychological developments to a theory of the therapeutic process; however, although by their very nature, process theories may guide the therapist, they are not as useful in stimulating interpretive metaphors. Freud was a better metaphor generator than modern ego psychology or object relations theorists, although the latter may have scientifically more comfortable, and logically more coherent, systems of understanding patients. We need more metaphor generators as we may be in somewhat short supply.

CONCLUSION

Perhaps the most valuable contribution that borderline patients have made to psychoanalytic psychotherapy has been the enrichment of the dialogue regarding what therapy is and how it works. By doing so, they have contributed to the quality of the therapy that we provide all patients, both borderline and otherwise. I believe that at this point it is far more convincing that the dialogue they have stimulated has greatly enriched the quality of treatment that we provide other patients and, therefore, they have made an altruistic contribution to the psychotherapy of patients in general. Perhaps now we are beginning to give some of that back to this patient group.

6.

Treatment of Borderline States: An Intersubjective Approach

Bernard Brandchaft, M.D., Robert D. Stolorow, Ph.D., and George E. Atwood, Ph.D.

In a recent discussion of the nature of truth in medicine and psychiatry, Wallace (1988) raises searching questions about the degree to which diagnostic categories "refer to actually existing entities versus the extent to which they are products of reigning medical fashions and social constructions of reality" (p. 138). He suggests that, throughout the history of medicine and psychiatry, such categories have to an important extent arisen as a product of predominant theories, and he cites as examples neurasthenia, pseudoneurotic schizophrenia, and involutional melancholia, among others. A similar argument can be made for the borderline personality organization (BPO), a diagnostic category that, in recent years, has succumbed to enormous popularity. We believe that there is substantial room for skeptical

This chapter is a modified and expanded version of chapter 8 in Stolorow, Brandchaft, and Atwood (1987), *Psychoanalytic Treatment: An Intersubjective Approach*. Hillsdale, NJ: Analytic Press.

    Earlier versions also appeared in J. Lichtenberg, M. Bornstein, and D. Silver, ed. (1984), *Empathy*, Vol. 2. Hillsdale, NJ: Analytic Press, pp. 333–357, and in J. Grotstein, M. Solomon, and J. Lang, ed. (1987), *The Borderline Patient*. Hillsdale, NJ: Analytic Press, pp. 103–125.

questioning as to precisely what, if anything, the term *borderline* describes. In this chapter, we present a critique of the currently prevalent view that the term *borderline* refers to a discrete pathological character structure rooted in pathognomonic conflicts and defenses, and we propose an alternative understanding of borderline phenomena that emerges when they are viewed from an intersubjective perspective. First, however, we present a brief overview of the development of our intersubjective framework.

THE INTERSUBJECTIVE CONTEXT

In our[1] previous work (Stolorow, Brandchaft, and Atwood, 1987), we defined the essentials of an intersubjective approach to psychoanalytic treatment as follows:

> In its most general form, our thesis . . . is that psychoanalysis seeks to illuminate phenomena that emerge within a specific psychological field constituted by the intersection of two subjectivities—that of the patient and that of the analyst. . . . Psychoanalysis is pictured here as a science of the intersubjective, focused on the interplay between the differently organized subjective worlds of the observer and the observed. The observational stance is always one within, rather than outside, the intersubjective field . . . being observed, a fact that guarantees the centrality of introspection and empathy as the methods of observation. . . . Psychoanalysis is unique among the sciences in that the observer is also the observed. . . .
>
> Clinical phenomena . . . cannot be understood apart from the intersubjective contexts in which they take form. Patient and analyst together form an indissoluble psychological system, and it is this system that constitutes the empirical domain of psychoanalytic inquiry [p. 1].

---

[1] We will use the words "our" and "we" in referring to works written by one of us, two of us, or all three of us.

We applied the intersubjectivity principle to the developmental system as well:

> Both psychological development and pathogenesis are best conceptualized in terms of the specific intersubjective contexts that shape the developmental process and that facilitate or obstruct the child's negotiation of critical developmental tasks and successful passage through developmental phases. The observational focus is the evolving psychological field constituted by the interplay between the differently organized subjectivities of child and caretakers . . . [p. 2].

The concept of intersubjectivity evolved in our thinking through a series of stages. The significance of the intersubjective perspective first became apparent to us in a study of the interplay between transference and countertransference in psychoanalytic therapy (Stolorow, Atwood, and Ross, 1978). There we considered the impact on the treatment process of phenomena arising out of the correspondences and disparities that exist between the analyst's and the patient's respective worlds of experience. An attempt was made in particular to characterize the conditions under which such phenomena may obstruct or facilitate the unfolding of the psychoanalytic dialogue. At this early stage we already were focusing on interactions between patients' and therapists' subjective worlds, but the more general concept of the intersubjective field within which psychoanalytic therapy takes place had not yet been articulated.

We then were led to an investigation of the situation that arises in treatment when there is a wide but unrecognized disparity between the relatively structured world of the analyst and an archaically organized personal universe of the patient (Stolorow, Brandchaft, and Atwood, 1983). Such a disjunction, we showed, often results in chronic misunderstandings wherein the archaic experiences communicated by the patient cannot be comprehended because of the analyst's unconscious assimilation of them to his own, differently organized subjectivity. The analyst's responses may then be experienced as grossly unattuned, precipitating a spiral of reaction and counterreaction that is incomprehensible to both parties. When the analyst fails to decenter from the structures of experience into which he has been assimilating his patient's communications, the final result is a view of the patient as an intrinsically difficult, recalcitrant person whose qualities perhaps render him unsuitable for psychoanalytic treatment. We thus had begun to understand in a very specific context how the analyst's picture of the patient's attributes crystallizes within the interplay between two personal universes.

The intersubjectivity concept is in part a response to the unfortunate tendency of classical analysis to view pathology in terms of processes and mechanisms located solely within the patient. Such an isolating focus fails to do justice to each individual's irreducible engagement with other human beings and blinds the clinician to the profound ways in which he is himself implicated in the clinical phenomena he observes and seeks to treat. We have now come to believe that the intersubjective context has a constitutive role in all forms of psychopathology, ranging from the psychoneurotic to the overtly psychotic. This role is most readily demonstrated in the most severe disorders, wherein fluctuations in the therapeutic bond are accompanied by dramatically observable effects. The intersubjective context is of equal significance, however, in less severe forms of psychopathology; for example, in anxiety neuroses, depressions, and obsessional and phobic disorders. The exploration of the particular patterns of intersubjective transaction involved in developing and maintaining each of the various forms of psychopathology is in our view one of the most important areas for continuing clinical psychoanalytic research. To that end, we turn now to an examination of the intersubjective contexts in which borderline symptomatology takes form, both in early development and in the therapeutic situation.

THE "BORDERLINE PERSONALITY ORGANIZATION"

The term *borderline* is generally used to refer to a distinct character structure that predisposes to faulty object relations, in which the fundamental difficulties are ordinarily attributed to the patient's pathological ego functioning. Typically the borderline personality organization is pictured as a direct structural consequence of the patient's use of certain primitive defenses—splitting, projective identification, idealization, and grandiosity—to ward off intense conflicts over dependency and excessive pregenital aggression (which dependency presumably mobilizes). But what is the clinical evidence that supposedly demonstrates the operation of these primitive defenses? And what is the meaning of the excessive aggression to which primary etiological significance is ascribed in the genesis of borderline psychopathology?

THE QUESTION OF SPLITTING

The experience of external objects as "all good" or "all bad" is generally regarded as a clear manifestation of splitting, resulting in sudden and total reversals of feeling whereby the view of the object is shifted from one extreme to the other. Oscillation between extreme and contradictory self concepts is similarly seen as evidence of splitting. This fluid and rapid alternation of contradictory perceptions of the self or others is presumed to be caused by an active defensive process whereby images with opposing affective valences are forcibly kept apart in order to prevent intense ambivalence. But is this assumption warranted clinically? Splitting as a defense actively employed to ward off ambivalence conflicts can come into play only after a minimum of integration of discrepant self and object experiences has been achieved through development (Stolorow and Lachmann, 1980). A defensive split into parts presupposes a prior integration of a whole. It is our contention that such a presupposition is not warranted when treating patients who are ordinarily diagnosed borderline. Their fragmentary perceptions do not result primarily from defensive activity, but rather from an arrest in development, which impairs their ability reliably to synthesize affectively discrepant experiences of self and other. Their rapidly fluctuating views of the therapist, for example, do not primarily serve to prevent ambivalence toward him. They are, in part, manifestations of a need for the therapist to serve as an archaic containing or holding object whose consistently empathic comprehension and acceptance of these patients' contradictory affective state functions as a facilitating medium through which their varying perceptions and feelings can eventually become better integrated (Winnicott, 1965b; Modell, 1976; Stolorow and Lachmann, 1980).

It is our view that the lack of synthesis of self and object experiences characteristic of so-called borderline states is neither defensive in nature nor central in the genesis of these disorders. In our experience, the intense, contradictory affective states that these patients experience within the transference, and in particular their violent negative reactions, are indicative of specific structural weaknesses and vulnerabilities rooted in specific developmental interferences. Archaic mirroring, idealizing, and other self–object needs are revived in analytic transferences, together with hopes for a resumption of development. When these needs are responded to, or understood and interpreted empathically, intense positive reactions occur. Similarly, when these needs are not recognized, responded to, or interpreted empathically, violent negative reactions may ensue. If these angry reactions are presumed to represent a defensive dissociation of good and bad aspects of objects, this in effect constitutes a covert demand that the patient ignore his own subjective experiences and appreciate the "goodness" of the analyst and his interpretations. It precludes analysis of the patient's subjective experience in depth, the elements that go to make it up, and their special hierarchy of meanings for the patient. In contrast, when we have held such preconceptions in abeyance, we have found that the intensity of the angry reactions stems from the way they encoded and encapsulated memories of specific traumatic childhood experiences.

We are familiar with the experience of becoming the target of a patient's intense and suddenly shifting affect states, of one day being perceived as almost godlike and the very next as all but totally malicious. We are also aware of the threat such shifting perceptions pose to therapists' sense of self sameness, and we can therefore understand their tendency to attribute such perceptions to distorting mechanisms operating within the patient. In an earlier work (Stolorow, Brandchaft, and Atwood, 1987), however, we questioned the assumption of an objective reality known by the analyst and distorted by the patient. We argued:

> The only reality relevant and accessible to psychoanalytic inquiry . . . is *subjective reality*—that of the patient, that of the analyst, and the psychological field created by the interplay between the two. . . . Analysts' invoking the concept of . . . distortion obscures the subjective reality encoded in the patient's productions, which is precisely what psychoanalytic investigation should seek to illuminate [pp. 4–5].

Eschewing the concept of distortion helps therapists gain empathic access to the archaic experiences that underlie borderline states, and thereby comprehend the patient's rapidly changing transference feelings as reactions to shifting elements within the intersubjective field.

THE CASE OF JEFF

A clinical vignette illustrates our idea of specific vulnerability. When Jeff, a young man of twenty-three, entered treatment, he was in a state of marked overstimulation. He could not sit still for more than a few minutes at a time; his eyes darted from object to object; and he spoke under constant pressure. Although enrolled in college, he had not been able to attend classes or concentrate on his work. Increasingly frightened when alone at night, he had recently begun to take to the streets. There he had been approached for homosexual purposes several times, and this made him more fearful of his own unrecognized wishes and heightened his agitation. In the sessions he gave the impression of wanting desperately to cling to something around which he might begin to reorganize and restructure himself. Consequently, during the first months of treatment it was very difficult to bring any session to a close. His initial resistances centered on fears of being used to fulfill the analyst's needs. When these were interpreted, an early idealizing transference developed. This enabled Jeff to confront the area of primary defect—a failure to have attained a cohesive self and a vulnerability to recurrent states of protracted disorganization. The analysis thus resumed a developmental process that had been stalled.

Jeff's relationship with his father had always presented difficulty for him. The father reacted to any weakness or shortcoming in his son with impatience and contempt. This situation directly entered the analysis because Jeff's father had assumed financial responsibility for the treatment. The arrangement became a source of greater and greater tension between the two, for the father resented the burden of payment, as well as what he saw as evidence of his son's weakness, and simultaneously a source of shame for himself. The difficulties in this area increased whenever Jeff made it clear that the analysis was not leading in the direction of making Jeff the son his father had always wished for, but was instead increasing Jeff's determination to develop in his own way.

Although the analyst realized the complications that might ensue, after two-and-a-half years he notified Jeff that he was raising his fees generally. He wanted to discuss the matter with Jeff to see if and how it might be worked out. The request came at a time when Jeff's relations with his father were already strained, though it did not appear likely that this would change within any foreseeable period of time. Jeff's initial response was one of some anger about the unfortunate timing, followed by a remark to the effect that of course he knew how the analyst felt because everything was going up in price. Recognizing Jeff's frequent tendency to substitute an understanding of someone else's position for an expression of his own, the analyst interpreted this, together with Jeff's fear of the analyst's reaction to his expressing his own feeling. (We would emphasize that in our experience such genuine emotional expression is always obstructed, and with it an essential aspect of an authentic relationship, when a patient's affective states are incorrectly interpreted as defensive transference distortions.)

Gradually, over the course of the next few sessions, Jeff was able to come out with his feelings—feelings of hurt, disappointment, and violent anger. The hurt seemed to center on the analyst's failure to ever (Jeff's words) consider him first, and the extent to which this experience revived feelings of always having been a burden, a supplicant, someone standing in the way of other people's plans or enjoyment. Jeff was a twin, and he recounted a welter of experiences in which his twin had preempted his parents' attention by being exactly the child they wanted and one who caused them no difficulty.

Jeff's anger at the analyst was related mostly to the poor timing and what that meant to him. He spoke of the bind the analyst's request put him in. Things were already going badly between him and his father. Jeff had started a new job and had been forced to ask his father for money for new clothes. Each encounter of that kind was humiliating for Jeff. Now he would have to face a review of how long he had been in treatment and how much longer it was to continue. How could the analyst, knowing all this, choose to put Jeff through it!

Frequently, after expressing himself unabashedly, Jeff would huddle up, as if in a corner, his arms protectively wrapped around himself. In response to questions, he confirmed that he was terrified. He was certain that the analyst would be furious with him, call him selfish, and berate him for his lack of appreciation for the analyst.

There now emerged a host of memories in which the timing of Jeff's life (and, indeed, his life itself) had to conform to someone else's wishes. He had to go to bed when his father told his mother he should. He had to wait until his father was done with the evening news before speaking to him, and then he could only talk about what his father was interested in. Monday night, football night, was especially sacrosanct—not an occasion when a pleasurable interest might be shared, but one more occasion when Dad was not to be disturbed.

Jeff's mother told him when, what, and how to eat. She chose his clothes for him, where and how he was to sit or stand. He was not to sit on the couch lest the cushions be messed up, nor on his bed for similar reasons. He had to renounce his own inclinations and adopt her wishes regarding what music he was to like. Always before the family left on an auto trip, he was instructed to urinate, and his mother checked to make sure he didn't put anything over on them. Otherwise they might have to stop along the way. And Jeff recalled that whenever he attempted to protest or assert himself, perhaps because something was especially important to him, he was squelched, accused of selfishness and a lack of consideration. He was told that his father wouldn't want to come home at all if he kept this up.

For Jeff, the most significant aspect of these repeated experiences was a feeling of absolute powerlessness. Once, when he could not stand it anymore, he went to his room and packed an overnight bag. When he appeared in front of his parents to declare he was running away, no one said a word or made a move to stop him. He then realized that he was stuck—that no one else would want him and that he had to give in.

These experiences formed the background of Jeff's reaction to the analyst's request for an increase. Jeff retained, in its most imperative form, the longing that someone would put his wishes first, and he was highly sensitive to the specific configuration of others' needs being put before his own. He therefore responded acutely and intensely to that configuration when it entered the transference. This response was covered over by a more moderate reaction, in which he apparently attempted defensively to "synthesize" good and bad object concepts. What was crucial, however, was for Jeff to recognize the underlying intensity of his hurt and the experiences behind it, rather than having his reaction regarded as an instance of splitting or a lack of appreciation for the analyst. This recognition opened up an entire area of the transference to analysis and ultimate resolution. Jeff and the analyst came to see clearly the extent to which Jeff had found it necessary to define himself around what was expected, what would please, and what would not offend in order to maintain his object ties. They were able to comprehend the threat constantly posed by any authentic experience of self—the threat of estrangement and isolation Jeff had encountered whenever he asserted himself or attempted to act on his own behalf. The analysis, then, brought out into the open and allowed Jeff to work through the enormous resentment such subjugation of self had aroused.

THE QUESTION OF PROJECTIVE IDENTIFICATION

First coined by Klein (1946) to describe an archaic fantasy, the term *projective identification* is now widely used to designate a primitive defense mechanism that is presumed to be characteristic of patients diagnosed borderline (Kernberg, 1975, 1987a). In projective identification, it is claimed, there is a blurring of the distinction between the self and the object in the area of the projected content. Such states of self–object confusion are assumed to be the product of an active defensive effort to externalize all-bad, aggressive self and object images. Once again, we question whether this assumption is clinically justified.

Projection as a defense actively employed to ward off conflict can come into play only after a minimum of self–object differentiation has been reliably achieved (Stolorow and Lachmann, 1980). Defensive translocation of mental content across self–object boundaries presupposes that those boundaries have been for the most part consolidated. Our experience contradicts such a presupposition for patients diagnosed as borderline. Their states of self–object confusion arise primarily from a developmentally determined inability to maintain the distinction between self and object. In the treatment context it is not useful to view such states as examples of either defensive projection or general ego weakness. Indeed, the analyst's insistence that what the patient is perceiving in the analyst is a disowned aspect of the patient is likely to undermine further the patient's

tenuous self-boundaries and thereby exacerbate the confu-
sional states. In contrast, the investigation of the patient's experience from within the perspective of the patient's own subjective frame of reference helps to consolidate the precariously
established boundaries. In general, these partially undifferentiated states are best understood as manifestations of revivals
with the therapist of a specific need for immersion in a nexus
of archaic relatedness, from within which formerly thwarted
developmental processes of self-articulation and self-demarca-
tion can be revitalized and once again resumed (Stolorow and
Lachmann, 1980).

Frequently we have encountered in the literature a second,
and to our minds even more questionable, use of the term
projective identification. There is presumed to be not only a projective distortion of the patient's subjective experience of the
object, but also a purposefully induced alteration in the external
object's actual attitude and behavior toward the patient:

> The subject projects intolerable intrapsychic experiences
> onto an object, maintains empathy with what he projects,
> tries to control the object in a continuing effort to defend
> against the intolerable experience, and, unconsciously, in
> actual interaction with the object, leads the object to expe-
> rience what has been projected onto him [Kernberg,
> 1987a, p. 796].

This formulation is based on the observation that intense reactions frequently occur in analysts who are treating borderline
patients. Because such reactions are experienced similarly by
most "reasonably well-adjusted therapists," the reasoning goes
"countertransference reactions in these cases reflect the patient's problems much more than any specific problems of the
analyst's past" (Kernberg, 1975, p. 54). It is also suggested that
if the analyst is reacting intensely to the patient, such countertransference is a clue to the patient's hidden intention. Kernberg (1975), for example, writes:

> If the patient systematically rejects all the analyst's inter-
> pretations over a long period of time, the analyst may

recognize his own resultant feelings of impotence and point out to the patient that he is treating the analyst as if he wished to make him feel defeated and impotent. Or when antisocial behavior in the patient makes the analyst, rather than the patient, worry about the consequences, the analyst may point out that the patient seems to try to let the analyst feel the concern over his behavior because the patient himself cannot tolerate such a feeling [p. 247].

In such formulations, the analyst's reactions to the patient at crucial points in the intersubjective dialogue are regarded as reliable, conclusive, and objective sources of data about the patient's motivations. These formulations fail to take into account that when the analyst, in his interpretations, insists that the patient's perceptions of him as threatening or damaging are the consequence of projections of the patient's own disavowed aggression, the only alternatives open to the patient are to agree with the premises being put forward or to find himself in the position of inadvertently making the analyst feel defeated and impotent. To us, this state of affairs seems to reflect the extent to which the analyst's self-esteem depends on the patient's acceptance of the correctness of his theoretical position, rather than necessarily reflecting any unconscious hostile intention on the part of the patient. Similarly, the analyst's concerns about a patient's antisocial behavior seem to us to reflect the analyst's difficulties in sufficiently demarcating himself from the patient so as to be able to devote himself to the investigation of the meaning of the actions in question.

A description of a typical clinical application of the concept of projective identification is contained in Kernberg's (1975) reference to Ingmar Bergman's movie *Persona*:

A recent motion picture . . . illustrates the breakdown of an immature but basically decent young woman, a nurse, charged with the care of a psychologically severely ill woman presenting what we would describe as a typical narcissistic personality. In the face of the cold, unscrupulous exploitation to which the young nurse is subjected, she gradually breaks down. She cannot face the fact that the other sick woman returns only hatred for love and is completely unable to acknowledge any loving or human feeling expressed toward her. The sick woman seems to be able to live only if and when she can destroy what is valuable in other persons, although in the process she ends up destroying herself as a human being. In a dramatic development, the nurse develops an intense hatred for the sick woman and mistreats her cruelly at one point. It is as if all the hatred within the sick woman had been transferred into the helping one, destroying the helping person from the inside [pp. 245–246].

We hold that conclusions such as this are unjustified and that the underlying assumptions are unwarranted and antitherapeutic. In the first place, there is no evidence that the sick woman is "able to live only if and when she can destroy what is valuable in other persons"; there are only indications that the sick woman does not respond in a way that the nurse–therapist wants or needs. We are familiar in our own practices with many cases in which patients who have recently experienced traumatic loss and disintegration resolutely protect themselves against any involvement until some spontaneous recovery has set in. Second, there is no evidence that "the hatred within the sick woman has been transferred into the helping one, destroying the helping person from the inside." There is, instead, every indication that the patient's responsiveness was required in order for the nurse to maintain her own self-esteem and to regulate her own psychological functioning. When frustrated, the nurse demonstrated her own narcissistic vulnerability and propensity for rage reactions. We have observed such factors at work in ourselves and regard them as to some degree universal in therapeutic relationships. In our view, their near universality does not warrant their being ignored as originating in the personality structure of the therapist. Nor does it warrant the assumption that these responses are an indication of pathological projective mechanisms on the part of the patient. We have found that the assumption that the patient wishes the therapist to feel impotent or infuriated is much more often than not directly contradicted in our own work. Such wishes, we suggest, occur only when the patient's disagreements, assertions, and primary wishes to have his own subjective experiences empathically understood have been consistently unresponded to. Far more often, the patient's fear of the analyst's narcissistic vulnerability and of being held responsible for the analyst's feeling of frustration constitutes a severe resistance to free association and is a prominent motive for defense. In essence, the patient fears that he is required to serve as an affirming self–object for the therapist, much as he had felt required to serve that function for a parent during childhood.

The concept of projective identification is used extensively to explain why patients are so regularly afraid of their analysts. It specifically neglects the potentially devastating threats posed to the patient's sense of self by the perceptions of him that are conveyed in the analyst's theory-rooted interpretive stance. We have found that the analyst's insistence that negative reactions in analysis are to be explained by the patient's innate aggression or envy, or by his projection of aggressively distorted internal objects, can be damaging to the patient, to the unfolding self–object transference, and to the analysis (Brandchaft, 1983). The application of the theory of projective identification carries with it the real danger of depriving patients of a means of defending themselves when they feel that the analyst is cruel, distant, controlling, or demeaning. This danger is increased if the analyst, for whatever reason, is unable or unwilling to become aware of his actual effect on the patient, or if he minimizes that effect because of a conviction that he has the ultimate best interests of the patient at heart. Frequently, this conviction in the analyst takes the form of a conception of a "more normal dependent" part of the patient, which is being dominated and excluded by the aggressive part. Such unwarranted, if reassuring, concepts notwithstanding, the tendency to fall back on interpretations of projection to the detriment of the subjective experience of the patient, even where such mechanisms exist, can in practice be shown to foster a dependence on the analyst's perceptions at the expense of the patient's. These interpretations encourage, indeed require, a pro forma belief in the analyst's "goodness" and correctness at the expense of the self. They impair the patient's sense of his own self and belief in himself, and they encourage an agreement that necessary and understandable efforts to protect a vulnerable self are indicative of severe pathology and should be given up.

FURTHER MISCONCEPTUALIZATIONS

Closely allied with the developmental disturbances discussed so far are the idealizations and grandiosity that often pervade the treatment of patients who are called borderline. Such perceptions of the self or others are regularly interpreted as being defensive against dependency and the attendant subject-centered or object-centered aggression. Our experiences indicate that most often the idealizations and grandiosity are manifestations of self–object transference (Kohut, 1971, 1977). They are not pathological defenses, but rather revivals with the therapist of the archaic idealizing and mirroring ties that were traumatically and phase-inappropriately ruptured during the patient's formative years and on which he now comes to rely for the restoration and maintenance of his sense of self and for the reinstatement of a thwarted developmental process.

Having argued that much of the clinical evidence cited for the operation of primitive defenses is actually evidence of needs for specific archaic self–object ties, and of disturbances in those ties, how shall we understand the "excessive pregenital aggression" that many authors believe is the etiological bedrock of borderline pathology? We contend that pervasive primitive aggression is an inevitable, unwitting, iatrogenic consequence of a therapeutic approach that presupposes that the psychological configurations we have been discussing are in their essence pathological defenses against dependency and primitive aggression. A patient revives an arrested archaic state or need, or attempts a previously aborted developmental step within the therapeutic relationship, and the therapist interprets this developmental necessity as if it were a pathological defense. The patient then experiences this misinterpretation as a gross failure of attunement, a severe breach of trust, a traumatic narcissistic wound (Stolorow and Lachmann, 1980). When vital developmental requirements reexperienced in relation to a therapist once again meet with traumatically unempathic responses, is it surprising that such misunderstandings often bring intense rage and destructiveness in their wake? We are contending, in other words, that the pervasive aggression is not etiological, but rather a secondary reaction to the therapist's inability to comprehend the developmental meaning of the patient's archaic states and of the archaic bond that the patient needs to establish with him (Kohut, 1972, 1977; Solorow, 1984).

AN INTERSUBJECTIVE VIEWPOINT

At this point we are in a position to formulate our central thesis regarding the borderline concept. The psychological essence of what we call "borderline" is not that it is a pathological condition located solely in the patient. Rather, it refers to phenomena arising in an intersubjective field—a field consisting of a precarious, vulnerable self in a failing, archaic self–object bond. In order to elaborate this thesis further, we must clarify the nature of the self disorder that contributes to the emergence of borderline phenomena.

We view the various disorders of the self as arbitrary points along a continuum (Adler, 1981) rather than as discrete diagnostic entities. The points along this continuum are defined by the degree of impairment and vulnerability of the sense of self, the acuteness of the threat of its disintegration, and the motivational urgency of self-reparative efforts in various pathological states. The degree of severity of self disorder may be evaluated with reference to three essential features of the sense of self: its structural cohesion, temporal stability, and affective coloration (Stolorow and Lachmann, 1980).

In certain patients, the sense of self is negatively colored (feelings of low self-esteem) but is for the most part temporally stable and structurally cohesive. One might refer to such cases as mild self disorders. In other patients, the sense of self is negatively colored and its organization is temporally unstable (experiences of identity confusion) but, notwithstanding fleeting fragmentations, it largely retains its structural cohesion. These cases might be called moderately severe self disorders.

In a third group of patients, the sense of self is negatively colored, temporally unstable, and lacking in cohesion and thus subject to protracted structural fragmentation and disintegration. Such cases can be termed very severe self disorders. Roughly speaking, patients who are called "borderline" fall within the moderate to severe range of self disorders.

The concept of self disorder as a continuum or dimension of psychopathology enables therapists to maintain a stance of empathic inquiry toward archaic states of mind that might otherwise seem too alien and thus refractory to such inquiry. This concept of self disorder as a continuum is somewhat at variance with Kohut's (1971) early view of "borderline" as a discrete diagnostic entity that is sharply distinguishable from the narcissistic personality disorders. The borderline personality, according to this view, is chronically threatened with the possibility of an irreversible disintegration of the self—a psychological catastrophe that is more or less successfully averted by the various protective operations characteristic of borderline functioning. This vulnerability to a permanent breakup of the self is the product of a traumatically crushing or depriving developmental history that has precluded even minimal consolidation of the archaic grandiose self and the idealized parent imago. Consequently, unlike the narcissistic personality, the borderline patient is unable to form a stable mirroring or idealizing self–object transference and is therefore unanalyzable by the classical method.

In contrast with Kohut's conceptualization, our observations are consistent with those of other analysts who have reported analyses of borderline personalities in which the therapist was eventually able to help the patient form a more or less stable and analyzable self–object transference (Adler, 1980, 1981; Tolpin, 1980). It is true that the self–object ties formed by those patients who are called "borderline" tend initially to be far more primitive and intense, more labile and vulnerable to disruption, and therefore more taxing of the therapist's empathy and tolerance (Adler, 1980, 1981; Tolpin, 1980) than those described by Kohut as being characteristic of narcissistic personalities. Furthermore, when the self–object ties of a patient with a moderate to severe self disorder are obstructed or ruptured by misunderstandings or separations, the patient's reactions may be much more catastrophic and disturbed, for what is threatened is the patient's central self-regulatory capacity—the basic structural integrity and stability of the sense of self, not merely its affective tone (Adler, 1980, 1981; Stolorow and Lachmann, 1980). Nevertheless, when their archaic states and needs are sufficiently understood, these patients can be helped to form more or less stable self–object transferences, and, when this is achieved, their so-called borderline features recede and even disappear. As long as the self–object tie to the therapist remains intact, their treatment will bear a close similarity to Kohut's descriptions of analyses of narcissistic personality disorders (Adler, 1980, 1981).[2] When the self–object tie to the therapist becomes significantly disrupted, on the other hand, the patient may once again present borderline features. What we wish to stress is that whether or not a stable self–object bond can develop and be maintained (which in turn shapes both the apparent diagnostic picture and the assessment of analyzability) does not depend only on the patient's nuclear self pathology. It will be codetermined by the extent of the therapist's ability to comprehend the nature of the patient's archaic subjective universe (Tolpin, 1980) as it begins to structure the microcosm of the therapeutic transference.

THE CASE OF CAROLINE

Our conception of borderline as phenomena arising and receding within an intersubjective field is exemplified by the case of Caroline. The "borderline" symptoms that led Caroline to enter analysis were immediately precipitated by severe disturbances in her relationship with her husband. In other words, they arose within a specific intersubjective field—that of a precarious, vulnerable self in a failing, archaic self–object tie. The analyst, however, did not

---

[2] In a personal communication (1981), Kohut stated that he had long held views compatible with those developed here. He wrote: "Insofar as the therapist is able to build an empathic bridge to the patient, the patient has in a way ceased to be a borderline case . . . and has become a case of (severe) narcissistic personality disorder."

sufficiently recognize this when the treatment began, and his lack of understanding complicated and prolonged the treatment. We have since observed that often patients enter treatment when there is a breakdown in an archaic self–object bond, which has hitherto served to maintain, however precariously and at whatever cost, the structural cohesion and stability of the self and the patient's central self-regulatory capability.

Caroline spoke with a Southern accent, which became more pronounced when she was tense. She was somewhat overweight and attempted to cover this with loose-fitting clothes, which only made it more obvious. For some time she had been in a state of more or less constant anxiety, at times hyperactive and at other times withdrawn, apathetic, and unable to get moving. Early in her treatment, she displayed a frightened, little-girl look, expressing her evident discomfort and, not infrequently, her terror. She avoided the analyst's eyes almost completely. In the first weeks, she openly voiced her disbelief that anyone could help her and said she saw no way out of her difficulties. Gradually it was reconstructed that her present intractable state dated from about ten years earlier and had followed a deterioration in her relationship with her husband (to whom she had then been married for about a dozen years). Although Caroline had been a reasonably attractive young woman, her shyness and lack of confidence, in concert with a puritanical upbringing, had constricted her social and sexual development. Thus, her husband was the first man with whom she had had a serious relationship. She had been an outstanding student—her remarkable intelligence was to become clearer as the treatment progressed—but she left college when she married, in order to support and further the career of her husband, then in law school. Subsequently, when he set up practice, she kept house for him, assisted him in many ways, reared their child, and operated a small business so that they could prosper financially. In spite of this, their relationship became more strained and conflicted, as her husband became ever more displeased with and critical of her—of her accent, her weight, her anxiety, and depression. This culminated in a "borderline" state, with progressive lethargy, hypochondriacal symptoms, feelings of deadness that began in her extremities and threatened to engulf her whole body, and frightening delusions about her husband harming, poisoning, or killing her.

Caroline recovered from this early episode in a matter of weeks, but many of the symptoms recurred (though not the delusions) and other symptoms took hold. She began to eat compulsively, and there were periodic withdrawals during which she remained preoccupied with puzzles or needlework for long periods of time. In the early months of treatment, Caroline appeared so distraught and disorganized that the analyst believed that only by seeing her six times a week could he avert a prolonged hospitalization or suicide (to which she made several references).

Whatever the content of the sessions, Caroline reacted to their ending with enormous anxiety and clung to the analyst as the hour drew to a close, speeding up her associations so that he could not interrupt her. When he succeeded in calling the session to a halt, she either continued the conversation until he closed the door behind her or, enraged by his interrupting her, walked out in a sullen pout. Weekends and more prolonged separations produced severe regressive states and numerous dreams filled with disaster—flooding and drowning, houses perched precariously on a cliff edge, supports crumbling, black men pursuing her, and imagery involving a variety of mutilations.

In the first dream that Caroline reported in the analysis, she described her husband and her analyst sitting in the living room. She went to the freezer and took something out. It was the trunk of a frozen corpse with no limbs. She showed this to the men, but they began to have sport with it—tossing it around and laughing.

The early sessions were marked by an almost uninterrupted stream of associations. The analyst found it hard to think, let alone formulate a coherent understanding of any underlying meaning. As this continued for some time, it was difficult for the analyst to escape the conviction that she was projecting her anxiety and helplessness into him in an attempt to rid herself of these feelings.

Gradually, however, it became clear that she was terrified of the analyst and the treatment—terrified that she would be treated cruelly, driven mad, or abandoned as a hopeless case. These fears were interpreted to her as indications of a lack of trust and reluctance to depend on the analyst. Such interpretations seemed for a time to calm her, and they evoked memories of her early experiences.

Caroline was her parents' first child. They had married when her mother was approaching forty. Her father, four years older and a widower with two teenaged sons, was a hard-working accountant who needed someone to take responsibility for their upbringing. As a young woman, Caroline's mother had wanted desperately to escape from the drudgery of her small town life, and her love of music seemed to offer her the opportunity. But she realized rather late that her hopes of becoming an opera singer or the coach of an operatic prodigy were destined to disappointment. By that time her chances for a good marriage had passed her by, and she settled on Caroline's father, more with resignation than ardor, a bird in no gilded cage.

The parents had been married two years when Caroline was born, after what she was repeatedly told was an extremely difficult labor. Three years after her birth a brother was born. This birth was even more difficult and resulted in severe damage to the mother's pelvic tissues. Afterward the mother took to her bed in a depression that lasted for many months during which time she was preoccupied with an assortment of hypochondriacal and somatic symptoms. When she recovered, she treated Caroline as if the little girl were an extension of her own defective, diseased self. She reacted to every sneeze as if it were a harbinger of death, took Caroline from doctor to doctor, and kept her out of school for two years. As Caroline and her health became her mother's sole preoccupation, intense conflicts arose. These centered on what foods Caroline was to eat, how much and at what intervals she was to sleep, and especially her bowel habits.

As the treatment progressed, the analyst noted that Caroline was somewhat better as each week proceeded, but then regressed toward its end. Weekends remained disasters, with the patient unable to think or function except at a minimal level. The analyst thought that the material indicated Caroline's inability to retain any image of a good object built up during the sessions—she and it underwent a nearly complete deterioration during separations. When she returned to analysis, it was in a state of helplessness. Repeatedly, she then complained that the analysis was not helping her, and frequently, apparently forgetting her condition when she entered treatment, she angrily asserted that the analyst was responsible for her pain and lack of progress.

It was easy for the analyst to conclude that the archaic states of confusion and disintegration into which Caroline lapsed came about because of persistent splitting, that her good internal objects were being kept widely apart from the bad, that synthesis was being actively prevented from occurring, and that she could not simultaneously accept the analyst's goodness and his separateness. She reacted to his unavailability on weekends and to what he believed were thoughtful and helpful interpretations as if they were purposely meant to make her suffer. Attacking him in that way, she anticipated being attacked in return. And she experienced every attempt on his part to explain this situation to her, no matter how cautiously, tactfully, and empathically phrased, as a renewed attack on her.

Another "symptom" appeared in Caroline's treatment. One day, in striking contrast to her usual outfit of jeans and tennis shoes, she appeared in a lovely skirt and jacket, a pretty blouse, and fashionable shoes and purse. Greatly embarrassed, she revealed that she had gone on a spree, bought three outfits, several pairs of shoes, and an assortment of matching accessories. She confided that she did this every once in a while, in spite of herself. She knew that when she went home she would have to hide all the things she had bought and might never be able to wear them, for her husband would be furious with her. He would be frightened and horrified by her excesses. He maintained absolute control over the family finances and regarded her buying binges as symptoms of insanity or as inconsiderate breaches of contract. Moreover, now he would have further grounds for his understandable concern over her treatment.

The analyst felt that if her purpose was to project into him her anxiety over behavior for which she wished to escape responsibility, she could not have devised a more effective means. He was also struck by the excess, the suddenness, and the lack of control, and he tried without success, to investigate the spree from that perspective. He was to learn later that Caroline did not buy another stitch of clothing for three years.

Caroline's fears of the analyst and the analysis kept recurring. Her dreams were filled with scalding suns, Chinese tortures, and monstrously cruel people. Such images were generally interpreted as transference projections. Gradually some small progress seemed to occur. Her anger subsided somewhat, her anxiety assumed more manageable proportions, and she was able to read and to socialize to a greater extent. Yet whenever her old symptoms returned, she thrashed herself mercilessly. Repeated working through of these themes seemed to the analyst to leave no alternative to the explanation that something in her was opposing success, making it impossible for her to benefit further from treatment, her marriage, and, indeed, her life. She made many starts in many directions, but invariably her enthusiasm disappeared, to be mourned and to become the focus of renewed disappointment and anger with herself. It seemed that continued treatment would only confirm an omnipotent fantasy that somehow some experience would magically solve her difficulties without her having to change.

The analysis, then, appeared to have reached a stalemate. Although basic problems had not been solved, the prospect of termination loomed unmistakably, for it seemed to the analyst that more analysis would only serve to keep Caroline from utilizing the considerable insights she had attained. Rationalizations appeared like weeds after a rain. After all, her background had left her with a considerable toll. The difficulties of her attachment to or detachment from her husband, especially at her age, were all but insurmountable. Yet her gains, looked at in a certain light, were not negligible, and it seemed certain that she was no longer so vulnerable to the threat of collapse that had brought her into treatment.

However, at this point, in the fourth year of treatment, the analyst decided to take one last look. It had long been apparent that Caroline was disappointed and felt herself to be a failure, but it was now also becoming clear that she felt that the analyst was disappointed in her and that he considered her and himself failures. This factor—Caroline's responsiveness to cues of the analyst's feeling about her—had been grossly underestimated. In fact, as was later understood, her imperative need to be liked and approved of and the devastating effect on her of the analyst's disapproval, which she sensed, had been crucial in structuring the first phase of treatment. Her depression, her attacks on herself, and her lack of sustaining motivation all became understandable from this perspective. The analyst could not continue to maintain that her perceptions of him were all projection, for he began to recognize in himself what she had been responding to. This dawning awareness ushered in the second phase of the analysis.

In a subsequent session, in response to Caroline's expression of weariness and thoughts about terminating, the analyst commented that he realized that the process was becoming wearing. But could they take one more good look at what had been occurring before deciding to terminate? Perhaps there was something he had not understood, something that might prove helpful. Perhaps he had conveyed an increasing disappointment in her and in himself, especially around her continuing symptoms, and perhaps that had contributed in an important way to her

dejection and disparagement of herself. Caroline responded enthusiastically. Yes, she exclaimed, she had felt
awful about the analyst's disappointment, which she had
sensed. By this time she should be able to feel better and
to control her diet, for she had learned so much. She had
attacked herself mercilessly for not having tried hard
enough. She was weak and self-indulgent, she said, and
must want to spite both her husband and the analyst as
she had always defied her mother. When she was on her
diets, she could somehow kill her craving for food and not
be hungry. But something always happened and she again
felt the urge to eat. Then she felt she was a failure and
tried harder and harder. When she was finally unable to
stick to her diet, she hated herself, for she had let the
analyst and her husband down. Once that point had been
reached she was absolutely unable to restrain herself—the
more alone she felt, the more she hated herself and the
more she felt compelled to eat.

The analyst was now able to glimpse the transference
configuration that had actually determined the course of
Caroline's analysis. Together they began to look at what
happened to her when she was alone, paying increasing
attention now to her subjective experiences and trying to
understand them in a different way. There seemed to be
a complex and thoroughgoing alteration of her state of
mind—a slipping away of self-esteem, feelings of accelerat-
ing disorganization and disconnectedness, an inability to
concentrate, and increasing feelings of deadness, involving
coldness and loss of sensation in her limbs, so that they no
longer seemed to belong to her. All these symptoms the
analyst came to recognize as signs of a fragmenting process
and of an underlying defect in her self-structure. It became apparent how much Caroline had looked to the analyst to maintain her sense of self, needing from him what
had not been acquired in her childhood. When the analyst
had interpreted her archaic states and transference needs
as expressions of pathological splitting and projection, she
had become intensely ashamed and self-hating. In their

impact on Caroline, the interpretations of pathological defenses had repeated the fragmentation-producing effects
of her mother's view of her as defective and diseased.

It was especially important to Caroline that the analyst
be pleased with her. She had tried valiantly to get this
across to him early in the analysis, but he had regarded
this as defensive. He had not recognized as primary her
specific need to establish him as a self–object who would
be a source of the mirroring, affirming responsiveness that
her self-absorbed, depressed and hypochondriacal mother
had been unable to supply during her early formative
years. Behind this specific need lay the vulnerability to
fragmentation that had pervaded Caroline's analytic experiences. When the self–object tie to the analyst was disrupted by a failure of the analyst to understand her subjective experience in its essence or by a loss of connectedness
during weekends or vacations, she could not maintain the
cohesion, stability, and affective tone of her precarious
self. She fell apart, eating compulsively in an effort to
strengthen herself and to fill the defect in her sense of
self—trying to recover through oral self-stimulation the
feeling that she existed at all.

As the disturbance in the transference tie was seen
and analyzed in this new way, with focus on the fragmented states and the underlying structural deficit, Caroline became more alive, friendlier, much more enthusiastic, and increasingly capable. Her desire to understand her
states of mind grew in direct proportion to her sense of
the analyst's desire to help her acquire this understanding.
She expressed appreciation that the analyst now recognized her vulnerability and the legitimacy of her fears.
"The first thing I had to get across to you," she explained
when she was certain that he would understand her, "was
how important what you thought of me was. Until that
happened nothing else could happen. I couldn't disagree
with you because I was afraid of worse consequences. So
I tried to see and use and apply what you said, even when
it made me hate myself. I tried to think you were opening
up a new world for me, a new way of seeing things that

would work out better in the end. And when it wasn't
working out that way, I blamed myself."

With the working through of her fragmented states in
relation to their triggering experiences within a disrupted
self–object tie, Caroline's borderline symptomatology and
paranoidlike fears dropped away, together with what had
previously been regarded as splitting, projection, and a
failure to internalize a good object. She and the analyst
could now better understand her dream of the frozen
torso and her expectations of being laughed at. She had
often been terrified as a little girl, but her fears had always
been mocked. She could not, for example, let her mother
bathe her or wash her hair, and her mother would be
furious with her. No one understood why she was afraid
of her mother—indeed, afraid of almost everything. She
was teased mercilessly by her brothers for being so afraid.
"Girls can't do anything," they would say.

As Caroline's vulnerability decreased, there were increasing signs that she was turning once more to the analyst to help her understand her early relationship with her
mother, its effect on her, and how crucial elements were
being replicated with her husband and the analyst. The
analyst could now understand the symbolism of an earlier
turning, which he had missed. Her buying binge had contained both her fear and her intense need to be noticed.
As a girl, she had turned to her father to be noticed, for
it was only through connecting herself to him that she felt
she might be able to extricate herself from the traumatogenic enmeshment with her mother. "But he was remote
and embarrassed by emotion—even by mother's emotion,
and even though he loved mother," she remarked. "When
feelings were expressed, he would look away. Then, after
a point, he would introduce another subject, as if what had
taken place before did not exist." Caroline remembered
wanting her father to pick her up, but he never did, except
as part of a game. She didn't play right, she felt, so she
couldn't be held. And she so wanted him to want to be
close to her. She realized now that when the analyst spoke
to her gently and smiled when he greeted her, she felt real

and warm, not frozen. If she had been feeling bad and hating herself, that made her feel all right.

Caroline had blamed herself when her father hadn't noticed her or loved her. In particular, she had blamed her anger. The anger evoked by her father's unresponsiveness had been enormously threatening to her because of her desperate need for him. Thus, she exonerated him and blamed her reactive anger for his faulty responsiveness. A similar sequence could be observed in reaction to unattuned responses from her husband and the analyst. Her idealizations were not primarily a defense against her anger. Rather, she preserved the vitally needed idealizations at the expense of her anger and of her ability to assert herself when her interests were disregarded.

Caroline had turned to her father not primarily as an oedipal love object, but as an idealized self–object whose responsive interest in her might open a compensatory path along which her thwarted development could resume. When this developmental thrust was revived in the transference, her associations led her back to her fourth and fifth years. Her memories clearly showed that what she most needed her father to notice and understand was what she was going through with her mother. In the analysis she realized that she had to return to that time because something had happened then that had made her life thereafter almost unbearable. She remembered herself before this time as a well-dressed little girl; afterward she felt like a ragamuffin.

When Caroline was four her mother, then recovering from a prolonged depression, had resumed her involvement with the church as an organist and choral leader. The church and the little girl largely made up the boundaries of the mother's restricted world. Even then her mother would often go to bed for the day, saying, "I know I can't get out today." Caroline remembered that during this period she had wanted to learn to play the piano. Taking it as an affront that Caroline might want anyone else to teach her, her mother undertook the task. Caroline recalled that as with everything else, her mother insisted on a strict routine—first, months of finger exercises away from the piano, and only then the real thing. Her mother was an overwhelming teacher. When Caroline tried and said, "I can't," her mother flew into a rage. Later, Caroline came to understand that the rage was toward her mother's own recalcitrant self, indistinguishable from that of her daughter. The mother desperately wished that her daughter would not give up, as she herself had done, that Caroline would not become a nobody doing the things in the kitchen no one else wanted to do. She insisted that Caroline did not care about her, did not value her. Caroline could see that her mother believed this, and it scared her. But then she told herself perhaps her mother was right, perhaps she would never be able to care for anyone (as she was also told) if she couldn't care for her mother. It was so frightening to think that her mother didn't understand her that she found it a relief to believe that she herself was bad.

Why couldn't she practice, her mother would ask. It was just a matter of moving her fingers. Her mother would demonstrate and then take Caroline's fingers and show her. It could only be rebelliousness, Caroline was always so stubborn. Then her mother would get out the whip as the little girl froze and cowered. It was a black, braided leather affair with a number of thongs, perfect equipment for not spoiling the child. Although it was only used three or four times, Caroline would remember her fear and humiliation for the rest of her life. That ended her career in music.

One of the most terrifying aspects of these childhood experiences was that something was glaringly wrong, but nobody seemed to know it or do anything about it. When Caroline went to her father, he would change the subject. When she went to the maid, she was told how it was to be an orphan as the maid had been. Caroline had to find some way to live with her mother, so she made herself responsible, telling herself that if she were better her mother would love her. "It is terrifying to be in the power of another person," she observed. The feeling that something was wrong and nobody seemed to know or do anything about it was replicated in the analysis when the analyst failed to respond to Caroline's assertions of the threat to herself posed by many of his interpretations.

There was something even worse than whipping, Caroline realized one day. One of the major methods by which her mother controlled her was by continually threatening to leave her. That was always, and still remained, the ultimate whip, both with her husband and in the transference. She realized that the threat may have been completely false objectively, but it was very real to her. Even now, anyone she needed could reduce her to submission by threatening to leave her. Her mother had simply walked away from her when the little girl had "misbehaved" or acted cranky. "It is almost as if you have a choice of existing or your mother existing, but not both," Caroline explained.

She often imagined running away from her mother's ruthless training. One day, in the analysis, she spoke of this, remarking, "If I had had a father to run to, I would have." It was when she saw all her little friends playing and going places with their fathers that she began to feel like a ragamuffin.

At this stage of the analysis, Caroline remarked on a feeling of being better integrated. The analyst had allowed her to revive in the transference the longed-for self–object bond to an idealized father, who would help her understand and separate from her pathological enmeshment with her mother. Everything she thought about now seemed more vivid, she commented. Her thoughts and feelings made more sense to her. She felt more self-confidence, although she was still worried that this would disappear and not return. Still, she felt she was stronger, as she put it, than the threat to her was. Moreover, she noted an increased ability to stick to her moderated diet. Slowly but noticeably, she began to lose weight. It was apparent both to her and to her analyst that a decisive corner had been turned in the reinstatement of her development.

To summarize this case: Caroline's adult "borderline" characteristics and paranoidlike distrust had arisen in the intersubjective field of her vulnerable, fragmentation-prone self within a failing, archaic self–object tie (with her husband). These borderline characteristics remained and were periodically intensified in the new intersubjective field of the psychoanalytic situation when the analyst's mis-attuned interpretive stance and faulty responsiveness un-wittingly triggered and exacerbated her states of self frag-mentation. The failures in her marital relationship and in the first phase of the analysis replicated the specific, traumatogenic self–object failures of her early childhood years. Caroline had adapted to these failures by attempting to serve the archaic self–object needs of her mother and pushing herself even harder when her mother found her wanting in that role. This was repeated with the analyst. In contrast, in the second phase of the analysis, when the analyst became able to comprehend the actual meaning of Caroline's archaic subjective states and needs, thereby permitting her to revive and establish with him the specific self–object ties that she required, her so-called borderline features dropped away.

CONCLUSIONS

We have criticized the view that the term *borderline* designates a distinct pathological character structure, rooted in pathogno-monic instinctual conflicts and primitive defenses. Instead, we propose an alternative conceptualization of so-called borderline phenomena from an intersubjective perspective. In particular, we believe that the clinical evidence cited for the operation of primitive defenses against pregenital aggression is better un-derstood as an indication of needs for specific archaic self–ob-ject ties, and of disturbances in those ties. As the case of Caro-line suggests, the psychological essence of what is called "borderline" does not rest in a pathological condition located solely in the patient. Rather, it lies in phenomena arising in an intersubjective field, consisting of a precarious, vulnerable self in a failing, archaic self–object bond.

We wish to clarify some potential sources of misunderstanding of our point of view. Conceptualizing borderline phenomena as arising in an intersubjective field is not equivalent to claiming that the term *borderline* refers to an entirely iatrogenic illness. As seen in the case of Caroline, the failing, archaic self–object bond is not always with a therapist or an analyst, although this will become increasingly more likely as the patient's self–object needs are engaged in the therapeutic transference. More importantly, the claim of an entirely iatrogenic illness would be markedly at variance with our concept of an intersubjective field and would overlook the contribution of the patient's archaic states, arrested needs, and fragmentation-prone self to the formation of that psychological field. If we view the therapeutic situation as an intersubjective field, then we must see that the patient's manifest psychopathology is always codetermined by the patient's self disorder and the therapist's ability to understand it.

We are aware of the difficulties regularly and inevitably encountered in the attempt to treat patients whose severe developmental deprivations predispose them to intense distrust, violent affective reactions, or stubborn defensiveness. In particular, we have become familiar in such patients with the pervasiveness of an underlying unconscious and invariant principle into which all experience tends to be assimilated. From their early history has crystallized a certain conviction that nothing reliably good could happen to them in relation to another person. Every experience of disappointment tends to confirm this principle and thus to produce violent affective reactions. This can stir the analyst's fears of impending therapeutic failure, leading, in turn, to further negative spiraling of the intersubjective system. We are aware, in other words, that the predisposition of borderline symptomatology is rooted in the patient's own structural vulnerabilities and preformed organizing principles. On the other hand, the concept of a fixed, intrinsic character organization that alone determines the course of the therapeutic interaction is rooted in the *analyst's* psychological organization and itself makes a decisive contribution to the course of treatment.

To be specific, our claim is not that borderline symptomatology is entirely iatrogenic, but that the concept of a "borderline personality organization" is largely, if not entirely, an iatrogenic myth. We believe that the idea of a borderline character structure rooted in pathognomonic conflicts and defenses is symptomatic of the difficulty therapists have had in comprehending the archaic intersubjective contexts in which borderline pathology arises.

We wish to emphasize that self–object failures are developmentally codetermined subjective experiences of the patient and that therefore their occurrence in treatment is not to be regarded as an objective index of the therapist's technical incompetence or inadequacy. They are revivals in the transference of the patient's early history of developmental deprivation and interference. Thus, the therapeutic task cannot be to avert such experiences of self–object failure but to analyze them from within the unique perspective of the patient's subjective world.

From the standpoint of the archaic nature of the arrested needs revived in the transference, it is inevitable that the therapist will "fail" the patient, and that under such circumstances borderline symptoms may appear. In our experience, it is only when the subjective validity and meaning for the patient of these disjunctions and self–object failures go chronically unrecognized and unanalyzed (often because they threaten the therapist's self organization requirements), and the reestablishment of the therapeutic bond is thereby prevented, that borderline phenomena become encrusted into what has been described as a "borderline personality organization." This formulation of borderline symptomatology illustrates the general psychological principle that psychopathology cannot be understood psychoanalytically apart from the intersubjective contexts in which it arises and recedes.

7.

Borderline:
An Adjective Still in Search of a Noun

Hagop S. Akiskal, M.D.

The diagnosis of borderline conditions enjoys great clinical popularity in North American psychiatry. The most prevalent opinion is that these are primitive disorders of developmental origin, characterized by an unstable sense of self and low-level defensive operations (Kernberg, 1981). It is also thought that borderline patients have an unusually high liability for transient breaks with reality (Gunderson and Singer, 1975). Despite criticism by phenomenologically oriented clinical investigators (Guze, 1975; Klein, 1975; Rich, 1978), the borderline concept has been introduced into *The Diagnostic and Statistical Manual of Mental Disorders* (DSM-III) (American Psychiatric Association, 1980). DSM-II had recognized such conditions only as "dilute" or "latent" forms of schizophrenia. In restricting the operational territory of schizophrenia to "process" or Kraepelinian schizophrenia, DSM-III has now pushed the borderline concept into the domain of personality disorders, where it is listed

*This paper is updated from the *Journal of Clinical Psychiatry* (1985), 41–48 (with permission). Dr. Akiskal's coauthors were Shen E. Chen, M.D., Glenn C. Davis, M.D., Vahe R. Puzantian, M.D., Mark Kashgarian, M.D., and John M. Bolinger, M.D.

The adverb "still" added to the present title embodies Dr. Akiskal's assessment, expressed in a new appendix at the end of this paper and written especially for this volume, that observations in the literature in the ensuing five years have provided little further clarification to the nosologic status of borderline conditions.

155

under two overlapping rubrics: (1) *borderline personality disorder* (BPD), manifested by such unstable characterologic attributes as impulsivity, drug-seeking, polymorphous sexuality, extreme affective ability, boredom, anhedonia, and bizarre attempts at self-harm, and (2) *schizotypal personality disorder* (STP), the hallmarks of which are oddities of communication or perception and other soft signs of "micropsychosis," typically, although not exclusively, associated with a schizoid existence.

Despite efforts to identify a distinct schizotypal disorder (Spitzer, Endicott, and Gibbon, 1979; Khouri, Haier, Rieder, and Rosenthal, 1980; Kendler, Gruenberg, and Stauss, 1981a; Siever and Gunderson, 1983), considerable overlap exists between schizotypal, schizoid, and avoidant types. Likewise, borderline patients are not easily discriminable from antisocial and histrionic personality disorders. One is reminded of Mack's (1975) suggestion that "borderline" refers to a personality disorder without a characterologic specialty. Implicit in the DSM-III position is that schizotypal disorders, believed to be on the border of schizophrenia, should be separated from the more nebulous mélange of unstable characterologic attributes constituting borderline conditions. In line with these developments, recent research, exemplified by Stone's (1980) work, has suggested a shift of the borderline concept from a subschizophrenic to a subaffective disorder. Gunderson, however, who was among the first to attempt to bring operational clarity to this murky psychopathologic area, in recent collaborative work with Pope et al. (Pope, Jonas, Hudson, Cohen, and Gunderson, 1983), seems to espouse the view that the characterologic pathology of borderline patients is distinct from any concurrent affective episodes. Monroe (1970), who subscribes to the existence of a third (neither schizophrenic nor affective) psychosis related to epilepsy, has postulated that "episodic dyscontrol" manifested by unmodulated affects is at the core of borderline psychopathology. Kernberg's (1981) concept, probably the broadest of all, embraces a wide spectrum of subpsychotic temperamental and polysymptomatic neurotic disorders tied together by identify diffusion and common, primitive defensive operations like splitting and projective identification, in the presence of grossly intact reality testing.

Despite a considerable amount of empirical work in the past few years, several controversies regarding the nosologic status of borderline conditions remain unresolved:

1. Is borderline a personality disorder?
2. Does it refer to *formes frustes* or interepisodic manifestations of affective, schizophrenic, or epileptic psychoses?
3. Is it an intermediate mode of functioning between neurosis and psychosis?

Several interview schedules for a descriptive identification of borderline and schizotypal personality disorders have been developed. Khouri et al. (1980), in their attempt to focus on subschizophrenic disorders, have excluded affective symptoms from their inventory. By contrast, the Gunderson, Kolb, and Austin (1981) diagnostic interview for borderlines (DIB) casts a wider net which includes circumscribed psychotic, affective, acting out, interpersonal and social areas. Pope et al. (1983) attempted to validate DIB borderlines by using the Washington University approach to validating psychiatric entities. Soloff and Millward (1983b) and Loranger, Oldham, and Tulis (1982), who used the same instrument, focused on the familial aspects of the disorder. Perry and Klerman (1980), using a related instrument, examined the phenomenologic features of the disorder. The data from these studies indicate (1) lack of relationship of the disorder to schizophrenia; (2) failure to discriminate from antisocial and histrionic character disorders; and (3) at least some degree of overlap with primary affective disorder.

Considering the general confusion in this area, the substantive findings of these studies are quite impressive. Nevertheless, one must bear in mind the following limitations: first, they were not generally conducted in outpatient settings, where the largest number of borderlines are encountered clinically. Second, proband Axis I diagnosis and family history were often based on chart review. Third, a control group of bipolar affective disorder was not specifically provided. Fourth, repeated evaluations at follow-up were not instituted, minimizing the chances of detecting hypomanic episodes. Finally, the degree of overlap of borderlines with antisocial and histrionic personality disorders could not be estimated in the absence of a control group consisting of such personalities.

We have elsewhere reported preliminary family history and follow-up data suggesting substantial overlap of borderline personality disorders with dysthymic and cyclothymic temperaments and atypical bipolar II disorder (Akiskal, 1981). Our findings were tentative because data collection on control groups had not been completed when our report was published. In the present article, we attempt to address the methodologic issues raised above and provide comparisons with schizophrenic, bipolar, unipolar, and personality disorder controls. Furthermore, we explore the possibility that childhood object loss and an unstable home environment due to assortative parental psychopathology may form the developmental background of borderline conditions. The overall aim of this exercise is to prospectively delineate the range of psychopathologic conditions for which the adjective "borderline" is currently applicable.

Our main hypothesis is that borderlines are heterogeneous groups of patients who meet specific criteria for more explicit Axis I psychiatric diagnoses. Based on prior work, we also hypothesized that borderlines would show high rates of familial affective (but not of schizophrenic) disorders, and would develop full-blown affective (rather than schizophrenic) breakdowns during prospective follow-up similar to affective, but unlike nonaffective controls. Because borderline patients are often considered to have complicated biographies, we wished to test the possibility that increased rates of early separations and broken homes—associated with assortative parental psychopathology—might underlie their character pathology.

METHOD

Selection of Subjects

We selected 100 borderline patients from a large pool of general psychiatric outpatients by examining *consecutive* admissions in two urban mental health centers. These subjects met at least five of the six Gunderson and Singer (1975) criteria. (This study was conducted prior to the availability of the DIB [Gunderson et al., 1981].) Most probands had extensive psychiatric histories dating back to adolescence or early adulthood, and had been considered complex diagnostic problems by referring clinicians. They had often been presented at diagnostic staff conferences and had received such diagnoses as borderline and mixed personality disorder, as well as "latent" and "pseudoneurotic" schizophrenia. Although 40 percent had had one or more psychiatric hospitalizations prior to the index outpatient interview, none had received the diagnosis of a definite affective or schizophrenic disorder.

Four control groups were selected from consecutive admission in the same outpatient settings: fifty-seven schizophrenic subjects, fifty nonaffective personality disorders (definite or probable somatization and antisocial), fifty classical (bipolar I) manic-depressives, and forty episodic major (unipolar) depressives.

Diagnostic Procedures

All probands and control subjects were evaluated in semistructured diagnostic interviews based on the Washington University criteria (Feighner, Robins, Guze, Woodruff, Winokur, and Munoz, 1972). Since DSM-III is more widely known to practicing psychiatrists, we have translated diagnoses to the corresponding DSM-III terms.

All Gunderson and Singer borderline probands also met the DSM-III criteria for borderline personality, but only sixteen fully met those for schizotypal personality. Borderline, schizotypal, and antisocial personalities were the only Axis II diagnoses used in this study; all other diagnoses were based on Axis I. Since DSM-III does not specifically distinguish hypomania from mania, we found it useful to set the following threshold for hypomania: (1) symptomatic criteria for mania of at least two days; (2) absence of querulous belligerence; (3) no psychotic symptoms; and (4) no hospitalization.

Each proband received principal and, when applicable, concurrent diagnoses. "Principal diagnosis" refers to the chronologically primary or most incapacitating disorder which usually brought the patient to clinical attention. "Concurrent diagnoses" include all additional diagnoses, which often followed the principal disorder chronologically.

Substance (including ethanol) use disorders were so prevalent in our borderline probands (unsurprisingly, because these are among the Gunderson and Singer and DSM-III defining criteria) that it was more meaningful to consider them independently from descriptive diagnoses. They were classified as sedative–hypnotic abuse or dependence, alcohol abuse or dependence, or psychedelic (hallucinogen – cannabis – psychostimulant) abuse or dependence.

Patients were seen at one- to eight-week intervals (as warranted clinically), and followed over a six- to thirty-six-month prospective observation period. Mean duration of follow-up was comparable for study and control groups. Pharmacologic, psychotherapeutic, and sociotherapeutic interventions were provided as deemed clinically appropriate. Schizophreniform, hypomanic, manic, and major depressive episodes, as well as mixed states, were carefully noted during follow-up. Hypomanic responses to antidepressants were considered pharmacologically occasioned if they occurred within six weeks after administration of tricyclic antidepressants or monoamine oxidase (MAO) inhibitors.

Criteria for Familial and Developmental Factors. One-third of affected family members were patients in our mental health clinics; one-third were directly interviewed to ascertain their diagnoses; and, in the remaining third, diagnostic information was obtained from other family members, using the Research Diagnostic Criteria—Family History version (Andreasen, Endicott, Spitzer, and Winokur, 1977). Except for familial schizophrenia (which included both first- and second-degree relatives), all other family history items refer to *first*-degree biologic relatives. Assortative mating (i.e., where both parents suffered from psychiatric disorders) was noted in particular. Of the 100 probands, three were adopted and were unable to provide family histories.

Developmental object loss was assessed by the following criteria, modified from Amark (1951): (1) proband born out of wedlock and parents not subsequently married or living together; (2) one or both parents lost by death before proband reached age fifteen; (3) parents separated or divorced before proband reached age of fifteen; (4) proband adopted or lived in foster homes or orphanages.

Statistical Techniques. Except for age distribution, which was analyzed by ANOVA, comparisons between groups were made by chi-square analysis, with Yates' correction when appropriate.

RESULTS

Demographic and Family History Characteristics

Borderline and control probands were preponderantly from Hollingshead-Redlich classes III and IV. The mean age at index evaluation was twenty-nine years for borderline probands, thirty-four for schizophrenics, thirty for nonaffective personalities, thirty-eight for the bipolar controls, and forty-seven for recurrent major depressive controls; these differences in age were not statistically significant. About two-thirds of the subjects in each group were women.

Borderline probands, when compared with schizophrenic controls, had a significantly higher rate of familial affective disorders (35% vs. 9%, $X^2 = 11.76$, p < .001) and a significantly lower rate of schizophrenia (3% vs. 21%, $X^2 = 11.21$, p < .001).

Borderlines and control groups did not differ in family history for major depression (see Table 7.1). However, with respect to familial bipolar disorder, borderlines were similar to bipolar controls but significantly different from personality disorder and unipolar controls.

TABLE 7.1

Family History for Major Depression and Bipolar Disorder
in Borderline and Control Groups

Family History	Borderline Group (N = 97)		Personality Controls (N = 50)		Bipolar Controls (N = 50)		Unipolar Controls (N = 40)	
	N	%	N	%	N	%	N	%
Major depression	17	17.5	5	10	11	22	8	20
Bipolar disorder	17	17.5*	1	2	13	26	1	3

*Significantly different from personality controls, X^2 = 6.03, p < .02; and from unipolar controls, X^2 = 4.36, p < .05.

Diagnoses at Index Evaluation

Table 7.2 provides diagnostic information on the 100 border-line probands at index evaluation. These probands can be categorized into five groups based on principal diagnosis. The largest group (N = 45) consisted of affective disorders, primarily cyclothymic or dysthymic and atypical (bipolar II) rather than "classic" forms. The next largest group, personality disorders (N = 21), consisted of probable or definite somatization disorder and antisocial personalities. An almost equal category was the polysymptomatic neurosis group (N = 18), consisting of panic, agoraphobic, and obsessive–compulsive disorders. There were nine patients with schizotypal personality and no concurrent disorders. The organic group is represented by two epileptic patients and one with adult (residual) attention deficit disorder.

The remaining four probands were considered undiagnosed at index evaluation; they had some affinity to adolescent identity disorder as defined in DSM-III, except that their condition had persisted beyond adolescent, was chronic, and had its basis in physical defects or abnormalities that could be expected to produce an irreconcilable identity conflict. For example, one subject was an albino girl born to black parents, and another was a very intelligent college-educated woman with multiple congenital abnormalities and short stature. The profound identity disturbance in these patients was based on realistic anatomic factors.

Also displayed in Table 7.2 are the concurrent diagnoses given to thirty-seven cases. Of these, secondary or superimposed dysthymia with chronic fluctuating course was the most common (N = 21). Of the remaining patients with multiple diagnoses, seven met the criteria for schizotypal personality disorder, two for epilepsy, two for adult (residual) attention deficit disorder, and five for somatization, sociopathic, and panic disorders. Patients with multiple concurrent diagnoses were not uncommon (e.g., an agoraphobic woman who suffered from preexisting somatization disorder and superimposed or secondary dysthymic disorder).

Substance abuse/dependence occurred in 55 percent of the probands and was equally distributed across all diagnostic groups (Table 7.2). Sedative–hypnotics were the most frequent drugs of abuse (46%), followed by alcohol (21%) and psychedelics (19%); many patients abused multiple drugs.

Follow-Up Course

As shown in Table 7.3, major depressive episodes with melancholic features developed in twenty-nine borderline probands; eleven others had brief hypomanic excursions (6 on tricyclic challenge); four had manic episodes (1 of which was on tricyclic administration); and eight evolved into mixed affective states (coexisting manic and depressive features). Four probands were known to have committed suicide after dropping out of treatment; their diagnoses ranged from obsessive–compulsive to somatization, schizotypal, and epileptic disorders.

Schizophreniform episodes (nonaffective psychotic symptoms that cleared within weeks) occurred in four borderlines and one personality disorder control. One borderline proband developed full-fledged paranoid schizophrenia, and two others (who at follow-up satisfied the Hoch and Polatin [1949] description of pseudoneurotic schizophrenia) were classified as chronic undifferentiated type. Thus, 8 percent of the borderline group developed "schizophrenia-related" disorders (assuming schizophreniform illness is related to schizophrenia), compared with 2 percent of personality disorder controls (X^2 = 1.19, .05 <

TABLE 7.2

Diagnoses in 100 Borderline Patients at Index Evaluation*

Principal Diagnosis	Concurrent Diagnosis	Substance Use Disorders	
Affective Group (N = 45)			
Recurrent Major Depression (6)		Sedative–Hypnotics	(2)
Dysthymic Disorder (14)	Schizotypal Disorder (3)	Sedative–Hypnotics	(2)
		Alcohol	(1)
		Psychedelics	(1)
Cyclothymic Disorder (7)	Somatization Disorder (1)	Sedative–Hypnotics	(4)
		Psychedelics	(2)
		Alcohol	(1)
(Atypical) Bipolar II	Sociopathy (1)	Sedative–Hypnotics	(4)
Disorder (17)	Somatization Disorder (1)	Alcohol	(1)
	Residual (Adult) Attention	Psychedelics	(2)
	Deficit Disorder (1)		
Personality (N = 21)			
Sociopathy (9)	Residual (Adult) Attention		
	Deficit Disorder (1)	Sedative–Hypnotics	(8)
	Schizotypal Disorder (1)	Psychedelics	(6)
	Temporal Lobe Epilepsy (1)	Alcohol	(5)
	Dysthymia (3)		

Disorder/Condition	Specific Disorder	Substance	(N)
Somatization Disorder (12)	Panic Disorder (2)	Sedative–Hypnotics	(12)
	Sociopathy (2)	Alcohol	(2)
	Temporal Lobe Epilepsy (1)	Psychedelics	(2)
	Schizotypal Disorder (1)		
	Dysthymia (7)		
Polysymptomatic Neurosis Group (N = 18)			
Panic and Agoraphobic Disorders (10)	Dysthymia (6)	Sedative–Hypnotics	(8)
	Sociopathy (1)	Alcohol	(2)
	Somatization Disorder (1)	Psychedelics	(1)
	Schizotypal Disorder (1)		
Obsessive–Compulsive Disorder (8)	Dysthymia (5)	Sedative–Hypnotics	(1)
	Schizotypal Disorder (1)		
Schizotypal Group (N = 9)			
Schizotypal Disorder (9)		Sedative–Hypnotics	(2)
		Alcohol	(1)
		Psychedelics	(2)
Organic Group (N = 3)			
Grand Mal Epilepsy (1)		Alcohol	(1)
Temporal Lobe Epilepsy (1)		Sedative–Hypnotics	(1)
Residual (Adult) Attention Deficit Disorder (1)		Psychedelics	(1)
		Alcohol	(1)
Undiagnosed Group (N = 4)			
"Chronic Identity Disorder" (4)		Alcohol	(3)
		Psychedelics	(2)
		Sedative–Hypnotics	(2)

*Numbers in parentheses refer to the numbers of patients with given disorder or condition.

TABLE 7.3

Prospective Follow-up Outcome in Borderlines and Nonaffective Personality Disorder Controls

Outcome	Borderline Group (N = 100)		Personality Controls (N = 50)		$X^2(df = 1)$	p
	N	%	N	%		
Affective Episodes						
Major Depression	29	29	2	4	11.22	<.001
Hypomania or Mania*	15	15	0	0	6.75	<.01
Mixed States*	8	8	0	0	2.79	NS
Suicide	4	4	0	0	0.80	NS
Schizophrenia–Related Outcome						
Schizophreniform Psychosis	5	5	1	2	0.20	NS
Pseudoneurotic Schizophrenia	2	2	0	0	0.06	NS
Paranoid Schizophrenia	1	1	0	0	0.13	NS

*Includes full episodes during antidepressant drug administration which did not remit upon reduction of drug dosage and required lithium administration.

p < .1). This nonsignificant trend for borderlines to develop schizophrenia-related outcomes should be contrasted with their highly significant liability for affective breakdowns ($X^2 = 19.1$, p < .001).

The link of borderline personality to affective disorder was further strengthened when we examined rates for pharmacologically occasioned hypomanic switches: 20 percent of the forty-five affective borderlines and 35 percent of bipolar controls had such switches as compared with no personality controls and 2.5 percent of unipolar controls ($X^2 = 29.02$, p < .001).

As expected, most of the affective episodes occurred in those given primary affective diagnoses at index evaluation (26 of 45). It is also noteworthy that 20 percent of those without primary affective diagnoses, including the four completed suicides, developed major affective episodes. Schizophreniform episodes were equally distributed in the nonaffective groups, but a chronic schizophrenic denouement was strictly limited to the pure schizotypal group (3 out of 9).

Developmental Object Loss and Parental Assortative Mating

With respect to childhood object loss, borderlines were intermediate between affective and personality controls (Table 7.4). Borderlines were not different from personality controls on parental assortative mating, but differed significantly from affective controls. Parental units with alcoholism and affective disorder were the most common, followed by alcoholism and sociopathy. These data suggest that many borderlines had troubled home environments due to psychiatric disorder in both parents (roughly two-thirds of patients with early breaks in attachment bonds had assortative parental psychopathology) that led to frequent separations, foster care, or adoption.

DISCUSSION

The major finding of the present study is that the borderline rubric encompasses a heterogeneous group of psychopathologic conditions lying predominantly on the border of affective,

TABLE 7.4
Developmental Factors in Borderline and Control Groups*

History	Borderlines		Controls				Comparisons			
			Primary Affective		Personality Disorder		Three-way		Pairwise**	
	N	%	N	%	N	%	X^2	p	Groups	p
Parental Assortative Mating	40	41	5	13	14	47	12.29	<.005	BL vs PA	<.01
									PD vs PA	<.01
									BL vs P	NS
Developmental Object Loss	36	37	7	18	18	60	13.46	<.005	BL vs PA	<.05
									PD vs PA	<.01
									BL vs PA	<.05

* N = 97 for borderlines (three cases of early adoption excluded);
N = 30 for personality controls because of unavailability of reliable data in 20 subjects.

**BL = borderline; PA = primary affective; PD = personality disorder.

anxiety, and somatization–antisocial disorders, and, to a minimal extent, that of schizophrenic and organic disorders.

The Border Conditions

The Affective Border. Our data favor the notion that borderline disorders are located predominantly on the border of affective rather than schizophrenic psychoses. At index evaluation, nearly half the sample met criteria for subaffective disorders, and two-thirds had a strong affective component, if concurrent or follow-up episodes are taken into account. The relationship to affective disorder is also supported by high rates of pharmacologic hypomania and of familial affective disorder, especially bipolar illness. This finding is in line with earlier reports by our group regarding a lowered threshold for pharmacologic hypomania in cyclothymic (Akiskal, Djenderedjian, Rosenthal, and Khari, 1977) and dysthymic disorders (Akiskal, 1983), and suggests a common neuropharmacologic substrate for subaffective and borderline disorders. The relatively young age of the borderline group is also in keeping with the insidious onset of bipolar disorders in adolescence or early adulthood. Many seem to suffer from life-long cyclothymia and dysthymia, and make transient shifts into melancholic, hypomanic, manic, and mixed affective episodes, with rapid return to their habitual temperaments. Hence, their diagnosis is best described as borderline manic–depressive psychosis. The 20 percent rate of depressive episodes with melancholic depth—including four suicides on follow-up in the fifty-five borderline probands who were placed into nonaffective subgroups at index evaluation—suggests that the entire cohort of borderlines suffers from intense affective arousal. This is not surprising, since six of the eight DSM-III criteria for borderline personality are affectively loaded. In brief, the clinical data on the close link between borderline and affective conditions reported here support other findings that have emerged from the application of neuroendocrine (Carroll, Greden, Feinberg, Lohr, James, Steiner, Haskett, Albala, de Vigne, and Tarika, 1981; Garbutt, Loosen, Tipermas, and Prange, 1983; Baxter, Edell, Gerner,

Fairbanks, and Gwirtsman, 1984) and sleep electroencephalographic techniques to borderlines (Akiskal, 1981; Bell, Lycaki,
Jones, Kelwala, and Sitaram, 1983; McNamara, Reynolds, Soloff, Mathias, Rossi, Spiker, Coble, and Kupfer, 1984).

The Border with Anxiety Disorders. These disorders conform
to what the British literature describes as atypical depression
(West and Dally, 1959) or phobic–anxiety–depersonalization
syndrome (Roth, 1959). Intermittent depression occurs in the
context of a chronically anxious multiphobic, usually agoraphe-
bic, illness with spontaneous panic attacks characterized by fears
of cardiac catastrophe or total mental collapse and associated
helplessness and dependency. The highly idiosyncratic manner
in which depersonalization and derealization (as part of a panic
attack) are experienced, coupled with strong histrionic or obsessional elements, may simulate bizarre but short-lived reactive
or schizophreniform psychotic episodes. Work by Klein, Gittelman, Quitkin, and Rifkin (1980) suggests that some of these
patients may represent affective variants with a history of childhood school phobia, dependent and histrionic features in adulthood and positive response to imipramine or MAO inhibitors.

The Schizophrenia Border. Nine percent of our sample appears to lie on a schizophrenia spectrum identified in the Danish adoption studies (Khouri et al., 1980; Kendler et al., 1981a).
This modest affinity to schizophrenia is evidenced by clinical
schizotypal features with familial background for schizophrenia, and progression to "soft" schizophrenic illnesses (schizophreniform and "pseudoneurotic") and, in three instances, to
process schizophrenia. All three patients with chronic schizophrenic denouement on follow-up belonged to this schizotypal
group. Seven other patients, who had other principal diagnoses, also met the criteria for schizotypal disorder. None of these
patients had family history for schizophrenia, suggesting that
many of the schizotypal features defined in DSM-III may be
nonspecific accompaniments of chronic psychiatric or affective
disorders, and that they have diagnostic value in suggesting a

subschizophrenic disorder only when they occur in the absence of validated psychiatric disorder.

The Personality Border. This subgroup consists of a spectrum of histrionic and sociopathic individuals (Guze, 1975) who have parents with similar or related disorders, who have suffered the developmental vicissitudes of unstable parental marriages, and who complain of lifelong intermittent dysphoria. Brief dysphoric psychotic episodes are often precipitated by substance abuse, but may also result from other organic factors (described next).

The Organic Border. This very small subgroup in our study is similar to patients described by Andrulonis, Glueck, Stroebel, and Vogel (1982) in their larger inpatient sample of borderline men. These authors suggest that subtle temporal lobe pathology underlies the impulsivity, affective lability, and anger outbursts of some of these patients. Until the nature of this pathology is defined in a more rigorous fashion, it may be preferable to limit the concept of episodic dyscontrol to those who evidence electroencephalographic (EEG) findings of a seizure disorder or who show unequivocal response to anticonvulsant medication such as carbamazepine.

The Nature of Micropsychotic Episodes

Our data suggest that schizophreniform episodes are the exception in borderline patients. Grandiose or irritable forms of hypomania, which are sometimes mobilized by antidepressant treatment, as well as depressive delusions, are more common. Drug-induced psychoses (i.e., secondary to ethanol, sedative–hypnotic, psychedelic, and stimulant abuse, or withdrawal states) represent another plausible explanation for micropsychotic episodes. Finally, depersonalization, derealization, and brief reactive psychoses, which are not uncommon in panic, sociopathic, and somatization disorders, could easily simulate schizophreniform symptomatology.

The Origin of Character Pathology

Borderline patients appear to suffer from early breaks in attachment bonds, largely because of assortative parental psychopathology. In this respect they seem intermediate between nonaffective personality disorder and unipolar affective controls. There is some evidence that among the affective disorders, history of assortative parental psychopathology is most common in bipolar II disorders (Dunner, Fleiss, Addonizio, and Fieve, 1976). Such findings strengthen the link between borderline and atypical bipolar disorders. More importantly, our findings suggest that borderline probands are at a double disadvantage: they may inherit the illnesses of one or both parents, and may develop exquisite vulnerability to adult object loss as a result of the troubled early home environment. As stated in Bowlby's (1977) latest formulations, childhood object loss may not predispose to affective disorder per se, but to character-based affective expressions. Since loss of parents is not an uncommon experience in the early life history of affective probands (Akiskal and Tashjian, 1983), their adult affective illnesses can be complicated by separation-related characterologic disturbances, similar to the hysteroid dysphoric women described by Liebowitz and Klein (1979). It is also likely that when one parent has affective disorder and the other a sociopathic or somatization disorder, their children may inherit both illnesses and thereby exhibit manifestations of both disorders. Another possible source of characterologic pathology in borderline disorders, such as cyclothymia or bipolar II, is in the hindrance to optimal ego maturation due to the high-frequency episodes beginning in early adolescence (Akiskal, 1981). Indeed, in an adolescent sample studied at Cornell (Friedman, Clarkin, Corn, Aronoff, Hurt, and Murphy, 1982), borderline personality disturbances generally *followed* affective episodes. Thymoleptic therapy or long-term lithium stabilization can bring many such patients to a level of ego stability that had not been achieved in years of psychotherapy and nonspecific pharmacotherapy (Akiskal, Khani, and Scott-Strauss, 1979). However, this outcome is not universal, suggesting that maladaptive personality patterns may become irreversible after many years of inadequately treated affective disorders. The reversability of "conduct disorders" in depressed children treated with thymoleptics illustrates the importance of early energetic and specific pharmacologic therapies in preventing postdepressive personality disturbances (Kroll, Sines, Martin, Lari, Pyle, and Zander, 1981). In brief, the characterologic disturbances of borderline patients sometimes represent primary character pathology but more often are secondary to or concurrent with an affective disorder (i.e., to be coded on an axis orthogonal to the phenomenologic diagnosis).

Lack of Predictive Utility

Borderline conditions emerge as an enormously heterogeneous group of disorders that embrace the gamut of psychopathology. Proportions of specific subtypes in different studies are probably a function of the different populations sampled. Borderline conditions do not seem to represent a definable personality type and, therefore, do not belong on Axis II in DSM-III. We suggest that the potential utility of the concept might be explored on a distinct psychodynamic axis. Despite an unwieldy degree of diagnostic heterogeneity, the concept may still prove useful in setting the stage for a psychotherapeutic intervention geared to the common developmental vicissitudes and ego functioning of patients with certain low level defenses as described in Kernberg's (1981) work.

It would seem, however, that the very heterogeneity of disorders within the borderline realm argues against a unitary therapeutic modality. For instance, if the clinician were to consider pharmacologic approaches, one could make the case for tricyclics, MAO inhibitors, lithium carbonate, neuroleptics, stimulants, and anticonvulsants—as well as for avoidance of pharmacotherapy—for the various subtypes.

In summary, the current nosologic use of the concept of borderline seems to map a large universe of chronically and seriously ill "difficult" patients outside the area of the classical psychoses and neuroses (Kroll et al., 1981). It is necessary to look beyond the characterologic "masks" in order to appreciate the phenomenologic diversity of these conditions. A specific personality type or psychopathologic entity as the proper noun for the borderline adjective has not been found yet. Nor is it likely to be found, because, similar to the imprecise adjectival use of terms like *neurotic* and *psychotic*, it has no place in modern descriptive psychopathology; there are simply too many neurotic and psychotic conditions which render futile all descriptive efforts to identify a specific "border" (Dickes, 1974; Rich, 1978). In a very literal sense, borderline personality can be considered to be a borderline diagnosis.

ADDENDUM[1]

The data from the present and a subsequent psychopathologic and sleep EEG study (Akiskal, Yerevanian, Davis, King, and Lemmi, 1985b) on borderline personality without concurrent affective episodes have led to the formulation of borderline as a heterogeneous group of disorders that fall on the border of more familiar psychiatric conditions such as mood, neurotic, schizophrenic, and epileptic disorders. This viewpoint is not too dissimilar from that of Stone (1980). I further submit that borderline represents a nonspecific cluster of unstable and "primitive" personality disturbances that are activated when young individuals develop a variety of nonclassical psychiatric disorders most of which belong to the affective realm. Data supporting the link to affective illness is so extensive that such authorities as Gunderson, Kroll, and their associates—who are skeptical of this association—wrote major reviews (Gunderson and Elliot, 1985; Kroll and Ogata, 1987) to explain away its significance.

The diagnosis of borderline is typically entertained during the symptomatic phases of the affective and other disorders listed above and, in part, reflects clinicians' countertransference to the disorganizing affective storm created by these patients. Our research suggests that the affective dysregulation of such patients is in turn correlated with retrospective reports of unstable object relations during their early developmental years; this

---

[1] Written by Hagop S. Akiskal, January 1989.

finding has been replicated (Links, Steiner, and Offord, 1988b). Finally, we have observed concurrent substance abuse which appears to contribute significantly to the affective instability and many of the observed "micropsychotic" experiences; this too has been replicated (Pope, Jonas, Hudson, Cohen, and Gunderson, 1985).

Nothing new since the publication of our work in the early and mideighties has emerged on the psychopathology of borderline conditions to suggest that the viewpoint expressed above should be modified. We obviously need more systematic data in complex areas such as the present one, not more reviews (Gunderson and Elliot, 1985; Kroll and Ogata, 1987).

From the clinician's perspective, the most promising systematic data on borderlines that has emerged over the past five years has come from controlled blind psychopharmacologic studies (Goldberg, Schulz, Schulz, Resnick, Hamer, and Friedel, 1986; Soloff, George, Nathan, Schulz, Ulrich, and Perek, 1986; Cowdry and Gardner, 1988). These studies provide evidence that neuroleptics, MAO inhibitors (specifically tranylcypromine), and the thymoleptic antiepileptic carbamazepine are useful in the clinical management of many patients meeting the DSM-III criteria for borderline personality. Low-dose neuroleptics might be especially relevant acutely for those borderlines that simultaneously meet the criteria for schizotypal personality and are more likely to be overrepresented in inpatient samples. The absence of significant response to a tricyclic antidepressant (e.g., amitriptyline) is also noteworthy. Taken together, these findings are compatible with the proposal that the "affective border" of borderlines is constituted by such nonclassical mood disorders as dysthymic, atypical depressive, cyclothymic, bipolar II, and rapid-cycling conditions and protracted bipolar mixed states now believed to have relative resistance to, and even worsening with, traditional antidepressants (Akiskal and Mallya, 1987; Wehr and Goodwin, 1987). I wish to point out, however, that the selectivity of a given drug for a small subgroup is often missed in placebo-controlled studies; systematic clinical experience does suggest that tricyclic antidepressants would be beneficial for some clinically depressed borderlines (Sternberg and Lawrence, 1987), especially those suffering from panic and unipolar depressive disorders. Lithium, which remains untested in a blind prospective controlled trial in a borderline population, might also offer stabilization for some borderlines in the bipolar realm (Akiskal et al., 1979), possibly in combination with an MAO inhibitor or thyroid hormone (Akiskal, 1987). Finally stimulants deserve controlled trial in those borderlines with residual attention deficit disorder in early adulthood (Hooberman and Stern, 1984).

The treatment considerations discussed above underlie the heuristic value of the position espoused by the author's research team which predicts treatment response to specific interventions based on a more precise subtyping of conditions in the borderline realm. A similar sentiment has been recently expressed by a Canadian research team (Links and Steiner, 1988).

It is to be wished that psychiatrists replace nebulous personality constructs such as borderline—which carry little or no predictive validity (Dahl, 1985a)—with nosologic entities that can be characterized with greater precision relative to their membership in the more traditional mental and nervous disorders. This suggestion to eliminate borderline from the descriptive nomenclature does not imply that the concept of borderline should be entirely abandoned. As suggested in the discussion section above, borderline can retain its (currently limited) psychodynamic utility that is best examined on a well-defined operationalized axis of defense mechanisms generic to a variety of psychiatric disorders. Therein lies the challenge for psychodynamic psychiatry.

8.

Borderline Disorders: A British Point of View

Alex Tarnopolsky, M.D., F.R.C.Psych.

In Great Britain, "borderline" is a battered concept. Traditional psychiatrists believe that borderlines are, at best, ill-diagnosed schizophrenics or atypical manic depressives; and at worst characters who should be allowed the right to their eccentricity and be left alone. Forensic psychiatrists have become interested in a psychodynamic concept of borderlines (Gallwey, 1985; Jackson and Tarnopolsky, 1989), but most other clinicians, grounded in biological models, seem to stall in impotence, perplexity, and dislike for borderline personalities.

Psychoanalysts, for their part, think that the current American diagnostic schema bastardizes and dilutes the richness of their formulations, that *The Diagnostic and Statistical Manual of Mental Disorders* (DSM-III) category is a "pseudo condition," and that research conducted with it only means "a multiplication of the basic error" (Gallwey, 1985). Therefore, in Britain, the attitude to the various concepts of the borderline ranges from hostility to prejudice to disbelief.

This is in part due to a certain degree of ignorance. Many psychiatrists answering a survey on the diagnosis of borderlines

Acknowledgment. I am grateful to the B. Rosenstadt Foundation of the University of Toronto for their support which allowed me to write this chapter.

confessed to being largely unfamiliar with the concepts (Tarnopolsky and Berelowitz, 1984); and of those who were familiar,
some rejected its usefulness very forcefully. Only 25 percent of
British psychiatrists use the borderline concept; of those using
the term, half are psychoanalysts. In contrast, the little empirical research that is available indicates that 15 to 20 percent of
DSM-III or Diagnostic Interview for Borderlines (DIB) borderlines are found among British inpatients (Kroll, Carey, Sines,
and Roth, 1982; Bateman, in press).

This situation perhaps simply reflects the unequal division
in British "psychological medicine." The mainstream consists of
biological and social psychiatry, with psychodynamic psychiatry
relegated to a thorn in its side. Proposals for hospital management or specific psychotherapy for borderline patients (such as
Masterson and Rinsley's in the United States) have not been
produced in the United Kingdom; what is found is a restricted
number of papers which were highly influential in their equally
restricted circles; exceptionally, some have reached a wider au-
dience (e.g., Main's "The Ailment" [1957]).

The vista from psychoanalysis is quite different. Yet, how
can a psychoanalytic theory be presented? Goethe wrote "All
theories are grey, green is the golden tree of life." Novelists
and playwrights can describe convincingly those stripes of life
that are as poignant and elusive as the psychoanalytic sessions
from which theories are derived. In *Uncle Vanya*, Elena com-
plains of the deadly effect that her aged, ailing, and lofty husband has on all of them. Chekhov makes her whine that he is
ill—yet he makes her feel so bored. In this way Chekhov has
captured the interpersonal aspect of projective identification.

An added problem for the North American reader is that
the most classical psychoanalytical paradigms and metaphors,
the structural model and the theory of instincts, have been
relegated to an unobtrusive position by the British writers. The
three strands of British psychoanalysis are represented by Anna
Freud, Melanie Klein, and the "Independent Tradition" of
which Donald Winnicott is the most popular writer. In a simpli-
fication of what is a complex ideological and technical spectrum,
the British views on borderlines will be presented under two
names: Klein and Winnicott. They were different in their views,

in their personalities, and in their relation to their followers—while Mrs. Klein was the founder and head of a movement, Winnicott shunned leadership and wished to remain "independent" with a lower case "i."

Broadly speaking, their writings are presented at different
levels of abstraction. Winnicott is mainly experiential, existential, at times macroscopic, and at times closer to introspection.
His concept of a true and false self, for instance, is evocative
enough to reach most of his lay readers, although they would
read in it something different from what he meant. Klein's
writings refer to a microscopy of the mind, a detailed world of
mechanisms and fantasies less accessible to the world at large
in the same way as the language of modern physics is incomprehensible except to a few of the initiated. Her design of an inner
world fueled by inexorable destructiveness is bound to create
particular resistances, independent of scientific criticisms.
These differences are clear in Winnicott's own statement: "It is
work with borderline patients that has taken me to the early
human condition, and here I mean the early life of the individual rather than to the mental mechanisms of earliest infancy"
(1963, p. 235).

In the following sections I will present some features of
these psychoanalytical theories aiming at what is more immediately relevant to borderline psychopathology; then I will answer, for each of them, "what is specifically borderline" in their
propositions. Finally, I will discuss some of their differences
and their clinical implications for British practitioners of today.

KLEIN

Melanie Klein's theories have been the subject of past and contemporary expositions (Segal, 1973; Hinshelwood, 1989). A
framework for the understanding of borderlines necessitates
reviewing the concepts of early superego and Klein's "positions"
with special reference to schizoid mechanisms and projective
identification.

Early Superego

Klein (1936) antedated the origins of psychopathology to the very beginning of life, "pushing backwards" the effects of instinctive pressures to the immediacy of birth, and also placed trauma, like weaning, in the first months of life. Her view on the origins of the superego illustrates her fundamental conviction that very early anxieties and defenses determine the organization and quality of later, oedipal, psychological structures.

Soon after Freud's (1923) formulation of the superego as the heir to the Oedipus complex, Klein put forward the view that a persecutory structure was present much earlier, from the beginning of the second year or even since the time of weaning (1926, 1933, 1975); and that this core of persecutory experience related to Freud's superego but was also qualitatively different from it. The late superego is moral and inhibiting; the early superego is aggressive rather than ethical, annihilating rather than restrictive. Forerunners or precursors of the superego, archaic or preoedipal superego, and Fairbairn's antilibinal object (1952), are related concepts.

Rosenfeld (1962) offered a clear clinical exposition of such structure in a female patient with hysterical character and severe symptoms, who presented extremes of idealization and persecution, unexpected peremptory shifts in attachments, and suffered a quasi-delusional persecutory episode during the analysis. The behavior ascribed to the ordinary latency superego is clearly shown by this attractive patient: she was tenacious, submissive, and an excited admirer of father and teachers. Her oedipal attachment to father involved an uncritical acceptance of his severity and his impositions. Mother was a shadowy figure. With a precision of detail that characterizes much of Kleinian writing, Rosenfeld describes how the analysis of these dynamics lead to the unearthing of a layer more persecutory than restrictive, more related to mother than to father, and antedating the oedipal phase. Dreams, life reports, and the vicissitudes of the transference demonstrated the coexistence of aggressive impulses and persecutory fears around mother's breast, and pointed to a traumatic weaning in the context of a severe whooping cough that worsened those feelings. Rosenfeld goes further to formulate that once such primitive hostility is mobilized, the target of aggression also becomes, by projection, the repository of aggression. A vicious circle is established because the subject is excited into further violence to annihilate it. This is the level of functioning of the "paranoid–schizoid position" described below, a situation that prevents reflection, restraint or reparation. Raskolnikov, in *Crime and Punishment*, hurts the old woman but then feels so tormented, probably with "persecutory guilt" (Grinberg, 1964), that goes on until he kills off both the woman and a possible witness. The alternative, reparative guilt or contrition, are not yet available and will only appear in the higher echelon of development of the "depressive position." Accounting for etiological factors, Rosenfeld weaves instinctive aggression and real frustration, the traumatic circumstances of weaning worsening the patient's assumed innate destructiveness.

Paranoid–Schizoid and Depressive "Positions"

Melanie Klein organized unconscious mental life in terms of defenses, anxieties, and internal object relations that result in broad mental constellations called psychological "positions."

The paranoid-schizoid position involves persecutory anxiety; a restricted ego and partial object relations (both of which result from the predominance of splitting mechanisms); and evident projective identification distorting the perception of the objects. Prejudice is a suitable example: the racist or the anti-Semite lives in dread of his objects (a type of persecutory anxiety) and in consequence gets involved in complicated and emotionally costly operations to defend himself from them; the object of fear and hatred, as found in racial stereotypes, is constructed on the basis of dissociated and projected parts of the self. As an immediate consequence, the self is impoverished or weakened. The projection has particular qualities and has been named "projective identification." This means that what is projected is not simply "abandoned" in the object; on the contrary, the subject maintains an agonizing relationship with it, combatting it, avoiding it, controlling it, and keeping his mind busy with it. Furthermore, the projection is not completely arbitrary and those who actively project may engage in unconscious collusion with their persecutors, in the manner of an unhealthy marriage, victim/victimizer, overprotectiveness/ dependence, and so on. Kleinians do not distinguish this from "projection" proper because they have cast the clinical phenomenon in a different theoretical net. Projective identification may be "used" to communicate, to disown, or to control unacceptable parts of the self; and as it leads to a confusion between subject and object it may result in considerable pressure in the interpersonal relationship.

By contrast, in Klein's "depressive position" the prevalent anxieties are guilt or remorse (Winnicott [1963] described it as the "stage of concern"). There is a feeling of responsibility for one's emotions and projections (i.e., an integration of previously dissociated destructive parts of the self); or guilt for the fate of one's objects, which are felt to have been damaged or lost (i.e., an acceptance of the value of the object). Varieties of mourning take place for the fantasized or actual loss of the object, or for the loss of the subject's totalitarian omnipotence. The ego is enriched by the recovery of projections, by the possibility of realistic relating, and by symbolic thinking. Ambivalence, nurturing rather than parasitic dependence, and a grasp of reality become possible. This awareness and this modesty allow a holistic appraisal of others and self, as they are brought to the "total object" level.

Paranoid–schizoid and depressive constellations of anxieties and defenses are normal ways of functioning that may become pathological. Paranoid–schizoid functioning is present in any process of alertness, discrimination or action; depressive functioning is present in any process of responsible concern or decision making. The resolution of mourning illustrates a normal depressive position process. Furthermore, the movement from one position to the other is constant.

In every case of pathology, the subject reverts rigidly to mechanisms of the paranoid–schizoid position: splitting, projective identification, idealization, denial. Clinically, they may appear as a manic triad: control, triumph, and contempt. If the dynamics are of the paranoid–schizoid type, these defenses operate against persecution, fear of dissolution, and awareness of the object. If the dynamics are of the depressive type, the same defenses operate against guilt, dependence, ambivalence, or loss. All these constitute, in the Kleinian viewpoint, the arena common to all psychopathology, the level of the "psychotic anxieties."

Schizoid Mechanisms and Projective Identification

Klein's (1946) basic formulation of psychopathology is elegantly applied in a short, didactic paper by Segal (1954) describing the "psychotic anxieties" underlying apparent neurotic problems. The patient, undoubtedly borderline, was a woman over thirty plagued with interpersonal difficulties and severe symptoms.

First, this paper illustrates schizoid mechanisms. Particular attention is given to projective identification, used in this case to deny separateness, with the ensuing impoverishment of the ego. The patient was depersonalized and unable to contact people in any meaningful way; for instance, having projected such capacities into the analyst, she assumed that Segal would "know" her dreams and initially felt no need of reporting them. Likewise, she could not recover parts or "bits" of herself projected into mother, hence she could not structure her own self sufficiently to separate and be autonomous. Here, "bits" of the self mean concrete representations of attitudes, emotions, and thoughts projected into the mother, functions that are felt to be lost and hence impoverish the ego. From an object relations standpoint affects or impulses carry with them a part of the ego, and necessarily imply a tie with an object (a point already made by Fairbairn [1952]). Clinical kinship and conceptual differences with the phenomena of "fusion" or with "self objects" will be evident.

Reintegration and growth of the ego become possible when the particular function or feeling that has been projected is identified and progressively reintegrated. The process is slow and complex because the anxieties that initially determined the projection also have to be worked through. Projective identification is initially a defensive mechanism of the budding ego used to preclude invasion by unmanageable anxieties. Premature reintrojection may force disintegration of the ego. Such types of anxieties mobilize very rigid schizoid defenses and paralyze the natural oscillation between the psychic positions. Inner life is frozen in a painful or unproductive impasse. It is precisely in the vicissitudes of such oscillations where some Kleinian writers find a specific characteristic of borderline personalities.

Is This Specifically Borderline?

The question that follows is whether these descriptions specifically address borderline psychopathology, or are simply the general Kleinian psychodynamic postulate. The answer is, first, that the position described encompasses the Kleinian universal viewpoint on pathology; but, second, that this functioning is glaringly clear among "schizoid" or "borderline" patients. It was precisely in the course of their analyses (as well as of children and psychotics) that these ideas were formulated. However, more recently there has been some attention given to specifying a metapsychology of borderline patients (Rosenfeld, 1978; Steiner, 1979; Gallwey, 1985).

Rey (1979) illustrates the early trend. Whilst addressing clinically identifiable borderline personalities, Rey's descriptions hinge on "schizoid phenomena," and then his examples straddle diagnostic boundaries into frank schizophrenic and manic depressive psychosis. For Rey, following Fairbairn, "schizoid phenomena" indicates an endopsychic rather than a phenomenological structure. Fairbairn's (1952) dictum that "the basic position of the ego is a schizoid position," meant that a profound split between acceptable and unbearable experiences in early infancy establishes the foundation of psychic structure, and at the same time indissolubly binds subject with object. In the same vein Rey describes the borderline's agora–claustrophobic dilemma and extends it "from a specific syndrome to a basic universal organization of the personality" (p. 474).

The agora-claustrophobic conflict is a particular type of relationship with people, time, and space. "Inside an object the schizoid character is claustrophobic, outside he is agoraphobic" (Fairbairn, 1952). In one way or another this conflict has been adopted or identified by many other writers, who have spoken of the in and out program, the need–fear dilemma, the avoidance–closeness struggle, the core conflict of perverts, and so on.

In the proximity of the object (and the object may be a person, a job, or an ideology) the borderline is terrified of closeness, which implies engulfment, loss of self, psychic annihilation. Away from the object, the borderline is terrified of distance, which implies isolation, abandonment, or premature separateness. Aggression is a possible response to both terrors, and this response throws the patient into the other situation, thus creating the known instability of borderline patients.

Explanations will vary according to the writer's persuasion: longing for or repetition of particular early experiences of merging, fusion, establishment of self objects, possessiveness of mother, specific difficulties in the rapprochement phase, have all been invoked. The Kleinian explanation speaks of unretrievable projective identifications. When objects are populated by projective identification a "particular kind of bond" is formed between the subject and the objects (or the spaces containing the objects). This bond results in the symptomatology of a given case. Thus, projection of greed would create fear of a threatening, devouring, grabbing object; projection of a wish for an exclusive intimacy would produce the fear of an engulfing, overwhelming object, with the concomitant erosion of identity, and so on. Such fears force the patient to escape, attack the object, quarrel with it, or simply withdraw from a relationship. This evasion, however, is not successful: for the borderline the outside is equally terrifying due to another projection. Life "outside" the object means annihilation, starvation, or psychic disintegration, a result of the projection of a stagnated self or of an object eviscerated of all vitality. Thus, the patient is forced into a pressurized, sometimes violent, return into the object.

The clinical presentation and chaotic lives of borderlines reflect these pressures: stormy marriages punctuated by rows and reconciliations, promiscuous relationships with unending change of partners, job instability, even emigrations. Their inability to solve the conflict results in their unsteady sense of identity. They cannot occupy psychological realms and therefore feel neither masculine nor feminine, sane or crazy, grown-up or childish, but exist in the frontier oscillating between two poles (Rey, 1979).

But, if the schizoid conflict and projective identification are part of a universal disposition, what is specifically borderline about them? It is the type of equilibrium achieved. For example, a withdrawn personality has stabilized in his rejection of external objects; the paraphiliac has solved the conflict by erotization and investing a sexual organ with some attributes (e.g., maternal) so that he localizes and controls his agora–claustrophobia around a sexual practice (Glasser, 1986). The specific borderline solution consists in an unending oscillation where the fears are not resolved. In theoretical terms, an unceasing vacillation occurs between the psychic positions. The feelings projected and retrieved are insurmountable and prevent working through of the depressive position. Borderlines may fleetingly step into the depressive position (Steiner, 1979) but they cannot tolerate concern, sadness, or loss. In clinical interviews they may have their eyes wet but they soon regress to a depersonalized state. The pressure of inordinate "depressive" feelings is such that the borderline violently and defensively pulls back to schizoid mechanisms—splitting, projection, and so on —with the clinical consequences of depersonalization, panic, and impulsive action. Thus he fails in achieving internalization, integration, reality testing, and symbolic thinking. Borderlines exist, metapsychologically speaking, in the border between the schizoid and depressive positions (Steiner, 1979, p. 390).

The assembly of objects populating the inner world differs, in these descriptions, from the neat "good/bad" split classically attributed to borderlines. It is seen (Rosenfeld, 1978; Steiner, 1981) as a malicious arrangement, with a false appearance that hides its true nature. Thus, "good" may conceal corruption, and "bad" may contain hidden valuable parts of the personality.

The difficult task of the analysis is to disentangle, clarify, and reorganize this puzzle.

While achieving such discrimination, the borderline also moves from concrete (paranoid–schizoid) to symbolic (depressive) thinking. In symbolic thinking an ill pet may *represent* or substitute for an ill child; in concrete thinking the pet *is* the child and commands immoderate reactions. For Klein such a "pet" is not a symbol but a "symbolic equation" (Segal, 1957), an amalgam created by projective identifications. When the projections have been reduced, proper symbolic and abstract activities are possible, and the thinking self has been discriminated from the object. Borderlines remain attached to external figures and to their original objects without demarcation between fantasy ("my infantile self is ill") and reality ("my pet is ill"). They lack an inner structure or symbols mediating and making stable their commerce with reality.

Pathological Organizations

The borderline solution may be transcribed into a general model of disorders furnished by the concept of "pathological organizations." These are structures of a defensive nature that, in the Kleinian model, freeze the natural to and fro between the psychic positions. Different organizations have been described (Spillius, 1988). The best known is perhaps Rosenfeld's (1971) "narcissistic organization," a structure that hijacks the libidinal parts of the self, paralyzes development, and causes negative therapeutic reactions. The patient may describe this organization as an association, or gang that terrorizes the patient while pretending to protect him and give him a false sense of security. The theme of severing links with dependable objects frequently represents the actions of such organizations. A patient who managed to keep a frightening balance between her isolation and her anorexia began to experience some symptomatic improvement. Simultaneously she turned to drinking and smoking in bed, burning her linen, and had to be hospitalized. At that stage she produced a dream with a striking manifest content. She appeared dissociated in two figures: herself as a witness, and a "twin sister" lying in a hospital bed. An elegant and accomplished nurse presided over the scene with a group of colleagues, reviewing the case. The nurse finally passed some scissors to my patient and ordered her to cut the intravenous feed which ensured the survival of the sick woman. The witness–patient felt forced to obey while the nurses burst into a crazy operatic laughter.

There are other presentations: the organization may exhibit a clinical overcoat of psychotic symptoms, obsessive control, erotic excitement, manic triumph, masochistic surrender, and so on (Steiner, 1987), all of which are sustained by the pillars of Kleinian psychopathology: splitting and projective identification. O'Shaughnessy (1981) described an anxious, fragmented, quasi-psychotic borderline man who acquired some balance with a restricted, controlled style of existence that allowed minimal inter- and intrapersonal contact: he swerved from chaotic into deadened. This paper provides a close look into a structure which, from another perspective, is an extreme form of "false self," and illustrates what I earlier called the "microscopic" quality of Kleinian writing. This will be exemplified further.

Gallwey (1985) has classified borderlines in two broad groups. One type represents a development of Winnicott's false self concept and is referred to as having a "false personality organization" which covers a hollow, improperly developed ego. Like Rosenfeld before him, and in contrast with other Kleinian authors, Gallwey hypothesizes that maternal deprivation has affected the inchoate ego. The current "false" ego can display a very convincing pseudonormality, and is likened to a brittle eggshell supported by primitive fantasies. To cover up these restrictions, men may rely on fetishes or other perversions; women may show extreme concern for their bodies, dieting, using cosmetics, and the like. Thus, subjects avoid awareness of their reduced capacity to face conflict, to overcome separations, or to tolerate emotional hunger. The impulsive or violent behavior sometimes exhibited by such patients "can be as much a desperate attempt to establish some supportive link with an object of over-dependency as an expression of pure destructiveness" (Gallway, 1985, p. 136). I am quoting these lines in anticipation of the discussion, sometimes extremely polarized, between instinctive and reactive aggression that has technical implications for the psychotherapy of borderline patients.

Gallwey's second type of borderline is explained drawing from Bion's (1957) model of psychotic and nonpsychotic parts of the personality. This paradigm allows for the coexistence of advanced and primitive modes of psychic functioning without recourse to the notion of regression. These borderlines have split personalities that enable them considerable successful adaptation whilst a powerful psychotic domain remains encapsulated or strictly dissociated from the apparent forward ego. The eruption of the psychotic part into the socially adaptive one may result in unpredictable violence, sometimes of a criminal quality, or in paranoid psychotic breakdowns. Although Bion's language may be unfamiliar to classical psychoanalysts, it allows Gallwey to participate in the experience of the borderline's thought processes and in their instinctive pressures. Grinberg, Sor, and Bianchedi (1985) have published a useful introduction to Bion's writings.

WINNICOTT

If projective identification and psychotic mechanisms are trademarks of the Kleinian theory, the transitional object and false self capture Winnicott's conception of borderline psychopathology—and are basic to his overall psychoanalytic position.

Transitional describes the passage from total dependence toward independence, but it also refers to the inner change between merging with the mother and individuality or separateness that accompanies that movement. Thus, Winnicott assumed "that the infant's mode of experiencing at these times was transitional between the earliest stage of total subjectivity and unawareness of external reality, and the later stage of objectivity where external reality was recognized and accepted" (Macaskill, 1982a, pp. 350).

In these circumstances a "thing" (a thumb, the archetypal blanket, the teddy bear) may come to embody the experience

and has been called a transitional "object." But transitional phenomena go beyond the possession of such objects. The blanket
and the teddy bear are only concrete pointers to the inner
experience it is assumed the baby is having. Paraphrasing Winnicott, Padel (1988) states that "the use is transitional, not the
object itself" (p. 10). A game, a dream, or later in life any other
expression of artistic and scientific creativity may represent
such transitionality. If in such experience, the central feature
is an object, "then it represents the mother or part of her, but
it also represents the self as infant or some part of the self" (p.
9). "The teddy bear is sometimes treated as part of the
mother—to fall asleep against—and sometimes as the child's
own self, which . . . may have to be taught things which the
child has just learned" (Padel, 1988, p. 10). For the infant in
this stage of experience, mother is neither his possession under
complete infantile omnipotence nor is she distinct, but is somehow both. So, transitionality has many meanings: a stage of
relationship with mother; a stage of appraisal of the object
between merging and separateness; a dual relationship where
subject and object imply each other in a single moment or a
single activity or a single thing; and finally the "thing" on which
such experience hinges.

Development will challenge such omnipotent convictions
but before they are eroded, mother is believed to be owned
when in fact there is a progressive awareness that she is not.
Necessarily, some degree of "disillusion" is setting in.

What is Specifically Borderline?

Macaskill (1982a) has sympathetically reviewed Winnicott's
writings, extricating the essence of his position with regard to
borderlines: "He proposed that borderline disorders arose
from a sustained empathic failure in the transitional relationship" (p. 351).

What is this failure about? In what ways was mother not
"good enough" to the future borderline patient? It means that
mother was not suitably reassuring or supportive during the
difficult transitional phase, and therefore no sense of continuity

could grow or even exist. Winnicott (1960, p. 52) thought that such failures in care result in interruptions of being and in weakening of the ego. The existence of a continuous, reliable, predictable maternal presence, "holding" the child physically and emotionally, is a precondition of mental health. For Winnicott, in his particularly suggestive but elusive style, "being" and "reacting" were antinomies. He also saw an alternative between the sense of being and the feeling of psychic annihilation. "The holding environment therefore has as its main function the reduction to a minimum of impingements to which the infant must react with resultant annihilation of personal being" (p. 47).

There is a further specification. Those who miss such care massively at early stages may develop psychoses; for the borderline such deficiency happened somewhat later in life when the mother could not adapt gradually to the changing and expanding needs of the infant. In the merged or totally dependent state the mother has to guess and provide; the child cannot explicitly request her help. Later the mother has to respond to clues, and allow the child the possibility of producing signals. In this process:

> [T]here is a very subtle distinction between the mother's understanding of her infant's need based on empathy, and her change over to an understanding based on something in the infant or small child that indicates need. This is particularly difficult . . . because children vacillate between one state and the other; one minute they are merged with their mother and require empathy, while the next they are separate from her, and if she knows their needs in advance she is dangerous, a witch [1960, p. 51].

Winnicott adds, poignantly: "This detail is reproduced in psycho-analytic work with borderline cases." Such specificity in the mother's response has interesting coincidences with Mahler's view that the borderline pathology stems from failures in the rapprochement phase, and with Kohut's (1971) account of "phase appropriate" maternal responses.

In Winnicott's view, such maternal failures cause a true "developmental arrest," and as a result, borderlines never reached any sense of inner security. Neither can they provide reassuring, soothing, creative, or constructive experiences for themselves; that is, the extensions of sustaining transitional phenomena in adult life. Stuck in this path, without achieving a sense of being a personal agent, the borderline reacts to impingement rather than responds to stimuli, and chronically exhibits the vulnerability and instability that result from his lack of "internal cohesiveness."

The logical consequence of these propositions was the prescription of a therapy where the transitional phase would be recreated and renegotiated, including a new experience of "disillusionment" under the empathic vigilance of the therapist.

This notion of transitionality involves a considerable departure from Kleinian theory. For the latter there is no normal stage of merging with the mother, nor an objectless state. The Kleinian view is that subject and object are separate from the start and any fusion or confusion between the two is due to an excessive display of projections (initially, a projection of the death instinct into the breast). From this the child, and, if he were unsuccessful, later the patient, will have to recover his distinctiveness. Freud's narcissism is for Kleinians a narcissistic object relation preventing awareness of separateness. The object (or part of it) has become incorporated into the self; or the self or part of the self has been projected into the object; but in either case they are not acknowledged to any degree as different from each other. Under these rules, when the patient says "I" or "You," who is the "I," who is the "You"? Who is the subject or the object? The "transitional object" is, therefore, in Kleinian terms, a pathological solution rooted in a presymbolic, concrete, part object state of affairs. Britton (1988) summarily stated that the transitional object would be a clinical manifestation of Segal's (1957) "symbolic equation." For the Kleinian analyst this is a stage to be dissolved interpretatively, thus undoing the projective identifications. Another Kleinian review, comparing transitional objects in normal and pathological development, was offered by Isaacs Elmhirst (1980).

Implications for Technique

Macaskill (1982a) has described how the Winnicott-based thera-pist conceives of treatment for borderline patients.

First, there should be an attitude of "maintaining empa-thy." Wolff (1971) regarded this as being partially a gift, and partially a result of education. It starts from the therapist's capacity for "being with the patient," of displaying what Fair-bairn (1952) called the receptive, "feminine" function of ther-apy, and is enhanced by knowledge. Winnicott, says Macaskill, understood that borderline patients, given their shaky selves, will experience their therapist as intrusive, and at the same time as an essential lifeline they cannot dispense with. They will react to some interpretations with rage, withdrawal, and narcissistic fantasy, and to others with a feeling of being soothed and reas-sured.

The second issue is how to distinguish one type of interven-tion from the other, or how to talk to the borderline patient. Acceptable interpretations are reflections of the experience of the patient. They are called mirroring or holding interpreta-tions, reflections and clarifications of feelings and experience. Unacceptable interpretations refer to psychodynamisms, de-fenses, splits, search for meanings, implicit requests for reflec-tion, and the like. Wolff (1971) referred to them as a "doing to the patient" function of the therapy. Bollas (1978) developed the issue and argued that for a long time patients are incapable of such introspection (they exhibit a paranoid–schizoid type of response, in Kleinian terms) and that such implicit requests may make them feel dismissed in their sense of personal exis-tence. In this vein Macaskill sees symptoms, negative self-im-ages, and even self-destructive acts as having a function in maintaining the patient's sense of self or asserting his individu-ality. He argues that interpreting them exclusively as an expres-sion of a destructive pulsion is likely to destabilize the patient further. In one of his cases, challenging the omnipotent func-tion of grandiose fantasy threw the patient into disarray. (Gall-wey [1985] says something similar about the function of certain fantasies that cover up an essentially hollow self.) In another example, the insistence on the aggressive qualities of self-cutting led to some relief, but the abandonment of the behavior was reached only when the underlying experience of meaninglessness after separations was addressed.

Macaskill refers to this protective function as the "transitional value" of symptoms. He proposed that interpretations reflecting on the patient's experience and including an affirmation of the patient's self, invest the therapist with a transitional function and therefore promote the missing sense of continuity in the patient. In this way symptoms lose their function. Macaskill's dictum, "Maintaining empathy and avoiding the destruction of personal meaning" (1982a, p. 354), entails interpreting, as was explained, although sometimes references to psychodynamisms or meanings may be included. About the latter, Winnicott (1968) stated: "It appals me to think how much deep change I have prevented or delayed . . . by my personal need to interpret" (p. 101).

Repeated appropriate empathic experiences create what Macaskill called a "therapeutic transitional state," a state of lack of interpersonal pressure where patients discover the feeling of authenticity and aliveness which are indicators of ego integration. In the beginning such states are only possible in the presence of the therapist, but with time patients learn to evoke the relaxed accepting atmosphere on their own, they learn to "soothe" themselves (Silver, Glassman, and Cardish, 1988).

Winnicott (1953) felt that mothers must "fail" their children if any separateness and growth will take place. In the same way, in therapy the disruption, disappearance, and recovery of the transitional states constitute the necessary bridge to the next stage of disillusionment. Absences, unavoidable failures, and misjudgments spontaneously recreate this state. Early in the therapy they only threaten the patient's cohesiveness (i.e., they are experienced as an attack on the self, in a paranoid–schizoid manner), but progressively the patient will identify them and tolerate their existence. Then, they determine a mourning reaction where sadness and anger are likely to occur. This is the stage of disillusion. Although the therapist must relentlessly acknowledge the validity of the anger addressed to him (Macaskill, 1982a, p. 357), it is here that more ordinary therapeutic work is possible. In Kleinian terms, the patient has reached a more stable contact of a depressive type. It is fascinating to note how this stage of integration is achieved by therapists working with very different assumptions and techniques, in both Britain and North America.

COINCIDENCES AND ALTERNATIVES

On Technique

In Great Britain there is no tradition of hospital treatment for borderline patients, except isolated examples; differences on the psychotherapeutic approach fade into wider differences in conceptions of psychoanalysis.

Kleinians advocate the adherence to classical psychoanalytic norms irrespective of particular clinical presentations, because they hold that the working through of primitive anxieties is only possible in that setting. However, Rosenfeld (1978, 1979b) has offered some sobering advice on the management of the transferential psychosis and subsequent impasse. He writes: "I then asked the patient to sit up and encouraged him to go over all the criticisms and grudges he felt against me. . . . I did not give any interpretations and adopted an entirely receptive, empathic, listening attitude to him. I also examined, as much as possible, my countertransference, for he constantly complained of some tension in me which disturbed him." And later, "it was difficult to distinguish whether the patient made envious, destructive attacks on my mind . . . or whether I made mistakes in interpreting and handling his anxieties" (Rosenfeld, 1978, pp. 219–220).

The reality that once-a-week psychotherapy is the only one widely available in the National Health Service has led other Kleinian writers to develop a psychotherapeutic technique based on transference (Gallwey, 1978), and to appraise how much relief can be attained in less than ideal circumstances (Steiner, 1979).

Writers of the "Independent" tradition associated with Fairbairn, Winnicott, and Balint also practice other psychotherapeutic approaches (family, marital) and accept some modifications for the individual treatment of borderlines, such as fewer than five sessions per week, face-to-face contact, and confrontations between fantasy and reality. Some writers have discussed more controversial measures: the feasibility (Little, 1986; Stewart, 1987) or disadvantage (Casement, 1982) of loosening the rule of abstinence. Little (1986, p. 93), who thinks that borderlines are fixated in an undifferentiated phase, says that the therapist, in given circumstances, may involve the body (holding a hand, preventing a movement) or may openly express opinions or feelings ("I am glad you have had a good holiday"). She argues that such measures have prompted a shift from delusion to reality, from preverbal to verbal or, in her own terms, from "basic unity" to object differentiation.

On Patient Populations

Is it possible that the different psychotherapeutic propositions might have grown out of the treatment of different types of cases? Rosenfeld (1979a) has described five varieties of borderlines but has added with wry humor: "They all have an important factor in common: they are difficult to treat!" (p. 195). Gallwey (1985) studied severe forensic borderlines and has cautioned that strict support may be advisable for those who have very weak egos, and that others may require strong institutional protection to face any intervention.

Macaskill (1982a) has outlined the differences between Winnicott's proposed therapy and others that accentuate the use of confrontation, limit-setting, and deep interpretations. He argues that they are dealing with different types of borderline cases, that Winnicott's patients were characterologically schizoid and controlled, while the borderline cases described by Kernberg and Masterson were impulsive and self-destructive and therefore necessitated considerable confrontation and limit-setting to ensure the survival of the treatment. Among the latter group, he writes, "interpretations seem to have a significant confronting role and value in maintaining reality testing and preventing acting out . . . this function seems largely unnecessary in the schizoid type of borderline case treated by Winnicott. For this latter group of patients the need to undo the sense of compliance and to create a sense of aliveness and creativity are the key issues" (p. 359).

However, the theoretical differences that prescribe divergent handling of the same cases should not be overlooked.

On the American Schools

It is frequently asked whether the Kernberg/Kohut debate in the United States is equivalent to the differences between followers of Klein and Winnicott in Britain. I will take up this issue here and in the next section on aggression.

First, some have affiliated Kernberg with Klein, and Kohut with Winnicott. The work of Klein and Rosenfeld is one of the pillars of Kernberg's position, even allowing for his known disagreements. But the Kleinian analyst, with his sense of scholastic purity and group loyalty, winces at bowdlerized or partial versions of the theory. As such Kernberg is not a popular writer in Britain; for different reasons, neither is Kohut widely read. Both Winnicott and Kohut addressed the same type of phenomena, and it is surprising that Kohut made so little reference to British theoreticians who had worked or were working on parallel lines to his (for a discussion of this, see Bacal [1987]). Kohut's and Winnicott's clinical languages are, at times, strikingly similar with their references to phase-appropriate maternal responses, maternal failures, mirroring, cohesiveness of the self, and the prescription of a therapy that sets out to correct a developmental fault. On the other hand, Kohut's metapsychology is quite strange to the British psychoanalytic schools. There is little space for a line of thought that in some ways overlaps and in others is so alien to Winnicott's. Kohut's self objects are understood from the Kleinian perspective to refer to narcissistic object relations created by projective identification, and this, coupled with the dismissal of aggression, makes Kohut also unattractive to Kleinian potential readers.

Second, a seemingly incidental geographical matter: followers of Klein and Winnicott coexist in London and debate continually within the same psychoanalytic society. Klein's and Winnicott's ideas are certainly known and to some extent used by every British analyst, irrespective of his affiliation. How much this is acknowledged in public is another matter. Closeness may also breed polarization, the need to be distinct, and the use of ideas as political emblems. Sandler (1983) has aptly described the differences between the private and public ideologies of psychoanalysts; and Wallerstein (1983) has shown the existing differences between technique as professed and technique as practiced.

On Aggression

In his incisive critique of self psychology, Kernberg (1974) wrote that Kohut had "almost total disregard for the vicissitudes of aggression" (p. 262). This certainly would not apply to Winnicott (1950, 1968), who struggled with the many developmental varieties of aggression and their sources, and framed the issue very succinctly: "In its simplest form the question we ask is: does aggression come ultimately from anger aroused by frustration, or has it a root of its own?" (1950, p. 210). The polarizations on this matter transcend psychoanalysis, because ultimately they refer to conceptions of man that have not been reconciled: whether man is, or contains an essentially beastly core harnessed with difficulty by society, or whether man is an essentially benign creature deformed and made aggressive by social life. Such views can be traced from philosophy through to ethology.

In psychoanalysis, those who think in terms of "response to frustration" are primarily concerned with deficiencies, impingements, deprivations, separations, abandonments, and specifically with the role of the mother who failed the child in early infancy through misfit, misjudgment, or misdeed. Fairbairn should be remembered as the theoretician who developed ideas about maternal mismatch into a metapsychological construct. The adherence to primary envy, destructiveness, or the death instinct is the psychoanalytic version of the "intrinsic badness of man" position. Melanie Klein thought that the earliest relation to the breast was the projection outwards of the death instinct, a necessary defense because it was experienced by the baby as an annihilating attack on his self. More recently, Segal (1987) wrote: "The concept of the death instinct is, to my mind, indispensable to clinical work" (compare with Guntrip [1971]: "In twenty-five years of psychoanalytic therapy . . . I have always found that all forms of aggressive reaction were defensive. . . . The frustration–aggression theory is the only one supported by clinical observation" cited by Bacal [1987, p. 89]). The death instinct is assumed to operate blatantly as in envious attacks, or it is supposed to exist behind a variety of phenomena, ranging from insurmountable negative therapeutic reactions to subtle misinterpretations that distort the meaning of the analyst's interpretations.

Although the affiliation of Klein with instinctive and of Winnicott with reactive destructiveness is clinically valid, none of them denied completely the existence of "the other root." Winnicott was very aware of the incompleteness of each position: "The work of Klein on splitting defense mechanisms and on projections and introjections and so on, is an attempt to state the effects of the failure of environmental provision in terms of the individual. This work on primitive mechanisms gives the clue to only one part of the story, and a reconstruction of the environment and its failures provides the other part" (1960, p. 50). "The other half of the theory . . . concerns . . . the qualities and changes in the mother that meet the specific and developing needs of the infant towards whom she orientates" (1960, p. 42). His axiom "there is no such a thing as a baby" meant one should always consider baby-and-mother together.

Melanie Klein did not formulate at any length a theoretical understanding of the maternal role but referred to the important consequences of weaning as a prototype of object loss. It was Bion ([1962]; see also Grinberg et al. [1985]) who articulated within the Kleinian framework of a theory of the function of the mother, with his concepts of container/contained, alpha/

beta functions, and maternal "reverie." Reverie refers to the capacity of the mother to perceive, process, and return to the infant the impact of those inner raw experiences that were unbearable for him and necessitated projecting. It is the counterpart, at the level of thought processes and intrapsychic mechanisms, of what Winnicott described as an intuitive, and even physical, capacity of the mother to hold the baby. The isomorphisms and differences between Winnicott's "holding" and Bion's "containing" were addressed by James (1984).

To Contain and To Confront

The literature on borderlines frequently discusses whether conscious and unconscious aggression should be met with empathy or with confrontation. What type of interventions would bring relief, curtail acting out and breakdowns, and eventually promote insight? In other words, what would "contain" the patient?

I will start with a quotation from self psychology about empathy: "it is not to be confused with being nice to someone. Empathy is to intrinsically comprehend the experience of others" (Baker and Baker, 1987, p. 2). In a similar vein, to contain does not mean to listen passively and respond with platitudes, nor to condone or collude with whatever the patient does. To contain means first to sustain the considerable pressure of the borderline patient (Heimann, 1950). It means to stand those feelings as a prerequisite to understanding them, without rushing into "interpreting away" the experience (Joseph, 1983). Next, to contain includes identifying and naming the type and quality of the emotions involved. This requires an intuitive and imaginative freedom of the therapist's mind (Bion's reverie, Winnicott's holding), so that the patient will hear a reflection of his experience in precise words. The patient will not only feel relieved, he will also incorporate the memory of an object that alleviates, and will incorporate the function of making sense and giving relief. But this is not all: to contain means also to remain emotionally available to work through. Therefore, to contain the patient is neither quick nor simple nor passive.

It will be evident that containing includes some of the processes of interpreting. This raises certain questions. Which of the patient's conscious or unconscious experiences will the therapist take up? How much will be described of the origins and consequences of such feelings, actions, and fantasies? Where it fuses with interpreting, containing will be shaped by the analyst's convictions. For some analysts these allude prominently to the unconscious hostility of the patient and they would describe such interpretations as essentially "containing." This is the activity that from other quarters is called "confronting"; it means confronting the patient with his destructiveness. As no amount of clinical detail is likely to alter a deep-seated persuasion, I will just give a snippet of a discussion between therapists of different convictions as a reminder of endless similar examples. A borderline woman who was away from home had the fantasy of stabbing the pregnant belly of her hostess. Troubled, increasingly panicky, and finally depersonalized, she interrupted the trip and went back to her hometown and her therapy. The interpretations offered in a seminar ranged from a consideration of her jealousy and envy ("confrontation"?), which for some participants was thought to be stimulated by her own uprootedness; to the idea that the stabbing "only" represented the pressure to make contact with her mother and the therapist ("empathy"?).

Each view has its merits and its shortcomings. Adopting one or the other requires considerable clinical finesse and intellectual freedom. Etchegoyen, Lopez, and Rabih (1987) have asked what happens when the patient is misunderstood, when the analyst misses either the envious root or the frustration root of the behavior? A vicious circle or an impasse; and I will add that with borderlines a quick decompensation may occur. There is a risk of a self-perpetuating vicious circle because frustration leads to envy; and envy of the object prevents taking from it to alleviate frustration. If the therapist misjudges the case and speaks of frustration where there is envy, the envy will be repressed and the patient will deteriorate. On the other hand, if the therapist implies destructiveness ignoring trauma or frustration, the patient will be further frustrated, persecuted by the interpretation, and may end up masochistically submissive or more disturbed. There seems to be no way of relinquishing a precise diagnosis of each situation because in the course of a long analysis both destructiveness and frustration are to be repeatedly addressed. In my experience patients clearly indicate their need and readiness to attend to one or the other.

EPILOGUE

This selective exposition on borderline psychopathology addressed developments that largely occurred in the context of wider theoretical issues on psychoanalysis. Are they reconcilable or incompatible? In Great Britain their isomorphisms have not been explored with the eagerness with which differences have been developed. Sometimes, as it was said with reference to another psychoanalytic debate, "an opposition is created where an articulation should be found" (Bleichmar, 1986, p. 11). Freud (1900) wrote that the unconscious speaks more than one language—and perhaps many dialects?

PART III

Therapeutic Issues and Treatment Modalities

9.

The Assessment Process

Daniel Silver, M.D., and
Michael Rosenbluth, M.D.

INTRODUCTION

The increasing emphasis on the assessment process results from accumulating evidence that familiar or accepted approaches of treatment for borderline patients can be either unsuccessful or even become intolerable to either the patient or the therapist (Skodal, Buckley, and Charles, 1983; Waldinger and Gunderson, 1984). While the heterogeneity (Akiskal, Chen, Davis, Puzantian, Kashgarian, and Bollinger, 1985a; Andrulonis, Glueck, Stroebel, and Vogel, 1982) of the borderline patient population still prevents us from identifying "the" treatment of choice, the assessment process should, nevertheless, attempt to minimize undue negative effects throughout the treacherous road of therapy with these patients (Frances and Clarkin, 1981; Crown, 1983; Mays and Franks, 1985).

For borderline patients an inept assessment and therefore subsequent poor treatment choices can prove disastrous. A poorly assessed neurotic patient may get worse, or leave therapy, but has supplies from within and without to draw upon to reestablish the pretreatment state. The borderline patient usually does not enjoy these supplies in the same proportion and his or her anxiety can quickly grow to psychotic proportions and lead to severe regressions, disintegrative experiences, or even suicide.

The purpose of the assessment process is essentially to provide the information necessary to choose appropriate treatment strategies. What clinicians extract from the assessment is based on their training, clinical experience, and familiarity with the literature describing similar patients. The assessment process should help the clinician to avoid both treatment mania (Main, 1957) and temper the excessive need to treat (Lerner, 1979).

The assessment process for this group of patients is always difficult because of the complexities of the presenting clinical picture. The major concern of the assessment is to sort out the varying aspects of the pathological personality organization that has been the patient's life-style as a result of biological, social, and psychodynamic factors; clarify Axis I issues; sort out the social factors which may influence the course of treatment; and particularly evaluate the capacity of the patient to engage in psychotherapy. Because of the diversity of influencing factors, it is particularly important for the clinician to approach the assessment with an open-minded and eclectic attitude. This attitude should prevail throughout. Whenever the therapeutic process bogs down or becomes too difficult, treatment should not be paralyzed by the adherence to one particular theoretical model or the pronouncements of one therapeutic guru or another. The clinician who feels he can conceptualize a borderline patient primarily within one social, biological, or psychodynamic model is advised to choose his patients very carefully so that they fit his particular biased belief system.

The assessment process for a borderline patient should not take more than two to four interviews—the less the better. The assessment process inherently puts the clinician in a very idealized light. For many borderline patients, this can be conducive to their developing an almost instantaneous idealized transference–attachment. During the assessment, the therapist is not infrequently experienced by the patient as easy going, very congenial, rather interactive, and most empathic. If at the end of the assessment the therapist decides to refer the patient on, for any number of reasons, the "rejection" can have devastating consequences. Similarly, in the case when the assessment is a consultation for a colleague due to a therapeutic stalemate, the assessment should be kept preferably to one session, never more than two. The consultative process is frequently experienced as being what the patient would wish his therapy to be like. This can only further devalue the current therapist and the ongoing therapeutic process.

Finally, a "pitfall" that can occasionally be disastrous is to uncover or dig too deeply during the assessment process for material which one is not prepared to follow up; or when one is not able to ensure that an immediate transfer to a competent psychotherapist will take place. This can be a disastrous process. These vulnerable and fragile patients, who may have managed to get along in their own particular way, may seriously disintegrate during the course of an insensitive assessment process. (In one case a patient suicided after a very difficult assessment interview. This can occur even when a very experienced consultant is there to "demonstrate" the usefulness of the assessment process to a group of residents or colleagues.) While the assessment process must be used to explore as many areas as possible, it must nevertheless bear in mind that the patient also has to continue functioning after the assessment is completed. It is not unlike the responsibility of a surgeon who embarks on a difficult operation only to realize that it is more complicated and complex than he had anticipated, and then walks away leaving it to his novice assistant to "close up." When these patients are subjected to a very intensive assessment, one must make sure that there is some closure after the assessment process.

THE "BORDERLINE" PATIENT POPULATION

The Diagnostic and Statistical Manual of Mental Disorders, revised edition (DSM-III-R) (American Psychiatric Association, 1987) is extremely useful for research purposes, making it possible for various centers to compare and contrast similar patients in treatment or follow-up studies. However, day-to-day clinical practice still challenges exact attempts to classify the borderline patient. One of us (D.S.), has labeled the heterogeneous group of borderline patients as characterologically difficult patients. This includes those with a significant number of traits usually ascribed to the DSM-III-R borderline patient, the histrionic personality disorder, the narcissistic personality disorder, and some of the milder antisocial personality disorders. The patients are very similar to Kernberg's (1975) borderline personality organization classification. They are the kinds of patients who seem to lack many of the intrapsychic capacities and interpersonal skills necessary to maintain stable, satisfying enough, interpersonal relationships or occupational pursuits. They all seem to suffer to varying degrees from feelings of dissatisfaction, futility, and despair. In addition, they are self-destructive and/or mutilative; frequently suicidal; involved in endless streams of unsatisfactory experiences in all areas in their lives; and have been seen, more often than not, by more than one or two therapists.

This heterogeneous patient population ranges from the highest functioning, hardworking, apparently "successful" professional person, whose personal life feels empty, futile, full of despair, and devoid of any meaningful personal relationships, to the more volatile, clinging, demanding, and chronically suicidal, self-mutilating patient frequently blacklisted from hospital emergency rooms and shunned by most psychotherapists.

Identity confusion and conflicts are a major concern for these patients: "Who am I?"; "What do I really want?"; "I am never satisfied with whatever I resolve." These are frequent questions and statements that this patient population struggles with. While these issues are not totally uncommon problems in the general population, the degree to which they are paralyzing and destructive to these patients is quite striking. Their job histories, academic pursuits, and interpersonal relationships are usually erratic and inconsistent. Initial satisfaction with new "challenges" invariably changes eventually to disappointment, boredom, frustration, and rage.

In therapy, therapeutic impasses are common; stalemates occur, often marked by threats of suicide which can become therapeutically paralyzing; and frequent threats of ending therapy precipitously are usually the rule. The most prominent overall feature for this group remains their exquisite general vulnerability and fragility which must be diligently assessed and scrutinized in the initial phases of the assessment phase. Many are indeed "psychic bleeders" (Stern, 1938). This fragility will color every aspect and almost every moment of the therapeutic relationship. It is not always apparent, but one must bear in mind that it can easily surface with any real, fantasied, or perceived assault and/or disappointment.

For these reasons, regardless how the patient presents initially, it is prudent to conceptualize the borderline patient as changeable in terms such as mild, moderate, or severe, and to expect that a given patient at any time can dissolve into one or the other of these states. Thus, a patient who may present as a "mild" borderline patient in the assessment phase can in therapy present a "moderate" or even "severe" clinical picture. The opposite is equally true; that is, often a patient presents as a "severe" borderline and, with the holding environment that the therapeutic process can provide, may show only mild disturbances.

SHIFTS IN THEORETICAL EMPHASIS

The major shift in theoretical emphasis from drive theory to object relations theory and self psychology has greatly influenced the usefulness of the assessment process both of the initial and the ongoing phases. This shift from a one-person to a two-person psychology has changed the foci on conceptualizing and assessing the borderline patient.

Thus, a patient's rage does not necessarily or primarily have to be conceptualized as only instinctual but can also result from frustration, particularly from an unempathic "therapeutic" intervention. Nor is acting out necessarily a fantasy "acted out" of the transference situation while the original wish remains hidden. It can also be, probably even more so in the borderline patient, a reliving of a childhood situation evoked unintentionally by the therapist which provokes an impulsive act reminiscent of an earlier period of development.

The concept of resistance has also broadened. It can be understood not only as a psychic force in patients which prevents pathogenic thoughts from becoming conscious, leading to stalemates in therapy, but rather, appreciated empathically by the therapist as a signal, albeit unconscious, that the patient is experiencing the therapeutic process as too intrusive, overwhelming, and threatening to his very sense of self. The therapist must respect this and "back off" to prevent unnecessary regression and disintegration.

Similarly, the compulsion to repeat experiences which are self-destructive (relational or otherwise) need not necessarily be understood as primary masochism but as attempts to resolve earlier unsatisfactory experiences satisfactorily.

As we move from drive theory to object relations theory, that is, from a one-person psychology to a two-person psychology, the onus of responsibility for lack of therapeutic progress or success, or untoward effects occurring during therapy, is focusing more on the therapist and the patient rather than the patient only. It is becoming more acceptable currently to pay more attention to patients' grievances about previous therapists' style or technique, and to consider that the patient may indeed be right. In more recent years, the literature on psychotherapy has increasingly reexamined the issues of negative therapeutic reactions, stalemates, precipitous endings, and treatment failures as not only being the patient's problem. Thus the implication for the assessment process is to consider closely the patient's complaints about previous therapists. Basic transference constellations regarding frustration, disappointments, and defenses against these affects can be elicited in the assessment process by reviewing previous therapeutic relationships. (The borderline personality disorder [BPD] patient has often seen several previous therapists [Gunderson, 1984].) Similar basic patterns can be elicited in reviewing other important relationships. Attention can be paid to how these are manifest in the assessment interview in how the patient reacts to a perceived or actually inaccurate interpretation or empathic failure.

ASSESSING SUICIDAL POTENTIAL

It is during the initial assessment phase that any previous suicidal behavior must be discussed frankly and in some detail.
We too feel very strongly that "any psychotherapeutic relationship that [is going to] extend over many months under unrealistic conditions without honest communication and clearly delineated and accepted responsibilities on the part of both
participants, may also be playing into the patient's suicidal potential" (Kernberg, 1984, p. 263).

Every therapist who has had any experience with borderline patients is all too aware of the therapeutic chaos that is
frequently encountered by their suicidal threats and attempts.
(And there are also successful suicides amongst them.)

The feelings among therapists regarding the suicidal potential among these patients probably range from categorical
condemnation to conditional acceptance if not approval. Regardless of one's position on this issue, "the management of the
person for whom suicidality has become a way of life requires
a willingness to take risks and an acceptance of the fact that
one cannot prevent all suicides" (Schwartz, Flinn, and Slawson,
1974, p. 204). Nevertheless, the rights of the suicidal patients
remain a most vexing moral question for the clinician (Sakinofsky and Swart, 1986).

We agree that "the more respectful the therapist is of the
patient's right to take his own life, the more open will the patient be about his suicidal intent" (Birtchnell, 1983, p. 34). We
try to impress upon the patient, however, that respect for his
rights must not be misinterpreted for a callous or cavalier attitude. While we admit that if the patient is bent on killing himself
we do not have such omnipotent therapeutic powers necessary
to prevent this outcome, we make it very clear that we will take
whatever steps are necessary to prevent it if we can.

In practice, the degree to which a patient has come to
depend on suicidal threats or attempts as the only "dependable"
care-eliciting behavior will determine the kind of therapeutic
course to embark upon. These are the most difficult patients
to treat. Yet it must be made abundantly clear that "reasonable

therapy cannot take place under the gun of suicidal threats"
(Meissner, 1988, p. 343). These patients must be made aware
that should continued threats of suicide and its prevention become the major preoccupying focus on the therapeutic process
then therapy will cease and suicide prevention procedures, such
as hospitalization, will then be instituted.

It is important to know the history of previous suicidal
behavior. One must never feel that previous attempts which
seem blatantly "manipulative" guarantee that the next attempt
may not be fatal. While there are no "guaranteed" predictors,
there are, however, additional indicators to those already mentioned which can be helpful in predicting more realistically
the degree and seriousness of suicidal problems which will be
encountered during the course of treatment.

Some authors (Buie and Maltsberger, 1983) emphasize the
need to appraise in the assessment such factors as the degree
of intolerable aloneness; fragmentation and annihilatory experiences; the reliance on self–object relationships; work gratification; and the degree of absence or presence of self-esteem
and self-confidence. They also emphasize the importance of
assessing how the patient has been affected in the past by shifts
in family attitudes; the impact of change of work; or serious
loss of one kind or another. Additional significant predictors
and dimensions are discussed in this volume in Chapter 15
(Maltsberger and Lovett). Other authors (Schwartz et al., 1974)
stress that a history of a life-style in which frustration and anger
in response to deprivation of narcissistic supplies leads to overt
suicidal behavior points to a high-risk patient. In these cases it
becomes almost a race against time between the chances of
suicide and the development of a tenable, trusting working
relationship between the patient and the therapist. Birtchnell
(1983) has emphasized how a therapist who has established a
strong, holding relationship can sustain a patient with powerful
suicidal urges.

Finally, where suicidality determines a large part of the
clinical profile in the initial assessment phase, it is important to
see the spouse, the parent, or some other person with whom
the patient is close. There are several reasons for this. First,
collateral information is very useful. Second, it provides an

opportunity to assess the family and social supports that may be available during treatment. Finally, it is important to share with the family that therapy does not guarantee that the patient will cease being a high suicide risk.

Interviewing other people must be done only with the patient's consent. In the event that the patient refuses to allow any other person to be interviewed where the clinician feels it is important, then the assessment process should stop. No therapist should ever be expected to decide on treatment strategies without the availability of all possible information he deems necessary. This stance may raise various doubts with some clinicians but in our experience many therapists have, regretfully, paid too heavy a price because of insufficient history during the initial assessment phase prior to embarking on a long-term therapy course.

SPECIFIC ASSESSMENT ISSUES

The serious substance abuse borderline patient addicted to alcohol or drugs should never be treated in psychotherapy alone. The number of therapists who still feel they can somehow, through psychodynamic interpretation approaches alone, deal with substance abuse is rather amazing (see Chapter 25, and Mays and Franks, 1985). Presumably, they are convinced that the discovery of the "true" underlying psychological causes can make the abuses disappear. "The well-known failure of insight-oriented psychotherapeutic approaches to these patients could well be compared to the futility of expecting a starving person to delve into the reasons why he lacks food, or the marooned desert traveler how he got himself into a waterless environment" (Rinsley, 1988, p. 6).

Substance abuse must be treated by specialized treatment programs before psychodynamic therapy begins or, occasionally, concomitantly with it. Immediate gratification from drugs allays any anxiety aroused in the therapeutic process, making the patient unavailable to work through conflicts or any discomforts. In almost all cases, severely addicted patients secretly continue abusing drugs and ultimately end up sabotaging the therapy and the therapist.

If an addiction problem is discovered during treatment and is minimized because it is not openly confronted, the patient will frequently become worse as he or she begins to feel that no one is able to intervene and set limits. Instead, they may talk for months or years about their difficult wife or husband, mother or boss, without ever referring to the substance abuse problem or how they tyrannize others. Thus, it is in the assessment phase that these difficulties must be sought out and confronted. The patient must agree to specialized treatment for addiction beginning prior to, or occasionally concomitantly with, individual psychotherapy. It must also be understood that if the specialized treatment program ceases, the individual psychotherapy will also be terminated. When these problems are ignored or minimized, serious deleterious side effects of the psychotherapy process occur and negative therapeutic fall-out is inevitable.

The severe antisocial behavior borderline patient also poses special problems during the assessment phase. Usually, they present themselves during a crisis. In these cases, it is the motivation for seeking treatment that must be carefully explored. We have found that the best test for sincere motivation for change is, after the assessment process has been completed, to tell the patient that therapy will only begin after all current legal difficulties have been resolved one way or another. Regardless whether the patient is guilty or innocent, the preoccupation, anxieties, pressures, and interruptions brought about by legal processes make any meaningful psychotherapy almost impossible.

Frequently, treatment is sought as a means of pacifying colleagues, family, or friends; at other times, it is used to demonstrate repentance to the courts. On some occasions the courts decide that treatment can magically cure long-standing maladaptive, self-defeating, self-injurious behavior, and render decisions with the understanding that the patient will enter treatment.

Perhaps the most important single factor to determine is the patient's capacity to feel depressed. The depression we are referring to here is what Kohut referred to as "guilty man" rather than "tragic man" (Kohut, 1977). Careful inquiry into past losses and how the patient dealt with them is very important. The history of relational capacities (see below) can also be very helpful in assessing the patient's motivation for therapy.

Finally, as with all borderline patients in general but with the antisocial borderline patient in particular, even a favorable assessment should only encourage a trial of therapy.

Experiences of severe abuse during childhood must be carefully examined in the assessment period. Sexual abuse, brutal physical abuse, or severe neglect and deprivation predict a variety of difficulties in any psychotherapeutic undertaking. The object hunger in some of these patients is frequently so great that therapy rather than ameliorating this problem only increases it. This leads to severe transference–countertransference difficulties, with all the ensuing complications of excessive demands and inevitable rejections.

A hopeful clue for some success in therapy with these patients lies in uncovering a forgotten good object during the patient's early development regardless of how brief the relationship may have been. This may include a grandparent or other extended family member, a grade school teacher, a family friend, or sibling. Where there is no such evidence, or more ominous, where the other siblings have suffered equally and are now suffering similar or more severe difficulties, any intensive therapy contemplated, other than a very supportive kind, or case work, must be considered in the realm of heroics.

SPECIAL MODALITIES OF TREATMENT

In the assessment process for individual psychotherapy of the borderline patient, there are those within this heterogeneous population that can benefit from various modalities of treatment. Some modalities of treatment may take place concomitantly with individual therapy while others may occur separately.

Family therapy can be a very useful concomitant or alternative treatment modality for the borderline patient (see Chapter

19). This form of treatment is often indicated for the borderline adolescent, who frequently serves the role of the family scapegoat, and addressing this issue in particular along with other family dynamic issues in general can be extremely helpful.

Similarly, couple therapy with the spouse of a borderline patient can assist individual therapy and sometimes avoid the unnecessarily long periods of little therapeutic movement that occur for lack of awareness of "real" situations in the family and otherwise.

The editors of this volume have had different experiences in their approach to adding or introducing family or couple therapy to individual treatment of the borderline patient. The more traditional approach is to have someone other than the patient's individual therapist, usually a social worker, treat the family or couple. The experience of one of us (D.S.) has been to do both the family (couple) and individual therapy. For example, the adolescent would be seen once or twice a week individually, and with his parents or whole family once a week. Similarly, a spouse would be seen once or twice a week individually and once with the husband or wife. While this creates certain transference and countertransference problems, it addresses various resistances more quickly and incisively, as well as the defenses of splitting, denial, and projective identification.

However, there is no "right way" of doing this. These issues are inevitably decided by the influence of one's teachers, training, and clinical experiences.

Group therapy has become a helpful treatment modality for the borderline patient. Dr. Leszcz discusses the pros and cons for this treatment approach in Chapter 18. For some borderline patients group therapy can be most useful either by itself or in combination with individual therapy.

If there is more than one therapist involved in the treatment, it is particularly important that from the outset, with the patient's permission and complete knowledge, that the therapists may discuss common problems from time to time and with the assurance that this would be brought back into therapy. All too often the therapists do not consult with each other. While this is traditional and perhaps appropriate for individual therapists doing analysis with neurotic patients, it is not suitable for the multimodal treatment of the borderline patient.

PREDICTIVE AND PROGNOSTIC INDICES

A review of the literature (Silver, Glassman, and Cardish, 1988) on those factors useful in the assessment of the borderline patient, both from a prognostic and treatment point of view, reveals numerous clinical and theoretical papers on treatment outcome and its prediction.

The importance given to particular predictor and prognostic variables depends very much on the differing patient populations, the theoretical bias of the therapist, and the difference in measurements used.

Some stress the importance of the relationship to the therapist (Woolcott, 1985). Others emphasize ego strengths and weaknesses (Bellak and Meyers, 1975; Kernberg, 1975; Goldstein, 1985), various capacities (Paolino, 1981), the inability to tolerate ambivalence (Adler, 1985), and goals and processes of psychotherapy (Weiner, 1986). However, empirical verification has still been very slow in coming. It is apparent that in our present state of knowledge the assessment process is still less than optimal in predicting variables for treatment outcome.

Whichever indices are used, the assessment process is aimed essentially at attempting to determine the degree to which therapy can achieve such treatment goals as effecting a feeling of a more cohesive sense of self by strengthening the borderline patient's sense of identity; increasing the capacity for relationships; decreasing feelings of emptiness, despair, annihilation, and disintegration; decreasing the degree of chronic feelings of rage; decreasing needy, clingy, demanding stances; and decreasing the paranoid stance, while increasing the capacity for trust.

The traditional indicators, such as anxiety, depression, impulsiveness, suicide attempts, precipitate termination of therapy, have proven neither accurate as predictors of outcome nor helpful with treatment decisions with this group of patients.

Our own clinical impressions and recent research endeavors seem to indicate that assessment of certain relationship capacities, many of which are widely described in the literature, may be more useful for treatment decisions (Silver, 1985; Silver et al., 1988).

TABLE 9.1

Primary Capacities
Interpersonal Relations:

a. Capacity for psychological soothing
b. Empathy
c. Trust versus paranoid stance
d. Engaging versus distancing thermostat
e. Intimacy

Secondary Capacities

1. Psychological mindedness
2. Depression versus life-long feelings of empty futility
3. Pleasure versus excitement
4. Creative accomplishments
5. Fantasies

The relational capacities we have described can be divided into primary and secondary ones (Table 9.1). The primary capacities can be subsumed under the heading of interpersonal relationships which includes the capacities for soothing, empathy, trust (versus a paranoid stance), intimacy, and the engaging–distancing thermostat. The secondary capacities consist of psychological mindedness, depression, pleasure (versus excitement), and creativity of fantasies. This chapter will discuss at greater length the capacity for soothing as an important index for psychotherapeutic engagement and only briefly mention some of the other capacities.

Clinically, we have found that the presence of the capacity to be soothed appears to have a very important association for psychotherapy outcome, while its absence seems to correlate with very poor outcome.

In everyday parlance, to soothe is understood as meaning to alleviate or to bring comfort, solace, or peace. What we mean by soothing in our clinical practice is that when a patient is greatly distressed or in turmoil, one often finds that through the natural course of psychotherapy, without having to resort to "special" interventions, the patient derives soothing and comfort. It is this capacity to experience feeling psychologically soothed or comforted, in all its vicissitudes, that is most important for predicting psychotherapy outcome.

In a review of the literature on predicting outcome with borderline patients, Woolcott (1985) indicated that the most important prognostic factor is the capacity for developing a relationship with the therapist. It is our impression that the capacity to be soothed is an important component that the patient must bring to the relationship, particularly for successful long-term psychotherapy and establishing an important relationship with the therapist.

The nature of the relationship with the therapist, generally subsumed under the concept of the therapeutic alliance, is generally viewed as being of crucial importance in prognosis, and the capacity to feel soothed by the therapist is, we believe, an important aspect of this. A number of studies have examined the therapeutic alliance and attempted to measure it. Luborsky (1976) distinguished two aspects of the alliance: type 1 was characterized by the patient's experiencing the therapist as warm, supportive, and helpful. In type 2 alliances the patient had a sense of working with the therapist in a joint effort. It would appear that this concept of a type 1 alliance is closely related to the capacity to be soothed.

While the psychological capacity for soothing is based on Winnicott's ideas of transitional relatedness (Winnicott, 1951), we have found it more useful to focus on the psychological experience of being soothed rather than on one of transitional object usage or relatedness, because the former is more readily defined and quantified (Silver et al., 1988). In attempting to assess transitional relatedness, the therapist or researcher must make difficult inferences, subject to unreliability and definitional idiosyncrasies, about, for example, "a mode of experience and relatedness in which the internal reality of wishes, desires, or convictions, are blended with internal physical reality in the contemplation of an object" (Horton, Louy, and Coppolillo, 1974, p. 618). Although this conceptualization may indeed accurately describe the psychological experience of a child with his teddy bear, to infer the operation of a similar mechanism in an adult listening, for example, to a favorite piece of music, is premature. On the other hand, an adult can usually describe the psychological experience of feeling "better," "soothed," or "comforted," and what strategy was used to achieve this state.

In those patients for whom no relationships, personal, therapeutic, or otherwise, seem to provide any comfort or solace, intensive uncovering therapy is usually contraindicated. Facilitating a deep awareness of this irreparable defect, without providing other alternatives or supports, can make the patient feel dangerously despairing, empty, and futile, and even increase the suicidal risk. However, a very careful history is important because frequently there has been some relationship in the distant past, such as a concerned and interested teacher, loving grandmother, or some other adult who provided at least one important experience of soothing, comforting, and solacing which, after many years of difficulties, may have been forgotten. If this is so, the capacity for soothing can become available during the psychotherapeutic process.

The potential capacity to develop a good therapeutic relationship can be predicted in the very beginning of the assessment process from the vicissitudes of the capacities for interpersonal relationships with the previous therapist(s), and significant others. If, for example, the borderline patient has been unable to sustain at least one meaningful and not self-destructive relationship in either a personal, work, or social situation for a minimum of one year between adolescence and the current assessment period, then intensive, uncovering type therapy should rarely be undertaken initially.

The assessment of the capacity for empathy requires the therapist to explore fully the patient's thoughts, feelings, and perceptions of significant others. The term *empathy* has suffered from overuse in the psychiatric literature. As a relational capacity, it is used here in the context of determining whether an empathic therapeutic bridge between therapist and patient can be established. Empathy is defined here as the patient's interpersonal capacity to "tune in" to others and be "tuned into" by others cognitively and affectively. Its total absence results in complete self-absorption or severe narcissism or schizoid withdrawal.

The question of whether severe empathic inhibition is an irreparable developmental defect, or whether, with sufficient therapeutic effort, the capacity for empathy can be developed or restored in even the most narcissistic patients, is interesting (Easser, 1974). Our clinical experience seems to indicate that for most borderline patients it is as if damage experienced at particular critical stages of early development destroyed this capacity forever. Those patients who indeed fail to demonstrate a capacity for empathy do poorly in long-term, intensive psychotherapy, and frequently get much worse or even experience psychotic episodes. Their tenuous hold on reality is repeatedly strained by their distortions of the therapist's interventions resulting from an inability to tune in to the therapist's underlying empathic concern. Typically, these patients do much better with crisis intervention strategies or by utilizing social agencies. In attempting to assess this capacity clinically, the therapist usually finds that the patient is unable to demonstrate any concern for other family members who may have experienced similar or even greater hardships or deprivations than themselves in the past, or who cannot admit any appreciation of a former therapist's efforts. The likelihood of an empathic bridge developing between these patients and the therapist is very low.

In those patients where there is a marked paranoid stance, a hypervigilant attitude toward the surrounding environment, and a general mistrust of all relationships, embarking on an intensive uncovering psychotherapeutic voyage is not indicated. While these patients can sometimes do very well in intensive psychotherapy, a long period of time is needed for an educative and supportive process to evolve, whereby the patient can slowly develop a sense of trust in the therapist. This sense of trust comes from the continuing dependability, consistency, and safety of the therapeutic process and the even-handedness, nonjudgmental stance, and holding environment provided by the therapist. Patience in developing this sense of trust, both in the patient and in the therapist, will be very rewarding, while impatience or forcing too intensive a therapeutic relationship too early will only increase the sense of mistrust and general paranoid stance.

In terms of the secondary capacities, the capacity for psychological mindedness refers to the patient's desire to learn the possible meanings and causes of internal and external experiences. The therapist's task is to assess the borderline patient's capacity to conceptualize the relationship between thoughts, feelings, and actions, and a willingness to at least entertain the notion that one's behavior may in some ways be determined by forces other than those at the level of awareness. However, the capacity for psychological mindedness should never be overestimated as a positive indicator for change. Therapists are all too aware of the patients who are exceptionally good at intellectually understanding the numerous processes involved in how they perceive, experience, and respond to their internal and outer environment, yet seem unable to effect much change despite many years of treatment.

The quality of the capacity for real depression in the sense of Kohut's (1977) notion of guilty man versus lifelong feelings of emptiness, anguish, torment, and despair, is a very important differentiation to make in assessing the advisability of long-term intensive psychotherapy. These latter feelings, which Kohut labeled "tragic man," are not a contraindication to long-term, intensive psychotherapy but should forewarn the therapist that it will be a very long time before the patient will show any improvement in these empty, despairing, and anguished feelings. However, patience and concern over a long period of time will gradually allow the patient to work through many of these feelings, and many who were once felt not to be candidates for long-term, intensive psychotherapy in fact do very well.

The capacity for pleasure seems to be a positive prognostic characteristic. Clinically, many borderline patients seem to lack the capacity for pleasure, but primarily enjoy excitement; that is, experiences which are rather short-lived, new, and exciting challenges that are sought out repeatedly. This is in contrast to pleasurable experiences which can be stored and conjured up as comforting and soothing memories in times of distress.

Assessing the patient's hypothetical engaging–distancing "thermostat" is very helpful in informing the therapist how the beginning of the process of therapy should evolve. The sensitivity of the individual patient's thermostat corresponds to the degree to which the patient must control the closeness or distance of relationships, therapeutic, social or personal. The therapist must respect this. Too early interpretation and uncovering of unconscious processes can be experienced as very threatening, intrusive, and aggressive. This can lead to early precipitous endings, or serious, self-destructive acting out. These patients, generally, should begin therapy on a once-a-week basis only and the frequency gradually increased to two or three times per week as gauged by the patient's decreasing fear of the therapeutic process.

AXIS I DIFFERENTIATION

One of the main difficulties in making an Axis I diagnosis in borderline patients is the clinician's relative lack of interest in the existence and importance of this axis in this patient population. Many clinicians, particularly of a psychodynamic perspective, tend to regard borderline disorders as almost precluding an Axis I diagnosis. Once the diagnosis of borderline is made, less effort is expended in determining if other diagnoses can be made. This reflects how common anxiety, panic, and depression are in the borderline presentation, and how these affects are seen as reflective of the characterological vulnerability of the borderline patient and thus diminish interest in them as Axis I comorbid diagnoses.

Yet clinical experience, outcome studies (e.g., Stone, 1987), and the heterogeneity of borderline patients (Andrulonis et al., 1982), indicate that intensive psychotherapy is not for all borderlines. In addition, work on completed psychotherapies of borderline patients suggests that a great number of patients do not remain in intensive psychotherapy beyond six months (Waldinger and Gunderson, 1984).

Thus the difficulty in engaging these patients in intensive psychotherapy and the uncertainty whether such treatment is indicated for most borderlines serves to emphasize the importance of determining if there is an Axis I diagnosis present so that other treatment options can be considered.

Although a more difficult task in the borderline patient, the general principles of Axis I diagnosis pertain. It is essential to take a descriptive history emphasizing not only the cross-sectional presentation but eliciting a past history of discrete nontransient episodes of depression, anxiety, panic, substance abuse, and other symptomatology. The family history of psychiatric disorder is relevant, as is previous medication response in the patient and family members. Lastly, reviewing the history for signs and symptoms suggestive of an organic component is essential. These include trauma, encephalitis, epilepsy, learning and/or attention deficits, and birth trauma. Andrulonis et al. (1982) indicated that some borderline patients have an organic component to their disorder.

With regard to affective disorder, this is a critical diagnosis to identify. Outcome studies indicate that on follow-up, up to two-thirds of BPD patients had one or more affective episodes (Akiskal et al., 1985a; Stone, 1987). More reliable than the quality of the depression are the descriptive indices of discrete nontransient episodes on current or past history characterized by a depressive profile—cognitive, affective, vegetative, and motor signs and symptoms of affective disorder. Family history and medication response are also contributory. Thus such patients may benefit from a pharmacological treatment of the Axis I affective disorder, restoring them to their previous level of functioning at the borderline level, for which they may more appropriately be treated with a more supportive approach rather than an intensive approach.

The search for Axis I diagnoses is not without its difficulties. As noted, some of the central affects of Axis I diagnoses are part of the main expression of the borderline patient's diagnosis. Furthermore, the dynamic assessment of the borderline patient is difficult enough without the attendant responsibility of taking a descriptive history. Nonetheless we feel it is advisable to take a careful history searching for an Axis I diagnosis.

While we have emphasized Axis I diagnosis, it is interesting to note that psychopharmacological research strategies hold some promise for different approaches in the future. While preliminary, they are of interest. Cowdry (1987) has called for further research directed at specific symptom complexes (e.g., suspiciousness, anhedonia, affective lability, or behavioral dyscontrol) which may be preferentially responsive to certain agents. This correlates with findings that low-dose neuroleptics may be of help for a wide spectrum of symptoms including hostility and psychotic-type thinking, even though no formal Axis I diagnosis exists (Kutcher and Blackwood, 1989). Thus this line of investigation emphasizes symptom complexes rather than Axis I diagnosis.

At the present time, the consideration of individual borderline patients for the presence of Axis I disorders is a worthwhile endeavor. While not all patients can benefit from the use of medications, pharmacotherapy provided in the context of careful diagnosis and a consistent relationship can benefit some patients. The whole issue of introducing medication must be carefully dealt with psychotherapeutically as would introducing any other parameter of treatment. The use of pharmacotherapy either alone or concomitantly with individual therapy is further discussed in Chapter 20 by Dr. Cowdry.

ASSESSING THERAPIST/PATIENT SYSTEMS

In addition to assessing the different aspects of the patient's life and functioning, some consideration should be given to the therapist and the system in which he or she works. This can contribute to the therapist's efficacy with borderline patients, or diminish it by making him less responsive and more reactive to them.

The context in which the therapy occurs colors the therapist's capacity to be therapeutic. A relatively therapeutic system facilitates the therapist's responsiveness and involvement with the borderline patient. A system which is not therapeutic negatively affects the therapist's capacity to respond to the patient. We would suggest that this is mediated through the countertransference process. Where therapeutic capacity is diminished by system variables, there simply is less capacity to tolerate the feelings that are projected into the therapist. As a result, the therapist is less able to sustain and subordinate these feelings to the therapeutic task.

With regard to system variables, where we work can affect our capacity to be involved therapeutically with borderline patients. Systems, particularly hospitals but also office groups, analytic societies, and so on, which value therapeutic work with borderlines, and where there is some therapeutic standard which is defined and protected, facilitate our work. Conflicts such as differing mythologies, research versus clinical priorities, or biological versus dynamic frameworks, all color our satisfaction with our fit with the system which we are part of. Ultimately, this translates into an enhancing or diminishing effect on the therapeutic process.

There are several different situations that can cause a system to become less therapeutic. Working with too many borderline patients at one time, or at a time when our personal lives are such as to negatively affect our capacity to be maximally therapeutic, affects the therapeutic dyad. Our entire caseload is part of the system in which work with the particular borderline patient occurs. When we exceed the number of borderline patients that we can treat, we diminish our individual responsivity to each particular patient.

The presence and relative availability of a like-minded inpatient unit is a necessary ingredient. Lacking this, therapists consciously or unconsciously work less often or not at all with these patients; or engage in less intensive work.

The other aspect of the therapist's system is our previous experience with borderline patients. The legacy of often unresolved feelings about previous borderline patients can influence our readiness to work with these patients. Furthermore, when a new patient is assessed, treatment decisions can be unduly influenced by previous experience rather than the actual capacities and needs of the current patient.

The patient's social support system must be assessed. The impact of shifts in family and friends' attitudes toward the patient, and the changes at work, may have a significant effect on the patient's presentation and ongoing treatment. To what extent do important friends or relatives care about the patient; or are they exhausted and fed up, almost wishing him dead? Has there been significant change at work or school which affects the amount of structure the patient has? What shifts in other therapeutic structures are occurring (e.g., group therapy or social agency involvement) that affect the patient's relative cohesiveness and stability (Buie and Maltsberger, 1983).

The presence of sustaining people and structure, or the ability to obtain and maintain this, has a crucial effect on both the patient and therapist's capacity to weather the difficult storms which work with borderlines entails. The state of the patient's external world can influence the patient's neediness and the treatment modality chosen.

THE CONTRACT

As the assessment process unfolds, it is important for the therapist to assess the capacity for the patient to accept and internalize a realistic therapeutic contract. This should be individualized and deal frankly with the dual responsibility of both the patient and the therapist; and assess the changes the patient and therapist are realistically expecting from the therapeutic process. This is particularly important for this group of patients because they typically experience their therapists as possessing omnipotent powers and therefore bestow upon them the ability to offer magical improvements or cures. This parameter is totally unlike the usual open-ended arrangements made with the neurotic patient. Treating borderline patients has taught us that we cannot transfer a treatment model intended for one group of patients to another without modifications.

Characteristically, their problems are long-standing and quite crippling. The patient must, therefore, be sensitively confronted with the clinical realities and with realistically achievable improvement expectations. Explicit negotiation and understanding of the therapeutic contract can minimize magical "cure" expectations and reduce reunion fantasies with the idealized original nurturers.

Other contract terms include frequency of sessions, confidentiality, consultations, medications, and hospitalization. In some instances, therapy is linked to whether the patient engages and then continues in a specialized concomitant treatment program or some other commitment such as a part-time or full-time work situation (Silver, 1985). The latter four issues, if discussed frankly and openly during the assessment phase, will decrease the need to introduce, in the future, hasty limit-setting strategies. Moreover, in our opinion, introducing these issues during the assessment phase will prove most helpful in establishing a more accessible empathic bridge between therapist and patient should therapy be undertaken.

Discussing the contract during the assessment process emphasizes that attempts to accomplish real characterological change are always ambitious and occasionally even heroic. However, if the patient can be helped to see that even modest improvement can make an enormous difference in the comforts of his life-style, then therapeutic disillusionment for patient (and therapist) will be greatly lessened (Cameron, 1963).

CONCLUSION

In summary, the assessment process for the borderline patient should be more thorough and leave less "to chance" than one might with a neurotic patient. A careful history of the patient's life-style reflecting his or her interpersonal relationships, work history, innermost personal feelings, and self-destructive behavior must be accurately elicited. The clinician must also attempt, with critical care, to assess his own feelings about the patient as the assessment process unfolds; for example, the degree of rage and forgiveness at an inappropriate or unempathic intervention; or the magical expectations the patient wishes to impose upon him. The inability to pay heed to such issues and the frequent negative feelings these patients can evoke in the clinician even after the initial first or second meeting can only result in inappropriate treatment strategies or referrals, precipitous endings even during the assessment phase, or increased self-destructive acting out by the patient.

A careful history; frank discussions of assessment findings; sensitive attention paid to the fragility of the patient; assessing the feasibility of negotiating a treatment contract; evaluating the patient's and therapist's "real" systems; and considering carefully Axis I diagnoses, will all tend to minimize undesirable negative effects should psychotherapy be indicated. In addition, maintaining an eclectic stance, regardless of one's personal theoretical persuasion, will greatly facilitate the appropriate choice of alternate or concomitant treatment programs.

10.

The Psychological Assessment of Borderline Personality

Rex Collins, Ph.D., C.Psych., and Edward J. Glassman, Ph.D., C.Psych.

The concept of borderline personality has gained wide currency and acceptance since Knight's seminal papers (Knight, 1953a,b). Receiving a measure of formal recognition by the inclusion of the diagnostic category of borderline personality disorder (BPD) in *The Diagnostic and Statistical Manual of Mental Disorders* (DSM-III) (American Psychiatric Association, 1980), the concept represents the culmination of three major lines of psychological inquiry: psychoanalytic object relations theory (Kernberg, 1967, 1975), infant observation studies (Mahler, 1968; Mahler, Pine, and Bergman, 1975), and phenomenological approaches (Grinker, Werble, and Drye, 1968; Gunderson, 1977; Perry and Klerman, 1978).

The acceptance of the concept has generated a considerable body of literature that has sought to establish the validity and reliability of the borderline syndrome and to further delineate and clarify its characteristics. Kernberg (1975) and Carpenter, Gunderson, and Strauss (1977) have advocated using psychological testing to assist in assigning a diagnosis of borderline personality, and, indeed, the use of psychological test procedures has become an integral part, not only of the diagnostic process in daily clinical practice, but of ongoing research efforts in the field. This chapter will provide a survey of current contributions to the area of psychological assessment of the borderline syndrome: specifically, the development of structured interviews, the use of self-report measures, and the increasingly sophisticated use of the Rorschach test as a means of understanding the patient's internalized world of object relations.

STRUCTURED INTERVIEWS

The diagnostic structured interview is a method whereby the presence of symptoms of a specific psychiatric disorder or syndrome may be assessed in a detailed and systematic way. Because the interviewer is required to follow the sequence of questions unerringly, and to read them verbatim, diagnostic reliability and therefore validity are thought to be enhanced beyond that achievable with an unstructured clinical interview. Typically, structured interviews take longer to administer than a standard clinical interview precisely because they must systematically query every symptom or criterion for the particular disorder(s) in question. For this reason, they are rarely used in everyday clinical practice. Rather, their primary application is in clinical research, where homogeneous diagnostic groups are a prerequisite.

    Not all structured interviews follow the same format. For example, some are referred to as "semistructured" because the interviewer is not limited only to the questions provided but may further probe the subject's response when deemed appropriate. Some interviews recommend that only experienced clinicians should use them, while others are designed for use by lay interviewers (e.g., the NIMH Diagnostic Interview Schedule).

    Not surprisingly, the growing interest in borderline conditions has yielded several structured interviews directed toward their investigation and refinement. They fall into two broad categories. Historically, the first developed were those that assessed BPD exclusively. More recently available are those that assess BPD in the context of all the DSM-III Axis II personality disorders.

Of those instruments exclusively addressing borderline personality, by far the most widely recognized in North America is Gunderson's Diagnostic Interview for Borderlines (DIB) (Gunderson, Kolb, and Austin, 1981). In its original form, the interview assessed five major content areas—social adaptation, impulse action patterns, affects, psychosis, and interpersonal relations—thought by Gunderson to be pathognomonic of the borderline personality. The DIB, utilizing a pyramidal scoring system, consists of 123 items or questions, the responses to which are used by the interviewer to make judgments on twenty-nine summary statements (yes = 2, probably = 1, or no = 0). These statement scores are in turn added together by section to provide a scale score for each content area. The final score, a possible 0 to 10, results from the addition of these scaled section scores. A score of 7 or greater is considered indicative of a borderline personality.

The data relevant to the DIB's reliability and validity have been amply documented elsewhere (Reich, 1987; Widiger and Frances, 1987). To summarize briefly, the DIB has consistently demonstrated good interrater agreement (Soloff and Ulrich, 1981; Gunderson, Kolb, and Austin, 1981). As well, good test–retest reliability over a two-week span has been reported (Cornell, Silk, Ludolph, and Lohr, 1983). Evaluation of the DIB's validity is a more complex question. Specifically, with respect to discriminant validity, the DIB has successfully differentiated borderline personality patients from patients with schizophrenia and major depression; however, the results have been mixed with respect to other Axis II personality disorders (Widiger and Frances, 1987). At issue here is the relationship between Gunderson's BPD and BPD as codified in DSM-III and DSM-III-R (1987). The primary difference between the two systems is that the DIB includes quasi- or minipsychotic features, which DSM-III(-R)[1] relegates to the schizotypal personality disorder (STP). Also important are two DSM-III(-R) criteria—affective instability and identity disturbance—which are not incorporated in the DIB. Lastly, there is no equivalent

---

[1] The designation DSM-III(-R) is used when reference is being made to both DSM-III and DSM-III-R.

in the DSM-III(-R) for Gunderson's social adaptation section. The impact of these discrepancies is perhaps minimized because no single feature is necessary to define the syndrome in either system. Nevertheless, it is not surprising that the research reveals a range of concordance values between the two. With one exception (McGlashan, 1983b), the evidence indicates that the DIB casts a somewhat broader net than the DSM-III(-R) BPD. It identifies a borderline population that includes DSM-III(-R) STP patients.

In response to the empirical data generated by the original DIB, Gunderson and Zanarini (1987) developed a revised version of the instrument. The major difference is that the social adaptation section has been eliminated. Additionally, the affect section now contains questions related to the experience of anxiety and the interpersonal relations section has added questions about repeatedly experienced fears of abandonment, engulfment, and annihilation, and demanding and entitled behavior. Finally, the psychosis section, which has been relabeled the cognitive section in the revised DIB, now places less emphasis on depersonalization and derealization, and instructs the interviewer to distinguish between "true" and "quasi" delusions and hallucinations.

Because the changes in the newer version are substantial, it would be imprudent to make inferences about the performance of the revised DIB based on the original. Unfortunately, there has been little empirical research published with the revised version. This seems hardly surprising given the recent shift in borderline research. It is now recognized that because there is substantial comorbidity for DSM-III-defined BPD and other Axis II disorders such as histrionic, narcissistic, dependent, and schizotypal, the former should not be investigated in isolation, but rather must be considered in relation to the broader community of personality disorders. (Here it will be recalled that the DIB's performance was mixed with respect to discriminating borderlines from other personality disorders.) Consequently, researchers have been busy developing and testing structured interviews which assess the full range of DSM-III(-R) Axis II disorders.

There are now four major DSM-III-based personality disorder interviews available, each with a DSM-III-R version in progress or already available. These include the Structured Interview for DSM-III Personality Disorders (SIDP) (Pfohl, Stangl, and Zimmerman, 1982); the Structured Clinical Interview for DSM-III-R Personality Disorders (SCID-II) (Spitzer, Williams, Gibbon, and First, 1988); the Diagnostic Interview for Personality Disorders (DIPD) (Zanarini, Frankenburg, Chauncey, and Gunderson, 1987); and the Personality Disorder Exam (PDE) (Loranger, 1988). It is beyond the scope of this paper to focus on each interview in depth. The discussion will be restricted to issues relevant to all the instruments, and to the PDE specifically, because of our first-hand experience using this particular interview. The reader is referred to Widiger and Frances (1987) and Reich (1987) for more comprehensive reviews of the instruments and issues relevant to the measurement of borderline and other Axis II disorders.

A number of critical issues confront any researcher developing an interview to assess the Axis II disorders. For example, should questions be grouped together by content area such as relationships, affects, and so on (as in the PDE and SIDP) or by disorder, that is, borderline, histrionic, and so on (as in the SCID-II and DIPD)? Widiger and Frances (1987) suggest that the latter organization may "encourage halo effects in which the subsequent ratings are influenced by prior diagnostic assessments" (p. 52). Also, they suggest that grouping the questions by content area makes for an interview that flows more naturally and smoothly.

Perhaps the most crucial concern which bears directly on the issue of validity is whether the interview relies on the judgment of the patient or the clinician. That is to say, are the subject's responses accepted at face value or is the interviewer instructed to probe and formulate his or her own opinion? Some kinds of personality traits, such as interpersonal exploitiveness, are socially undesirable and unlikely to be endorsed by an interviewee. Other traits, such as interpersonal empathy, require a degree of psychological sophistication too frequently absent in personality disorder patients to be accurately assessed. Still other qualities, such as perfectionism, are routinely endorsed by almost all subjects. Furthermore, numerous researchers have noted the potentially distorting effects on a patient's self-perceptions of state anxiety and depression attributable to an Axis I disorder (Reich, 1987). Finally, a number of DSM-III-R Axis II criteria are inherently difficult to judge regardless of whose perspective is relied upon. For example, the borderline criterion of "a pattern of unstable and intense relationships" is difficult to operationalize. How many relationships are required to constitute a "pattern"? How are intensity and instability measured? Are a series of "superficial" relationships applicable?

It is instructive to consider some of the issues raised above with respect to the development of the PDE. Both the DSM-III and DSM-III-R versions organize the Axis II criteria into six sections labeled work, self, interpersonal relationships, affects, reality testing, and impulse control. The earlier version consisted of 249 questions, typically two per criterion, as well as seventy-nine more items to score based on observed behavior during the interview. Commenting on this version, Widiger and Frances (1987) noted that "Although the PDE provides a balance of structured and open-ended assessment, it may at times rely too heavily on the patient's opinions and self-evaluations rather than obtaining more objective, behavioral data. . ." (p. 51). Given this reliance on the patient's stated opinions, it is not surprising that the PDE produced excellent interrater reliability for all the personality disorders (Loranger, Susman, Oldham, and Russakoff, 1987). However, its validity is another question.

The revised PDE (Loranger, 1988) was designed to be compatible with DSM-III-R. It comes with a manual which provides guidelines for scoring each Axis II criterion. In addition, the interview includes a number of "probes" which require the subject to substantiate their self-perceptions with examples. As well, the interviewer is directed to further query any given criterion until they are satisfied that they can make a valid rating. Although published data are not yet available, one can predict that these changes may lead to a slight decrease in interrater reliability because of the increased need for subjective judgment, but by the same token may augment the PDE's validity because of the increase in data available to help formulate the ratings.

In closing this discussion on Axis II structured interviews, several points remain to be addressed. Apart from issues of reliability and validity, clinicians and researchers will also be concerned with an instrument's utility. One consequence of the changes to the PDE is that, in our experience, the interview can take between two and three hours to administer properly. The other interviews may proceed more quickly, but it seems likely that a positive correlation exists between interview length and validity. Thus, it probably requires a lengthy interview to accurately assess the multitude of personality traits. Parenthetically, the revised SCID-II utilizes a prescreening self-report questionnaire. The interviewer then directs his questions only to those items positively endorsed on the questionnaire. Though this should dramatically shorten the interview, the validity of this approach has yet to be substantiated.

It is, at this time, premature to render judgment on the Axis II structured interviews. Reliability data is just becoming available, while validity data will take years to accumulate. In the final analysis, the structured interviews can be only as valid and useful as the diagnostic system which spawned them (a comprehensive discussion of which would be inappropriate in this paper). However, it is worth noting that there are data which indicate that it is not uncommon for interviews such as the SCID-II and PDE to diagnose inpatients with character problems as meeting the criteria for anywhere from three to five Axis II disorders (Skodol, Rosnick, Kellman, Oldham, and Hyler, 1988). These data raise the question of the relative usefulness of a behaviorally oriented personality disorder classification scheme in which patients can meet the criteria for so many disorders simultaneously. It is suggested here that although borderline and other personality disorders can be described in terms of overt symptoms and behaviors, this should not be at the cost of ignoring underlying psychodynamic formulations. That is to say that structured interviews provide only one source of data relevant to the assessment and investigation of borderline conditions. It is necessary to turn to other psychological instruments to fully explore borderline pathology and clarify the relationship among borderline and other DSM-III-R personality disorders.

SELF-REPORT MEASURES: MMPI, MCMI

The development of the Minnesota Multiphasic Personality Inventory (MMPI) predates the inclusion of borderline personality disorder in DSM-III by some forty years. It has emerged as the most widely used self-report measure of psychopathology in psychological assessment and it is firmly grounded in a vast body of research literature (Butcher, 1977). Empirically derived from the item responses of patients grouped according to specific psychiatric diagnoses, the instrument is used extensively to assist in the identification of major psychiatric disorders and personality patterns. The current version of the MMPI consists of ten basic clinical scales, as well as three validity scales. Clinically researched code types expressing the two or three prominent scale elevations are used to generate diagnostic statements with regard to the subject's psychopathology.

Since the inclusion of BPD in DSM-III in 1980, MMPI researchers have sought to establish a "borderline profile." The most consistent finding to date has been that borderlines typically attain an 8-2-4 code type (i.e., elevations on the schizophrenia, depression, and psychopathic deviancy scales), with an elevation on the F scale, a validity scale related to reported level of distress (Kroll, Sines, Martin, Lari, Pyle, and Zander, 1981; Snyder, Pitts, Goodpaster, Sajadi, and Gustin, 1982; Gustin, Goodpaster, Sajadi, Pitts, LaBasse, and Snyder, 1983; Lloyd, Overall, Kimsey, and Click, 1983; Resnick, Schulz, Schulz, Haymer, Friedel, and Goldberg, 1983; Abramowitz, Carroll, and Schaffer, 1984; Evans, Ruff, Braff, and Ainsworth, 1984; Patrick, 1984; Hurt, Clarkin, Frances, Abrams, and Hunt, 1985). Edell (1987), in a study examining the differential characteristics of BPD and STP, has found that schizotypal subjects presented an 8-2-7 profile (schizophrenia, depression, and psychasthenia scales).

As Edell points out, clinical descriptions of these two particular three-point code types developed by researchers such as Gilberstadt and Duker (1965) and Marks, Seeman, and Haller (1974), although written some years before DSM-III criteria for BPD and STP were developed, are remarkable in the way they outline essential features of these disorders. Individuals with primary elevations on scales 2, 4, and 8 have been described as quite paranoid, extremely irritable, hostile, and tense, fearful of emotional involvements yet having an exaggerated need for affection and attention, and guilt-ridden. They are immature, lacking drive and responsibility toward occupation, unpredictable, relationally and sexually maladjusted, and often display superficial and manipulative acting out. They are unable to express their emotions in any modulated or adaptive way. Those with elevations on scales 2, 7, and 8 are described as anxious, depressed, fearful, schizoid, shy, quiet, and withdrawn, with feelings of inadequacy, inferiority, and ambivalence. Their thinking is often bizarre and displays ideas of reference, and there are difficulties in concentrating, despite superior intelligence. They are lacking in social skills and are particularly inept at developing heterosexual relationships.

Despite the apparent consistency over numerous studies and the compelling nature of the findings, major concerns and criticisms have been expressed with respect to the methodology of the above research, the overlap of BPD with other personality disorder diagnoses, and in particular the polythetic nature of the diagnosis as it stands in DSM-III (Patrick, 1984; Widiger, Sanderson, and Warner, 1986).

Widiger et al. (1986) argue that the research to date has failed to yield an MMPI profile that is either sensitive or specific to the borderline diagnosis. They point out that the 8-2-4 profiles described in the literature are group mean profiles and that this code type typically occurs in less than a third of the individual borderline patients (Kroll et al., 1981; Gustin et al., 1983). Further, the 8-2-4 code type occurs in other diagnostic groups such as hysterical and paranoid patients and the borderline profile does not differ in pattern but only in the degree of elevation.

Widiger et al. point out that efforts to develop a sensitive and specific MMPI profile for BPD are frustrated by limitations that are inherent in the DSM-III diagnostic criteria themselves. They point to the prototypal model of classification employed here, that is to say, a model which uses multiple and optional criteria to assign a diagnosis. They note that any five out of eight criteria satisfies the diagnostic requirements and have calculated that there are in fact ninety-three different combinations of the criteria possible in the assigning of the borderline diagnosis. Further, they point to research that demonstrates the overlap of the diagnosis with schizotypal, histrionic, and antisocial disorders, as well as the dependent, narcissistic, passive-aggressive (Clarkin, Widiger, Frances, Hurt, and Gilmore, 1983; Pope, Jonas, Hudson, Cohen, and Gunderson, 1983; Gunderson, 1984).

In summary, the evidence to date suggests that, while the 8-2-4 code type is a profile that is quite consistently related to BPD, the limitations and criticisms cited by Widiger et al. preclude its use in assigning a definitive diagnosis of this disorder. However, the profile may be useful in the initial screening of patients for more comprehensive diagnostic workups, and as part of the cross-validation process when a battery of psychological tests is employed.

The Millon Clinical Multiaxial Inventory (MCMI) is a self-report inventory developed with more specific reference to the DSM-III Axis II personality disorders. Its proponents (Antoni, Tischer, Levine, Green, and Millon, 1985) view it in this regard as a superior instrument to the MMPI, which, as they point out, was not designed to provide information regarding Axis II personality disorders. It is not within the scope of this chapter to critically examine the relationship of Millon's scales to the entire set of Axis II personality disorders, but it is relevant to note that the criteria used to develop the borderline scale are different from those of the DSM-III. Millon states "the borderline personality was formulated to be a disintegrated Dependent, Histrionic and Passive-Aggressive mix" (Millon, 1983, p. 812). The forty-four items comprising the borderline (or, in Millon's terms, the cycloid) scale, are subsumed under five broad criteria: intense endogenous moods, dysregulated activation, self-condemnatory conscience, dependency anxiety, and cognitive–affective ambivalence. While the scale appears to provide some useful information on the cognitive, affective, and interpersonal life of the patient, it contains no items relating to impulsivity or identity disturbance, two key criteria of the DSM-III diagnostic schema. Approximately half of the forty-four items relate to symptoms of depression and anxiety. Thus, the utility of the scale in the diagnosis of BPD remains in some doubt and awaits the requisite empirical investigations. While some of Millon's colleagues (Antoni et al., 1985; Levine, Tischer, Antoni, Green, and Millon, 1985) have conducted some interesting work combining the MCMI with particular MMPI code types, the validity of this approach with respect to the identification of BPD as well remains uninvestigated.

THE RORSCHACH

The structured interviews and self-report measures described above, while comprehensive in their assessment of symptomatology and unquestionably useful in assisting in the development of some degree of consensus as to what precise symptoms and behaviors constitute the borderline syndrome, remain limited in that they measure only conscious phenomena and manifest features. Psychoanalytic theory has contributed significantly both descriptively and theoretically to the understanding of borderline personality. Psychoanalysis is, if anything, a theory of the unconscious, and to examine the unconscious intrapsychic structure and conflicts of the borderline syndrome through psychological testing we must turn to the projective techniques, in particular, the most widely used of these, the Rorschach.

The history of the Rorschach test reflects its continuing and close connection with developments in psychoanalytic theory. In the 1940s and 1950s, Rapaport, Gill, and Schafer (1945) and Schafer (1954) established a solid basis for the understanding of Rorschach phenomena from an ego psychological perspective. Schafer (1954) in particular delineated the Rorschach correlates of ego defenses while Holt (1977) has developed an exhaustive manual for scoring manifestations of primary process and related defenses.

However, with the shift in emphasis in psychoanalytic thought from the drives and their vicissitudes to object relations theory and self psychology, Rorschach researchers have increasingly focused on Rorschach phenomena as a means of understanding normal and pathological manifestations of the individual's internal world of self and object representations.

Mayman (1967) postulates that when a person is faced with the task of making sense of stimuli that are ambiguous, vague, and strange, even alien, as is the case with the Rorschach, he will attempt to reconstitute the apparent formlessness with people, animals, and things that make up his "real" phenomenal world. Mayman further suggests that "A person's most readily accessible object representations called up under such unstructured conditions tell much about his inner world of objects and about the quality of relationships with these inner objects towards which he is predisposed" (p. 17).

Blatt, Brenneis, Schimek, and Glick (1976), in a landmark longitudinal study of normal development in subjects followed from age eleven to age thirty, found a significant increase in Rorschach percepts of well-differentiated, highly articulated, and integrated human figures seen in constructive and reciprocal interactions. When normal protocols were compared to those of a hospitalized group of adolescents and young adults, the hospitalized group gave human figures that were significantly more inaccurately perceived, distorted, and partial, and that were seen as inert or engaged in unmotivated, incongruent, nonspecific, and malevolent activity.

Similarly, Urist (1977) studied the way in which Rorschach images reflected developmentally significant gradations in the individual's capacity to experience self and others as mutually autonomous within relationships. He developed a seven-point rating scale on a continuum ranging from responses in which relationships are characterized by an overpowering, enveloping force through figures seen as reflections of each other, to figures leaning on each other, to figures that are engaged in some relationship or activity in such a way that conveys a reciprocal acknowledgment of their respective individuality. The results of his study support the argument that individuals tend to experience self–other relationships in consistent, enduring, characteristic ways that can be defined for each individual along a developmental continuum ranging from primary narcissism to empathic object relatedness.

It is from this background and within this context of interest in the Rorschach phenomena as reflective of the individual's internal world of self and object representations, that a good deal of the current work in Rorschach correlates of borderline psychopathology may be viewed. The theorists and researchers whose work is described below view borderline pathology as an expression of an enduring character structure and would subscribe to Kernberg's notion that borderline personality *organization* (our italics) may exist in a variety of personality types (Kernberg, 1970). From this perspective, borderline personality *disorder* (our italics) is viewed as a manifestation of borderline personality in an infantile and impulsive personality.

In 1980, Lerner and Lerner developed a Rorschach scale, conceptually derived from Kernberg's formulations of object relations in borderlines, which rates the human percepts in a protocol as they manifest the use of the major defense mechanisms characteristic of this pathology. The manifestations of these defenses—splitting, devaluation, idealization, projective identification, and denial—were operationalized, with the added requirement that responses reflecting devaluation, idealization, and denial were ranked on a continuum of high versus low order. Subsequent investigations (Lerner, Sugarman, and Gaughran, 1981; Lerner, Albert, and Walsh, 1987) have supported the utility of the scale in discriminating borderlines from other diagnostic groups.

However, Smith (1980) and Cooper and Arnow (1986) have suggested that while Lerner and Lerner's scale has made a valuable contribution to the assessment of defensive structure in borderlines, it is unnecessarily narrow in that it restricts itself to the human percept. Cooper and Arnow argue that Rorschach responses of animal percepts and percepts consisting of parts of objects, animate and inanimate, may contribute vital

information to the understanding of an individual's object relations. As well as broadening Lerner and Lerner's approach in
this way, Cooper and Arnow have further refined and extended
the ways in which manifestations of splitting and projective
identification may be scored.

Following Stolorow and Lachman (1980), they identified
two divergent forms of splitting: defensive splitting in which
good and bad object images are linked to at least two separate
objects, and "pre-stage" splitting where polarized views of the
same external object rapidly fluctuate in a fluid and uninte-
grated way. "Pre-stage" splitting is thus seen rather as reflecting
a developmental arrest. An example of a Rorschach response
showing defensive splitting would be one used by Lerner and
Lerner to illustrate the splitting criteria in their scale: "Looks
like an ugly criminal with a gun" immediately followed by "A
couple sitting together cheek to cheek." Rorschach percepts
such as "A knight in shining armour, one half is majestic and
the lower part is ugly and worn, he's mounted on an ugly horse"
(Card IV) are indicative of pre-stage splitting in their inability
to integrate contrasting affects to a single object.

The concept of projective identification is a complex one,
but in psychoanalytic theory, it remains a central mechanism of
defense in borderline pathology. The notion, originally developed by Melanie Klein, is seen essentially as a defensive process
in which "parts of the self and internal objects are split off and
projected into the external object which then becomes possessed by, controlled, and identified with the projected parts"
(Segal, 1974, p. 27). In the development of their scale, Lerner
and Lerner attempted to operationalize three subprocesses that
they assumed to be involved in projective identification: an externalization of parts of the self with a disregard to real characteristics of the external object; a capacity to blur boundaries
between self and objects; and a compelling need to control
the object. Two scale criteria are used as indices of projective
identification: confabulatory responses involving human figures in which the form level is FW- or F- (i.e., perceptually
inaccurate), and human or human detail in which the location
is Dr (small, rarely used, and arbitrarily delimited detail), the
determinant F(c) (i.e., nuances of shading in the interior of the

blot are used to outline the form of the response), and the figure is described as either aggressive or as the object of aggression.

Cooper and Arnow (1986) conceive of projective identification as subsumed in the following three processes: fantasies of concretely putting a dangerous or endangered part of the self into another object in order to control or harm the object, or to safeguard part of the self; fearfully empathizing with objects bearing projections of aggressive self-images; and hyperalertness to external threat or attack coupled with expressions of primitive rage. Cooper and Arnow, particularly in the first criteria, thus extend Lerner and Lerner's conceptualization in a manner perhaps more consonant with original Kleinian theory than with Kernberg's somewhat more narrow view.

As noted earlier, Cooper and Arnow have extended the range of percepts which may be scored according to their scale beyond the human percepts necessary for assigning scores in Lerner and Lerner's scale. Their criteria, operationalizing their conceptualization of projective identification, place somewhat less weight on the formal aspects of the percept and more on the content. A Rorschach response reflecting the first subprocess of projective identification, for example, would be (Card X) "these tarantulas are injecting their poison into these grasshoppers." It is perhaps worth underscoring that aspect of this subprocess which speaks to projection into the object of a vulnerable part of the self which needs to be safeguarded, as exemplified in Cooper's example (Card X): "These little innocent, weak looking creatures seem to be trying to get inside these pink things. Maybe they are trying to find refuge from this world of vicious looking crabs and insects." Cooper and Arnow here remind us that projective identification need not be solely employed as a means of projecting the aggressive, destructive bad parts of the self.

Taken together, Lerner and Lerner's scale (now referred to as the Lerner defense scale [Lerner et al., 1987]) and Cooper and Arnow's work provide a rich matrix for the assessment of borderline defenses and internal object relations as they are manifested in Rorschach protocols. While Lerner and Lerner's scale offers the more precise and specific criteria and enjoys a greater measure of empirical validation, Cooper and Arnow's work offers rich conceptual extensions of the Lerners' work.

Other contributions to the understanding of the internal world of the borderline patient have been made by Kwawer (1980), Spear and Sugarman (1984), and Coonerty (1986).

In their research, Spear and Sugarman used Blatt et al.'s scale measuring the differentiation and articulation of human percepts and the integration of the human object in a context of action and interaction with other objects, together with a modified version of Urist's scale. They point out that Blatt's scale represents a more structured approach to the categorization of the human percepts, where Urist's offers a more thematic approach in its measurement of relatedness. They suggest from their findings in a research study comparing two types of borderline pathology (the obsessive–paranoid and the infantile) with schizophrenics, that both approaches to the measurement of the object in the Rorschach are necessary in order to obtain the most comprehensive understanding of the patient's inner representational world.

Kwawer's conceptual framework, while essentially remaining within the object relations paradigm, focuses more on the vicissitudes of separation and individuation as delineated by Mahler and her followers. He examines Rorschach responses as they reflect themes of merger, fusion, separation, and individuation as well as manifestations of boundary disturbance and symbiotic longings. In the same spirit, but anchoring her criteria more specifically in the three subphases Mahler postulates as comprising the separation individuation period (differentiation; practicing; rapprochement), Coonerty (1986) has developed a scale, the separation individuation theme scale, which she has demonstrated distinguishes borderline from schizophrenic patients.

Recently, Carr (1987), whose own Rorschach research is usually associated with the ego psychological approach (Spear and Sugarman, 1984), in a trenchant criticism of a recent study undertaken by Lerner et al. (1987), questions the validity of a Rorschach approach to the discrimination of borderline pathology based exclusively on defensive operations as reflected in human and quasi-human responses. While his criticism is directed specifically at the Lerners' work, he does provide a useful reminder that many of the object relations approaches outlined above rely heavily on the content of the Rorschach to the virtual exclusion of the more formal scorings, such as location, form level, and determinants, in particular the various manifestations of thought disorder identified by earlier writers (e.g., Rapaport et al., 1945). Given the reported frequent occurrence of minipsychotic episodes in some borderline patients (Gunderson and Singer, 1975) and the overlap between BPD and STP, it would seem only appropriate that Rorschach manifestations of thought disorder also be considered in clinical and research investigation of the syndrome.

Sugarman (1986), in a closely reasoned paper, argues for a synthesis of ego psychological and object relations perspectives, citing Blatt's reconceptualization of Rapaport's major thought disorder indices as representing a continuum of boundary disturbance (Blatt and Ritzler, 1974; Blatt and Wild, 1976). Disturbances in reality testing as reflected in the contamination, fabulized combination, and confabulation responses are viewed as also representative of pathological levels of self and object representations. (In contamination responses, percepts are fused in response to a single area of the blot so that the boundary between the separate images is lost, for example, percepts of "blood" and "an island" become "a bloody island"; fabulized combinations are unlikely combinations of percepts based on spatially contiguous images, for example, "two beavers climbing on a butterfly"; in confabulation responses, partially accurate percepts are highly elaborated in an unrealistic and/or idiosyncratic fashion.)

Finally, Exner (1986), whose approach is a structural one reflected in the summaries, percentages and ratios of the Rorschach protocol's more readily quantifiable perceptual cognitive features, reports that the major differences between individuals with borderline personality compared to those with schizotypal personality disorder and schizophrenia involve variables related to the experience or discharge of affect.

In summary, the richest and most compelling work comes from those researchers who base their assumptions on the object relations model, whose theoretical framework it both validates and extends. However, as Carr (1987) and Sugarman (1986) remind us, a more comprehensive and complex understanding of borderline pathology requires not only that we do not discard the contributions made by the earlier ego psychological model, but that we continue to work toward a more fruitful integration of this model with the insights of the object relations approach.

CLINICAL APPLICATIONS

In closing, some comments on the practical relevance of the above work to the practicing psychotherapist and clinician are in order. In institutional settings, in particular, a frequent question asked of the psychologist providing testing is, "Is this patient borderline or schizophrenic?" While this question is certainly valid and usually capable of being answered by psychological testing, a too exclusive view of psychological testing as contributing only information relevant to the assigning of diagnosis can lead to a wealth of other psychological information being ignored or overlooked. It is important to keep in mind, however, that while essentially the Rorschach, in a manner of speaking, does not lie, neither is it always completely exhaustive in its reflection of a patient's internal world, particularly with those guarded and defended patients who offer constricted records. As well, the familiarity of the testing psychologist with psychoanalytic theory and his or her experience clinically with borderline patients will be a factor in the complexity and richness of the clinical hypotheses generated.

Nonetheless, a careful examination of the Rorschach protocol, along with information from other projective tests such as the Thematic Apperception Test (TAT), can usually provide much useful information for the psychotherapist in areas such as potential transference and countertransference manifestations, the patient's affective life, the nature and level of his or her reality testing, and the level of impulsivity.

The following Rorschach responses, taken from protocols of borderline patients, provide us with some direct clinical examples upon which the testing psychologist may begin to develop hypotheses which relate to the above areas. While such hypotheses would typically require a measure of cross-validation from other test material, the comments on the responses will provide the reader with some sense of the inferential processes involved in developing an understanding of the individual's psychodynamics, and proposing treatment recommendations.

A thirty-four-year-old male borderline inpatient offered the following response to Card II. "Looks like two animals . . . nose to nose with each other . . . pushing up on each other . . . seems like there's combat . . . there's a few blood splashes . . . holy Christ, now I see . . . looks like two animals actually . . . or kissing each other . . . rubbing noses, probably." In this response, we can observe the oscillation between the "bad" aggressive representation and the "good" nurturing and intimate one, from "combat" to "kissing." The defensive splitting is effective in that the aggression is contained and denied by the "kissing." In developing hypotheses with respect to transference manifestations, the examiner might note the following: the response involves animals rather than humans, the oscillations between "bad" and "good" occur in the context of the same percept (two animals), and there are "blood splashes." A clinician attempting psychotherapy with this individual may thus find that there are quite rapid and polarized shifts in the way the patient perceives him or her and, indeed, in the way the patient views himself (the oscillation between "bad" and "good" occurs in the context of the same percept); these oscillations may be experienced as rather primitive and intense and may not be particularly accessible to the patient's awareness (the response involves animals rather than humans) and there may be impulsive and angry outbursts (the color response "blood splashes" is not form dominated, that is to say that color is the primary determinant of the response rather than the contours of the blot). However, while this man may provoke some irritation in the therapist by the level of denial of his aggression—angry outbursts followed by a bland "everything's fine now"—the effectiveness of the splitting defense may allow him to maintain a connection with the therapist upon which a more effective therapeutic alliance may be built.

Compare his response to that of a twenty-three-year-old borderline woman to the same card. "They look like two bears dancing, because they've got their hands clasping at the top . . . the red looks like blood . . . there's been some struggle . . . down at the bottom they're both wounded and there's red throughout their fur . . . and they're both leaving blood behind." In this response, a mutually pleasurable and cooperative interaction ("bears dancing") becomes spoiled by the aggression which emerges. The potential for an intense negative transference after an initial therapeutic honeymoon is high, as is the potential for a stormy and impulsive end to therapy.

Consider, too, this response to Card IV, offered by a twenty-six-year-old male borderline. "This way I see a head of a man with a crown on in a distorted body or whatever." Here, abortive attempts may be made by the patient to develop an idealizing transference in the Kohutian sense, efforts which will likely be extremely difficult to sustain as the idealization will become spoiled and "distorted." The reader will note that this response provides an example of what Cooper and Arnow (1984) refer to as "pre-stage" splitting.

Rorschach responses can provide important information on the nature of the individual patient's depressive affect. This may be particularly useful in differential diagnosis in the light of observations (e.g., Kernberg, 1975) that the depressive affect of borderlines has to do more with experiences of emptiness and loneliness than with experiences of guilt.

Consider the following two examples, the first from a twenty-four-year-old borderline man and the second from a twenty-eight-year-old borderline woman. In response to Card IV, the man says, "Looks like a pair of Canada geese . . . they look sort of sad and forlorn . . . they have to leave each other or something." The woman says, in response to Card VII, "I think they were short of ink on this one, a big empty space in the middle . . . that could be the caricatured outline of a girl's face with a ponytail standing up on its end . . . kind of dumb." In the first response, the relation of depression to abandonment fears is evident. The regressive wish for merger is underscored by the patient's remarks in the inquiry that there "seem to be a group of them clustered together . . . overlapping." The young woman's sense of self is depreciated ("kind of dumb") and has an "as if" quality ("caricatured outline") which serves to mask the "big empty space in the middle."

Other questions that the Rorschach can provide useful information on might be as follows. Are self and object representations organized along sadomasochistic lines? Are human percepts distanced in time and space (e.g., astronauts, medieval figures, famous figures) thus implying narcissistic issues? Does the individual's reality testing become impaired mainly on the affectively arousing colored cards or on cards which might elicit sexual themes? If there are significant lapses in reality testing, can the individual reconstitute as the test progresses or is the regressive process more malignant? When self-injurious acts occur are they likely to have stemmed from a relatively conscious attempt to manipulate and control the individual's environment, or do they represent failures of impulse control? Or are they attempts, in the face of unbearable emptiness or dissociative episodes, to feel "real"?

As Michels has pointed out elsewhere in this volume (see Chapter 3), diagnosis of Axis I disorders generally indicates an appropriate treatment intervention, usually of a psychopharmacological nature, whereas with the Axis II disorders such as BPD much less consensus exists as to what constitutes the most appropriate treatment intervention. In the light of this, psychological assessment will continue to remain extremely helpful, not only in ongoing research efforts, but in providing a means of understanding the complexity of those characterologically disturbed individuals whose suffering we seek to mitigate.

11.

The Myth of the Therapeutic Alliance with Borderline Patients Revisited

Gerald Adler, M.D.

The concept of the *therapeutic alliance* has been utilized for many years. Zetzel's (1956) use of the term and Greenson's (1965) discussions of the working alliance brought more forcefully to the therapist's and analyst's attention ideas that had been previously described in the literature in defining work with neurotic patients. In the past several decades, as more clinicians work with and write about more "primitive" patients, such as those with a borderline or narcissistic personality disorder, the alliance concept has been readily applied to these patients, too. However, in my clinical work with these borderline and narcissistic patients over the years, I have questioned the validity and utility of a formulation that places the therapeutic alliance on center stage in treating these patients (Adler, 1979, 1980, 1985). In this chapter, I shall review my original discussions briefly, and then define some of the ways I am currently conceptualizing the therapeutic alliance concept and the problems it poses for therapist and patient in the treatment of borderline psychopathology.

DYNAMIC DESCRIPTION OF THE BORDERLINE PATIENT

In order to place the therapist alliance in a proper perspective in relation to borderline patients, I shall first describe the difficulties of these patients and the dilemmas that they face, which also rapidly involve their therapists.

At the core of the borderline disorder is the patient's inability to count on his internal resources to allay separation anxiety. Buie and I (Adler and Buie, 1979; Buie and Adler, 1982; Adler, 1985) have characterized this difficulty as the borderline's defective evocative memory capacity, which we also conceptualize as his or her inability to maintain holding and soothing introjects when faced with the rage that accompanies separation. The clinical manifestations of these difficulties are evident in the midst of an intense regressive transference in which the patient is angry, feels abandoned, and cannot tolerate the separations that occur between sessions or during therapist vacations. At such times, the patient may phone the therapist, stating that he has lost the ability to remember the therapist *with feeling* as someone who cares, soothes, or holds. Although the object representation of the therapist is present, allowing for the possibility of the phone call, the patient has lost the holding and soothing introject, the felt presence of the therapist that the patient can use during the time of separation. Buie and I have related this core borderline difficulty to the themes of absolute or relative abandonment in the patient's history and experiences of aloneness, emptiness, and despair, which are relived in the current dyadic relationships, including the one with the therapist, as feelings of neediness emerge.

In addition to aloneness difficulties, borderline patients have two other important features that help clarify the psychodynamic understanding of them: the need–fear dilemma and primitive guilt. Burnham, Gladstone, and Gibson (1969) described the need–fear dilemma problems of schizophrenic patients. Borderline patients also manifest the need–fear dilemma, but, in contrast to schizophrenics, do not become psychotic in the presence of the other important person. As Kernberg (1975) and Jacobson (1964) have defined, psychotics can readily lose the distinction between self and object representations when involved in intense relationships. Borderlines can largely maintain this distinction, except for transient breakdowns, manifested clinically by short-lived psychotic episodes during an intense transference. Instead, a major difficulty for borderline patients is their inability to integrate positive and negative affects associated with self and object representations (i.e., their difficulty with splitting [Kernberg, 1975] and an inability to tolerate ambivalence [Adler, 1985]). Their need–fear dilemma problems also relate to their terror in the face of their devouring oral hunger. For them, closeness is often equated with swallowing up the person they need, experienced as the destruction of that person. For these reasons, they feel danger in the presence of someone who becomes important to them. They can alternate between intense neediness, hunger, and rage, followed by a flight from that person in order to maintain their ego boundaries, which they experience as tentative and fragile. These need–fear dilemma problems also explain one of the difficulties in treating borderline patients: they flee from the therapist as their longings and anger emerge.

Primitive guilt is manifested by the ease with which borderline patients project aspects of their superego onto the other person as well as the fact that their superego is unremittingly cruel and relentless. Thus, they may readily shift between hating themselves and maintaining the conviction that their therapist cannot stand them. It may alternate with their loss of holding and soothing introjects, leaving them with the internal feeling, which they may also project, that the world is either unpeopled, or full of malevolent people who will punish and destroy them.

THE BORDERLINE PATIENT'S VULNERABILITY IN TREATMENT

The borderline patient's limited capacity to maintain holding and soothing introjects in the face of separations, his need–fear dilemma problems that do not allow him to be safely in the presence of the therapist, and his ease in punishing himself or

seeing his therapist as malevolent, lead to a very shaky therapeutic situation. As needs emerge in the transference, accompanied by disappointments and anger, the patient may feel the
emptiness and panic that follow the loss of holding and soothing introjects, the fear of his destructiveness or the danger of
engulfment by his therapist, or an overwhelming belief in his
badness or in the hatred of his therapist. This description of
the borderline patient is most visible at those times when longings and anger are escalating in the transference. At other
times, the patient's higher level defenses and capacities to maintain a relatively stable relationship with the therapist obscure
this vulnerability to regress in the transference.

Thus far I have been utilizing a framework that combines
an object relations model with that of structural theory and
ego psychology to explain the borderline patient's difficulties in
treatment. In order to define further these patients' problems
as they emerge in the transference, I shall now utilize aspects
of Kohut's (1971, 1977) self psychology. Kohut's work is particularly useful in defining the bond between patient and therapist
in the treatment situation, especially with those patients who
have difficulty in maintaining a therapeutic bond. The concept
of the self–object, and its utilization in elaborating self–object
transferences, offers an explanatory framework for aspects of
patients who have a borderline or narcissistic personality disorder, related to their need for the other person to supply functions missing in them. The person who is the self–object per-
forms a needed function for another while being experienced
as part of the self by the person who requires that function.
Borderline patients require others to perform functions for
them in the areas of soothing and holding as well as in the
maintenance of their self-worth. Narcissistic personality disorder patients require self–object help, particularly in the area of
self-esteem regulation. Kohut defined the narcissistic personality disorder patient essentially as someone with manifestations
of significant incompleteness in his capacity to regulate his sense
of his self-worth, and required the therapist or analyst to perform that function for him in the treatment. As Kohut has
elaborated, these self–object transferences are both mirroring
and idealizing, recreating situations of parental failures in the

person's past life, and setting the stage of therapeutic growth through the reliving and analysis of these transferences in the current treatment. A major aspect of the treatment is the exploration of the ruptures in these self–object transferences through the "empathic failures" of the therapist (e.g., his not providing the understanding that the patient wishes for or needs at any particular moment). These therapeutic ruptures or experiences of "fragmentation" reveal the relative instability of the patient's self cohesiveness, which can be healed through the analysis of the transference and the reworking of past parental failures. The result, as Kohut defined, is the development of the patient's stunted grandiosity into mature ambitions (through the working through of the mirroring self–object transference) and the taking in of missing self-esteem regulating functions (through the process of transmuting internalization in which these functions from the idealized therapist are internalized).

I have found that Kohut's descriptions of self–object transferences with narcissistic personality disorder patients is also applicable to borderline patients. As already stated, borderline patients do form self–object transferences both in the areas of self-esteem regulation and holding and soothing. However, these self–object transferences are particularly vulnerable to regression as the described problems with aloneness, the need–fear dilemma, and primitive guilt emerge. Kohut's discussion about the narcissistic personality disorder patient's problem with regression to the core area of stunted grandiosity needs to be broadened to understand the borderline personality disorder patient's further regression to the core area of aloneness and inability to maintain holding and soothing introjects (Adler, 1984).

Clinically, the therapist may find that initially in treatment borderline patients are capable of forming self–object transferences which may appear to be similar to or identical with those of patients who have a narcissistic personality disorder. With some borderline patients, only a careful history will reveal characteristic borderline psychopathology which has emerged in important past dyadic relationships. In the current psychotherapy, the relatively stable-appearing self–object transferences will rupture as separation issues, with their attendant anger, occur, revealing the borderline problems and the regression accompanying them. For the clinician, what may appear at first as a relatively stable narcissistic personality disorder patient whose problems were largely around feelings of incompleteness and self-worth, is revealed to be a very vulnerable borderline patient who is in a panic and rage with lost holding and soothing introjects and the other accompanying manifestations of the borderline disorder, as feelings of separation emerge.

TRANSFERENCE OR ALLIANCE WITH BORDERLINE PATIENTS

The description I have elaborated about borderline patients in treatment spells out the relative instability of their self–object transferences: their desperate return to annihilatory fears of aloneness, as well as feelings of destruction and self-destruction, which may be accompanied by the experience of the therapist and the world as malevolent. Is it possible that such patients can form a therapeutic alliance? Although able clinicians have described a major task of therapists in work with borderline patients as one of establishing a therapeutic alliance with them, has an "alliance" occurred? My question has been whether indeed a therapeutic alliance has been formed, or whether a more valid and useful explanation is that there is the formation of an initially relatively vulnerable self–object transference which only gradually over time will become more stable, and ultimately begin to resemble the therapeutic alliance described by Zetzel or the working alliance elaborated by Greenson.

When we observe the "therapeutic alliance" described in work with borderline patients, we can note the short period of time that this "alliance" may be present. It can quickly dissolve in the face of the therapist's "empathic failures" or escalating patient needs, resulting in the patient's rage, terror, acting out, flight, or self-punishment. I find it difficult to be comfortable in calling such an unstable and potentially chaotic situation a therapeutic alliance. In Zetzel's use of the term, a *therapeutic alliance* largely describes a stable, mature collaborative relationship between analyst and analysand which also involves the patient's capacity to maintain an observing ego. I feel that a more accurate and useful explanation is one that utilizes our understanding of the fragile self–object transference of these patients and the therapist–patient interaction that aids either in its maintenance or breakdown.

My clinical and supervisory experience supports the formulation that it is the self–object bond and its vulnerability that determines the therapist's sense that an "alliance" exists with the patient at any moment in the treatment. The therapist who talks with the patient about their work together may quickly be disappointed, frightened, and enraged when the momentarily "collaborative" patient no longer remembers any such experience of collaboration following an interaction of feeling misunderstood by the therapist. Instead, the therapist may have a patient who is in a frightening or self-destructive rage.

Understanding that the self–object bond between therapist and patient has been ruptured can help the therapist find ways to address the breakdown in the transference and help the patient bear and understand it, as well as require that the therapist acknowledge to himself, and when appropriate, to the patient, his role in the rupture. Such a formulation places the issue where it most accurately is and allows for the possibility of productive therapeutic work. Stressing the therapeutic alliance concept misses the mark by not focusing on the centrality of the transference breakdown. It can also lead to the greater likelihood of therapist and patient despair that "alliances" fail so often. Of particular importance is the fact that stressing the alliance concept with the patient can be experienced as an empathic failure, leading to further breakdown in a tenuous self–object transference: the patient may feel that the therapist's wish to have a collaborative, mature, observing relationship is a demand that he cannot fulfill. An angry though compliant patient, who develops a false self in order to remain with the therapist, may result. In actual clinical work, true therapeutic

alliances are the result of long periods of successful psychotherapy with these patients.

THE THERAPEUTIC ALLIANCE AS A COMPANION

Why has the therapeutic alliance concept so persistently and
tenaciously remained in discussions of borderline personality
disorder (BPD) patients? I believe that the answer lies in part
in the therapist's or analyst's experience in working with this
group of patients. Countertransference responses to the
aloneness, emptiness, rage, and self-destructiveness of these
patients, and the intensity of their demands on the one hand,
matched on the other hand by their tendency to run, act with
total self-sufficiency, or merge with the therapist in ways that
keep him from feeling that he is relating to another human
being, are painful experiences for the therapist to bear. The
intensity of these patients' neediness, as well as their inability
to use the therapist as a separate person through their self-
sufficiency defenses or merger fears and needs, create a situation in which the therapist requires something to fill his inner
world. If he only pays attention to the patient, he is faced with
nothingness, merger, nonrelationship, or devouring hunger
and rage. In the face of such untenable alternatives, the therapist can summon his wishes for an "alliance" with the patient
and with others in his life to survive such painful situations.
Either he can remember interactions with supervisors and colleagues who have been useful, or appreciate the literature written about the understanding and treatment of these patients.
The literature on therapeutic alliances not only offers such
help, but allows the therapist to feel that he is not alone in what
he is experiencing. He can also believe that his patient has
greater capacities and has levels of maturity that he can readily
tap in contrast to his current countertransference helplessness
and hopelessness. The concept is useful to the degree that it
helps the therapist bear his countertransference pain. However, as discussed, through its inaccuracies, it can provide serious obstacles to maximally useful therapeutic work, and even
be destructive.

PROJECTIVE IDENTIFICATION, AMBIGUITY, AND THE THERAPEUTIC ALLIANCE

In my current thinking about the therapeutic alliance problems with borderline patients, I have been elaborating and utilizing the concepts of projective identification, transitional phenomena, and ambiguity in the treatment situation.

Projective Identification

I have been increasingly impressed with the usefulness of understanding projective identification in work with borderline patients (Adler, 1984, 1989; Adler and Rhine, 1988). The concept was first used by Klein (1946), and elaborated by Bion (1967), Grotstein (1981), and Kernberg (1975). Kernberg stressed the need of the patient to rid himself of self or object representations with a specific positive or negative affective charge by placing that constellation in another person. The patient then had to control the person in order to remain in touch with the valued or feared parts which were placed into that person.

Bion was the first contributor who emphasized the interpersonal aspects of projective identification. He described the analyst as the container and the patient's "excessive" demands on the analyst who attempts to provide that function for the patient. He also implied that the patient will intensify the projective identifications if the analyst cannot tolerate them. Since Bion's work, the interpersonal significance of projective identification has been elaborated by a number of workers (Malin and Grotstein, 1966; Ogden, 1979; Shapiro, 1982b). They elaborate a series of steps that make up the process (Adler, 1989).

As these workers describe, the patient first attempts to remove an unacceptable or cherished part of himself by placing it into the therapist. The patient then interacts with the therapist in a way that provokes the therapist to respond to him in consonance with the projected fantasy. The therapist's primary function is to contain the projection; although provoked, the therapist *ideally* can use the projection and provocation as a source of "empathy" so that he can interpret to the patient the nature of the projection and his understanding of the reasons it is projected. However, in unsuccessful or partially successful containment, the therapist has unresolved, conflictual, or split-off aspects of himself that are vulnerable to the patient's projections and interpersonal provocations.

The successful or relatively successful containment process allows the patient to reinternalize the modified projection. Ogden (1979) has stressed the importance of projective identification in understanding the process of change in patients. I (Adler and Rhine, 1988; Adler, 1989) feel that the concept is particularly important in clarifying how the aloneness problems in borderline patients are resolved. For example, the repeated experiences of the therapist surviving the patient's rage by containing it, interpreting it, and not acting out by retaliating or abandoning, can also be conceptualized as part of the process that allows the patient to modify deficits by internalizing new structure. These may consist of introjects of the therapist, including memories of interactions with him as a holding, soothing, and containing person in the face of the patient's projections and enormous provocations.

In order to understand the relationship between projective identification and the problems with the therapeutic alliance concept, I shall spell out two further elements of projective identification: its relationship to transitional phenomena, and the distinction between constructive and destructive projective identification.

Transitional Phenomena and Ambiguity

Winnicott has made major contributions to our understanding of child development and the creative aspects of psychotherapy and psychoanalysis. His elaboration of the concepts of transitional phenomena and transitional objects (1951) has helped explain experiences that were relatively unclear in psychotherapeutic encounters. The capacity of patient and therapist to have a "space" in which to work and be "playful" and creative, all qualities of a good therapy session, relate to these concepts.

The transitional object, whose creation is unclear, provides the basis for understanding these experiences. Is the "blanket" provided by the mother, or does the child select it, in part to deal with separations and to evoke a mother who is not present all the time when the child has a vulnerable evocative memory capacity (Adler, 1989)? As Winnicott notes, the good-enough mother never asks the child whether she provided the blanket or whether the child chose it for his needs. The mother's capacity to tolerate this ambiguity ultimately allows the child the opportunity for illusion, creativity, and play. Comparably, as I shall discuss later, the therapist who can feel comfortable with many of the ambiguities of the psychotherapeutic situation can create with the patient an environment that encourages comfort, safety, and creative work.

The concept of transitional phenomena is related to that of projective identification. As discussed, projective identification, when it is successfully contained, provides the setting for significant change in psychotherapy. This successful process (constructive projective identification), in contrast to the intensity of the patient's projective identifications coupled with the therapist's failure to contain them adequately (destructive projective identification) is also a situation of uncertainty, ambiguity, and creativity. The therapist can never be certain how much comes from the patient and how much from himself, what role he is playing in reactivating old issues in the patient and in himself, whether the projections are so insistent that they are uncontainable by any therapist or are difficulties more related to his own unresolved problems, as well as how much is transference or how much is the "real" relationship with the patient. The therapist's capacities to contain not only the patient's projections and provocations, but also his own uncertainties about the ambiguity of the situation determine to a large extent whether the projective identification experience will be constructive or destructive. In the latter instance, so common in the treatment of borderline patients, the creative space, safety, and relatively stable self–object transferences will disintegrate, with a recrudescence of the well-known borderline disorganization and its repetition of such negative experiences from childhood to the present. With constructive projective identification, a situation of containment has developed which is akin to that of the transitional phenomena experience with the creativity it allows.

The concept of the therapeutic alliance can now be viewed in the context of the discussion about transitional phenomena and constructive projective identification. The intensity of the experience of projective identification for both patient and therapist is well known. The projection of painful affects and interactions, and the provocation of them in the therapist who may have vulnerabilities in similar areas, can and does cause obvious distress in therapists, regardless of their relatively successful capacity to contain them. I emphasize the intensity of affects experienced by the therapist in order to contrast it with a wish to find some way out of such potential or momentary actual chaos. I feel that the therapeutic alliance concept can be grabbed by the therapist at such moments to attempt to provide some stability or distance in the midst of such chaos. When it is used in this way, it can communicate to the patient that the therapist is unable to bear (i.e., contain) the intensity of the experience. It can be felt by the patient as an aspect of the therapist's discomfort, defensiveness, and need to distance himself, and therefore, as an empathic failure. Under these circumstances, the therapist, in utilizing the therapeutic alliance concept, is destroying the creative space that may have been present to allow the patient to bring into the treatment such intense projective identification experiences. The result can be the breakdown of a self–object transference as a result of the therapist's failure as a self–object who contains the projective identification, thus becoming an example of destructive projective identification (Adler and Rhine, 1988).

Clinical Vignette

A clinical illustration of this misuse of the therapeutic alliance concept occurred in a therapist's work with a thirty-four-year-old borderline man in the fourth year of twice weekly therapy. The patient had been repeatedly angry at his therapist for six months, stating that therapy and the therapist were useless. In addition, he felt that he was stuck in a hopeless despair that nothing would ever change, and that he would always have to live with his feelings of isolation, emptiness, and despair. The therapist, who had been interpreting this material as a manifestation of the patient's anger at him, and as a reliving of the hopelessness and despair of the patient's childhood, began to feel increasingly stuck and hopeless about the treatment himself. He was increasingly uncertain that much progress had occurred over four years, and that he and the patient would ever get beyond this impasse.

On four occasions in the last two sessions with his patient, the therapist emphasized the importance of their collaborative work to understand the patient's feelings of anger and despair. After the therapist's last statement about the need for more collaboration, the patient became very angry, stating that he felt that no collaborative relationship existed, and that the therapist was tired of him because he also felt that treatment was hopeless. The therapist remained silent for the moment, but began to acknowledge to himself that the patient was correct: indeed, he was feeling angry and hopeless, and wished that he did not have to see the patient any more. He was uncertain about the "impasse." Were they really stuck, or was this the nature of the transference with this patient at this time; which he had seen in other borderline patients and which could require many months to analyze and resolve further?

In his work with his patient, the therapist explored the patient's fantasies of the therapist's anger and hopelessness, and acknowledged to the patient that he could understand the patient's concerns, based upon the patient's observations of the therapist's statements about collaboration. The therapist did not make further acknowledgment of the correctness of the patient's observations. The therapist was able to return to his previous position of bearing his uncertainty about the "impasse" while continuing to explore the meanings of the patient's anger and hopelessness and their possible relationship to the patient's past. After several more months, the patient's anger and despair abated at a time that he was considering a creative job offer that he now felt he was ready for.

This clinical example demonstrates the therapist's wavering capacity to contain the projective identification experiences. It was only after the patient's confrontation of him that the therapist could acknowledge, to himself, the validity of his patient's statement and the fact that he was using a therapeutic alliance statement at a point that he was overwhelmed by the intensity of the patient's feelings. His recognition allowed him to regain his containing capacity, and prevented the projective identification experience from becoming destructive. This vignette also illustrates the ambiguity and uncertainty that is often present at the height of intense projective identification, as will now be discussed.

Ambiguity and Uncertainty

In a comparable way, the therapist who utilizes the therapeutic alliance concept at such charged moments may be destroying the ambiguity present in the therapeutic situation. Paradoxically, the patient at the height of rage at and provocation in the relationship with the therapist may talk with certainty and condemnation about the inadequacy of the therapist. It is often at those moments that the therapist is most uncertain and lost in the ambiguity of his role in the treatment. I would formulate that the therapist, through projective identification, is simultaneously the repository of the patient's as well as his own feelings of uncertainty and ambiguity that the patient cannot tolerate. The therapist's creative capacity to tolerate the uncertainty and ambiguity is threatened by the patient's assaults about the certainty of the situation, the "wrongs" of the therapist in the eyes of the patient at that moment. Overwhelmed by these rageful attacks, the therapist can respond to the patient's simultaneous projective identification of old relationships and experiences of certainty, and provoke the therapist into a position of stating with certainty that among the issues is a need to have a therapeutic alliance. To the degree that the therapist presents it as a hypothesis which he allows the patient to accept and utilize or dismiss, the possibility remains for the therapist to continue to work within the framework of painful projective identification which he is having some difficulty in containing. However, if the therapist is provoked to summon up the therapeutic alliance concept with insistence and certainty, the painful, but potentially creative experience with constructive projective identification is destroyed.

Shapiro (1982b) has described pathological certainty in families of disturbed adolescents, manifested by a lack of curiosity within those families. Many of the borderline patients we see have come from backgrounds in which they experience pathological certainty with one or both parents. Through projective identification, they recreate those experiences in their therapy, and place the therapist in the role of someone who can either contain and rework the projected experiences of pathological certainty, or allow it to be pathologically and destructively relived. Simultaneously, the therapist who can contain the patient's creative feelings of ambiguity and uncertainty, which can be conceptualized as being placed by the patient into the therapist for safekeeping, can allow it to be ultimately reinternalized as a permanent part of the patient. The therapist's defensive use of the therapeutic alliance concept in the middle of such moments can be a part of the pathological situation that interferes with such change.

CONCLUSION

Although the therapeutic alliance concept has been important and useful in the treatment of neurotic patients, its application to borderline patients may often be a manifestation of countertransference difficulties or part of an experience of projective identification which is in the process of becoming destructive. It is crucial that the therapist recognize the problems in working with borderline patients that can push him to evoke alliance concepts. The therapist's failure to acknowledge these difficulties can compound impasses in the treatment and result in experiences of destructive projective identification, as well as the loss of ambiguity, creativity, and "play" in the treatment.

12.

A Borderline Treatment Dilemma: To Solace or Not To Solace

Paul C. Horton, M.D.

INTRODUCTION

Borderline patients have been labeled the "most difficult" (Gutheil, 1985, p. 9) of patients because of their rage, entitlement, manipulativeness, impulsivity, and other features of their condition. They have also been called most "dangerous" from a medicolegal point of view due to their seductiveness and ability to get the therapist to deviate from professional standards. For example, in twenty-two instances of alleged sexual misconduct by therapists the "overwhelming majority" of plaintiffs were "borderlines" (Gutheil, 1988). Findings such as these have led Gutheil to caution therapists against "lesser" deviations from professional standards "such as lending money, offering rides, or socializing with borderline patients" (Gutheil, 1988, p. 14).

The medicolegal hazards in treating the borderline patient are an ironic symptom of the borderline's most basic and unsatisfied psychological need, which is to find appropriate solace, comfort, and nurturance (Horton, 1977; Arkema, 1981, 1988). What the borderline patient needs most desperately is what poisons the doctor–patient relationship if it is not given in an exactly correct and proper manner. With many of these patients it is not clear that it is even *possible* to "appropriately" solace them, that is, to comfort them in a way that is both potentially satisfying to the patient and in accordance with professional standards of conduct.

The pivotal developmental and therapeutic issue to be examined in this paper is the borderline patient's difficulties in finding solace. A number of studies over the last three decades have delineated the borderline patient's special use of solacers. Arkema (1981) has described the rigid, regressive, and maladaptive efforts which borderline patients make in seeking comfort. The apparently unique way in which borderline patients seek solace has led to the suggestion that this characteristic may be a diagnostic marker (Horton, 1977; Arkema, 1988). Before looking more closely at these difficulties and their implications we will find it helpful to consider the capacity for self-soothing in a broader, normative, and developmental context.

INFANT STUDIES

Winnicott (1951) was, of course, the first to call direct attention to a crucial developmental role for solacers in early childhood (Horton, 1988a). His concept of the transitional object has been invaluable in allowing theorists and researchers to conceptualize new approaches to understanding the function of soothers. However, there were important earlier studies by Spitz (1945, 1946b), the results of which suggested that solacing relationships in infancy were necessary not only developmentally but for sheer physical survival as well. Lack of comforting maternal care leads to a progressive deterioration, "hospitalism," which frequently culminates in death.

Provence and Lipton in their pioneering *Infants in Institutions* (1962) began their monograph with the story of the King who, in order to find out which language children "naturally" spoke, ordered foster mothers and nurses to have limited, impersonal, nonlinguistic contact with the infants in their charge. However "he laboured in vain, because the children all died. For they could not live without the petting and joyful faces and loving words of their foster mothers" (Provence and Lipton,

1962, p. 3). In their study of seventy-five institutionalized babies, Provence and Lipton observed that none of the children learned to find comfort from other people or from soft or hard toys. This deficit proved at least partially irreversible, even after several years in more satisfactory home environments:

> The areas in which there were residual impairments of mild to severe degree were in their capacity for forming emotional relationships, in aspects of control and modulation of impulse, and in areas of thinking and learning that reflect multiple adaptive and defensive capacities and the development of flexibility in thought and action. A lessened capacity for the enjoyment and elaboration of play and an impairment of imagination were also evident [Provence and Lipton, 1962, p. 158].

Gaensbauer (1980) described anaclitic depression in a three-month-old infant suddenly deprived of maternal care, demonstrating how early the need for specialized comfort arises.

Horton and Sharp (1984) presented clinical evidence and reported numerous studies supportive of the idea of a connection between the experience of psychologically internalizable soothing and the acquisition of linguistic competence. Adams-Silvan and Silvan (1988) also demonstrated a relationship between internalizable soothing and meaningful use of language, as well as the ability for empathy. These and many other studies (Horton, 1988a) lead to the conclusion that solacing experiences during infancy and early childhood are developmentally essential.

NORMATIVE STUDIES

In a survey of 144 mothers of public school children (N = 76) and outpatients at a child guidance clinic (N = 68), 97 percent of the subjects were reported by their mothers to have used or to be using a solacing object (Horton and Gewirtz, 1988). A subsequent study of 890 children ranging in age from five through thirteen showed that 99 percent of the sample were currently using a soothing object, activity, or sound. The average number of solacers observed to be used in a twelve-month period was approximately 7. In both studies these were essentially middle-class children residing in central Connecticut.

There are a number of formal studies of transitional object usage which have relevance to the issue of solace-ability in childhood because of the soothing function of the transitional object. However, the notion of the transitional object is too metapsychologically encumbered to lead to consistent findings. It seems that everyone has their own idea or interpretation of what Winnicott meant by "transitional object." Thus, we elected to avoid definitional dispute by focusing on the capacity to be *soothed*, "transitionally" or otherwise. In any case, it appears that frequent solacing object usage in childhood is a ubiquitous and normal occurrence.

NONBORDERLINE PERSONALITY DISORDERS

Studies of adults with severe personality disorders confirm the developmental importance of solacing object attachment not only in childhood but adulthood as well. Horton, Louy, and Coppolillo (1974) demonstrated that none of a group of nineteen severely personality disordered males related transitionally in the present and that only 16 percent had a history of childhood transitional object use. This was in marked contrast to a group of normal controls, 94 percent of whom reported attachment to solacers. Morris, Gunderson, and Zanarini (1986) studied five subgroups including fourteen subjects with nonborderline personality disorders vis-à-vis their use of transitional objects. They concluded: "The most specific and discriminating pattern of transitional object use was, in fact, found in our nonborderline (other personality disorders) axis II sample. . . . This finding is consistent with Horton et al.'s report . . . of the absence of transitional relatedness in an antisocial diagnostic group" (p. 1537).

THE ROLE OF SOLACE IN EMOTIONAL DEVELOPMENT

Feelings may be divided into those which are instinctually based and those which are essentially neocortical in origin (Horton, 1988b). The former are derived principally from the temporal–limbic system. These are feelings such as fear, rage, and sexual appetite. They are demonstrable in the stimulation and ablation experiments of the neurophysiologist. However, the feelings which are usually of greatest interest to us clinically—often because of their absence—and which are of greatest significance culturally are the *positive* feelings exemplified by love, generosity, forgiveness, gratitude, interest, fascination, happiness, awe, joy, bliss, and ecstasy. These are the feelings which separate the psychopath from the creative artist. They appear to arise in the activity of the parietal neocortex of the right hemisphere and are not elicitable in limbic stimulation and ablation studies (Horton, 1988b).

Nowhere is the capacity for solace more crucial than in the development of the positive emotions (Horton, 1988b). The most basic of all of the positive emotions is solace. In its simplest form, observable in the first few weeks of life, it is an emotional response to the optimally agreeable state of the self. With growth and development this feeling comes to embrace elements of the external world leading to love and eventually to other *derivative* positive feelings. We (Horton et al, 1974) said of this ability to soothingly blend aspects of the internal and external worlds:

> [It] take[s] its origin, in part, from the time a child is able to imbue a toy or other concrete object with the life he feels stirring inside of himself. . . . Even as he recognizes that the teddy bear is indeed cloth, stuffing and buttons, he suspends that aspect of reality just enough to permit himself to ascribe to the object those traits and qualities he needs to see in himself at the moment. In this way, *that* teddy bear becomes *his* teddy bear. Unique in the world and irreplaceable, it is the psychological area of the personal universe where the external reality of cloth, stuffing

and buttons becomes inseparably interwoven with the internal life of its owner [p. 621].

As important as the above process is it is just the beginning in terms of the development of positive emotions. The "derivative" (Horton, 1988b) forms of solace are called such because these feelings all contain a solace core which is added to and modified. For example, a primary or near-solace derivative such as peace or happiness adds to or combines with solace certain ideas about oneself, the world, and the goodness of fit between them. Love is an example of a "secondary" derivative and consists subjectively of the feeling of solace blended with instinctual yearnings and desires and is further differentiated by companion ideas—loving ideas about the self, the other, and the relationship between. A comforting feeling of uniqueness or specialness blends solace with aggression and certain ideas about one's place in the world. "Tertiary" derivatives are even further removed from the basic solace core by modifications in feeling and ideas; penance and suffering for a greater purpose are examples of solace blended with painful feelings and ideas in the service of reaching a hoped-for comforting ecstasy. The details of the relationships between solace and its derivatives and to the instincts have been discussed elsewhere (Horton, 1988b). What is underscored here is that the relationship–valuable–facilitating feelings such as love, generosity, forgiveness, a sense of responsibility, and patience *depend* on solace both subjectively and developmentally. To highlight this we can note that a chronically anxious, frightened, enraged person cannot feel and behave in a consistently affectionate, caring, loving, responsible way toward those closest to him, let alone toward those whose only claim on his attention is that of being a fellow human being.

THE BORDERLINE PERSON AND THE ABILITY TO FIND SOLACE

In 1977, using Grinker, Werble, and Drye's (1968) concept of the "borderline syndrome," Horton published a paper showing that borderline persons on the psychotic border could be differentiated from acting out psychopaths by determining whether or not the patient related "transitionally"; that is, was able to find psychological solace in things external. The "pseudopsychopathic" borderline person was shown to be in search of comfort, often tangible and fixated or regressive but nonetheless comfort. The true psychopath, on the other hand, was not only not looking for solace but demonstrated obliviousness to even the possibility that solace might exist.

Following this article, Arkema (1981) studied forty-five hospitalized borderline patients, most of whom were on the personality disorder border, and found that all showed past and present use of transitional objects. Subsequently, Cooper, Perry, Hoke, and Richman (1985) compared borderline, antisocial, and bipolar subjects and found that this borderline group used "more activities for soothing purposes." Morris, Gunderson, and Zanarini (1986) found that their sample of borderlines "had a relatively high level of transitional object usage . . . in line with the previous report by Arkema."

All in all, it appears that borderline patients, whether at the psychotic border or at the personality disorder border use a relatively high number of easily identifiable "transitional objects." This brings us to the issue of the *quality* of transitional object usage shown by borderlines.

BORDERLINE TRANSITIONAL–SOLACING OBJECT USAGE

Before discussing the borderline patient's use of transitional or solacing objects, a few words about the similarities and differences between "transitional" and "solacing" object are necessary. As mentioned earlier, the transitional object concept has become bogged down with disputes over its meaning. It seems that every theorist or researcher who has written on the subject has given his own special emphasis or meaning to Winnicott's idea (Horton, 1988a). I would like to suggest that many of the inconsistencies in the literature (e.g., frequency of transitional object usage by various populations) have to do with how the transitional object is defined. For example, one study of "transitional relatedness" includes transitional "phenomena" (more subtle, less tangible examples of transitional relatedness) whereas, at the other extreme, another study restricts transitional relatedness to the child's first stuffed animal or blanket. In the face of this confusion we (Horton, 1981; Horton and Gewirtz, 1988; Horton, Kreutter, and Gewirtz, 1988) have decided to focus on the principal experiential feature of relationship to a transitional object or phenomenon, that is, its *soothing* quality, and to explore other nontransitional solacing modes as well. Silver, Glassman, and Cardish (1988) have nicely summarized a principal reason for the shift in research strategy we are recommending:

> In our own work with characterologically disturbed patients, we have found it more useful to focus on the psychological experience of being soothed rather then on one of transitional object usage or relatedness, because the former is more readily defined and quantified. A patient, or any adult for that matter, is unlikely to describe his or her experience as one of transitional relatedness (as opposed to, for example, symbiotic relatedness). . . . On the other hand, an adult can usually describe the psychological experience of feeling "better," "soothed," or "comforted," and what strategy was used to achieve this state [p. 110].

Let us turn now to what has been shown about the quality of *borderline* solacing object usage. Modell (1963) was one of the first to explore borderline patients' use of soothing transitional objects and described their "cocoon" transference by which they create a comforting "illusion" of safety. Horton (1977) suggested that characterologically disturbed patients at the psychotic border could be separated from those at the severe personality disorder border by assessment of transitional relatedness; like schizophrenic patients, true borderlines use highly visible, often concrete and tangible age-inappropriate solacers, whereas psychopathic patients do not use transitional objects of any kind.

Arkema (1981) was the first to formally study solacing transitional object usage by borderline patients. Every one of a group of forty-five borderline inpatients reported past and present use of transitional objects. Frequently, this information (about soothers) "appeared spontaneously and always emerged easily" (Arkema, 1981, p. 174). Regarding qualitative issues Arkema stated:

> Generally, they used transitional objects rigidly and maladaptively. They returned repetitively to a potentially soothing world, wrung from it everything they could get, and occasionally, when the transitional object failed them, they experienced rage and demonstrated tantrum-like or self-destructive behavior [p. 175].

More recently, Arkema (1988) has extended his studies of borderline psychopathology to include patterns of bonding in families of borderline patients. It is perhaps significant to note that the frequency and quality of transitional object usage by borderline patients reported in the earlier study (Arkema, 1981) was duplicated in this proband of twenty subjects.

Silver, Glassman, and Cardish (1988) have discussed many of the conceptual and methodological problems existing in the published studies on soothing transitional object usage by borderline patients and have made astute recommendations for future research. These limitations notwithstanding, the collective evidence of the last two decades points strongly, I believe, in the direction of the borderline's difficulties in self-solacing as basic to the disorder. Given that the clinician cannot always wait for the results of elegantly designed prospective studies and must sometimes rely on case report and seasoned clinical judgment, it is suggested that we contemplate some of the treatment implications of the information we now have on the borderline patient's problems in self-soothing.

THERAPEUTIC HURDLES WITH THE BORDERLINE PATIENT

Problems the borderline patient has in finding solace are of several kinds: (1) attachment to inappropriate solacers; (2) narrowness or inadequacy of the solace base; (3) use of paradoxical solacers; (4) use of addictive substances for solace; and (5) reliance on anger for solace. I will discuss each of these in turn.

Attachment to Inappropriate Solacers

Case Example: A physically attractive thirty-two-year old computer sales representative has been attached for several years to a philandering, alcoholic ex-football player who cheats on her and, when drunk, slaps her around. She flies into almost daily rages, accusing him of unfaithfulness—which is true—but her accusations are off-target and she is easily proven wrong. For example, she stews for days about his having had an affair on a recent business trip. Finally, she presents her "evidence"—telephone numbers on his hotel bill. He readily and legitimately explains the telephone calls. With characteristically twisted logic, she "forgives" him completely, initiating another cycle of trust and disillusionment. What she steadfastly refuses to let herself see is that her boyfriend is indeed destructive to her. Following a drunken fight at the airport in which they were both arrested, I began to question her insistence on relying mainly, if not solely, on her antisocial boyfriend for comfort and nurturance. She became frightened at this line of inquiry and broke off treatment.

Many borderline patients become attached to animals—dogs, cats, and horses—for their main solace. These are "inappropriate" solacers because the exclusive attachment to them serves as a barrier and a defense against substantial, reciprocal involvement with adults. A particularly common borderline pattern is that of the "horsewoman"—the woman who, as an adolescent, became attached to horses and never outgrew this dependency. These women dedicate their lives to dominating, training, manipulating, and nurturing their horses. Frequently, these animal addicts become "woods-queer"; that is, think, behave, and feel as they imagine their animals do, further exacerbating their sense of aloneness and isolation.

Narrowness of the Solace Base

Here, the borderline patient relies mainly or exclusively on one solacer which may be lost or disappoint.

> *Case Example:* A single, forty-five-year-old research assistant idealizes and "loves" her remote and distant boss—a confirmed bachelor who has no interest in women in general and none in her in particular. Secretly, she fantasizes about him, that he loves her, will come to her eventually, and that they will live happily ever after. When finally she makes an overture to him he shows disgust and she reacts by overdosing. Her world "collapsed" when she found that he did not care for her; she had put all of her solace-eggs in a romantic-dream basket.

Typically, the borderline patient who has only one or two solacers tends to choose inappropriate solacers as well; all too often, psychotherapists are "loved" exclusively by the primitively idealizing borderline patient.

Use of "Paradoxical" Solacers

These solacers are called paradoxical because few people other than borderlines would find them soothing. Giovacchini (1988) has explored the unconscious reasons why patients find solace in "pain," "traumatic situations," and in "inner agitation" (p. 414). A fairly common example in my experience, referred to by Giovacchini, is that of the adult in his late teens or early twenties who finds his main comfort in painfully loud, raucous, "heavy metal"-type music. While many teenagers listen to such music as a cultural fad—an adolescent passing phase—the borderline patient finds a kind of identity in the auditory-nerve destroying, antisocial screeching and wailing about the virtues of suicide, murder, sadomasochism, and Satanic worship.

Wrist-cutting is another example of a paradoxical solacer; whereas a more normal person might, for example, weep to find comfort, the angry, danger-seeking borderline patient injures herself.

Use of Addictive Substances for Solace

> *Case Example:* A twenty-two-year-old machinist uses pot to reduce tension. He looks like a refugee from the heady sixties—long scruffy hair, a Fu Manchu beard, crude tattoos, and dirty jeans. He beats his wife and abuses his child. Becoming increasingly paranoid, he refuses to stop his pot smoking—it's "the only thing that relaxes [him]."

The use of addictive substances for solace points up the need for a more "overarching" (Grotstein, 1988) concept than transitional relatedness to describe essential borderline psychopathology. As Morris, Gunderson, and Zanarini (1986) have said, "There is a tendency in the literature to reserve the term 'transitional object' for what is viewed as normal development and to apply other terms to objects that are used in pathological ways" (p. 1537). While many solacers used by borderlines are like safety valves or life-savers, that is, they may stand between the patient and suicide, they are not "healthy" or psychologically progressive. Alcohol and drugs may seem to be "necessary" to the borderline—the borderline patient may claim that he "cannot live" without pot—but his use of it may be a case of slow, de facto suicide or of psychological water-treading and thus not "transitional."

Reliance on Anger for Solace

For many borderline patients being angry is a kind of addiction, a prime, if not sole, way of finding comfort. As with all borderline strategies for self-solace, getting angry does not work very well—it is accompanied by anxiety, creates disturbing, even self-destructive situations, and further isolates the patient from potentially more healthy relationships.

Case Example: A thirty-eight-year-old schoolteacher and father of four is chronically angry and short-fused. Over the years he has disrupted virtually every Thanksgiving dinner and family Christmas celebration by "flying off the handle" over imagined slights. After he blows up he sulks and pouts rehearsing the justifications for his behavior. When his mother is present, she tries to mediate and placate the family, reminding them that, "It is just John's way." It is clear that the patient finds a perverse solace in being offended and in retaliating with verbal abuse in the case of adults, and with physical abuse as well if the offender is a child. The angry outbursts occur two or three times a week, suggesting the addict's need for a fix.

THOSE WHO CANNOT BE HELPED

Each of the foregoing delineated problems present special challenges to the therapist. Given our present state of knowledge about the solacing process we must, I think, concede that in some instances we cannot be of much help. The rigid and stubborn patient, exemplified by the thirty-two-year-old woman who was attached to an antisocial man, will not let the therapist or anybody else suggest or bring about change; no substitute is good enough; she clings tenaciously to her destructive source of solace like a drowning person to a life buoy in a stormy sea.

The use of paradoxical solacers such as nerve-damaging rock music may place the patient in an insulator, immune to the therapist's attempts, especially if attachment to the solacer is part of a larger, angry, hostile, paranoid, addictive and destructive life-style. Every therapist should attend at least one "heavy-metal" concert at a local coliseum to gain a full appreciation of the subculture in which many borderline patients are immersed.

Rarely, in my experience, can the psychiatrist compete with the comforting effects of drugs—pot, cocaine, alcohol. While it is true that drug solace is unreliable and not very satisfying, its

effect is immediate—appealing to the borderline's impulsivity—and can be passively achieved. Nothing the therapist offers
can take the place of the comforting drug; nor can the relationship with the doctor become significantly solacing as long as
there is a chemical barrier.

The addiction to tension-reducing anger may also keep the
patient in his or her proud fortress.

> *Case Example:* A sixty-five-year-old borderline patient
> fights with everybody. He gets a little solace from me be-
> cause I am the only person who will listen to his tirades.
> He visits me every week or two, and has been doing so for
> more than a decade. My office is clearly a safe haven for
> him, but he *does not change.* I learned early on that it was
> a mistake to challenge him except in the most indirect,
> subtle way. He had broken off treatment with several pre-
> vious psychiatrists when they had begun to question his
> assumptions and behavior. He wants someone—any-
> one—to share his rage with him, and my willingness to do
> this helps to keep him from experiencing micropsychotic
> episodes with dangerous acting out, and from overusing
> virtually every clinical service at the Veteran's Hospital.

Finally, there is the borderline patient, described by Silver,
Glassman, and Cardish (1988, p. 97), who cannot tolerate the
realization that she is in a solaceless state and who may react to
this jarring insight by quitting treatment or becoming suicidal.

> *Case Example:* A thirty-five-year-old clinical psycholo-
> gist was doing poorly in her practice and hating every
> minute of it. She did not like patients and felt that most
> of them were "stupid" but felt "trapped" in her chosen
> profession. None of her patients cooperated with what
> she saw as her eminently good, but wholly unempathic,
> behaviorally oriented advice, and she spent much of her
> personal therapy time venting her rage at them. Gradu-
> ally, I brought her to the realization that it was *she* who
> needed to change; specifically, to develop a more comfort-
> ing, loving attitude toward others and toward herself. This

was not good news to her, and I was not prepared for the intensity of the negative therapeutic reaction. When she began to see how empty she was when not angry, and how little she gave to others (despite her strident demands for payment), it was more than she could stand. She abruptly terminated treatment with intimations that she might kill herself if "somehow" things did not improve. It was crucial to her self-esteem that she always know more and be in control of others—including me.

SOLACING STRATEGIES AND ISSUES

The treatment of the borderline usually involves the following steps: (1) allowing the patient to express negative feelings; (2) inquiring about sources of solace; (3) helping the patient to see the need for solace and to find appropriate ways of getting it; (4) exploring the patient's way of loving and helping him to move beyond the "teddy-bear" stage.

1. Expressing negative feelings: Typically, the borderline patient enters therapy with a lot of angry, hurt, vindictive, negative feelings. It is difficult to focus on much else until he feels that he has been fully heard. In the worst case scenario the borderline patient may demand that the psychiatrist agree, at least tacitly, with his enraged view of things. (This was the case with the 65-year-old veteran described earlier.) The duration of this phase may range from a few sessions to years. This, of course, can be very psychologically wearing on the psychiatrist. If the doctor starts getting impatient or angry or begins to press too soon for closure on the rage phase, the patient frequently quits treatment or the treatment gets bogged down in a struggle for control.

2. Inquiring about sources of solace. In 1976 I recommended the following steps to be taken in the treatment of severe personality disorder:

1) [T]he therapist must identify the inability to relate transitionally as a core ego deficit; 2) he must interpret this to

the patient, calling on the latter's observation of transitional object usage by others and explain in non-technical language its relevance to the patient's relationships; and 3) he must then help the patient to contemplate various interactions, the outcome of which depends on his ability to experience transitionally or to permit others to do so. The therapist thus *orients* the patient to perhaps the most basic ingredient in human interaction.

This educative approach is attempted in tandem with the therapist's efforts to create a soothing atmosphere. I did not, for example, discuss the adult patients' difficulties without acknowledging their assets. The therapist must constantly scrutinize the transference to eliminate painful, frightening, or hostile distortions of present reality [p. 264].

The job is theoretically a bit easier with the borderline than the nonborderline personality disorder because the former has already demonstrated some capacity for self-soothing however distorted, fixated, regressive, or ineffective. The above prescription requires revision to replace the idea of "transitional relatedness" with the broader idea of solacing-object relatedness as discussed earlier.

I usually employ a solacing methods questionnaire (see appendix, this chapter) to help pin down, for the patient and myself, what her sources of solace are. The questionnaire consists of various objects, activities, and sounds which a cross-section of patients and nonpatients alike have reported using for comfort. There is room for the patient to indicate other solacers as well. Typically, the borderline patient already realizes that there is a problem in the area of self-soothing and immediately expresses interest in how to do it better. About this often preconscious insight Arkema (1988) has commented, "Interestingly, patients sometimes wondered why they had not been asked about these important experiences previously" (p. 126).

3. Helping the patient see the need for solace and to find appropriate ways of getting it. This is the "educative" aspect

referred to above (Horton, 1976). Once I have gotten the patient's attention to his way of solacing himself and have encouraged him to compare and contrast it with how others do it, I explain how the ability to solace oneself fits in with the larger scheme of feelings. I explore with the patient the differences between the instinctual feelings—anger, anxiety, sexual appetite, etc.—and the solace-based feelings (Horton, 1988b). While acknowledging that a certain amount of anxiety, aggression, and sexual desire is normal and necessary, I point out the inverse reciprocity of extreme instinctual affects, such as rage, with the condition of being solaced. If they want to feel better and to live a more rewarding life, I tell them, they need to shift the emphasis in their feelings from hostile–aggressiveness to solace and its derivative feelings.

Sometimes I find it helpful to talk with the patient about the emotional differences between the reptile brain, the lower mammalian brain, and the human brain (Horton, 1988b) suggesting that we have potential for behavior at all three levels and that it is important for us to be able to *choose* which level we will function at.

If the patient requires some chiding to stimulate movement away from the horse–crocodile brain emotional mentality and the pride that sometimes accompanies being able to get angrier than anyone around, I may say something to the effect, "*Anybody* can have a rage attack; it's *easy* to destroy things . . . anybody can get sexually excited—dogs do it; but it's *hard* to be constructive, to build things, to comfort another person; it's even harder to love another person unselfishly." I emphasize the distinction between feelings that are mere *givens* (aggression, anxiety, sexual appetite) and those which must be aspired to (love, generosity, forgiveness, patience, curiosity, happiness, joy, etc.). The more intelligent borderline patient may like the challenge of learning a new way of thinking and feeling and will accept the implied criticism of his behavior if it is proffered in a solacing therapeutic context (see Greben [1988] for a description of the solacing features of the therapeutic setting).

4. Beyond teddy bear love. The borderline patient is typically a "teddy-bear" lover: he loves another person the way a child loves a teddy bear. The child turns to the teddy bear for

comfort when upset, hurt, or frightened. He talks to the bear believing that the bear understands his every utterance and shares his every feeling. When he feels better he throws the teddy bear on the bed or in the closet, comforted by the aware- ness that the bear will be there waiting for him when it is needed again. The bear has no needs, makes no demands, and issues no challenges. This is how the baby viewed the mother—as big and powerful with no needs of her own. About this pattern of loving we (Horton and Sharp, 1984) stated:

> [Borderline patients] use another person regressively, de- mandingly, and exclusively as their primary comforter. All is well as long as the other person can tolerate this one- way relationship. However, when the solacing person eventually wears out emotionally—much as the proverbial teddy bear wears out literally—the borderline person be- comes flooded with anxiety and requires an immediate solace-fix. He or she may then turn relatively indiscrimi- nately to anyone or anything for the needed comfort [p. 182].

The borderline patient who is being encouraged to seek com- fort in new, more varied and mature ways needs to be apprised of the ultimately self-defeating nature of teddy-bear loving. As they seek solace for themselves I point out the necessity of comforting others. This is one of the hardest lessons for border- line patients to learn and the success of the treatment hinges on their ability to grasp this deceptively simple notion. The case of the thirty-five-year-old clinical psychologist, a Ph.D., exemplifies how one can be idea-smart but feeling-dumb.

I recently attended an American Psychiatric Association course on neuropsychology given at the annual meeting. The instructor told a story about a medical student who was failing surgery. The student was given a battery of psychological tests and it was discovered that his verbal IQ—presumably reflecting mainly left-brain activity—was very high. His performance IQ, however, reflecting mainly right-brain activity, placed him nearer the average range of intelligence. The recommendation: Encourage the student to go into psychiatry since he was good with words but not with spatial and visual-motor concepts! It had not occurred to the neuropsychologist to ask about the young doctor's intonative capacities, his communicative competence, his ability to see the emotional woods for the trees—also cardinal functions of the right brain. I tell this story because it exemplifies the tendency even by those who should know better to overemphasize the role of abstract intelligence in human relationships while neglecting the crucial importance of emotional intelligence.

THE PSYCHIATRIST'S ATTITUDE ABOUT SOLACE

There is in fact a prejudice against comforting patients. Greben (1988) has written eloquently of the "resistance" among psychotherapists, "especially psychoanalysts" to the idea "that people not only deserve but require solacing . . . within the therapeutic situation" ([p. 439]; see also Horton [1981, 1988a]). After comprehensively reviewing the ways in which solacing transitional objects come into play in therapy, Greben concludes that it is through the therapist's role as a "solacing figure" that the patient is able to change and mature vis-à-vis psychotherapy (p. 447). Greben is among a growing number of therapists and researchers who are helping to correct the traditional psychotherapeutic neglect of the role of solace in developmental, healing, and maturational processes (Horton, 1988a).

THE DILEMMA: TO SOLACE OR NOT TO SOLACE

If the psychiatrist is able to bring the patient to the point of exploring the nature of solacing love there is at least one more very high hurdle to leap. The experience of reciprocal love is new to the patient—an emotional first. In reality, the borderline patient, as Arkema (1988) has shown, has not been adequately solaced and loved. The solacing psychiatrist becomes a real person to the patient not just an object of transference love.

The psychiatrist himself may come to feel loving and protective toward the patient as though the patient were a cherished family member. In one instance, an older psychiatrist permitted violation of conventional boundaries when he developed "fatherly" feelings toward an adolescent borderline girl. In another case, a psychiatrist assumed the roles of father, uncle, and benefactor in helping a young disadvantaged borderline woman to realize her career potential. In both of these cases the psychiatrists experienced uneasiness about the extent of their involvement in the patients' lives. However, they both elected to compromise professional decorum in an effort to support and protect their patients' continued emotional growth.

Because the borderline patient is new to these powerful solacing and loving feelings and because of her borderline style of relatedness (all-or-nothing, impulsive, etc.) she may seek to express them in concrete, tangible ways toward their apparent source (i.e., her psychiatrist). For example, she may want to give him gifts and to praise him. She may want to learn about his family and his personal habits and interests. She will expect clear signs of reciprocal regard; she may want to use his phone and to be given a ride to a service station when her car battery has gone dead in the parking lot; she may want him to serve as a job reference and to call him by his first name; eventually, she may want to have sex with him. The psychiatrist may begin to wish that he were back dealing with her anger.

Solace is the immediate precursor of love. The infant is solaced and before long—within a few weeks or months—comes to love its primary solacer. This is the natural sequence, solace followed by love. It is probably not possible to share solacing feelings with someone—anyone, patients included—without simultaneously feeling, and stirring up, the first intimations of love.

The borderline patient's tacit complaint of being insufficiently solaced is not mere "splitting" or "manipulativeness." The patient cries out, usually angrily, for comfort and soothing and the sensitive therapist tries to relieve the pain. In reality, he may be the first "good-enough" mother that the patient has ever had.

Loving feelings tend to recruit sexual urges. Unfortunately, the sexuality of the borderline patient is characteristically sadomasochistic—a potentially all-or-nothing maelstrom that may have a hypnotic appeal to the repressed therapist who has become a witness to these volcanic changes. The patient, not having had experience with the whole gamut of positive feelings—a range of feelings which includes the sense of duty, loyalty, and other moral sensibilities—now blends her fledgling positive feelings with familiar aggressive and sexual impulses. The resulting demand is intense and insistent. Indeed, sexual excitement, especially sadomasochistic excitement, is a kind of brain drug, the experience of which soon eclipses solace and its derivative feelings. One cannot be lusting to go down in a vortex of virtual or actual suicidal sexual gratification and simultaneously remain committed to, and know the essentially instinct-free positive feelings which unfold from a solace base. Though the positive feelings—solace, love, happiness, or generosity—do normally coordinate with instinctual activity, the anger-laden, sadomasochism of the borderline is incompatible with the experience of constructive solace and its derivatives.

If the therapist is successful in solacing the patient, while neutralizing or deflecting the sexual surge which accompanies the first solace–love–fascination phase of treatment, he will still not be out of the woods. As the primary and secondary positive feelings unfold and develop, sexual wishes will reemerge, but this time at a more compassionate, tender level. Now, the therapist may find the patient more interesting and trustworthy. He, himself, may not be ready for or accustomed to feelings of awe, passion, and rapture and may begin to think that he has found a new soul mate. However, the therapist is wise to remember that his borderline patient is just beginning to find out about positive feelings and is insecure and weak in their expression. Sexualization of the relationship threatens to bring the positive feeling structure tumbling down and the doctor may be left with a sadomasochistic partner who is disillusioned to boot.

Borderline patients usually invite lesser transgressions than a suicide pact or marriage. However, the experience of shared solace may open an emotional Pandora's Box for the therapist; he may not be ready for the feelings of love which come next in the sequence of unfolding positive feelings. The shared feeling states—love, generosity, curiosity, happiness, joy, etc.—may cause suspension of customary points of view and lead to well-intentioned actions which may be later regretted. In fact, in only one of several cases of therapist–patient sexual involvement, which I have been able to study, were the therapist's motives primarily sexual; he was sued. In the other instances of boundary violations—not motivated by lust—there were no legal ramifications but there was a lasting sense of puzzlement, awkwardness, and torment about "where to draw the line."

In the face of these very considerable obstacles to the successful treatment of borderline patients and the element of personal risk involved, it is understandable that many psychiatrists would simply wish to avoid such patients, referring them to younger colleagues who have "more energy"; or, if one has the temerity or necessity to take such patients on, to do so in a guarded, legalistic way making sure not to let the patient "get to [him]" whether with anger or love. However, the failure to attend to the borderline patient's needs for solace may be as clinically damaging as sexual and other boundary violations.

A great deal of work needs to be done to complete the solace picture of borderline pathology. We are just beginning to collect the kind of data we need to map out the "normal" use of solacing objects and to delineate the connection between solace and other positive feelings. Standardized questionnaires and other formal procedures will help. However, as this chapter may suggest, much additional, intensive clinical research by psychiatrists working from a solacing perspective will be essential to provide a basis for the structuring of meaningful formal research strategies.

APPENDIX

Solacing Methods Questionnaire

Below is a list of some of the methods individuals use to solace, comfort or soothe themselves. You may have used some of these or others. Please check off only the methods you have used *DURING THE PAST YEAR*. Where an item that you have been using does not appear in the list, describe it in the section labeled "OTHER." Check *only* if your use of this object activity or sound was *primarily* for soothing purposes at the time you used it.

1. _____ Another person
2. _____ Sailing
3. _____ Talking to yourself
4. _____ Food
5. _____ Building something
6. _____ Humming
7. _____ Book/s
8. _____ Gift-giving
9. _____ Playing a musical instrument
10. _____ Collections/ (stamps, coins, dolls, etc.)
11. _____ Dancing
12. _____ Singing
13. _____ Crucifix or other religious artifact
14. _____ Listening to music
15. _____ Doll/s
16. _____ Meditating
17. _____ Mantra
18. _____ Prayer/s
19. _____ Artistic activity e.g. painting
20. _____ Crying
21. _____ Good luck charm (rabbit's foot, etc.)
22. _____ Praying
23. _____ Imaginary companion
24. _____ Spending
25. _____ Pet/s
26. _____ Getting ill
27. _____ Drug/s
28. _____ Rocking
29. _____ Poems
30. _____ Writing (poetry, journal, stories, etc.)
31. _____ Religious figure/s (St. Jude, Virgin Mary, etc.)
32. _____ Bicycle riding
33. _____ Walking
34. _____ Stuffed animals
35. _____ Fishing
36. _____ Pillow
37. _____ Exercising so hard that it hurts
38. _____ Gambling
39. _____ Reading

40. _____ Blanket
41. _____ Cuddling
42. _____ Eating too much or the wrong thing
43. _____ Sexual Activities
44. _____ Memories
45. _____ Gardening
46. _____ Taking warm baths or showers
47. _____ Cooking
48. _____ Watching T.V.
49. _____ Talking on the telephone
50. _____ Whistling
Other: _____
       _____

13.

Studies of Borderline Patients in Psychotherapy

John G. Gunderson, M.D.

BACKGROUND

My interest in psychotherapy with borderline patients goes back to the important early years during residency training. The term *borderline* was considered a wastebasket category and it wasn't used much. Nevertheless, each first-year resident had a patient to whom they were deeply attached, with whom they were highly involved and preoccupied, as were the nursing staff that were associated with their treatments. Near the end of that period I did a survey asking fellow residents to describe the nature of those patients. That was the beginning of my interest in the descriptive aspects of borderline personality. In order to study the effective or ineffective treatment of borderline patients, I first had to have a way of identifying the sample. My primary interest, however, remained that of a distraught first-year resident, wondering whether and how such people could be treated.

When I was a resident I also became interested in the psychotherapeutic treatment of schizophrenia. Major teachers in our residency program (and many others) had developed reputations and teaching programs that featured doing dynamically informed psychotherapy with schizophrenic patients. That led to my involvement in a related long-term empirical study (Gunderson, Frank, Katz, Vannicelli, Frosch, and Knapp, 1984; Stanton, Gunderson, Knapp, Frank, Vannicelli, Schnitzer, and Rosenthal, 1984). The field of psychotherapy with borderline patients is now in a very similar state to the field of psychotherapy with schizophrenic patients twenty years ago. Many people now write about intensive, dynamically informed psychotherapy with borderlines. Implicit in most of that literature is the idea that this is the ideal treatment, and that it can be extremely effective if done well. The experience of having done an empirical investigation into the similar claims about psychotherapy with schizophrenic patients taught me a number of lessons. One lesson was that when clinicians talk about treatment (especially long, extensive, highly involved treatments), they will both generalize from the sample of patients that they have seen, which is small, and they will generalize about effectiveness from a case of their own that has done well. That sets a standard in their mind by which they measure what can be done, and by which they measure what their students and colleagues are doing with patients receiving similar diagnoses. There are many hazards in this.

Most of the quite extensive literature about psychotherapy with borderline patients has reflected a dynamic orientation and has implied that more intensive treatments are better. Nevertheless, the experience on which most of this literature is based is suspect, because of the limits of the generalizability from accounts by experts who are seeing relatively small samples, and because of the idiosyncracies of both the patient samples and the therapists' conceptual and clinical backgrounds. An example of this would be Abend, Porder, and Willick's book on psychoanalytic perspectives of borderline patients (1983). The arguments which they build from looking at a very idiosyncratic and nonrepresentative sample are illustrative of some of the problems. They conclude that modern psychoanalysts are underestimating the oedipal conflicts of borderline patients and they suggest that traditional psychoanalysis is, indeed, a good treatment for such patients. Even a relatively naive observer who reads this book will note that the authors used a very narrow range of literature and that the patients that they describe are too healthy to meet any modern criteria set for borderline personality disorder.

Another, less dramatic example comes from Masterson. When Masterson first began to write about treatment of borderline patients, they were hospitalized adolescents, and his accounts of the treatment problems accurately reflect the kinds of things you would see in borderline patients by any kind of modern criteria (Masterson, 1972). Yet Masterson himself has moved from that inpatient setting into an outpatient clinic setting in which he is supervising the work of other people. His most recent writings reflect this change. The patients are getting healthier. The patients he is now writing about would not be considered borderline using DSM-III criteria. He uses the term *borderline* to refer to those people who have severe separation problems and abandonment concerns independent of the associated ego strengths and weaknesses.

Another issue in examining the literature, which confounds generalizability, has to do with the close interface between the personality of the author, the belief systems which they espouse, and the techniques which they employ. The contrast of two prominent psychotherapists for borderline patients is illustrative. Gerald Adler is by his nature reconciliatory. What he emphasizes in his conceptualization of borderline patients is their deficits, and what he emphasizes in his model for their treatment is the need for the therapist to provide a soothing model for introjection (Adler, 1985). That is quite a contrast with Otto Kernberg, who is by his nature challenging. His description of borderline psychopathology emphasizes the marked polarities within such people, and his treatment recommendations emphasize the need for confrontation. What clinicians believe is to some extent a projection of their personalities. That, of course, is true for me, too.

THE ISSUE OF FINDING SUCCESSES

A project that Bob Waldinger and I completed retains many of the problems of generalizability (Waldinger and Gunderson,

1987). It nonetheless offers conclusions about the processes of change which are an advance—you can trust them as being better informed hypotheses than the conclusions the prior reports have reached. We started out by seeking dynamically treated cases that had gone particularly well. These proved not so easy to find. Despite the enormous amount of staff experience in doing intensive analytically informed psychotherapy with borderline patients at McLean Hospital, relatively few people could confidently point to a case that they had seen from beginning to end in a continuous therapy where they felt the patient had had a dramatic resolution of character pathology. That would have been very surprising to me if I had not already gone through a similar process with respect to psychotherapy with schizophrenic patients. There, too, many clinicians made their living from this type of work. Yet, when you get down to actual cases, despite their obvious investment and intense involvement, few clinicians could claim to have seen a patient through to a dramatic resolution of their psychopathology. We found about eight or nine cases, and of those we could get access to five for the purposes of writing them up. Some problems encountered were: one therapist didn't want to write up a case under circumstances where the patient might reappear; a second therapist hadn't seen the patient for some years and felt it could be destructive to get in touch with her; and another therapist didn't know how to reach the patient. (One needs to get in touch with the patient to get his or her consent.) After the therapists wrote up the case reports, and independent of our ratings of these reports, we asked the patients to review and make any corrections to them.

THE ISSUE OF NATURAL COURSE VS. THERAPY EFFECTS

The successful therapies were never less than once a week when patients were in therapy, and never more than four times a week. On balance, most patients were seen about twice a week throughout the period of their treatment. The durations of the treatment were a minimum of four years and a maximum of seven.

The usual length of more definitive treatment effects raises an interesting methodological problem. When you study long-term treatments, you have to differentiate change that is part of the natural course from change due to treatment. There have been multiple studies which have been done on the three- to seven-year course of borderline patients. Those studies have shown that over these periods of time borderline patients generally do poorly. For example, they continue to be in and out of hospitals, their relationships remain very intense and unstable, self-destructive acts are recurrent, they remain depressed. There are exceptions, of course; nevertheless, such studies provided some framework against which to evaluate case reports. If a borderline patient does dramatically well in this period, there is a good chance it is a treatment effect—it is not the usual or expected course.

The five therapists had all been in psychoanalytic training at the time these treatments were undertaken, or had recently completed it. The youngest therapist was a year or two out of residency and the oldest was about eight to ten years out of residency when these cases were initiated. This, in itself, raised a question in my mind as to whether there isn't an optimal phase of professional development during which people have the motivation—the enthusiasm and the optimism—to undertake and persevere in such treatments. I'll return to that question.

The patients themselves were all young adults. The youngest began treatment at nineteen, the oldest at twenty-six. All of them were unemployed and/or school dropouts; all were alienated from their families; all of them met both diagnostic interview of borderlines (DIB) and *Diagnostic and Statistical Manual of Mental Disorders* (1980) (DSM-III) criteria for borderline personality disorder (BPD). The patients were not representative in some respects. This was a brighter than usual group of patients and none of the five was extremely impulse-ridden, although all were self-destructive, and three abused substances.

THE ISSUE OF DROPOUTS

The five patients in this study were also exceptions insofar as they remained in a long-term course of psychotherapy, quite aside from the fact that they allegedly had good outcomes. An extraordinary fact about the literature on psychotherapy with borderline patients is that although there have been many books and papers written on the subject, there is not a word in any of them about dropping out. Yet, in the first empirical examination, Skodal, Buckley, and Charles (1983) showed that two-thirds of the borderline sample dropped out within three months. With other coworkers I have recently completed another naturalistic study (Gunderson, Frank, Ronningstam, Wachter, Lynch, and Wolf, 1989). In both outpatient clinic and our inpatient setting we found somewhat better but still very sobering results. Amongst inpatients at McLean Hospital, about 40 to 50 percent will drop out within six months. About half of them drop out because of impasses with the therapist (they find the therapist cruel and/or misunderstanding, so they leave angrily). Some of the other dropouts leave because of lack of support once they get out of the hospital. Their families, who were ostensibly in favor of therapy, become rather passive if not overtly antagonistic to its continuation. That presents both financial and logistical obstacles to continuing. A third subgroup of dropouts were people who were poor candidates for psychotherapy from the beginning. They had serious antisocial features and their motivation was never good. They were never really interested in self-examination or saw themselves as having serious problems, and hence treatment failure was almost predictable for that group.

When I first reported on the frequency with which borderline patients drop out of psychotherapy, Kernberg was initially skeptical because his own patients had not dropped out in any large numbers. But then when he and his colleagues started to look at the issue systematically, they also found a very high frequency of borderline patients dropping out of treatment. As a consequence, Kernberg (Kernberg, Selzer, Koenigsberg, Carr, and Appelbaum, 1989) now emphasizes the importance of setting up a contract before starting any psychotherapy with borderline patients. Contracts simply put into a more formal, operationalized form the need to educate borderline patients about what to expect and what not to expect, and set up advance provisions for dealing with crises. This depersonalizes the conditions of therapy—they are less apt to be experienced as cruel or thoughtless. In the midst of crises, the things therapists do can seem awful, but if patients have been prepared and know why this is being done, that it isn't simply the therapist's angry reaction to them, they are more likely to accept and learn from the limits or other interventions.

It is again worth noting that the patients in our small sample whose course of treatment we examined cannot easily be generalized from. What you can generalize from is the more common experience that if you often undertake treatment with borderline patients, you often get dropped. Therapists in this situation can experience a profound sense of discouragement or guilt. Guilt that you have behaved poorly is aggravated when borderline patients fire you with vehemence, and with personal accusations about your failures. Sometimes there is just enough truth in the accusation so that it cannot easily be discounted. We are usually a part of a "bucket brigade" for such patients. Many borderline patients go from one therapist to another to another, all of whom are left feeling disheartened, and most of whom are left feeling like they failed. It is easy to lose sight of the fact that borderline patients may use such people in very constructive and important ways. Therapists rarely get the satisfaction of knowing that they helped the recently departed borderline patient survive a crisis which might otherwise have resulted in self-destructive or suicidal behavior. Longer-term follow-up studies show that by the time they are in their mid-thirties a good number of these dissatisfied patients will be doing fine—certainly much better than when you typically see them in their early twenties. A significant fraction of borderline people achieve a steady job, a place to live, no longer go in and out of hospitals, and have steady relationships. Dr. Paris' follow-up on borderline patients with variable intelligence and modest socioeconomic assets suggests that such good "outcomes" don't seem to be related very much to their treatment experience (Paris, Brown, and Nowlis, 1987). If that is sobering, it is also encouraging. It confirms that those therapists who have been dropped may still be doing something very important if they just help the borderline patients stay alive and allow natural developmental processes to occur.

THE PATTERNS OF CHANGE

Year 1

The first year of treatment was primarily marked by a broad range of acting out activities. The most noteworthy of these were, of course, self-endangering acts which required sustained hospitalizations in two instances and short-term hospitalizations in two others. For patients who were outside the hospital, the involvement of their significant others was required by the therapists. Limits were set on a variety of behaviors such as absences from treatment, unpaid bills, and failures to relate meaningful content in the sessions. In all instances but one, the patients initiated a pattern of contacting their therapist between sessions on an unscheduled basis. Another feature of the first year of treatment was that all five patients relied heavily upon the defensive use of externalizing their problems and devaluing both previous caregivers as well as their present therapist. This was also a period in which rapid fluctuations were seen in their view of the therapist and of themselves. Therapists were generally seen as powerful people who were beseeched to provide care and nurturance or, alternately, they were seen as cruelly withholding and denounced for this. The significant power consistently attributed to the therapist was also accompanied by significant levels of distrust as to their genuineness, care, and ability to be useful. While the clearly distrustful aspects were evident, the hopefulness which sustained them in treatment was usually covert. They didn't speak about that, but you could infer that they had to have some hope, otherwise they would not have continued. This can be a difficult perspective to bear in mind when you are weathering this phase of treatment.

Year 2

Year 2 saw a continuation of significant acting out problems, including ongoing self-destructive behavior in four cases. For

the two patients who had previously been protected by prolonged hospitalizations, there were measurably increased instances of action problems (e.g., bill payment, attendance, and
substance abuse) once they left the hospital. All five patients
continued to explore the boundaries of the treatment by either
extratherapeutic contacts or within-therapy behaviors which
tested the limits of the therapist's tolerance for either their
defiance or for their demands for care. In three instances,
meetings with the patients' families were instituted by the therapist to help sustain the patients in treatment. As noted in our
study of dropouts, the failure of therapists to involve and solicit
the support by significant others is an important factor in treatment failure. The second year was accompanied by a diminished craving for actual love or nurturance, but was associated
with more explicit acknowledgment of the patient's dependence upon the therapist. Therapists continued to manage separation by scheduled contacts or the provision of substitute
interim therapists. The second year witnessed a clear improvement in role performance. Within therapy, there was a notable
increase in the willingness of the patients to talk voluntarily
about important issues and to utilize memories and dreams.
All the patients returned to stable, albeit low-level employment
during this second year. The nature of this employment usually
involved routine tasks rather than those expanding or testing
intellectual or social abilities.

Year 3

In Year 3 there was a continued diminution in the severity and
frequency of acting out behaviors, but a continued and perhaps
even intensified level of testing within sessions. At this time,
the sessions themselves remained largely preoccupied with an
examination of the patient–therapist interactions, with increasing attention being paid to the indirect expressions of anger.
Therapists were more active in interpreting the sadistic and
controlling motives behind manipulative and self-destructive
acts. In most instances, the patients were able to accept and
own some of their sadism. By the end of the third year, all but
one of the patients were comfortably expressing their anger

quite directly at the therapist for both those limitations inherent in the therapeutic relationship and for the real failures in attention, reliability, or understanding. By this time, the patients had established a relationship with their therapists in which a rudimentary trust was evident, based on the belief that the therapist was interested in them and based on their therapist's usual reliability and consistency.

Year 4

By Year 4 there were only rare instances of acting out which necessitated interventions beyond interpretations. There were only rare instances of limits being set on behaviors within or outside the therapy, and no use of either hospitalizations, family meetings, or medications. Absences by the therapist were now managed without substitutions, and, with few exceptions, without recourse to phone contacts. The patients now consistently saw their therapists as people who really cared about them, and it was possible to identify a stable, collaborative working alliance. An expression of this was the emergence of humor in the exchanges between patients and therapists. Outside of therapy the fourth year was a time when, in most cases, friendships became a significant part of the patients' lives, often of a quality which was more stable and intimate than ever before. This was also a time at which a second incremental advance occurred in the employment of the five patients. There was some variation in this from the third to fifth year, but the patients shifted from the stable, low-level vocational tasks they had been involved in, into vocational situations which were oriented toward the possibilities of advancement and long-term satisfaction. Indeed, their performance at work now was equal or superior to that at any time in their past histories. These shifts in the patients' orientation toward their future and in their views of the therapists as caring, reflected underlying shifts in the patients' views of themselves as worthwhile. There was a clear diminution in the fluctuating views of themselves and their therapists which had been evident earlier.

Year 5+

In the years following the initial four, a gradual increase in the interest in and quality of heterosexual relationships was evident. In some instances this became an explicit and major focus within the transference, whereas in other instances the patients terminated without this being worked through as a transference issue. It is safe to say that the latter terminations were associated with their having established a stable heterosexual relationship and it was difficult for the therapists to tease apart the degree to which this change reflected what they had learned, or was an enactment of transference which was adaptively "too good" to be interpreted. During these later years, the patients could openly express feelings of a caring, positive nature toward their therapist. It was only in these years that they could and did feel guilty and concerned about either past or present transgressions toward the therapist. In addition, in three cases more attention came to be focused on what might be considered issues related to grandiosity. Their more grandiose self representations were evident in beliefs about how special they believed themselves to have always been to the therapist, and/or were evident in their ongoing sense of responsibility for things which were outside their influence. In short, it can be said that as pervasive and characteristic as the anger was in the early years of treatment, during these later years a positive ambience pervaded the treatment. There were still some identity diffusion problems, clear in one patient, and possibly in a second. One of the patients remained very angry but was very adaptive in other respects.

THE QUALITY OF OUTCOME

At the end of the five years of therapy, there was very little evidence of the features of borderline psychopathology by which the diagnosis might be made. According to either DIB or DSM-III criteria, none of the patients would have fulfilled those or come close to fulfilling them (see Table 13.1). They felt generally good about themselves and their functional roles

TABLE 13.1
Number of the Five Patients Rated as Meeting Criteria

DSM-III Criteria	Baseline	Outcome
1. Impulsivity or unpredictability	3	1*
2. Unstable and intense interpersonal relationships	4	0
3. Inappropriate, intense anger	4	0
4. Identity disturbance	4	1*
5. Affective instability	4	1
6. Intolerance of being alone	5	1
7. Physically self-damaging acts	4	0
8. Chronic emptiness or boredom	4	2*

*The persistence of the criterion was questionable in these instances, i.e., they may be false positives.

were stable. They all had achieved stable relationships and they were no longer self-destructive or impulsive. These changes, then, seem to reflect that basic resolution or modification had occurred in the psychopathology of this group of patients. By Kernberg's criteria (1975), there were no problems in reality testing, and the reliance on typical primitive defenses (in particular, the use of projection or splitting) were largely absent. There were, however, some identity problems, as I noted, in several of the patients.

Again, we cannot say for sure that these changes were due to the therapy these patients received, yet the changes were sufficiently tied to an intense therapeutic process and were sufficiently consistent across cases that they provide at least face validity for the argument that an intensive, well-informed psychotherapy can bring about major character change in borderline patients.

ASSESSING PROGRESS AND COUNTERTRANSFERENCE

The clinical implication from this study that I use most often in daily work has to do with the indices of change that the clinician should look for in the course of treatment; namely, at what point the clinician should conclude that something is going wrong, or at what point impatience or discouragement should be viewed as countertransference problems. An example occurred just this week: after a year in therapy, I could not speak to my patient, Hazel, without her responding with an abusive outburst. This wasn't psychotherapy; I couldn't even speak. She could see I was discouraged and I, in turn, acknowledged this. I said I didn't feel that this was very useful, and she said she couldn't agree more; it was not only not useful, it was really distasteful! I suggested that we get a consultation, and Hazel immediately agreed to it, but she also became a bit alarmed. She then called before the next appointment to say she wasn't coming. I indicated that the consultation had already been started and suggested that she come for her session to discuss it. She came. The consultation had really begun when I noticed my impatience and my discouragement. When I stood back from this and considered what, with reference to these particularly successful cases, it was realistic to expect from her, this was helpful. My impatience derived from expecting her to collaborate in terms of examining her acting out behaviors. As an analytic therapist I felt that such examining was what I was being paid for, what I was good at, and what I liked to do. It was easy to lose sight of the fact that behaviorally she was generally doing much better and to infer that she was under a lot of added stress from recently resuming school. Rather than actively supporting her I was getting preoccupied with the fact that she would not/could not look at herself with me. That kind of alliance wasn't realistic even in cases that go well.

Another side of the guideline for assessing progress offered by the study is also illustrated by Hazel. If the patient hadn't shown some change in the first index of change (i.e., diminution in self-destructive behavior by the end of a year), that ought to cause discouragement. Failure to see that change is quite likely to be a signal that there is something wrong within the therapy. If in the second year of treatment a patient has not formed a more positive dependency upon the therapist, that too is a signal that something has gone wrong. Hazel, for instance, was and remains very dependent on me but she does not acknowledge it and possibly does not even recognize this. That will change, I would hope, during the course of the next year or so; she should become more open, more comfortable in acknowledging what is already clearly there, and when this takes place, she should be freer to talk about what frightens her so much about a separation. There is a movement, then, from a sort of counterdependency (a negation of dependency) into its more open acknowledgment, that makes it much more workable within the therapy. That is the second index of change that emerges from one study of successes, which is often very helpful clinically.

A third implication concerns the work on negative transference. Productive, sustained work on negative transference really didn't occur early in the treatments. From Kernberg, one gets the sense that such work can and should start early (Kernberg, 1975, 1984). Early in the treatment you sometimes do need to be able to identify and confront borderline patients about negative transference behaviors. For example, "You know, it worries me that a reason that you say you want to cut your wrists is because you'd like to see me suffer on account of it." That would be a good interpretation in the first year. I'd probably even cushion it by indicating that I would not expect the patient to agree with me. It is not negative transference work; it is simply drawing out into the open something that was already there and would otherwise have been more likely to be acted upon. I think Kernberg is right about the value of identifying that kind of issue with some borderline patients early on. But for sustained negative transference work, a reliable, stable relationship is essential, one in which the patient has already come to count on the clinician's commitment and durability. Then the patient's experimentation with expressions of negative transference can be more openly experienced and owned, and can have corrective significance for them. That is because they learn that the therapist doesn't disappear and doesn't retaliate as a result of their being angry at him. To be angry at the clinician when they don't rely on his presence the next week and whose resilience they are testing, is just water off a duck's back so far as such corrective changes are concerned.

Let me close by returning to an issue that I mentioned earlier (p. 295), that has to do with the professional development of therapists. Looking back after writing up these successful cases, the therapists often felt that if they had known when they were treating the patient, what they know now, they would have done things differently. Four therapists would have been more confrontative and set limits more rapidly, and they would have been more interpretive about negative transference. They learned about those things as they went along with these patients. On the other hand, with the exception of one of the five, none of them could point to subsequent cases that they treated successfully. That one was the therapist who learned by experience to become more supportive. I think there may be several lessons in that. First of all, not only is it possible, but I think it is often desirable to switch from more supportive techniques early in the treatment toward more exploratory, more interpretive techniques as therapy goes along. I recognize that is in contrast to what Kernberg has written about the dangers of trying to shift from more supportive to more exploratory methods. I think that the failure to make such shifts may lead to what Kernberg refers to as negative therapeutic reactions, and, hence, more premature dropouts than are necessary.

CONCLUSION

This paper has attempted to place psychotherapeutic work with borderline patients into some historical and scientific perspective. Even the modest studies on dropouts and successful cases that I have described offer significant revisions to existing beliefs. The modesty of these studies precludes strong credibility for the results. Nonetheless, they dramatically underscore the imposing logistical problems of such empirical efforts and their possibly imposing clinical importance. I hope, and I believe, that more definitive research on the effects of psychotherapy with borderline patients will further clarify its role, its benefits, and its limits.

14.

The Borderline Patient: Psychotherapeutic Stalemates

Joshua Levy, Ph.D., C.Psych.

After listening for a while to my informal presentation on "Psychotherapeutic Stalemates," a seasoned and feisty colleague commented: "Is there any other kind?" This spontaneous and rhetorical question was meant to highlight the frequency with which we are mentally prepared to encounter stalemates in our current clinical practice with characterologically difficult patients. Furthermore, the affects that accompanied my colleague's comment indicated the psychic pain and agony that therapeutic stalemates rekindled in the therapist (Kernberg, 1977b; Silver, Cardish, and Glassman, 1987; Robbins, 1988; Gunderson, Chapter 13).

The signs of the impasse or treatment that has become bogged down, have been recognized for a long time, and every student of psychotherapy has experienced them during his or her training. Therefore we would have expected voluminous literature that would enlighten us in understanding and coping with this troublesome outcome. But on the whole, the literature on psychotherapeutic stalemates has remained disjointed and piecemeal. We find many articles that concentrate mainly on relatively general, abstract, and theoretical issues. Bellak (1981) touched briefly on a host of factors that could contribute to this therapeutic outcome. He also offered some general suggestions as to how to resolve it. In the literature on psychotherapy supervision, there are numerous references to stalemates, but they lack detailed clinical data; without this data the essence of the therapeutic interactions that contributed to the stalemate are missing. As an exception to this general trend, I would like to single out Saretsky, Fromm, Bernstein, Wong, and Bernstein (1981) who presented the kind of psychotherapeutic interactions that address some of the specific reasons that produce stalemates and their attempted resolutions. Congruent with my emphasis on the psychotherapeutic interactions in depth, Saretsky and his collaborators focused on the subtleties of the destructive transference–countertransference binds that result in pathological interactional patterns and offer us constructive solutions (see also Levy [1985]).

I shall rely mainly on detailed clinical material, based on one case study, to outline the specific dynamics in therapist–patient interactions that produced the stalemate, and the particular kind of consultation that facilitated its resolution. Although only one case, it nevertheless contains, in my experience, recurrent themes underlying therapeutic stalemates, and it highlights typical struggles that patients and therapists go through in long-term therapy with the characterologically difficult patient. By illustrating both the nature of the therapeutic stalemate as well as outlining a method that facilitates the resumption of the therapeutic movement, the readers will have the opportunity to evaluate the clinical material, and draw their own conclusions as to the phenomenon of stalemates, its dynamics, and possible resolutions. No one illustration can shed sufficient light on this complex phenomenon. The readers may, justifiably, be left dissatisfied. However, each therapist has material on only a small number of detailed cases regarding stalemates. Therefore by putting together our accumulated knowledge, we may arrive at a better integration of the clinical data and its theoretical underpinning, in order to find ways to facilitate the resolutions of these recurrent therapeutic outcomes.

THE CHARACTERISTICS OF THE THERAPEUTIC STALEMATE

While in the midst of a therapeutic stalemate, an introspective and articulate patient said: "I feel like one of those small hamsters stuck in a cage and running inside a wheel that spins with great speed but is always in the same spot" (Maldonaldo, 1984, p. 264). Though the patient intended only to present his own conscious internal experience during the therapeutic stalemate, he at the same time highlighted his correct perception of his therapist's complementary internal experiences. He thus captured vividly a therapeutic couple locked in automatic, repetitive therapeutic interactions that are extremely boring and lead nowhere. The expected freshness and dynamics that accompany at least some of the therapeutic explorations have gone completely stale. Understandably, both therapist and patient who are involved in the therapeutic stalemate experience paralysis, psychic pain, struggle with intense conflicts over anger, frustration, guilt, depression, and even despair.

The stalemate period may take place at any stage of the treatment. The length of this period may vary. What is characteristic of this period is that the therapist's interventions, based on what he considers to be proper understanding of the patient's history and psychodynamics, result in disappointments to both parties. There may be no movement, or even deterioration. This is a stalemate at its extreme. For this reason the therapeutic stalemate should be regarded as a warning signal to the therapist: "Handle with care or you are going to have a serious crisis on your hands."

The stalemate period may be an indicator that both parties have proceeded as far as they can go at that point. If the termination for this patient is achieved by mutual agreement, with a proper working through, the patient may return for further treatment at a later date either to the same therapist or to another one. However, the intense emotions experienced by both therapist and patient may result in abrupt and premature termination of treatment, to the detriment of both. Quite often, however, both the therapist and the patient share the wish to continue treatment. They can discuss the situation quite openly and decide to seek consultation. This will be illustrated in my clinical material.

THE DYNAMICS OF PSYCHOTHERAPEUTIC STALEMATES

While clinicians seem to agree on what are the overt manifestations of psychotherapeutic stalemates, there is a divergence of viewpoints regarding their psychodynamic understanding. For a general orientation, I shall propose to classify these viewpoints along a continuum. It will range on the one hand from those who emphasize the patient's intrapsychic structures as the primary factors leading to stalemates. On the other hand it will extend to those who stress that the psychotherapeutic stalemates are primarily the byproducts of the patient's reactions to incorrect psychotherapeutic interventions. Somewhere in the middle, there are those who hold the viewpoint that psychotherapeutic stalemates (PS) are the products of the interactional outcome between intrapsychic factors of both therapist and patient.

Freud emphasized the patient's intrapsychic factors as the source for PS. The Wolf Man (Freud, 1918), one of Freud's more significant and celebrated case histories, would qualify as a classical case of psychotherapeutic stalemate. At one point in the treatment, Freud's patient became preoccupied with his symptoms and repetitively brought up the same associations and complaints. After many failed attempts on Freud's part to get the treatment moving again, he became irritated with his patient. He interpreted the stalemate as stemming from the patient's attempts to paralyze the therapeutic process because of his very early traumas and pregenital fixations. Indeed, from our current perspectives, the Wolf Man's early development and symptoms may place him squarely within the borderline character pathology (Blum, 1974). Therefore, a period (or periods) of PS would not be unexpected in his treatment.

Freud later (1923, 1937) identified a certain group of vulnerable patients who because of intrapsychic factors tended to reach not only stalemates but negative therapeutic reactions.

Their response to correct interpretations was further deterioration and worsening of their psychological conditions (for recent critical reviews of negative therapeutic reactions, see Gorney [1979]; Levy [1982]; Lane [1984]). Freud did not clarify the distinctions between stalemates and negative therapeutic reactions. For this reason, subsequent authors tended to regard the two outcomes as synonymous and interchangeable. I have found it helpful and clarifying to distinguish between them. The negative therapeutic reaction by definition involves a period of stalemate and deterioration. In contrast, stalemate is not necessarily a negative therapeutic reaction, because it may not involve deterioration in the patient's psychic condition. The stalemate is a period of no therapeutic movement. It may escalate into worsening of the patient's condition depending in part on the therapist's understanding and response to the patient.

Segal (1964) and Riesenberg Malcolm (1980–1981), associates of Melanie Klein (1957), represent those who emphasized the patient's psychopathology as the primary factor in paralyzing the therapeutic situation. "Unconscious envy," for example, was regarded by them as the major determinant that produced psychotherapeutic stalemates. They argued that good and effective interpretations were repeatedly destroyed by a certain group of patients, rendering the interpretations useless. This paralyzed the therapeutic process and brought it to a standstill or even dragged it downhill. These writers stressed that particularly after good sessions, certain patients tended to feel fragmented, confused, and severely attacked from within.

In contrast to the emphasis on intrapsychic factors that produce psychotherapeutic stalemates, some self psychologists have concentrated on an entirely different approach. Kohut (1971) and particularly some of those who continued to develop his ideas such as Stolorow, Brandchaft, and Atwood (Brandchaft, 1983; Stolorow, Brandchaft, and Atwood, 1987) have found that the therapist who tended to focus on intrapsychic factors, such as innate aggression and envy, would in all likelihood be, unknowingly, the major contributor to the paralysis of treatment. They stated that these therapists failed to comprehend the essence of the patient's transference needs and therefore their interpretations constituted "empathic failures." The therapist, by his continued misunderstanding of the patient's needs, repeatedly inflicted narcissistic injuries and was responsible for the therapeutic stalemate.

Thus there are two perspectives: those who emphasize the patient's psychopathology as the motivational forces for PS; and representatives of self psychology who concentrated primarily on the therapist's contributions to this therapeutic outcome. I would like to suggest that a basic similarity exists between these two approaches. What is common is that they both place primary emphasis on intrapsychic factors and structures; one stressed those of the patients and the other those of the therapists. Both tend to give insufficient attention to the specific interactions in depth between the personality dynamics of the therapeutic dyad. I would like to suggest that potentially the most fertile treatment context for the development of the therapeutic stalemates is when the patient's specific transference needs that represent aspects of his early traumatic experiences reactivate in the therapist his own unresolved conflicts. Under these circumstances, the therapist may have to struggle to maintain his general level of adequate functioning in the therapeutic situation. The therapist's responses, after processing the enormous emotional pressure that is exerted on him, would make the difference between potential and actual PS. The implications of this suggestion are broad. It opens the way to studying how the personalities of the therapist and his patient are reciprocally affecting each other. Levy and Epstein (1964) presented a method for investigating the sequences of overt and covert, step-by-step interactions between personalities and the various outcomes of these interactions, including "developmental stalemate," of the child within the family. In the process of this investigation, we specified how aspects of each participant's psychopathology are consciously and unconsciously communicated and responded to by the other members, and the results of these communications on their psychological functioning. One finding that is especially relevant to PS is that the individual's unresolved emotional conflicts exert specific emotional pressure on the individual with whom he is in close emotional contact. This may stimulate his own unresolved developmental conflicts and mobilize lower level defense mechanisms.

Characterologically difficult patients may exert intense emotional demands on the therapist, specifically when their regressive powerful transference needs are revived in the treatment. In those periods, their emotional demands can tax the therapeutic capacity of the vast majority of therapists and may bring out intense personal struggles within the therapist himself. The therapist must process his responses so that his contributions will not aggravate the therapeutic situation. Despite the efforts of the competent therapist, when a stalemate has been reached, it is likely that the treatment touches on the patient's rock-bottom defenses (Freud, 1937), which may signal the limits to benefits from therapy for these patients. As well, it may signify the limits and limitations of the therapeutic couple. Guntrip (1968) stressed that PS, for the schizoid personality, are inherent in his intrapsychic structure, which is expressed in the treatment by recurrent, inherent, and inevitable impasses that bring about premature disruption.

Therefore the therapist's contributions to stalemates, regardless of the patient's psychopathology, must be carefully considered and assessed at all times. Under the emotional difficulties described, these particular dynamics and sensitivity may promote, unknowingly, less than optimum therapeutic conditions. Freud has given less than adequate weight to the therapist's countertransference contributions to PS.

Let us concentrate for the moment on the patient's affective expressions that are known to contribute significantly to PS. Among those repetitive and automatic reactions, we may include stormy and violent affective expressions (experienced by the therapist as "too much, too fast"), such as relentless attacks and depreciations ("you are incompetent, phoney, masquerading as a therapist"); cold, sadistic rejections of the therapist as a person in the form of denying ever having established any relationship with him because of the therapist's "personality" and "body language"; overly polite and silent patients who insidiously and repetitively complain about their symptoms; and varieties of sexual seductions. Although these patients' reactions (labeled as "transference resistances") are part and parcel of what one would expect from the difficult patient, they nevertheless are most likely to affect the therapist's personality and lower his therapeutic efficacy. The ensuing interactions may result in transference–countertransference binds as others have amply demonstrated and applied to the therapeutic situations (Langs, 1976; Gorney, 1979; Saretsky et al., 1981).

Freud (1914), Loewald (1971), and Giovacchini and Boyer (1975) suggested a way of conceptualizing and intervening in the therapeutic situation in order to keep the therapeutic momentum. They emphasized that these repetitive and automatic modes of relating to the therapist are unconsciously attempts to relive and reenact in the transference infantile traumatic experiences. Unconscious forces that are reactivated in the therapeutic situation compel the patient to recreate infantile helplessness and rage, with the tacit hope of receiving appropriate therapeutic interventions that would bring these forces under the patient's ego organization. Therefore, the therapist's awareness of the patient's conscious and unconscious impact on him becomes crucial in lessening potential therapeutic stalemates. However, by consciously and unconsciously colluding with the patient and resorting to an automatic and repetitive line of interpretation that mirrors and reacts in kind to the patient's affective expressions, the therapist and patient jointly set up the fertile ground for the impasse. This type of therapeutic stalemate is exemplified by Riviere (1936), who over fifty years ago sounded a warning signal to the therapist that is still valid and worth emphasizing. She described a group of patients who needed to rely heavily on denial of their "psychic reality" and their therapists, who automatically and consistently (and relentlessly, as experienced by the patient) confronted them with their defense of denial and other primitive defenses. These repeated interactions not only brought the treatments to a standstill but the patient's psychic condition deteriorated. Riviere concluded that the therapist's insufficient understanding of his patient's psychic reality resulted in traumatizing of the patient by incorrect responses to the patient's tacit signals and intense needs.

RESOLVING PSYCHOTHERAPEUTIC STALEMATES

Let us return to Freud's Wolf Man (Freud, 1918) to discuss how he dealt with his psychotherapeutic stalemate. In its midst, he felt hopeless and emotionally exhausted, and was convinced that the patient had paralyzed the treatment process, and that no interpretive effort on his part would have remobilized it. He saw no point in continuing the treatment, and therefore he issued an ultimatum to the patient, by setting a time limit for the termination of the treatment. The patient soon realized that Freud was in earnest, and once more began to produce the clinical material that Freud expected of him. This allowed Freud to resume the treatment. However, twenty years later (1937), Freud reviewed this case, and was skeptical of utilizing a termination date as a standard technique for overcoming therapeutic stalemates. Yet, how many therapists since Freud have relied on ultimatum techniques as a method for "resolving" the psychic pain that is so characteristic of this therapeutic outcome? Unfortunately, it is still a fairly common, but clandestine solution to stalemates, because no therapist is proud of resorting to it. Freud did not present his clinical material to a consultant. Had he done so, the consultation would probably have brought out not only the patient's contributions to the stalemate, but also how Freud's overt interpretations and unconscious messages colluded with the patient's psychopathology to paralyze the process. Freud did not give sufficient weight to his own countertransference influence on the treatment and its share in the stalemate. Consultation has since become a well-accepted and frequently used method that facilitates the resolution of psychotherapeutic stalemates (Silver, unpublished).

The role of these consultations is to scrutinize the clinical material in order to discern the factors that produced PS. Numerous interrelated issues must be examined. These include: the patient's history; the dynamic hypothesis that guided the treatment (whether the techniques and therapist's interventions were adapted to the patient's personality); how unconscious processes—in both therapist and patient—affected the treatment processes; the degree to which transference manifestations influenced the interventions; whether specific therapist's interpretations interfered with the treatment progress; and when the stalemate became apparent.

Rosenfeld (1987) in his comprehensive book, *Impasse and Interpretation*, pointed to a number of factors that interlock to produce an impasse. He demonstrated how the therapist specifically colluded with his patients, which resulted in the therapist acting out what was assigned to him by the patient. Being absorbed and overwhelmed by these powerful and unconscious forces, the therapist misunderstood the patient, became distant, lost his emotional contact and relied on intellectual interpretations. Rosenfeld's consultations aimed at bringing out the essential factors that led to this outcome.

In "The 'Bogged Down' Treatment: A Remedy," Cooper and Wittenberg (1985) emphasized that the stalemate was related to the therapist's failure to formulate a cohesive overview of the patient. They suggested that even prior to recognizing the stalemate, the therapist was essentially disorganized about the patient and comprehended only fragments of the patient's personality. To guide the treatment and put it on the right track, their consultations focused on producing a coherent overview that was flexible enough and may be modified during the subsequent treatment.

When the therapist comes for consultation, he usually is in psychic pain, frustrated, ridden with self-doubts regarding his therapeutic capacity ("I am no good"; "I have nothing of value to give to the patient"). Identity crisis, diffused anger, and therapeutic despair are frequently experienced just below the surface. Often the therapist has tried to comprehend the dynamics of the stalemate and to rectify the situation, but found himself stuck in a vicious circle. Both his self-esteem and observational capacity are diminished. The wish to abandon the patient or to transfer him to another therapist is likely to be intense. During the stalemate period, the therapist is functioning far below his therapeutic capacity. When this happens, it raises the possibility that the patient's psychopathology reactivated the therapist's conflicts which resulted in his contributing significantly to the stalemate. I have found it helpful to form a collaborative working relationship, aimed at restoring the lost confidence. The goal is for the consultant and the therapist to set up conditions to explore together as candidly as possible the details of the clinical data in an atmosphere of trust, closeness, and compassion. The consultation becomes a period of assessing the actual therapeutic interactional patterns in order to highlight how the patient's transference needs may have affected the therapist's interventions.

To explore clinical material that is representative of this stalemate period, I have found it necessary to scrutinize in detail a taped session of therapeutic interactions. The therapist is encouraged to express his second thoughts, give free rein to his feelings, and recall subjective experiences related to specific interactions, images, and personal memories. This process facilitates the therapist's increasing awareness of what specific emotions the patient aroused in him, how he responded to them silently, and to what extent his overt interventions were determined by his own conflicts and needs, as mobilized by the patient's fluctuating transference needs. Interactions between the therapist and the consultant uncover the therapist's tacit hypotheses that determined his interventions and the covert messages he communicated to his patient. During this type of consultation, the similarity between the therapist's covert messages and those of Freud's with his patient, the Wolf Man, becomes apparent. Freud then was particularly interested in developing his theories of infantile sexuality, and his patient, by his somatic preoccupations, frustrated his ambition. Freud demanded that the patient put aside his needs and supply him with the kind of material that would strengthen his theoretical orientation. Like Freud, the therapist in the midst of a therapeutic stalemate finds himself tacitly communicating to the patient, "If only you were different." The therapist becomes disturbed by the patient's need to repeat his traumatic past and refuses to be a representative of the patient's infantile environment. Instead, the therapist acts out what is induced in him. During the consultation, it should be determined whether the therapist was responsive to or blocked the patient's tacit appeals, and perceived correctly or misunderstood the patient's central anxieties. In addition, were the patient's needs to repeat and recreate his childhood environment taken as attacks which resulted in counterattacks and/or withdrawal, because of the therapist's vulnerability. Frequently, for example, the patient's appeal, "Take care of me as a maternal figure," or "Respond to me and help me and hold me in my attempt to develop separateness" may reactivate the therapist's complementary un-resolved struggles which is likely to influence his interventions.

Consultation gives the therapist an opportunity to process the patient's associations to his interventions and to realize that the patient responds to unconscious messages. Thus, he learns how the patient, indirectly, points out what the factors were that contributed to the stalemate. When the consultation process has proceeded well, the therapist is likely to gain insights into his own contributions and make new discoveries about himself and his patient. Perhaps of greater importance, the therapist learns to separate off the patient's problems from his own and thus free himself from unnecessary entanglements. In summary, this process may result in deepening the therapeutic relation-ship by reestablishing therapeutic closeness and releasing the therapist from his blocks.

While this type of consultation is helpful for many thera-peutic stalemates, there are certain blocked treatments that will not benefit from adequate consultation on an outpatient basis. In these cases hospital treatment that provides a "holding envi-ronment" (Winnicott, 1951) should be considered.

CLINICAL EXAMPLE

A relatively experienced psychotherapist reached PS and sought consultation. She described her dread of the sessions, rage at the patient, and self-doubts over her therapeutic capaci-ties. She agonized over endless repetitions and stagnation in the treatment, and despaired over the outcome. It is to her credit that she overcame her feelings of inadequacy and help-lessness, and sought consultation. Specifically she was asking to examine which of her therapeutic interactions contributed to the PS. We discussed the feasibility of a taped session, which was agreeable to both her and the patient. The tape and its transcription provided us with a basis for the consultation. These are presented below; though disguised, the essentials were preserved.

The patient was a thirty-year-old, single, professional woman who came for therapy because of mood swings, panic, anxiety, dizziness, and head spinning. She also described difficulty in establishing and maintaining satisfactory relations with men, feelings of not being real, and being emotionally detached. She exercised tight control over her impulses. Significant signs of identity disturbances were evident. For several years she had been treated by several psychiatrists, GPs, a neurologist, acupuncturist, behavior therapist, and also had diet therapy. With the present therapist, she expressed the wish to "understand what is behind my symptoms." Some of her symptoms had been present since early childhood, but were exacerbated after she left home to go to university. There she was attracted to friends who were heavy drinkers and used drugs. The freedom of the university atmosphere was in sharp contrast to her home environment where her parents exercised rigid controls and enforced high moral values. This conflict deeply disturbed her, resulting in schizoid withdrawal from social life. The patient was the younger of two children, having a sister three years her senior. Both the parents and her sister were high achievers with whom she compared herself, and felt that she could never come closer to their standards. She always wanted to be like her older sister, but felt that she could never be as good as her. The dynamic formulation made by the therapist centered around major conflicts stemming from unresolved separation–individuation anxieties.

After about ten months of dynamic psychotherapy on a twice-a-week basis, the symptoms that brought the patient to treatment lessened considerably, but the signs of the therapeutic stalemate began to appear. The therapeutic interactions were characterized by mutual anxiety over premature termination; boringly repetitive material frustrating to both participants; and intense anger and despair just below the surface. In what follows, the transcriptions of the tapes, both of the therapist–patient interactions and the discussions during the consultations, are presented. This clinical material is divided into segments; each segment includes both the self-evaluations and records subjective experiences in response to the patient's associations as well as the interactions and spontaneous comments during the consultations. There were three consultation sessions.

Segment 1

The Therapeutic Interactions: This session took place after two weeks of Christmas vacation.

Therapist: How are you?

Patient: Fine. I got snowed in for five days. I couldn't get out so I couldn't do much.

Therapist: That's right, the roads were closed down, weren't they?

Patient: Leaving B was hard because I really enjoyed it. Last night I started getting into a sort of panic. I found I was going through about five or six different mood changes pretty quickly, starting just to worry about one thing or another. I am worrying about the future a little. . . . I was really dizzy the last time I was here. After getting to B the dizziness had gone. I haven't felt dizzy since coming back. I started to try to figure out what it was I was running away from. I guess I had been thinking again about feeling normal and feeling worried about feeling anxious, feeling resentful that I had such trouble going back to work and from work to holidays, that I worry over little things, feeling dissatisfied with myself and feeling unhappy. And then I started thinking that what was really bothering me was that a lot of my anxieties and my fears aren't really based on reality, that I cannot really point to specific things that are making me feel anxious. I can't see why I don't have much confidence in myself. Then I started thinking that all of my lack of confidence is not based

on reality, there is something in me and therefore I cannot do anything about it, so I go
about thinking that there is nothing that I can
do about feeling the way I feel; so I try to be
something that I am not and it's this conflict
that builds up and I get in this real panic state,
almost feeling that I should be different.

Therapist: Feeling that you are not good enough, unless
you are like someone else.

Consultation:

Therapist: I sounded annoyed . . . I was frustrated by the
patient repeating the same thing. The patient
was going on and on and I didn't know what
to interpret. I wanted to focus on what had
become a familiar and repetitive theme: when
you are with someone, I didn't say with me,
you feel strong and together. By yourself, you
feel weak, you race on one spot, there is no
movement on your own.

Consultant: What comes to your mind about "not saying
with me"?

Therapist: I wanted to continue from the point where we
had left off. That's perhaps why I ignored the
vacation–separation. The panic was an example of the patient's chronic dissatisfaction with
herself and her trying to be like someone else,
to imitate. But this is not good enough either,
because it does not make her feel real, she gets
panicky. I now realize that I did not respond
to the patient's attempts to be connected with
me after a period of separation. To reestablish
the bond. I am wondering why I didn't realize
this in the session. I was repeating the same
theme . . . how did I feel about not seeing her
for two weeks? . . .

Consultant: The patient said: "It's not based on reality . . ."

Therapist: She keeps saying that . . . it blocks me.

Consultant: Is it based on psychic reality?

Therapist: Yes, of course.

Segment 2

The Psychotherapeutic Session Continued:

Patient: It was really clear to me last night, and now it's not so clear.

Therapist: But it sounds like a dissatisfaction with yourself.

Patient: Yes, little things will happen during the day where the dissatisfaction with myself will come out. When I was in class I think that's where part of it started. Yesterday we got the exams back. The professor had already told me before that I had done well and therefore better probably than most, if not all the other people in the class, so that should have been something that should have given me confidence in my ability, and then I started getting nervous. It is a seminar class so it is participation, it is in my work area, which gives me advantage over the others so you'd think there again that I should have more confidence. But it was really hard for me to speak out in the class. It's always hard for me the first time after being away for a long time. I was feeling very self-conscious and then almost a rash breaks out on my neck, not my face, and that happens to me a lot when I am really nervous. So I worry about not having control over things like that, about feeling not confident and self-conscious. So in a way I was in the class feeling like I hadn't done that well, but I also knew that . . . what I don't understand is why I should react that way.

Therapist: It sounds like you are almost feeling depressed about having won, having been better than the others. It is almost as if you are trying to avoid the feeling that you have done better than the others.

Consultation:

Therapist: In the session I did not understand why when she wins she is so uncomfortable. I know that the patient needs to get the highest mark in the class. There is so much competition. I stressed the need to outperform others and did not respond to the rash, fear of loss of control and embarrassment.

Consultant: What else didn't you respond to?

Therapist: Why did she bring up the teacher and the classroom? Perhaps they were her indirect references to me in the therapeutic situation. This did not occur to me during the session.

Consultant: Perhaps she was alluding to her affects and blocks in the treatment . . .

Therapist: She said, "It always is hard for me the first time after being away for a long time." She needed me to respond to her wishes to be close to her . . . I was annoyed by her intense need to be the best. . . . She gave me another chance to return to the break . . .

Consultant: What was she trying to communicate to you by recalling her experiences with her teacher and classroom?

Therapist: I don't know . . .

Segment 3

The Therapeutic Session Continues:

Patient: I don't know. I sometimes think it is not feeling perfect or resenting not being perfect, not accepting that I cannot be perfect. That's the only reason why I can think of that I focus so much on my inner criticisms.

Therapist: It is almost as if you are trying to avoid the feeling that you have done better than others by sort of trying to distract yourself. I guess you have spent so much time trying to please other people that you have lost touch with what makes you feel really good.

Consultation:

Therapist: The patient became vague, scattered, less focused; I sounded angry, I felt critical; and I told myself, "Here we go again." This is where we often got stuck. She tells me "I can't be perfect," and then I don't know what to say. I don't know what to do with that. My inclination is to say you don't have to be perfect. The patient would then say, "Yeah, I know, I was told that before." I don't know what else to say. The patient may say "Yeah, that's the way I am." Whatever you say it's not going to be the perfect answer.

After a pause, the therapist continued:

Who is she trying to imitate? Who is she comparing herself to? She had a successful vacation without any symptoms, which means that she does not need me as much. She was starting to individuate. Therefore she has to present herself as a helpless wimp in front of me, getting sick just before the session. "I really didn't do so well in the exam, I got 80s instead of 90s." The symptoms tie her up to me. She has to present herself as less competent in front of me. I am not so sure, I did not interpret that.

The therapist's associations and recall of subjective experiences were accompanied by genuine affects. The therapist got in touch with personally disturbed experiences aroused by the vicious circles in the stalemate treatment.

Consultant: Let's continue to focus on the patient's association as indirect references to the therapeutic relationship.

Therapist: Was the patient expressing her dissatisfaction with me—the imperfect session? Is she saying you aren't perfect—you have not taken away my symptoms? . . . Oh, yes, I now see that I'm disturbed by her oscillations—one minute she's the best, then she's helpless. . . .

Segment 4

Patient: I am not feeling confident enough in being able to determine what I like and don't like, since I have always been swayed by whatever others like. It gives me a feeling of panic when I think about my job and can't figure out whether I like doing it or not. I am really feeling at a loss, too, about what I do with my time . . . I get that feeling about having moved with my boyfriend. I don't know why I did it. . . . All is fine with my boyfriend . . . I don't know how to feel about things and that makes me panic too. I am scared to find out that I don't like piano. I am scared to find out that I don't like my job.

Therapist: You might feel that if you don't agree all the time with other people you will have a feeling of being disconnected from them, like, for instance, your boyfriend. If you don't like to do the things he likes, then there won't be any connection.

Patient: I was worrying about my future relationship with my boyfriend. When I start looking at the future, I worry that we are not enough alike for there to be a connection. I think it's got to the point that I no longer know what myself is. Am I lying by trying to be alike? I guess I really do feel isolated. I feel unconnected, that I cannot seem to be able to make bonds between people. Maybe I did before because I became like them, but I am feeling more and more that I don't want to become like other people. I would rather be isolated than have to compromise.

Therapist: You seem to feel that you either have to be like someone else or be isolated. That no one would like you the way you are with your own ideas and interests; that you are only likeable by the way you imitate others.

Patient: I just can't get those kinds of close relationships I remember having with friends in high school and university. I think one of the reasons that I was able to have close relationships was we became totally one, I became totally submerged in a group.

Therapist: It's almost like a fusion.

Patient: Yes.

Therapist: You are wondering how to be close but still retain your own identity I guess. Well, I suppose there is a feeling of loss, isn't there, that you will never feel as close as you used to because you are not as willing to lose your identity; you feel that the alternative is isolation.

Consultation:

Therapist: The patient's chronic dissatisfaction with herself makes her feel that she has to keep achieving, namely imitate either her sister or mother. But that imitation makes her feel false to herself. Since the patient spends so much time complying with others, when she tries to be true to herself, she becomes confused and ambivalent. She either complies and feels false, or she rebels and feels empty and isolated. My aim has been to help her develop a sense of self, but the patient is afraid because she sees it as being destructive, telling everyone to screw off. She wants to tell her boyfriend not to force her to say yes or no to canoeing. This is going to result in disconnectedness, aloneness, and emptiness.

While listening to this segment, the therapist became aware that she was repeating herself and said, "Oh my god, I don't know what's going on, that's why I repeat myself. I must have been wrong. Because she is so confused, I go over it again and again. This results in disconnectedness between me and the patient."

We discussed the last interpretation, that focused on "feeling of loss." We realized that the therapist's tone and content indicated compassion and closeness. We anticipated the patient's next associations would be responsive to the therapist's attempts to be connected with her.

The consultant also commented that the patient seems to have "ins and outs" of connectedness with her boyfriend and how her real life parallels the therapeutic relationship.

Segment 5

Patient: I can't seem to overcome it. My sister and I were really close. I started resenting having to do everything her way, that I depended on her more than she depended on me. I found myself wanting to be like her. That feeling of loss is part of the panic feeling. Feeling like I once had closeness and I no longer can have it. I keep thinking that if I knew myself better, or liked myself better, I could figure out who I was and if I liked who I was, then I would have an easier time getting close to people. I am really anxious in social situations now, not as bad as I was a year ago. A year ago I couldn't even go to a party without feeling anxious and I can do that now, although I still feel like I'm going through the motions. Every once in a while I'll hit on somebody and have a really good time. A feeling of real warmth and then it will be gone. I don't know where the warmth comes from but perhaps I should just stop worrying and talking about it.

Therapist: You get confused. What's you and what's them, and what's close and what's fusion.

Consultation:

Therapist: I missed it. . . . The patient really responded to my previous interpretation . . . I realize now that tacitly, unconsciously, the patient connected me with her older sister—she has formed a connection between how she has felt about her sister and me. Perhaps I have resented this connection. Obviously I have had sufficient material to make a "transference interpretation." This would have made us closer . . . be connected. It did not occur to me in the session. . . .

Consultant: Try and say more about it.

Therapist: I don't like her ambitious sister. . . . She reminds me of my own sister. . . .

DISCUSSION

The aim of this manner of consultation was to broaden the therapist's awareness of the possible determinants that contributed to PS. It pinpointed specific factors that contributed to the binds. A spirit of collaboration prevailed that encouraged the therapist to bring out subjective experiences during the review of the selected session. To get to the underlying determinants of the stalemate, some of the therapist's personal vulnerabilities had to be exposed, though I have been careful to respectfully preserve the boundaries between the consultation and therapy.

I would like to outline some of the factors that might account for the constructive effects of this manner of consultation. By herself the therapist was unknowingly repeating the snags that led to the therapeutic stalemate. Being away from the "heat" of the therapeutic interaction had a calming effect, which is a necessary first step in the process of resolving the stalemate. Although the therapist demonstrated intense affects during the consultation, they were contained (and it seemed that she felt "held" and "contained"). It was essential that her affects were reawakened during the consultation, which allowed her to be in touch with personal associations, affects, and memories that were unknowingly influencing her responses to her patient. In the process she was beginning to listen differently to the clinical material, to verbalize what she was learning, and to indicate new perspectives. Thus the consultation became a period of reflection and contributed to a better harmony with the patient. The end result of this relatively short experience was that the immediate crisis was lessened and the treatment could proceed.

We shall now concentrate on the processes that were uncovered during the consultation that facilitated the resumption of the therapeutic movement. These are related to highly personal determinants which were revealed in the interaction and mutual involvement between the therapist and the consultant. The stalemate in this treatment was reached somewhere at the beginning of the working through phase, where the patient's symptoms that brought her to treatment had lessened. In order to go beyond symptom improvement, the patient sensed she would need to deepen her understanding of what happens to her when she is involved in intimate relationships (e.g., older sister, boyfriend). This required first becoming emotionally closer to the therapist. Specifically, at this stage in therapy, the patient, via her transferences, needed to work through her traumatic and pathological aspects of her relationship with her older sister by working through processes within the therapeutic relationship. When these painful, earlier struggles with her sister were emerging, they reactivated the therapist's unresolved emotional conflicts with her own sister. The therapist unknowingly relied on a number of protective devices to ward off both the patient's needs and her own contributions to becoming disconnected and distant from the patient. In this manner, the therapist became a partner in colluding and blocking the therapeutic movement. This illustrates the hypothesis that the therapeutic stalemate in this case (and other cases) was the consequence of interaction in depth between the patient and the therapist. It indicated the patient's implicit needs for reliving in the transference pathological earlier experiences with significant persons in her life. When the therapist, for whatever reasons, was not responsive to those needs, the treatment became blocked.

The opportunity to examine closely the sequence of interactions facilitated her realizing how she actively participated in bringing about the stalemate. In Segments 4 and 5, for instance, the therapist had an "aha" experience. She made an emotional contact with the patient and expressed it by an interpretation; the patient responded to that in a spontaneous manner by bringing forward memories, hopes, and needs, implicitly asking for a deeper therapeutic relationship. But now the therapist was not responsive; she returned to a general theme related to the patient's struggles outside the therapeutic relationship. This blocked the development of deeper layers of psychic experiences. It resulted in repetitive, mutual frustration and despair, the hallmarks of PS. This patient and others whose capacity for symbolic representation is intact require the therapist to facilitate the working within the transference.[1]

During the consultation, the therapist developed insight into the implications of her therapeutic interventions. She sensed that she was pushing the patient to individuate (from her sister-therapist) but did not present the patient with a substitute person with whom the patient could relive her conflicts. The patient was losing the sister as a love object, but now the therapist was afraid to establish a secure context for mourning and working through of the loss. During the consultation, the therapist became aware that she was afraid of the patient becoming closer and even more dependent on her. She was telling herself, silently: "You have already exhausted me, what do you want more from me?" The therapist had known the value of

---

[1] After the consultation, we noted that the patient's initial associations to the blocked road were perhaps an allusion to the therapeutic situation. "Being confined," "being in a cage," "hemmed in," are frequent representations of the therapeutic stalemate.

focusing on the therapeutic relationship as among the most useful and alive aspects of treatment. But during the stress of the stalemate period, the therapist had lost this knowledge. She had to regain it during the consultation.

One of the therapist's protective devices against forming a close therapeutic relationship was her relying on theory and dynamic formulation. While reviewing subjective experiences around her first intervention (Segment 1), she said that after two weeks of Christmas vacation she wanted to pursue the theme that they had explored before the break. In response to the patient's associations that included revival of symptoms stimulated by resuming the treatment, the therapist said: "Feeling you are not good enough unless you are like someone else," a repetitive theme derived from the therapist's attempts to bring out the "pathology of separation–individuation." The therapist admitted that she was confused and needed to fall back on an organizing formulation. It sounded like a prepared interpretation, which is a common experience in PS. It is as though the therapist in between sessions had been determined that during the next session she would give a better interpretation. The prepared interpretation is usually derived from theory and is intertwined with the patient's psychopathology. It is experienced by the patient as a forceful maneuver to comply with the therapist's orientation. In this case, it diverted them from their work on the dynamics of the here and now, from the patient's associations and affects that were stimulated by her implicit struggles with the therapist after the two-week break. The therapist repeated unnecessarily the patient's negative attributes and accentuated the patient's weakness in an imbalanced manner. Thus the therapist unknowingly became a sadist who colluded with the patient's masochistic components. Generally speaking, this pattern of therapeutic interactions might have escalated into a negative therapeutic reaction. During the consultation, the therapist realized that an alternative line of inquiry would have been their understanding why the patient's symptoms returned as she was resuming treatment.

We tried to pinpoint the specific interactions where the therapist was experiencing boredom and emotional withdrawal, common therapist experiences during stalemates. We realized that the patient's oscillations between two psychic states, "gran-diosity" and "competition," and "helplessness" and "defeat," disturbed the therapist. The therapist said that it confused her and resulted in unhelpful interventions. What the therapist tried here (and in other sessions) was to confront the patient with "objective reality." She said that she drew the patient's attention to the fact that her chronic dissatisfaction was incongruent with her achievements. The therapist hoped to reduce the patient's drivenness and fierce competition, which inevitably followed by experiencing defeat and suffering from her chronic symptoms. During the consultation, the therapist began to recall what she had known and lost; namely, to explore the patient's intense needs and sources of living up to infantile expectations and her falling short of perfection. In listening to the tape, the therapist had an exciting discovery when she noticed that the patient was vague as she was switching from one psychic state to the other. This irritated the therapist; she inwardly called the patient a "wimp," and unknowingly became more directive and authoritarian. Thus the therapist had a glimpse of how the patient's unconscious struggles affected her and reduced her therapeutic competency. The therapist seemed to achieve an emotional understanding that to help the patient integrate the oscillations between the two psychic states, the therapist had first to contain them inside her.

In the follow-up to the consultation, the therapist presented evidence that the sources of the stalemate had been clarified, integrated, and applied in subsequent sessions. Gradually, by appropriate focusing on the therapeutic relationship, the therapeutic movement was resumed. The patient's significant change was in her relationship with her boyfriend, which was also at a stalemate during the consultation. The boyfriend, as an intimate relationship, was in a "bogged-down" phase. Through the therapeutic relationship, the patient worked through her intense struggle to be emotionally "in" and "out" of contact with him. They decided to get married. The last I heard two years later was that the treatment ended satisfactorily. The therapist remembered the consultation as a significant learning experience that facilitated her getting over the stalemate treatment.

We know that stalemate treatment is a common experience in our current therapeutic endeavors with the characterologically difficult patient. When this therapeutic outcome occurs, the therapist is under enormous emotional strain and his colleagues are asked to find methods to facilitate the resolution of the impasse. The kind of consultation presented in this paper is only one of the methods. When we scrutinize the process of this consultation, it becomes abundantly clear that the interactions between therapist–patient and therapist–consultant revolve around relatively simple and at times even elementary issues. To expose such issues as problematic for the experienced therapist can stimulate intense shame. Nevertheless these issues are common to the therapist who is in the grip of a therapeutic stalemate. Intense emotions and conflictual attachments to his patient are blocking him from adequately processing and managing his own personal contributions to the impasse. In order to become meaningfully aware of his personal involvement in the stalemate, the therapist is invited to participate actively in finding out how specifically he and his patient have reached the impasse.

However, this is only one method. Therapists are keenly interested in learning from their colleagues the intricacies of the varieties of stalemate processes, and methods of resolving them. But to the detriment of our therapeutic efficacy, the details of this kind of treatment outcome and its resolution have been confined to the privacy of our offices. Understandably, presenting the details of a therapeutic stalemate and how it was resolved would likely expose the therapist and possibly his consultant to vulnerable personal areas and may bring limitations to light. Narcissistic vulnerabilities notwithstanding, we need to learn from each other and bring out these experiences into the open and compare notes in order to facilitate the resolution of therapeutic stalemate. Each clinician's experiences are limited to a small number of cases. Thorough case studies have added substantially to our knowledge. By learning to recognize the signs of therapeutic stalemates and work through our contributions to them, we facilitate their resolution.

The type of consultation discussed in this paper may not result in solving stalemates with certain therapeutic dyads.

When the impasse is not resolved, termination of the therapeutic relationship may be indicated. The separation may be worked through with the help of the consultant in order to effect a constructive break-up of the treatment at the time when the two individuals are quite vulnerable. Referral to another therapist or evaluating other therapeutic modalities for a particular patient, such as group or couple therapy, are the natural outcome of unresolved stalemates. With the more primitive patients, inpatient consultation may be most useful (Bernstein, 1980; Carsky, 1985–1986). These varieties of consultations are beyond the scope of this paper.

SUMMARY

This paper focuses on the salient features of a therapeutic stalemate and how a specific method of consultation processes facilitated its resolution. The consultation revolved around a detailed examination of a therapeutic session and it highlighted the interactions between therapist and patient, and therapist and consultant. The consultation process restored the therapist's capacities by realizing in an emotionally convincing manner how her various interventions contributed to the therapeutic stalemate.

15.

Suicide in Borderline Personality Disorder

John T. Maltsberger, M.D. and Christopher G. Lovett, Ph.D.

Defining and clearing out the thicket known as the borderline personality disorder (BPD) has been one of the principal activities of psychiatric and psychological workers for the past twenty-five years. A particularly thorny area of this thicket has to do with suicidal and parasuicidal phenomena in such patients. Is suicide common in this group? If it is, how is it different from suicide that befalls patients in other diagnostic categories? To what extent can suicide be anticipated, to the extent that it occurs? What can we do about it?

Although self-destructiveness is a cardinal feature of borderline psychopathology, surprisingly little is known about suicide in these patients. We know little about how suicide in borderline patients may differ in motive or means from suicide occurring in those with other diagnostic labels. Had we clearer, better answers to such important questions, clinicians could better anticipate self-destructive activity and intervene more effectively. Our present ignorance lulls many into a view that well may be incorrect—that suicide and suicide attempts by borderline patients merely demonstrate "typical" borderline random impulsivity and unpredictability.

These sharp questions, as any clinician confronted with a problematical borderline patient will recognize, are typical of those with which we must struggle in our work. While at the present time definitive answers, firmly established by statistical study and analysis, are not yet to hand, we offer here a clinical opinion, informed by our work with borderline patients, by published studies, and by discussions with other workers in the same prickly territory. The questions surrounding suicidal phenomena in borderline patients not only require careful study as a specific clinical problem, but they also map out important avenues for understanding the critical issues regarding borderline psychopathology and its treatment. How are borderline personality disorder and depression related? How can our knowledge of narcissism and masochistic phenomena illuminate our understanding of these patients? What are the interconnections between states of depersonalization, depression, and self-destructive acts which borderline patients carry out?

We believe that an increased understanding of such relationships can be obtained by examining how borderline psychopathology is influenced by the transformations of narcissistic structures, body image, and object relations which occur during adolescence, a developmental period during which the risk of suicide increases dramatically and when borderline phenomena often make their first appearance.

THE INCIDENCE OF SUICIDE IN BORDERLINE PERSONALITY DISORDER

Suicidal behavior and related forms of self-destructiveness are prominent features in current descriptions of the borderline personality disorder (BPD). These behaviors constitute a major diagnostic criterion for borderline psychopathology, and they are often the most anxiety-provoking for the clinician involved in the treatment of these patients. One encounters impulsive, indirectly self-destructive actions such as reckless driving, as well as suicide threats and gestures, and self-mutilation. All these phenomena are included as subcriteria among the diagnostic specifications for the borderline personality disorder in the revised third edition of *The Diagnostic and Statistical Manual of Mental Disorders* (DSM-III-R) (American Psychiatric Association, 1987). Other prominent features of the borderline personality disorder (hostility, aggression, depression, and loss-sensitivity, for example) have long been viewed as important factors related to suicide (Kullgren, 1988). There is, however, no mention in DSM-III-R of the potential for serious suicide attempts, the intent of which is to put an end to life. This reflects a general lack of serious attention paid to this aspect of the treatment of borderline patients throughout the literature.

Recent empirical studies show that clinicians should be briskly alert to the risk of outright suicide in borderline patients. The long-term outcome of BPD disorder had not been systematically examined until recently, and for this reason the dangers, incidence, and predictors of suicide in this population have been poorly understood. The reported percentage of suicide in follow-up studies has varied from 3 percent (McGlashan, 1986a), to 7.6 percent (Stone, Hurt, and Stone, 1987a), to 8.5 percent (Paris, Brown, and Nowlis, 1987). The mean age of suicide in borderline patients has been found to be twenty-seven (Stone et al., 1987a). Other research shows that borderline personality disorders may well comprise 12 percent of all suicides among psychiatric patients (Kullgren, Renberg, and Jacobsson, 1986). The prevalence of BPD has been reported as 14 to 20 percent in hospital settings (Kroll, Sines, Martin, Lari, Pyle, and Zander, 1981; Kroll, Carey, Sines, and Roth, 1982); thus borderline patients would not appear to be seriously overrepresented among those who commit suicide as inpatients. Nevertheless there is reason to believe that the proportion of borderline suicides among psychiatric patients in general is increasing—this has been shown in a Swedish study of psychiatric suicides between the years 1961 and 1980 (Kullgren, Renberg, and Jacobsson, 1986).

In addition to the above findings, several studies have shown that borderline patients improve if followed for as long as ten to fifteen years (McGlashan, 1986a; Plakun, Burkhardt, and Muller, 1986; Paris et al., 1987; Stone et al., 1987a). Overall this research indicates that after some years borderlines grow significantly less impulsive, their interpersonal relationships less chaotic, and their affective experiences less miserable and errat-ically changeable. One may conclude that borderline personal-ity disorder is a condition which decreases in intensity over time to a point of quite significant improvement if the patients can be kept from suicide (Paris et al., 1987). In reviewing the results from the various follow-up studies of borderline patients, Paris (1988) states, "One could conclude from these studies that the main thing to worry about in a borderline patient is suicide. We do not know, however, whether the suicides in these patients are preventable. . . . The question of which borderlines com-plete suicides remains unanswered" (p. 195). That question we shall address below.

DEFINING SELF-DESTRUCTIVE PHENOMENA IN BORDERLINES

There is some disagreement in the literature regarding the scope across the character disorder continuum to which the term *borderline* may be appropriately applied. We agree with those colleagues who would reserve the term for one class of several distinct, reasonably discrete personality disorders. We differ from Kernberg (1975), who raises the umbrella of his structural concept, "borderline personality organization," over all the major forms of character pathology. Kernberg's (1980) emphasis upon underlying weaknesses in the borderline's ego and superego functioning, particularly the selective failures in reality testing and use of primitive defenses, is nevertheless useful in understanding suicidal phenomena in patients who meet the criteria for "borderline personality disorder" diagno-sis in DSM-III-R.

Let us now turn our attention to the self-destructive behav-ior of patients who satisfy the narrower criteria for the diagno-sis of "borderline personality disorder." As character structure and pathology are intricately involved in all significant acts in-cluding suicide, it would be well to notice those psychological features of the borderline which play major roles in generating such behavior.

The intimate relationship between borderline pathology and self-destructive acting out, including suicide, has been noted from the very first as one of the fundamental aspects of this group of patients. When Stern (1938) first introduced the term *borderline* into the psychiatric–psychoanalytic literature, he remarked that the tendency toward negative therapeutic reactions in such patients may be dangerous. "Patients may develop depression, suicidal ideas, or make suicidal attempts," he said (p. 473). Among the other symptoms and character features which Stern described in these patients were injured and depleted narcissism, pervasive masochistic tendencies, inordinate hypersensitivity, readily mobilized anger and depression, and a trait which he described as *psychic bleeding*. (This latter term refers to a tendency to sudden dramatic regression in response to a painful or traumatic experience, during which the patient "goes down in a heap, so to speak, and is at the point of death" [p. 471].) Published over fifty years ago, Stern's original observations included many details which remain essential to the understanding of suicidal phenomena in borderline patients: he noticed their narcissistic sensitivity, their mercurial, unstable affect, and their tendency to regress when emotionally overwhelmed by painful feelings. More recent efforts to define the distinguishing descriptive features of borderline patients have again demonstrated the importance of self-destructive behavior as a discriminating characteristic (Gunderson and Kolb, 1978; Spitzer, Endicott, and Gibbon, 1979; Perry and Klerman, 1980). Manipulative suicidal gestures and masochistic interpersonal relationships remain on the list just where Stern placed them (Gunderson and Kolb, 1978; Gunderson, 1984).

The diagnosis of BPD is also most frequent among self-mutilative patients (Grunebaum and Klerman, 1967; Graff and Mallin, 1967; Schaffer, Carroll, and Abramowitz, 1982) and among adolescents who attempt suicide (Crumley, 1979). In addition, the more frequent presence of impulses to self-injury statistically discriminates depressed borderline patients from other kinds of depressed patients (Conte, Plutchik, Karasu, and Jerrett, 1980). Similarly, suicidal behavior is more prominent in depressed patients who carry a concomitant diagnosis of BPD

(R. Friedman, Aronoff, Clarkin, Corn, and Hurt, 1983). Even within a sample of borderline patients, one of the best predictors for poorer long-term outcome is self-damaging acts (Plakun et al., 1986).

If it is obvious that borderline patients are egregiously self-injurious, the significance and psychological nature of their injuring is not. To understand what the injuring is about requires us to notice the different ways in which the patients hurt themselves, and in what differing circumstances. Their self-injuring repertory reaches from impulsive but unconsciously driven self-destructive acts such as reckless driving or substance abuse, self-mutilative acts such as wrist-cutting or head-banging and suicidal gestures, to deadly suicide attempts and suicide itself. In comparison to the true suicide attempt, the suicide gesture is more common in patients with BPD, and has received more attention in the literature. Gunderson (1984) found that over 75 percent of a sample of hospitalized borderline patients had made at least one manipulative suicide attempt. He defined attempts as manipulative in quality based upon their having been carried out with an aim to coerce some desired response from a specific other person and in which rescue was likely. The three most common explanations given by the patients for these acts were rage at another person, a wish to punish oneself, and a state of panic.

Although it is our purpose here to concentrate on actual suicide and deadly suicide attempts, for purposes of clarity we will first notice the various kinds of parasuicidal behavior which are common in these patients. *Parasuicide* (like the vernacular but more ambiguous terms *suicide gesture* and *suicide attempt*) refers to behavior which is equivocally suicidal in its nature. It has been defined as a "non-fatal act in which an individual deliberately causes self-injury or ingests a substance in excess of any prescribed or generally recognized therapeutic doses" (Kreitman, 1977, p. 3). Most self-injuries or self-poisonings, often referred to as "suicide attempts," really are not intended to put an end to life at all. For this reason it is not appropriate to refer to the majority of such episodes as suicide attempts. Clarity and precision make it desirable to reserve the expression "suicide attempt" for comparatively unambivalent efforts toward self-killing, lethal in nature, and certainly likely to succeed unless sidetracked by some unexpected and unpredictable quirk of the moment that preserves the patient's life by chance.

The relationship between suicide attempts and parasuicidal behavior is a complex one, and the two are frequently confused with each other. While overdoses and self-cutting are generally not as lethal as suicide attempts, unintentional suicide can occur as a result of unconscious lethal forces or true accident. In addition, an increase in the frequency and severity of parasuicidal acts may augur an approaching true suicide attempt (Gardner and Cowdry, 1985). The clinical wives' tale that patients who have engaged in numerous parasuicidal acts are at lower risk for completed suicides has been repeatedly disproven (Kullgren, 1988).

In an effort to clarify the phenomena of self-destructiveness in borderline patients, Kernberg (1975, 1987c) described a group of patients with manifest self-destructive behavior who tended to discharge aggression indiscriminately toward the outside or toward their own body. Psychoanalytic exploration found them to be characterized by a severe lack of superego integration, conscious or unconscious pleasure connected with the pain they inflicted on themselves, and the general characteristics of BPD. In Kernberg's view such patients typically relieved their anxiety by cutting themselves, by committing some other form of self-mutilation, or by parasuicidal acts carried out in fury and with almost no depression. He sorted this primitive self-destructiveness into three groups: first, patients described as "infantile," corresponding quite closely to BPD as described in DSM-III-R, who injure themselves under conditions of great frustration, dysphoria, or rage in an apparent effort to reassert control over the environment; second, chronic mutilative and/ or suicidal trends which mark out a syndrome of "malignant narcissism"—patients with borderline personality organization and a narcissistic personality disorder (NPD) functioning on an overt borderline level, he describes as malignantly narcissistic. In these patients the self-destructive behavior expresses "cold rage." It is accompanied by a sense of triumph over pain and death and reasserts an omnipotent independence and power over pain and death. Third, there is psychosis: bizarre self-destructive behavior in this last class outwardly manifests a primitive, idiosyncratic fantasy world that mimics borderline psychopathology.

Gardner and Cowdry (1985) sort the self-destructive borderline activities somewhat differently. They describe four categories, separable by differences in underlying drive, intent, course, and outcome. Their categories are: (1) true suicidal acts related to melancholia and despair; (2) self-destructive acts which are impulsive, nihilistic, or based on retributive rage; (3) commonplace parasuicidal gestures; and (4) self-mutilation or overdose to relieve "dysphoria."

Gunderson (1984) points out that it is important to understand whether the borderline patient's self-destructive behavior is designed to reassert a sense of control over an important person or to delineate or destroy the patient's "bad self."

Perhaps more simply than most others we recognize two varieties of parasuicide: self-injury to influence, coerce, or punish others who are emotionally important to the patient, and self-injury to relieve subjective distress. No veteran of a general hospital emergency ward will be unfamiliar with parasuicide of the first kind, *manipulative parasuicide*. Commonly enough a patient will take an overdose or superficially wrist-cut, often in the presence of someone else, when an important person threatens to break away. Self-injury of this sort is never lethal except by accident, and it is intended to provoke guilt, make the departing person change his mind, and, by asserting a bloody control, to relieve a painful sense of helplessness. Manipulative parasuicide is provoked by narcissistic injury; it is usually accompanied by some combination of such feelings as anger, fear, frustration, agitation, and anxiety (Gardner and Cowdry, 1985). It not only asserts the need intrusively to control others. It further communicates a desperate need to connect with someone in order to stave off painful feelings of aloneness and emptiness. Under different circumstances such behavior can be driven by the need to demonstrate that one is not under the control of another (Cooper, 1988).

Patients often carry out manipulative parasuicidal acts to punish others for not fulfilling their psychological needs—parasuicide is sometimes a kind of sublethal revenge. A patient in our experience, a young woman in her twenties, flew into a rage at her boyfriend, doused her upper torso with eau-de-cologne, and set herself afire in his presence to punish him for what she experienced as a persistent want of sympathy and hardness of heart. She said she had wanted "to teach him a lesson." The lesson she wanted to teach him was that he should conform his behavior more closely to her needs for relief from emotional tension. In the borderline patient's perception, the failure of an important person to meet such needs is experienced (with the operation of projection and distortion defenses) as a sadistic, willful attack, and the relief experienced through parasuicide may derive from a symbolic enactment of revenge (Kernberg, 1987c).

Apart from manipulative parasuicide we recognize one other type—*depersonalization parasuicide*. It is usually self-mutilative. Although wrist-cutting, self-burning with cigarettes, banging, or biting oneself are its usual forms, some patients hurt themselves more idiosyncratically. Dripping acid on the hand, sandpapering the face, and trying to break an arm with a hammer have been reported (Liebenluft, Gardner, and Cowdry, 1987). Whether the self-injury performed is ordinary or exotic, however, the purpose is the same—to relieve depersonalization and derealization.

Patients suffering from BPDs are particularly subject to episodes of depersonalization and derealization, especially when stressed. These experiences are extremely unpleasant, and patients sometimes feel that such states are being visited on them from outside themselves. (One woman said that her depersonalization episodes made her feel that the body she inhabited was not hers, that it was an imitation, even a good imitation, but not the real thing.) The patients commonly grow angry during such states, and repeatedly report that a physical self-attack, commonly in the form of cutting, puts an end to the depersonalization episode. Such dissociative states are often accompanied by an eerie lack of feeling and nihilistic fears. "Am I dead?" the patient may wonder, and then cut himself to make sure he is alive. Pain, it would seem, is the only trustworthy assurance that life goes on (Gunderson, 1984). Patients often say that the cutting itself is anesthetic, that normal body-sense returns in a wave of relief when blood is seen welling up in a cut, when its warmth is felt on the skin. At least half the patients who self-mutilate feel nothing painful during the act (Liebenluft et al., 1987). Instead they may experience a "numbness" or a sensation of cold washing over them.

Gardner and Cowdry (1985) refer to a related variety of self-destructiveness which they call "dysphoria-related self-injurious behavior" (p. 396). This they connect to borderline patients' extreme sensitivity to separation, loss, rejection, and failure. They define dysphoria as, "a rapidly escalating mixture of depression, anxiety, and anger often with depersonalization, emptiness, and psychotic-like symptoms" (p. 396). The psychotic symptoms they describe encompass inner voices commenting on the patient's behavior, auditory hallucinations, and delusions of possession by the devil. Feelings of rage and hopelessness may appear, with wishes to get revenge on frustrating others.

Gardner–Cowdry parasuicide embraces such a wide range of subjective experience and mental state variety that it encompasses virtually the entire borderline experience, and for that reason, cannot help much in discriminating between types of patients and their inner experiences. To their credit these authors try to define what they mean by "dysphoria," although they mix together feeling states and psychotic phenomena that belong to a different order in descriptive psychiatry.

We believe the time has arrived to abandon such words as *dysphoric* and *anhedonic*. They are high sounding but in fact convey little. "Dysphoric" means no more than feeling ill or dissatisfied; "anhedonic" means insensitivity to pleasure or lacking the capacity for happiness. They mean no more than the plain English "miserable" or "blue." Describing the wretchedness of our patients with polysyllables that carry no precision will help neither them nor us. "Clear your mind of cant," said Samuel Johnson.

We are nevertheless prepared to admit that the imprecision in our clinical language may in part reflect something about the emotional experiences of the borderline patients themselves. Gardner and Cowdry point out that although these patients can readily differentiate their dysphoric moods from depression, they still have difficulty describing the mixed mood state they experience. The dysphoria they discuss seems to have a primitive, poorly differentiated quality. Perhaps this points to roots in the archaic periods of child development (Liebenluft et al., 1987). It is closely tied to body feeling. The patients commonly say such things as this: "My heart seemed to be pounding through my body . . . it feels like my heart is racing outside myself. Emotionally I just want to feel . . . I feel unreal and out of touch and I can't get connected with anyone."

Does our descriptive difficulty arise from the incapacity of most clinicians to empathically experience psychotic affect? The automatic tendency to ward off empathic resonance with the suffering of an agitated depressed patient, for example, is widely appreciated. Gardner–Cowdry dysphoria includes psychotic experiences. Derealization, depersonalization, psychotic depression, paranoid experiences, hallucinations, and delusions are commonplace in these patients (Chopra and Beatson, 1986).

Hallucinations and delusions are not feelings, and paranoid experiences are not either, but such mental experiences are often eerie, terrifying, crushing, exhausting, and invite despair.

Our patients may be inarticulate or reticent in describing to us the feelings of madness. Most of us would rather not know how madness feels. If we are really to understand borderline (or other) suffering, however, we must pluck up our empathic courage, refine our interviewing skill, and press our patients to describe their inner feelings as clearly and precisely as they can.

Self-injury is often strikingly effective in relieving "dysphoria"; as an episode of suffering escalates, the impulse to self-mutilate intensifies. The patient may recognize the signs that he is about to mutilate, but in general, he feels he has no control over what is about to happen. Another "force" has taken over, the patients may say. They may later explain, "I felt like another person." "I don't feel like myself," they complain beforehand (Gardner and Cowdry, 1985). The injury itself may have a ritualistic or ceremonial quality. After it has occurred the patient will have a sense of "physical relief" and, sometimes, feelings of remorse, shame, self-hatred, and confusion. The circumstances which triggered the crisis, commonly rage at some frustrating other person, is no longer of focal concern to the patient after the parasuicidal act (Liebenluft et al., 1987).

Depersonalization parasuicide (and Gardner-Cowdry dysphoria parasuicide, presumably) is frequently mistaken for manipulative parasuicide. Sometimes it is convenient to forget that depersonalization parasuicide even exists when one is feeling angry at a patient. It is easier to justify an attitude of moral indignation against the patient who self-mutilates in order to manipulate or punish others. Angry countertransference reactions are easily rationalized once the parasuicidal patient is labeled (and devalued) as a manipulator.

Any tendency to class all parasuicidal behavior as manipulative can obscure serious and sometimes ominous meaning which the behavior betrays. Parasuicide, especially depersonalization parasuicide, can point to a crescendo of despair and the imminence of suicide itself (Gardner and Cowdry, 1985).

Commonly enough manipulative and depersonalization suicide are mixed. To complicate the matter further, mixed parasuicides of this sort are not always easy to distinguish from genuine suicide attempts. It can be difficult clinically to decide whether a given mutilation is primarily hostile and manipulative, whether it is primarily intended to relieve depersonalization (or a psychotic affect of some kind), or whether the patient is primarily trying to feel alive, or to demarcate his self boundaries. More than one intent may drive a given episode. One self-mutilating patient said, "I feel like I have no outlet and hurting myself is a physical relief as well as a message to other people to know what pain I have inside me when I can't reach them any other way" (Liebenluft et al., 1987, p. 318). More than one meaning may be expressed by a given parasuicidal episode. Mutilation can relieve a sense of depersonalization; it may also concretely symbolize revenge against a frustrating object. An unconscious sadomasochistic drama can be played out in which the patient's temporarily depersonified and victimized body stands for the object who is being punished (Kernberg, 1987c).

The multiple determinants of any self-destructive act were demonstrated by Woods (1988) who described a number of aims for self-cutting in one patient. That patient cut to relieve

tension and depersonalization, to obtain perverse sexual gratification, to express a preoccupation with loss or damage, to
draw blood as a way to feel clean and purified, to relieve feelings
of emptiness and disintegration, to cut off feelings, to cut the
self off from the world, and to cut the world out of her mind.
Suicide itself may be driven by wishes for rebirth, wishes to rid
the self of an unwanted part, wishes to punish others or get
revenge, or wishes to fuse with a lost object (Maltsberger and
Buie, 1980).

Gunderson (1984) has suggested that the thorough assessment of self-destructiveness in borderline patients should take
into account three interlocking factors. First, the most prominent affect in the patient's experience. (This may vary between
depression, anger, depersonalization, or some mixed state of
so-called "dysphoria.") Second, the particular intrapsychic and
interpersonal dynamic wishes associated with the act (such as
wishes to expel a "bad" internal object through self-mutilation
or to punish a frustrating person). Gunderson's third and central factor for assessment is the nature of the patient's relationship to some sustaining object.

Much light can be shed on parasuicide in borderline patients by examining the availability of sustaining resources
(Maltsberger, 1986). All of the "danger situations" described by
Freud in "Inhibitions, Symptoms and Anxiety" (1926) have in
common the theme of separation from a source of comfort
external to the core of the self. Such comfort sources may be a
person or some structural derivative of a human relationship,
for example, a comforting introject, but a sense of psychic closeness to a comforting presence is essential throughout life if
regression to states of anxiety of agonizing proportions is to
be avoided. The failure of borderline patients to develop, via
internalization, sufficiently stable capacities for self-regulation
leaves them vulnerable to feelings of emptiness, fears of abandonment, and the crises of aloneness, worthlessness, and rage
that can precipitate suicide. In order to minimize distress and
vulnerability, borderline patients must rely on such sustaining
resources as they can find outside themselves for narcissistic
survival. Among these are relationships to others, to work, or
to poorly integrated, archaic introjects.

Gunderson (1984) believes that all the manifest psychopathology of the borderline can be organized according to whether it is carried out in relationship to a sustaining object perceived as present and supportive, frustrating or absent. According to this scheme, the central issues for the borderline personality involve convictions of inner badness, the wish for an available sustaining object, and the need to feel able to control that person. The rapid, unstable changes in functioning are not related to changes in core dynamics, but rather to regressive changes in defenses and the behavioral expression of the efforts to preserve a sense of contact with and control over the sustaining object.

When such sustaining objects are present and supportive the borderline's functioning is at its highest level. This state of affairs corresponds to what others have referred to as the libidinal availability of the object (Masterson and Rinsley, 1975) or to the presence of the holding self–object (Adler and Buie, 1979). Depressive, masochistic, and lonely features are present but not dominant. They relate to conflicts around frustration over wanting more from the object and distress with the aggressive greediness of their wishes. Intentional self-destructive behavior, however, is unlikely to occur.

When a sustaining object is frustrating to a borderline person or when a loss is threatened, then the angry, devaluative, and manipulative features come more prominently into play. Under these circumstances self-destructive acts directed at others—manipulative parasuicidal behavior—often appear. These represent attempts at preventing the other person's leaving, and are undertaken in order to stave off the dreaded narcissistic collapse which follows object loss, and to sustain an unconscious belief in the ability to exert omnipotent control over others as well.

When a borderline patient feels he is losing or has lost a sustaining object, brief psychotic episodes, states of rage and panic, intolerable experiences of "aloneness" (Adler and Buie, 1979), and the experience of total inner "badness" may be suffered. This corresponds to Masterson's "abandonment" (1972). Defensive measures to ward off the inner states which follow the failure of exterior sustaining resources are often dangerous and usually impulsive. The patient may begin to abuse drugs or alcohol, become sexually promiscuous or perverse, generate dissociative experiences, and turn to parasuicide. It is important to remember that the combination of substance abuse and depressive episodes in borderline patients has been found to increase the risk for successful suicide (Stone et al., 1987a).

At these moments the patients may hurt themselves in ways which are outwardly identical to what they did formerly in manipulative frames of mind, but the same behavior now has different or additional purposes and meaning. Parasuicide is now depersonalization parasuicide, which must be understood and treated differently. Above all, depersonalization suicide is closer to true suicidal behavior than manipulative suicide.

In Gunderson's (1984) view the components of self-destructive behaviors of borderline patients reacting to the absence of an object are different in intent and reflect more intrapsychic unbalance than the parasuicidal acts that occur when ongoing contact with a sustaining object still seems possible or coercible. The abandoned patient feels overwhelmed by the subjective horror of aloneness. Often they say that they are dying. Their underlying conviction of total inner badness rises like a dark and drowning tide. These experiences of "alone-badness" (Gunderson, 1984, p. 37) reflect the poorly integrated, archaic, and cruel nature of the borderline's superego (Kernberg, 1975). Brief psychotic episodes organized around morbid convictions of being evil, feelings of unreal emptiness, and nihilistic ideas (e.g., "my body is dissolving") can give rise to bizarre forms of self-mutilation and suicide itself.

Further differences between suicide and parasuicide are evident when the patients' feelings, attitudes, and relationships to their bodies are examined. All sorts of harmful behavior apart from suicide can be self-directed, or more precisely, directed against one's own body. Laufer (1987) has correctly pointed out that suicide itself is unique: "Suicide can be related only to a very particular form of violence, that of murder . . . it is only in a suicidal action that the aim of the violence contains the wish to annihilate an object rather than hurt or injure it" (p. 1).

Because of the confusion between parasuicidal and suicidal behavior to which we have alluded previously, there is a tendency to apply conceptual models that apply to suicide to parasuicidal phenomena, and here the models do not always fit. In particular suicide models may fail correctly to describe the meaning of cutting of wrists or other body parts. The symbolic meaning of the choice of method or anatomy is often overlooked (Daldin, 1988). While suicide attacks the entire physical self of the patient and can express an overwhelming sense of badness (this we meet in suicidal crises of total, inundating inner badness), selective self-mutilation may mean something quite different. Injuring certain parts of oneself, the genitalia, for instance, may reflect guilt about certain impulses associated with the injured part, or hostility toward an introject for which the physical part has come to stand (M. Friedman, Glasser, Laufer, Laufer, and Wohl, 1972). Chronic self-mutilation may express an unconscious masturbatory fantasy, as well as punishment for such activity (Joffe, 1982; Daldin, 1988).

Any self-destructive act may arise from multiple determinants, of course, most of which are hidden in the unconscious. For example, the borderline patient's sense of calm following self-mutilation may derive from a fantasy that part of the "inner badness" has been purged from the body or self. Similar wishes, although more extreme in form, are evident in suicide attempts where the conscious intent is to attain a state of peace, while the motivating unconscious wish is to destroy a hated internal object and expel the "badness" forever.

One borderline patient, a young woman who often engaged in cutting her arms, had multiple fantasies concerning the meaning of her blood. Often it represented an internalized mother serving as a transitional object, so that she resembled the patient described by Kafka (1969). Her intense ambivalence toward her internal mother, however, was reflected in her highly charged suicidal fantasy of death through exsanguination.

DEPRESSIVE ILLNESS AND SUICIDE IN BORDERLINE DISORDERS

There is general agreement in the psychiatric literature that the definition of BPD as set forth in DSM-III-R describes a discrete nosological entity, and that patients so diagnosed are not to be understood as subtypes of schizophrenia or major affective disease (American Psychiatric Association, 1987). Nevertheless, there is much evidence to suggest an important link between borderline disorders and affective disturbances of various types. The criteria for BPD in DSM-III-R emphasize affective disturbance, such as the items describing inappropriate, intense anger or lack of control of anger, affective instability, and chronic feelings of emptiness or boredom. In addition, patients with this diagnosis are extremely likely to develop serious depressive illnesses (Pope, Jonas, Hudson, Cohen, and Gunderson, 1983; Gunderson and Elliot, 1985; Perry, 1985; Stone et al., 1987a). This is of the utmost clinical importance, because borderline patients are even more likely to commit suicide when depressed than those with major depression who do not suffer from a personality disorder (R. Friedman et al., 1983). In light of the marked mood lability, sustained dysphoric feelings, and periods of intense depression characteristic of the borderline, it has been suggested that the essential difficulty for these patients is in the process of affect regulation and that they represent a subgroup or atypical form of the affective disorders (D. Klein, 1975, 1977; Stone, 1980; Akiskal, 1981; Stone, Kahn, and Flye, 1981).

The reported lifetime prevalence of major depressive disorder in patients with borderline personality disorder varies between 67.6 percent (Stone et al., 1987a) and 74 percent, or 87 percent if subjects with a history of previous psychotic symptoms are included (Perry, 1985). In hospital and clinic populations a 40 to 60 percent overlap between major depressive illness and BPD has been reported (Gunderson and Elliot, 1985). In a prospective study it was found that over the course of a one-year follow-up, borderline patients averaged more than two mild exacerbations of depressive symptoms and nearly 0.4 exacerbations severe enough to warrant a diagnosis of major depression (Perry, 1988). In this same study it was found that acting out and the use of defenses characteristic of borderline patients, such as splitting and projective identification, were correlated with higher depression rates, especially following stressful life events. Despite such findings, however, it does not appear that BPD is merely a subclinical affective disorder (Pope et al., 1983).

Depression is characteristic of borderline patients, but many other diagnoses have associated depression and borderline pathology can occur without any evidence of depression (Gunderson, 1984). Certain features of the borderline, however, contribute to a vulnerability to both depression and suicide.

That patients suffering from significant depressive illnesses account for a third to a half of successful suicides is a clinical commonplace (Dorpat and Ripley, 1960; Barraclough, Bunch, Nelson, and Sainsbury, 1974; Robins, 1981). Furthermore we know that approximately 15 percent of patients with major depressive illnesses will die of suicide (Sainsbury, 1986a). There is some evidence to indicate that the prevalence of affective disorders is no more frequent in borderline patients than in other personality disorders (Fyer, Frances, Sullivan, Hurt, and Clarkin, 1988). Yet depressed borderline patients have been found to attempt suicide more often and make more seriously lethal attempts than depressed patients with other personality disorders or with no personality disorder (R. Friedman et al., 1983). The presence of borderline psychopathology accelerates the onset of depressive symptom formation and increases the risk of suicide (McGlashan, 1987). In one study 92 percent of depressed borderline patients, most of whom were adolescents or young adults, had already made one or more suicide attempts, and 6 percent of these patients committed suicide during or immediately after the index hospitalization (R. Friedman et al., 1983). This risk continues to disrupt the treatment and threaten the lives of these patients for many years. Over a fifteen-year follow-up, patients comorbid for BPD and depressive illness were found to be twice as likely to commit suicide than depressives without a personality disorder and eight times as likely than borderline patients without a concomitant depressive illness (McGlashan, 1987a). It is for this reason that the concurrence of BPD and major depression has been described as exerting an "ominous pathosynergistic effect" [sic] (R. Friedman, Clarkin, Corn, Aronoff, Hurt, and Murphy, 1982, p. 519).

Schmideberg (1947, 1959) invented the oxymoron "stable instability" to describe the functioning of borderline patients, and in large measure, it refers to affective instability. This affective dysregulation is characterized by intense and negative affects, usually depressive or hostile, and by a propensity for rapid affective shifts. In various long-term follow-up studies, affective instability has been found to be the most consistent predictor of poorer outcome (McGlashan, 1985; Plakun et al., 1986; Paris et al., 1987) and suicide (Kullgren, 1988), while the presence of felt affect without affective dysregulation predicted better outcome (McGlashan, 1985). It is the combination of this deficit in affective regulation, and the intensely painful affect experienced in depression, that makes these patients so vulnerable to self-destructive acts and deadly suicidal behavior. As the above studies clearly demonstrate, patients with borderline character pathology are incapable of tolerating depressive affect; indeed, they tolerate it much less well than those with uncomplicated diagnoses of major depressive illness. Stressed with the development of significant depressive pain, borderline patients are likely to react impulsively and to destroy themselves.

Individuals whose object relationships are stable, who have the capacity to renounce an omnipotent self-image, and who can accept the necessary limitations of reality, may develop extremely painful depressions, but ego regression into a frank suicidal crisis is unlikely. Where object relations are unstable, where self-esteem has been dependent either on outstanding performance or the reassurance of a narcissistically stabilizing object, the vulnerability to depression and suicidal regression is great. By definition, patients suffering from BPD fall into the vulnerable group.

Contained anxiety and contained depression need not interfere seriously with object relations. When these affects cannot be contained, however, ego regression of a lesser or greater degree will take place. Demands for increased external support will crescendo and become increasingly unrealistic so that frustration and disappointment become inevitable. Borderline patients are likely to defend against the consequent rage by projecting it onto those who fail them, and as their reality testing falters in the deepening regression, objects are devalued as fickle and false. With the abandonment of significant objects, aggression, guilt, and hopelessness rise and a suicidal crisis appears.

In any patient group, but particularly in the borderline realm, the potential for suicide is not solely related to depression. Suicide is an act of self-destruction, and certain personality features promote or reinforce suicidal actions as solutions to states of psychic pain. Depressed borderline patients are different from other depressed patients because they are more impulsive and resort to depersonalization–"dysphoric" parasuicide to ward off depressive affect and feelings of total badness or worthlessness (Conte et al., 1980).

THE BORDERLINE DEPRESSIVE EXPERIENCE

The capacity to bear depression demands tolerance for the hurts and losses that inevitably afflict every adult. Every adult must from time to time suffer, and resign himself to helplessness in the correct perception that emotional injuries which cannot be undone must be endured. That is mature suffering, and it is not possible for those persons whose ego ideals do not permit surrender. To passively submit to the inescapable pain of grief or of a depressive experience and to hope for recovery in the future is not consistent with self-respect in some people, especially in those with a more masculine–active ideal self (Zetzel, 1965). This may account in part for the fact that more men than women commit suicide. It may also have some bearing on the impulsive reactions of patients with borderline disorders when beset with depressive affect.

The sadistic and masochistic fixations which afflict borderline patients also play a part in their incapacity to bear depressive affect. Some patients cannot bear to surrender passively to depressive affect and to suffer it. Instead they are driven to fight it, sadistically turning against their own bodies, as though their bodies contained the depressive enemy, and fighting the enemy within with such ferocity that they may choose to die rather than give in. Other patients seem to hear a call for masochistic submission in the rising fog of a developing depression; the attempted suicides that follow represent "lethal surrender" (Krystal, 1978). These attitudes suggest that the patient is resisting or submitting to an attack from outside the core of the self; that is, the depressive suffering is experienced in the form of an attack from without.

Clinical lore has it that those patients who describe the depressive experience as a malignant influence coming on them inexplicably from without (they may say they feel seized by it, as in the talons of a predatory bird, or that it surrounds and comes into them, like a black fog) may be more suicide prone than those who do not. Although untested, this proposition makes a certain amount of psychoanalytic sense, inasmuch as a depressive experience of invasion from "without" suggests the operation of an introject highly charged with unneutralized aggression not integrated into a harmonious ego–superego system through identification. The patient with a better integrated superego is less likely to experience depression as an invasion from without, but will instead recognize it as arising from within himself, however painful the experience may be.

Many depersonalized patients have parallel experiences—they feel that something is being done to them from the outside; sometimes they feel robbed of their feelings, or that a false body has been substituted for their true body. Similarly, during states of escalating subjective distress some patients may perceive that a self-destructive act is about to occur, but they feel they cannot prevent it. The patient may report that an outside "force" has taken over; after they have hurt themselves they may say, "I felt like another person" or "I don't feel like myself" (Gardner and Cowdry, 1985). Taken together these observations reflect poor ego and superego integration in borderline patients, as well as the interplay between shifting primitive defenses and unstable ego states.

Depersonalization was described by Jacobson (1959) as the pathological result of a conflict within the ego. She understood the conflict as taking place between the part of the ego that has accepted and the part that attempts to undo an identification with a degraded, threatening object representation, often the image of an infantile, sadomasochistic self. The ego endeavors to reaffirm and restore its intactness by opposing, detaching, and disavowing the existence of the "bad" part of the ego and the corresponding regressed sadomasochistic self-image. The peculiar quality of depersonalized states corresponds to an internal situation in which a detached, intact part of the ego observes the unacceptable part or pretends it does not exist.

The relationship between depersonalization, attacks on the self, and attempts to reject parts of the self is illustrated in dramatic form by those patients whose ego integration is so notoriously diffuse, the so-called "multiple personalities." For example, Gardner and Cowdry (1985) describe a self-mutilating patient whose dissociative episodes corresponded to the emergence of different personalities. This woman increased her self-destructive behavior, particularly head and arm banging, when she sensed that a new personality was about to emerge. She said she did these things to prevent the new personality from coming on, and to relieve her sense of panic. Parallel dynamic phenomena are sometimes evident in suicide; patients may do away with themselves when convinced that the only way in which the "good" part of the self may be "saved" from a cruel submission and corruption is through total bodily destruction. Such a situation is depicted at the conclusion of the film *The Exorcist,* when a priest who has been invaded by the devil hurls himself out of a high window.

Jacobson (1971) also understood that depersonalization may develop within the psychic framework of depression. She believed this happens when the primitive, ill-integrated ego and superego join forces in the struggle against a worthless, degraded self-image. A state of depersonalization, like the depression against which it often serves as a defense, represents an attempt to solve a narcissistic conflict. Both depression and depersonalization may follow object loss or narcissistic injury and both are preceded by primitive identification processes.

Kraepelin (1921) was very explicit in describing depersonalization phenomena in depressed patients. Depersonalization occurs only in a minority of depressed patients, and in these, complaints of blunting, deadness, or unreality dominate the mental state (Slater and Roth, 1977). Although we cannot prove it statistically, we and other observers believe that depression with a strong depersonalization–abandonment color is most typical of patients with BPD.

In any patient group, including the borderline group, the potential for suicide is not solely related to depression. Suicide is an act of self-destruction, and certain personality features promote or reinforce suicidal actions as solutions to states of psychic pain. The depressions of borderline patients differ from those of uncomplicated depressives in that they are more marked by impulsive activity, often self-destructive in nature (Conte et al., 1980). The impulsivity is a defense against the depressive affect they cannot endure, and against feelings of total badness or worthlessness.

The most common form of affective disorder found in borderline patients is unipolar nonmelancholic depression (Charney, Nelson, and Quinlan, 1981). Brief psychotic depressive experiences are common in borderline patients, often in combination with depersonalization or derealization (Chopra and Beatson, 1986). Sustained depressions of psychotic proportions, however, are unusual (Gunderson, 1984). Borderline patients more typically resort to defenses such as splitting, projective identification, externalization of feelings of failure, depersonalization, and impulsive acting out to avoid or moderate the depressive experience.

Because of the specific deficits in ego and superego functioning typical of the borderline functioning, it is not surprising that the depression from which borderline patients suffer differs as a subjective experience from that which patients with uncomplicated major depressive disorders must endure. To describe the borderline's depressive experience Masterson (1972, 1976) invented the term *abandonment depression*. He compared it to Spitz's (1946a) "anaclitic depression," a phenomenon encountered in infants deprived of caring human contact. Masterson differentiates between "superego depressions" and abandonment depressions. He holds that abandonment depressions spring from the loss of narcissistic supplies, or the loss of a part of the self necessary to narcissistic integrity. Research on the subjective, interior affect, and mood experiences of depressed patients lends support to such a distinction.

For instance, Grinker and his coworkers (Grinker, Miller, Sabshin, Nunn, and Nunnally, 1961) differentiate between depressions marked by guilt and the need for restitution, and depressions where feelings of deprivation dominate. In deprivation depressions they noticed how commonly patients attempt to manipulate others to obtain emotional comfort.

Contemporary efforts to characterize the specific depressive experience of borderline patients intersect with earlier attempts to separate depressions based on guilt from those based on a predominance of conflicts around dependency. Fenichel (1945) described two "subjective formulas" for depression: (1) "I have lost everything; now the world is empty" (characteristic of depressions in which the loss of self-esteem arises mainly from a failure of external narcissistic supplies); and (2) "I have lost everything because I do not deserve anything" (p. 391) (characteristic of depressions wherein the superego deprives the ego of narcissistic supplies).

A further intersection between earlier and present work is to be found in a distinction drawn by Jacobson (1943). She differentiated depressions marked by loss of self-esteem, feelings of helplessness, weakness, and inferiority, from those dominated by a sense of moral worthlessness and sinfulness. More recently we find Kohut (1977) and Tolpin (1978) differentiating "guilt depressions" from "depletion depressions"; the latter in their view arise more from the sense that the self is depleted and empty than from the sadistic action of the superego. Superego depressions in the classical sense would belong in the guilt category.

Anthony (1970) has pointed out that a similar two classes of depression can be discerned in adolescents. Adolescence is a developmental stage in which psychic structures are being reshaped and reformed. Conflicts relating both to separation–individuation and the oedipal phase are revived in the course of this restructuring, and force it along its course. Adolescent developmental reorganization is proceeding at the time Anthony's two depressive types first become discernable, and they are theoretically the consequences of it.

Depressed patients of Anthony's first type exhibit a psychopathology with marked preoedipal features. These patients appear never to have surrendered a symbiotic tie to their seemingly omnipotent, need-satisfying mothers. These young patients suffered primarily from shame, humiliation, inferiority, inadequacy, and a sense of weakness, and their object relations were narcissistic, dependent, and masochistic. Anthony's second variety of depression is more oedipal in nature; the patients suffering from it have punitive superegos, feel deeply guilty, and are morally masochistic. Second-type patients are more prone to self-disgust, tend to turn hostility against themselves, and condemn themselves. Anthony implies that second-type adolescents, hating themselves so much more than first-types, will be at greater hazard to commit suicide.

Four years later, thinking along similar lines, Blatt (1974) introduced yet another term, *anaclitic depression,* to describe a depressive subtype in which patients suffer from helplessness, weakness, depletion, intense fears of abandonment, a sense of inner emptiness, and marked object hunger expressed through wishes to be cared for, loved, fed, protected. He contrasted "anaclitic depression" with another type, "introjective depression." He found patients with introjective depressions to be self-critical and guilty. These patients blame themselves and feel worthless for not living up to expectations and standards; they fear the loss of approval, of recognition, of love from those to whom they are attached (these fears reflect superego projection). Such patients are driven to atone for their imagined shortcomings, wrongs, and failures.

Blatt's "anaclitic depression" is quite obviously very like Masterson's "abandonment depression," and Anthony's first depressive type. Furthermore, Blatt is now suggesting that depressions of this sort may have something to do with the patients most of us are content to class as borderline personality disorder—he recently has suggested that there is an "anaclitic type of personality disorder" (Blatt and Auerbach, 1988).

In practice many depressions are mixed, displaying both "anaclitic" and "introjective" features (Blatt, D'Afflitti, and Quinlan, 1976). The most severe clinical depressions appear to combine both poles of narcissistic pathology, preoedipal and oedipal, the patients feeling at once depleted, empty, impoverished, as well as evil and contemptible (Blatt, Quinlan, Chevron, MacDonald, and Zuroff, 1982). This clinical fact and the contributions of Masterson, Anthony, and Blatt are all quite congruent with the older work of Jacobson (1953). She believed that depressive illnesses evolved along a continuum that began with "simple depression" (Bibring, 1953), marked by dejected mood and feelings of inferiority, reaching on into melancholia where profound guilt and despair appeared.

Plainly, many workers agree that there are two poles of the depressive experience, and we concur in this impression. Nevertheless an essential descriptive task is waiting to be done. We badly need more precise and clear descriptions of the inner experience of depressed patients, along with better descriptions of their clinical behavior and styles of relatedness. Now that more precise diagnostic criteria are available, it will be possible to sort out the details of differing depressive experiences according to diagnosis. Anticipating that this work will soon be underway we suggest the term *abandonment depression* is preferable to *anaclitic depression*. We prefer the word *abandonment* because it describes many of the experiences and fears of patients near to one of the depressive poles. Furthermore it does not imply that the depressive difficulty arises primarily from deprivation experiences, which the word *anaclitic* does, even though we continue to believe that emotional injuries in the first three years of life are etiologically important. Similarly, we would prefer to describe patients nearer the other depressive pole as suffering from *melancholic depression* instead of "introjective depression." The adjective "introjective" implies a psychological mechanism and begs important questions by giving special emphasis to a mechanism of defense in the illness. We do not doubt the importance of introjection in melancholia, but prefer descriptors that are closer to observable clinical phenomena.

Abandonment depression still needs to be carefully described. The depressive experience of patients with borderline personality disorders is commonly close to the abandonment pole, however, and we feel that certain aspects of their suffering may most correctly be included under that rubric. Their wishes to be cared for, loved, fed, and protected are pronounced, and they complain of a sense of inner emptiness which they look to others to fill. The sustained pleading, yearning, suffering of many borderline patients suggests that they feel abandoned and afraid. The form of their chronic depression would seem closely related to their intense object hunger, and related too to their common conviction that life can only be empty and futile because they are inhibited or prevented from deriving any gratification (Perry and Cooper, 1986).

Patients with abandonment depressions feel not only helpless, but specifically helpless against a vague and terrible danger which seems to threaten something like death or disintegration. They do indeed fear abandonment; close proximity to others who serve as sustaining objects seems vital to them, because separation implies not only death or disintegration, but the loss of personal reality. The disintegration dread which haunts these patients is closely related to the quite common depersonalization and derealization experiences which harrow them.

The depressions of many borderline patients are of course distinctly melancholic in quality. The patients are self-accusatory and guilty. They exhibit the classic vegetative signs of weight loss, sleep difficulty, and failure of appetite.

In many patients careful mental-state examination will disclose a mixture of abandonment and melancholic miseries. Keller and Shapiro (1982) have described a group of patients suffering from "double-depression," where an acute depressive episode is superimposed on a chronic depressive mood. We suspect that this group of "double depressives" includes many borderline patients with chronic depressions of the abandonment type. The superimposition of a melancholic depression upon a chronic abandonment state would be highly likely to overwhelm a borderline individual whose capacity to tolerate painful affect of any sort is limited at best. The summation of melancholia onto abandonment suffering can be enough to trigger suicide.

PERSONALITY DEVELOPMENT AND VULNERABILITY TO SUICIDE IN BORDERLINE PERSONALITY DISORDER

The borderline patient's vulnerability to depressive regressions and self-destructive bursts arises from an accumulation of developmental failures and the deficits that arise from them.

These patients have a poor capacity for self–object differentiation, their capacity for sustained object relatedness is limited, they exhibit sadomasochistic fixations, their capacity for bodily self-love is deficient, they have great difficulty in tolerating mental pain or depression, and they are unstably moody (a reflection of their primitive superegos and their prominent use of splitting as a defense).

Each one of these difficulties has its roots in poor mastery of the developmental challenges that pertain to the separation–individuation phase (Mahler, Pine, and Bergman, 1975). These difficulties in turn interface with oedipal and later childhood development. As the child moves toward adulthood many structural transformations occur in the effort to establish some degree of self-stability in a narcissistically defective personality system. That is why the borderline's chaotic adaptations and frequent regressions reflect not only difficulties arising from the failure to master separation anxiety, but difficulties that reflect distortions in oedipal development as well. In addition, the usual structural reorganization that belongs to adolescence (especially reorganization in the superego system) does not proceed in a normal way in these patients. Pathological phenomena that can be related to all phases of development, ranging from the separation–individuation phase onward, are discernible in the adult borderline's behavior.

Parasuicidal and suicidal acts reflect an early disruption in the individual's relationship to his body (Laufer, 1987). The developmental histories of these patients will often show that in very early childhood nobody was interested or able to show much consistent loving warmth in caring for the little child physically (Furman, 1984). This often interferes with the child's development of a good capacity for caring for and protecting his body.

Systematic investigation of the developmental histories of borderline patients compared to depressed and schizophrenic patients showed a significantly greater incidence of broken families and parental loss (particularly the father) in the borderline group, and further reflected a pathologic pattern of overinvolved mothers and underinvolved fathers (Soloff and Millward, 1983a). The incidence of early maternal separation (between 0 and 5 years) has also been found to be higher (Bradley,

1979) in borderline children and adolescents in comparison to psychotic or delinquent patients.

Bodily self-love is the earliest form of self-love, and it is an essential part of the primitive matrix in which healthy narcissistic development is rooted (Spruiell, 1975). Failure to receive an adequate amount of early loving bodily contact can result in an insufficient libidinization of the bodily self (Kaplan, 1980). Difficulty integrating the body representation and the self representation may occur; many of these patients grow up suspicious of their bodies, uncertain that their bodies are really a part of them, limited in their capacity to care for and to protect their bodies. Indeed, their self-mutilations reflect body hatred. Gunderson and his colleagues (Gunderson, Kerr, and Englund, 1980) have demonstrated that the families of borderline patients may be discriminated from those of controls specifically by the absence of a maternal erotized relationship with the child who will grow up to be borderline. The more deficient the child's early experience of loving body investment by the mother, the more disposed he will be later to carry out parasuicidal or suicidal attacks on his body.

The incapacity these patients have to love themselves physically (not having been physically loved as small children) is only part of the picture. Their readiness to hurt themselves is compounded by sadomasochistic fixations as well. The histories of these patients frequently will show that they have had unusual and frequent painful childhood body experiences, and that these experiences often pertain to the skin. The skin and the sensations arising in it are important in the development of body image and in the establishment of body boundaries (Cooper, 1984).

The adult borderline's object relations are notoriously sadomasochistic (Abend et al., 1983). In addition, the persistence of primitive, unfused aggression in the context of a sadomasochistic model of "doing-and-being-done-to" in relationships fuels the self-destructiveness of these patients (Furman, 1984).

The importance pain assumes in children with a borderline destiny, struggling for self-definition, longing for bodily contact that is denied, probably contributes to a masochistic orientation in development. By masochistic orientation we refer to the active seeking of psychic or physical pain, suffering or humiliation, including subjugation of the self and its needs, in the service of adaptation, defense, and gratification (Novick and Novick, 1987; Stolorow, Atwood, and Brandchaft, 1988).

The masochistic pattern of pleasure-in-unpleasure develops during the earliest stages of self–object differentiation (Cooper, 1984, 1988). Sometimes it appears to arise from an empathic mismatch between the mother and infant; sometimes the mother experiences difficulties in relation to her child's activity and dependency needs. The mother may have difficulty in containing her child's anxieties and impulses—through an ambivalent sequence of intrusive control and sudden withdrawal she actually intensifies the child's aggression (Novick and Novick, 1987). Under such circumstances the child's need for his mother can override his need for pleasure, and a pattern of struggling toward a relationship through the giving and receiving of pain can be set up.

The early experience of having bodily or emotional needs rejected or ignored also interferes with the development of the capacity for self–object differentiation. In order to maintain a sense of closeness to the mother and adapt to her emotional needs, the child fails to learn that he is fully separate. This seems to be especially true in terms of a sense of full physical separation. Many borderline patients feel that their bodies belong to their mothers, or that their bodies are in fact their mother. Self-cutting can stand for cutting mother. The borderline's self-mutilation is usually accompanied by restitutive fantasies in which an important object is believed to be performing the act or being punished (Gunderson, 1984).

The transferences borderline patients develop in the course of psychotherapy repeat these difficulties. They have great trouble in discerning where they leave off and their therapists begin. Portions of their mental life are experienced as taking place in the therapist (they project across the unstable and shifting self–object boundary with great facility), and sometimes their bodies, or portions of their bodies, seem to belong to someone else. McGlashan (1983c) has published clinical examples of these phenomena, illustrating how their sense of self is organized around a primitive, fused self–object which he calls the "we–self." In treatment many of his patients could only experience themselves as real in the context of the relationship; the symbiotic self–object was actualized in the transference.

The difficulty borderline patients have in maintaining a sense of object permanence has been clarified by the contributions of Adler (1985) and Adler and Buie (1979). They have pointed out that the achievement of evocative memory, belonging more or less to the eighteenth month of life (in the rapprochement subphase), is a necessary step in the development of the capacity for self-soothing. Without it the child cannot move beyond the phase of relying on transitional objects; of course, borderline patients make extensive use of transitional objects because of their disturbance in this area. Without reliable evocative memory capacity the child has an inadequate basis to form permanent reliable object representations, soothing introjects, and the mental structures necessary for maintaining reliable adult narcissistic equilibrium.

Problems in object permanence are a critical factor in disposing these patients to suicide. Even when reliable and loving others are available the patients may not be able to make use of their care. Because of the difficulty they have in normally forming object representations and maintaining stable libidinal investments to them, borderline individuals, especially when crushed under the weight of depressive affect, do not feel loved, cannot love, do not have an affective sense that others are there, that others care, or that others matter. At such moments the patients feel utterly alone and without connection to the object world. Indeed, the frequent complaints of these individuals that the world seems empty, meaningless, or unreal reflects their unstable capacity for relatedness. Object investment is not abandoned entirely in a sustained way by borderline patients (such is the case in schizophrenia), but it may be abandoned from time to time during periods of regression. Suicide is, we believe, most likely to occur during these isolative, comfortless regressive episodes.

When enough data is available about a suicidal act it is usually possible to discern an underlying masochistic fantasy in which the victim and the executioner are destroyed and die together (Asch, 1980; Maltsberger and Buie, 1980). The borderline patient's deep sense of victimization and fears of abandonment, his chronic depressive mood and proneness to acute depressive episodes, and his tendency to impulsive self-destructive behavior all may be viewed as related to early narcissistic injuries and a primitive masochistic core within the personality.

Depression and masochism are closely related phenomena, and appear to develop out of similar early experiences of pain and disappointment (Cooper, 1984). Early experiences of separation or deprivation give rise to emotional pain, and, if the child feels helpless to undo the loss, can generate a depressive reaction (Sandler and Joffe, 1965).

If the mother attempts to resolve her conflicts and feelings of failure through the projection of hated, devalued parts of herself onto her child, then the important pathogenic components of the borderline's "basic fault" (Balint, 1968) are in place. The mother communicates to the child that its anxiety and aggressiveness are unbearable, that she cannot survive its needs without withdrawal, and that all of the "badness" and hatred in the relationship is located within the child. The borderline patient's "bad self," poor capacities for tolerating anxiety and depression, a deep sense of victimization, and fears of abandonment, have their origins in such early pathological object relations.

During the rapprochement subphase of separation–individuation (from the 15th through the 24th month) early difficulties become consolidated during the disappointing realization of separateness that occurs (Mahler, 1972b). Ambivalence in object relations emerges, along with the capacity to retain narcissistic injuries and harbor a sustained sense of failure and hopelessness (Pine, 1980). The crystallization of self-awareness during this time causes self-esteem to become a focal conflict for the first time. Even in normal children the characteristic self-experience here is likely to be one of smallness, aloneness, and a generally saddened or depressed mood (Mahler, 1966). In children destined for a borderline development a negative outcome of the rapprochement crisis may take place and can be expected to include the establishment of a basic depressive core and a predisposition to later depressive episodes.

When the realization of separateness and the accompanying feelings of helplessness during rapprochement emerge too abruptly and painfully, painful self-consciousness and despair will follow. Masochistic defenses emerge as a means of coping with the frustrations experienced in the child's realization of his dependence on the mother and his inability to control her. The child's initial acceptance of his mother's projections coalesces with any early deficits in bodily self-love so that the process of turning aggression against the self appears and develops as a defense (Novick and Novick, 1987). Masochistic defenses come into play as the child defends against destructive impulses directed at the mother and tries to repair the narcissistic injury incurred through feeling helpless and alone. The child attempts to restore damaged self-esteem by erotizing his suffering, learning even to like it, as he struggles to maintain an idealized image of his mother. When his mother disappoints him and his rage is stimulated, he blames the disappointment on himself, entertaining fantasies that his anger is omnipotent, that it is his own badness which causes mother to be cruel and rejecting (Cooper, 1988).

The regressive pull of the child's intense ambivalence during this time can aggravate archaic splits in the mother's internal object relations, prompting her to respond either by withdrawing or by engaging in an aggressive, intrusive way. Often she will oscillate unpredictably between the two extremes. The mother's changeability mirrors the child's infantile splitting of object images, and distinctions between reality and fantasy, or between self and other, are difficult to establish and remain obscure (Ross and Dunn, 1980). The use of splitting and projective identification is reinforced, and experiences of disappointment that bring about a hostile devaluation of the parents become more likely. The struggles for separation and autonomy which first occur around bodily activity are experienced by both the mother and the child as aggressive attacks. There is now added to the child's fears of losing the mother a diffuse unconscious guilt around normal wishes to separate from her and achieve some independence, which Modell (1984) has referred to as "separation guilt."

An ambivalent, clinging dependence on an object felt to be both intrusive and rejecting becomes characteristic of the child's relationships. This conforms with the clinical observations of Freud (1917) and others who noticed that depressed patients were intensely dependent on ambivalently loved objects.

In defending against aggressive impulses which have become associated with normal strivings toward activity, separation, and autonomy, the child develops a masochistic quality. The child is attempting to maintain the familiar, "receptive relationship with the intrusive object" (Novick and Novick, 1987, p. 368). A hypersensitivity to the mother's moods or attitudes develops, and this hypersensitivity is carried over into the adult relationships of borderline patients (Stern, 1938).

Although much attention has been given to borderline patients' use of projective identification, there has been comparatively little notice given to their intensified vulnerability and responsiveness to what others project into them.

The sensitivity of borderline individuals to the hateful and sometimes murderous wishes of others is a critical factor in provoking their suicides. It originates in their early experience with intrusive, aggressive projections in mother–child interactions. Krohn (1974) refers to this selective, pathological sensitivity in describing "borderline empathy," a heightened sensitivity to the primitive levels of inner experience in others. Another person's immediate unconscious conflicts are sensed with exquisite sensitivity by borderline patients. Their intuitive radar especially picks up hateful impulses and primitive superego contents in others. These perceptions are not integrated well with a correct perception of the full, balanced character of others. Loving, caring aspects of the other person who is being "scanned" are likely to be dismissed as unreliable or pretended. Only what is hostile is credited as genuine. The combined effect of sensitive receptiveness to hateful projections, and the long-established preparedness to abandon self parts in response to the perceived needs of others, furnishes lethal power to the murderous wishes of the borderline's relatives or other love objects. Because of this malignant sensitivity, borderline patients can be thrust toward suicidal acting out by unconscious countertransference hate in therapists or others who are responsible for their care (Maltsberger and Buie, 1974).

The incapacity to tolerate anxiety or depression has long been related to the vicissitudes of the separation–individuation phase of development. Gitelson (1958) suggested that certain borderline traits were related to the failure to develop the capacity for signal anxiety, so that repeated experiences of unmodulated traumatic (separation) anxiety would persist into adult life. The adult capacity to endure painful separations without despair also depends on the mastery of separation anxiety in childhood. This mastery cannot evolve unless the distress of separation is consistently and reliably modulated by soothing caretakers who see to it that fear does not become too overwhelming, and who help the child learn that separation is followed by reunion. Repeated soothing experiences of this sort color the pain of separation with hope and make it more endurable. In the absence of a consistent, empathic helping adult who may later be replaced with a comforting transitional object, the child left alone too roughly, too often, or too unpredictably, is likely to experience separations or threatened separations as abandonments and will be prone to react with panic and despair.

The disposition to depressive, pessimistic moods as a character trait stems in part from the precocious superego formation likely to arise from intense ambivalence felt toward frustrating objects during separation–individuation (Mahler, 1966). Superego formation has a fundamental influence on the development of affect and mood control. The excessive harshness and poor integration of the primitive superego is evident in general moodiness, chronic deficits in the regulation of self-esteem, and unstable, shifting affect states that pervade the self and lend it a dark color.

Separation–individuation difficulties of the typical borderline kind invite the premature onset of the phallic–narcissistic conflicts that belong to the oedipal period (Kaplan, 1980). Premature castration anxiety makes the child's poorly contained separation anxiety, his ambivalence, his fear of abandonment, and his masochistic investment in disappointment worse. A pattern of provoking rejection from others develops, and rejections are followed by rage and projected contempt. Unresolved preoedipal and oedipal sadomasochistic conflicts interfere with the processes of organization and structuralization which normally occur during latency. Ego consolidation is impaired and the synthetic functions of the ego are never well established (Nunberg, 1931). Finally, the failure to achieve some satisfactory oedipal resolution makes it more likely that the reworking of the oedipal situation during adolescence will become a source of tremendous anxiety.

Adolescence is a developmental crucible: separation–individuation issues and the problems of the oedipal period are reexperienced and reworked. This is the time of life when borderline psychopathology is likely first to emerge in clear form (Masterson and Costello, 1980). That adolescence is the period in which the frequency of suicide increases dramatically is no coincidence (Hawton, 1986). The maturational issues of adolescence organize around the surge of puberty when new modes of relatedness to others and body changes and impulses must be integrated. This process often brings to light vulnerabilities in ego development which previously had lain dormant. When boys and girls move into adolescence with crippled ego–superego organization from earlier phases, the developmental process is likely to undergo a catastrophic derailment. Pathological organizations become consolidated and reach into adulthood (Laufer and Laufer, 1984).

Recent clinical investigation has demonstrated that the diagnosis of BPD can be reliably established in adolescents (McManus, Lerner, Robbins, Alessi, and Barbour, 1984). Manipulative parasuicide, chronic depressed mood, and hostile devaluation are familiar parts of the adolescent borderline syndrome. Adolescents so afflicted are highly susceptible to painful depressive episodes, and they are quite likely to try to escape from their suffering by suicide and parasuicide. The diagnosis of borderline personality disorder is most frequent among adolescents who attempt suicide (Crumley, 1979) and who meet criteria for major depression (R. Friedman et al., 1982).

There are several reasons why borderline adolescents are more self-destructive and vulnerable to depressive regression than younger children. They experience a renewed dependency and ambivalence as normal adolescents do, but with much greater intensity. The same may be said about the specific vulnerability of bodily self-love during this period, and the central place of feelings of helplessness and loneliness that belong to adolescent experiences of separating from parents and sexual development. Borderline adolescents are sorely compromised in tolerating solitude and at the same time they are more likely to experience the age-appropriate sexual impulses of adolescence as hostile acts of separation and sadistic oedipal triumphs (Novick, 1984).

Furthermore the adolescent must get used to feeling alone with a sexually mature body, whereas before he could depend on his parents to protect and help him with physical needs (Laufer, 1987). For those who have not mastered the demands of separation–individuation and the Oedipus complex this may be impossible. Their maturing bodies appear to force on them a traumatic loss which is unendurable.

These troubled young people, experiencing increasing dependent longings but needing to separate, can be alternatively clinging and intensely repudiative toward their parents. While the adolescent repeats the shifting, clinging, and pushing away of the rapprochement phase, the parents are once again tested in their capacity to bear the feelings of rejection and failure which their child's behavior evokes. When the parents are too ambivalent or too narcissistically crippled they are likely to retaliate with devaluing attacks of their own, or else to withdraw. The whole family may then fall into a pattern of mutual projective identification and regressive hate (Shapiro and Freedman, 1987).

When parents withdraw emotionally, the borderline adolescent is particularly likely to feel that, just as he had feared, the bad, destructive, and envious parts of himself have caused it, and that he deserves to be rejected and abandoned. His poorly integrated ego, excessive aggression, poor self–object boundaries, and receptive–masochistic orientation make him extremely vulnerable to his parents' aggressive projections. Lightning regressions into moods of depression and hate can take place. When impulse control is poor, parasuicide and suicide can follow. Behavior of this kind is an effort to escape from pain that arises from the repetition of earlier abandonment experiences. It is driven by hostile, devaluating introjects from earlier childhood, now reinforced by the hateful behavior (retaliatively sadistic or aversive) of the parents.

The parasuicidal or suicidal borderline adolescent has commonly unconsciously assigned all his feelings of worthlessness and shame to his body (Laufer, 1987). The influence of external objects at the moment of self-hurt is much less than that of the internal objects. It is the internal objects which dominate the patient's attitude toward his body and it is primarily they who are involved in the narcissistic regression which is an essential aspect of any attack on the self. As Asch (Panel, 1984) has pointed out, suicide is a paradigm that links depression, masochism, and pathological narcissism. In each condition the patient is dominated by an internal object on which he relies as a source of narcissistic supply and as a defense against the feelings loss arouses.

Many borderline adolescents have established a pattern early in development wherein hostile impulses toward the frustrating mother are turned against the self as she is introjected. When girls begin to mature sexually an unconscious hatred and rejection of their bodies appears; the mature sexual body is identified with the devalued, damaged, and hated parts of mother. Boys probably experience a parallel development, but in that case, the hated body may be identified with the father as well as the mother. In both sexes it is the sexual body that takes the blame for the loss of the mother of early childhood. Deficient in body self-love in the first place, these adolescents are prone to treat their physical selves contemptuously, to expose themselves to danger, to mutilate themselves, and sometimes, to commit suicide.

Their suicide attempts often follow events that seem to prove failure, especially the failure to separate, to become autonomous, and to function in a mature heterosexual way outside of mother's control (Laufer, 1987; Novick, 1984). Failures in these ways confirm old fears that one is abnormal and unacceptable, that the body (its sexual strivings in particular) is repellent and revolting. The danger associated with the unconscious wish to surrender and submit totally to the powerful mother seems intense.

The essential dilemma of the borderline patient as it is experienced in adolescence is clearly in place. Because these adolescents long to maintain the infantile dependent relationship to mother (nothing else seems safe), they deny hostile wishes and find themselves blocked from moving toward autonomy. To integrate their sexuality and acknowledge themselves owners of their bodies is "bad," because such wishes are infused with the primitive rage directed toward the mother. They repudiate their sexual strivings and cannot develop the core sense of personal identity essential for adult well-being. Attempts to find a solution to this predicament can lead to suicide along two different pathways. We understand these to be organized around deadly variations of the two mechanisms of defense Anna Freud (1936) called "altruistic surrender" and "identification with the aggressor."

The self-destructive behavior of some borderline adolescents is organized around the unconscious masochistic fantasy that surrender to total dependency on the powerful preoedipal mother will satisfy their yearning for closeness and blot out hating her. They are prepared to cast off parts of themselves for mother's sake—their autonomy, their sexuality, the right to have a separate existence; they believe she requires it; that unless they comply, they will be abandoned. The unconscious fantasy is that self-sacrifice and subjugation of self parts will transform the pain-giving mother into a loving, caring mother (Novick, 1984). This preparedness for self repudiation explains in part the chameleonlike quality of borderline adaptation so often described in the literature. But the self repudiation, one must remember, is often experienced as a "little suicide."

Of course self repudiation as an adaptive maneuver can never succeed in its end except for short periods. The experience of complete dependence on the mother increases anxiety over hostile wishes which might provoke abandonment, and this conflict becomes more fraught with danger with the mother's failure to change. What the child perceives as her escalating, sadistic demands for more and more self-sacrifice stirs up and intensifies the child's hate.

Suicide may follow, and in such cases it represents what Novick (1984) has called "the ultimate sacrifice of a separate self." Suicide attempts in such patients are accompanied by the fantasy of reuniting and fusing with the wished-for, all-loving mother of infancy. Unconsciously these patients believe that they can be accepted and loved only by relinquishing any sense of identity and separateness.

What we have here is malignant, masochistic altruistic surrender, described by Anna Freud (1936) as combining projection of instinctual impulses, identification with the person onto whom the instincts are projected, and the seeking of vicarious gratification through others instead of reaching toward pleasures of one's own. She described it as a method of overcoming narcissistic mortification, and related its use to the development of a severe superego which forbids the gratification of wishes belonging only to the subject. She also connected it to the fear of death in the following passage:

> We may for a moment study the notion of altruistic surrender . . . in its relation to the fear of death. Anyone who has very largely projected his instinctual impulses onto other people knows nothing of this fear. In the moment of danger his ego is not really concerned with his own life . . . When his impulses have been surrendered in favor of other people, their lives become precious rather than his own [pp. 144–145].

The theme of death is ubiquitous in the conscious and unconscious fantasy life of the self-destructive borderline patient. Fear of dying, the experience of rejection as death, abandonment of the self as death, or complaints of a pervasive feeling of "deadness," all point to a powerful unconscious fantasy of the self as a dead object who has sacrificed all feelings of aliveness and separate selfhood.

Identification with the aggressor is a second defensive complex that can bring borderline patients to suicide. Although Miss Freud (1936) described it as a special form of defense, it is in fact a combination of several—identification, turning passive into active, and projection.

As we have seen, the intensification of regressive dependent longings toward the mother following a failure to separate can arouse overwhelming anxiety in some borderline adolescents. The yearning to submit to the omnipotent, intrusive, yet rejecting mother of early childhood is warded off with narcissistic defenses such as devaluation and the maintenance of an illusion of self-sufficiency (Modell, 1984). Failure of these mechanisms, however, may lead to suicide as the only possible way to separate from the mother and to resolve the sadomasochistic struggle over ownership of the patient's body. Suicide in this case destroys the self part which seems to contain the wish to remain a baby (the body self) and asserts control over the mother who seems to draw the patient toward her like a dangerous magnet.

Inasmuch as the patient wishes to deprive his mother of her little child as the patient felt deprived by her; inasmuch as he is attempting to undo the sense of helplessness and passivity; and inasmuch as the patient projects his sense of failure and worthlessness onto the parents he abandons, such suicides represent identification with the aggressor.

Although any close exploration of a suicide attempt or parasuicide often reveals that both altruistic surrender and identification with the aggressor are at work, the distinction remains useful; one should be prepared to explore in detail both patterns as they may be uncovered in treating patients. Most patients will be influenced to some degree by both defensive complexes. Some suicides are more masochistic and others more destructive–narcissistic in nature, but in a suicidal or parasuicidal act the patient plays out his identification with both the aggressor and the victim.

VICTOR TAUSK'S SUICIDE

Victor Tausk, a psychoanalyst and a student of Freud's, committed suicide by simultaneously shooting and hanging himself on July 3rd, 1919. He was forty years old at the time of his death, and his suicide occurred only eight days before the scheduled date of his marriage. Tausk was a gifted, restless, and troubled man who had tried several different careers before becoming a psychiatrist and a psychoanalyst. Between 1909 and

1919 he was the author of twenty-eight psychoanalytic papers. It is one of the ironies of his life that the memorial note of his death appeared in the same volume of the *Internationale Zeitschrift fur Psychoanalyse* as the paper on psychosis for which he is still held in such high esteem, "On the Origin of the 'Influencing Machine' in Schizophrenia." We discuss his suicide here because it illustrates many of the phenomena involved in borderline self-destructiveness.

Tausk had at first idealized Freud, but after a time he began to display a paranoid, embittered, yet desperately dependent attitude toward him. Tausk repeatedly claimed that Freud was stealing his ideas and not acknowledging him as their true source. It was well known, however, that Tausk often repeated in his lectures ideas which Freud had presented one day earlier. Although over time Tausk had become deeply ambivalent toward Freud, about seven months before the suicide he asked Freud to take him into analysis. The biographical record makes it plain that Tausk's object relationships were unstable, that he made use of splitting as a defense, and that toward Freud, at least, there were alternating attitudes of primitive idealization and devaluation. The equation of self-recognition with self-destruction points to poor ego–superego integration. Feelings of confusion and dread suggest the persecutory, overwhelmed experience of borderline patients when they are trying to reintegrate previously split-off self parts.

Tausk as a child had a history of impulsive, murderous tantrums directed toward his mother whom he both hated and adored. Once in a rage he pierced the heart of a picture of his mother which hung on the wall in his family home. For a long time afterward Tausk did not dare enter the room, behaving as though an actual murder had taken place there. Eissler (1983) has pointed out that destructive outbursts of such intensity indicate primitive, unfused aggression, and that Tausk's avoiding the "scene of the crime" suggests difficulty in separating fantasy from reality.

Freud had good reason to feel uncomfortable about the intensity of the ambivalence and the paranoid attitude Tausk had developed toward him. He refused to accept Tausk for analysis himself but sent him instead to Helene Deutsch, who herself was in analysis with Freud at the time.

Tausk remained in analysis with Deutsch for three months, from January through March of 1919. He spent his hours reiterating his grudges against Freud and sending him entreaties—he knew full well that Deutsch would be forced to detail them in her own analysis. During his analysis with Deutsch it became clear that Tausk's identification with Freud was extremely primitive in nature, if not psychotic. Tausk did not merely wish to be like Freud; unconsciously he wanted to become Freud (Eissler, 1983). Magical, massive identification wishes of this sort defend against intense hate. They involve fantasies of total incorporation of the object in which the object as a separate person is destroyed, with the result that the self is globally transformed (Jacobson, 1954). Tausk was obviously experiencing an ego regression in which his capacity for self–object differentiation was breaking down. Finally, Freud intervened: he told Deutsch that if she was to continue analysis with him she must stop her analysis of Tausk; that the work was leading nowhere, and it was interfering with the treatment Freud and Deutsch were attempting to do.

Deutsch informed Tausk of the termination in his next session, and the treatment ended immediately (Roazen, 1985). Tausk then approached Freud once again, but Freud remained steadfast in his refusal to treat him. Very soon after this double rejection by Freud and Deutsch, Tausk became engaged to a former patient whom he had made pregnant. On the night before he was to obtain his marriage license, following a probable incident of impotence with his fiancée, Tausk killed himself (Eissler, 1983).

The controversy over the circumstances and causes of Victor Tausk's suicide has been vigorously debated through a series of publications by Paul Roazen (1969, 1982, 1985) and K. R. Eissler (1971, 1983). Roazen's central thesis is that Freud was ultimately responsible for Tausk's death because he at first encouraged his magical expectations and then abandoned him. In unflagging defense of Freud, Eissler underlines Tausk's psychopathology as the root cause of his death, emphasizing his narcissistic vulnerabilities, sadomasochistic relationships with women, and tendency to lapse into depressive, paranoid states when he felt he had lost control of his love objects.

We suggest a third formulation informed by a contemporary understanding of suicide in borderline patients. We would contend that Roazen is wrong in contending that Freud, in effect, killed Tausk. Psychoanalysis was still young when Tausk died, and neither Freud, Deutsch, or the other analysts of the time were yet aware that transference psychosis in a borderline patient could be so dangerous. We further believe that Eissler has underestimated the devastating effect that Freud's devaluative comments and gloomy remarks must have had on Tausk who was in so many respects functioning at a borderline level. As we have seen, borderline patients are exquisitely sensitive to projections from others, particularly when what is projected is hostile and aversive. Freud plainly wanted Tausk to go away and leave him alone; Freud's loving approval had become necessary to Tausk for maintaining narcissistic equilibrium. Without it he lay at the mercy of hateful inner objects and would turn against himself. His bitter complaints and entreaties as he lay on Helene Deutsch's couch indicated his incapacity to maintain self-integration without help from the external objects he had chosen.

Freud had been both emotionally and financially supportive of Tausk, but after Tausk's attitude began to change, quite understandably he began to feel uncomfortable, disappointed, and annoyed. When the analyst Ludvig Jekels asked Freud why he declined to take Tausk as a patient, Freud replied, "He is going to kill me!" (Roazen, 1982). Ultimately Freud came to view Tausk as worthless and dangerous. In a letter to Lou Andreas-Salome after Tausk's death Freud wrote, "I confess I do not really miss him; I had long taken him to be useless, indeed a threat to the future" (Roazen, 1985).

In our view Tausk was a fair representative of the class of patients for whom Stern (1938) invented the term *borderline*. Referred for psychoanalysis because superficially they appeared to have intact egos and to maintain a neurotic level of adaptation, such patients, once on the couch, experienced ego regressions in the transference that frequently required interruption of analysis and, sometimes, admission to a hospital.

Stern pointed out that such transferences could lead to suicidal crises.

Tausk was psychologically brilliant, and central to his brilliance was a deep understanding of ego-regressed and ego-fragmented states. About these painful states he appears to have known much from his own suffering. The paper on the "influencing machine" introduced the concept of loss of ego boundaries in psychosis, and discussed a notion quite similar to projective identification or identification with the aggressor, referred to as "identification with the persecutor." It is clear, furthermore, that Tausk's moods were unstable and that he was subject to spells of marked despair and burning feelings of rejection.

Freud and Deutsch had quite reasonably concluded that they could not help Tausk—the "analysis" with Deutsch was going nowhere, and Freud, sensing a hopelessly sticky situation, declined to take Tausk as a patient himself. These disappointments Tausk must have experienced as a double and devastating oedipal defeat and narcissistic humiliation; he could not, on his own, find or accept another analyst, and neither Freud nor Deutsch appears to have appreciated that their double refusal was more than Tausk could endure.

Tausk next impulsively tried to preserve his ruined self-esteem by action in the phallic–narcissistic mode. He was regressed; his dependency needs were intense, his body narcissism unstable. He needed reassurance, and he must have been exquisitely sensitive to any further failure. Thus, as already noted, he began an affair with a patient, made her pregnant, and asked her to marry him. Then he apparently became impotent, and went on to kill himself.

His suicidal regression began with an attempt to find a woman to idealize who might then counteract his inner sense of fragmentation and bolster the denial of his sadistic wishes. His self-destruction, however, may have become unavoidable if the safety of this idealized union was invaded by regressive fears and longings for total dependence and submission to an omnipotent preoedipal mother in the person of his pregnant fiancée.

His suicide probably took place in an acute depressive spell wherein he had abandoned hope of holding himself together with the aid of an idealized exterior sustaining object. His incapacity to care about the difficulties and needs of the woman and child he abandoned by committing suicide reflects the depth of his narcissism, but the suicide quite probably reflects a parallel conviction that he could never be of any real use to anybody in this world. In his suicide note, he referred to his death as an act of "decency and health," and his sense of worthlessness was reflected in his request that he should be speedily forgotten.

Tausk's suicide would seem to have followed a sadomasochistic regression which escalated into a determination to die and disappear into nothingness. He wished, in essence, that he would be blotted from the memory of everyone—in other words, that all the projected parts of himself should be relinquished and disposed of. One can see here an indication of the role which projective identification (M. Klein, 1946) and the failure of its containment (Bion, 1962) played in Tausk's death.

As Ogden (1982) has pointed out, projective identification includes a component of provoking others. The patient attempts to induce in the recipient of the projection behavior which is consistent with that which is being projected. The psychotherapeutic relationship provides a laboratory where this phenomenon can be studied. The therapist's capacity to bear and to contain the patient's projections and provocations helps the patient reintegrate parts of himself previously felt to be unbearable. However, as the intensity of the patient's interpersonal provocation increases, the therapist finds it increasingly difficult to contain the projection without slipping into a destructive countertransference response (Adler, 1989). If the safety of the therapeutic environment begins to give way because the therapist cannot tolerate the provocations and projections, what the patient projects will become more primitive, an even more intense interpersonal coercion arises, and the patient's capacity to differentiate himself from the therapist may crumble (Shapiro, 1982a).

Tausk's relationship with Freud and its influence on Tausk's suicide shows what can happen when the object of excessive projective identification, in both its projective and provocative aspects, fails to endure and modify the patient's warded-off aspects, but instead withdraws and is felt to return the feared, negative projections. Tausk was certainly not Freud's patient, but he behaved and felt as though he were Freud's patient, or should have been Freud's patient. Freud's refusal to treat him must have made Tausk feel abandoned and confirmed as "bad," destructive, and alone. We know that in actual therapies the dangerousness of the patient's violent impulses and fantasies is reinforced by the therapist's negative counterprojections (Marziali and Monroe-Blum, (1987). Tausk's self–other confusion between himself and Freud, along with his complaints of having things stolen from him, indicates the operation of projective identification of an excessive nature.

COUNTERTRANSFERENCE PROBLEMS

The importance of countertransference hate as a factor in suicide, particularly in the treatment of borderline patients, has long been appreciated. The emotional assaults that such patients level against the therapist are certain to evoke troublesome responses. These patients project hateful, rejecting attitudes into the therapist and treat him as though the patient's unwelcome attitudes belonged to him. The devaluated therapist, reacting to a concentrated attack on his self-esteem, is likely to be sadistically stimulated toward the patient. Unless the therapist's superego is sufficiently mature so that his sadism can be consciously experienced but contained, aversive acting out is likely to take place. The patient will be rejected because the therapist cannot tolerate the impulses in himself that the patient provokes.

Countertransference hatred of borderline patients is not only a problem in their psychotherapy, but in their ward management. Kullgren (1988) has reported on a group of fifteen patients with a diagnosis of BPD who committed suicide, comparing them with a control group of borderlines who did not. Eleven of the suicides took place in an inpatient setting, and countertransference reactions on the part of the staff which led to punitive or rejecting behavior were important factors in

Therapeutic Issues and Treatment Modalities

more than half of those cases. (These suicides were discussed in greater detail in an earlier article he published in the Scandinavian literature [Kullgren, 1985].) His examples of countertransference acting out included premature discharge from the hospital against the patient's wishes, unwillingness to accept a patient for treatment, inappropriate restriction, unnecessary medication, and transfer to other institutions.

Krohn (1974) has discussed the borderline patient's disturbed subjective experience of others. His incapacity to integrate the positive, enduring ego traits of others into his inner images of them, coupled with an exquisite sensitivity toward their primitive superego contents and aggressive impulses, can hurt the self-esteem of excessively vulnerable therapists and give rise to destructive acting out. Self-love and self-esteem injuries inflicted on a therapist can give rise to unconscious narcissistic rage reactions that imperil the treatment.

Obviously, and from the previous discussion, this kind of interaction between the patient and the therapist can be, and often is, explained in terms of projective identification. While the notion of projective identification is useful in understanding how borderline patients need to split off and attribute to others aspects of their own mental life which they cannot tolerate (sometimes evoking in those others noxious reactions), it is insufficient to explain fully all countertransference phenomena that arise in treating borderline cases.

To explain the phenomena of hate in the countertransference solely on the basis of projective identification overlooks the fact that therapists themselves have a psychological homeostasis in which there are complex interactions of impulse and defense intimately connected to the therapist's superego system and the maturity of his narcissism. There is more to the mind of the therapist than a passive reflex system which reacts automatically to what the patient projects into it. The target of any projective identification has certain conflictual or unacceptable feelings that may be repressed, split off, or denied. These feelings, to the extent that they remain unconscious, are the targets at which the projective maneuver is aimed. If the problem feelings cannot be acknowledged, contained, and placed in perspective by the therapist, countertransference acting out is likely to follow.

We hope that previous discussion in this essay will have shown why borderline patients must resort to manipulative, controlling, and hateful behavior, projecting their own hate and destructiveness into others, provoking others to punish and attack them for their "badness." Now let us have a look at why this psychological activity of the borderline patients causes such difficulty for those who are responsible for their care.

Semrad (Semrad, Buie, Maltsberger, Silberger, and Van Buskirk, 1969) and his coworkers have pointed out how over-stimulating deeply disturbed patients may be to those who spend long periods of time with them. Trainees, especially, who sit hour after hour with borderline individuals, experience an assault against their defenses to the point where sexual, but most especially, aggressive, impulses threaten or in fact break through to consciousness. If clinical workers cannot tolerate aggressive reactions in themselves, acting out against the patient is likely to occur.

These difficulties and their potential in promoting professional development are illustrated by the history of Dr. P., a colleague, who has given permission for us to report a painful experience in his residency and how he made it an occasion for growth.

> Dr. P., a first-year psychiatric resident, was subjected to protracted periods of freezing silence over many hours in his psychotherapy of an aggressively parasuicidal border-line woman. He felt at first quite restless and uncomfort-able, but ultimately experienced a conscious breakthrough of wishes to slash the patient's neck with a knife. The experience was extremely shocking to him and the treatment would certainly have ended by a rejection of the patient had not a skillful supervisor been available. The resident also was able to integrate and profit from this experience in the course of his personal psychoanalysis.

Maltsberger and Buie (1974) have examined in some detail the defenses against and reactions to countertransference hate in therapists. They distinguish two principal components of transference hate—malice and aversion. Dr. P.'s difficulties with his punishing borderline patient show how countertransference malice and aversion are called into play.

Some months after his alarming countertransference experience Dr. P. was able to share with his supervisor the following understanding: he understood the restlessness and discomfort he experienced with his patient before the aggressive breakthrough to be the consequence of a weakening defense against the sadistic impulses the patient was arousing in him through her rejecting behavior. When Dr. P. had been feeling restless and fidgety the impulse to attack the patient remained unconscious; he was only aware of looking frequently and furtively at the clock, and wanting the session to end so he could leave the room. When the conscious wish to attack her came fully into consciousness, Dr. P. was horrified and had difficulty in making himself sit still until the end of the session.

This countertransference experience shows both aspects of countertransference hate at work. The countertransference of malice is obvious in Dr. P.'s wish to cut his patient's throat. The countertransference of aversion is also plain in this example—Dr. P. wanted to get away from the patient who was making him so uncomfortable. During his restless phase he wanted to leave the room. When his sadism broke through into consciousness, he wanted to run out. Generally speaking, aversion in the countertransference expresses the wish to take flight from what the patient is stimulating in oneself by getting rid of the patient.

Although the patient's part in provoking this impulse to cut is obvious (one may call it an example of projective identification), there was, Dr. P. believed, another factor at work: the patient had injured his self-regard, and he came to identify his wish to attack her for it as an example of Kohut's (1972) "narcissistic rage." This patient had injured his self-regard in at least two ways.

First of all, Dr. P. had chosen to go to medical school to help sick people. In the course of his internship he had derived great satisfaction from prescribing effective medicine for pneumonia, for congestive heart failure, and other illnesses, and had enjoyed the grateful responses of his medical patients. His

borderline patient, however, denied him the narcissistic gratification he needed in order to feel good about himself; that is,
to improve under his care and to thank him for it. This patient
even seemed to get worse (the frequency of her manipulative
parasuicidal episodes had increased), and instead of thanking
him for his very earnest efforts, she treated him with silent,
cold contempt. This was too much for him to bear, and he
wanted to take a bloody revenge on her for showing him up,
for making him look a failure according to his inner standards.

Dr. P.'s ego ideal, like that of many trainees (and quite a few
more mature practitioners), required him to cure his patients in
order to feel good about himself. He had not matured sufficiently to come to terms with the fact that some patients do not
get better. As the months of the residency passed he developed
a wiser if sadder set of self-expectations, renouncing his previous self-requirement of therapeutic omnipotence. He came to
see that a therapist's merit is not determined by the cures he
effects, but by how loyally and faithfully he puts at his patients'
disposal the best of the knowledge and art of his craft that he
can command.

His maturing ego ideal had to develop yet further. Before
his residency experience it had been unacceptable to Dr. P. to
have sexual or hostile impulses toward patients. His personal
therapeutic ideal resembled Sir Galahad. Psychoanalysis helped
him reach a more physicianly perspective. The identification
he was able to form with the supervisor who helped him at the
time of his countertransference eruption was also very helpful.
From the supervisor he received support: an explanation that
such primitive emotional moments were commonplace in the
minds of sensitive, mature therapists, and that all manner of
feelings and ideas must be expected. He was reassured that a
homicidal impulse was not a signal he was going mad, or that
he was a bad doctor. Dr. P., over time, was able to take the
tolerance and acceptance of his supervisor and of his analyst
into his superego. He came to understand that at the level of
his impulse life the Latin maxim, "Nothing human is alien to
me," must apply. To feel a homicidal impulse, he learned, is
part of being human, and that to acknowledge without quailing
the dark and primitive aspects of his impulse life could not only

be interesting but helpful in treating psychotic patients. He even came to feel that he was courageous in being able to do so.

Psychotherapeutic, psychoanalytic, and supervisory work with other clinical professionals has shown that countertransference aversion can also be generated as a defense against empathic experience of psychotic and suicidal affect. To feel what suicidal patients feel, to share, even for an hour, the subjective sense of worthlessness, eerie aloneness, and despair, can be very painful indeed. Even to have a fully empathic experience of profound sadness is exquisitely painful for some clinical workers. The tendency is to get away from the patient in one way or another. Good clinical work with borderline patients requires of us the willingness and capacity to suspend defensive and avoidance operations sufficiently to empathize with their inner experience to the extent they can permit it. It is empathy which they need to repair the structural deficiencies and malformations which have made them borderline in the first place, and it was deprivation of empathy, early and late in life, that made them sick.

CONCLUSION

While suicide remains a special hazard in patients with borderline personality disorders, enough is now understood so that times of special danger can be identified and particular risks and vulnerabilities recognized.

We have shown that parasuicide needs to be distinguished from the true suicide attempt, and that their purposes are different. The manipulative parasuicidal act which fails in its aim to coerce the needed narcissistic relief from others in the patient's environment can indicate a genuine suicide attempt may follow. Borderline patients are exquisitely sensitive to the loss of those on whom they rely for support and self-regulation; we need to keep alert to the danger of suicidal crises when losses occur.

The development of melancholic depressive symptoms in a borderline patient who is already suffering from a characteriologic abandonment depression signals the appearance of "double depression" and an increase of suicidal danger. A history of dangerous previous true suicide attempts heightens the danger. Since borderline patients have so little capacity to tolerate depressive pain it is essential that their depressive symptoms should be aggressively treated by whatever possible means (including drugs and electroconvulsive treatment) if the risk of suicide is to be reduced.

The sensitivity of borderline patients to hostile projections from others, and their readiness to introject what is projected into them (projective identification), makes it important to monitor the attitudes of those on whom the patient depends to keep in narcissistic balance. Evidence that important others want to get rid of the patient, or that the patient is provoking them to devalue him, should alert the clinician to the danger of an impending suicide crisis.

In a corollary way the clinician must be alert to what the patient excites in him, whether by projective identification or by narcissistic assault. When the caretakers unconsciously want to destroy the patient and act out their countertransferences so as to reject the patient (aversive acting out) suicide may follow.

16.

Medicolegal Issues Between the Borderline Patient and the Therapist

Thomas G. Gutheil, M.D., and Victoria Alexander, B.A.

The experience of clinical work with borderline patients has qualities that set it apart from work with patients who have other kinds of disorders. Borderline patients can mobilize intense feelings in those who treat them, and these feelings may at times interfere with the use of sound clinical judgment. In addition, such patients are prone to impulsive behavior in the form of violence toward themselves or others or destruction of property. These features of the borderline syndrome make both the treating clinician and the patient particularly susceptible to legal scrutiny. The clinician who allows intense responses to the borderline patient to undermine clinical judgment may be the target of malpractice litigation, and the patient who behaves violently may likewise come under the scrutiny of the court—a result that may in turn involve the clinician. Indeed, borderline patients appear in a disproportionate percentage of suits against therapists (Gutheil, 1985, 1989).

This chapter outlines the primary areas of medicolegal vulnerability for therapists treating borderline patients and suggests approaches to clinical management designed both to promote the alliance between clinician and patient and to protect the clinician against malpractice litigation (Gutheil, 1985, 1989). The discussion is illustrated by hypothetical case vignettes and by actual cases (the details of which have been disguised to protect the privacy of the individuals involved), all based on extensive clinical and forensic consultation.

THE LEGAL CONTEXT

That borderline patients, many of whom do not appear to be very ill, are disproportionately overrepresented in certain kinds of medicolegal cases may seem counterintuitive: one expects sicker patients to be involved in such cases. This curious finding merits a brief examination of the legal context in which medico-legal issues are played out.

Malpractice Liability

The issue of malpractice liability is discussed in more detail elsewhere (Gutheil and Appelbaum, 1982), but the essentials can be summarized as follows.

The legal definition of malpractice has four elements. First, it must be shown that the clinician owed a duty to the patient (i.e., the patient claiming malpractice must be the clinician's patient). Second, the clinician must have breached that duty by deviating from—falling short of—the standard of care (i.e., the care given by the average reasonable practitioner of the same discipline). Such a deviation by omission from standard practice is considered "negligence." Third, damages—physical, emotional, or economic—must have resulted from that negligence. Fourth, a direct causal link must be established between the negligence and the damages. All four elements of malpractice—duty, negligence, damages, and causation—must be established on the basis of a preponderance of the evidence.

Suicide: Suicide is the most common ground for malpractice claims against mental health professionals. The legal action may be styled "wrongful death"—wrongful because death allegedly occurred through negligence. While threats of suicide and manipulative attempts are familiar phenomena with borderline patients, actual deaths by suicide are also a common basis for litigation in this population of patients. Closely related clinical issues are impulsive self-harm or self-mutilation, impulsive harm to others, and overt criminal behavior (e.g., drug-related crimes).

Failure to Commit: With the wisdom of hindsight, the claim may be advanced that a suicidal or self-mutilating borderline patient should have been committed.

False Imprisonment (Unjustified Commitment or Seclusion): Conversely, a borderline patient may claim that his or her involuntary commitment (or seclusion while hospitalized) was inappropriate and unjustified. Although many clinicians are particularly fearful of this claim, in modern practice it is rarely successful in court, as long as the clinician can demonstrate good faith in the decision to commit (or seclude) the patient.

Abandonment: While, in theory, clinicians may stop work with any patient at any time for any reason, two practical exceptions to this rule have medicolegal significance. First, a therapist may not stop treating a patient in the midst of a crisis; the crisis must be weathered or the patient contained (e.g., hospitalized) before the therapist can "pass the baton." Second, in situations other than mutually agreed-on terminations, the clinician must arrange for a transfer of care or offer referrals to alternative services, so that the patient is not left without recourse. Failure to heed these exceptions may bring a claim of abandonment. The sensitivity to rejection that so many borderline patients demonstrate may trigger valid or specious claims of abandonment.

With this background, we now turn to an examination of the borderline patient from the attorney's perspective.

Patient and Attorney

Attorneys who specialize in mental health litigation are familiar with the symptoms and behaviors associated with such diagnostic categories as schizophrenia, mania, depression, and psychopathy. The borderline syndrome, however, is comparatively new to mental health law—as it is to psychiatry itself—even though it was one of the diagnoses entertained in the trial of John Hinckley for the attempted assassination of President Reagan in 1982.

The borderline syndrome constitutes a somewhat murkier diagnostic category than, say, schizophrenia or bipolar disorder. Indeed, the term *borderline* is itself rather ambiguous, particularly in the legal arena, where an effort is made to use language in a strictly denotative capacity, avoiding the ambiguities of connotation. Attorneys encountering the diagnosis in a case record generally lack a clear picture of the symptoms and behavior associated with the borderline disorder (Gutheil, 1985).

Moreover, many borderline patients, unlike those with other serious disorders, do not appear to be sick. A patient with schizophrenia, for example, often has symptoms of illness, such as psychotic delusions or hallucinations, that are evident to the lay observer as well as the experienced clinician. A borderline patient, in contrast, may seem quite normal, and the attorney representing such a patient might even wonder why he or she is under psychiatric care. Similarly, the attorney may be deceived by a borderline patient's distorted perceptions, because they are expressed by a seemingly rational, lucid individual. Whereas a more overtly paranoid patient may voice wild and unlikely accusations, a borderline patient's complaints appear to be more plausible. Thus, unfamiliar with the clinical manifestations of the borderline syndrome and misled by the patient's apparently normal demeanor and plausible complaints, the unsuspecting attorney may become the catalyst in the transformation of a clinical conflict into a formal adversarial proceeding.

The problem is complicated by the attorney's professional mandate, as the patient's legal advocate, to represent the patient's view of the situation at hand (Gutheil and Magraw,

1984). If the attorney believes that the client's complaint is unrealistic, he or she may of course express that opinion and advise the client not to pursue the matter. However, the situation is not always so clear-cut.

Case 1

A borderline patient who had been involuntarily committed to a psychiatric hospital requested that her attorney seek her release. She was able to convince the attorney that a recent overdose had been accidental rather than intentional, and that her physician was simply overreacting out of anxiety. The attorney, persuaded by the patient's picture of the situation, succeeded in obtaining her release from the hospital. Shortly after being discharged, the patient again overdosed.

The otherwise experienced attorney may also be confused by the apparent disparity between the borderline patient's clinical demeanor and the recommended treatment. Some patients, as noted above, seem too healthy to be hospitalized, medicated, or otherwise treated; others, particularly those undergoing a transient but severe regression, appear to be too sick for discharge, even though this course of action may well "cure" the regression.

RELEVANT PSYCHODYNAMIC FEATURES

The psychodynamic workings of the borderline syndrome are discussed elsewhere in this book. Here the discussion is limited to the effects of certain psychodynamic characteristics on the relationship between the borderline patient and the therapist, as well as the potential medicolegal repercussions.

Borderline Rage

Clinicians in training are often reluctant to work with borderline patients because of the contagious quality of their intense affect, especially rage, which is typically directed at the therapist. Even the experienced therapist, feeling undeserving of the patient's anger, may respond in kind. If not acknowledged and controlled, this reactive anger can cloud clinical judgment, leading to abandonment of the patient—whether overtly, through termination, or indirectly, through distancing and failure of empathy. In the event that these maladaptive responses result in a bad outcome, there may be grounds for a claim of malpractice against the therapist (Gutheil, 1985).

For example, consider the hypothetical case of a borderline patient who is hospitalized because of suicidal behavior. The patient directs her rage toward her primary clinician, as well as toward other members of the clinical staff on the unit, quickly establishing a reputation as a "difficult" patient. The staff respond by avoiding her and thus fail to observe her behavior closely. When she requests a pass, her primary clinician and the treatment team grant it without sufficient evaluation of her suicidality. While away from the hospital, the patient throws herself in front of an oncoming train and is killed. In the wake of her suicide, the patient's family takes on her rage at her treaters, suing the primary physician and the hospital for negligence. In this case, they may well be found negligent for failing to exercise sufficient caution in granting the pass.

Though hypothetical, this case is by no means exaggerated. It suggests the kinds of clinical responses to borderline rage that can be so detrimental to treatment. The staff's decision to grant the patient a pass may well have derived in part from an unconscious wish to be rid of her (Maltsberger and Buie, 1974). Their response amounted to a form of abandonment, however subtle or unintentional, which might conceivably have contributed to the patient's final despair.

Another characteristic response to borderline rage is reactive overinvolvement on the clinician's part. Although the effect of this response is quite different from that of abandonment, it springs from the same feeling of coercion—the therapist "dares not" refuse the patient's wishes. Thus, the therapist who is ordinarily quite strict about remaining within the boundaries of the therapeutic relationship may feel pressured into transgressing those boundaries in the face of angry demands, hostile threats, or persistent personal inquiries from a borderline patient. At its extreme, this type of response has led to a sexual relationship between patient and therapist, as we discuss in some detail later in this chapter.

Narcissistic Entitlement

Many borderline patients are convinced that they are special and therefore entitled to special treatment. They tend to view any therapeutic result that falls short of perfection as less than they deserve. At an extreme, this narcissistic entitlement, and the inevitable disappointment it fosters, may prompt the patient to sue for malpractice as a punitive measure against the therapist, either for "less than perfect" results or for the feelings of rejection associated with termination.

Borderline patients often combine an overpowering sense of entitlement with strong manipulative skills, which may serve feelings of entitlement. Even patients who have become dysfunctional in many areas of their lives may remain surprisingly adept at manipulating other people in order to obtain what they are convinced they deserve. Clinicians in training and even those who are seasoned professionals may fall prey to the borderline patient's sense of specialness (Main, 1957; Pollack and Battle, 1963), making exceptions that they would never make with other patients. Like rage, this sense of specialness can be contagious, particularly when combined with an idealizing transference. Some of the most destructive relationships between patient and therapist begin as a mutual admiration society. The therapist, already idealized, is invited to partake of the patient's specialness as well. The narcissistic isolation of the resulting misalliance may account, at least in part, for the failure of so many therapists to obtain consultation in such cases or even to exercise their own critical judgment.

Conversely, clinicians and staff may respond to the borderline patient's sense of entitlement by bending over backward to *avoid* treating the patient as special. In doing so, they may actually withhold appropriate care or fail to provide sufficient observation. This too can lead to litigation, but with more substantial grounds for a finding of negligence than in the case of an entitled patient suing for less than perfect treatment results (Gutheil, 1985).

Victimization and Dependency

Another expression of narcissistic entitlement is the borderline patient's posture of victimization. This stance tends to evoke an overgiving rather than undergiving response from the therapist, yet it can be just as detrimental to treatment. Feeling protective of the patient, the clinician may be tempted to make exceptions to the usual therapeutic rules governing fees and scheduling of sessions, for example. Taken to an extreme, such special dispensations may violate the boundaries of the therapeutic relationship between clinician and patient, in the form of inappropriate social or sexual interactions (Gutheil, 1985).

Case 2

A suicidal borderline patient lamented his "imprisonment" in the hospital in such a pathetic yet persistent manner that he made the clinical staff feel like his sadistic jailors. Out of guilt, they granted him a pass, during which he made a serious suicide attempt.

Victimization and dependency may engender the fantasy that the therapist is the one person who can gratify all the patient's needs, not just therapeutic ones (Smith, 1977). In some cases, a reciprocal narcissistic fantasy motivates the therapist: the wish to "be everything" to the patient (Gutheil, 1989).

Psychotic Transferences

Borderline patients are highly susceptible to psychotic transferences to their therapist. Often intense and abrupt, these transferences make clinical work with borderline patients particularly taxing. Unlike a neurotic transference, a psychotic transference is not bound by any tests of reality on the patient's part. For example, a neurotic patient might articulate feelings toward the therapist and recognize that they are like certain feelings about a parent: "I feel toward you *as if* you were cold and withholding like my mother." A borderline patient expresses the parallel feelings but does not recognize their origin in transference: "You *are* cold and withholding" (Gutheil, 1985). In the case of a change in therapists, the psychotic transference can shift rapidly to the new clinician, however intense the transference with the previous clinician.

Inexperienced clinicians are often dismayed by the rapidity with which the borderline patient forms a psychotic transference, as well as by the intensity of its expression. The medicolegal implications are apparent. The patient tends to view the treatment—and the treater—as "the problem" or, often, "the *only* problem." It is also easy to see how this essentially transferential view of therapy can reinforce some of the other psychodynamic features of the borderline syndrome, especially rage and entitlement, leading to an accusation of negligence.

Case 3

A patient was admitted to the state hospital at night. At the treatment planning conference the next morninng, the patient was interviewed by her primary clinician. Asked what she thought the problem was, the patient complained bitterly about the night staff's insensitivity and neglect. The startled therapist exclaimed, "But surely things were going wrong for you even *before* you came to the hospital! Otherwise, you wouldn't have been admitted."

Two other features of psychotic transference in borderline patients add to the medicolegal repercussions. First, a psychotic transference often tends to be expressed in a manner that devalues the object of the transference, as Adler (1970) has emphasized. The patient who is convinced that his or her therapist is cold and withholding may react by claiming that the therapist is no good and perhaps even negligent. Second, a borderline

patient is frequently psychotic *only* in the transference, otherwise behaving in an apparently rational and credible manner
(Gutheil, 1985). Thus, the devaluing opinions issue from a patient who may not appear to be "merely crazy."

Splitting

The psychic mechanism of splitting, which Kernberg (1967)
describes so well, provides fertile ground for acting out clinical
conflicts in a medicolegal setting. Not only can the idol be
abruptly transformed into the pariah, in the eyes of the patient,
but the patient can cast two different people—such as therapist
and attorney—in these roles simultaneously. Consider the following case:

Case 4

A severely ill woman with the borderline syndrome idealized her attorney and denigrated her therapist. She told
her attorney that her therapist was "sadistic, vicious, and
full of rage." The attorney, both flattered by his client's
compliments and incensed at her depiction of her physician, tried to arrange for a new therapist. Threatened now
by the possible loss of her therapist, the patient suddenly
turned on the bewildered attorney and accused him of
sabotaging her treatment. The attorney was astounded at
his client's "change of heart."

In this case, the attorney does not realize that the
patient's feelings toward him are directly influenced by
her opposite and equivalent feelings toward her therapist.
Faced with the threat of losing the therapist, she turns on
the attorney, reversing the roles she has assigned them
and thus maintaining her external enactment of the split
that she experiences within herself (Gutheil and Magraw,
1984).

Boundary Confusion

Some borderline patients lose sight of the boundaries between themselves and others when they are under stress. In combination with certain other psychodynamic mechanisms, such as fusion and projective identification, the patient's confusion over the boundaries between patient and therapist may engender a reciprocal confusion in the clinician, a disturbingly common prelude to legal trouble. When boundaries are blurred on both sides, the relationship between patient and therapist is particularly vulnerable to distortions resulting from the patient's intense affects and wishes and the therapist's collusion in these feelings. For this reason, clinical work with borderline patients, over and above their treatment needs, calls for the most scrupulous attention on the therapist's part to the preservation of clear boundaries delineating the roles of patient and clinician within the therapeutic relationship (Gutheil, 1989).

REGRESSION AND LIMIT-SETTING

It is no coincidence that much of the literature on limit-setting in response to regression is illustrated by examples from clinical experience with borderline patients (Cohen and Grinspoon, 1963; Gutheil, 1977). A clinical response to regression in patients with various kinds of psychiatric disorders, limit-setting is particularly appropriate as a means of managing regression in the context of the borderline syndrome. As Friedman (1969) has observed, patients with this disorder are prone to a dangerous form of regression that occurs not in the service of the ego but as a response to libidinal or aggressive flooding. By setting limits, or external controls, on the patient's behavior, the clinician helps thwart, and hence contain, the destructive impulses or wishes that might otherwise overcome the regressed borderline patient. Examples of limit-setting include verbal sanctions, restriction of space (at an extreme, commitment, seclusion, or restraint), and even involuntary discharge or transfer (Gutheil and Appelbaum, 1982), which is the most problematic in terms of medicolegal ramifications. The latter two forms of limit-setting may be particularly effective in managing regression in borderline patients, since such patients tend to distrust verbal communication but are likely to accept communication through physical action (Friedman, 1969).

Of course, limit-setting as a means of managing dangerous regression in borderline patients carries certain dangers of its own. Inexperienced staff may lose sight of the different functions of regression, setting limits indiscriminately in an effort to avert all regressive behavior (Peteet and Gutheil, 1979). If unexamined, moreover, milieu countertransference may prompt angry staff to label "difficult" behavior as borderline regression in need of control.

From a medicolegal perspective, limit-setting may appear to be arbitrary deprivation of the borderline patient's rights and freedom.

Case 4

A severely regressed borderline man was put in seclusion and allowed to go to the bathroom during scheduled breaks when a staff member was free to accompany him. The patient's attorney demanded that her client be allowed to go to the bathroom unaccompanied whenever he wished. She discounted the staff's concerns about the patient's frequent impulsive suicide attempts, claiming that her client was healthy enough to take care of his own bodily needs and that the requirement that he be accompanied at scheduled times was an infringement of his rights.

In this case, limit-setting seemed unduly harsh to the attorney because of the patient's apparently rational state. Yet the clinical means of managing the patient's regression (telling him that he would have to wait for a staff member to accompany him) represented an appropriate intervention for an impulsive, suicidal patient who felt entitled to an immediate response to his demands, despite the needs of sicker patients and limited staff availability.

Considering this kind of misunderstanding, limit-setting in the form of involuntary discharge may be interpreted as a violation of the patient's right to hospital care. In addition, some voluntary discharges, however well negotiated and clinically sound, cause anticipatory regression, and in some cases, an involuntary discharge temporarily intensifies the regressive behavior it is intended to control. If the patient acts out, instead of pulling together, the staff may be vulnerable to a charge of negligence.

BOUNDARY VIOLATIONS AND PATIENT–THERAPIST SEX

It should be apparent from the discussion thus far that clinical work with borderline patients is particularly susceptible to boundary violations. The psychodynamic forces underlying such violations vary, but certain patterns are much more characteristic of therapy with a borderline patient than of work with patients who have other kinds of psychiatric disorders. The borderline patient may act out of rage and entitlement or neediness and dependency, and the therapist may respond from reactive anger or narcissism. When this occurs, the interaction between the two is more perilous in the sense that there are greater temptations, on both sides, to lose sight of the standard limitations imposed on the therapeutic relationship. If these psychodynamic patterns remain unexamined, errors in therapy and countertransference responses may result in violations of the boundary between patient and therapist. These violations can range from social interactions that overstep the limits of the therapeutic relationship to sexual intercourse (Gutheil, 1989).

The Legal Perspective

All the mental health professions view sexual relations between clinician and patient as unethical. Recent case law reflects this position. Such relations are viewed as a deviation from the standard of care and therefore malpractice, provided the other requisite elements of malpractice can be demonstrated (dereliction of the clinician's duty to care for the patient and harm suffered by the patient as a direct result of the clinician's deviation from the standard of care) (Gutheil and Appelbaum, 1982). Yet the scope of this problem is much broader than the case law would suggest (Kardener, 1974; Kardener, Fuller, and Mensh, 1976; Perry, 1976; Gartrell, Herman, Olarte, Feldstein, and Localio, 1986), since many episodes are never reported, much less litigated, and many filed legal claims—perhaps even the majority—are settled out of court.

Whether litigated or settled, a large number of these cases involve borderline patients. Stone and others have examined the characteristics of therapists who become sexually involved with their patients (Stone, 1984; Gartrell et al., 1986). Here we are more concerned with the particular features of the borderline syndrome that influence the relationship between patient and therapist, making it vulnerable to sexual and other boundary violations.

THE CLINICAL CONTEXT

In this section we present a series of cases that illustrate boundary violations, including sexual misconduct, by therapists treating borderline patients (Gutheil, 1989). Some cases involve false accusations of sexual misconduct by the therapists, but in most cases the accusations were true. In fact, most claims of sexual misconduct brought by patients against their therapists turn out to be substantiated. Borderline patients figure prominently in these claims, whether true or false. For our purposes here, "true" accusations are those that were acknowledged as true by the therapists involved, and "false" accusations are those that the patients subsequently revealed to be false.

All the cases presented here have been disguised to protect the privacy of the parties involved. Taken from actual case law and from forensic consultations, these cases all involve male therapists and female borderline patients, reflecting the most common pattern. All the legal cases have been settled out of court, resolved in court, dropped, or dismissed, and more than a year has elapsed since each consultation.

Whether the accusations were true or false, these cases have certain features in common. They were all clinically mismanaged, in that the therapist failed to maintain boundaries between himself and the patient and also failed to recognize the patient's specific need for clarity about these boundaries. In some cases this mismanagement seemed to represent a lapse in clinical judgment by an experienced therapist dealing with a difficult patient. In other cases, boundary violations were the result of inexperience, ignorance of the appropriate clinical management for borderline patients, or unrecognized countertransference problems.

False Accusations of Sexual Misconduct: In the comparatively small number of cases involving false accusations of sexual misconduct, the patient seems to be motivated by rage and the wish for revenge. Overwhelmed by the intensity of these feelings, the patient apparently feels justified in disregarding the truth or is simply blinded to it. This type of pathological lying, or "pseudologia fantastica," as Snyder (1986) terms it, may involve sexual fantasies and may serve the function of primitive denial or projective identification; alternatively, it may represent a transient loss of the ability to engage in reality testing. As the following cases demonstrate, it is essential to consider the clinical context in which an accusation occurs.

Case 5

Enraged at her therapist for treating her "like a welfare case," a borderline patient claimed that he had sexually molested her during a therapy session. She later confided in her attorney that she had fabricated the claim as a way of getting back at her therapist for treating her disrespectfully.

Case 6

Responding to his patient's helpless demeanor and acute loneliness, a psychiatrist became excessively, although not sexually, involved with her. For example, over a period of several weeks, while she was without a car, he drove her home after each therapy session. On one occasion, she asked to see him on the weekend. He refused, explaining that he had plans with his family. Enraged, the patient sued him for sexual abuse but later told a friend that she had lied.

In the first case, the patient's false accusation was a response to her feeling of being mistreated, although the therapist did not act in any manner that might realistically have been interpreted as mistreatment, clinical or otherwise. In the second case, specific errors in clinical judgment fed the patient's fantasy that her therapist had "special feelings" for her that took precedence over his feelings for everyone else (his other patients and his family). She accused him of sexual abuse after experiencing his refusal to see her on the weekend as an explicit rejection. Thus, although neither therapist appeared to be guilty of actual sexual misconduct, the second therapist, unlike the first, violated the boundaries of the therapeutic relationship with the patient and in doing so fed her disappointment and rage. In some sense, then, he invited the accusation. Other cases of false accusation have been prompted by borderline rage at bill collection efforts and termination of treatment.

Boundary Violations: As we have discussed in earlier sections of this chapter, borderline patients often have problems with boundaries, whether intrapersonal (ego boundaries) or interpersonal (the boundaries of the relationship between the patient and the therapist, or between the patient and other persons with whom he or she interacts). Thus, clinical work with borderline patients requires considerable vigilance on the clinician's part in clarifying and maintaining boundaries that might otherwise become blurred (Kernberg, 1975).

In addition, borderline patients frequently seem to have the uncanny ability to seduce or provoke therapists "who know better" into boundary violations (Stone, 1976). As the case below suggests, the countertransference with such patients is often at the root of these missteps (Gutheil, 1989).

Case 7

A psychiatrist lent money to his borderline patient and gave her medication that he had prescribed for himself. When she had to move out of her apartment and was temporarily without a place of her own, he invited her to stay at his house. While she occupied the guest room, he slept on the floor just outside her room, so that he could be aware of, and prevent, any attempt she might make to leave. He rationalized all these measures as necessary responses to the patient's need for extra support and protection.

This is an example of the therapist's rescue fantasies gone wild. Borderline patients are prone to distorted expectations of the therapist's role, requiring careful and sometimes continual clarification of the limits of that role. In the case above, the therapist colluded in the patient's fantasies about her specialness and need for protection, overstepping the limits of the therapeutic relationship as he acted out his own fantasies of rescue and omnipotence.

In some cases boundary violations made in a misguided effort to "rescue" the patient reflect the therapist's conflict about setting limits and fear of the patient's reactive rage (Gutheil, 1989). A similar conflict may engender boundary violations in the form of favors exchanged between patient and therapist.

Case 8

A psychiatrist agreed to accept calls late at night from his patient, because talking with him helped her get to sleep.

Eventually, he began to initiate some of these calls, while his wife and children slept. During the conversations he would occasionally discuss his own personal problems.

Case 9

A psychiatrist who was treating an editorially talented borderline patient asked her to help him improve a paper he was writing for publication in a professional journal.

Sexual Relations Between Patient and Therapist: Sexual relations in therapy are the most extreme form of boundary violation between patient and therapist. Yet the traumatic effects on the patient and his or her future treatment (Collins, Mebed, and Mortimer, 1978; Ulanov, 1979; Apfel and Simon, 1985) and the medicolegal ramifications set this particular violation apart from the others (Gutheil, 1989).

Many therapists assume that sexual relations with a patient are acceptable as long as the therapy has been terminated, with or without a referral to another clinician. This assumption, however, is false: the therapist who stops treatment with a patient one day and has sexual intercourse with the same person the next day is violating the fiduciary relationship with the patient just as severely as if the therapy and sex had occurred on the same day (Gutheil, 1989).

Some therapists believe that sex with a former patient is acceptable after a "suitable" interval has elapsed since termination of the therapy, but there is no clear agreement on what period of time, if any, is appropriate under these circumstances. This matter has received some legislative attention. A new law in California (SB 1406) addresses the question of timing by stating, "A cause of action against a psychotherapist for sexual contact exists . . . if the sexual contact occurred . . . [during] the period the patient was receiving psychotherapy . . . [or within] two years following termination of therapy . . ." (Lymberis, 1988). Unfortunately, this effort to define illegal sexual relations with patients (or former patients) may instead have opened the way for further confusion by suggesting that sexual relations between a therapist and a former patient become legal two years after the therapeutic relationship has ended. Both the legality and the ethics of such relations, even after two years, remain questionable (Lymberis, 1988). For the purposes of durable liability prevention, therefore, the most prudent policy is to refrain altogether from engaging in sexual relations with a former patient, whether weeks, months, or even years have elapsed since the therapy was terminated (Gutheil, 1989).

Case 10

An experienced clinician on an inpatient unit was treating a borderline patient with a history of sexual abuse by a family member. In recent years she had suffered several major psychotic regressions and was known to confuse fantasy with fact and intimacy with sexuality. She had also made a previous accusation of sexual misconduct, which she subsequently confessed having fabricated for attention. Despite this background, her therapist acknowledged giving her, on several occasions, a variety of hugs, including "social" hugs, "reassurance" hugs, "goodbye" hugs, and "congratulatory" hugs. On the occasion in question, the patient had threatened suicide in the face of a planned termination and was being seen for a second appointment on the same day as her regular one. During this second session the patient's condition was marked by impulsivity, loose associations, and serious regression. At the end of the session, she requested a "goodbye" hug, which the therapist provided. The patient suddenly began heavy breathing and pelvic thrusting, and she drew a vibrator from her purse, leading the therapist to disengage. The patient broke down in tears and threatened suicide but refused hospitalization. She asked the therapist instead to take her home so that she wouldn't have to face the "unsavory characters" at the bus station. After several delays, he agreed to drive her home and told her that he would call her later to make sure she was okay and see whether she wanted to make an appointment for one additional session. She subsequently accused her therapist of initiating sexual intercourse in his office and in the car on the ride home (Gutheil, 1989).

The patient later retracted her claims of sexual intercourse. Yet in this case, even the hugging was sexual from the patient's perspective and thus represented a clear boundary violation by her therapist. In view of her tendency to confuse sexual and other kinds of behavior, the hugs—no matter how carefully labeled—were bound to be misinterpreted. Moreover, the patient's previous accusation of sexual misconduct should have put the therapist on alert.

Case 11

A psychiatrist gave his borderline patient "anatomy lessons" on their naked bodies to help allay her fears about engaging in a sexual relationship with a man. He thought that as long as they refrained from actual intercourse, their behavior was "not really sex." Not surprisingly, however, the "anatomy lessons" eventually led to intercourse.

Case 12

Claiming an overbooked daytime schedule, a psychiatrist arranged to see his hospitalized borderline patient at night for many sessions. They met in her room, sometimes quite late at night, and for two to four hours at a time. These meetings eventually came to include sexual intercourse.

SUICIDE, MANIPULATION, AND IMPULSIVITY

Clinical work with borderline patients is particularly vulnerable to medicolegal difficulties because of the tendency for such patients to engage in manipulative or impulsive behavior, some-times resulting in suicidal gestures or even serious attempts.

Olin (1976) and Schwartz, Flinn, and Slawson (1974) have distinguished between two types of suicidal states: acute and chronic. An acute suicidal state, in which the patient feels over-whelming guilt and despair, is a short-term emergency requir-ing immediate clinical intervention. The acutely suicidal patient needs to be guided through the crisis, with somatic or psycho-therapeutic support, until the self-destructive urge has sub-sided.

Chronic suicidality, on the other hand, represents a dis-turbed, yet consistent adaptation to life, requiring therapeutic intervention that assists the patient in assuming responsibility for herself or himself. To complicate matters, these two differ-ent states may coincide in the same patient at a particular point in time. That is, a chronically suicidal individual may suffer an acute exacerbation of the self-destructive urge.

Chronic suicidality is quite common in borderline patients, and the appropriate clinical response may be misconstrued by the lay person as callous or uncaring. For example, after careful evaluation of an apparently desperate person, the clinician may decide that hospitalization is not in that person's best interests because it is likely to precipitate a severe regression. In arriving at this decision, the clinician has weighed the short-term risk of suicide against the longer-term benefit of changing the patient's adaptive style (Gutheil, 1985). The decision is by no means an easy one, and it is much more complex than the lay person might imagine. The critical challenge that the clinician faces is to assess the patient's condition accurately and to identify the suicidal state correctly.

Borderline patients are characteristically manipulative in their interpersonal relationships, sometimes resorting to threats of suicide to obtain the response they want. Largely a learned skill, manipulativeness may often reflect lack of entitlement: the feeling that one deserves nothing from anyone and there-fore will get nothing without resorting to more or less subtle forms of coercion (St. Clair, 1966; Fontana, 1971; Bursten, 1972). Even a borderline patient who is clearly threatening sui-cide as a means of manipulation, however, may be genuinely at risk of acting on that threat. Careful observation, evaluation, and documentation, which are always necessary, are critical under these circumstances.

The greatest challenge to the clinician is to respond correctly to a clear case of manipulation by setting a limit on the behavior, which may mean refusing hospitalization (Gutheil, 1985). In the majority of cases, this decision initially elicits rage on the patient's part, followed by a resolution of the crisis. Infrequently, however, the patient responds by acting out in a self-destructive manner. The clinician must recognize and weigh this risk, however small.

Impulsivity, noted earlier as a characteristic feature of the borderline syndrome, can also complicate the assessment of suicide risk. Sensitive to rejection, borderline patients with a history of self-destructive behavior may be particularly susceptible to suicidal impulses after they have experienced rejection. Unfortunately, the subjective experience of rejection is highly variable, both from one patient to another and within the same patient over time, making the clinical assessment particularly difficult.

Case 13

A hospitalized woman who had slashed her wrists told the staff that she felt rejected by them. They were puzzled by this, since they had just decided to keep the patient on the ward rather than transfer her to another hospital. Further discussion with the patient revealed that when she was moved to a different room (necessitated by a longer stay), she felt rejected by the staff, although she could not explain why or how.

The sometimes intersecting problems of impulsivity, manipulation, and suicidality in borderline patients are most effectively addressed when both clinician and patient acknowledge the need to predict that which seems unpredictable, within the context of the therapeutic alliance (Gutheil, 1985). The following case suggests how the clinician might initiate such an approach:

Case 14

In response to his therapist's efforts to help him assume responsibility for his actions, a chronically suicidal patient insisted that his self-destructive impulses were abrupt and unpredictable. The therapist responded by saying, "I realize that you don't know now when you might suddenly feel suicidal in the future. You can't predict when those feelings will strike you, and neither can I. With this problem in mind, let's figure out how the two of us can plan for your safety."

The clinician acknowledges the problem of predicting impulses that are largely unpredictable and, more important, casts it as a joint problem. Neither the patient nor the therapist can predict the timing of his suicidal urges. Working collaboratively within the context of the therapeutic alliance, however, the therapist suggests that they plan together how to manage the patient's impulsive behavior whenever it might occur. The therapist is thus inviting the healthy side of the patient to join in a partnership devoted to managing that which otherwise (i.e., without the active participation of both patient and therapist) might well be unmanageable (Gutheil, 1985). The partnership requires certain sacrifices on both sides. The clinician must put aside any desire to rescue or control the patient by taking over responsibility for his or her life, and the patient must give up the effort to thrust the responsibility onto the therapist's shoulders. To put it another way, each must forsake fantasies of certainty and join forces to manage a situation that is inescapably uncertain.

ETHICAL ISSUES

This subject is really too broad to cover comprehensively here; it may, indeed, be said that all the medicolegal issues described above have identifiable ethical dimensions—elements best understood in terms of goods and harms—as well. But two important areas of ethical concern merit particular attention in the treatment of borderline patients.

As some authors have pointed out (Friedman, 1969; Olin, 1976), clinical work with borderline patients may dramatically heighten the ethical tension, widely relevant in the mental health field, between paternalism (or protection) and autonomy, between responsibility and freedom. When should one hospitalize the suicidal borderline patient? When should one accept the calculated risk of a suicide attempt in the service of helping the patient develop a mature responsibility for himself or herself? The labile condition of such patients, the often ephemeral suicidal ideation, and the equally common interminable or chronic suicidal state, the use of suicide threats as a manipulative device or a real intention to die—all these ambiguities should sharpen the clinician's focus on the ethical underpinnings of decision making.

A second source of ethical tension is the personal strain that many clinicians experience in working with borderline patients—strain resulting from countertransference issues, personal antipathy toward such patients, difficulties in coping with their extreme neediness and demands, the destructive effects of splitting on relationships with one's colleagues, and the like. To escape the strain, clinicians often seem eager to terminate work with such patients. In fact, the query, "How can I get rid of this borderline patient without abandoning him or her?" is one of those most commonly asked in liability prevention seminars.

The underlying ethical issue might be posed in this way: is it ethical for a clinician to discontinue work with a patient for reasons that may actually represent manifestations of the very illness for which the patient is seeking help? Should the clinician instead attempt—through supervision, self-analysis, consultation, and other mechanisms—to overcome the negative feelings that are interfering with the alliance, in the service of advancing the clinical work?

While both these areas of ethical tension require individualized responses and defy generalization, we might call attention here to the durable observation that when supplies of clinical wisdom have been exhausted and the legal viewpoint offers no useful approach, the ethical analysis of a problem may provide some guidance for the clinician trying to find a pathway toward a decision.

CONCLUSION

Patients with the borderline syndrome are widely considered the most "difficult" to work with in therapy. Prone to expressions of rage, narcissistic entitlement, psychotic transferences, regression, impulsivity, and suicidal behavior, they also tend to be skilled in the art of manipulation. Even experienced therapists have made serious errors of clinical management with borderline patients that they would never have made in treating patients with other disorders. Too often—whether or not the therapist is guilty of mismanagement—the potent clinical material that the borderline patient brings to therapy ends up being played out in a legal arena.

The best clinical approach to the borderline patient, as well as the best protection against medicolegal repercussions, is to promote a strong therapeutic alliance, enlisting the healthy side of the patient in an active collaboration to manage the unhealthy (enraged, entitled, suicidal) side. Documentation and consultation go hand in hand with this approach, both contributing to and providing evidence of sound clinical practice.

Countertransference is especially potent with borderline patients, requiring an extra measure of vigilance on the therapist's part. Rage toward the patient or fantasies of rescue, if unrecognized, can lead to abandonment or boundary violations—forms of clinical mismanagement that may result in malpractice litigation. For this reason, the therapist must possess a thorough knowledge of the transference and countertransference feelings that tend to permeate clinical work with borderline patients, as well as a practical alertness to the incipient blurring of boundaries. In addition, consultation with colleagues or supervisors can help elucidate potentially dangerous countertransference responses and clarify the boundaries of the relationship between therapist and patient.

17.

Behavior Therapy, Dialectics, and the Treatment of Borderline Personality Disorder

Marsha M. Linehan, Ph.D.

Treatment of borderline personality disorder (BPD), to date, has been dominated by psychoanalytic and biological approaches. Until recently, behaviorists have not addressed the treatment of individuals meeting criteria for BPD. There are a number of historical reasons for this lack of attention by the behavioral community, including problems in BPD diagnostic reliability and validity as well as a theoretical bias against personality diagnoses. Although behaviorists have developed effective treatment strategies for many of the behavioral syndromes associated with BPD, they have only recently integrated these strategies into comprehensive treatment programs designed specifically for the borderline patient. Improvements in diagnostic validity as well as the inclusion of BPD in *The Diagnostic and Statistical Manual of Mental Disorders* (DSM-III) have had a marked effect on the interest of behavior therapists and applications of behavior therapy to personality disorders are receiving increasing attention within the behavior therapy community (American Psychiatric Association, 1980; Turner, 1983,

Acknowledgment. Preparation of this chapter was supported in part by National Institute of Mental Health Grant MH34486 to Marsha Linehan.

1984; Padesky, 1986; Young, unpublished; Young and Swift, 1988; Pretzer, in press, 1983).

Suicidal behavior, especially parasuicide, is particularly associated with BPD. The term *parasuicide* as used here includes all instances of acute, nonfatal, intentionally self-injurious behavior. Thus, it includes actual suicide attempts as well as self-injuries (including self-mutilation, self-inflicted burns) with little or no intent to cause death. Suicide attempts are a subcategory of parasuicide. Parasuicide also includes behaviors commonly labeled "suicide gestures" and "manipulative suicide attempts." The term *parasuicide*, however, is preferred for two reasons: first, it does not confound a motivational hypothesis with a descriptive statement. Terms such as *gesture, manipulative,* and *suicide attempt* assume that the parasuicide is motivated by an attempt to communicate (gesture), to influence others covertly (manipulate), or to suicide (suicide attempt). There are other possible motivations to parasuicide, however, such as affect regulation (e.g., to reduce anxiety). In the particular case careful assessment is needed, a necessity obscured by using descriptions assuming such an assessment has already been conducted. Second, *parasuicide* is a less pejorative term. It is difficult to like a person who is labeled a manipulator. This is a particularly salient issue with respect to borderline patients. The difficulties in treating these individuals effectively makes it particularly easy to "blame the victim" and consequently dislike them. Yet liking one's borderline patient is correlated with helping them (Wollcott, 1985). Furthermore, up to 70 to 75 percent of borderline patients have a history of at least one parasuicide (Clarkin, Widiger, Frances, Hurt, and Gilmore, 1983; Cowdry, Pickar, and Davies, 1985). However, although there are substantial literatures on both parasuicidal behavior (Kreitman, 1977; Maris, 1981) and BPD, there is virtually no overlap between the two areas of study.

The purpose of this chapter is to describe a biosocial (behavioral) theory of BPD and a behavioral treatment approach I have been developing over the past ten years designed specifically for suicidal and parasuicidal individuals meeting criteria for BPD. The treatment, dialectical behavior therapy (DBT), has been found in preliminary studies to be effective in reducing parasuicidal behavior and number of days of inpatient hospitalization, improving maintenance in treatment, and is marginally effective at reducing self-reports of depression (Linehan, 1987, unpublished).

Dialectical behavior therapy is defined by its philosophical base (dialectics), theoretical perspective (biosocial/behavioral), treatment targets (seven), treatment strategy groups (eight), and treatment modes (individual, group, phone). There are, as well, a number of specific, behavioral treatment protocols covering crisis management, suicidal behavior, and compliance issues. Space here is too brief to give a detailed description of each component of the treatment. The interested reader is referred to the detailed treatment manual and associated updates (Linehan, unpublished).

DIALECTICAL PHILOSOPHICAL BASE

Dialectics

A dialectical world view has been applied to socioeconomic history (Marx and Engels, 1970), the development of science (Kuhn, 1970), biological evolution (Levins and Lewontin, 1985), analyses of sexual relations (Firestone, 1970), and more recently to the development of thinking in adults (Basseches, 1984). Wells ([1972], cited in Kegan [1982]) has documented a shift toward dialectical approaches in almost every social and natural science during the last 150 years. Although clinicians do not commonly use the word *dialectics* in conceptualizing psychotherapy, the psychotherapeutic relationship between the opposites embodied in the term has been regularly pointed out since the early writings of Freud (Seltzer, 1986).

Dialectics can be defined in a number of ways. Definitions coming closest to the use here include the following from Webster's New Collegiate Dictionary (1979). "The Hegelian process of change in which a concept or its realization passes over into and is preserved and fulfilled by its opposite"; "Development through the stages of thesis, antithesis, and synthesis"; "Any systematic reasoning, exposition, or argument that juxtaposes opposed or contradictory ideas and usually seeks to resolve their conflict"; and "The dialectical tension or opposition between two interacting forces or elements." Dialectics can be used in two contexts: that of persuasive dialogue and that of the fundamental nature of reality. When viewed from the point of view of dialogue, it refers to change by persuasion rather than by formal impersonal logic. Thus, unlike analytical thinking, dialectics is personal in that it takes into account and affects the total person.

A dialectical perspective on the nature of reality and human behavior has three primary characteristics. From an analysis of these characteristics, BPD can be viewed as instances of dialectical failures in each of these three areas. (1) Dialectics stresses the fundamental interrelatedness and wholeness of reality. From a dialectical point of view, identity itself is relational because no element has a priori independent existence. Rather existence of a particular element occurs only as it relates to a particular whole. In this sense, it is similar both to systems and to feminist theoretical perspectives. The commonly observed difficulties among borderline patients with self-identity and tendencies to scan the environment for guidelines on what to think and feel, arise from failure to maintain in mind their essential relationships both with other people and other moments in time. Without such relationships, both to other individuals and other moments in time, identity becomes defined in terms of each current moment and, thus, is variable and unpredictable rather than stable. (2) Reality is not static but is comprised of internal opposing forces (thesis and antithesis) out of whose synthesis evolves a new set of opposing forces. From this perspective, all propositions contain with them their own oppositions. Or as Goldberg (1980) put it, "I assume that truth is paradoxical, that each article of wisdom contains within it its own contradictions, that *truths stand side by side*. . . . Contradictory truths do not necessarily cancel each other out or dominate each other, but stand side by side, inviting participation and experimentation" (pp. 295–296). The tendency toward dichotomous, rigid thinking among borderline individuals can be viewed as the tendency to get stuck in either the thesis or antithesis, unable to move toward synthesis. (3) The interconnected, nonreducible nature of reality leads to a wholeness continually in the process of change. Thus, change is a fundamental aspect of reality. As noted by many, borderline individuals have great difficulty with change.

The term *dialectical* with respect to DBT is meant to convey both these coexisting multiple tensions that must be addressed within the therapeutic relationship, as well as the emphases in DBT on enhancing comfort with ambiguity and change and teaching dialectical thinking patterns to replace the rigid, dichotomous thinking characteristic of suicidal and borderline patients. The overriding dialectic for the therapist is the necessity of acceptance of the patient as she[1] is within the context of trying to help her change. Treatment strategies are polarized into those most related to *acceptance* and those most related to *change*. Dialectical behavior therapy requires that the therapist balance use of these two types of strategies within each treatment interaction.

BIOSOCIAL/BEHAVIORAL THEORY

Dialectical behavior therapy is based on a biosocial theory of BPD, similar to a diathesis/stress model. From this point of view, the primary dysfunction of BPD is one of inadequate affect regulation, largely due initially to biological factors, including genetics, intrauterine experiences, and environmental effects on development of the brain and nervous system. The social or environmental stress component is the invalidating environment; that is, a social environment that invalidates the experiences of the individual and does not take seriously the individual's communications, especially when they have to do with nonpublic events and with difficulties in meeting social expectations. Given this initial affective dysregulation, together with an invalidating social environment, dialectical behavior theory specifies both how BPD develops and which behavioral

---

[1]Although both males and females are diagnosed as BPD, our research is mainly focused on females and, thus, the feminine pronoun will be used throughout.

patterns are central to it once it has developed. The behavioral patterns can be organized along three dialectical poles: (1) emotional vulnerability versus invalidation; (2) active–passivity versus the apparently competent person; and (3) unremitting crises versus inhibited grief. Patterns first in each pair are more heavily biologically influenced; patterns second in each pair are derivatives of invalidating environments. These patterns have been described in detail in other places and will be only briefly described here. A key point about these syndromes is that the discomfort of the extreme points on each of these syndromes insures that the borderline individuals vacillate back and forth between the polarities. They are unable to move to a balanced position representing a synthesis.

EMOTIONAL VULNERABILITY VERSUS INVALIDATING SYNDROME

Emotional vulnerability refers to the high sensitivity to emotional stimuli, intense response to even low-level stimuli, and slow return to emotional baseline characteristic of borderline individuals as well as the individual's personal sense of this vulnerability. The mechanisms of this emotion dysregulation are unclear but difficulties in attention control and limbic system reactivity may be important. Invalidating families of origin, especially physically and sexually abusive families, contributes both to the development of emotion dysregulation, as well as fails to teach the child how to label and regulate arousal, how to tolerate emotional distress, and when to trust his or her own emotional responses as reflections of valid interpretations of events. The invalidating syndrome refers to the adoption by the individual of characteristics of the invalidating environment. Thus, borderline individuals tend to invalidate their own affective experiences, look to others for accurate reflections of external reality, and oversimplify the ease of solving life's problems. This oversimplification leads inevitably to self–hate following failure to achieve goals.

These two interrelated syndromes might give us a clue as to why therapy with the borderline patient is sometimes iatrogenic. To the extent that the therapist creates an invalidating environment within the therapy, one would expect the patient to react strongly. For example, with respect to suicidal behaviors, an invalidating therapy environment can lead to parasuicide and/or suicide via several paths. Recognition of the discrepancy between one's own capacities for emotional and behavioral control and excessive demands, and criticism on the part of the therapist can lead to both anger and attempts to prove to others, including one's therapist, the error of their expectations. Such communication can be essential if one is to get the help one believes is needed. Also, borderline persons do not have clear guidelines as to what they should believe, their own experience, or that of their invalidating therapists. Suicidal behavior not only self-validates the individual's own sense of vulnerability, reducing the ambiguity of the double messages coming from her own experience versus those coming from the therapist, but it also proves to the therapist that she is as desperate as she says she is. Additional help is often forthcoming, or at least the therapist communicates understanding directly.

On the other pole, the patient adopts the invalidating attitude of the therapist, but in a typically extreme manner. Aspirations are lowered by the patient but not by the environment. When both the individual and the therapist are invalidating the individual's own experience, then she is the failure the environment (and often, not so subtly, the therapist) says she is and she deserves self-injury or death. The dialectical balance that the therapist must strive for is to both validate the essential wisdom of each patient's experiences, especially as it relates to her vulnerabilities and sense of desperation, as well as teach the patient requisite capabilities such that change can occur. The recognition of this state of affairs requires the combining and juxtaposition of validating treatment strategies with capability enhancement strategies (skill training). The tension between alternating excessively high and too low aspirations and expectations relative to their own capabilities offers a formidable challenge to the therapist, requiring moment-to-moment changes in the use of validating–acceptance versus behavioral–change strategies.

ACTIVE-PASSIVITY VERSUS THE APPARENTLY COMPETENT PERSON SYNDROME

Active-passivity refers to the tendency of borderline individuals to approach problems passively and helplessly, as well as a corresponding tendency under extreme stress to actively demand from the environment (and often the therapist) solutions to life's problems. This syndrome is very similar to learned helplessness except that there is some evidence that a passive style of self-regulation is correlated with a tendency to high autonomic arousal (Eliasz, 1985). Thus, it may not be entirely a result of learning, although a history of failing in efforts to control both themselves and aversive environments are very likely important. The apparently competent person syndrome is the polar opposite of the active-passivity syndrome and refers to the tendency of borderline patients to appear deceptively competent. The deception is that the very real competencies of the individual do not generalize across all relevant situations and across different mood state. For example, the person may be appropriately assertive in work settings but unable to produce assertive responses in intimate relationships. Or, the individual may appear very competent interpersonally, all the while experiencing extreme distress privately. Impulse control while in the therapist's office may not generalize to settings outside his or her office. Thus, there is the frequent experience of the patient who seems to feel good, or at least in control, leaving the office only to end up in the emergency room for parasuicide several hours later.

The active-passivity versus apparently competent person presents a dialectical challenge for the therapist. If therapists see only the competence of the apparently competent person, they may not only be too demanding in terms of performance expectations, but may also be unresponsive to low-level communications of distress and difficulty. An invalidating environment ensues. The tendency to attribute lack of progress to resistance rather than inability is especially dangerous. Not only is such a stance, adopted uncritically, invalidating, it also prevents the therapist from offering needed skill training. But it is also important that the therapist recognize patients' existing capacities.

Otherwise, the therapist falls into the active-passivity pattern with the patient, offering too much help when help is not needed. Inducing active participation on the part of the borderline patient can be a continuing struggle. Generally, adept use of contingencies is crucial here. The mistake the therapist must avoid is oversimplifying the ease of change, and assuming too soon that the patient can cope with problems alone. Such an assumption is understandable given the apparently competent syndrome. However, such a mistake simply increases the passivity of the patient. Otherwise the patient risks going out on a limb and being left alone to climb down. The role of the therapist is to balance both the patient's capabilities as well as deficiencies, once again flexibly synthesizing supportive–acceptance strategies with confrontational–change strategies. Exhortations to change must be integrated with infinite patience.

Unrelenting Crises versus Inhibited Grieving. Unrelenting crises refers to the seemingly never ending personal crises that borderline individuals present with, and their inability to return to a baseline of neutral emotional functioning. These unending crises are the result of the vicious cycle set up by individual vulnerabilities and stressful environments. The crises often interfere with any treatment planning the therapist may engage in, as critical problems change too fast for either the patient or the therapist to deal with them effectively. The inhibited grieving syndrome refers to the pattern of repetitive, significant trauma and loss, together with an inability to experience and personally integrate these events. The individual is in bereavement overload, so to speak, and avoids all negative emotions. Thus, the necessary process of grieving is inhibited and personal change is blocked.

In my experience, unrelenting crises make predetermined, behavioral treatment plans almost impossible to follow. This is especially so if the treatment plan includes teaching the patient skills which, while useful for long-term gains, do not promise immediate stress reduction. It is a bit like trying to teach someone with a tent how to build a house in the middle of a raging hailstorm. It is understandable if the person insists on waiting out the storm in the tent. The solution to this dilemma has been to develop psychoeducational group treatment modules which focus on teaching specific behavioral skills. The role of the individual therapist is to help the patient integrate these skills into daily life. However, skill acquisition is not dependent on the individual therapist. Although in our treatment program, skill training is usually accomplished in groups, we have at times used a behavioral technician. Groups are simply more efficient. In the structured setting of a skill training group, patients are often able to inhibit emotionality enough to attend to the task of learning coping skills.

Borderline patients vacillate back and forth between emotional crises states and inhibited emotionality. This inhibition is quite adaptive as the individual usually has no previous history of succesfully negotiating extreme emotional states. It is the task of the therapist to help the patient learn to experience affect in such a way that it is dissipated, or extinguished. The constant emotional avoidance, typical of borderline individuals, virtually insures that extinction does not occur. But extinction of negative emotional responses requires that the experience of emotions must be reinforcing; in other words, that the environment reinforces rather than punishes affective experiencing and expression. Sufficient help must be given to achieve this outcome.

TREATMENT TARGETS

Treatment goals or targets in individual DBT are hierarchically arranged as follows: (1) high-risk suicidal behaviors (parasuicide, high-risk suicide ideation); (2) therapy interfering behaviors; (3) behaviors serious enough to substantially interfere with any chance of a reasonable quality of life (e.g., severe substance abuse, risky criminal behaviors, dysfunctional work behaviors, poor judgment); (4) behavioral skill acquisition (skills in mindfulness, emotion regulation, interpersonal effectiveness, distress tolerance, self-management); (5) post-traumatic stress; (6) respect for self; (7) other goals the patient wishes to focus on. By targeting a behavior or goal, I mean that particular behavior is addressed directly and openly in the session. Thus, the first, and at times continuing task, is to obtain the patient's commitment to work on the behavioral goals at hand. In my experience, this is rarely difficult for the first two targets. We simply do not accept patients in treatment if they do not agree that a therapy goal is to reduce suicidal behaviors. Generally, I am clear that my goal is not to keep patients alive, but rather to help them make life worth living. With respect to parasuicide, however, I am equally clear that the behavior most likely has to stop before we can address the misery that surrounds the behavior. With respect to each target, the task of the therapist is to elicit the patient's collaboration in working on the target behavior, then to apply the relevant treatment strategies described below. Attention to each target is determined by the behaviors and problems that surface during the particular week preceding a session and/or during the current session. Thus, treatment is oriented to current behaviors. The order of attention is determined by the hierarchical list above. Therapy is somewhat circular in that target focal points revolve over time.

TREATMENT STRATEGIES

Dialectical behavior therapy addresses all problematic patient behaviors and therapy situations in a systematic, problem-solving manner, which includes conducting a collaborative behavioral analysis, formulating hypotheses about possible variables influencing the problem, generating possible changes (behavioral solutions), and trying out and evaluating the solutions. There are eight basic strategy groups which are combined to deal with specific problematic situations. Not all strategies are necessary or appropriate for a given session and the pertinent combination may change over time. These are more fully described in the treatment manual (Linehan, unpublished).

Dialectical Strategies: The role of the therapist in using these strategies is both to focus upon the dialectical issues in the therapist–patient relationship, as well as to explicitly promote dialectical thinking on the part of the patient. The therapeutic task is to facilitate growth by bringing out the opposites appearing both in therapy and the patient's life, and to guide the patient through synthesis after synthesis. The key idea guiding the therapist's behavior is that for any statement, an opposite position can be held. Thus, synthesis and growth require attention to balance, searching for what is left out of both the therapist's and patient's current ways of ordering reality, and then assisting the patient to create new orderings which embrace and include what was previously excluded. Need for this strategy comes up at every point; for example, when patients are seeing reality in extremes, when struggles about who is right and who is wrong arise, when tension arises about whether to push the patient harder or be more supportive and nurturing. Dialectically, the therapist might highlight the extreme the patient does not take while not rejecting the point the patient is trying to make. Or, the therapist might search for how both points of view can be right. Or, the therapist might combine nurturing with pushing, alternating between the two so quickly that they blend into one strategy. Strategies include extensive use of metaphor, myth, and paradox, nonresolution of ambiguity, focus on reality as constant change, cognitive challenging and restructuring, and reinforcement for use of intuitive, nonrational knowledge bases. We have at times begun a metaphor with a patient and then continued it across many sessions. Dialectical strategies, especially a dialectical framework on the part of the therapist, is essential in every interaction with the patient and also informs the treatment supervision and staff meetings.

Problem-Solving Strategies: Problem solving with borderline patients is a two-stage process involving first an acceptance of the problem at hand and second an attempt to generate, evaluate, and implement alternative solutions which might have been made or could be made in the future in similar problematic situations. In DBT, all dysfunctional behaviors, in and out of sessions, are viewed as problems to be solved or, from another perspective, as faulty solutions to patient problems in living. The acceptance stage employs both insight and behavioral analysis strategies; the second stage, targeting change, employs solution analysis and environmental intervention strategies. Behavioral analyses requires a very detailed chain of analyses of the events and situational factors leading up to and following the particular problematic response at hand. The analysis is conducted in great detail, with close attention to the reciprocal interaction between the environment and the patients' cognitive, emotional, and behavioral responses. For example, if a patient has parasuicided, the therapist would closely question the patient until every detail leading up to the act and following it, including environmental events, thoughts, beliefs, expectancies and feelings, are elicited. Insight strategies include observing and labeling patterns of behavior and situational influence over time. For example, one might note that parasuicide seems to happen every time the patient feels angry at an important person but does not express it directly. Problem solving proceeds in a nonjudgmental fashion, with attention to the tendency of the borderline patient both to experience panic and to engage in ruthless, vindictive evaluative judgments whenever behavior or behavioral outcomes are less than expected or desired. Typically, the target of these patient judgments shifts, sometimes with lightning speed, from the self as generating the problems, to other people or the environment as the sole source of the problem. The behavior analysis strategy is repeated for every instance of parasuicide, behavior seriously interfering with therapy, and other problematic behaviors, until the patient achieves an understanding of the stimulus–response patterns involved (the insight strategy).

The second stage requires the generation of alternate response chains, that is, adaptive solutions to the problem, as well as an analysis of the patient's response capabilities. The process usually leads into one or more of the strategies described below. For example, it may become clear that the individual does not have the requisite response capabilities (skills) to produce alternate adaptive solution behaviors. The therapist then moves to the capability enhancement strategies. Or the patient may have the needed skills but be inaccurate in predicting outcomes of various responses to the problem. In these cases contingency strategies are employed, where the therapist would discuss with the patient and highlight the likely consequences of different courses of action. For example, the therapist might discuss how a mother's child is likely to react if she suicides. At other times the therapist must use consultant strategies to teach the patient how to elicit needed help from others. When the therapist–patient relationship is the source of the problem, relationship strategies are employed. Finally, direct environmental intervention by the therapist may be needed to effect immediate changes which are both essential and which the patient cannot yet produce. For example, the therapist might intervene directly with the mental health system if involuntary commitment seems likely, or a therapist might go and pick up a teenager whose car has broken down on the way to a session.

Validating Strategies: The essence of the validating strategies is that the therapist searches for, recognizes, and reflects the current wisdom of the patient's response. I stress current in that highlighting how a response was functional in the past but is not now would be an instance of invalidation, not validation. Nor does validation simply involve making patients feel good or building up their self-esteem. If a patient says she is a terrible person, saying you think she is wonderful invalidates the experience of being terrible. If a patient says you don't like her and you respond that you do, but given the patient's experiences with *other* caregivers, it is reasonable that she misinterprets you, you are invalidating her by not searching openly for your own behavior that might be rejecting. There are three steps in validation; the first two are part of almost all therapy traditions, the third step, however, is essential to DBT. First, the therapist accurately hears or observes the patient's responses. This step is similar to hearing with a third ear, or seeing with a third eye. The second step requires the reflection back to the patient of her emotional response, thoughts, or assumptions, or behavior as observed by the therapist. In this step, a nonjudgmental attitude is fundamental. Finally, the third step is the communication to the patient that her response has essential wisdom in the moment, that it is understandable in the current context. It is this latter step that takes the most searching by the therapist and that defines the strategy. At times it is much like searching for a nugget of gold in a cup of sand. The attention to the wise rather than the dysfunctional sets this approach apart from other cognitive and behavioral strategies. The attention to wisdom-in-the-moment (rather than transferentially) sets the strategy off from more psychodynamic approaches. Validating is done in every session.

Capability Enhancement Strategies: These strategies are drawn primarily from standard behavior therapy techniques and include skill acquisition strategies (e.g., instructions, modeling), skill strengthening strategies (e.g., behavior rehearsal, feedback), skill generalization (e.g., homework assignments, discussion of similarities and differences in situations), and reduction of factors inhibiting skill performance (e.g., cognitive restructuring, environmental restructuring). In individual therapy, skills needing remediation are derived from the behavioral analyses described previously. Other more generic skills are taught in group therapy. It is this emphasis on teaching, for example giving advice, role-playing difficult interpersonal situations and giving feedback, teaching relaxation skills, etc., that differentiates DBT from many nonbehavioral approaches to treating borderline patients.

Consultation Strategy: The consultation strategy is simple in concept and very hard to carry out. Essentially, the strategy is a simple rule that states that the goal of the DBT therapist is to teach the patient how to interact effectively with her environment, not to teach the environment how to interact with the patient. Thus, the role of the therapist in carrying out this strategy is that of a behavioral consultant. As a general norm, DBT therapists don't intervene to adjust environments for the sake of the patient. For example, when patients are admitted to an inpatient setting it is their responsibility to both get a pass to come to individual and group sessions and to keep enough control over their medications that they don't get put on drugs they know won't help (or that are not allowed in our program, e.g., the anti-anxiety drug alprazolam). We do not consult with the inpatient staff; we teach the patient how to be effective in that environment. As a rule, the DBT therapist does not meet or consult with other professionals about how to treat the patient (unless the patient calls the meeting and sits in on it).

The exception here is when the patient is being treated by a therapeutic unit (e.g., our suicidal behaviors clinic, an inpatient unit, an agency). In these instances, various therapists working with the patients consult in order to obtain information about the environment the patient is trying to be effective in. For example, our patients are in both individual and group therapy. In individual therapy we might teach them how to interact effectively with group members. In group therapy we often help members learn how to interact with and modify the behavior of their individual therapists. It is never the job of one therapist to defend another therapist, nor is treatment consistency particularly valued in DBT. For example, as in the real world, rules may change depending on who is enforcing them. In staff meetings each therapist obtains information about the "other side of the story," so to speak, not to influence the other therapist but, rather, for use in working with the patient. (One can immediately see why this is easy in concept and difficult in practice!) The single exception to using the consultant strategy is in the following circumstance: the environment has high power relative to the patient, the outcome is important, the patient does not have the requisite capability to influence the environment, and the therapist can influence it. In this instance, the therapist uses the environmental intervention strategy described above.

Irreverent Communication Strategies: This strategy is a communication style characterized by a matter-of-fact attitude, where the therapist takes the patient's underlying assumptions or unnoticed implications of the patient's behavior and maximizes or minimizes them, in either an unemotional or overemotional manner to make a point the patient might not have considered before. The strategy is similar to being the "straight man" in a comedy team. Humor and a certain apparent naiveté are characteristic of the strategy when it is used well. The essence of the strategy is that it "jumps track," so to speak, from the patient's current pattern of response, thought, or emotion. To be effective the strategy must have two components: (1) it must come from the therapist's "center," that is it must be genuine, and (2) it must be built on a bedrock of compassion, caring, and warmth. Generally, this strategy is used whenever the patient is "stuck" in a particular emotional, thought, or behavior pattern.

Contingency Strategies: There are a number of contingency strategies. In contingency clarification, the therapist gives the patient explicit information about the process and requirement of therapy as well as what can be reasonably expected from the therapist. The professor strategy involves giving information about factors that are known to influence behavior in general and theories and data which might cast light on a particular patient's behavior patterns. Observing limits (with an emphasis on observing rather than setting) requires each therapist to carefully monitor his or her own limits with respect to what is acceptable patient behavior in the therapeutic relationship and to observe these limits in the conduct of therapy. Limits can change due to therapeutic relationship factors, therapist's goals for the patient, personal factors in the therapist's life, and characteristics of particular patients. The key idea here is that therapist limits are not presented as being for the good of the patient but rather for the good of the therapist. Of course, the dichotomy is artificial since the good of both parties is essentially linked in the course of any therapeutic relationship. The contingency management strategy requires, as far as possible, the arrangement of therapist responses to reinforce adaptive, non-suicidal behaviors and extinguish maladaptive and suicidal behaviors. Due to the life-threatening nature of suicidal behavior, the therapist necessarily walks a dialectical tight rope, so to speak, neither reinforcing suicidal responses excessively nor ignoring them in such a manner that the patient escalates to a life-threatening level. The DBT therapist takes some short-term risk to enhance long-term advantage. For example, generally hospitalization (a reinforcer for many, but not all, borderline patients) would not occur following parasuicidal behavior (unless, of course, medical care were needed). A key ingredient of applying contingencies is the notion of shaping, where gradual approximations to the target (or goal) behaviors are reinforced. Shaping is essential with borderline patients. Due to past histories favoring hopelessness and passivity, even small steps are sometimes hard to come by.

Relationship Strategies: There are six specific relationship strategies: relationship acceptance, reciprocal vulnerability, relationship enhancement, relationship problem solving, relationship contingencies, and relationship generalization. Relationship acceptance highlights the need for the therapist, at each successive moment, to accept the current state of the patient–therapist relationship, including the level of therapeutic progress or lack thereof. Patience, a high tolerance for rejection, criticism, and hostile affect, and an ability to react nonjudgmentally are requisite therapist characteristics. Reciprocal vulnerability simply requires that the therapist comes into the therapeutic encounters nondefensively and openly shares his or her own reactions to the patient and to the therapeutic relationship. A high level of therapist self-disclosure is encouraged, with a focus maintained on the relationship of self-disclosure to patient needs for feedback, modeling, and so on. Relationship enhancement involves a direct attempt to create both a strong, positive patient–therapist relationship as well as a perception by the patient that the therapist is competent and able to be helpful. For most borderline patients it is difficult to find effective reinforcers. In the relationship contingency strategy, the therapist highlights and uses the relationship itself as a contingency for patient behavior. For example, a DBT therapist might communicate to the patient that as her interpersonal skills vis-à-vis the therapist improve, the quality of the relationship itself will improve or therapist's limits may expand. Generally, this strategy is the behavioral consequence of the observing limits strategy. Relationship problem solving is simply the application of the general problem solving strategies to difficulties in the therapeutic relationship, either from the patient's or the therapist's point of view. This strategy is useful both to repair the patient–therapist relationship and to improve via generalization the patient's ability to successfully problem solve in other relationships. Thus, the therapeutic relationship is dealt with as a "real" relationship rather than as a transferential relationship. Generalization from and to other relationships of capabilities and dispositions acquired in the therapeutic relationship is not assumed. Instead, as in all behavior therapy, generalization of behavior is an active focus of assessment and treatment.

SUMMARY

This chapter has described a biosocial (behavioral) theory of borderline personality disorder and a behavioral treatment approach (dialectical behavior therapy) for suicidal and parasuicidal individuals meeting criteria for BPD. From this perspective, the primary dysfunction of BPD is one of inadequate affect regulation. Etiological factors include biological irregularities together with an invalidating environment, i.e., a social environment that invalidates the experiences of the individual and does not take seriously the individual's communications. At the adult level, behavioral patterns of borderline individuals can be organized along three dialectical poles: (1) emotional vulnerability versus invalidation; (2) active-passivity versus the apparently competent person; and (3) unremitting crises versus inhibited grief.

Dialectical behavior therapy (DBT) is based on a dialectical philosophical orientation which has three primary characteristics. (1) It stresses the fundamental interrelatedness and wholeness of reality. (2) Reality is viewed as comprised of internal opposing forces (thesis and antithesis) out of whose synthesis evolves a new set of opposing forces. (3) Change is seen as a fundamental aspect of reality. The overriding dialectic for the DBT therapist is the necessity of acceptance of the patient as she is within the context of trying to help her change and be different than she is.

Treatment goals or targets in individual DBT are hierarchically arranged as follows: (1) high-risk suicidal behaviors; (2) therapy-interfering behaviors; (3) behaviors serious enough to substantially interfere with any chance of a reasonable quality of life; (4) behavioral skill acquisition (skills in emotion regulation, interpersonal effectiveness, distress tolerance, self-management); (5) post-traumatic stress; (6) respect for self; (7) other goals the patient wishes to focus on. There are eight basic strategy groups which are combined to deal with specific problematic situations. Strategies include dialectical focusing, irreverent communication, validating strategies, consultant strategies, capability enhancement, problem solving, relationship strategies, and contingency strategies.

18.

Group Psychotherapy of the Borderline Patient

Molyn Leszcz M.D., F.R.C.P.(C)

INTRODUCTION

This chapter will explore some of the potentials and limitations in the treatment of patients with borderline personality disorder (BPD) in group psychotherapy. Utilizing relevant contributions of current psychodynamic conceptualizations of this disorder, the chapter will elaborate the context in which the therapist can respond to the articulation in more manifest interpersonal terms of the patient's latent internal world. The idea of context—what he attends to—is essential to the group therapist as it determines what he is able to observe, how he understands it, and how he can respond to it. There are relevant implications for the group therapist in terms of each aspect of the group psychotherapy experience for the borderline patient, beginning with pregroup assessment and indications for treatment, the nature of therapist interventions, and the general and specific ways in which group psychotherapy is to be conducted. There are factors intrinsic to group therapy that are beneficial in the treatment of the borderline personality, and other factors that emerge only through specific therapeutic intent.

THE BORDERLINE PERSONALITY IN GROUP THERAPY: OVERVIEW

Interest in the use of group therapy with the borderline personality dates back nearly to the beginning of the practice of group therapy in North America. Clinicians such as Fried (1954) and Spotnitz (1957) reported on the beneficial effects of adding group therapy to the individual therapy of severely disturbed patients. They believed, as many do now, that there are certain inherent attributes of group therapy that contrast with individual therapy, and thereby account for this beneficial effect. These findings are largely clinically based, and research in the area of process and outcome is sorely lacking. Some supportive research findings include the results that patients with BPD treated in structured short-term inpatient groups valued group psychotherapy highly (Leszcz, Yalom, and Norden, 1985); in fact, they often preferred it to short-term individual therapy. In looking at long-term treatment, Kretsch, Goren, and Wasserman (1987) reported that group psychotherapy has specific advantages over individual psychotherapy, as reflected by measures of ego functioning. The borderline patients showed significant improvement in the area of defenses, reality testing, and object relations, as measured by the Bellak Ego Function Assessment Scale. Kretsch et al. conclude that long-term psychodynamic, interactive group therapy had specific attributes, which they could not clearly identify, that accounted for this improvement. This stood in contrast to long-term individual psychotherapy for the borderline patients and long-term group psychotherapy with nonborderline patients.

Reviewing the relevant literature, it appears that the particular constellation of difficulties presented by BPD that get activated in individual therapy may, in some instances, be better illuminated, contained, and treated in the group psychotherapy setting. These central difficulties and the current explanations regarding their etiology are detailed elsewhere in this volume, and by this writer (Leszcz, 1989). For present purposes the emphasis will be on clinical and therapeutic issues.

The tendency to split and the ego syntonicity of certain character traits produce treatment blind spots and factual distortions, which are greatly reduced when the focus of therapy is not the patient's reportage, but rather the recreation of his characteristic difficulties in the group, in vivo, here and now, in words as well as behavior (Bellak, 1980). At the same time, participation in the group dilutes the intensity of the patient's transference and potential regressions (Horwitz, 1980). The patient becomes subject to the group's reality orientation and group pressure to work things through, rather than use avoidance or denial. This may modulate aggressiveness and abrasive behavior, as the group members may offer alternative models for expression of emotion (Horwitz, 1977). This can broaden the patient's repertoire beyond the dichotomy of passive over-compliance or impulsive discharge. Indirect and self-destructive protests of hurt and anger may be rechanneled as the patient sees that comembers can be angry with one another without destructive consequences, retaliation, or abandonment.

The scrutiny and feedback of multiple observers make it hard to refute the group's feedback about one's behavior, and feedback from peers cannot be readily dismissed as a professional ploy or devalued enviously. Working through intense and divergent affects is more possible as well because of the positive attachments within the group and the greater scrutiny by the peer group of the patient's disavowed affects (Glatzer, 1965). Transference distortions are more readily challenged by the contrasting perspective of other group members. This may contrast with individual therapy, in which the patient may not be able to feel simultaneously supported and confronted by his therapist. Both intense transference and countertransference reactions can be cooled down due to the reduced exclusivity of the therapeutic relationship. Patient and therapist can pull back from each other temporarily, and yet maintain the treatment. Additionally, the therapist may be better able to analyze the patient's intense interactions with added objectivity in the group, because unlike the situation in the individual setting, he may well not be at the center of the heat.

The provision of a stable, nondeviant, and affirming group with real and positive relationships, coupled with the presence of an accurately empathic therapist, is for many such patients a unique opportunity to relate. The patient's real object hunger can be met with less fear of engulfment due to the reduced exclusivity of the therapeutic relationship (Grobman, 1980). The dilution of exclusive dependence on the therapist, coupled with the opportunity to observe him in the more active, real, and therapeutically transparent fashion of the group therapy, encourages the patient to view the group therapist as a separate individual, in contrast to the experience of individual therapy, in which instance the patient may see the therapist as existing only for that particular patient (Horwitz, 1977). The therapist's active presence, coupled with the support of peers, can diminish the risk of an erotization of the transference developing in response to intense object hunger being frustrated. There are other available and accessible people with whom it is possible to relate in order to decrease the pain of the lost fantasied relationship.

It is possible to be involved with the comembers of the group, helping them in their therapy, and thereby building one's self-esteem, while not being the central focus of therapy. The importance of the therapeutic factor of altruism in the group therapy experience of the borderline patient appears substantial (Macaskill, 1982b). Group therapy provides a greater zone of neutral territory, useful in enhancing the therapeutic alliance. This deintensified zone also provides an opportunity for enhanced cognitive functioning as affective experiences can be examined indirectly and vicariously, rather than only directly at the height of the storm.

The more actional orientation of the group appeals to more action-oriented and impulsive patients; they may welcome the greater opportunity for translating the group's feedback into behavioral action (Fried, 1961). The patient has a direct opportunity to practice behaviorally what he is learning, in a relatively safe and supportive milieu. The group becomes a vehicle for exploring and reconstructing the patient's failure in maintaining a clear and stable sense of himself, and the interpersonal consequences of his defensive efforts to protect himself. Interpersonal learning may ensue that further modifies the overtly maladaptive behaviors.

Clinical Vignette

Marg, a forty-two-year-old woman, was referred to group therapy by her individual therapist, after a year of frustrating and stalemated treatment. She initially sought treatment for symptoms of incapacitating social anxiety and depression, precipitated by the end of a ten-year stormy, hostile–dependent relationship with a man. She had few close friends, often rupturing relationships in response to perceived slights. She described herself as very isolated and almost always angry. There were associated difficulties with alcohol use and a dangerous attraction to speeding her car, resulting in several near-collisions. She described her early childhood as one of quiet anger, living in fear of her religious and dominating mother. Marg described the mother as a woman who tolerated no expression of affect, impulse, or desire. A prototypical description of the patient's childhood relationship with her mother is the patient's description of being fitted for a dress with mother silently poking and jabbing at her. There was no interaction, and the patient felt that her mother handled her coldly, without love, as though she were a bag of potatoes.

Individual therapy began with much positive anticipation, but quickly fell into a rut, with the patient unable to describe or explore any essential experiences. The individual therapist felt alternately her rage at him and her hunger for him. No headway, however, was made on these fronts. He felt he had nothing to offer her, and planned to discontinue individual therapy if group therapy took hold.

Upon entry into the group, Marg refused to talk for several meetings, asking for time to determine how the group ran. After four meetings, her silence was punctuated by a ferocious attack on one of the group coleaders whom she addressed as though he were the "mother" of the group—cold, powerful, and rejecting of her, with no further elaboration of how or why. She attributed it only to her "feeling." She expressed contempt for some of the other group members because of the apparent affection they showed this group leader. She cited this as further evidence of his domination and their submissiveness. In contrast, she liked the other group leader because he was soft, warm, and caring. Copatients in the group were startled by her black-and-white view of the coleaders, and began to explore with her how these perceptions were derived. Although she recognized it was linked to her relationship with her mother and father, she offered no further information other than that she would attempt to work with it.

Her attachment to the one leader and to some comembers allowed her to tolerate her intense, hostile feeling to the other coleader, and she was able to work with the group on other issues, intermittently returning to denounce the coleader. Her anger was not met with retaliation but rather with continued exploration of the observation that anger appeared to always be her reaction to any unpleasantness. This and her specific, fixed anger at the therapist, which was described by her as immutable, continued to be the foci of her therapy when she felt able to speak without being paralyzed by her "anxiety."

A notable change occurred with the "bad" therapist's vacation, when reaction to his absence emerged in the group. Marg's first reaction was a fantasy of wanting to kill him—or at least see him suffer—she joked. This led a comember to suggest that perhaps she hated so much because she wanted so much to be closer and was convinced it would never be forthcoming, as was the case with her mother. This feedback had immediate and dramatic impact on Marg in softening the anger and leading for the first time to a description of her longing for a different kind of relationship with her mother and perhaps with the therapist she appeared to hate. She began increasingly to show a capacity to express some sadness at her isolation and a wish for more closeness with other members of the group. Upon his return from vacation, the members of the group commented on some important work that Marg had done, but did not push her to speak about it in any way until she chose to several meetings later. She felt the anger was softening a bit, and it was evident in her interpersonal interactions with members of the group and the therapist.

In this instance, treatment was facilitated by the presence of peer supports, a strong positive attachment, albeit an idealized one, to one group leader, and the presence of the group diluting the intensity of her very strong negative transference, to the point that it could be talked about and explored. These were issues that appeared not possible for her to approach in the individual therapy. As treatment proceeded, the tendency to split lessened. In her second year of group therapy her mother developed a malignancy, and when she reported this to the group, she became quite sad. In fact, Marg brought in photos of her mother and expressed the wish that her mother not suffer. She was confident that her mother's tremendous strength would help her get through the illness. Her newfound sense of balance was reflected in her statement, "If I've represented my mother to you as being evil, I was wrong. I was just a victim of a victim."

The group therapy may be experienced as a much less regressive experience than is the situation with individual therapy. This last statement leads to examination of Horwitz's statement (1977) that groups may both diminish or enhance regression. How are the potential benefits of group therapy facilitated? Three relevant factors include: (1) group composition; (2) the orientation of the group; and (3) the role of concurrent therapy.

Group Composition

Most clinicians agree with Wong (1980) and Rutan and Stone (1984) that many of these therapeutic advantages require a heterogeneous group, composed ideally of no more than one or two more severely character disordered patients and four to six less disturbed patients. A homogeneous group of borderline patients may exacerbate regression because of the patients' impaired ego boundary maintenance, primitive competitiveness, and the lack of alternative and less pathological viewpoints that can clarify distortions and challenge projections. Furthermore, the primitive demandingness of such a group can place enormous demands upon the therapist, producing intense countertransferential reactions of confusion, defeat, and demoralization (Roth, 1980). Nonetheless, some clinicians, such as Slovinska-Holy (1983), advocate the treatment of the borderline personality in homogeneous groups. At the present time, this approach is probably most aptly viewed as a highly specialized technique; more the exception than the rule.

Orientation of the Group

The issue of context emerges at the level of the therapist's orientation to the group, shaping his attitude and focus. Bion (1961) was the first to theorize about group therapy from an object relations perspective. His model—the Tavistock approach—is a group-centered, unstructured model, in which the group leader is abstinent and serves only as an interpreter of group-as-a-whole phenomena. This model clearly illuminates patients' pathological internalized object relations as they regress substantially when faced with participation in an unstructured group experience. Anxiety about attachment and acceptance surge. It is a powerful technique and an excellent model for learning about the dynamics of groups. However, it is not an effective therapeutic technique in and of itself, as concluded by Malan, Balfour, Hood, and Shooter (1976). By his abstinent posture, the therapist places himself as the central and only object of a strongly regressive transference, depriving the group of the tremendous value of multiple transferences and peer interactions. Rigid adherence to only group-centered interventions may result in intensification predominating over dilution. The borderline personality is vulnerable to loss of ego boundaries, contamination by group contagion, and the narcissistic injury of having his personal experience regularly linked to that of other group members in what may feel to him to be a homogenizing fashion (Stone and Gustafson, 1982).

In contrast, Yalom's interpersonal group model (1985) is less regressive. Group-as-a-whole phenomena are explored only if they serve as resistance to the group members' engagement with one another. The emphasis is on each interaction within the here and now of the social microcosm of the group, providing an opportunity to explore and learn about each individual's characteristic way of dealing with engagement and intimacy. This model is rooted in Sullivan's interpersonal theory (1953), making the unit of clinical study the individual's interpersonal interaction at any particular time. As such, this model is allied with object relations theory, but it attends insufficiently to the internalized aspects of interpersonal relationships. It is essentially a model based upon whole object relatedness. For the borderline personality, such an approach, emphasizing interpersonal learning, addressing only the objective reality of the group, may result in confrontations that are so painful and assaultive as to lead to further entrenchment of the patient's split, rather than to integration, with the potential for negative outcome or premature dropout. This is especially so if the manifest interpersonal behavior is not viewed in its entirety and linked to its core or disavowed components (Horner, 1975). The denied and split-off elements must be brought into the treatment focus. Each patient interaction within the group here and now can be understood in terms of its link to the promotion, expression, or obstruction of development of self. Basch (1987) argues that the individual's here and now interpersonal contact is indissolubly linked with the internalization of past relational experiences. One cannot focus on the self without conceiving of the impact of the object, and vice versa.

In order for the group to achieve maximum effectiveness, the group leader should be sufficiently active to reduce unnecessary regressogenesis. The group composition should be heterogeneous. The therapy should focus on the interpersonal interactions within the group but the understanding and depth applied to the interpersonal interactions ideally should be informed by object relations theory (Rutan and Alonso, 1984). Sense can be made of the confusing, contradictory presentation of the patient if the therapist is able to analyze the moment-to-moment, here and now variations of the patient's transferences in terms of the activation of antithetical units of self and object representation. In other words, the context of treatment begins with an understanding of the individual patient's internalized object relations, extends to its expression in part and in whole within the interpersonal interaction with the group, and further effects and is effected by the entirety of the group process. Peer transferences are perceived to be mutative in and of themselves and are not, by definition, resistance to the development of the transference to the group leader (Kibel and Stein, 1981).

Concurrent Group and Individual Therapy

The role of concurrent individual therapy is often pivotal. Horwitz (1980) cites the failure to add individual therapy to the borderline person's group therapy as the commonest cause of premature termination of the group treatment. In general, prior or concurrent individual therapy increases patient tenure in group therapy (Stone and Rutan, 1984), and this model of treatment has shifted from being controversial to being accepted practice (Ormont, 1981; Rutan and Alonso, 1982). There are a number of important considerations for the therapist (Horwitz, 1977; Wong, 1980; Rutan and Alonso, 1982).

Concurrent group and individual treatment may be combined (same therapist) or conjoint (two therapists). The borderline patient's propensity to distort and split is perhaps better contained when the same therapist does both the individual and group therapy, generally beginning with a period of individual therapy and adding group therapy once the individual therapy has stabilized somewhat. A logistical limitation is that the group should be homogeneous for the combined approach, in order to reduce the iatrogenic production of envy and destructive rivalry. Conjoint therapy offers the opportunity of tailoring each patient's specific needs, thereby maintaining a heterogeneous psychotherapy group. Group therapy may begin, or individual therapy may begin. However, more is not necessarily better. A treatment should not be added haphazardly, and the first treatment should be well established before the second one is begun.

In both instances, one of the modalities is more intensive and the other is more supportive. Often the group therapy provides illumination and confrontation, and the individual therapy provides containment, crisis management, and support. Where management issues will be prominent, relating to medication, acting out, and potential hospitalization, concurrent individual therapy is imperative. Groups are not effective or able managers. Each treatment facilitates working through in the other, and it is important to ensure that the patient deals with the relevant issue in the relevant setting. There must be clear consensus between the therapists regarding diagnosis and the direction of treatment. As well, they must be able to have open and regular contact to ensure that distortions and splitting are contained immediately. The therapeutic right hand must know what the therapeutic left hand is doing, and patient agreement should be obtained for communication between therapists at their discretion.

If the two therapists can indeed work collaboratively and offer the patient no fertile ground in which his idealizing and devaluing projections may grow, a powerful therapeutic technique is accessed. Conjoint psychotherapy can serve as a form of peer consultation as well, helping each therapist with the potentially difficult and disruptive countertransferential responses that commonly arise.

Confidentiality is never absolute and is best left to the therapists' discretion, again with the patient's explicit agreement prior to starting treatment. It is preferable that the patient and not the therapist introduce relevant information from the other therapeutic modality. If it is patently being avoided, it may be gingerly broached at the lowest level of inference in order to safeguard against the situation in which the patient regressively relies on the therapist to know what is important and relevant.

Clinical Vignette

Barb, a twenty-four-year-old borderline woman with prominent narcissistic features, was referred for conjoint group psychotherapy by her individual psychotherapist. Although a talented artist, she was unable to organize herself, and intermittently was self-destructive, with impulsive wrist-slashing. Her individual therapy essentially focused on the frustrations of her external world, and the way in which her opportunities were sabotaged by people around her. The individual therapist felt it would be useful for Barb to see first hand what her contributions were to this unsatisfactory situation.

Barb frequently dominated and monopolized the group with her in vivo elaboration of her tendency to overwhelm people in her interpersonal world, through her raw and affect-laden expression of intense needs and repeated rejections from her mother and the world at large. She attributed being overwhelming to her large physical stature, a condition impossible to change, hence likely to cause her considerable ongoing rebuff. She lamented that no one ever gives her a chance, and she fails to get the credit due her. For several months, Barb intermittently paralyzed the group when she talked. Her response to very ginger confrontations about her monopolizing the group led to her explosions that she was only talking because no one else was. It was her way of helping the group. On several occasions, she ended sessions suggesting she was feeling suicidal, which further inhibited the group's willingness to confront her. A number of such crises were managed by the individual therapist, knowledge that safeguarded the group from being further controlled by Barb.

During this early phase of treatment, her continued tenure in the group always seemed fragile. This persisted until, after a long, typical exposition, a comember responded to Barb that in fact what made her overwhelming, alienating, and likely to incur rejection, was her repeated broadcasting of her vulnerability and the crimes committed against her. It made him afraid to broach her at all, and he found himself turning off to her. Barb dissolved into tears and started for the door in a panic, at which point the therapist requested that she stay. With much encouragement from comembers, she did, and the copatient went on to say that he chose to give her this feed-back because he was indeed fond of her and couldn't stand to see her continue to self-destruct. Furthermore, he felt confident she could hear him out without inducing a sui-cidal reaction, thereby in fact bolstering her much desired need for recognition of some real strength. Barb settled, and it was that point in her treatment that marked the beginning of any movement in therapy. The frequency of crises diminished substantially, and her tenure in the group became less precarious. She began to assume more responsibility for her therapy, both in individual and in group therapy.

THE BORDERLINE PATIENT IN GROUP THERAPY: SPECIFIC TREATMENT CONSIDERATIONS

A backdrop to the further elaboration of the group therapy of the borderline patient is the idea of the group serving as a developmental matrix (Leszcz, 1989). Its objectives include: helping facilitate for the patient integration of his split parts; consolidation of a stable sense of self; clarification of distor-tions; the capacity to modulate and regulate affects; the experi-ence that intimacy with another is manageable and that he will not be attacked or usurped for engaging; as well as the expan-sion of the range of the observing ego; and limiting maladaptive ego syntonic character traits. Accordingly, the therapist will be attuned to any patient articulation at the level of content or process that expresses or blocks these developmental tasks. Such an orientation both provides the treatment with an abun-dance of material for exploration and working through, and an overall general direction. I will now focus on several relevant issues that may facilitate group therapy in specific fashion.

Pregroup Assessment

The very patient characteristics that warrant group therapy also may impede it; therefore entry into an ongoing group must be

explored in detail in a pregroup assessment. Group psychotherapy generally involves a long-term commitment typically consisting of a once weekly session, and an individual's tenure
ranges in successful cases from between one and four years.
Indications and contraindications are relative, as in almost every instance the borderline patient remains vulnerable to premature termination from group psychotherapy and is often not
easy to integrate into groups. Patients in acute crises, who are
acutely suicidal, or actively abusing drugs or alcohol, generally
fare poorly in the standard long-term psychotherapy group.
Their entry is often better delayed until these difficulties can
be resolved (Yalom, 1985). The patient requires a detailed diagnostic, psychodynamic, and ego function assessment to determine whether the patient and the group will be able to tolerate
one another (Horwitz, 1977).

More than other diagnostic entities, the borderline personality is likely to be referred to the group therapist from an
individual therapist. This may follow the occurrence of one of
the following three developments in the individual therapy: (1)
the patient's transference is too intense and needs to be diluted
by participation in the group; (2) the patient is defensively isolated and unengaged in psychotherapy and requires the group
to mobilize engagement; or (3) the individual psychotherapy
has been effective but the patient requires further interpersonal
and interactive experience to move beyond the gains achieved
in the dyadic relationship. On occasion, the referral may also
reflect therapist demoralization or a wish to get disentangled
from an apparently untreatable patient.

Group therapy should not be considered if it involves explicitly bypassing a central issue of resistance or transference–countertransference impasse without a thorough evaluation. It is necessary to avoid the iatrogenic situation in which
the patient leaves one therapy for another, having had the
experience of being rejected and abandoned. If this is not
worked through to its fullest potential, the second treatment
may well be contaminated by the impasse of the first.

Regarding assessment for individual therapy, Silver (1983)
recommends assessing the patient in terms of his level of object

relations, as reflected in the history of interpersonal relationships, the capacity for feeling guilt, being empathized with and
being soothed. Other important considerations before group
therapy include determining how vulnerable the patient will be
to stimulation in the group. What is the risk of the patient being
flooded or overwhelmed by affect, or group contagion, without
even being directly involved in the group interaction? A propensity to decompensate in strongly paranoid fashion bodes
poorly for group tenure. On the other hand, clear evidence of
a consolidated area of strength or consistency either in the area
of career, hobby, or a relationship, speaks to a greater realm of
nondisturbed ego functioning that may be a useful resource in
psychotherapy.

The level of ego functioning, hence, is a more important
consideration than the specific nature of the patient's symptomatology in determining entry into the group. The importance
of such an assessment is heightened for the group situation,
because of the mutual and reciprocal effects of the group on
the patient. The therapist needs to assess the risk of premature
dropout if the patient is unable to tolerate the group, as well
as assessing the group's capacity to deal with such a patient at
a particular point in time in the group's life (Kibel, 1980). A
mature group will be better able than a newly formed group to
deal with the anticohesive effect of the borderline patient. In a
newly formed, beginning group, the tension that emerges related to cohesion and intimacy that is part of the typical development of groups may well lead to scapegoating of a borderline
patient. The patient's internal sense of badness and worthlessness makes him a fertile target for these group projections,
and hence a high risk to drop out.

Preparation includes both general features and highly specific aspects tailored to each individual. Proper pretherapy
preparation enhances tenure in treatment and task adherence
in group psychotherapy (Yalom, 1985). Information about the
workings of group psychotherapy provides a cognitive backdrop to an otherwise highly charged affective situation. In addition, the pretherapy assessment may provide an opportunity to
identify ego syntonic character traits, for instance a trend toward aggressive bullying, devaluation of others, or a tendency

to flight. Early identification and prediction that these character traits will emerge within the group can increase the patient's ability and willingness to work with them and make them more ego alien. It may also facilitate the development of a therapeutic alliance by virtue of the opportunity it provides to later return, in the midst of therapy, to the baseline difficulties that were identified. Instead of panicking in the face of "here I go again," the patient may have the chance to reach a more adaptive resolution by recognizing these identified difficulties. The patient's wish for a guarantee regarding relationships may best be modified to a form of "warranty." In other words, when things go awry, as they inevitably will, every effort will be made to understand, work through, and repair, and the patient can either help or block the responsiveness of the group members or therapist.

The group therapy contract of coming regularly, coming on time, no extragroup contact, and dealing with group issues only inside the group, is relevant for all patients, but particularly so for this patient group. The pathology of breaking the contract is much less easy to conceal or rationalize in the face of the group reality that everyone else experiences the contract as reasonable. This can mitigate against unnecessary regressogenesis and patient wishes for special treatment that could undermine the psychotherapy. Seltzer, Koenigsberg, and Kernberg (1987) highlight the necessity of establishing an appropriate and specific treatment contract with the borderline patient. The contract underscores the fact that psychotherapy is a partnership in which both parties have responsibility. It can only proceed and succeed under certain circumstances, such that the patient and therapist retain a realistic, nonidealized, and nondevalued perspective on its potential. The mutual knowledge that therapy can be stopped if the contract is broken puts a floor beneath the potential regression and protects against sadistic–masochistic enmeshment. It is advisable to explain to the patient that the treatment contract emerges not from an authority-based injunction, but from the realistic need to protect the treatment from any antitherapeutic forces that could undermine it. Background information and a history of prior therapy relationships may provide useful clues as to what kind of antitherapeutic behavior or acting out may emerge.

A specific instance in the group is that the borderline patient is liable to impulsively storm out from an intense group meeting. It is helpful to discuss with the patient prior to treatment that integral to group functioning is the premise that people stay and, if they leave, return. If there is an impulsive walking out, obviously specific clinical considerations need to be addressed for each individual, but it is useful for all concerned to know that there is an expectation of the patient returning—either to that meeting or the next meeting. If telephone follow-up is necessary after the group, it should be brief, serve to enable the patient to return to the group's next meeting, and this extragroup contact will be brought to the attention of the group at the next opportunity. A clear protocol and group norm in this instance reduces the group's anxiety and may also mitigate against the patient blackmailing the group into providing "special treatment." The role of concurrent individual therapy should be determined as well, including obtaining the patient's explicit permission for contact between therapists at their discretion.

Group Cohesion

In general, group cohesion serves a function parallel to the therapeutic alliance in individual psychotherapy. It is a whole object derivative function—the patient's membership is acceptable and desired by the group and group membership is acceptable and desired by the individuals. Ambivalence can be expected. It is the backbone of all group work, promoting real engagement and the tolerance of divergent opinions, feedback, and interpersonal learning (Yalom, 1985). Group cohesion takes on added complexity with the borderline patient. As Masterson (1978) and Adler (1985) have both commented, the therapeutic alliance with such patients is tenuous due to the patient's aggression, impulsivity, and tendency to split, with the resultant loss of the memory of the prior positive object relational unit of patient and therapist. There may be little distinction between transference and therapeutic alliance, and the self-observing component of the patient may be quite minimal at times. In the same way that it is useful to always attend to the therapeutic alliance and work to maintain it in individual therapy, in the group therapy setting, attention must be paid to the individual's experience of group cohesion. The therapeutic alliance of the patient in group therapy may be fostered by the greater opportunities for real relatedness, which may be nontreatment specific. For instance, group meetings often have a brief period outside the formal "door-closed" treatment during which more lifelike social interaction is present. Humor, discussion of movies, books, and the like, are a form of play that is a prominent feature of these prologues and epilogues. This can be clearly distinguished from antitherapeutic subgrouping or extragroup socialization, by virtue of the absence of any secretiveness or privacy attendant to it.

In the group, cohesion may be experienced as threatening or engulfing and hence need to be resisted. This may be transient or permanent. Where it is transient, a patient's sense of self may be predicated at times upon differentiating himself from the group, through denigration of the group, or blatant disregard for group norms (Stone and Gustafson, 1982). However, where it is an unchanging element it may not be manageable within the group, because of its anticohesive effect on the group. Although every effort needs to be made to encompass the patient in this situation, sooner, rather than later, the issue requires resolution. Neither the patient, who will likely be scapegoated, nor the group, which will likely be furious and obstructed, benefits from persistence with an unworkable situation.

Other paradigms may include the patient who sees himself as special or above the group. This may reflect narcissistic issues of specialness or it may reflect the disavowal of one's needfulness, holding one's own dependency in contempt and unconsciously projecting it into other members of the group. The group experience may be of use for the patient who wishes for more closeness with his therapist, but fears either his rageful consumption of the relationship or the imagined retaliation of the therapist. Participation in the group dilutes the intensity of this. The group serves as a kind of transitional object being both part patient and part therapist and yet existing separately from both (Kosseff, 1975). Alternatively, the cohesion experienced in the group by a patient may be a pseudocohesion based upon compliance and splitting off of elements of the self that are protectively and shamefully kept hidden.

A whole range of subjective experiences of belonging can emerge from the same objective phenomena. Accordingly, the therapist must be attuned to the range of possible subjective experiences of his patients. He may need on occasion to advocate on a patient's behalf to safeguard a vulnerable patient from the group demanding more real engagement than he can tolerate. Similarly, the patient cannot be cajoled to be more objective, or more realistic, or more practical, without again first understanding the patient's subjective experience. This may include exploration of the patient's fear, vulnerability, or at times his wish to master and dominate the group through his passivity, dependence, or manifestation of being "out of control." The self-protective aim must be understood before it can be successfully altered. Generally, groups are quite supportive to individuals whom they perceive to be trying but unable to do more, as opposed to their intolerance of patients who seem more able but are unwilling or denigrating of the group process. The therapist may need to intervene to help the group distinguish between these two possibilities. The patient's vulnerable core may be very hard to keep in perspective at times when the manifest interpersonal defenses may infuriate the group through devaluation or denigration of the group.

The therapist is often the main integrator, the anchor who is able to link objective and subjective realities. He may need to be the advocate for both the group and the individual; for both the attacked and the attacker. As the group matures, other members of the group will assume this function, modeling for the borderline patient a respect and appreciation for the requirements necessary for emotional growth.

Ruptures in the feeling of connectedness to the group occur regularly with borderline patients and need to be examined each time in the context of the subjective experience of the event that induced the rupture. Often this is a perceived disappointment, empathic failure, or rage-inducing frustration.

Linking prior object relational units with current ones, and linking affect to behavior promotes the necessary repair. This is more readily done when the patient's tendency to split and make abrupt shifts in his relatedness is well appreciated and understood. Unlike the situation with a patient who uses higher level defenses, in which instance the patient's unfettered associations will provide the necessary material for proper understanding, with the borderline personality the split-off material—the alternate pole of affect and interpersonal experience—is unlikely to be brought forward by the patient. The therapist must actively pursue it and integrate it.

This trend is further exacerbated by the use of the defense of projective identification. This concept is an important one in the treatment of character disordered patients in all kinds of treatment, but in particular in group therapy. It is an unconscious mechanism that enmeshes people, unlike simple projection of a disavowed part, which estranges people. It is both a defense and an interpersonal phenomenon and has the effect of shaping the behavior of the recipient of the projection in particular ways. Therefore, as a concept, it is a clear bridge between internal object relations and interpersonal relationships (Horwitz, 1983).

It may have a profound effect on group cohesion, either promoting it or more typically obstructing it, correlated with the nature of the projection. The mechanism is most accessible in an environment in which there is either substantial intimacy or some reduction in self–object differentiation, both of which can occur in any intensive psychotherapy. The essential mechanism is that an internal, disavowed part of the self's inner world is projected into another person. What follows is the self linking with (the identification with) the disavowed part. This increases the pressure to control and master the person(s) into whom the projection has been made. The final component is that of the self, "taking back," or reintrojecting, the "part" projected out, with the unconscious hope that the formerly unacceptable part has been neutralized and modified within the other person, such that when it is taken back in it will be made less noxious. How the projection is contained or handled by the target of the projection is cardinal. The cycle of fearful disavowal and projection is broken only if the recipient does not complement the projection by responding in a way that corroborates the projecting patient's view of the world. Ideally, the recipient is able to contain it, by empathically understanding why it has needed to be projected out by the subject. This is not to say that one greets hate with love in a superficial or manipulative way, but that one greets hate without retaliation, and with an integrated memory of the prior object relational unit. Groups offer exceptional opportunities for reversing the chaotic new reality the borderline patient can create by the use of projective identification.

Clinical Vignette

Ann was attending her third to last scheduled meeting in the hospital after an intensive inpatient treatment of several months' duration. The group normally met three times a week and was composed largely of severely character-disordered patients. Ann had been an integral, valued, and valuing member of the group but had been aggressively distancing herself from the group prior to her impending discharge. She abruptly began the meeting in a cruel and devaluing way, announcing to the group her realization that the experience of being in the group with them turned out not to be worth much at all. She acknowledged her previous involvement as having been nothing more than a "vacation relationship." It had no real substance or meaning. Ann's aloofness and devaluation was crushing to a copatient, Norma, her roommate for the past several months. She withdrew and began to cry quietly, while a third member of the group agreed loudly and angrily, saying that it was indeed a meaningless relationship and that Ann, in fact, could drop dead on the spot.

What evolved was an escalating competition to see who could hurt the other most, ripping apart in minutes, weeks of cohesive work. The therapist intervened, asking each person to stop and reexamine the process of what had just happened, before they continued to damage each other and turn valuable relationships into garbage. Ann calmed considerably when the therapist confronted her with the idea that the reason she attacked the others today was because she feared that she would be meaningless to them after she left. She responded saying, "I don't know how or why I began to believe it, but I felt very strongly that no one here cared for me any more."

In the face of the abandonment of discharge, her internalizations of the prior relatedness began to fragment. Abandonment, and her rage at the abandoning objects, made her feel worthless, ugly, and unlovable, in relationship with devaluing and rejecting part-objects. She devalued others in the face of feeling devalued. Until it was confronted in the group, it remained split off and disavowed. Ann then proceeded to project into the group members her own fear of being unlovable and her own difficulty in sustaining the positive memory of the group, but in such a way that she almost succeeded in leaving the group bereft of the positive relationships and memories she had worked so hard to generate. By perceiving the group members as though they were fully her own projection, and by treating the comembers badly—as dependent, needy, and therefore contemptible—she invited their rage, thereby confirming her internal perception of not being cared for or valued. The relationship subsequently was repaired in that meeting with the group's understanding that it was Ann's fear, beneath this haughty defense, that was generating this attack. Linda, a comember, apologized for having been in fact cold and intolerant of Ann recently, having failed to see what was going on inside of her.

Ann's separation from the hospital became more manageable and, also of importance, it was possible for her and for the group to be angry and to work it through rather than have it only amplified and lead to greater destruction. Ann expressed her gratitude prior to leaving, stating, "I didn't want to leave the hospital the same way I came in—carrying nothing of no one inside of me." Her temporary loss of the evocative memory of the positive experience of the hospitalization and the group needed to be rekindled by active confrontation. During the last week of her hospitalization she was able to grieve and leave with a warm, expressive goodbye. This illustrates the negative potential the borderline patient has to translate an intrapsychic experience into a new, pathological interpersonal reality.

Simultaneous with the need to assess the patient's subjective experience is the therapist's need to assess the impact of the borderline patient on the rest of the group. In addition to the impact of projective identification, the patient's tendency to split presents an ever-present challenge to the group. Failure to recognize and address the presence of splitting will lead to a perplexing and discouraging therapeutic impasse.

Clinical Vignette

Lois, a twenty-eight-year-old woman, was initially very angry, monopolistic, and intimidating in the group. She described a long-standing view of herself as bad, noxious, and greedy, repeatedly expecting the group to reject her. She had joined a group that had just begun and was effectively utilized by the group to carry its affect—thereby allowing them to remain only superficially involved with one another. Her characterological style meshed with the group's developmental resistance. The stunting effect on the group was addressed by the therapist's repeated confrontation that the group members were afraid to really engage and were using Lois to this end—it damaged the group and was damaging to Lois as well. Repeated exploration of the group's passivity proved of little use, as they often encouraged Lois to continue speaking and praised her for her forthrightness, mistaking discharge with working through.

The situation changed for the better when Lois was hospitalized by her individual psychotherapist for a pharmacological assessment of her lability and eating disorder. During this two-month hospitalization, the group began to mobilize itself in her absence, and when she returned both she and the group were different. She felt calmer, less out of control on a low dose of a major tranquilizer, and the group was more active, spontaneous, and engaged. As Lois experienced herself to be less overwhelming and noxious to the group, positive changes in her mood and self-esteem regulation ensued. She in fact continued to do well, and reported valuing the group, and could, much to her surprise, begin to feel valued by the group.

This continued apace until the group regressed with the entry of two new quiet, passive members. The whole group was slowed, a fairly usual reaction to the entry of new members, but one that resulted in Lois resuming her former domineering position in the group. This time, members complained. Lois experienced this as a major empathic lag, coming on the heels of her tenuously consolidated improvement. She regressed completely. She distorted feedback, to put it into its worst light, utilizing members' comments to angrily flagellate herself. She began to yell, "I'm sick—I can't function—I'm no good for anything. Years of treatment and I'm nowhere." The more group members tried to challenge her distortion and repair the rupture she experienced, the louder she became, refuting any statement of valuation, ultimately storming out of the group abruptly. Feedback that would have been reparative for a patient who had achieved object constancy and the capacity for ambivalence, had the antithetical effect on this patient, widening her internal and interpersonal rupture.

Later, in consultation, the group therapist reported that she felt throughout the session that something was "missing," and she felt unable to contain and encompass Lois. Removed from the intensity, it was possible to see that Lois experienced a massive regression and fragmentation in her object relatedness with the initial perceived attack of the group members. She had felt previously that she was finally doing well, and when criticized instead of praised, she became enraged, having felt seduced and misled. Intimacy indeed was just an invitation to sadistic attack. She lost all contact with the more positive and balanced object relational unit of the previous period, and instead experienced herself and the group members in part object fashion. She was bad and ugly, in relationship with bad and attacking part-objects. The emotion that linked them both was one of rage. Attempts at repairing the injury succeeded only in making her more fearful that she would trust and get close only to be attacked again. Hence the more valuing and caring the group members were, the more Lois angrily renounced herself and the group.

Unchecked, this process can degenerate into the group actually beginning to attack the patient, confirming the patient's worst fear. They may even agree that she is untreatable and unhelpable because of how she destroys their care, precipitating a heightened sense of aloneness and feeling of abandonment for the patient, with the concomitant risk of self-destructive acting out. As well, the patient may drop out of therapy. Both these deleterious effects can be reduced if the treatment is able to encompass the patient's unconscious persistence, recapitulating her object relational experience, as opposed to working it through. These recapitulative experiences present crises in treatment. They are both dangerous and yet offer the best opportunities for making significant change.

An additional difficulty is that of the borderline patient making special requests of the group therapist. This may involve telephone calls outside of group sessions, a wish to speak privately with the group therapist at the end of the group, or any of a host of possibilities that involve some form of special relatedness between the patient and the therapist. Often these special requests are made suddenly and may take the therapist by surprise. His response, ideally, should be one that melds the requirements of understanding empathically where the request originates from within the patient, but limiting without rejecting the patient for his wish for specialness, ensuring that undue envy is not stimulated in other group members.

Continuous rages with persistent angry devaluation of the group or therapist serve no useful function for the patient, group, or therapist, and the attacking patient should not be allowed to ride roughshod over the group. If this occurs repeatedly or persistently, it may reflect the group's utilization of the patient to carry their own affect, be it anger or be it a protection against engagement. In this instance the context needs to shift from the interpersonal world of the patient to the group as a whole. Alternatively, at a more practical level, some members of the group may be terrified of engaging in a rage battle with the borderline patient who may be more willing to raise the ante than they are, as well as less vulnerable to feeling guilt over the threat of injury than they would be. If this is not encompassed, the group will inevitably move toward placation and passivity, with associated feelings of demoralization and futility. Occasionally the group may have the experience with such a patient that they end up in an untenable position, reached imperceptibly. This can be likened to watching a movie frame-by-frame, each frame shifting so slightly from the preceding frame, that one's senses are not triggered until one sees the entire footage and realizes how much of an irrational position has been reached.

The Group as a Holding Environment

Elaborated by many authors (James, 1984) is the idea of the group functioning as a holding environment, containing affect, confronting and clarifying without retaliation, prior to the establishment of true cohesion or real engagement with the borderline patient. Many of these ideas stem from Winnicott's (1965b) original conceptualization of the holding environment being that early, developmentally necessary period in which the infant is protected from severe environmental threats that threaten to destroy the emerging sense of self. Modell's (1976) elaboration of the holding environment as a kind of background safety net in which the therapeutic environment is made as reliable and predictable for the patient as possible has relevant application to the group. The group presence is constant and reliable. It meets regularly and is rarely canceled. It has a history that antedates the patient and will likely go beyond him. The patient is accepted and his affects are tolerated, and generally he will not be extruded. Pines (1983) describes the group serving as a container for the patient's painful and distressing affect. It tolerates, absorbs, identifies, and finds words for it, neutralizing and detoxifying it, only *then* sharing the painful affect with the patient. This promotes a heightened capacity for the patient to tolerate the affect and integrate it, rather than split it off in order to expel it. The patient's capacity for integration is enhanced the more he is responded to in a concordant and empathic fashion rather than a complementary one. Holding is not gratification by any stretch, nor should it reward clinging or regressive behavior. Rather, it is a realistic encompassing of the patient.

For more withdrawn patients, the holding function of the group includes the provision of an opportunity to be involved in a seemingly nonrelated way, building up fundamental trust without overtly having to leave the protective cocoon of self-sufficiency. Instead, the patient can observe how people are treated in the group, how affect is responded to, how rage is dealt with, and how object hunger is addressed. Frequently, patients who are silent for long stretches at the outset of their therapy appear hypervigilantly involved, taking in everything but saying nothing. Yet they value the experience enormously and comment on its value when it becomes more possible for them to speak. Part of the holding function is to allow them to relate in a nonrelated way, in a steady, ongoing way, until they develop to the point of ascertaining that it is safe to let the object world in, and expect self and object resonance and not mismatch with the dread of being overwhelmed. Myerson (1979) comments on the necessity of tolerating this without demanding more engagement, in order to safeguard the patient from feeling once again that his agenda and self-need have been supplanted by the object's. Ultimately, treatment needs to move beyond this level, however, or the cocoon will be self-perpetuating. There can be no true, stable acceptance without some expression of self. Similarly, a sense of separateness only follows from the experience of self-expression being met with response rather than a perpetuation of intuitive resonance with nonverbal experiences.

Later, as the patient begins to reveal more of himself and his self needs, the group can often respond in a much fuller and animated way than can the therapist. The therapist's task is to identify the change and revelation of the more true and real elements of the self to ensure that it is not missed or bypassed by the group. As more growth and disclosure proceeds, the group provides a substantial opportunity for mirroring (Kohut, 1977), or for communicative matching (Masterson, 1976). Both of these activities reflect back to the patient that what he carries and feels inside of himself is valued and worthwhile.

There are five other elements in the group psychotherapy of the borderline patient that warrant further comment and specific notation. These include the use of confrontation and clarification; the acquisition of empathy; dealing with object loss; the opportunity for new internalizations and new introjections; and countertransference.

Confrontation and Clarification

A potential pitfall in the psychotherapy of the borderline patient is making premature genetic interpretations, the consequence being premature regressogenesis. This risk is lessened in the group because the very nature of the treatment process is here and now feedback, and confrontation and clarification of distortions. The emphasis on self-awareness is dynamic and not genetic. The patient regularly demonstrates in vivo those aspects of his behavior that need to be challenged. They are less easily lost by his avoidance of their reportage. Focusing on confrontation and clarification illuminates the patient's distortion and the distinction between the objective reality and the patient's expectation of response. However, confrontation does not mean an angry attack. It is a forceful, but supportive pressure on the patient to acknowledge something that is conscious or preconscious, but avoided or denied because of the distress that it involves (Adler and Buie, 1972). The objective of confrontation and clarification should not be solely to stop a maladaptive behavior or alter a patient stance. Rather, its objective should include promoting understanding of how and why it has emerged the way it has; again, linking the objective reality to the subjective experience of the patient (Stone and Gustafson, 1982). Groups have some added clout in this regard because group members are less restricted in their range of responses and may be better able to use humor, cajole, or shock one another to force attention to a disavowed issue. The group's multiple observers serve as a check and balance to ensure that confrontation and clarification is not misused in punitive fashion.

Acquisition of Empathy

In addition to the causes of interpersonal upheaval mentioned earlier, an additional factor is the distortion of empathy by projection, and the consequences of ego boundary blurring. Borderline patients are highly tuned into interpersonal cues, at times seemingly able to read their therapist's unconscious mind. Yet they do not always do this empathically, as everything is redefined in terms of their own internal experiences. This results in further isolation and estrangement, as it is difficult to relate to another person without being able to have a sense of what his internal experience is. The group promotes an opportunity to sharpen these perceptive skills, but objectify the meaning attribution component, by encouraging clear self and object differentiation, through the articulation of the actual internal experiences of group members. The group provides multiple opportunities for checking out intuitions and countering antitherapeutic assumptions. Patients also have the opportunity of exercising their empathic awareness by trying to ascertain what others might be feeling as they are relating to the group and checking this out with the group.

Peer interaction can be used to establish boundary maintenance and to diminish merger anxiety by encouraging patients to identify their own internal state, in order to differentiate it from others in the group. Often the borderline patient ultimately becomes a very important and effective catalyzer of group work because of his perceptiveness. At the same time, the group norms of understanding rather than reacting may be internalized by the patient as well. Group therapy is one psychological treatment that insists on a certain degree of altruism—of attending for the benefit of others and not always only for one's own (Mullan, 1987), serving to further the realization that not only the patient has needs.

Dealing with Object Loss

A third consideration is the role of group psychotherapy in dealing with the experience of separation and object loss. These are ever-present threats to the borderline personality and to his sense of self. Much of the regressive fragmentation and pathological defensive alignments arise in response to these events. The departure from the group of senior members who have successfully ended therapy induces strong reactions in all the group members. This is particularly so for the patient who is vulnerable to feelings of abandonment and associates object loss with the devaluation of self, and the fantasy that the relationship could have been preserved if only the patient had been more deserving of it. The group may be the first opportunity in which the patient can experience object loss and not have it end in an all-or-nothing fashion—feeling rejected and worthless with no memory of having loved or been loved. Due to the fact that the remaining group members are mourning the departures, the experience of loss is less easily denied. The dual realities of loss and of continuity are solidly confronted. The support and care offered to one another fosters an access to mourning—one hopes with enhanced tolerance for real sadness. Such opportunities are vital for the promotion of self integration and the development of object constancy.

Opportunities for New Internalizations

The group offers opportunities for new internalizations, ones that can be used for growth and not for defensive purposes. The process of internalization of interpersonal relationships in the group is achieved in an environment that is less exclusive, less intense, and in which there is less dependency of the self on a single significant other (Stierlin, 1973). The group provides not only multiple real opportunities for relationships but also serves a mirroring function, reflecting back to the patient various parts of himself as illustrated in others' behavior and style of relating. Both through the affective intensity of direct interaction and, at other times, the cognitive intensity of indirect and vicarious involvement, alternative self and object interactions are vivified. The repetitive relationship circuit of engagement and separation, of rupture and repair, promote the internalization process as well, when it occurs in an overall stable treatment framework.

The group may also provide the first significant opportunity for relating to a nondeviant milieu with models of healthy communication and engagement (Horwitz, 1980). This is enhanced further by the patient's behavioral practice in the group of the interpersonal facets of his acquired skills. Each emerging feature of the integrated self needs reinforcement and bolstering, and the here and now of the interactive group provides such opportunities repeatedly. I refer here to such developments as interpersonal sensitivity, empathy, tolerance to criticism, progroup behavior, appropriate assertiveness, reduced impulsivity, and the whole range of interpersonal behavior that mirrors the patient's increased self-integration. Not the least such opportunity is the process of feedback and reorientation that occurs in the group with the addition of new members who are able to reflect back to the patient how he comes across to them *now*, without the influence of the behaviors that marked the initial phases of treatment. This further mitigates against regressive adherence on the part of the therapist or old group members to a potential role lock.

Countertransference

At both the level of therapeutic intervention and the level of countertransference, the borderline patient makes strenuous demands on the group therapist. The therapist often needs to be proactive rather than reactive, and active rather than abstinent. He must continually integrate the process of the therapy in terms of the overt and subtle ways in which the patient's core sense of self is influenced progressively or regressively by the group. In order to fully utilize the potential benefits of group therapy, the therapist must be able to accept the responsibility for these integrating, modulating, and, at times, advocacy functions. This latter posture can only be taken if the therapist genuinely believes that the patient and the group can survive and grow together. The group will accept this intervention if some end is in sight and some progress can be seen. This complicates the already abundant countertransferential issues that emerge in any psychotherapy of the borderline patient.

The countertransferential difficulties that borderline patients arouse have been graphically titled and described. Feelings of helplessness, demoralization, rage, and submissiveness alternating with omnipotence, are some of the reactions authors cite in their description of this phenomenon (Adler, 1972; Maltsberger and Buie, 1974). The therapist's therapeutic and personal narcissism is often on the line. However, when the individual therapist embarks upon treatment, he need consider only himself and the patient. The group therapist faces additional challenges in that he is also involving all the other members of the group. Not only is he responsible for the provision of the most suitable treatment opportunity for the group at large, his own therapeutic failures are now public events. The group therapist will often be faced with his concern, or even guilt, about the difficult patient's impact on the rest of the group. Is their therapy obstructed? Or is it even being damaged irreparably? The wish to extrude the difficult patient in this instance may be powerful and may be fueled by a group contagion. At times it may be very difficult to distinguish between an accurate clinical decision and a countertransferential reaction to the borderline patient's projective identification of a disavowed part of himself. Analysis of the countertransference therefore involves exploration of the patient's experience in its entirety and not just the more dominant components present at the moment. At the same time, the group and the therapist's contribution to the interaction must be explored. As with the intensive individual psychotherapy of the borderline patient, ongoing supervision or the availability of consultation can be very helpful and at times absolutely necessary in retaining an appropriate therapeutic perspective.

Inpatient Group Therapy

Although grounded in the therapeutic issues elaborated heretofore, the short-term inpatient group psychotherapy of the borderline patient necessitates further consideration. Patients with borderline personality frequently require hospitalization, and their number in absolute terms is quite substantial (Gunderson, 1989), reaching between 8 to 25 percent of all inpatient admissions in many general hospital settings. Substantial differences exist between short-term inpatient group therapy and long-term outpatient group psychotherapy (Yalom, 1983; Leszcz et al., 1985). By definition, the shorter-term nature of the group experience—days rather than months—and the more severe condition of the individual patient, warrant utilization of more structured models with realistic and limited goals. Characterological change should not be pursued. If the therapeutic alliance in the ideal situation is difficult to maintain, in the acute, rapid turnover setting of the inpatient unit the therapeutic alliance may be next to impossible to establish. The opportunities for working through are very limited.

Realistic goals may include provision of support, problem identification, and linking of behavior to affect, recognition of the idea that talking and engaging may be useful and indeed safe, and a reduction of the strain of interpersonal distortions as they occur in the hospital milieu, and as they are influenced by milieu events. This recognizes that the patient in the group, and the group itself, are integrally linked to the entire hospital and ward, and neither stands in isolation. This consolidates reality testing and boundary maintenance for the borderline personality, and may accordingly decrease the patient's feeling of estrangement and isolation (Kibel, 1978, 1981). Ideally, the group should be sufficiently encouraging to the patient that he will be prepared to continue in group psychotherapy after discharge from hospital.

Here and now approaches that are structured to be supportive and are affect-deintensifying are useful in this regard. The emphasis in this instance should be on improving communication, clarification of distortion and misassumptions, and quick repair of ruptures. The limited resources for working through require firm regulation and modulation of the degree of affect that can be stimulated, especially anger and aggression. Patients will continue to have contact with one another on the ward after the group; hence it is useful to contain the antagonistic feelings within the group. The group therapist may need to actively limit potentially destructive interactions, always seeking the invitation for what is desired behind the rebuff of what is rejected (Leszcz, 1986). In this regard, management substantially overlaps with treatment. Some seemingly rich areas for exploration will need to be patently avoided because of the risk of opening up more than can be realistically addressed within the time constraints of the short-term hospitalization. If effective, the group may free the patient to make more effective utilization of other therapeutic aspects of the hospitalization experience.

Kibel (1978, 1981) advocates the specific focus of dealing with the borderline personality's rage, attempting to defuse, normalize, neutralize, and externalize it. He recommends protecting the patient from the deterioration that would likely follow if the patient were confronted forcefully with his rage within the group. The objective in his model is the return of the patient to his precrisis level—even if this necessitates not confronting the patient's splitting. To this end, Kibel finds it useful to address the group as a whole, with direct interventions to individual patients being quite limited. He believes this helps to further normalize aggression and bolster whatever positive feelings of cohesion and trust may exist within the group.

CONCLUSION

Group psychotherapy provides a valuable, albeit challenging modality of treatment for the borderline patient. Treatment effectiveness is enhanced when the entirety of the patient is kept in focus and the patient's relative lack of self-integration and tendency to relate to the world in split, part-object fashion is appreciated. When the self needs are addressed effectively, growth and maturation may ensue for both the individual and the group, reflected in a greater sense of integration, modulation, and moderation. This affects every level of the patient's internal world including his sense of self, his affective world, and his view of the external world. Within the group, and in the adaptive spiral that follows from the group, the patient develops a greater empathic awareness of the requirements for emotional growth, and enhanced respect rather than devaluation for the emotional needs of the people in the group and in his external world.

19.

Family Dynamics and Borderline Personality Disorder

Edward R. Shapiro, M.A., M.D.

I have been involved in the study of borderline adolescents and their families in an inpatient setting for over fifteen years. Beginning with a seminal collaboration with Roger Shapiro and his colleagues John Zinner and David Berkowitz at NIMH from 1972 to 1974 (Shapiro, Zinner, Shapiro, and Berkowitz, 1975; Shapiro, Shapiro, Zinner, and Berkowitz, 1977) I have developed (with colleagues at the Adolescent and Family Treatment and Study Center at McLean Hospital) an application of group and object relations theory to the treatment of these patients and their families which has been presented in a number of clinical papers (Shapiro, 1978a,b, 1982a; Shapiro and Kolb, 1979; Kolb and Shapiro, 1982a; Shapiro and Carr, 1987; Shapiro and Freedman, 1987) and brought together in the book, *Lost in Familiar Places* written in collaboration with Wesley Carr from England, with applications of the clinical work to the study of organizations and society (1991). In the book there are numerous case studies and illustrations of these ideas. What follows in this chapter is a synthesis derived from these publications of our clinical thinking about the family of the borderline patient.

The current increase in the diagnosis of "borderline" is a striking phenomenon. A generation ago, when the intact nuclear family was assumed to be a stable institution in Western society, holding many of its core values, the diagnosis of "neurotic" was the familiar manifestation of psychopathology. This diagnosis referred to individuals who experienced their conflicts as internal to themselves and who presented themselves to mental health professionals with *symptoms,* such as anxiety, guilt, and depression. Neurotics were able to manage relatively competently in the world and looked to themselves as the source of their own difficulties. They had internalized from their family experience a structure of personality which allowed them to take responsibility for their lives and to develop a complex fantasy life. The development of individual psychotherapy and psychoanalysis as a primary treatment modality made sense for such relatively autonomous individuals.

In contemporary society, where families can consist of people in untraditional relationships, and thus where the notion of "family" has become much broader, less stable, less nuclear, and less predictable, the diagnosis of "borderline" is increasingly made. These patients are characterized by problems with *behavior.* They find themselves in a world made up of people they believe they know but do not; they have difficulties in controlling their impulses and in taking responsibility for themselves; and they have limited capacities to develop complex internal fantasies. They manage reasonably well in situations where external structure is provided, where limits and tasks are clear, authority is well delineated, and psychological interest and support are available. But in unstructured environments they become disorganized, and act chaotically and impulsively, exhibiting poor judgment. They cannot tolerate anxiety and possess no clear goal orientation. They are often not symptomatic, that is, they do not complain of internally experienced anxiety, guilt, or depression. They look to others rather than themselves as the source of their problems, and people around them often have difficulty in tolerating their behavior and their demands. In many ways, these patients have difficulty in experiencing themselves as separate from others, having powerful needs for others to supply psychologically missing aspects of themselves. In other words, borderline patients are exquisitely sensitive to their interpersonal environment, which they readily find disruptive. Because they have been unable to develop an inner psychological structure from their family lives which allows them to function well autonomously, they are extraordinarily vulnerable to any lack of structure in their interpersonal environments.

The lack of structure, a poorly defined sense of developmental tasks, and irrational roles taken up in these patients' families, as well as the psychological vulnerabilities of the parents, contribute to and exacerbate the borderline child's difficulties, particularly during the critical childhood separation periods of ages two to three and adolescence. Our ongoing study of family process and interaction in these families suggests that in adolescence family treatment may well be the most useful approach.

The relationship between borderline patients' family structures and the problems these persons have during adolescence is striking. A number of clinical investigators have studied this interaction with a view to defining both the developmental contributions of the family context and describing ways of providing treatment. The basic clinical concepts used in this approach have been: projective identification, pathological certainty, the holding environment, shared unconscious assumptions, task and role, countertransference and interpretation.

PROJECTIVE IDENTIFICATION

The central bridging concept that allows a scrutiny of the connection between the individual with his internal conflicts and the family group is that of projective identification. Initially described by Melanie Klein (1946), the notion of projective identification has been elaborated by a number of workers, and is now widely used to encompass a variety of group and family dynamics. With an understanding of this mechanism, it is possible to grasp the ways in which individuals use relationships with others to manage conflicted aspects of themselves. These dynamics are particularly evident in families with borderline adolescents because of the child's exposed and troubled efforts at reworking earlier identifications with the parents as he or she begins to separate and individuate. Similarly, parental identifications with the child increase during this time, as the child's adolescence reawakens aspects of earlier parental childhood conflicts and as they attempt gradually to relinquish their parental authority while the adolescent takes up his or her own.

The central questions which led to the elaboration of our understanding of projective identification were: first, how do we understand the nature of interpersonal influence; and second, in what ways are unconscious collaborative links between people expressed and transmitted? The basic emotional connection between people derives from empathy. Since we cannot be in another's body, how does empathy work? When empathy is accurate, it is not a mystical phenomenon. It is because we know our *own* feelings, learn to recognize elements of similarity in the bodily communication of others (tears, smiles, tremors), and accurately estimate similarities in their internal states. The notion of projective identification begins with accurate empathy and takes it a step further. It has eight components, which I will list, focusing on their interpersonal meanings.

1. The projection or disavowal of an uncomfortable aspect of ourselves.
2. The discovery (through a kind of empathic recognition) of another person who has a part of himself which corresponds to that aspect of us that we are attempting to disavow.
3. The willingness, conscious or not, of the other person to accept the projected attribute as part of himself.
4. The development of an enduring relationship between the two individuals in which the projections are sustained by unconscious collusion.
5. The other (now seen as possessing the disavowed characteristics) is consciously identified as *unlike* the self, while an unconscious relationship is sustained in which the projected attribute can be experienced vicariously— "I'm not like that, *she* is!"
6. The use of manipulative behavior that is unconsciously designed to bring out feelings and behavior from the other

that confirms the idea that the projected attribute belongs to him or her.

7. Selective inattention to any of the real attributes of the other person that may contradict or invalidate the projection.
8. A complementarity of projections—both participants project.

So, for example, if a parent has an internal conflict between his dependent wishes and his autonomous strivings, it can be managed by developing a relationship with another person, say, a child, onto whom conflicted and aggressively tinged aspects of his dependency are projected. A child is particularly usable for such a projection since the child is dependent and the projection is therefore directed onto an actual attribute. The parent then angrily experiences the child as clinging and demanding and consciously withdraws from him or her, while maintaining an unconscious connection with that projected (and hated) dependency. The parental withdrawal and lack of responsiveness to the child's dependency contributes to an exacerbation of the child's dependent needs, and the child's behavior then confirms the parental projection. Similarly, the abandoned child projects his own autonomous capacities onto the parent and ultimately identifies with the monochromatic (and hated) parental autonomy which contributed to the abandonment. This identification serves as a defense against the feelings of abandonment engendered within the relationship. In the absence of collaborative interpretation of the enacted conflict, each member of the pair (and subsequently the family as a whole) is stuck with disconnected aspects of what inevitably becomes an interpersonal fight.

Case Example

A mother of a borderline adolescent describes herself as a "superficial kind of person, always upbeat." She cannot relate to her daughter's depression, rage, and outbursts of panic; she experiences them as alien. In the family treatment, she remembered how she locked her drunken husband in the basement in the child's early years, piling furniture against the door and screaming, "You can piss in the sink for all I care!" Her daughter, awakened, came out in the hall and cried, "What the matter?" Mother remembers how she smiled calmly and said, "Nothing, dear, everything is fine." In the presence of her daughter, she denied her fury and terror and could not see or respond to the panic she evoked in the girl, leaving her daughter to bear these affects alone. In response to this affective abandonment and projection, the child could not mobilize her own resources and competence, and was left sustaining angrily a complementary and fragile image of an unflappable (and unavailable) mother.

Important aspects of how people behave and interact are, then, not necessarily specific to them as individuals alone. Projective identification and its use as an interpretive notion directs us to see both individual *and context* simultaneously. People are intrinsically complex. It is likely, therefore, that different interpersonal contexts may evoke strikingly different aspects of individuals. It is for this reason that James Masterson's earlier notion (subsequently revised) that borderline patients' mothers are all borderline was too simple (1972). While these mothers may demonstrate borderline phenomena within their family *in relation to their particular child,* in other contexts they often show more complex personality functioning, and the dynamics of the family that evoke borderline functioning in the pair (mother and child) can shift under different emotional pressures.

We cannot, therefore, consider the borderline individual apart from his or her context. The concept of projective identification is one means of facing this problem without surrendering the importance of individual autonomy or sacrificing the reality that individual personality functioning is contextual. The family is a sufficiently small context in which the significance of each individual is in principle not in dispute. It is, therefore, a convenient (and familiar) place to examine the nature of this interlocking.

The marital situation is in some degree grounded in projective identification. The birth of a child offers new possibilities for the partners to project their internal conflicts onto another individual. Although it is not yet possible to determine the genetic or biological vulnerabilities of these children that might make them particularly susceptible to borderline behavior or more likely than others to be chosen by parents for particular projections, their dynamic roles in these families are repetitively reenacted in our population of hospitalized adolescents and their families. Our studies have indicated that in families of borderline adolescents major developmental conflicts about autonomy and dependency are experienced by both parents in different ways. These contaminate the parents' ability to respond to these issues in the child at appropriate developmental stages, particularly during separation–individuation. During these periods, parents relate to the child as an aspect of themselves and are unable to perceive the child's differentiated needs. Either dependency in the child is experienced as draining (contaminated by aggression) or his autonomous functioning is experienced as abandoning (similarly contaminated by aggression). What aspects of these aggressive projections fall upon actual aggressive aspects of the child remains unclear, although once these parental and shared family conflicts are interpreted and reinternalized, most of these adolescents (and their parents) are significantly freer to grasp and work with their own difficulties in an individual context.

The problems presented by the borderline child, therefore, do not just arise from within, nor are they the simple outcome of displacement by the parents into the child of some pathology of their own. There is a complex nexus of relationships which is exposed and disturbed by the absence of a sufficient family structure to contain anxieties at many levels.

The borderline phenomenon, therefore, directs us to a key distinction between "relationship" and "relatedness" (Shapiro and Carr, 1991). "Relationship" describes interaction between persons who are in actual contact in terms of the dynamic that is generated between them. "Relatedness" indicates that there is another perspective, no less personal in terms of the dynamic material, which examines the *structures* that such relationships create and their impact on and use by those involved. So, for example, although the parents and the child are in a series of relationships, they also carry in their minds some vaguely perceived, shared notion of a structure called "the family" which affects their behavior. The process of projecting within the boundaries of the family group creates this structure which is entirely in the mind. The notion of "the family," as it is collectively, emotionally, and largely unconsciously developed by family members, is a product of this shared projective process. It is in relation to this structure that shared unconscious assumptions about individuals within the family context evolve. Without a sense of this shared unconscious structuring we believe that it is not possible adequately to address problems in interpersonal relationships without getting locked into unworkable countertransference dilemmas of blaming and recrimination. Equally, of course, it is not possible to address family structures without a profound awareness of relationships.

The family may be defined as a group with a task. Following Roger Shapiro (Shapiro, 1968; Zinner and Shapiro, 1972; Shapiro and Zinner, 1975; Zinner, 1978b), we define the family's task as the facilitation of the mastery of developmental stages for each of its members. During adolescence, one major task of the family—to provide support for the individuation and identity formation of the child—is disrupted because of the revival of conflicted needs in family members. Through the use of projective identification, boundaries between individual members of the family are obscured. The period of adolescence itself is a time of major role change. The child is moving toward adulthood and the parents are undergoing shifts in their role relationships with the child and hence with one another. And because the major overt changes, bodily and emotional, are occurring in the adolescent child, he or she almost inevitably becomes the presenter of the family pathology. The adolescent's efforts to make new relationships outside the family threaten the integrity of the boundaries of the family unit by opening it to outside scrutiny.

Each of the key sustaining elements in the life of the family as a group—boundaries, structure, task, and roles—is in flux.

This is the case in every family, whether it produces a borderline adolescent or not. The usual, and generally reliable supports which enable people to manage new dependent needs, become unexpectedly unstable. The essential structural components of "the holding environment" of the family are thus exposed for examination.

THE HOLDING ENVIRONMENT

The "holding environment" was initially described by Donald Winnicott (1960). He studied the nature of the mother–child bond, focusing on the provision of an environment in which basic human development can take place. There are two basic aspects to this environment: accurate empathy and the containment of aggression. An empathic context affirms the individual's sense of himself as *good*. This word is not used in a moral sense; it describes a sense that the individual is understandable, can be known, know himself, and be of significance in human contact. The second aspect, containment of aggression, allows the individual to discover that his or her aggressive impulses and action on them do not necessarily have to be destructive. They can be mobilized to serve a task (in this case, development) without inevitably disrupting human relationships.

The use of the term *environment* suggests that the family is not simply a collection of individuals in complex relationships which sustains itself. Rather it is an organization which, through its various members and their liaison, interacts with its external world. Initially, when with the birth of a child the family comes to be, parents stand between the child and his world, providing links for the child through their help with communication, through their tolerance of his behavior, and through their interpretation of his or her feelings and needs. It is in this dimension of the family's life—the world of increasingly understandable, manageable, and interpretable feelings—that human development takes place. When this holding environment decays or is absent from the beginning, as in borderline cases, the child feels unsafe in the world and is forced into a premature maturation, developing what Arnold Modell (1975) calls an "illusion of self-sufficiency." In more schizoid cases, this illusory self-sufficiency appears as detachment; in other more flamboyant borderline cases, it is shown through a denial of dependency combined with a chaotic and seemingly unrelated series of outbursts that demand some kind of containing response from the environment.

Failures in the holding environment during the adolescence of a particular child are not simply the result of the various pathologies of individuals within the family. Each contributes to but also joins a shared family regression, which damages, and frequently destroys either or both of the facets of the holding environment.

Regression is a defense common to all of us. At times of stress, when our mature capacities cannot manage, we all have the capacity to shift in our functioning backwards toward the use of psychological mechanisms more appropriate to earlier periods of our lives. Regression may entail a shift from words as communication to action, from organized imagery in our minds toward fantastic images and simple metaphors more characteristic of the child. Or, in regression, we may alter our entire mode of relationship, from rational, organized perception toward primitive distortion and dependent clinging. In groups and families, a shared regression may evoke earlier modes of communication, loss of individual boundaries, and shared, sometimes psychotic defenses.

Failures of empathy, characteristic of families of borderlines in regression, are often due to a confusion about who the other person is. Images recalled from other, earlier circumstances so dominate the interactions that it becomes impossible to distinguish current feelings and locate them accurately. All concerned doubt their value, not the child alone. The second aspect of holding, the containment of aggression, fails when boundaries become so blurred that they cannot be clarified and explored. The family, for instance, may confuse itself with its external world, and import or export so much unmanageable feeling that not only is it unsure of its own definition but it also becomes uncertain whether it has a task at all.

The recognition of the existence of boundaries is a developmental achievement. The normal child first learns to recognize that the other is separate and that she has a life which persists outside of his or her needs. To accomplish this the child has to surrender his omnipotent feeling that he has control of the mother, that everything she does is related to him, in other words, that she is a part of him. Hand in hand with this discovery of separateness the child has to begin to recognize and tolerate his own anger at frustration. Once he realizes that the environment is separate, the child must give up the fantasy of commanding it and learn to negotiate with it. As this negotiation begins to take place, the child's familiarity with the environment, initially due to its connection with the self, changes. The interpersonal world becomes newly strange and separate. This experience and the learning which results from its mastery produces an ability both to tolerate delay and to take control of aggression. This development fails in families of borderline patients, resulting in idiosyncratic and often paranoid interpretations of reality and an inability to manage aggression; the responsibility for the failure belongs to all members of the family.

In these families there is no shared awareness that interpersonal negotiation of meaning is a way of life. Interpretations remain the prerogative of a parent or a child separately; they do not become the basis for negotiated interpretation of meaning between child and parent. Implicit in the notion of negotiation is tolerance of delay which is strikingly missing in these families. Also the child's need to protect fragile parental vulnerability does not allow him to recognize that the parental holding container for aggression can be vulnerable but not destructible. The child, therefore, cannot begin to become his or her own container for aggression; that is, become responsible for aggressive feelings. The discovery of individual boundaries, then, crucial for development, does not occur.

In normal families, in early childhood the child begins to be aware of group boundaries of similar importance. The young child's parents manage the external family boundary. To do this, they must be able collaboratively to define themselves as a couple and then as a family and begin to define others as "not us." This is similar to the individual's beginning boundary formation which defines "me" and "not me." To define such boundaries requires the adaptive use of aggression. Here, the notion of aggression refers to a quality of response used for differentiation as opposed to that used for linking. Again, therefore, at a most crucial developmental stage, we find it impossible to separate issues of the individual—his or her worth and the constructive containment of aggression—from issues of the group, the family. The family as a whole must manage its aggression so as to be able to differentiate itself and negotiate with its external world. And for the normal child the world external to the family must ultimately be recognized as separate, potentially discoverable, but requiring negotiation. In families of borderlines, aggressive projections of unmanageable conflict result in a failure of collaborative parental management of family boundaries, contributing to difficulties in the children's capacity for group identification and collaborative joining to a task. In conjunction with their own difficulties, this family dilemma leaves borderline patients emotionally isolated from others and engaging in repetitive reenactments of primary family dynamics in group after group throughout their lives.

Case Example

A mother of a borderline adolescent was raised in a family where her mother's narcissistic needs of her precluded attention to her differentiated talents—she felt unacknowledged and unrecognized. As a mother, she was committed to providing specialized schooling for her son's talents. Her husband's father abandoned his family when he was a child. As a boy, he denied his dependency and became the father figure for his siblings. His notion of education for his son was like his own, "the school of hard knocks," where the boy could learn to mobilize his own resources. Father aggressively interpreted his wife's school plans as "coddling," she interpreted his plans as unloving and ungenerous. Both interpretations were derived from their original families; they could not discern the strengths inherent in each other's ideas and could not therefore negotiate a shared parental approach to their son which would define the couple and consequently this new family. As a consequence, the boy felt battered about between them with no clear parental interpretation of his needs. When father would speak to the affective side of learning, mother would become cognitive, or they would unpredictably switch sides. The boy would often awake to hear his parents arguing about him, but when he asked they would say, "It has nothing to do with you." He could not find himself in relation to them and was filled with unmanaged aggression and lack of self definition. There was no negotiated sense of a family approach to the task of development.

For both the individual and the family there is an equation between this establishment of boundaries and the recognition of separation. However, membership in a family group requires that connectedness is also recognized. How is it possible to hold onto both at the same time? This is one of the earliest issues in life, since it is a primary issue of the family. The recognition of the capacity for connectedness and separateness is ordinarily initially negotiated around the care of the child's body.

It is our observation that borderline adolescents have difficulty in managing their own bodies. This is seen both in their concrete difficulties in caring for their bodies (suicide, eating disorders, promiscuity, violence), and in their more abstract difficulties in grasping their affective experience and translating this experience into words rather than action. Because of conflicts around their dependency on their own parents, parents of these adolescents have had similar difficulties in their own upbringing and they have consequently been unable adequately to manage the child's necessary bodily care. This failure is due to the chronic projection of unresolved aspects of their own conflicted bodily experience onto their children (projective identification) and resultant failures in responding to the child as he or she actually is. This impasse represents both a failure in recognizing differentiation (the child has a separate body with needs different than their own) and connectedness (the child is relatively helpless and cannot manage his or her body without them).

PATHOLOGICAL CERTAINTY

An important derivative of this parental difficulty in responding to the child's bodily needs occurs around what I have called "pathological certainty." I have previously suggested that

> [I]n families where individuals manifest severe personality difficulties, [there is] a striking lack of curiosity between family members about each other. Instead, they are often extraordinarily certain that they know, understand, and can speak for the experience of other family members without further discussion or question. The infrequent attempts on the part of individuals within such a family to challenge this certainty are regularly met by bland denial, unshakeable conviction, or platitudinous reassurance. Despite the fact that such certainty is usually incorrect and frequently leads to stereotyped arguments and escalating disagreements within the family, it is difficult to interrupt.
>
> In many disturbed families, parents act as if they have (and sometimes explicitly claim) a so-called "understanding" of the child's experience, which can interfere with his development. This pathological quality of parental certainty is based more on unresolved needs of the parent than on an accurate understanding of the child. The resultant lack of openness and curiosity contributes to feelings of isolation, emptiness and futility within the family group [Shapiro, 1982b].

Parents who are unable to tolerate ambiguity, uncertainty, and the relative helplessness that comes with the need for negotiated interpretation of meaning often struggle anxiously to control their interactions with their child. Parental outbursts of child abuse are often precipitated by the child's efforts to hold onto a separate experience. Vulnerable parents, overwhelmed by interactions with their child that they can neither control nor grasp, may react anxiously, telling the child in effect, "If I can't understand what is upsetting you, then I will do something to you so that you (and I) will *know* what you're crying about."

As a consequence of unmanaged internal conflicts which are projected, parents of borderline children are unable to be interested in their child's differentiated experience and become pathologically certain about the way they perceive their child. These rigid perceptions may evoke in the child a defensive constriction of his sense of himself. Motivated in part by his need to protect his parents from anxiety, the child may develop a "false self" that is organized around responses to his parents' needs rather than his own.

In normal families the recognition by the child that his parents' views of him and many of their responses to his needs may come about as a result of negotiated interpretation between them as parents presents an important step in his development. A derivative of the parents' sexual relationship, these negotiated interpretations about the child reveal the nature of the parental relationship to him. Unconscious recognition of this allows the child to learn about the creation of meaning as a product of negotiated interpretation between people in a given role (i.e., the parental role) in relation to a task (development). With this step, and with his parents' ongoing interest in his own interpretations, he is increasingly able to join the interpretive complexity of the family group. Again, because of marital and family conflicts due to unresolved elements of projective identification, it is here that the borderline child and his family fail.

In adolescence, there is a particular demand for parental interest and flexibility. Since both the adolescent's mind and body are more rapidly changing and developing, parental interest helps to provide the adolescent with the freedom continually to redefine himself as his adult identity evolves. For borderline adolescents, impoverishment in childhood experience or lack of parental support of current adolescent experience may interfere with their normal differentiation. As a consequence of an unstable marital coalition and a shared family regression, the entire family loses its capacity to negotiate shared meaning and interpretation in a mutually respectful way. The disturbed adolescent in such families appears to be chosen unconsciously, both by his parents and siblings, to represent disavowed aspects of unresolved conflicts. This occurs in a powerful, coercive manner that results in a remarkable certainty about who the adolescent is in specific areas of the family's interaction. These interactions have a profound impact on the adolescent's experience of himself and contribute to the weakening of his unstable boundaries as well as supporting stereotyped patterns of behavior between the adolescent and other family members.

The stifling nature of pathological certainty in family life is evident. Family members chronically exposed to such annihilating interactions develop stale, shallow, mechanical investments in themselves and in each other. The thin social veneer in these families is often shattered by eruptions of violence, barely concealed contempt, or flight from the family itself. This is the contextual background, I suggest, for the borderline patient's aggressive enactments with the outside world.

TASK AND ROLE

The family is an organization for the management of social experience, and it has a number of related tasks and individuals in different roles. These terms require definitions: *task* is the family unit's organizing structure. We have suggested that family members are deeply (though often unconsciously) connected around the family's task of facilitating development. The discovery that it is possible to recognize and value the separateness of individuals (including oneself) and still join others in a task, begins in the family. With such conscious joining to a task, both connectedness and separateness can be acknowledged. Thus they become manageable within the family. Through their management basic dependency needs can be met without either destroying the uniqueness of individuals or obliterating necessary linked work at the family's task.

Role is a more complex notion. In a family the usual roles are father, mother, son, daughter, brother, sister, and so on. In these roles, individuals experience themselves as individuals, but their personal behavior is restricted by these roles. For example, a father, as a man, can experience sexual attraction to a young girl. But because of his role as "father" he discovers in himself constraints in exploring these feelings in relation to a girl in a daughter role. Similarly, a woman in a mother role can feel competitive with another woman. But if that woman is in a daughter role, there are implied constraints on how she allows and acts on those feelings.

Such roles, however, do not originate with the individual. All family roles derive from there being a family in the first place. And the complex entity which is a family is essentially defined by its task. It is not constituted by a random set of relationships. It is a distinctive unit, the task of which contributes to the development of its members. Roles, therefore, we define as functions of a task. When a family loses sight of its task or adopts one that is inappropriate, as in borderline families, the consequential loss of roles on the part of each member produces pathological symptoms in individuals and degeneracy in the family unit.

In addition to these familiar, socially determined roles, unconscious conflicts and shared fantasies within families can create a further series of roles which are not obviously task related. These we may describe as "irrational roles," as, for example, the "good father" or the "rebellious adolescent." These, however, are not necessarily pathological, since they may have a key function as products of transitory, but necessary, family dynamics. For example, the irrational creation of a "good father" through the network of projective identification pervading a family ultimately may need disentangling and interpreting, if developmental tasks are to be pursued satisfactorily. But it may also for the moment contribute significantly and usefully to the holding environment that is needed. For example, the "good father" may be an important idealizing experience for a boy in the beginnings of his gender role development. Irrational roles, then, may perform a serious function in assuring family members that their individual and shared irrationalities are not unaddressable.

We may now link these ideas of task and role with the concept of the holding environment and its functions of containment of aggression and accurate empathic interpretation.

These are the underpinnings of normal family life, all of which are in disarray in families of borderline adolescents. They must, therefore, be developed within any successful family treatment. Breaking these two functions into smaller units provides a view of the holding environment as including *task, boundaries,* and *role* as basic containing structures, and *acknowledging* (curiosity), *bearing* (containing), and *putting in perspective* (empathic interpretation in context) as major action components. "Acknowledging, bearing and putting in perspective" were the basic tasks of psychotherapy as defined by Elvin Semrad [Semrad, Buie, Maltsberger, Silberger, & Van Buskirk, 1969]). The containing and interpreting in the holding environment (and, therefore, in family therapy) provides individuals, caught up in the inevitable human process of projective identification, with the opportunity to become aware of projections and to *reinternalize* them. Through so doing they recover and develop a more complex sense of themselves, a more empathic and richer view of others, and a strengthened ability to join with others in different roles in a shared task. In other words they grow and develop.

I have now summarized the significant dilemmas faced in families of borderline patients as well as the normal contextual needs for their repair. In any family treatment, projective identification occurs between family members and therapists as well as within the family. Indeed, since these patients have difficulty communicating affective experience in words, it is often in the therapists' countertransference that central family dynamics can be discerned. Acknowledging, containing, and interpreting countertransference becomes a central aspect of the work. A case history will illuminate these issues.

In the following, I will present a brief report from the hospital treatment of a family with a borderline adolescent. In this case, the presenting issue was the adolescent's rebelliousness, truancy, and aggressive acting out. The family presented itself as respectful, well organized, and "good," experiencing their child's behavior as "alien" to the family culture.

On our inpatient unit the adolescent patient is cared for by a nursing staff whose attention is focused on issues of behavior, a derivative of bodily care. Their effort is to help the adolescent contain his or her impulses and to translate affective experience into words. They spend a lot of time around issues of limit setting, and because of their spending day and night with the patients often develop very intimate relationships with them. In most cases, since nursing staff take on important aspects of the parental role, the adolescent and his or her family often project into the nursing staff unresolved and negative aspects of parental functioning. This results in heated encounters, with the parents often blaming the staff for things that they themselves have been unable to manage well. This displacement of parental functioning offers a unique opportunity to examine the complexities of family functioning one step removed. Interpretation of this displacement into the nursing staff allows for the reclaiming of projections and responsibility for traumatic behavior which contributed to the child's difficulties.

In our program, the individual therapist is also responsible for the management of limits in that he or she authorizes the behavioral care and chairs the treatment team. Having the therapist responsible for the management of behavior places behavioral communication at the heart of the encounter with the adolescent. By bringing the patient into the hospital, the family explicitly authorizes the therapist and the staff to take over aspects of parental functioning. In the individual therapy, therefore, the focus is often on the passionate interactions with the nursing staff, which are seen by the therapist (and often, in the beginning, not interpreted) as a displacement for what ultimately will become an organized and focused individual transference relationship as the patient leaves the hospital. Because of the joint authorization of the entire staff, the transference is initially spread out across the entire team, which meets to attempt an integration of the system.

Case Example

The patient is a fifteen-year-old adolescent, admitted because of escalating difficulties in school, prolonged running away from home, and most recently taking out a failed legal petition against his father with a charge of physical abuse. The family is an upwardly mobile, success-ful family. Both parents had emerged from impoverished, difficult childhoods to become established professionals, "pillars of the community." The boy is the youngest of three children. Both older siblings had difficulty around their adolescent separations, with impulsive departures from home and difficulty in maintaining relationships with both parents after they had left home.

Several years prior to admission, the family had adopted a boy from a deprived background, which had led to serious problems at home, with escalating violence. Father, whose mode of discipline always involved spank-ings of the children, found himself unable to cope in his usual manner. Previously, when he would get mad at his children, his response was to wait until he had calmed down. He would then proceed with a methodical spank-ing—not "out of anger," but out of "disciplinary needs." Though for much of the early hospitalization he denied this, the father began to lose his temper with the adopted and rebellious adolescent in the home and his discipline escalated to the point at which he was using a stick to hit the boys, including his natural son, who also began having difficulty. The patient's running away and school problems continued and worsened and he was admitted to the hos-pital.

Over several months of treatment, the patient re-mained apathetic on the unit, occasionally running away but always returning, speaking about his fear of his father, stating that despite father's denials, he had severely beaten the patient, asserting his reluctance ever to return to the family, and his worry about his own potential for violence. He refused to attend individual therapy and would only talk with his therapist on the open unit, where he could be surrounded by his peers and near the open door. He swore at the staff, subjecting them to verbal abuse and evoking angry responses in return, which left staff mem-bers feeling conflicted about their own aggression.

On one occasion, in the parental therapy, the therapist described the boy's abusive behavior on the unit to the parents. He pointed out that the staff were in the parental role and that perhaps the boy was really swearing at them. The mother said that she never used such language, it was not part of her world, they did not tolerate such language in the home and that she resented the therapist's articulating the details. She became very upset, screaming at the therapist to stop using that language—she felt abused by it. Though he had been initially convinced of the need to include the parents in the management of their son's behavior on the unit, the therapist began to experience in himself the role of abuser—of the narcissistically fragile mother, who threatened to quit treatment. He acknowledged his experience and presented his conflict to the parents: he found himself on the edge between abandoning them by abdicating his treatment role and abusing them by pushing too hard. Both parents recognized themselves in this conflict in relation to their children; they felt they had to respond to their children's behavior as parents, but they recognized that they, too, might have gone too far.

In the family meeting, the mother confronted the boy with his obscenities, asking him if he wanted to say such things to her. "Sometimes," he said. He then reported in great detail how his mother herself had screamed obscenities at him when she had lost control of herself in the middle of family fights. To her own surprise, she remembered that she had sworn at him, but that "it was unlike (her), and was (his) fault." The boy reported a scene in which he had awakened one morning in bed to a severe beating with a stick being administered to him by his angry father. The father, as usual, denied the story and picked on a single detail to correct the "facts." The therapist, recalling his own countertransference defensiveness in the couples' meeting about mother's accusation of him as an abuser, suggested that the father delay his response and consider the way in which the boy's story might be accurate. The father burst into tears suddenly recalling, with wrenching sobs, that he had in fact beaten the boy when he had lost control of himself. The memories seemed torn out of him as he illustrated the conflict between this "bad" self (previously projected into his son as "the alien") and the "good father" view he had constructed for himself, leading to repression of these painful memories and insistence on seeing his son as a liar and bad. All family members were in tears and father and son were able to face each other for the first time, lessening the boy's terror. The boy acknowledged that he had not attended individual therapy because the only safety in his mind was in public settings; he did not trust adults behind closed doors.

In the multiple family meeting on the same day, the issue of abuse was raised by several families. One boy recounted how his mother, while drunk, had locked him out of the house when he was ten, and watched fearfully through the window as a gang of boys beat him. A staff member commented that he felt he was in the same role as this mother when he discharged a patient (effectively "locking the hospital door" behind him) because of insurance limitations into a world the patient could not yet manage. The link between staff and patients around the experience of the abuser opened a deluge of discussion about sexual and physical abuse within families, with both sides (abuser and abused) acknowledging their roles and their resultant self-hatred and conflict.

In this case, aspects of early parental conflict were denied and projected onto the children, resulting in a failure of empathy about them and a lack of curiosity about their differing needs. The children similarly projected abusive aspects of themselves into their parents. The family was unable to define itself in a flexible manner and physical abuse resulted from their inability to see themselves as needing help. Since these dynamic issues could not be communicated in words, they were displaced, through projective identification, into relationships with hospital staff who provided containment and interpretation, linking their experiences to those which were being denied within the family.

DISCUSSION

In families of borderline adolescents, the chaotic and shared experience of boundary confusion coincides with the developmental family task of facilitating separation and individuation. In the resulting maelstrom, the adolescent is renegotiating his identifications with his parents as they are reexperiencing their identifications with him. Unresolved conflicts about autonomy and dependency originating in the parents' childhoods in conjunction with the adolescent's vulnerabilities precipitate a shared family regression in which:

1. The normal developmental task of the family is lost and family roles become based on shared irrational fantasies;
2. The family's capacity to manage accurate empathy and the containment of aggression (the holding environment) fails;
3. There is an inability to negotiate shared meaning amongst family members;
4. Pathological certainty becomes the mode of communication;
5. The adolescent becomes the bearer of family pathology.

Family treatment allows for a therapist to enter the family system and experience within himself aspects of dissociated and projected conflicts. Containment and interpretation of these previously unbearable issues provides an environment in which family members can reinternalize projections and rediscover the family's task. This frees individuals within the family to pay attention to themselves, and to each other, and allows the borderline adolescent to begin to take responsibility for his own behavior.

20.

Psychobiology and Psychopharmacology of Borderline Personality Disorder

Rex W. Cowdry, M.D.

Borderline personality disorder (BPD) is a complex, puzzling, and distressing disorder, characterized by a polysymptomatic presentation with prominent affective, cognitive, and behavioral disturbances. While psychodynamic and developmental theories provide useful formulations of the etiology of the disorder, and useful perspectives to guide the difficult course of psychotherapy of these individuals, these theories are less instructive about the constitutional factors which are widely thought to play a role in shaping the development of BPD. An alternative approach to understanding BPD intentionally underemphasizes the psychological and developmental issues to focus instead on phenomenology and biology—while recognizing that the ultimate task is a productive integration of these perspectives.

Attempts to integrate clinical observations, biological findings, and psychopharmacologic trials tend to be based on one of two models. The first model is categorical or diagnostic. In this model, careful clinical phenomenology is used to identify symptoms occurring together as a syndrome, a diagnostic group, or a diagnostic subgroup. Such an approach may emphasize clarification of the relationships between borderline

495

and schizotypal personality disorders and the relationships among personality disorders and Axis I disorders. Family history studies may provide further evidence of relationships among disorders. Such categorical groupings of patients may suggest shared hereditary, constitutional, or environmental factors. Biological studies may then be directed at finding biological differences between BPD and normals, biological differences among subgroups of patients, or biological similarities between BPD and clinically related disorders. Distinctive psychopharmacologic responses in particular subgroups, or similarities to the responses of patients with related disorders, may help confirm the existence of meaningful clinical subgroups, or suggest specific biological mechanisms on which the drugs act.

The second model which may be used to guide psychobiologic research is dimensional rather than categorical, focusing on identifying critical clinical dimensions which may cut across diagnostic groups and subgroups. Such dimensions may then be associated with specific biological mechanisms and pharmacologic treatments. Animal research linking behavioral dimensions to specific anatomical structures or neurochemical systems often guides the search for biological abnormalities associated with specific symptoms, and for psychopharmacologic agents which specifically affect a dimension of psychopathology.

CATEGORICAL APPROACHES TO THE PSYCHOPATHOLOGY OF BPD—SUBGROUPS AND BORDERS

Advances in biological research on clinical disorders depend in part on descriptive psychiatry. Most psychiatric diagnoses are symptom clusters which occur together and are presumed to share a common origin, course, or response to treatment; that is, most diagnoses are tentative hypotheses about "meaningful" groupings and subgroupings of individuals. Thus, *The Diagnostic and Statistical Manual of Mental Disorders* (DSM-III and DSM-III-R) (American Psychiatric Association 1980, 1987) defined and redefined descriptive diagnoses in the "borderline realm," and suggested that the emotionally unstable presentation ("borderline personality disorder") differed in significant ways from the withdrawn–eccentric presentation ("schizotypal personality disorder") (Spitzer, Endicott, and Gibbon, 1979).

This categorical approach also encouraged attempts to identify significant "comorbidity"—other diagnostic entities occurring together with BPD at greater than chance rates. Attempts to delineate and explore the clinical and biological implications of comorbidity have dominated much of the clinical and biological research in BPD. This emphasis on comorbidity is hardly surprising, since from its initial description, BPD has implicitly been placed on the border of another disorder. Initial formulations (Hoch and Polatin, 1949; Frosch, 1960) placed it on the border of schizophrenia, in part because of the prominent cognitive disturbances, including brief psychoses. However, recent research suggests that BPD, as defined in DSM-III, is not closely related to the schizophrenias. "Conversions" from BPD to schizophrenia are uncommon (McGlashan, 1986a), and family history studies do not demonstrate an increased incidence of schizophrenia in the relatives of BPD patients (Loranger, Oldham, and Tulis, 1982; Soloff, George, and Nathan, 1982; Pope, Jonas, Hudson, Cohen, and Gunderson, 1983).

On the other hand, schizotypal personality disorder (STP), originally included in the "borderline spectrum" of disorders and characterized by a greater degree of unusual thought process and content, may be related to the schizophrenias, as suggested by the Danish adoption studies (Rosenthal, Wender, Kety, Weiner, and Schulsinger, 1971; Kendler, Gruenberg, and Strauss, 1981a).

The strongest association between BPD and a classical Axis I disorder occurs with the major mood disorders. Forty to 60 percent of BPD patients have experienced at least one major depressive episode at the time they are studied (Carroll, Greden, Feinberg, Lohr, James, Steiner, Haskett, Albala, DeVigne, and Tarika, 1981; Soloff et al., 1982; Pope et al., 1983; Baxter, Edell, Gerner, Fairbanks, and Gwirtsman, 1984; Steiner, Martin, Wallace, and Goldman, 1984; Beeber, Kline, Pies, and Manning, 1984; Torgerson, 1984; Grunhaus, Kling,

Greden, and Fliegel, 1985). There is also an increased incidence of major mood disorders among relatives of BPD patients (Stone, 1979; Akiskal, 1981; Loranger et al., 1982; Pope et al., 1983); however, the increased familial incidence may only be present in relatives of those BPD patients who themselves have major mood disorders (Pope et al., 1983). Some authors report a specific association between BPD and bipolar disorder and suggest that many BPD patients have a "sub-affective disorder" (Akiskal, 1981), but most clinical and family history studies have not found a strong association.

The relationships between affective disorder (AD) and BPD must be complex ones. Gunderson and Elliot (1985) have provided a particularly lucid discussion of the possible relationships between the disorders. Clearly, depression does not invariably (or even strongly) produce BPD. Nor is the association between depression and BPD in any sense specific, since depression appears to be strongly associated with other personality disorders as well (Barash, Frances, Hurt, Clarkin, and Cohen, 1985). Finally, half the BPD population has not had a classical major depression. More specific research dealing with the differences between BPD patients with and without AD is needed to clarify whether a meaningful subgroup exists, either with regard to etiology or to treatment response.

Other research suggests that neurological dysfunction may play a role in BPD. Andrulonis, Glueck, Stroebel, Vogel, Shapiro, and Aldridge (1981) found a particularly strong association between attention deficit disorder (ADD) or learning disability (LD) and BPD in male adolescents, raising the question of whether the neurological underpinning produces both ADD/LD and affective–behavioral dyscontrol, or whether the early presence of ADD/LD exercises a secondary influence on developmental processes, producing difficulties with self-image, mood, and behavioral regulation as a secondary effect.

Other studies of comorbidity suggest connections among BPD, eating disorders, and affective disorders (Hudson, Pope, Jonas, and Yurgelen-Todd, 1983; Levin and Hyler, 1986), between BPD and substance abuse (Loranger and Tulis, 1985), and between BPD and multiple personality disorder (MPD) (Horevitz and Braun, 1984). The relationship with MPD may be of particular interest, since the development of MPD is so strongly related to traumatic early life events, raising the question of whether BPD could also result from such events. However, even in MPD, the occurrence of such events does not seem to be sufficient to produce the disorder; some form of early predisposition to utilize dissociative defenses may also be a necessary factor—a factor which has heritable or at least constitutional components, as shown by differences in suggestibility/ hypnotizability early in life.

DIMENSIONAL ISSUES IN THE PSYCHOPATHOLOGY OF BPD

A research approach implicitly derived from observed comorbidity with other disorders has significant limitations. For example, there is a risk that the predominant focus in biological research on the presence and meaning of AD in BPD neglects some of the fundamental clinical features/dimensions of the disorder. Unlike melancholia, in which abnormal mood states, once established, persist independent of environmental events, the "usual" mood disorder in BPD is not one of an autonomous dysregulation of mood but rather one of hyperresponsivity, with labile mood shifts precipitated by events or pseudo-events. The characteristic dysphoria of the borderline patient seems different than the classical depressive mood state, and the anhedonia in BPD usually fits Klein's characterization of "anticipatory anhedonia" rather than his characterization of "consummatory anhedonia" (which typifies melancholia) (Klein, Gittelman, Quitkin, and Rifkin, 1980). The behavioral dyscontrol characteristic of BPD is not particularly characteristic of classical depression. And finally, the dysfunctional attitudes observed in depressed patients, primarily during depressive episodes, are present to a profound degree in BPD, whether the patient is classically depressed or not (O'Leary, Cowdry, Gardner, Liebenluft, Lucas, and deJong-Meyer, unpublished).

Research efforts derived from observed comorbidity therefore need to identify not only similarities between disorders but also critical differences. An alternative approach involves the identification of critical dimensions of psychopathology which are prominent in BPD, but which may cut across diagnostic categories. Dimensions such as reactive affective lability, dysphoria, and impulsivity, may help delineate important aspects of the disorder and suggest biological mechanisms underlying the clinical phenomena.

BIOLOGICAL RESEARCH

Research exploring possible associations between BPD and schizophrenia is extremely limited. Unlike many studies of patients with schizophrenia, the existing studies of BPD patients do not demonstrate an increased incidence of structural brain abnormalities (Synder, Pitts, and Gustin, 1983; Lucas, Gardner, Cowdry, and Pickar, 1989). There is, however, some evidence for an increase in smooth-pursuit eye tracking (SPET) abnormalities, a biological abnormality found in patients with schizophrenia, and in individuals with schizotypal personality disorder (STP) as well, suggesting a possible biological marker for a predisposition to develop schizophrenia-spectrum cognitive disorders (Seiver, Coursey, and Alterman, 1984). Another study (Kutcher, Blackwood, St. Clair, Gaskell, and Muir, 1987) reports that patients with BPD and with schizophrenia show increased latency and decreased amplitude of the late (P300) evoked potential compared with patients with other personality disorders, patients with major depression, and normal controls. Such studies raise the question of whether there is a subgroup of BPD individuals with schizotypal features who have a distinctive biological trait and a distinctive pattern of response to neuroleptics.

A larger body of biological research in BPD is derived, explicitly or implicitly, from the observed comorbidity of BPD with affective disorders. A series of studies (Carroll et al., 1981; Soloff et al., 1982; Aguilar, Lemaire, Castro, Libotte, Reynders, and Herchuelz, 1984; Krishnan, Davidson, Rayasam, and Shope, 1984; Baxter et al., 1984) document a high prevalence of abnormal dexamethasone suppression tests in BPD. It has been suggested, however, that these abnormal results occur specifically in those BPD patients who also have a concurrent major depression (Krishnan et al., 1984; Baxter et al., 1984). Several studies (Akiskal, Rosenthal, Haykal, Lemmi, Rosenthal, and Scott-Strauss, 1980; Bell, Lycaki, Jones, Kelwala, and Sitaram, 1983; McNamara, Reynolds, Soloff, Mathias, Rossi, Spiker, Coble, and Kupfer, 1984; Reynolds, Soloff, Kupfer, Taska, Reshfo, Coble, and McNamara, 1985; Akiskal, Yerevanian, Davis, King, and Lemmi, 1985b) demonstrate abnormally short latencies to the onset of rapid eye movement (REM) sleep in BPD, a finding originally observed in major depression episodes. Again it is not clear whether this is a state finding specific to BPD patients with concurrent depression. There is one study (Akiskal et al., 1985b) suggesting that the abnormality persists during nondepressed periods, raising the question of whether REM sleep abnormalities are a trait rather than state phenomenon in BPD. Finally, there are reports of abnormal blunting of thyroid stimulating hormone (TSH) responses to TRH infusions (Garbutt, Loosen, Tipermas, and Prange, 1983; Sternbach, Fleming, Extein, Pottach, and Gold, 1983), although this abnormality was not associated with the presence or absence of major depression.

As suggested above in the section on dimensional issues in BPD, comorbidity per se may not provide the most meaningful avenue for clinical or biological research. An alternative approach would focus on distinguishing features of BPD—on postulated critical dimensions of mood and behavior which are characteristic of BPD, such as reactive mood, dysphorias, and behavioral dyscontrol. Thus, research would seek to identify biological (or psychological) traits which predispose to labile, reactive states.

Unfortunately, research tools to examine such regulatory phenomena are not well developed. Pharmacologic challenge studies may seek to identify poorly regulated, hyperresponsive biological systems in BPD, including neuroendocrine and neurotransmitter systems. Alternatively, pharmacologic probes producing states such as dysphoria may be used to understand pathways leading to the dysphoric states; much as lactate infusions have been used to explore another dysregulatory phenomenon, panic attacks. Functional neuroimaging may be used to identify neuroanatomical abnormalities predisposing to (trait findings), or involved in the expression of (state findings), abnormal mood or behavior. Finally, trials of psychopharmacologic agents may help to identify drug-responsive dimensions of psychopathology in BPD, as reviewed in the following section.

There is also a need for research on the perceptual–cognitive aspects of BPD, which may in turn shed light on the biological underpinnings of the disorder. Neurophysiological studies, such as event-related potentials, may contribute to an assessment of fundamental information processing problems. On a broader and more clinically relevant level, there is a real need for reports of the performance of BPD patients on a comprehensive array of structured neuropsychological tests, which might give some insight into the apparent defects in encoding, interpreting, and recalling information, which are observed both clinically and in projective psychological testing. Such studies may help clinicians comprehend and deal more specifically with aspects of the often-frustrating interactions with BPD patients.

Finally, it may be possible to develop meaningful animal models of aspects of BPD. For example, separation studies in primates are often thought to model classical depression. It can be argued that such studies are more likely to model various borderline phenomena, including the response to threatened or actual rejection or separation. In passing, it should also be noted that there are significant species differences in primate responses to early separation, suggesting that there are heritable individual variations in vulnerability to "psychopathology" which interact with life events. Such complex considerations of the interplay of nature and nurture are likely to dominate the next generation of hypotheses about the development of character and its disorders.

THE PSYCHOPHARMACOLOGIC REALM—DRUG TRIALS IN BPD

The preceding section mentioned the role that psychopharmacologic probes (brief infusion or oral administration studies of provocative drugs) might play in exploring the biology of BPD. This section addresses the more clinically relevant question of longer term attempts to treat the disorder with drugs.

The data base needed to assess fully the role of psychopharmacologic agents in BPD is neither broad nor deep. The number of well-controlled trials is small. Several studies of potential relevance antedate diagnostic criteria for BPD. More recent studies have involved limited numbers of patients treated for relatively brief periods of time, often during acute exacerbations of their symptomatology. Nonetheless, the literature provides some guidance in developing a rational approach to pharmacotherapy of BPD.

Two early studies focused on "pseudoneurotic schizophrenia" (PS), characterized as passive–dependent character with multiple neurotic and affective symptoms. A moderate overlap with current concepts of BPD is likely. As part of a larger study, Fink, Pollack, and Klein (1964) and Klein (1968) treated thirty-two PS patients with imipramine (to 300 mg/day), chlorpromazine (to 1200 mg/day), or placebo. Patients on imipramine showed a significantly higher rate of positive global outcome (9/13 patients) compared with placebo (3/12 patients). Chlorpromazine reduced agitation and some other symptoms, but did not produce a higher rate of positive outcome than placebo. Hedberg, Houck, and Glueck (1971) compared trifluoperazine (to 32 mg/day), tranylcypromine (to 30 mg/day), and the combination of the two in twenty-eight PS patients. Half of the patients responded "best" to tranylcypromine alone, with the other half evenly divided between the other two "best" treatments. These studies are somewhat difficult to interpret because of diagnostic issues and because of the high dosages of neuroleptic medication employed, but suggest possible benefits from antidepressant medication.

Patients with emotionally unstable character disorder (EUCD), characterized by rapid, relatively autonomous shifts of mood in young character-disordered individuals, predominantly women, were studied in two reports. The EUCD subgroup of the Fink and Klein study reported above showed a significant improvement on chlorpromazine, with particular improvement in affective lability. In a study of thirty-one patients with EUCD, Rifkin, Quitkin, Carrillo, Blumberg, and Klein (1972) demonstrated that lithium significantly attenuated the frequency and severity of mood shifts, compared with placebo. Extrapolation to BPD patients is problematic, however, since environmental reactivity rather than autonomy appears to characterize most BPD patients. These studies, coupled with those of Akiskal (1981), suggest the possible existence of a subgroup of BPD patients with relative autonomy of mood swings, treatable with lithium or neuroleptics.

Patients with "hysteroid (rejection-sensitive) dysphoria" treated with tranylcypromine for six months by Liebowitz and Klein (1979) showed a striking reduction in frequency and intensity of dysphoric episodes and an improvement in their ability to function in daily life and in psychotherapy. Of these three pre-DSM-III populations, hysteroid dysphoria probably most closely approximates BPD.

Several controlled studies of BPD suggest a beneficial role for low-dose neuroleptic treatment. Leone's study (1982) of 80 patients with BPD showed improvement in a wide range of symptoms including anger, hostility, and depression on either loxapine (14.5 mg/day) or chlorpromazine (110 mg/day), but there was no placebo control. Serban and Seigal (1984) treated fifty-two BPD and STP patients with low-dose thiothixene or haloperidol, without placebo control, and showed moderate to marked improvement in 84 percent of patients at three months, again with broad symptom reduction, most marked in cognitive disturbances, derealization, ideas of reference, anxiety, and depression. The inclusion of patients with STP and the absence of a placebo control may bias toward high improvement rates on neuroleptics.

Goldberg, Schulz, Schulz, Resnick, Hamer, and Friedel (1986) studied fifty outpatients with BPD or STP and "at least one psychotic symptom." Thiothixene (average dose 8.7 mg/day) produced significant improvement on a number of symptoms, particularly those from "psychotic" clusters on the rating scales, and on anxiety and obsessive–compulsive symptoms. Again, the inclusion of STP patients and the requirement of a "psychotic symptom" may bias toward improved response rates.

In the best placebo-controlled study to date, Soloff, George, Nathan, Schulz, Ulrich, and Perel (1986a) randomly assigned sixty-one patients with BPD and/or STP to haloperidol (4–16 mg/day), amitriptyline (100–175 mg/day with plasma level adjustments), or placebo. Haloperidol, but not amitriptyline, produced improvement on self-rated depression, anxiety, and hostility, on schizotypal symptoms, and on a global severity scale. Soloff, George, Nathan, and Perel (1986b) also found that amitriptyline was associated with an increase in behavioral dyscontrol in some patients. The authors also failed to find any association between presence or absence of a current major depression and response to amitriptyline (Soloff et al., 1986a). Improvement was described as "modest at best, but clinically and statistically significant" (p. 695). This study provides the strongest support for low-dose neuroleptics and casts doubt on the existence of a pharmacologically meaningful subgrouping of BPD based on presence or absence of a mood disorder.

Our group (Cowdry and Gardner, 1988) performed the only placebo-controlled multidrug crossover trial in sixteen patients with pure BPD. Alprazolam (2–6 mg/day) produced a variety of responses in different patients and in the group as a whole was not superior to placebo. It was associated with an increase in frequency of serious episodes of behavioral dyscontrol, possibly related to the behavioral disinhibition observed with other benzodiazepines and alcohol. Trifluoperazine (2–6 mg/day) was also not superior to placebo, but had a high discontinuation rate. Patients treated for at least three weeks showed a trend toward improvement across an array of symptoms. Carbamazepine (400–1200 mg/day) produced significant improvement in blind clinician ratings but not in blind patient self-ratings, and had a unique impact on behavioral dyscontrol, reducing the overall severity significantly. Although clinician ratings suggested a broad-spectrum effect on symptoms, the discrepancy with patient ratings and clinical observations suggested that subjective mood tended to improve little on carbamazepine. In contrast, tranylcypromine (20–60 mg/day) produced significant improvement across a wide range of symptoms in both clinician and patient ratings. Improvement in mood was clinically more striking than improvement in impulsivity. Overall, improvement on one medication did not correlate with improvement on another, and each drug had at least some patients who did "best" while on it. There was some suggestion that a past history of a major mood disorder was associated with response to tranylcypromine.

SUMMARY OF PSYCHOPHARMACOLOGIC RESEARCH

All placebo-controlled trials of medications in BPD and closely related disorders demonstrate at least modest improvement with at least one pharmacologic agent. The most consistent findings suggest that low-dose neuroleptics produce improvement, but it is unclear whether the improvement is more likely or more marked in individuals with "psychotic" symptoms, and whether "psychotic" symptoms are more likely to respond.

The use of antidepressants is more controversial. Imipramine in full treatment dosages was beneficial in pseudoneurotic schizophrenia but amitriptyline was not of benefit in the best controlled trial of a tricyclic antidepressant. Tranylcypromine was beneficial in pseudoneurotic schizophrenia, in hysteroid dysphoria, and in BPD. Monamine oxidase (MAO) inhibitors probably are the antidepressants of choice based on the current literature.

The anticonvulsant carbamazepine may have a special role in attenuating behavioral dyscontrol in BPD, but does not produce a robust subjective improvement in mood in most patients and may even be associated with the onset of melancholia. Possible benefits of other anticonvulsants with different mechanisms of action such as valproate or clonazepam have not been carefully investigated.

All in all, while pharmacotherapeutic trials suggest some drug responsivity, these trials have not proven to be terribly enlightening with regard to underlying mechanisms, in part because of the heterogeneity of response patterns and the lack of any clear-cut clinical or biological correlates of response. While drug trials have not yet succeeded in identifying meaningful subgroups, they have helped suggest several fruitful lines of related research: the possible role of the dopaminergic system in modulation of a variety of symptoms of BPD, the possible role of paroxysmal (epileptoid) discharges in behavioral dyscontrol in BPD, and the possible role of catecholaminergic systems in the atypical depressive syndrome so common in this population.

A CLINICAL APPROACH TO PSYCHOPHARMACOLOGIC TREATMENT

Given the limited knowledge available from controlled trials, the apparent clinical heterogeneity within the borderline realm, the heterogeneity (and lack of predictability) of drug responses, the prominence of complaints about side effects from drug treatment in this population in particular, and the clinical difficulties establishing and maintaining a therapeutic relationship with these patients, it is hardly surprising that no road map or decision tree exists for. pharmacotherapy.

Nonetheless, sufficient evidence for drug responsiveness exists to warrant judicious and well-structured trials of several medications in most patients with BPD. Stage-setting is, however, vital. Patient (and therapist) expectations need careful attention in order to develop realistic perspectives. Patients in particular need to be reminded that pharmacotherapy is a collaborative effort, that the trials need to be structured, and that changes should not be impulsive, that they need to bring their observing ego to bear on changes in mood and behavior, and that pharmacotherapy may be a useful adjunct to psychotherapy, but is very seldom a dramatic and lasting magic potion.

Certain indicators for specific approaches may be outlined, and are discussed at greater length elsewhere (Cowdry, 1987). For example, "psychotic" features, schizotypal symptoms, and uncontrollable rage episodes may bias toward a low-dose neuroleptic. Prominent behavioral dyscontrol, particularly when any symptoms suggestive of epileptoid phenomena are present, may bias toward an anticonvulsant. Current major depression, particularly when it has lasted more than a month, is circumscribed, and is autonomous, and particularly when there is a family history of major depression, may bias toward an antidepressant. Atypical depressive features, and possibly rejection-sensitive dysphoria, may bias toward an MAO inhibitor. Agoraphobia and panic disorder may also bias toward an antidepressant.

Seldom is the choice clear-cut, seldom is there a single agent worthy of consideration. Always there are significant side effects to review and discuss with the patient. Nonetheless, careful psychopharmacology can usually help attenuate the most disruptive symptoms of BPD, thereby contributing directly to a more therapeutic relationship with the therapist. Pharmacotherapy can also become useful grist for the psychotherapeutic process, as idealization and devaluation, transference issues, difficulties recruiting the observing ego, and difficulties negotiating and following through on planful action play themselves out in the context of drug treatment.

FUTURE DIRECTIONS

Currently, the gulf between biological and clinical perspectives on the character disorders appears wide. Biological research in this area is in its infancy. However, two lines of biological research show particular promise for enhancing our understanding of these disorders. The first examines the biological mechanisms involved in the expression of psychopathology, and the role of pharmacotherapy in modifying these biological mechanisms. The second involves an even greater challenge only alluded to in the presentation: understanding the complex interactions between biological predispositions and experience in shaping the developing organism, its cognition, its motivational states, its affective life, its mechanisms of defense, and ultimately its character.

21.

The Inpatient Treatment of Borderline Personality Disorder

**Michael Rosenbluth, M.D., and
Daniel Silver, M.D.**

The inpatient treatment of borderline personality disorder (BPD) is an often crucial yet frequently controversial phase in the care of the BPD patient. Clinical experience and longitudinal studies indicate that hospitalization is a frequent occurrence in the care of the borderline patient (Werble, 1970; Skodol, Buckley, and Charles, 1983; Gunderson, 1984).

Research into the issues of hospitalization of BPD has lagged behind the burgeoning interest in the outpatient treatment of this disorder. This reflects the relative lack of formal research into issues of hospitalization in psychiatry, and particular difficulties with regard to the BPD population.

Considerable controversy exists regarding the most suitable inpatient care of the BPD. The controversy involves the use or avoidance of the regression which can accompany hospitalization and how length of stay is subsequently affected. This central issue has considerable therapeutic implications, as the potentially negative effects of hospitalization for these patients have been described (Friedman, 1969). In addition, related to this issue, there has been controversy regarding whether the goals of inpatient treatment should be stabilization and attachment (Viner, 1983), or internalization of a new psychic structure (Kernberg, 1976).

The purpose of this chapter will be to review some of the basic premises regarding the hospitalization of BPD. The strengths and weaknesses of the various approaches will be discussed. In particular, research regarding hospitalization will be examined as well as research regarding long-term follow-up of BPD in general, in order to determine the proper indications for hospital treatment and length of stay. Four issues will be highlighted: (1) indications for hospitalization; (2) the different ways that countertransference and staff reactions to the BPD can be utilized on an inpatient service; (3) the critical effect suicidal behavior has on the hospital care of the BPD patient; (4) the central role of hospitalization in coordinating, evaluating, strengthening, and, when necessary, changing outpatient care.

PREMISES

The premises of hospital care of BPD reflect the differing conceptualization of treatment. Gordon and Beresin (1983) describe the two main approaches as structural and adaptational. In fact, the main distinction turns on the diagnostic and therapeutic implications of the inevitable regression that working with the BPD patient entails.

Those viewing the etiology as developmental and amenable to reversal through an intensive psychotherapeutic involvement favor a perspective where short-term hospital treatment is used occasionally, but where considerable emphasis is placed on long-term treatment as having an important and fundamental place in the care of the BPD patient. Those viewing the etiology as predominantly biological, stress shorter hospitalization with the emphasis on stabilizing the patient rather than achieving new internalizations and more profound psychic change.

Long-Term Hospitalization

The leading advocate of this approach is Otto Kernberg. His contributions represent an elaboration of how hospitalization of the borderline fits into a therapeutic approach which is based on his structural conceptualization of borderline psychopathology. He minimizes nonstructural changes in the patient, referring to them as merely behavioral (Kernberg, 1976).

Kernberg views the hospital as a relatively unstructured milieu that presents the patient with a host of possible relationships. In this context, the borderline patient rapidly develops numerous relationships that operate on and reflect his or her primitive object relations. This provides a diagnostic opportunity to view the patient's internal world of object relationships and to gradually change them using analytically informed understanding, confrontation, and clarification. The focus is on the interpretation, in the here-and-now, of the patient's impact on the social system of the hospital and how it is colored by primitive distortions caused by the patient's past. Thus the goal of Kernberg's approach is the integration of previously primitive, nonmetabolized object relationships. The diagnosis, interpretation, and resolution of primitive transferences that reflect primitive internalized object relations is seen as resulting in structural intrapsychic change.

Due to the centrality of observing and diagnosing these primitive object relationships and transference, Kernberg takes what may be termed a proregression position. He feels regression may be blocked by a highly regimented hospital routine, making it impossible fully to observe the regression. Pathological dependency and apathy may also be fostered by an overly structured hospital environment (Kernberg, 1976).

Short-Term Hospitalization

The therapeutic implications of the regressive process that occurs is a salient problem in treating BPD. Those favoring longer hospitalization see the regression as essential and ultimately positive, while those favoring a short hospitalization see the regression as counterproductive, nonessential, and perhaps iatrogenic.

Advocates of short-term hospitalization feel that regression to primitive object relationships manifest and utilized in the transference is undesirable and unworkable. Friedman (1975), developing positions previously taken by Anna Freud (1969, pp. 36–43) and Zetzel (1971), states that preverbal experience, while of great importance to development, cannot be fully recovered in the transference with successful therapeutic effect. He advocates an approach emphasizing the treatment alliance, not mobilizing negative transference yet clarifying and interpreting it when it develops and using limit-setting when necessary. Hospitalization is shorter and focuses on concrete goals rather than structural change.

Others have also contributed to a short-term antiregression position and to the evolution of a short-term hospital approach. Nunberg and Suh (1980, 1982) advocate time-limited hospitalization with rapid diagnostic assessment and the establishment of a firm discharge date whereupon transfer or discharge occurs. They emphasize the importance of this time-focused approach in combating the borderline patient's ahistoric tendency. Viner (1983) emphasizes the use of brief hospitalization for attachment and not internalization. He focuses on the self–object function of the hospital and its role in providing a holding environment for the patient. Wishnie (1975) emphasizes the rapid identification of the BPD patient, clear definition of goals, limits and expectations, and education of staff in terms of consistent responses. Sederer and Thorbeck (1986) have described the dangers of exploratory therapy in a short-term hospitalization.

RESEARCH AND ITS IMPLICATIONS

Three strategies can be employed to support the different approaches to the hospitalization of the BPD patient.

The Clinical Description Approach

The most common strategy has been for interested clinicians to describe their experience in the hospital treatment of borderline patients. This approach is a descriptive one based on considerable experience in treating BPD patients. The strength of the approach is the careful observation and documentation of the clinical phenomena that occur, and the elaboration of a conceptual framework to understand these phenomena. There have been descriptions of transference and countertransference issues (Book, Sadavoy, and Silver, 1978; Kernberg, 1987b), the role of the hospital as a holding environment (Adler, 1977), commentary on the need to set limits effectively (Adler, 1973), attendance to outpatient issues as they relate to hospitalization (Bernstein, 1980), and a description of the different approaches to the inpatient care of BPD (Rinsley, 1968; Kernberg, 1976; Hartocollis, 1980; Brown, 1981; Silver, Book, Hamilton, Sadavoy, and Slonim, 1983a).

The shortcomings of this approach have been considerable. This has been due to the difficulties in defining the term *borderline* itself, but also due to the lack of a standardized vocabulary to describe the issues relating to hospitalization, and the lack of a systematic approach to the issue of hospitalization of BPD patients. The observational approach all too often focuses on broad issues such as the dynamics, dangers, and length of hospitalization, while the complexities of the variables of hospital treatment and its effect on individual patients have been understated. Little consideration has been given to the diagnostic heterogeneity of the disorder or to the considerable modifying factors such as intelligence, social skills, age, ego strength profile, social support systems, and severity of the disorder.

While this approach is clinically rich and therapeutically relevant, it is a clinical rather than a research inquiry into the use of hospitalization.

The Research Approach

There is a more formal research literature on the hospitalization of BPD. While it is subject to some of the criticisms just described, it is still an interesting and important literature to consider.

Kernberg has based his view of long-term hospitalization on his clinical experience and on the Psychotherapy Research Project of the Menninger Foundation (Kernberg, Burstein, and

Coyne, 1972). The findings were that patients in expressive insight-oriented psychotherapy coupled with long-term hospitalization did better than those in supportive psychotherapy without hospital treatment. Comparison with an expressive insight-oriented psychotherapy and short-term hospitalization was not done. Thus the subject of this study was the different modes of outpatient psychotherapy, not the effect of short versus long hospitalization of BPD. Hospitalization, in fact, is described only as a parameter used in expressive, insight-oriented treatment. Thus, Kernberg's indications for long-term hospitalization, for those patients with (1) low motivation; (2) severe ego weakness; and (3) poor object relations are based on his clinical experience rather than research which supports these contentions (Kernberg, 1973).

Masterson and Costello (1980) describe a follow-up study of thirty-one of fifty-nine borderline adolescents. Mean hospitalization was fourteen-and-a-half months. While indicating considerable variation in outcome (from minimal to severe functional impairment), they conclude that 58 percent showed significant improvement at follow-up of approximately four years. However, their conclusions are based on: (1) follow-up on only 53 percent of the sample; (2) cases treated that were, by their own description, more suitable for psychotherapy; and (3) no control group of outpatient treatment and short-term hospitalization to compare with their sample of outpatient treatment and long-term hospitalization. Because of this, and because the authors themselves point out that their research was designed for hypothesis gathering and not testing, this outcome study is not sufficient for confirming the value of the long-term inpatient treatment of BPD. It is interesting to note, particularly in light of Kernberg's indication that the more severely disturbed patient may be a candidate for long-term hospitalization, that Masterson and Costello indicate that it was the healthier borderline who benefited from long-term inpatient treatment, not the more severely disturbed patient.

Similarly, Greben (1983), commenting on preliminary outcome data, indicates that of four patients studied intensively, the two who did well in follow-up were healthier borderline patients with better relationships and sense of self prior to admission; the two who did poorly were more severely affected borderline patients.

Tucker, Bauer, Wagner, Harlam, and Sher (1987), in a particularly careful and unique prospective evaluation of long-term hospital treatment of borderline patients, showed that, after the first postdischarge year, patients hospitalized for more than one year were more likely to remain in outpatient therapy and to avoid rehospitalization. However, despite the authors' expectations, follow-up after the second postdischarge year showed little difference between those hospitalized for shorter or longer stays.

McGlashan (1986a) describes the outcome of BPD patients treated with long-term in-hospital treatment averaging two years in duration. Although not described, the treatment was characterized as taking place in a milieu that was tolerant of regression and that utilized intensive psychotherapy (4 times per week). The outcome was assessed as being comparable with unipolar affective disorder and significantly better than schizophrenia. The author's conclusion regarding long-term inpatient treatment was that its clinical efficacy could not be considered to have been demonstrated by his study, due to the absence of a clinical trial methodology. However, he felt further study with controlled clinical trials was indicated. This study seems more a description of the course of an illness than the specific testing of long-term hospital care.

Elsewhere in this book, McGlashan summarizes his work on outcome. It is interesting to note that one of the three most frequent variables predicting outcome was longer hospitalization which predicted poor outcome. While this may be tautological in that sicker patients may require longer hospitalization, it is still of interest that long hospitalization predicted poor outcome.

Stone (1987) has followed up 254 borderline patients treated with intensive hospitalization. He found only one-third amenable to expressive psychotherapy. Improvement in the other borderlines was attributed to supportive therapy, the patients' personality characteristics, good fortune, or a combination of the three. Stone concluded that the efficacy of expressive psychotherapy was difficult to prove. As in McGlashan (1986a), Stone's work is by his own description a study of the natural history of borderline patients treated with intensive hospitalization rather than a study of the intensive hospitalization of BPD.

Thus the specific research studies raise questions about long-term hospitalization as a primary modality of treatment. In fact, the studies are rather consistent with other studies on long versus short hospitalization in general. Major studies on the effect of hospitalization show little effect of length of stay. While these studies do not deal with BPD in particular, the conclusion reached is of interest. They suggest that global outcome is better correlated with prehospital level of functioning rather than length of stay. In addition, the studies suggest that the amount of aftercare is a more important determinant than the length of hospitalization (Cournos, 1987). We will return to this point later.

Implications of Research on Outcome of BPD

The third strategy in evaluating the premises of hospital care is to consider the formal research on outcome of BPD.

General outcome studies of BPD patients (Werble, 1970; McGlashan, 1986a; Plakun, Burkhardt, and Muller, 1986; Stone, Hurt, and Stone, 1987b) suggest an interesting observation that may be made about the goals of intensive long-term hospitalization. There appears to be a marked dichotomy between what is sought in intensive hospitalization (structural change and internalization of new introjects), and what is obtained and measured in follow-up studies (general work and social adaptation, persistence of symptoms, and rate of rehospitalization). Silver attempts to bridge this dichotomy by pointing out that even patients who do well on the grosser measures of long-term follow-up appear to have strong remnants of the psychological fragility readily elicited on psychodynamic assessment when followed up years later (Silver, Cardish, and Glassman, 1987). Read this way, outcome studies of BPD raise questions about an approach focusing on sophisticated intrapsychic reorganization which longer hospitalization strives to achieve.

Intensive hospital treatment requires special staffing, skills, interest, and financial support that few facilities have (Klagsburn, Reibel, and Piercey, 1987; Silver et al., 1987). The absence of firm evidence demonstrating the superiority of longer hospitalization, the heterogeneity of the disorder, its uncertain etiology, and the economic realities of hospital care in the 1990s, all point to short-stay hospitalization as the hospital treatment of choice for borderline patients.

Long-term hospitalization, while useful for learning more about borderline dynamics and teaching psychotherapy (Silver, Book, Hamilton, Sadavoy, and Slonim, 1983b; Rosnick, 1987), should be regarded as an experimental treatment best reserved for a very small minority of patients, particularly those who cannot be contained outside of a hospital and for whom no alternative exists. Unfortunately, in practice, longer hospitalizations usually occur when the treatment staff extend the length of stay due to difficulties in discharging an acting-out patient. Thus the longer stay is reactive rather than proactive, and active treatment is often sacrificed as staff focuses on discharging the patient.

THE ROLE OF HOSPITALIZATION

There is an extensive literature on hospitalization, describing important issues such as assessing outpatient therapy (Bernstein, 1980), stabilizing the patient and the team (Wishnie, 1975), choosing a focus (Nunberg and Suh, 1982), combating an ahistoric tendency (Nunberg and Suh, 1980), and using self–object function for stabilization rather than internalization (Viner, 1983). These issues are reviewed elsewhere (Rosenbluth, 1987).

Rather, the focus will be on emphasizing and elaborating several important aspects of the hospital treatment of BPD that have been insufficiently described in the literature. These are: (1) the indications for hospitalization; (2) the different ways that countertransference and staff reactions to the BPD can be utilized on an inpatient service; (3) the critical effect suicidal behavior has on the care of the BPD patient; and (4) the central role of hospitalization in coordinating, evaluating, strengthening and, when necessary, changing the outpatient care of the BPD.

Indications for Hospitalization

The main indication for hospitalization of any psychiatric patient is suicidal risk. However, this is a more complicated issue for BPD where patients may be not only acutely but also chronically suicidal. Clinically the dilemma is twofold: (1) to distinguish between true suicidal risk and the wish of the patient to elicit caretaking behavior from the helping other—therapist, family, or friend (Gunderson, 1984); (2) to respond to the chronically suicidal patient.

Hospitalization may also be indicated in order to reintegrate the patient. The particular admixture of vulnerability, irritability, and impulsivity makes the borderline patient prone to need short hospitalization for crisis intervention during rage attacks and/or during a period of psychotic transference.

Besides suicidality and crisis intervention, an important indication and function of hospitalization is diagnostic clarification. Usually this occurs during a hospitalization necessitated by suicidality and/or a crisis. There are two main diagnostic functions that a hospital can fulfill—clarifying Axis I and Axis II diagnostic issues, and determining or confirming that the patient is a candidate for psychotherapy and/or other modalities of treatment (such as family or group therapy, and pharmacotherapy).

Frequently, borderline patients' Axis I diagnoses are overlooked in the chaos of the clinical situation and/or when there is an inclination to be preoccupied by the Axis II diagnosis. While the patient is in the hospital, it is important to identify the presence of a coexisting Axis I disorder such as major affective disorder, anxiety disorder, panic disorder, or substance abuse disorder. Treatment of previously unidentified Axis I disorders can have an important impact on a patient's overall course.

Another diagnostic role of hospitalization is the identification of a previously unidentified Axis II disorder. This is the converse of the previous situation; that is, due to the centrality of the Axis I pathology (e.g., severe affective disorder and/or an inclination to be preoccupied with biological disorders), an Axis II disorder is overlooked. In this instance, the hospital milieu acts as a culture bringing out previously overlooked signals of BPD, such as splitting, projection, or the regression that the BPD patient is subject to. The presence of BPD comorbidity is important to ascertain and has implications for the course of hospital treatment and the after care provided for the patient.

Lastly, once hospitalized, the patient may require examination of the psychodynamic profile to determine whether or not psychotherapy is a feasible undertaking and, if so, in what form. Not all borderlines can benefit from an intensive psychotherapeutic approach (Waldinger and Gunderson, 1984). A determination of whether the patient is suitable for psychotherapy should be influenced by developmental variables such as whether the patient has had a positive relationship in the past or present; demonstrates some capacity to empathize with the experiences of important others; has a history of being able to be soothed by something or someone; and how close the patient is able to get to others before withdrawing; that is, if there is a relationship thermostat that is set on "too distant" (Silver, Glassman, and Cardish, 1988). It is important to determine these variables while the patient is hospitalized, and this issue is discussed elsewhere in this book. More generally, hospitalization can also help by educating patients in the work of psychotherapy—increasing their awareness that much of their behaviors and feelings are determined by processes that are not always available to them at a conscious level, and that words rather than action can be used to convey feelings.

Different Uses of Countertransference in the Inpatient Treatment of BPD

A crucial aspect of the hospital care of the BPD patient is the full and effective use of the countertransference processes that are elicited. Considerable attention has been given to what can be learned about the inner world of the BPD patient by examining and understanding the feelings induced in the therapist and inpatient treatment team (Kernberg, 1976; Adler, 1977; Book et al., 1978). The main theme of this literature has been the effects of splitting on the patient–team interaction, with the emphasis on integrating the split and avoiding the acting out of the patient's inner world by the team.

There are other uses of countertransference which have been insufficiently emphasized. In addition to understanding the patient's inner world, the response of treatment staff to the patient can be used to clarify outpatient countertransference problems and the family's interaction with the patient. Friedman (1975) has discussed the signal function of countertransference in the dyadic outpatient setting. This concept can be elaborated to yield a new conceptualization and use of countertransference for the inpatient setting.

Attention to the feelings induced in the treatment team may reveal important information about general system features such as the team's history, needs, and capacity. As well, this signal function may also be important in increasing the team's understanding of the patient's diagnosis and management. The first step in using the countertransference is to learn how it reflects the individual patient's dynamics. The second step is to ascertain what reflection of general system factors is occurring.

A consideration of the system aspects of the inpatient setting permits an elaboration of the traditional views of countertransference. While the content of the feelings engendered in the team may be used to increase the understanding of the patient's dynamics, the rapidity and intensity of the countertransference response may raise more general questions about the patient–ward interaction and the patient.

Mental health professionals who have a broad concept of countertransference can more thoroughly utilize the feelings engendered in them when working with troubled and difficult patients. This awareness permits better patient care with a difficult patient population by facilitating a more thorough involvement with each patient. In addition, over time, it permits the team as a whole to continue to work with difficult patient populations, such as BPD, in an ongoing, creative manner. Failure to develop a means for the full identification and utilization of countertransference leads to increased staff turnover, burnout, and a less effective therapeutic involvement with each patient.

The Team's History. The countertransference response may reflect unresolved issues in the team's history of working with a certain kind of patient. Thus, the response may be indicative not only of one patient's dynamics, but may also be a signal that there are unresolved feelings within the team from previous patients which are being transferred to the current patient. These responses could elicit particular feelings or might disclose more general attitudes about working with certain kinds of patients such as the borderline personality disorder patient.

> Several months after the turbulent and unsuccessful inpatient treatment of a BPD female with somatic complaints and drug addiction, a patient with similar features was admitted. The team rapidly developed a rejecting, hostile response to the new patient. This response was reflective, in part, of certain relationships in the patient's past that were being elicited in the present. However, the response of the team also reflected unresolved feelings about working with the previous patient. These feelings were related to certain issues that the team was experiencing in dealing with borderline patients in general, particularly hopefulness versus despair. When these different issues were revealed, the second patient was found to be similar to but not the same as the first, and a more successful therapeutic engagement with the patient was thus facilitated.

The Team's Needs. The countertransference response may disclose important aspects of the team's capacity to be therapeutic as well as reflect the dynamics of the individual patient. The treatment staff, both individually and collectively, need to feel that their therapeutic contributions are acknowledged, respected, and valued. The relationship between the team, team leader, and the institution may serve to fulfill or heighten this need.

> In a Balint group discussion, the problem of being nurturing and involved therapeutically with a certain demanding patient was identified. Feelings of envy of the attention and care that the borderline patient was eliciting were noted in the staff's response to the patient. From a traditional point of view, the envy was seen as a projective counteridentification as the team was experiencing the feelings which the patient often felt, and which had a dynamic origin in the patient's past. However, the countertransference was also examined with reference to the system in which the treatment occurred. The nursing staff was involved in stalemated contract negotiations and was feeling ignored and undervalued by the hospital administration. The countertransference not only reflected the patient's dynamics but also reflected the staff's envy of the attention and caring that the patient received. The staff's feelings were impeding their capacity to be therapeutic with the patient.

The Team's Therapeutic Capacity. The response to an individual patient may reflect and/or be prejudiced by the team's global response to the particular inpatient population at the time. The countertransference noted may partially demonstrate that there are simply too many difficult patients with which the team must work in a therapeutic manner.

> A BPD patient was admitted to a ten-bed inpatient unit. Upon reflection, the particularly strong countertransference response was seen as being indicative not only of the particular patient's dynamics but also of the staff's difficulty with the patient population on the ward at that time. There were three other BPD patients in the unit. As well, two patients had anorexia nervosa and another was a bipolar affective disorder patient in the manic state. As a result, there were too many severely disturbed patients for the team to work effectively with the newly admitted patient.

The intensity and rapidity of development of the counter-transference reaction was a signal of this difficulty. Attempts were made to lessen the "load" for the team at the time. More importantly, the team was subsequently able to negotiate successfully the maximum number of difficult patients that could be admitted at any one time so that the care of any individual patient would not be similarly compromised.

Patient Management. The presence of an intense or unexpected countertransference response may reflect not only the individual dynamics of the patient but may also be a signal that there is a malignant regression occurring. Balint (1968) has described this situation as occurring when the patient seeks gratification, not understanding, and the neediness rather than the psyche of the patient grows. The patient's object hunger is increased rather than satisfied.

Dealing with such a situation depends on the team's treatment philosophy and may call for rapid patient and team stabilization so that this regression can be appropriately managed and not be allowed to remain malignant. The response to this signal countertransference is an examination of how the patient and the team are interacting. Insufficient structure for the patient may promote regression that is beyond a workable level. Increased attention must be given to the therapeutic alliance rather than to the transference. Responses include addressing clinical administration issues, such as passes and privileges, as well as defining the goals and expectations of the patient more clearly (Gutheil, 1982).

Diagnosis. A strong countertransference response may be diagnostic not only of the particular dynamics of the patient, as has been traditionally considered, but may also have general DSM-III-R diagnostic implications. These implications can be reflected in two different ways:

1. A particularly strong countertransference response may indicate that an Axis II diagnosis of borderline personality disorder has been overlooked:

A patient was admitted with a DSM-III-R diagnosis of major depressive episode. The countertransference response noted early in the admission was particularly intense and included splitting. This response was useful in understanding the patient's inner world but also pointed to the need for a diagnostic reevaluation. A careful review of the patient's history and ward behavior revealed an Axis II borderline personality disorder diagnosis which had been overlooked.

2. Conversely, when the usually intense countertransference response that the borderline patient elicits is recognized and utilized to stabilize both the patient and the team, an Axis I diagnosis that has been overlooked can be revealed.

During the course of the hospital treatment of a BPD patient, a strong countertransference response was elicited. This response was used to understand the patient better and to stabilize both patient and treatment team. When this occurred, the patient's course in the hospital was characterized by less acting out. As a result, an underlying affective disorder previously undiagnosed was noted and successfully treated with antidepressant medication.

Suicidality and Hospitalization

The acute suicidal risk of the borderline patient is probably the most common indication for admission to a hospital. While in a hospital the usual concerns and difficulties of dealing with suicidality in this patient population continue but the in-hospital context poses several new issues.

The common concerns about suicidal behavior in borderlines will be mentioned briefly, as they are described more fully elsewhere in this book. The central dilemma is whether the patient is indeed acutely at risk for harming himself, or is seeking to elicit caretaking behavior from the therapist (Gunderson, 1984). A related concern is whether the suicidal behavior is acute or whether it is chronic and therefore less likely to be acted upon. In the latter case, protecting the person from self-harm may interfere with the central therapeutic task of the chronically suicidal patient—the transfer of the responsibility for the patient's welfare back to the patient (Gutheil, 1982). Failure to do so impedes the therapy and causes treatment to flounder and become preoccupied with suicidal behavior.

In a hospital, these issues are colored by what may be termed the public domain of hospital care. What was a dyadic relationship becomes one involving many individuals—the resident, nursing staff, occupational therapists. The consequence is that certain conscious and unconscious determinations enter the decision-making process for the hospitalized BPD. Patients expressing suicidal ideation who would perhaps be deemed safe to be permitted to leave the therapist's outpatient office may be placed on constant care or close observation on the ward. Anxiety regarding public scrutiny can interfere with the containing function of the hospital. An overconcern with the sequelae of a patient's self-harming behavior can cause a regression in the therapeutic staff to a controlling, overprotective response or, alternatively, to an abandoning, rejecting response to the patient who may require the setting of limits.

Thus, concerns about how staff will be seen cause primitive fears of exposure and humiliation to increase. This in part reflects the consequence of projections from the patient having been inadequately processed and partly reflects the ambivalent nature our society has about psychiatric care (hospital wards are criticized for being too restrictive or too lax). Experiences with previous patients also color staff response. Recent suicides or attempts by other patients, particularly if not sufficiently processed, can increase the countertransference reactivity of treatment staff.

The problem of suicidality frequently becomes more of an issue as discharge nears. The patient who has made considerable progress may suddenly become suicidal. This frequently causes a short hospitalization to become longer, because the team is unable to discharge the patient. Several steps facilitate the staff's response to the suicidal inpatient:

1. An understanding of countertransference issues stirred up by the suicidal BPD patient, and a forum to process these

feelings in order to distinguish real concerns from anxieties projected into the staff is important.

2. A screening process is also essential so that more severe BPD patients who might undergo malignant regressions are identified and receive a more structured approach in order to avoid regression to unworkable levels.

3. Contracting can be useful. This is described in detail elsewhere (Bloom and Rosenbluth, in press). The negative effects of self-harming behaviors on the therapeutic process are emphasized, and the consequences are clearly spelled out, including transfer to another institution. Such transfer can occur if the patient's self-harming behavior does not stop. Often, a clear statement about the possibility of transfer acts as an effective limit, resulting in a decrease in the patient's self-harming behavior (Friedman, 1969).

4. In order to diminish the suicidal potential of BPD patients, it is crucial to identify the main issues of the discharge phase such as separating from the hospital (i.e., leaving behind significant figures) and reentry into the outside world (i.e., building and repairing relationships). Separation and reentry challenge the equilibrium achieved by patients in the hospital, once again threatening them with painful feelings, and may lead to an increase in suicidal ideation (Silver et al., 1987). A mutually agreed-upon initial discharge date is set, realizing that it may not be met. The first discharge date is set so that the anticipated regression and acting out can be worked through, particularly the attendant separation and abandonment feelings and some of the anticipatory anxiety about reentry. Anticipating this occurrence diminishes the staff's disappointment, and permits them to help the patient with the feelings evoked rather than to confirm the patient's fears of abandonment and rejection. A second firm discharge date frequently goes more smoothly.

5. After care planning is a central feature of hospitalization. Reentry must be concerned with addressing social and vocational issues and also the patient's chronic sense of inner alienation from the community. The outside therapist must resume or begin work prior to discharge.

6. A realistic sense of the BPD course, where readmissions are accepted and not viewed as signs of failure, permits the patient to reach out appropriately for help when difficulties are encountered in the postdischarge phase. Hospital units that have formal mechanisms such as holding beds for brief readmissions, or informal mechanisms such as the patient returning to the ward for brief visits, facilitate the discharge process.

After Care and Hospitalization

The borderline patient has been described as ahistoric in that he has difficulty looking beyond the present (Miller, 1964; Hartocollis, 1978). Elsewhere we have described how the literature on hospital care is similar (Rosenbluth, 1987). Rather than taking a longitudinal view of the borderline course, the literature is preoccupied with the index admission, and insufficient attention is paid to issues that arise from numerous rehospitalizations and that affect the patient, the family, and the hospital staff. The place of hospitalization in the course of the problem and the opportunity for the hospital to take a leadership, consultative role in the whole treatment approach, including after care issues, has not been sufficiently developed.

The development of the outcome literature on BPD (McGlashan, 1986a; Plakun et al., 1986; Stone et al., 1987) offers an opportunity to remedy this situation by stressing the need for a longitudinal approach and underlining how frequent hospitalization can be in the course of the BPD. Hospitalization needs to concern itself not only with the stabilization of the borderline patient, but must address the problems of the system into which the patient returns. Thus a longitudinal rather than cross-sectional orientation underlines issues of after care which must be addressed. These include stabilization of the referring therapist, stabilization of the family, and augmentation of supporting social, vocational, and/or therapeutic structure.

Hospitalization provides an opportunity for the outpatient therapy to be reviewed. Outpatient therapy of the borderline patient is often a difficult and demanding enterprise for the patient and the therapist. A longitudinally informed view of the inpatient treatment of the borderline patient sees the examination and stabilization of the outpatient therapy as critical. This involves assessing how transference–countertransference problems contribute to the admission. With regard to the role of the therapist, the hospitalization is seen by the inpatient staff as an opportunity for the stabilization of the therapist's relationship with the patient so that the treatment is not disrupted. Occasionally, the task is to aid in achieving termination when the therapy cannot proceed.

The stabilization of the outpatient treatment can be seen as having two phases—the inpatient and the outpatient phase. The inpatient phase involves checking for signs of strain and countertransference problems in the outpatient therapist. Signs of therapist strain include change in the frequency of the sessions, missed or changed therapy hours, the therapist's sudden vacation with little notice, or an alteration in the manner in which the therapist speaks to and about the patient (Bernstein, 1980). The critical countertransference constellations that need to be addressed include the polarities of masochistic submission to the patient's aggression, alternating with an inappropriate and excessive distancing from the patient (Kernberg, 1975).

It is important for the hospital staff to fully assess the state of the therapeutic relationship. In so doing, a tendency to devalue the outpatient therapist must be avoided. Similarly, a tendency to accept the ongoing therapy uncritically and uncreatively may also be problematic (Adler, 1977). Full consultation is required between hospital staff and the outpatient therapist with the goal of stabilizing the outpatient treatment so that it can proceed after the patient is discharged. The time the patient is in the hospital may be sufficient for the outpatient therapist to take stock and clarify the countertransference. On other occasions, the patient and/or therapist may refuse to continue with treatment. Termination and a new engagement must be facilitated. Ongoing outpatient therapy may benefit from the clarification of the Axis I diagnosis, and/or the addition of auxiliary therapeutic structure such as day hospital, drug clinic, or drop-in center. This can be particularly useful for the outpatient therapist as well as the patient.

Therapist burnout can be diminished if the therapist is in contact with other mental health workers involved in the care of the patient. The outpatient phase of stabilizing the referring therapist may involve ongoing postdischarge contact with the inpatient psychiatrist aimed at minimizing transference–countertransference whirls which result in hospitalization. Thus, by reinforcing the therapist's involvement and capacity to contain the patient and by stabilizing countertransference reactions, boundaries between outpatient therapist and patient are better maintained. The patient's disappointment and reactive rage are kept in workable proportions rather than allowed to be disruptive of the therapeutic relationship.

Winnicott (1965c) has described mothers who have the capacity to provide good enough care and who can be enabled to do better by being cared for themselves in a way that acknowledges the essential nature of their task. Outpatient therapists of BPD patients are similar in this regard. Ongoing postdischarge checking by the inpatient psychiatrist of the therapeutic situation can be of help to both the outpatient psychiatrist and the patient.

An after care contract can be an aid in stabilizing the postdischarge course, particularly for the patient with a past history of several admissions. This involves a review of previous interim functioning and treatment planning to determine the nature of the problems. Past failures of treatment are reviewed and analyzed, and a future-oriented plan is emphasized. Those patients who have had several admissions in the last few years prior to the index admission are invited to plan, with the staff's aid, an improvement in this pattern based on a dynamic understanding of what contributed to previous readmissions.

An attempt is made to help the patient form realistic goals and objectives for the next few years. The possibility of readmissions during that period is recognized. Assurance is given that such backup and support can be counted on. However, in addition to defining goals, the expectations of the patient are also defined as much as possible. Particularly, readmission criteria are explicitly discussed. These may include spelling out the patient's responsibility for taking medication, attending various programs, being involved in family meetings, and/or decreasing certain self-destructive behaviors. The target behaviors chosen as readmission criteria depend on a realistic reading of what can be expected of the patient at that point in treatment.

Also, the patient and the after care system are aided in differentiating between the true need for readmission and the patient's regressive wish to escape the pressures of daily life. With help the patient can resist this tendency.

Careful limit-setting that takes into consideration the patient's capacities and deficits stabilizes the after care and mobilizes the patient. Planning over time tends to help patients to develop a future orientation and a broader sense of their responsibility in treatment.

The family needs to be stabilized as well. Often demoralized and drained by the efforts of dealing with what they see as a tyrannical individual, members of the family may require treatment or at least some guidelines for relating to the patient. It is often beneficial to help the family develop ways of providing the external control the patient requires, rather than provoking and perpetuating negative behaviors.

Although there is controversy about the different family constellations, the literature suggests two major family styles. On the one hand are the families that exclude the borderline patient, and on the other hand the families that are enmeshed and overinvolved (Gunderson and Woods, 1981). Patterns similar to those relating to the therapist's countertransference, described earlier, may be noted in the family's involvement with these patients. The axis of involvement may revolve around either masochistic submission or inappropriate distancing and abandonment of the patient. In either case, attention to the connection of the patient to the family and the role of the family in the after care of the patient can contribute to after care stabilization. This involves clarification of the interactive dynamics of the patient and family. It may also include helping the family achieve an appropriate degree of involvement.

While the patient is in the hospital, attention must be paid to the social, vocational, and therapeutic network of the patient outside the hospital. From the beginning of the hospitalization, these networks are assessed so that important elements are maintained during the hospitalization and not jeopardized as the patient recedes into the cocoon of the hospital. Thus, where appropriate, the patient is encouraged to maintain external structure, such as returning to school or a job as soon as possible and continuing with outpatient therapy. This can stem excessive inpatient regression. Attempts are made, while the patient is in the hospital, to coordinate the different agencies that are involved in maintaining after care stabilization by making some aware of the presence of others or discontinuing redundant efforts. The role of the day hospital as an alternative to future hospitalization and as a mainstay of the after care program can be considerable (Pildis, Soverow, Salzman, and Wolf, 1978). Stable vocational, educational, and therapeutic structures are seen as important components of a holding environment.

CONCLUSION

The hospital care of the borderline patient can be an opportunity to protect the patient from his or her self-destructive impulses. It can be a time when the entire therapeutic enterprise is reappraised, with attention given to the outpatient treatment, social and vocational supports, the intervention with the family, and the clarification of diagnostic, psychodynamic, and psychopharmacological issues. In this way, the hospital can function as a base sustaining and facilitating the borderline patient's quest for help.

Or, it can mark the end of a therapeutic enterprise. Acting out, transference–countertransference whirls, malignant regression, and/or premature discharge and dropping out of treatment can be its characteristics. Rather than a beginning, hospitalization may be just another failed opportunity in the patient's search for peace, stability, and constancy in his or her life.

This chapter has described critical issues in hospital care—issues which may determine which path is taken. The premises of short- and long-term hospitalization of the BPD patient have been described. A consideration of the clinical and research experience suggests that short-stay treatment is the preferred modality of hospital care of BPD. Long-term treatment, while useful for learning more about borderline dynamics and teaching psychotherapy, should be regarded as a treatment best reserved for a very small minority of patients, particularly those who cannot be contained outside of the hospital and for whom no alternative exists.

The indications for and the role of hospitalization have been described. Particular emphasis has been placed on the stabilization of the patient; a full consideration of the after care system that the patient is discharged to; and the different ways the countertransference processes elicited can be used in the hospital care of BPD.

The hospital treatment of the borderline patient is never easy. A consideration of the premises and core issues of hospitalization may facilitate the patient's more successful engagement in treatment in the hospital and after discharge.

PART IV

PARTICULAR BORDERLINE POPULATIONS

22.

Borderline Personality Disorder in Adolescents: A Critical Overview, Novel Speculations, and Suggested Future Directions

Stanley P. Kutcher, M.D., and Marshall Korenblum, M.D.

The diagnosis of borderline personality disorder (BPD) in adolescents has evolved primarily from psychodynamic constructs which have linked a wide variety of behavioral, affective, and cognitive "symptoms" to presumed intrapsychic pathology (Ritvo and Solnit, 1958; Kernberg, 1967, 1972, 1978, 1979; Mahler, 1971; Masterson, 1972, 1973a,b; Schwartsberg, 1978; Giovacchini, 1978a,b; Rinsberg, 1982). Although of heuristic value, such an approach has tended to perpetuate tautologic reasoning in which defects in psychic structure are used both to infer and describe the syndrome. This approach negates a basic classificatory principle (Kendell, 1982; Frances and Widiger, 1986; Skinner, 1986), the separation of internal and external validity of defining a disorder in terms other than the symptoms used to describe it. With the advent of the DSM-III and DSM III-R (American Psychiatric Association, 1980, 1987), a relatively more atheoretical phenomenological nosology has been elaborated. This should facilitate the first steps in establishing diagnostic construct validity by ensuring reliable descriptive homogeneity. What is still lacking, however, is a comprehensive developmental perspective in applying this diagnosis to the adolescent age group. It is the purpose of this chapter to advocate such a perspective while critically examining the current state of knowledge in this area.

"BORDERLINE" AND ADOLESCENCE

The syndrome of BPD in adolescence must first be clearly distinguished both from normal developmental processes, and then from other adolescent psychiatric disorders. There are parallels between the tasks of adolescence and some features of borderline psychopathology (Giovacchini, 1978b), particularly in the areas of identity formation, affect and impulse modulation, and establishment of autonomy (separation and individuation).

As well, both "normal" and "borderline" adolescents share features which may obfuscate clear diagnosis. Both are characterized by incomplete ego development, fluidity, and ease of regression in functioning, incompletely consolidated defensive functioning, mood lability, and a high reactivity to interpersonal or social vicissitudes. These features may be normatively stage specific in the teenagers' progression from early to late adolescence (Stein, Golombek, Marton, and Korenblum, 1987). In a longitudinal prospective study of nonclinical subjects, for example, Korenblum, Golombek, Marton, and Stein (in press) noted that the prevalence rate of histrionic, narcissistic, or borderline features was 0 percent at age thirteen, 3 percent at age sixteen, and 17 percent at age eighteen.

In spite of these developmental issues, however, clear differences between normal and borderline adolescents do exist. Reality testing, object constancy, modulation of affects, and tolerance of ambiguity–ambivalence are all compromised in BPD but not in normals. Nonclinical teens can maintain memories of positive feelings toward their most significant others even in the presence of hostile affects—borderline patients often cannot. Contrary to normals, borderline teenagers are subject to dichotomous, "all or nothing" thinking, particularly in affect laden situations, which results in cognitive peculiarities such as confusing the unique for the universal and vice versa (Elkind, 1976; Kroll, 1988). Existential concerns may often be exaggerated, and the family or the school may be the settings in which many of these difficulties are most evident.

At this time, although BPD symptomatology in adolescence seems to be both qualitatively and quantitatively different from normative developmental processes, no well-conducted studies of this issue have been reported. As a result, the full range of BPD symptoms in teens has yet to be defined. As in many adolescent Axis I diagnoses, BPD in teenagers may well present in an "atypical" form. For example, the nature of the "psychotic" type symptoms may differ with fewer classic Schneiderian symptoms, and more commonly the occurrence of depersonalization or derealization phenomena reported. Such issues need careful documentation and study, which will potentially lead to a better delineation and understanding of the life cycle–specific features of this disorder.

DIFFERENTIAL DIAGNOSIS AND ASSESSMENT

Although DSM-III cautions against the use of personality disorder diagnoses in adolescents under eighteen years of age, the BPD diagnosis is frequently applied to much younger individuals who seem to exhibit a persistent pattern of BPD type behaviors. Bradley's (1981) survey of eighty-one child and adolescent psychiatrists found that over 80 percent used a "borderline diagnosis" in twelve- to eighteen-year-olds, although the reliability and validity of these diagnostic practices were not assessed.

Diagnostic criteria for BPD used in adults have been successfully applied to adolescent populations, and the use of structured diagnostic interviews such as the diagnostic interview for borderlines (DIB) (Gunderson, Kolb, and Austin,

1981) and the personality disorders examination (PDE) (Loranger, Susman, Oldham, and Russakoff, 1987) have improved
the reliability of this diagnosis. McManus, Alessi, Grapentine,
and Robbins (1984) reported that both DSM-III and DIB criteria could be used in hospitalized adolescents aged thirteen to
eighteen. Yanchyshyn, Kutcher, and Cohen (1986) successfully
applied DSM-III and DIB criteria to an older adolescent inpatient population (mean age 16.8 years). Both groups found high
rates of interrater reliability and a good congruence between
diagnostic systems. Concurrent Axis I diagnoses in both reports
tended toward major affective disorders.

     Although adult diagnostic criteria for BPD can be applied
to the adolescent population, and DSM-III-R recognizes the
BPD diagnosis in both children and adolescents, much work
yet remains to be done in determining: core versus related
symptomatology; the stability of the diagnosis over time; sex
specificity of symptoms such as other-directed violence in males
and self-directed violence in females; the concurrence of Axis
I and other Axis II diagnoses, and the applicability of these
criteria to outpatient populations.

     In adolescents, the assessment of character pathology must
take into account both time and contextual variables. Cross-
sectional diagnosis of BPD is to be discouraged, especially in
the presence of an Axis I disorder. Substance abusers may show
problems in reality testing, impulse control, mood lability, aggressive outbursts, and experience legal difficulties. Major depression in adolescents seems to exert a strong "state dependent" effect on borderline symptomatology. Korenblum,
Marton, Kutcher, Kennedy, Stein, and Pakes (1988) in a study
of depressed adolescents, for example, found that 24 percent
met DSM-III criteria for BPD. When assessed at least six
months later while euthymic, more than half of the initially
diagnosed BPDs no longer met BPD criteria.

     In addition to substance abuse and major depression, other
adolescent Axis I disorders may present with borderline-type
symptomatology. Hypomania often includes "classic" borderline behaviors such as limit-testing, projection of responsibility,
splitting, intrusiveness, affective lability, irritability, anger outbursts, and interpersonal hypersensitivity (Davis, Noll, and

Sharma, 1986). These behaviors may present in the absence of grandiosity (particularly in adolescents), and often revert to normal with proper pharmacologic interventions. Thus, great care must be taken to exclude or properly treat an Axis I hypomanic disorder (which can often present in atypical form in the adolescent) before a diagnosis of BPD is made.

Psychotic disorders (schizophrenia, schizoaffective disorder) may first present during adolescence with behavioral profiles similar to BPD. Disturbances of interpersonal relationships, difficulties in affective modulation, impulsivity, self-damaging acts, episodes of active psychosis, and the presence of dynamic defenses such as splitting, projection, and projective identification commonly form part of the early clinical picture of a developing adolescent psychosis. Overenthusiastic application of the BPD Axis II diagnosis without careful consideration of a developing psychotic illness may lead to incorrect and even harmful therapeutic interventions. A diagnosis of BPD in teens should therefore be made only if the clinician is certain that the symptom profile is not a reflection of an underlying psychosis. Often careful observation over a period of time is necessary before this is possible.

The effect of place on adolescent symptomatology has yet to be systematically and properly investigated, but both the school or family contexts may allow for more flagrant expression of BPD symptoms than those seen in an office setting. Erotic or idealized attachments to teaching staff, manipulative self-harm threats made to school counselors, declining grades in the context of decreasing classroom structure, or the development of intense dyadic relationships at the expense of peer group function may be signs of school-based BPD behaviors. In some families, issues of autonomy or separation may give rise to well-recognized BPD behaviors which are enacted more intensely in the familial context.

The diagnosis of BPD in the adolescent must therefore be based on consistent longitudinal observations and not merely on cross-sectional assessment. Family, peer, and school behaviors must be documented. Borderline personality disorder should not be diagnosed in the presence of an Axis I disorder which may "create" similar symptoms. The systematic use of semistructured interviews of proven utility in determining Axis I diagnoses, such as the K-SADS (Chambers, Puig-Antich, Hirsch, Paez, Ambrosini, Tabrizi, and Davies, 1985) or DICA (Herjanic and Reich, 1982), are of great value in clinical assessment and their routine use should decrease false positive BPD diagnoses.

POSSIBLE ETIOLOGIES

Although most authors speculating on the etiology of BPD in adolescents attribute its origins to early childhood trauma or fixations (see below), no investigators have adequately explained why this disorder emerges in adolescents, nor indeed have specific childhood antecedents to adolescent BPD been clearly defined. Organic, psychodynamic, familial, and sociocultural factors may all play a role, the exact weight of which may vary in individual cases.

Organic

Recently, the presence of subgroups of BPD has been suggested. Andrulonis, Glueck, Stroebel, Vogel, Shapiro, and Aldridge (1981) have described an episodic dyscontrol subgroup, a minimal brain damage (MBD) subgroup, and a nonorganic subgroup. This identification of a minimal brain damage or attention deficit disorder (ADDH) "subgroup" highlights the phenomenologic similarities between BPD and ADDH. Difficulties in modulating arousal, impulsivity, lapses in judgment, and idiosyncratic cognitive processes are common to both. Since the two diagnoses are coded on separate axes they are not mutually exclusive nor is it clear which may be primary. What may help in the clinical differentiation is the rather specific sensitivity to separation and abandonment fears of the BPD patient as opposed to the almost indifferent emotionality of the ADDH teen, and the presence of a learning disability, neurologic soft signs, or a positive behavioral response to stimulants in the ADDH adolescent.

   The ADDH and episodic dyscontrol subgroups suggest an organic basis for the concurrent Axis II BPD diagnosis, perhaps on the basis of reproductive misadventure, childhood head trauma, or a subclinical central nervous system (CNS) infection. However, even in Andrulonis' "nonorganic" subgroup a biologic basis to BPD was identified. The "nonorganic" subgroup was predominantly female and seemed to have a later onset of difficulties as well as a later mean age of admission to hospital. However, these "nonorganic" females were highly overrepresented in their susceptibility to intermediate degrees of motion sickness, suggesting a difficulty with central control of sensory processing previously associated with a schizophrenic illness. This suggests that even in the "nonorganic" subgroup there may be an underlying biological vulnerability.

   Blackwood, St. Clair, and Kutcher (1986) have described abnormalities in the P300 amplitude and latencies of adult BPD patients that differentiated them from other personality disorders. Kutcher, Blackwood, St. Clair, Gaskell, and Muir (1987) have demonstrated increased P300 latency in BPD which is indistinguishable from that found in schizophrenics. This abnormality distinguished BPD patients both from normal controls and depressives, and occurred in those BPD patients who also met DSM-III criteria for depression but not in those depressives who did not meet criteria for BPD. Further, although these abnormalities do not differentiate BPD from schizotypal personality disorders they do differentiate BPD from other personality disorders (Kutcher, Blackwood, St. Clair, and Muir, 1989).

   These findings suggest that subtle abnormalities in CNS information processing may be an underlying physiologic basis for the adolescent borderline. Such deficits may be associated with misinterpretation of internal and external stimuli and may lead the borderline patient to act on the basis of such misinterpretation. This incongruent behavior could certainly be understood as "splitting," "projection," mood lability, and cognitive distortion. Abandonment anxieties may then be a reflection of the borderline individual's confusion regarding the seeming incongruence between what she expects on the basis of her faulty misrepresentations and what the environment actually

delivers. Maladaptive behaviors may then become fixed following repeated enforcement by "unexpected" environmental responses.

An alternative approach to understanding the issue of BPD
in adolescents may be that of utilizing a more diagnostically
"dimensional" paradigm in which specific behaviors and not
syndromes are identified as the unit of analysis. One such "classic" BPD behavior is lack of impulse control. Suicidality, other-
directed aggression, impulsivity, lapses of judgment, and even
bulimic-type eating may reflect a common etiology such as a
disturbance of CNS serotonergic functioning.

Postmortem studies of adult suicide victims, for example,
suggest decreased brain 5-hydroxytryptamine turnover with
significantly lower levels of CNS and CSF 5-HT and/or 5 HIAA
being consistently reported (Shaw, Camps, and Eccleston, 1967;
Beskow, Gottfires, Roos, and Winblad, 1976; Cohen, Winchel,
and Stanley, 1988). Further, decreased tritated imipramine
binding sites in the frontal cortex (Stanley, Virigilio, and Gershon, 1982; Myerson, Wennogle, Abel, Coupet, Lippa, Rank,
and Beer, 1982) and "compensatory" increases in postsynaptic
serotonin receptor binding have been described (Mann, Stanley, McBride, and McEwen, 1986). Two studies of adolescent
and young adult male suicide attempters have both reported
low CSF 5-HIAA levels (Brown, Goodwin, Ballinger, Goyer,
and Major, 1979; Brown, Ebert, Goyer, Jimerson, Klein, Bunrey, and Goodwin, 1982). Further, in adolescents, suicidality
has been more significantly associated with a blunted growth
hormone response to intravenous desipramine than either a
diagnosis of depression or no psychiatric illness (Ryan and Puig-
Antich, 1988).

Other markers of disordered CNS serotonergic function
such as decreased platelet imipramine binding sites in children
with aggressive and impulsive behaviors have been reported
(Stoff, Pollack, Vitiello, Behar, and Bridger, 1987). Studies of
bulimic populations have suggested decreased CNS serotonergic turnover (Riederer and Kruzik, 1982; Kaye, Ebert, Raleigh,
and Laker, 1984), and recently, a blunted prolactin response to
fenfluramine has been described in a mixed affective/personal-
ity disordered population (Coccaro, Siever, Klar, Maurer,
Cochrane, Cooper, Mohs, and Davis, 1986).

Whether this approach to the study of BPD phenomenology will be more productive than previous biologic studies of the dexamethasone suppression test and the thyrotropin releasing hormone test yet remains to be seen. This symptom specific approach needs to be applied to homogeneous BPD populations. Such a dimensional behaviorally specific paradigm, however, may allow more careful differentiation of the BPD symptoms and lead to unique conceptual, diagnostic, and treatment constructs.

Psychodynamic

Early psychological trauma, particularly during the ages of eight to twenty months, has often been hypothesized to underlie the development of BPD (Ritvo and Solnit, 1958; Kernberg, 1967, 1972, 1978, 1979; Mahler, 1971; Masterson, 1972, 1973a,b, 1981; Giovacchini, 1978a; Rinsley, 1978; Shapiro, 1978a; Rinsberg, 1982). The presence of unpredictable or partially nurturing mothering during this developmental phase has been postulated to lead to the development of disturbed object relations in which "good" or gratified and "bad" or frustrated self representations are fixed. Adolescent borderline symptomatology is argued to be a recapitulation of this misdevelopment and is thought by some to be rekindled by the adolescent developmental tasks of independence and separation or sexual awakening.

Unfortunately, few studies have tested these hypotheses, yet much clinical work in adolescents is premised on their presumed veracity. Bradley (1979) compared fourteen child adolescent borderline patients with nonborderline psychiatric controls and found that borderlines had experienced significantly more separations prior to age five. No structured diagnostic interviews were used, no other personality disorders were included for comparison, depressive disorders were not controlled for, nor was the sample size large enough to allow discrimination between early separations and other significant early childhood events such as medical illness, abuse, severe family dysharmony, and so on. As well, the nature of the separations and the type of support received by the child during separations were not addressed. Greenman, Gunderson, Came, and Saltzman (1986) found that contrary to theory, strictly diagnosed BPD children were not more commonly from broken homes nor did they experience more maternal deprivation than non-BPD psychiatric controls. Thus, although heuristically appealing, the childhood rapprochement phase trauma hypothesis of BPD etiology awaits objective verification.

Family

Family studies of borderline adolescents have identified several possible dysfunctional interaction patterns amongst the BPD adolescent and the parents (Masterson, 1972; Shapiro, Zinner, Shapiro, and Berkowitz, 1975; Zinner and Shapiro, 1975; Shapiro, 1978b). Masterson's (1972) early suggestion that the mothers of BPD adolescents are themselves borderline, although widely accepted has, however, not been confirmed in properly conducted family studies. Shapiro's assertions that there are two types of "borderline" families (Shapiro et al., 1975; Shapiro, 1978b)—one in which parents are intolerant of their child's autonomy needs and another in which parents deny their child's dependency needs—are based on the theoretical construct that adolescent BPD is a result of the recapitulation of the separation–individuation issues of the early rapprochement phase. Although these authors present their clinical impressions as studies, research validity is lacking. Shapiro and Shapiro et al., for example (1975, 1978b), describe a study population in which no clear personality disorder diagnoses were assigned. The reader is asked to believe that the sample is indeed that of BPD on the suggestion that of the fifty families assessed "many had adolescents who fit descriptively in the category of borderline by Kernberg's definition" (Shapiro, 1978b, p. 349) of borderline personality organization. Sample bias is further complicated by a lack of objective diagnostic criteria and a lack of objective criteria independently applied to classify or categorize family function of BPD defenses. No control groups were used and the purpose seems not to have been the testing of the null hypothesis but the selective presentation of clinical vignettes designed to describe a predetermined hypothesis. Further, no data from the sample was presented. However, allowing for the deficiencies in study design, Shapiro (1975, 1978b) and Zinner and Shapiro's (1975) work suggests that certain adolescent BPD phenomena may "flower" most visibly within the family context. This is an observation requiring more detailed and careful analysis.

Gunderson, Kerr, and Englund (1980) have reported a more properly conducted analysis of twelve adolescent (ages 15–24) BPD families matched to twelve schizophrenic and twelve neurotic families. Although numerous methodologic difficulties make conclusions tentative, they did note that adolescent BPD families shared some characteristics that differentiated them both from schizophrenic and neurotic groups. Adolescent BPD families showed more maternal psychosis, poorer rule enforcement, and more parental neglect. Little support was found for the theoretical descriptions of maternal overinvolvement, projection of parental disturbance, maternal borderline illness, or excessive hostility and acting out. Whether these features are causal in the development of the BPD adolescent or a reflection of that adolescent's disorder on a family functioning, or a combination of both cannot be determined from this study. Further rigorous work remains to be done in this area.

Sociocultural

Societal factors may play a role in the development of adolescent BPD symptomatology. Millon (1987) suggests that an increase in "divisive and diffusing social customs," such as increased mobility, separation, divorce, drug abuse, and "capricious" TV role models; along with a decrease in "reparative and cohering social customs," and extended family associations play an important role in producing BPD. Adolescents given their semidependent developmental state may be particularly vulnerable to peer and societal influences (Levine, 1978;

Rakoff, 1978). Although appealing, such theories are difficult to validate and suffer from a general applicability which limits their explanatory utility. Whether unstable social structures and rapid social change perpetuate ongoing BPD disturbance otherwise determined is, however, a possibility that bears serious investigation.

Ongoing sexual abuse in childhood may lead to a variety of behavioral, social, and interpersonal disturbances. A neglected area of social and developmental study in the adolescent borderline is the relationship of sexual abuse to adolescent borderline pathology. In a detailed assessment of fifteen adolescent inpatients at Sunnybrook Medical Centre meeting DSM-III-R criteria for BPD (9 female, 6 male; mean age 17.1 years) 47 percent reported childhood sexual abuse. The effect of such trauma on personality development is unclear but needs to be addressed. Further, the symptomatic manifestations of sexual abuse in the adolescent also need to be clarified. Acting out, running away from home, substance abuse, self-damaging acts, mood lability, uncontrolled anger outbursts, and suicide attempts may reflect the adolescents' attempts to deal with ongoing sexual abuse in a society which denies, ignores, or even subtly condones it. Certainly this entire issue demands detailed study in the borderline adolescent.

Many populations of severely disturbed adolescents do not easily lend themselves to psychiatric study, but may have a wealth of important information not found in clinical samples. One such population is the "street kid"—the adolescent prostitute, hustler, pimp, and drug dealer who rarely if ever enters the mental health system. Studies of these populations have traditionally been the arena of sociologists or cultural anthropologists and as a result the psychiatric aspects of such groups are not well known. In an ongoing study of adolescent prostitutes in Toronto, Kutcher and Hillier (unpublished) using clinical interviews and detailed history reviews assigned DSM-III diagnoses to seventy-five "street kids"; forty-one females and thirty-four males, mean age 17.9 years. Eighty-six percent met DSM-III criteria for BPD, 89 percent of the females and 82 percent of the males. A diagnosis of BPD in both sexes was associated with drug and alcohol abuse, a history of sexual and physical abuse, school failure, suicide attempts, a family history of psychiatric illness, and in the females, an Axis I diagnosis of attention deficit disorder. Major affective disorders were not significantly associated with a BPD diagnosis.

Whether these populations of street kids are substantially different from clinic adolescent populations, or merely reflections of less stable familial or environmental supports, is not known at this time. The higher prevalence rates of male BPD in this group suggests that contrary to current prevalence estimates based on clinical populations which show female predominance, male borderlines may be equally common but simply do not come to psychiatric attention. Supporting this possibility is the report by McManus et al. (1984) which identified a high rate of BPD in incarcerated male juvenile delinquents.

Further in this street population the lack of association between BPD and an Axis I diagnosis of depression differs from the findings by investigators who studied adolescent inpatient populations. Perhaps it is the presence of a depressive disorder which defines entry to the mental health system, thereby skewing earlier study populations toward an association between depressive disorder and BPD, and when all adolescents with BPD (clinical and nonclinical populations) are studied, the depression/BPD relationship may disappear.

TREATMENT

There is no clearly effective treatment for the BPD adolescent. Instead there are a multitude of treatment approaches (Masterson, 1972; Rossman and Knesper, 1975; Zinner, 1978a; Kernberg, 1979; Kolb and Shapiro, 1982b; Green, 1983; Broden, 1984; Egan, 1986, 1988; Simon, 1986; Goodrich, 1987). Most often these treatments are based on presumed developmentally determined intrapsychic ego deficits and most often unvalidated, unevaluated, and delivered more on the basis of the therapists' beliefs than on any demonstrated therapeutic efficacy. Some commonly suggested treatments include: long-term analytic psychotherapy; long-term inpatient psychoanalytic therapy; day hospital; family therapy, and others. None of these treatments have demonstrated proven efficacy in carefully controlled treatment outcome studies, yet the treatment literature is often replete with assurances of certainty as to the correctness of the individual author's preferred approach.

Kolb and Shapiro (1982a,b), for example, argue that long-term inpatient hospital treatment is the preferred approach, but present no evidence to support this. Rossman and Knesper (1975) categorically state the BPD adolescent is "immeasurably helped by long term hospital treatment," again without valid supportive evidence. Simon (1986) argues for day hospitalization, in which he prescribes a mix of various therapies in a sort of "throw everyting at it and see if it is helpful" paradigm. No effort is made to distinguish essential from nonessential treatments. Green (1983) argues for a combination of long-term inpatient, family, and intensive analytic therapy, offering a nonsupported assertion of fact that the BPD adolescent is sicker than the BPD adult and asserting (again with no solid evidence) the BPD adolescents' parents are either themselves borderline or have failed their child during the developmental phases in which separation–individuation issues are paramount. As in many articles on treatment, Green (1983) argues the correctness of his approach from unvalidated etiological constructs supported solely by sketchy illustrations selected from a few cases.

In general the adolescent BPD treatment literature is of such poor quality that it provides few if any treatment approaches of proven validity. Treatment approaches are based on unvalidated hypotheses, operational outcome criteria are not defined, control groups are not studied, essential versus nonessential strategies are not clarified, diagnoses are not made using recognized diagnostic criteria with the assistance of structured interviews, and case material is selectively presented as proof of the effectiveness of the approach. The null hypothesis is conspicuous by its absence.

Rarely if ever are the costs of long-term inpatient treatments considered by the proponents of this view. At a daily private room rate of $2,166.00 (Province of Ontario figures) continued over a needed four years, as asserted by Goodrich (1987), the $3,162,360.00 cost per adolescent not only is not substantiated by any evidence of positive outcome but shows a degree of fiscal irresponsibility that brings discredit to adolescent psychiatric treatment in general. To then argue that this treatment is necessary "in order to prevent a severe adult mental disorder" (Goodrich, 1987, p. 283), without providing any evidence for this, lowers the credibility of adolescent psychiatry at a time when no further such lowering is needed.

As well, none of the generally quoted treatment literature considers the negative effects of psychiatric treatments for the BPD adolescent, yet clinical practice suggests that the behaviors of the BPD adolescent may worsen in a hospital or during long-term intensive treatments. Contagion-type suicidal behavior in such populations has been described (Kamirer, 1986), and the well-known patient–therapist struggles may themselves lead to self-destructive or other-destructive behavior. Advocates of any treatment approach not only must be able to show the benefit of their specific treatment by means of carefully controlled studies, but must also show their "treatment" does not do more harm than good. Indeed, particularly for those long-term therapies which foster regression, clear evidence is needed to show that they are not actually iatrogenic either in the exacerbation or perpetuation of the adolescent borderline disturbance.

Biological treatments of adolescent BPD are rarely if ever mentioned. Green (1983) offers the unusual and unsupported assertion that adolescent borderlines are often made worse by phenothiazines, but respond to relatively small doses of tricyclic drugs. Egan (1988), in a recent review of this topic, provides a cursory overview of some adult studies but offers no specific data for adolescents. Unfortunately, no studies of the pharmacological treatment of adolescent BPD that we are aware of have been reported to date. A review of the adult literature suggests that low dose phenothiazines may be helpful, while some tricyclics and benzodiazepines may actually worsen impulsive and self-destructive behaviors (Soloff et al., 1986; Cowdry and Gardner, 1988; Kutcher and Blackwood, 1989). To argue that the adolescent BPD patient be treated with tricyclics (Green, 1983) suggests a lack of knowledge of basic adolescent psychopharmacology in which tricyclic antidepressants have yet to be shown as efficacious in any disorder including depression (except for ADDH) (Ryan and Puig-Antich, 1987). This is a particularly irresponsible suggestion because tricyclics can be lethal in overdose, a not uncommon phenomenon in the adolescent BPD (Crumley, 1981). The area of psychopharmacologic treatment for the adolescent borderline remains one in which appropriately controlled studies are urgently needed.

CURRENT CANADIAN TREATMENT PRACTICES

To determine what treatment modalities are most commonly used in BPD adolescents we sent out a questionnaire listing seventeen possible treatments of a BPD adolescent without a concurrent major affective disorder to the 328 members of the Canadian Academy of Child Psychiatry. Of the questionnaires sent, fifty-five were returned because the addressee could not be located. One hundred-twenty-four of the remaining 273 (45%) were completed and returned. Of the seventeen treatment possibilities listed, the respondants endorsed an average of 5.6 different treatment modalities. The treatment approaches most frequently chosen were: supportive individual psychotherapy, 75 percent; acute care crisis hospitalization, 50 percent; collaborative family therapy, 48 percent; and social skills training, 45 percent. Intensive insight oriented individual psychotherapy (minimum twice weekly) was chosen by 28 percent while neuroleptics were endorsed by 40 percent.

These results illustrate the plethora of treatment approaches currently used by practicing child and adolescent psychiatrists. Supportive individual psychotherapy was the most frequently endorsed even though there is no clear evidence of its efficacy. Over one-quarter of the respondents endorsed the very costly method of intensive insight oriented psychotherapy—again with no clear evidence of its effectiveness. The two most likely conclusions from this survey are: that the psychiatric treatment of the BPD adolescent is largely a matter of personal preference; or that treatment is based on a "scattershot" approach in a "try anything and hope that something works" scenario. Both are very poor foundations on which to base psychotherapeutic treatment.

Essential questions about the treatment of the BPD adolescent remain unanswered. Should BPD adolescents even be treated by psychiatrists? Are some forms of psychiatric treatment actually harmful? What are the essential and necessary aspects of treatment and what are nonessential? How long should treatment be continued and what should the treatment goals be? What is the cost of treatment and what is the cost–benefit analysis of this treatment? Much carefully designed research in this area is urgently needed.

APPROACHES AND RECOMMENDATIONS

It is premature to suggest a specific treatment strategy for the adolescent borderline, given the lack of solid research in this area. Nevertheless, the clinical necessity remains—what should one do until the cavalry arrives? A number of general principles can be offered.

First, it is important to remember that treatment follows from proper diagnosis and formulation, meticulously arrived at, in which all Axis I disorders are carefully considered and longitudinal observation is utilized. Structured interviews, as previously noted, should be used whenever possible and DSM-III-R criteria rather than the broader concept of borderline personality organization should be followed.

Second, treatment should be tailored to the severity of the condition and a clear understanding of the adolescent's current ego strengths. The general approach may be a synthetic and not an analytic one, to help the adolescent build up ego strengths, often using islands of functioning such as academic or athletic success, which have been relatively spared, as a starting point. A cognitive approach in which the teen is taught to link cognitive distortions to maladaptive affect and behavior may help decrease impulsivity and improve social skills.

Third, the treating professional should be familiar with and willing to use different approaches when necessary. For example, short-term, nonregressive hospitalization for crisis management may be indicated, or referral to a vocational skills group to develop needed job abilities. Medications when used

should be for clearly defined symptoms and low dose phenothiazines (Kutcher and Blackwood, 1989) may be the first choice
for a variety of behavioral, affective, and cognitive difficulties.
Tricyclic antidepressants have not generally been shown to be
helpful in depressed adolescents, and because of their lethality
in suicide attempts should only be used if other approaches to
a clearly diagnosed Axis I depression, which has persisted over
three to four weeks, have proven ineffective. It may be helpful
for a treating therapist to utilize the services of a specialized
psychopharmcology treatment clinic, especially in cases where
conflict over interpersonal issues with the therapist is being
played out in medication misuse.

     Finally, and above all, it is important that treatment should
do less harm than no treatment at all. Treatment holidays may
help to clarify this, and well-timed consultations from "neutral"
colleagues can help when difficulties arise. Simple strategies
such as avoiding intimate contact with the patient or ensuring
that therapy appointments are during "regular working hours"
and occur in a clearly defined treatment location will diminish
the chances of therapeutic misadventure.

CONCLUSION

In conclusion, much has been done in the area of adolescent
BPD, yet much more remains. What is needed in current and
future work are innovative ideas that challenge long held beliefs
and subject them to critical empirical analysis. Only then will
the study of the adolescent borderline progress beyond the
level of the medieval debate as to the number of angels that
could dance on the head of a pin.

23.

The Aging Borderline

Joel Sadavoy, M.D.

Late-life borderline phenomena pose a variety of diagnostic and management problems. Although recent research has begun to define more clearly the boundaries of borderline personality disorder (BPD) in younger patients, we have very little research data, with the exception of incidental references (Snyder, Goodpaster, Pitts, Pokorny, and Gustin, 1985), on the natural evolution of borderline symptoms into old age. We have yet to begin to define systematically the similarities and differences in signs and symptoms of presentation. We need to know more about the nature of the stresses of old age that promote symptom expression. We also need data on the differentiation of BPD from regressive phenomena precipitated by decline, loss, and dependency, as well as identifying specific features of the management of these symptoms in the aged. Indeed, with regard to the latter issue of management, our inquiry is further confounded by the paucity of data on whether basic personality change is possible in late life. Does the personality remain rigid, unyielding to even the best therapeutic efforts, or is there a continuing plasticity of personality that can be exploited to induce change? Some authors (Rechtshaffen, 1959) have even suggested that defensive structures are more amenable to therapeutic intervention in old age, although they certainly were not writing about BPD.

In summary, discussion of personality disorder in old age is still at a rudimentary stage reliant upon clinical impression, bolstered by detailed case studies. Particularly for staff working in institutional settings the issue is of great interest. Often, the personality disordered patient and his or her family create the greatest demands on staff for care. Indeed, in our institution, when geriatricians express their highest priority for psychiatric consultation, the help requested relates to the management of these disorders. Institutionalization is probably one of the specific stresses of old age that stimulates regression and exacerbates borderline symptoms. This reaction probably arises from a combination of increased dependency conflicts, forced closeness and intimacy with others, and fears of abandonment. Hence, specific research on institutionalized versus noninstitutionalized patients would be useful.

The recent attempts to define personality disorders have resulted in the derivation of symptom complexes that reliably seem to differentiate BPD, as defined by *The Diagnostic and Statistical Manual of Mental Disorders* (DSM-III-R) from other diagnostic entities (American Psychiatric Association, 1987). On close inspection, however, considerable overlap remains among the personality syndromes, a feature recognized by the DSM-III-R "grouping" of personality disorders into three clusters: Cluster A, the odd or eccentric types (paranoid, schizoid, and schizotypal); Cluster B, the dramatic, emotional types (borderline, narcissistic, antisocial, and histrionic); and Cluster C, the anxious, fearful types (avoidant, dependent, obsessive–compulsive, and passive–aggressive). A fourth cluster is comprised of those mixed or otherwise unspecified types, a potentially large group which may be especially relevant in old age.

It is interesting, and perhaps not surprising given the paucity of research data, that factors of aging are mentioned very infrequently in the DSM-III-R section on personality disorders. In this section, it is noted that personality disorder begins early in adolescence or adulthood, that major depression may be more frequent as the person approaches middle age, and that features of personality disorder may become less evident after middle age.

BPD VS. BPO

Kernberg's term *borderline personality organization* (BPO) encompasses a wider field than the more narrowly defined syndrome of BPD. While less specific, BPO is perhaps more realistic in incorporating a variety of overlapping features that share common behavioral and psychodynamic properties. As Gunderson has noted (Gunderson, 1984), the narrowly defined BPD (DSM-III-R) would constitute a small proportion of Kernberg's classification of BPO. The core syndrome of the DSM-III-R (BPD) would probably correspond most closely to Kernberg's infantile subgroup. Indeed, BPO seems to encompass many features of all three clusters of the DSM-III-R. To reduce the confusion of overlapping terminology (i.e., BPO and BPD) and the growing body of data that convincingly define BPD as a reliably definable entity, it may be wise to follow Gunderson's suggestion that the term *severe character disorder* be substituted for BPO.

The paucity of research on the elderly in this diagnostic area makes it difficult, at this stage, to use highly specific terminology; hence, the concept of severe character disorder (BPO), while less rigorous, is more clinically applicable at this point. However, because BPO is in common usage, it will be used interchangeably with severe character disorder in this chapter.

DIAGNOSIS OF SEVERE CHARACTER PATHOLOGY IN OLD AGE

The process of aging imposes stresses that are derived from forces beyond the control of the individual but which interact with preexisting personality structures. These personality structures, while recognizable throughout the life of the individual, do not necessarily remain fixed. The behavior of the patient when young sometimes appears different on the surface than when he or she becomes old.

Based on present definitions, personality diagnosis is an amalgam of current behavior with evidence of its origins in early adulthood or adolescence. Until we can clarify whether or not behavior and personality structure remain constant into old age, this element of diagnosis remains tentative. We are probably on safe ground conceptualizing psychodynamic factors in the personality as being constant throughout life and into old age. However, behavioral expression may change, as I will discuss below.

Diagnosis in the elderly is further complicated by the need to distinguish between institutionalized patients and those who continue to live in relative independence. Moreover, the factors that influence behavior and that arise with aging are different, depending on the age cohort of the patient and other demographic variables, notably gender. The personal, emotional, and physical resources of the individual shift and evolve with the changing stages of old age, causing an alteration in the phenomenology of the behavioral manifestations of personality disorder. For example, the action-oriented and dramatic manifestations of borderline behavior may be best conceptualized as being phase-specific to the younger borderline. As old age gradually erodes both the capacity for aggressive, sexual, or other impulsive behavior, as well as the satisfaction that can be derived from such activity, these behaviors diminish in drama and intensity. Impulsivity is defined in DSM-III-R borderline criteria as comprised of erratic sexual activity, impulsive spending, shoplifting, reckless driving, and binge eating. Clearly, all of this behavior is much less common in the elderly. Physical incapacities, dependency on others for financial and social support, intellectual decline, reduced physical attractiveness, narrowed social and interpersonal contacts, and other similar factors all conspire to restrict the expression of impulsive, action-oriented behavior characteristic of Cluster B dramatic personality types. However, the dynamics which drove the patient to such behavior in youth still remain.

Diagnosis of severe personality disorder is sometimes further obscured because of difficulties in differentiating behavior associated with age-specific developmental adaptations from lifelong personality disorder. A variety of stressors affect all aging individuals, although they have greater impact on those whose basic personality organization has a borderline structure. These factors include major and frequent interpersonal losses, especially of close, sustaining relationships. However, for the aging individual with severe character disorder, the effect of these losses is compounded by their preexisting deep fears of abandonment and empty aloneness. For any aging person, with or without character disorder, loss of a spouse, sibling, or close friend creates intense emotions of loss, grief, and fear. Even the most cohesive person suffers feelings of loss of self-cohesion when longstanding relationships that have become incorporated into the fabric of the individual's sense of self are dissolved by death, illness, mental decline, and so on. Reconstitution may be a slow and painful process, accompanied by regressive behaviors easily misinterpreted as personality disorder. For example, even well-integrated, mature personalities may become very clinging and importuning; they may project their bitterness and become somewhat paranoid; they may withdraw and reject help, all the while complaining about their emptiness; narcissistic haughtiness and jealousy may develop along with exquisite sensitivity to any real or perceived rejections or criticisms; they may blame others for their misfortune. An important discriminating feature in diagnosis is that, in general, such symptoms do not become entrenched in the more mature personality. Such individuals regress temporarily but, with regenerated interests, redirection of affection, and so on, the behavior remits. The more borderline individual, however, tends to remain locked in these aberrant patterns. The reasons are multidetermined, arising from multifactorial psychodynamic features (Sadavoy, 1987a). However, these aging individuals are unlikely to escape experiencing prolonged grief reactions which sometimes become chronic and may be characterized by emotional features of intense narcissism, object hunger, help rejection, complaints, projection, splitting, and intermittent withdrawal. Often, these individuals first come to the family physician's attention as either desperate families or patients seek relief from intense affective states, often accompanied by somatized complaints. It is most important to differentiate between normal intense grief in a mature personality and borderline grief which will likely become prolonged and be very difficult to manage. Indeed, prolonged, or otherwise aberrant grief and inability to mourn, is a hallmark of BPO in the elderly.

Physical disability, loss of beauty and physical power, and alterations of social roles all lead to obvious narcissistic assaults in old age. They are accompanied by what may be called the normative intergenerational empathic lag (Sadavoy, 1988). This lag is a social phenomenon that has tended to stereotype the identity of the aging individual and leads to devaluation or idealization. Whichever polarity results, there is little awareness in those who are younger of the continuing vibrant, inner psychological life that persists in the aging person. Interestingly, clinical data repeatedly reveals that such internal states are generally rooted in a self-concept that is much younger than the individual's actual age and that is, therefore, inconsistent with the person's chronological age and capacities. Younger individuals generally lag behind in their understanding of the inner identity of the old, and unwittingly react in ways that become narcissistically assaultive and inherently rejecting. The more mature person can handle these assaults, albeit with sadness, anger, or surprise. The borderline individual may be devastated.

Earlier defensive modes of coping with narcissistic vulnerabilities and fears of fragmentation or basic aloneness may have been tied to structured activity, work, physical performance, or seductive sexual attractiveness. These specific defenses, so important to the maintenance of self-cohesion in younger years, are reliant on youthful, physical capacities, appearance, and so on, which, when lost in old age, may lead to the emergence of previously compensated borderline symptoms.

> For example, an eighty-two-year-old woman was referred by her family for "depression." She and her children had always had a mixed relationship strained by her intense narcissistic needs for admiration. She was famous for being the belle of the ball wherever she went—beautiful, fashionable, and theatrical. Indeed, in her early adult years, she had been successful briefly, as an actress and pianist. As she aged, some of her overt flirtatiousness and flamboyance was channeled into community activity, where appearance rather than substance remained the

stimulus for the admiration and envy of others. With advancing years, despite her attempts to hang onto her "prestige" and grandness, her beauty was transformed, her energy declined, and her admirers and suitors were lost. She tried to retain her old "look" but succeeded only in creating a caricature of her former self—inappropriate attempts at youthful dress and elegant hairstyles. Her gradual awareness of her losses led to symptoms. She began to abuse alcohol, drinking secretly and heavily. She threatened suicide and "languished" in her home. While still protesting her importance, she became uncertain, easily agitated, sleepless, and demoralized. Utimately, she had to be hospitalized to place some external structure and control on her symptoms. It was quickly evident to treatment staff that her "depression" was not a primary diagnostic concern. Treatment addressed her need to adapt to her new self-image and the shift in her interpersonal relationships that accompanied her evolving self-concept. She was successfully discharged home after several months of individual, group, and family psychotherapy.

This case vignette illustrates both one type of symptom picture that can evolve in old age as well as the natural history of some individuals with BPO. While circumstances in earlier life stages fortuitously permitted her to lead a compensated emotional life, old age led to specific assaults against which the patient could no longer defend. The case also shows that, while acting out behavior is much less common in old age than in youth, it is by no means unknown. In an earlier report of a severely borderline geriatric patient (Sadavoy and Dorian, 1983), the potential for acting out was well demonstrated.

Mrs. A., a seventy-one-year-old widow, was admitted to the hospital ten months prior to psychiatric consultation, after suffering a hip fracture. Initially, her physical rehabilitation progressed well until she took an overdose of several drugs that she had been secretly hoarding. This incident was precipitated by her being informed that she would not be able to return home to her apartment. After her overdose, Mrs. A.'s course was steadily downhill, complicated by grand mal seizures, episodes of bronchospasm, cardiac failure, and several admissions to the intensive care unit.

Past medical history included irritable bowel syndrome, psoriasis, hypothyroidism, and macrocytic anemia due to dietary deficiency. Her personal history revealed lifelong chaotic and transient relationships, especially with her husband and children.

When she was younger and less vulnerable, she demonstrated a narcissistic coping style. She was vain, proud, haughty, cold, and remote, even to those who were closest to her. Those she could control and who responded to her needs were idealized; all others were villified and rejected, including her children and mother.

Unlike many narcissistic personalities, however, this patient's coping ability was fragile and frequently broke down throughout her life to reveal aspects of the more primitive, borderline behavioral picture that was later seen in the hospital. These breakdowns revealed a fragmented underlying sense of self that was prone to easy temporary disintegration, especially under the strains of abandonment, physical illness, and institutionalization.

At the time of the initial consultation, Mrs. A. presented herself as a haggard, emaciated, chronically ill-looking woman. She was dressed in a hospital gown, sitting half in and half out of bed; she had an oxen mask dangling about her neck and was surrounded by an incredible clutter of papers, books, clothes, and trays of half-eaten food. Her hair was cut mannishly short and she was totally ungroomed. Her manner was dramatic, with an exaggerated range of affective responses. Her speech was circumstantial and vague and her mood was melancholy, although not depressed or suicidal. Mrs. A. characterized her state and that of the hospital as "bedlam." She reviled her roommate and her present doctors and nurses, while extolling those from the past whom she had equally vilified during their term of care. She had a litany of somatic complaints; yet, she stated that her life would be hopeless if she could not leave the hosptial. She desperately feared becoming demented like some of those around her.

The initial request for psychiatric consultation was based on Mrs. A.'s continued dependence on supplemental oxygen which she used inappropriately and irregularly despite her stable cardiorespiratory status. When attempts were made to remove the oxygen tank from her room, she became flooded with anxiety and threatened to commit suicide. Frequently this reaction was associated with severe apparent respiratory distress, raising staff concerns about the medical and legal implications of removing the oxygen. Moreover, Mrs. A. frequently and illicitly smoked in bed, which lead to an obvious risk of fire and explosion since she kept the oxygen mask with her and demanded control of the oxygen flow herself.

Subsequent discussion with the staff revealed many covert reasons for the consultation beyond the use of oxygen. These reasons included Mrs. A.'s hoarding of food; the filth and disarray of her room; attempts, often successful, to control her treatment regime; her refusal to get dressed or to leave her room; her sitting on the commode for hours in her room; and her abuse of her roommates, always ending in their transfer to another room at the insistence of their incensed relatives. The staff felt demoralized, angry, helpless, and terrorized. The true underlying reason for the consultation was the staff members' desire to have the patient transferred off their ward.

Using regressive defenses, she attempted to compensate for her inner emptiness by clinging to various comforting inanimate objects such as food, oxygen, cigarettes, and mementos—objects that could be viewed as serving a desperate but unsuccessful transitional role. Although this behavior had some limited success in controlling her environment, she was unable to control her underlying physical illness, the most potent symbol threatening her annihilation. As a result, she was under a constant sense of threat and helplessness which, at times, led to the breakdown of her perception of reality, with subsequent minipsychotic episodes of paranoia and visual hallucinations which often ended in her admission to the intensive care unit with associated acute respiratory distress.

It is common wisdom that personality disorder declines in frequency with advancing age (Solomon, 1981). Cluster B symptoms, dramatic acting out in particular, seem to decline (Reich, Ndvaguba, and Yates, 1988). In the young–old (60+ age) group of Reich et al.'s sample, however, there is a slight rise in prevalence of Cluster B symptoms. No information is yet available to tell us about the middle or old–old populations, nor is there a distinction between community- and institutional-living aged. Reich et al. were intrigued by the upturn in symptoms in the old-age group. They suggest this rise could be an effect of aging per se or, alternatively, an unmasking by late-life stresses of vulnerabilities already present: I favor the latter explanation. While dramatic and narcissistic features are uncovered in old age, the expression of these symptoms is different. Gone are the dramatic incomplete suicides, self-mutilations, serious drug abuse, and antisocial features such as stealing. Instead, the forum for acting out is more restricted and interpersonally directed—demandingness, verbal attacks, frequent pleas for help from physicians and family or sometimes other authorities, and increased alcohol or prescription drug abuse.

The Reich study showed even stronger trends for anxiety-cluster traits to increase with age; this finding makes clinical and intuitive sense. The upsurge in intense symptoms are likely to be concurrent with the more vulnerable individual's attempts to cope with anxiety.

Dramatic acting out is more often threatened than performed, although it can be alarmingly convincing.

For example, an eighty-three-year-old man was admitted to a geriatric psychiatric unit because of his uncontrollable behavior in a home for the aged. He was mildly demented but essentially intact. He had always been a man who experienced the world as dangerous and attacking, with much justification considering his Holocaust experiences. During that time, however, rather than passively accepting his fate, he resisted and met violence with violence. Controlled aggressive behavior continued in a somewhat adaptive form during his subsequent adult years, but led to crisis once he became dependent and forced into the intimacy of institutional life because of physical decline. To cope with the imposed and intolerable sense of helplessness he began to hoard razor blades, pins, scissors, and knives. On one occasion, he scratched himself, but generally, he just threatened suicide. He became too threatening for staff to manage when his suicidal feelings became complicated by paranoid ideation—someone had stolen his money from his room he thought—leading to physical threats against staff.

This patient's personality had always been difficult, in part because of his aggressiveness, and in part because of his narcissistic sensitivity and projective stance. In the old-age home, he played favorites with new staff, quickly becoming accusatory if they failed him. In other words, his personality structure had borderline features with a strong dramatic flavor. These behaviors were adaptive and controlled in younger years when they could be channeled appropriately, but became maladaptive and increasingly regressive and self-directed under the impact of old-age dependency needs and blocking of his previous channels of defensive expression.

Vulnerability to and intolerance of intimate relationships is a central diagnostic feature of BPO. These relationships are characterized by desperate seeking out of idealized relationships followed by deep disappointment and devaluation at the slightest perceived problems. At the root of these responses are unconscious fears of incorporation by the loved and feared object existing side-by-side with primitive rage and the fear of destroying the loved and needed object. The chaos seen in the relationships of younger borderlines is similar to that of old age, but it changes subtly in the older person. The "other" is no longer only needed and demanded in fantasy. Real dependency needs—physical, economic, and environmental—make these relationships essential.

A young borderline mother abandoned her children inter-mittently in her younger years. Advancing age caused her to reestablish a dependent link. The subsequent ambiva-lence on both sides led to a painful relationship, but one with which the patient could no longer cope by running and distancing. Instead, she focused on her physical needs and expressed her demands based on her failing capac-ities.

Breslau (1987) has described this particular form of symp-tom expression as the exaggerated helplessness syndrome.

Uncovering and understanding the special factors that lead to breakdown in elderly borderlines is one important factor in diagnosis. However, the clinician should be aware of the poten-tial for similar features to arise in highly stressed and regressed individuals whose underlying personality structure does not show borderline vulnerability. A careful longitudinal psychody-namic history is obviously essential to accomplish this. However, such histories are not always easy to elicit. Secondary sources may be necessary and may constitute the primary source of information. Yet, recent evidence from Steingart at Baycrest Hospital (personal communication) suggests that the family's descriptions of impaired and regressed parents (as measured by the Adult Personality Rating Scale) who are depressed are much more diagnostic of personality disorder during the acute phases of illness. Their recollections of behavior gradually change, however, as symptoms are treated and their descrip-tions of past behavior become less indicative of personality-based pathology. In other words, acute stress colors both the patient's story and appearance, as well as the memories of the family. In situations of chronic stress (e.g., institutionalization), initial reports of past behaviors should be accepted with some caution. Zimmerman, Pfohl, Coryell, Stangl, and Corenthal (1988) have reported on some of the discrepancies between diagnosis of personality disorder based on direct patient inter-views versus secondary sources.

BORDERLINE PERSONALITY AND DEPRESSION

One of the major difficulties in evaluating personality factors in old age is the overlap which occurs between symptoms of chronic depression and personality disorders. This issue has been addressed by Kocis and Frances (1987). It is clear that under the impact of external stress individuals may respond with long-standing depressive episodes, the components of which often contain elements that overlap with personality diagnoses, particularly dependent and mixed personality disorders as well as narcissistic disorders. These states are variably responsive to medication and other traditional interventions for affective disorder. In particular, in institutionalized patients, where the day-to-day stresses of aloneness, abandonment, and interpersonal intensity abound, the ongoing perpetuating factors interfere with the course of treatment.

Further preliminary work on the nature of dramatic symptomatology in patients who receive psychiatric consultation in the chronic care institution suggests that those patients who are the most "difficult" often have a long history of previous depressive illness. The retrospective diagnoses, once again, are highly suspect, but one must consider that major "personality problems" in the institution are the result of a continued vulnerability to chronic depression or dysthymia that have attached to it the well-recognized features of personality disorder that often accompany depression (Liebowitz, Stallone, Dunner, and Fieve, 1979; Hirschfeld, Klerman, Clayton, Keller, McDonald-Scott, and Larkin, 1983; Koenigsberg, Kaplan, Gilmore, and Cooper, 1985). The results of these studies promote caution in accepting the diagnosis of an entrenched long-standing personality disorder. Furthermore, based on clinical experience and the work of Zimmerman et al. (1988), it is evident that patients provide unrealiable data in their retrospective descriptions of their symptoms. This inaccuracy is due partly to the coloring of past experiences by the patient's current situation, which leads either to unrealistic idealization of the past or to depressive bleakness. Hence, the differential diagnosis of borderline personality in the elderly is confounded by a variety of factors, including the presence of massive external stresses altering the personality function on the basis of regression, the overlay of dysthymic or major depression producing artifacts of personality resembling the borderline spectrum disorders, and the difficulty of determining accurate diagnoses of personality, the most crucial feature of which is the capacity of the diagnostician to determine the presence of these symptoms from early adulthood.

Finally, in considering diagnostic and etiological factors, one must examine whether aging can have an ameliorating and not just an exacerbating effect on symptom expression. In youth, as has been pointed out above, the intrapsychic confrontation of the borderline with basic fears of abandonment, engulfment, destructiveness, and so on may be dealt with by utilizing dramatic defensive behaviors. Generally, there are few external limits that effectively prevent the often chaotic expression of such maladaptive attempts to cope with internal fragmentation, anxiety, and rage. In old age, this freedom of expression becomes restricted. Symptom expression then changes, and it may be viewed as a channeling or structuring of behavior induced by de facto external confrontations and limits set by the process of aging itself. Significant others also begin to see the aging person as more vulnerable and therefore more "controllable," leading them to feel freer to intervene and stop aberrant behavior, sometimes for the first time in the history of the relationship. This artificial "splitting" of the personality by age may reduce reliance on magical, denial-based defenses, and may further control impulsiveness by constant reinforcement of an image of old-age helplessness.

CLINICAL PICTURE IN OLD AGE

As has already been pointed out, the data is not yet systematically gathered to establish precise and reliable statements about reproducible symptom clusters in old age. However, certain features emerge with some consistency (Sadavoy, 1987b).

As stated above, the expression of pathology shifts from action-oriented, dramatic behavior to an interpersonal and somatic focus. Hypochondriacal symptoms become much more pervasive and are the prime vehicle for eliciting the needed responses of concern, availability, and caretaking. For example, a woman of sixty-nine, with a long history of documented personality disorder and affective illness, was admitted to a geriatric psychiatry inpatient unit for treatment of acute paranoid symptoms. Her paranoia quickly disappeared, without specific treatment other than the nurturing comfort of the milieu, and did not return. In its place arose intense but unverifiable somatic concerns and claims of physical illness. Despite her obvious vigor, she clung to nurses and physicians protesting that "all the others think they're sick, but I'm the sickest one on the ward."

Narcissistic features often become more pronounced in old age. These features are somewhat different in old age, however, because protestations of grandness, ability, and achievement, and demeaning, haughty attitudes toward others are in marked contrast to the visible effects of aging. Hence, this mode of defense provokes not only anger in caregivers and peers, but mocking ridicule. In the words of one group member responding to another who was protesting her specialness: "Who do you think you are? We are all the same here. Old, sick, and useless."

The often constant failure of the environment to provide rewards for dramatic symptom expression in old age drives behavior inward, producing the third major pathway of defensive expression in the aging borderline—depressive withdrawal. Because dysphoria, dysthymia, and depression are so common in old age, these states of borderline withdrawal are easily misdiagnosed as depressive syndromes and, as noted above, the reciprocal diagnostic dilemma also presents itself. Generally, however, personality disordered patients are more refractory to antidepressant medication, the most potent form of therapy being interpersonal and environmental.

Borderline Personality and Dementia

One additional aspect of symptom expression deserves further comment. Here I refer to the effect which dementing illness has on the symptoms. While some very primitive borderlines, in youth, are subject to "flooding of emotional response" (Volkan, 1976), the less emotionally chaotic members are able to defend against such states. Their relationship to reality remains basically intact although intermittently and temporarily disrupted. Paranoid symptoms flare and die like sunspots. Memories of painful and aberrant upbringing are suppressed and often "forgotten" as the individual deals with intense day-to-day involvements.

The capacity to defend against overwhelming emotion or to rechannel it into acting out behavior may be lost in old age, and particularly so when dementia supervenes. The dementing process is often accompanied by the return of unmodified and perhaps previously repressed feelings and memories of relationships that had not been worked through. These memories may be from early childhood or from traumatic adult experiences. Although not borderline, an instructive example is the vulnerability of Holocaust survivors who, when dementing, begin to reexperience concentration camp memories with renewed immediacy, vigor, and vividness. Similarly, there is the return of traumatic dreams which may have been quiescent for years. Dementing patients with severe character disorder are also vulnerable to a similar return of overwhelming affect, often experienced as unmodified anxiety. Because their capacity to distinguish past and present is gradually eroded, the memories are reified and take on an immediacy and reality leading to emotional flooding. The resultant panic is comprised of the reified past interacting with the conflicts of the immediate environment. For example, anger or disappointment with a caregiver, staff, or family member becomes enmeshed with images from nightmares and with long-past losses and hurts that are merged into a stew of past and present that has lost the orientation of time, place, and person. It is not surprising that such patients are viewed simply as having organic psychosis. In order to comprehend the patient's symptoms and behavior, it is necessary to examine the content of anxiety states, to sort out the features that connect with the past, and those associated with the present (Sadavoy and Robinson, 1989). This examination is perhaps most crucial when early experiences have been traumatic.

As second feature found in patients with BPO and dementia is frequent paranoid symptomatology. The projective stance of earlier years, under the influence of lost orientation and impaired capacity to link cause and effect, will predispose to increased reliance on suspicion and accusation of others. Unlike the more mature individual who develops concrete paranoid delusions when dementing, the personality disordered individual expresses his or her paranoia with an overlay reflecting the underlying character pathology—narcissistic accusation, aggressive and raging attacks, intense fear, and sometimes suicidal wishes.

In general, the BPO group handles dementia more poorly than others. The early awareness of cognitive decline at the onset of the illness provokes narcissistic injury and fears of loss of control that are expressed in vibrant conflict with those who are near. Help is demanded with intense guilt and fear-inducing anxiety, only to be inconsistently rejected as inadequate. These states of anxiety are very difficult to manage because they are a complex mix of premorbid abandonment–engulfment conflicts and current cognitive decompensation.

In summary, the basic clinical picture associated with dementia is given a drama and intensity when associated with BPO that is difficult to diagnose, more refractory to management, and places greater demands on the caregivers.

THERAPEUTIC ISSUES

Whether therapy is intense and continuous or intermittent (Silver and Sadavoy, 1976), a long-term perspective on treatment is essential for younger borderlines. Moreover, the crises that arise in therapy develop largely from the impulsivity and interpersonal problems inherent in the disorder. Additionally, while these patients are often in chaos, they are generally physically healthy adults whose dependency needs arise more from intrapsychic conflict than external "realities." These elements of time perspective in therapy, the impact of uncontrollable external events, and physical health are all obviously quite different in old age than in youth.

Time takes on different implications. Ten years in the life of a seventy-year-old woman, for instance, traverses several critical watersheds. If married, she is statistically likely to be or become widowed; she will encounter the watershed for average mortality; her chances of cognitive decline will more than double; and her physical health, as she approaches age eighty, is statistically more likely to lead to a disabling disorder. In other words, the life matrix of the aging borderline in therapy is in a state of flux and crisis impelled by external forces unconnected with the core personality conflicts.

When treating the elderly, therefore, the therapist cannot necessarily view time as an ally of therapy nor expect a progressive course in the direction of health. This does not mean to imply that therapy of younger patients with severe personality disorders always evolves in a direction of improvement or that the course is predictable. However, geriatric patients of this type will have an inherently more complex treatment course.

What then may the therapist expect when considering the potential for change? In summary, clinical experience suggests that age per se is not a limiting factor in inducing change. If all else remained constant, the older adult can be expected to engage in therapy in much the same fashion as a younger patient. Transference themes are often intense and unstable, easily shifting from positive idealization to negative rage and disappointment. Eroticization of the primitive transference occurs in the old just as in the young, but may not be easily understood as such unless sought out. Similarly, dream content may be vivid and express the basic conflicts of the therapy, just as it does with younger patients. One important difference is the frequent presence of a spouse and adult children in the transference relations which some developmental theorists suggest represent basic intrapsychic change in the patient's object world. Not only does the therapist confront parental and sibling transference figures from early life, he or she encounters figures internalized through deep adult relationships in marriage and parenthood.

The following vignette illustrates the richness of the material. It is comprised of elements of the therapy of a seventy-five-year-old woman who was in treatment for three years once a week. Therapy began at the request of her physician to help her deal with an overwhelming, unresolving grief-reaction which followed the death of her husband. As brief background, it is noteworthy that she had an early adult history of promiscuity, abortion, and suicide attempt preceded by a childhood characterized by withdrawal, emotional deprivation, and intense sibling rivalry. Internally, she experienced the world as unjust, a perspective that often provoked stormy rage.

Within two months of beginning therapy, the patient began to develop an idealized relationship with the therapist. While the content of her sessions was filled with a flood of emotionally significant events and descriptions of intense affect, particularly depression and rage, she began slowly to make reference to her relationship to the therapist. During an early session she spoke of the feeling that she could "now tolerate some of my symptoms" because she knew she could come in to speak to her therapist about them. This early idealization permitted a gradual freeing up of a variety of extremely painful early memories characterized by loss and abandonment. She had a great need to reveal these feelings although they caused her serious pain and sometimes released difficult-to-control affective symptoms. For example, she recalled in one session her painful relationship with her mother, and then cried unremittingly for the next two days.

Sessions were frequently filled with descriptions of her feelings of anxiety, emptiness, and despair, affects mobilized by the death of her husband, but clearly repetitions of frequent feelings that she had experienced throughout her life. As therapy progressed, it became possible to begin to link the current emotions that she was experiencing with long-standing patterns and to begin tentatively to make genetic interpretations. At first, the patient was fearful about her revelations and, at times, she angrily accused the therapist of not understanding the things that she was telling him. As therapy progressed, her affective expression began to change. The periods of noctural rage which characterized the early phases of therapy (during which she would pace around the house, cursing and swearing at her dead husband and other ambivalently held objects in her life) gradually remitted, and were replaced by softer states of tearfulness and depressive sadness.

As her anger diminished and rudimentary feelings of trust developed in therapy, the patient began to describe some of her dreams. Initially these were characterized by anxiety and searching. For example, she had a repetitive dream, which had continued uninterruptedly for most of her life and into her old age, in which she was running through halls trying doors on all sides but unable to open any of them. In another dream, she reported running through a railroad station looking for someone, she wasn't sure who, going through a door and being told that the person had just moved and was next door. The mood in the dream was anxious, although not panicky, and when she awoke she was always sad. It was suggested that this feeling was precipitated by her husband's death but, more importantly, was a feeling that went back to much earlier periods of her life, particularly her feelings of rejection by her mother. Following the intervention, she began to describe in more detail some of her childhood; she remembered how her mother went away to a TB sanitarium for one year when the patient was six years old, leaving her with her grandmother. During that time, she recalled that she had her tonsils out, staying in hospital for a week, lonely and in pain, but not daring even to ask for a drink. The pain and sadness of her childhood memories were revealed dramatically as she described these and other events. A flood of deprivation and loneliness then followed with memories of deprived poverty, never having had a toy, and lonely isolation from other children around her. It was at that time that she began to develop a fantasy life characterized by narcissistic grandiose fantasies of being admired by others. It would appear that this inner fantasy life had characteristics of a transitional object, her only one which converted her into her own mothering figure and nurtured her in the absence of anyone outside who she felt understood or cared for her.

It was only after the first year of therapy that the patient began to reveal other aspects of her earlier life. She spoke of her suicidal thoughts, her intense phobic anxiety in university classes, her suicide attempt, and sexual indiscretions. She was intensely ashamed of these events, not only because of her re-membered feelings but also because, in the transference, she was experiencing a return of many of these sexual feelings and, at times, impulses. She recounted a dream in which she was standing in a room when her husband came up behind her and put his arms around her. She felt intense sexual stimulation. The scene shifted and she found herself in a bedroom standing fully clothed, seeing her husband lying on the bed asleep. An-other man broke into the room and approached the bed where her husband was lying. She became terrified and began scream-ing to wake her husband. However, her voice was muffled in the dream and all she could do was feel immense pressure in her head as she tried to awaken him and realized that she could not. In relating the dream she spoke with uncertainty and then continued to describe some of the strong sexual feelings that she had experienced. She said that she had not intended to speak about sex in her therapy or about that part of this dream, but, in spite of herself, she revealed her feelings.

> She talked about her strong self-attacking moral feeling about sexuality and about her concern that her sexual feel-ings were still very powerful. She would find herself spon-taneously fantasizing sexually and having to control her-self through activity in order to bring herself "back under control." She struggled with the feeling that her sexual impulses were inappropriate to her age while, on the other hand, fearful that she might lose them. She said "they are after all a feeling of life." As she talked, she began to think for the first time that she would like to find a sexual partner for herself although she felt that people would be

outraged, not only at the lack of morality but also the fact that this was occurring in old age.

In this fashion, this bright, accomplished, but very troubled woman gradually worked through a variety of intense emotions and feelings rooted in early abandonment experiences which were perpetuated by failures of adult relationships and exacerbated by the stresses of old age. The case demonstrates the liveliness of conflict and primitive feeling into old age as well as the potential for intensive insight-oriented therapy with the patient of primitive character development. While the dangers of regression are present in this therapy, as long as the patient's ego capacities are relatively intact with regard to health and cognitive ability, the patient's age should not be a specific barrier to an attempt to deal with conflicts at an intrapsychic level in therapy. The temptation, when such a patient presents, is to characterize the symptom solely as intense aberrant and prolonged grief and perhaps to treat with tranquilizing or antidepressant medication. In this instance, medications were entirely avoided and psychotherapy alone instituted. Despite the difficulties, the premorbid personality problems, the regressive episodes during therapy, and the patient's age, she successfully negotiated the vicissitudes of treatment and made substantial life changes reflective of intrapsychic change. Toward the end of therapy, she spoke of feeling a sense of strength and personal value that had alluded her for the whole of her life. It would have been a major loss to have deprived this woman of the opportunity to explore herself and make these important gains. On follow-up, two years after therapy ended, the patient was well and had no return of the intense and decompensating affective states that had plagued her in the past.

INPATIENT TREATMENT

In general, it is good clinical practice to avoid hospitalization for the elderly unless it is clearly indicated, but there are a variety of reasons why hospitalization becomes necessary for the borderline elderly. These factors are not dissimilar to those of younger patients. A major destabilizing element is breakdown of support systems, leading to intense anxiety states, suicidal ideation, withdrawal from others, and extreme agitation, sometimes ending in brief psychotic episodes. Because elderly patients with BPO generally have markedly aberrant relationships with close family members, the family structure of the borderline elderly is not able to tolerate the increasing dependency needs of the parent. The therapist of such a patient is faced not only with the need to treat the individual but also with the generally long-standing conflicts inherent in his or her relationships with children and/or spouse. Helplessness, desperation, scapegoating, angry withdrawal, guilt induction, and overinvolvement all abound within such systems. It is these circumstances which frequently make outpatient care an impossibility and lead to the need for hospitalization.

Despite concerns about hospitalizing such patients, regression, and overdependency have not been seriously limiting features of therapy. Paradoxically, the greater the sense of caring, security, and reliability which the individual can experience from the institution, the greater his or her capacity to separate without panic if the dischargement process is handled with sensitivity and firmness.

The usefulness of hospitalization for this patient group is dependent on several factors. Simple custodial care and the utilization of medication, so often the major modalities of treatment for the hospitalized elderly, are insufficient. Indeed, they may well add to anxiety and depressive symptoms, exacerbating feelings of hopelessness. Unless symptoms can be alleviated, maladaptive defensive patterns altered, and family interaction addressed, hospitalization will only be a stop-gap measure. The important therapeutic elements in this treatment are: (1) an in-depth understanding of the nature of the patient's expressed behavior, based on psychodynamic understanding; (2) an accurate assessment of the specific stresses on the individual and, in particular, understanding what specific intrapsychic impact the stressors are having at this time; (3) a diagnostic evaluation of the family and social system of the patient, paying particular attention to the underlying unconscious conflicts which have

been exacerbated by the immediate stress situation; (4) implementation of a step-wise and phased treatment program which
includes the coordinated team approach leading to "relationship intrusion" (Sadavoy, Silver, and Book, 1979), integration
into the therapeutic milieu of the ward, intensive individual
psychotherapy, and appropriate utilization of family therapy.
While psychodynamic, interpersonal, and family treatment issues must be stressed in therapy, it is also of special importance
that treatment of the elderly borderline be flexible and include
all appropriate modalities, including the full range of organic
therapies where necessary. In this regard, one should recognize
the frequent need for integrated medical care and the utilization of rehabilitation facilities.

In any population, there are prerequisites for successful
outcome of treatment. Among these prerequisites are the availability to the patient of a source of outside relationships which
can be approached and embraced when the patient is ready; a
capacity for self-support and the development of essential skills;
physical health; and, finally, the cooperation of fate in maintaining a congenial environment in which growth can be encouraged and sustained.

In the geriatric population, regardless of the patient's diagnosis, there are obvious impediments to any intensive therapy.
For example, the fantasized dependent relationship that the
younger patient has in therapy, which may be successfully
worked through in therapy, is immeasurably complicated by
the reality that the older person is frequently dependent on
the therapist and/or the institution for basic life support. This
difficulty is especially true when there is no opportunity for
that individual to return to an independent living situation and
the end point of treatment thereby becomes adaptation to living
in a group setting of some sort. The therapist must also take
into consideration the reality that the patient's outlet for gratification is often extremely restricted. While this is by no means
always the case, the older person often does not have the resources or capacity to reach out to others around him in order
to form close, interpersonal ties. Similar impediments exist in
introducing occupational or other gratifying activities into the
patient's life. For inpatient therapy to be useful, therefore, goals

must be carefully established and realistically evaluated. The therapist must consider the real social situation that the patient faces, the capacities of that individual to take independent control of his or her life, the impact of real dependency needs on the patient and the therapeutic situation, and the requirements of the patient's family to alter their expectations and approaches to that individual.

In general terms then, the goals of hospitalization may be broadly stated as follows: (1) removal of the patient from a stressful situation; (2) reestablishment of internal homeostasis with attention to physical needs and concurrent reduction of anxiety and depression; (3) diagnosis of intrapsychic pathology, family pathology, and inappropriate behavior based on defensive maneuvers; (4) institution of individualized treatment; (5) appropriate discharge planning.

It is the final stage of therapy, the disengagement process, which is often most problematic in this age group. This is difficult not only because of the need to institutionalize certain patients permanently, but also because the process of disengagement is different in the elderly than it is for the younger patient. For example, rather than preparing a patient for continued long-term intensive psychotherapy, a useful goal in younger patients, a frequent primary goal of inpatient therapy is to prepare the aging individual for reintegration into a relatively dependent living situation, be this with family, spouse, or in an institutional setting. The inpatient treatment team must focus specifically on modifying the patient's defensive need to maintain control over others which is often expressed through a variety of manipulative behaviors reflective of abandonment anxiety and narcissistic needs. The patient often must be helped to adapt to a new level of dependency and to begin to tolerate the intense relationships inherent in institutional life or, at best, an increasing reliance on others.

CONCLUSION

In summary, we can conclude that the symptoms of personality pathology remain active and vibrant into old age. While they change in focus away from the more impulsive action-oriented defenses, the symptoms remain highly challenging to the treatment team. It is further evident that psychotherapeutic approaches (often in combination with necessary pharmacological treatment) can not only be effective but may be essential to the treatment outcome. It is most important that treatment units be aware of the necessity of this type of intervention and that it not be denied to patients because of the fear of promoting undue dependence or regression. Equally important, however, is the understanding that treatment units must consciously be designed to deal with these problems. Not every unit has either the interest or the capacity to do so. In such instances, it is probably in the patient's interest to provide focused symptom relief and rapid discharge.

24.

Eating Disorders and Borderline Personality Disorder

Paul E. Garfinkel, M.D., F.R.C.P. (C), and Ruth Gallop, R.N., Ph.D.

Anorexia nervosa (AN) and bulimia nervosa (BN) are complex disorders that have become common in the past fifteen years. Anorexia nervosa is characterized by an all-consuming pursuit of thinness which overrides the patient's physical and psychological well-being. The person begins to diet, ostensibly to alter her weight, but this desire masks a pervasive sense of helplessness (Bruch, 1973). Pursuing a thin body becomes an isolated area of personal control in a world in which the individual feels ineffective; the dieting provides an artificial sense of mastery and control. As the weight loss progresses, a starvation state ensues, which eventually develops a life of its own, leading to the features of AN.

Bulimia is characterized by episodic patterns of binge eating with a sense of loss of control, usually followed by extreme efforts to lose weight, and depressive moods. Bulimia can occur as a symptom in many illnesses, including AN, and as a separate syndrome, with little weight loss (BN). While this chapter will briefly review some of the features of these disorders, the main focus will be a discussion of the relationship between borderline personality disorder (BPD) and the eating disorders.

Anorexia nervosa occurs in about 1 percent of young women and BN occurs in 2 to 3 percent of women (Crisp, Palmer, and Kalucy, 1976; Pyle, Mitchell, Eckert, and Halvorson, 1983; Cooper and Fairburn, 1983). More mild variants of these disorders occur in about 5 percent. About 95 percent of cases are female. These eating disorders remain serious problems, causing significant mortality (about 5%) and morbidity (about 25% of patients develop a chronic form).

The hallmark of these eating disorders is the exaggerated desire for thinness and intense fear of fatness. The person states that she feels her body is too large no matter what she weighs, and she offers no explanation for this—merely that she feels better the thinner she is. There is often a denial of illness; the individual does not recognize her changed body is no longer beautiful or healthy. There is usually an associated dissatisfaction with one's body, which may reach a level of loathing.

The intensity of the drive for thinness generates a variety of eating behaviors. Food is hidden, avoided, or toyed with, rather than eaten. Many excuses for missed meals appear. An often complex set of rules regarding foods and their manner of consumption develops, with an unusual awareness of caloric content and magical beliefs about different food groups; many patients develop a long list of forbidden foods, which are frantically sought during binges—namely, high-calorie, carbohydrate-rich items. This is followed by efforts to prevent any gain in weight by vomiting, laxative or diuretic abuse, severe food restrictions, or intense exercising. Physical fitness becomes a means to avoid fatness.

Diminishing consumption of food is accompanied by an increasing preoccupation with it. Patients often collect recipes and work in food-related jobs. This increases the fear of yielding to the impulse to eat and further heightens the prohibitions against it. Characteristic thinking styles emerge, including a black-and-white pattern of reasoning called dichotomous thinking (Garfinkel and Garner, 1982). Patients believe that if they gain a small amount of weight—say from 80 to 85 pounds—they might as well be 200 pounds, since they've "blown the diet" and lost control; there is "no in-between." This type of thinking extends beyond food to intrapsychic and interpersonal beliefs. For example, the rigid exercise pattern must be followed exactly. If one must do 250 sit-ups per day, stopping at 249 will not do—it's all or nothing. Significantly, caregivers are viewed in this all-or-nothing fashion, as all good or all bad. Coupled with this thinking style is a profound sense of self-mistrust which has been termed intrapsychic paranoia (Selvini-Palazzoli, 1974). This mistrust relates to biological signals of hunger and satiety as well as to more purely emotional states. Bodily impulses are not to be experienced, but rather controlled artificially.

There are a number of features associated with BN and AN. These are generally the products of starvation or the effects of repetitive bingeing and purgeing. These have been described elsewhere (Goldbloom and Garfinkel, in press). There are no primary or trait-dependent physiological features of patients with eating disorders known at this time.

THE MULTIDIMENSIONAL NATURE OF THE EATING DISORDERS

Anorexia nervosa and BN can be viewed as illnesses with a variety of predispositions; these result in a particular individual being at risk (Garfinkel and Garner, 1982). As Weiner (1977) has described, illness often results from an interplay of predisposing forces acting upon an individual; many people in a population may have the predisposition to an illness, only some actually develop it. For particular individuals with a disease, the exact interaction of predisposing forces will vary. These predispositions help explain why a particular illness is "chosen." Such risk factors may be quite different from factors which initiate or precipitate the illness. These in turn may be quite different from circumstances which perpetuate the disorder (Weiner, 1977). Common sustaining factors include the presence of the starvation syndrome, relying on vomiting as a means of controlling weight, the familial relationships that change during the illness, and the person's social and educational skills (Garfinkel and Garner, 1982).

The likelihood of developing AN is related to the presence of a number of risk factors which may be conceived to arise from the culture, the family, and the individual.

The cultural component includes the pervasive emphasis on thinness in young women. This, in turn, is responsible for the increased risk for people in professions such as ballet, modeling, and certain competitive sports in which weight regulation is crucial. Pressures on women to perform, to achieve, and to please others rather than to please themselves are also important here (Garner and Garfinkel, 1980).

Familial risk factors include a family history of a depressive illness, alcoholism, or eating disorder, all of which are more common than in the general population (Piran, Kennedy, Garfinkel, and Owens, 1985). A genetic component is strongly suggested by the findings of twin studies which report a concordance rate of 50 percent in monozygous twins, versus a rate of 10 percent in dizygous twins (Holland, Hall, Murray, Russell, and Crisp, 1984). Particular family patterns in which independence is discouraged may also be a contributor. Family stresses, including separation and losses, often precede the onset.

Risk factors within the individual include fears of the demands of maturation and the increased independence this requires (Crisp, 1970). This, in turn, is related to an underlying sense of personal helplessness and fears of losing control (Bruch, 1973). Weight becomes the only aspect of the individual's life which she feels she can control.

Particular thinking styles may also serve as risk factors; the "dichotomous" thinking referred to previously, personalization and superstitious thinking, are common (Garner and Bemis, 1982). People with eating disorders also have an extremely low sense of personal worth. Frequently their self-worth is governed by external criteria such as parental approval, high grades, and a "look" or an image that is culturally sanctioned. Many people with AN also have a disturbance in self-perception in which they either do not recognize the extent of their weight loss or continue to feel a particular part of the body is too fat no matter what they weigh.

Chronic illness may serve as a risk factor to an eating disorder. Rodin, Johnson, Garfinkel, Daneman, and Kenshole

(1986) conducted a systematic study of female adolescents and young adults with insulin dependent diabetes mellitus (IDDM) and found that 6.5 percent met criteria for AN and 6.5 percent for BN, representing a sixfold and twofold increase respectively in the expected prevalence; a further 6 percent displayed a partial syndrome. Bulimic symptoms were closely associated with poor metabolic control as reflected in blood levels of glyco-sylated hemaglobin. Why adolescents with IDDM may be vulnerable to eating disorders is not known. It may relate to the heightened preoccupation with bodily control through eating that is fostered by attempts to improve metabolic control and reduce later complications.

HETEROGENEITY OF THE EATING DISORDERS

Subtypes of AN have been recognized since Janet (1919) de-scribed obsessional and hysterical forms. He differentiated these on the presence or absence of hunger; and this distinction was reintroduced by Dally (1969), but it has not been supported by research, which has shown that true anorexia is rare until late in the starvation process (Garfinkel, 1974). However, Ja-net's and Dally's observation that certain symptoms such as vomiting, bulimia, and mood lability clustered together in one group of patients was an important insight. It led to later differ-entiation of the bulimic subtype.

Bulimia as a symptom of various illnesses has been recog-nized at least since its description in the Babylonian Talmud (Kaplan and Garfinkel, 1984), written around the year 400 B.C. It was associated with AN in the nineteenth century. For exam-ple, Gull (1874) mentioned overeating in a patient with AN. He noted: "Occasionally for a day or two the appetite was vora-cious," but this increased appetite was rare.

Recent studies (Russell, 1979; Garfinkel, Moldofsky, and Garner, 1980; Casper, Eckert, Halmi, Goldberg, and Davis, 1980) have described the significance of bulimia in AN. The presence of bulimia has characterized a group of anorexic pa-tients with special features. Garfinkel et al. (1980) found that bulimic anorexics were more likely than restricters to have been premorbidly obese, to have mothers who were obese, to vomit, and to abuse laxatives. The bulimic subjects were more impulsive than the restricting group. They were more likely to use alcohol or street drugs, to steal, to mutilate themselves, to be more sexually active, and to have labile moods. They have also been found to have an impulsive cognitive style (Toner, Garfinkel, and Garner, 1987). Character differences between the two groups (Piran, Lerner, Garfinkel, Kennedy, and Brouillette, 1988) will be discussed below.

An important question that has arisen from these observations relates to the relationship between the bulimic form of AN and BN without appreciable weight loss. Garner, Garfinkel, and O'Shaughnessy (1985) found that when bulimics who never met weight loss criteria for AN (i.e., BN), anorexic–bulimic, and anorexic–restricter groups were compared on demographic, clinical, and psychometric variables, the normal-weight bulimic group closely resembled the anorexic-bulimic group. They argued that the presence or absence of bulimia could be of greater diagnostic and etiologic significance than a history of weight loss. While there is clinical value in considering patients with BN and the bulimic form of AN to have many similarities, there must also be differences between these groups which at present are poorly understood.

CHARACTER DISORDER AND THE EATING DISORDERS

Before reviewing what is known about the association of BPD and the eating disorders, a cautionary note is necessary. In addition to the usual problems of validity and reliability of personality disorder diagnoses (Dahl, 1985a) and construct validity of BPD relative to other Axis II diagnoses (Perry and Klerman, 1978), some specific problems exist here. First, many patients with eating disorders are quite young, and have not yet reached an age at which character fully matures (Morgan and Russell, 1975). Second, prospective studies do not exist; all studies to date rely on the assessment of personality in chronically ill patients, and chronic illness itself may affect certain features in the assessment of character. Also, patients with eating disorders frequently have a coexistent major depression (Piran et al., 1985) and this may highlight the validation problems of the BPD diagnosis, given the current controversy that exists between BPD and major depression (Pope and Hudson, 1988).

Moreover, patients with eating disorders develop a starvation state which has profound effects on their thinking, feeling, and behavior (Garfinkel and Garner, 1982) and this may alter the presentation of features related to character pathology. There is some evidence for this view from a study of psychotherapy by Garner et al. (1988). In comparing dynamic and cognitive–behavioral psychotherapies for patients with BN, Garner et al. (1988) noted significant changes in features of character disorder in both groups, when the symptoms of the eating disorder were brought under control. Finally, the studies which have been reported to date suffer from a bias in sample selection—most likely toward severity of character disturbance, since they have been generally derived from populations at tertiary referral centers, where the most seriously ill patients predominate (e.g., Piran et al., 1988; Johnson, Tobin, and Enright, in press) or they have relied on advertisements in newspapers and on radio (e.g., Levin and Hyler, 1986) which are also likely to produce a distortion toward severity of personality disorder.

Akiskal, Hirschfeld, and Yerevanian (1983) and Swift and Wonderlich (1988) have suggested several possible relationships between personality and psychopathology. One possible relationship considers personality to provide a predisposition to the development of a disorder. This will be considered in detail, below. A second possible relationship between personality and psychopathology emphasizes the modifying influence of personality on the expression of psychiatric disorders. As such, personality is not considered a risk factor to the disorder, but rather shapes its expression. To demonstrate this, Akiskal (1984) has used the example of differences in depressed people with obsessive–compulsive versus those with histrionic personality features. With regard to the eating disorders, there have been speculations that outcome may be affected by the presence of unstable and neurotic personality traits (Garfinkel and Garner, 1982) and by a borderline personality disorder (Johnson et al., in press).

A third possible way of understanding the relationship between personality and mental illness is to assume that personality disorders are primarily complications of the disorder. As noted above, Garner et al. (1988) have found that the symptoms of the eating disorder itself may alter personality characteristics. Finally, a fourth possible association suggested by Akiskal et al. (1983) is that personality characteristics are actually attenuated or subclinical forms of other psychiatric disorders. As Swift and Wonderlich (1988) have noted, however, it is difficult to view the personality traits associated with AN and BN (e.g., obsessionality, impulsivity) as subclinical forms of the disorders themselves, and of the four possible relationships, this final one is least relevant to the eating disorders.

Of the various possible relationships between personality and eating disorder, it is the first which considers the personality to be a predisposition to illness, which has received recent attention. Garfinkel and Garner (1982) reviewed the clinical features of bulimic anorexics and concluded that many also have a BPD. They based this on the frequent observation of lability of affect and sense of emptiness in bulimic anorexics, as well as their lack of pleasure and need to artificially control bodily functions. Poor impulse control was noted to be common. Interpersonal relationships were observed to be distorted with fluctuation between transient, superficial ones, and intense dependent ones that led to personal devaluation and anger. While performance at work or school could be maintained by superficial identifications with others, Garfinkel and Garner (1982) felt this often masked a severely disturbed personal identity. Based on these shared features, they concluded that many bulimic anorexics have BPD, and that the BPD serves as a risk factor to the bulimia through the special problems of the borderline in separation and achieving autonomy. They also emphasized that the BPD could not be considered as either necessary or sufficient for the later development of the eating disorder since not all borderline individuals develop an eating disorder with separation or other stress and not all anorexics, or even most, have BPD.

Garfinkel and Garner had based these suggestions on the observations of patients with the bulimic form of AN and on the formulations of several theorists. Especially important were Bruch's (1973) descriptions of the specific deficits in people with AN. In describing AN to be qualitatively different from culturally sanctioned dieting, Bruch emphasized three specific interrelated ego disturbances—in body image, in awareness of interoceptive cues, and in an overall sense of ineffectiveness, which she linked to disordered self-esteem and attempts at self-regulation. Selvini-Palazzoli (1974) and Sours (1974) independently evolved similar formulations on the genesis of AN which focused on the helplessness of the ego.

Masterson (1977) was able to combine views of object relations theorists, with Mahler's (1968) descriptions of the separation–individuation process for an understanding of borderline phenomena in AN. According to Masterson, there is a developmental arrest in borderline individuals in the separation–individuation phase, with the resultant lack of internalized good self–objects. This is presumed to be related to the mother's inability to tolerate the child's efforts to separate and become autonomous. The mother of the borderline patient is thought to reinforce the child's clinging dependency by withdrawing if the child attempts to separate. Through the preteen years such behavior may be quite acceptable and in fact, it has been repeatedly noted how compliant anorexics have been in childhood. After puberty, further striving toward individuation–autonomy tends to threaten this relationship. The child, whose sense of self depends on external confirmation or approval, has fears of abandonment or withdrawal of the mother's love. Viewed in this light, Masterson (1977) considered the borderline individual's development of AN to be adaptive by preventing separation and by substituting obsessional mechanisms for behaviors that encourage individuation. The symptoms may also represent a mechanism for expressing hostility to an ambivalently regarded parent. These issues with separation–individuation, which to some extent correspond to Minuchin, Rosman, and Baker's (1978) concept of the "enmeshed" family, help explain why borderline patients may be overrepresented in an anorexic population.

A recent study by our group attempted to determine whether these theoretical formulations could be empirically verified (Piran et al., 1988). Several earlier studies (Norman and Herzog, 1983; Pyle, Mitchell, and Eckert, 1981) had employed the Minnesota Multiphasic Personality Inventory (MMPI) and found a similar constellation of personality features in restrictive and bulimic anorexics and those with BN, with elevations on the depression, psychopathic deviance, and schizophrenia scales. De Silva and Eysenck (1987) reported on differences between AN subjects and various groups of bulimics, with the bulimic groups scoring high on an addiction scale based on the Eysenck Personality Questionnaire; they also scored higher on psychoticism and neuroticism and lower on social desirability than the AN group. Piran et al. (1988) were interested in DSM-III personality diagnoses, and so each of the bulimic and restricting anorexics in the study were seen by two clinicians who independently arrived at an Axis II diagnosis; this was repeated after patients were treated in the hospital. In addition, all subjects received the diagnostic interview for borderlines (DIB) (Gunderson, Kolb, and Austin, 1981) and the MMPI.

Restricting and bulimic anorexics displayed a differential distribution of DSM-III personality disorder diagnoses. Three-quarters of the restricters fell within the avoidant, compulsive, dependent, and passive–aggressive personality disorders. By contrast, two-thirds of the bulimic anorexics met criteria for the following personality disorders: borderline, histrionic, narcissistic, and antisocial. While the most common personality type for the restricters was an avoidant personality (in about 60%) suggesting the inhibition or control of action, almost half of the bulimics fulfilled criteria for BPD, reflecting a tendency toward discharging impulse through action.

While the bulimics and restricters showed marked differences in BPD diagnoses using DSM-III criteria, these differences did not occur when the groups were compared on the results of the DIB. Gunderson's criteria for BPD were fulfilled by 42 percent of bulimics and 36 percent of restricters; by contrast only 6 percent of the restricters had met DSM-III criteria for BPD. These discrepant findings reflect the fact that the DIB seems to include a wider range of psychopathologic conditions (Kroll, Sines, Martin, Lari, Pyle, and Zander, 1981;

Loranger et al., 1984), especially other personality disorders, as defined by DSM-III. Loranger, Oldham, Russakoff, and Susman (1984) have summarized the results of three studies where the percentages of DIB-positive individuals who are also DSM-III positive for BPD, ranged widely. The DIB appears to assess severe personality disturbance, but with less emphasis on poor impulse control than in the DSM-III criteria; impulsivity is one of the marked characteristics of the bulimic groups. Also the DSM-III criteria specify a series of pathological relationships; many restricters because of their distancing style, have not allowed this pattern to be expressed. It is for these reasons that many restricters were DIB positive in the study by Piran et al. (1988) while being in other personality disorder categories according to DSM-III. The findings from this study strongly suggest that both restricting and bulimic anorexics display major character pathology but that they exhibit differences, especially in the discharge of impulses through action in the bulimic group (Piran et al., 1988). It is the bulimics who meet DSM-III criteria for BPD.

While the Piran study involved only bulimics with AN, similar findings are beginning to emerge from studies of personality in patients with BN. Gwirtsman, Roy-Burne, Yaker, and Gerner (1983) administered an unstructured interview and reported that 44 percent of bulimics met DSM-III criteria for BPD. Levin and Hyler (1986) used structured interviews and found that 25 percent of their sample met criteria for BPO, and 46 percent met the criteria for either BPD or histrionic personality disorder. In the largest study to date, Johnson et al. (in press) reported that 41 percent of 95 consecutive referrals for BN met criteria for a borderline disorder, based on the self-report Borderline Syndrome Index. The BPD group in this study were readily differentiated from the other bulimics by their polysymptomatic clinical picture, more disturbed family environment, and greater psychopathology on the Eating Disorders Inventory (Garner, Olmstead, and Polivy, 1983). Johnson et al. speculated that this group was the most difficult to treat. In the only discrepant study to date, Pope, Frankenberg, Hudson, Jonas, and Yurgelun-Todd (1987) reported a greatly reduced prevalence (2%) of BPD in bulimics; however, their study was based on a revised scoring system for the DIB. Twenty-five percent of their sample would have met criteria for BPD if the previously published scoring procedures were used.

Many patients with eating disorders are admitted to the hospital, without the diagnosis being revealed to the attending staff; for example, a study by Kutcher, Whitehouse, and Freeman (1985) found that 15 percent of the psychiatric beds in Edinburgh were occupied by patients with an eating disorder. For about two-thirds of the patients, the diagnosis was not known to the attending staff, who were frequently treating the patient for features of a character disorder, depression, or alcohol abuse. It is not known with precision how frequently people with BPD have bulimia.

In this discussion we have presented evidence to show an association between BPD and bulimia, whether it be the bulimic form of AN or BN. We have suggested that the personality disturbance may be a risk for the eating disorder by virtue of problems such people have in separation and individuation; and problems with self-esteem and linking self-esteem to external phenomena. A lack of a core identity and certain familial interaction patterns may also contribute to why BPD puts someone at risk for BN. A shared genetic vulnerability may also occur, as can links between serotonin deficiencies and the presence of impulsivity (Van Praag, 1984).

TREATMENT

The treament of AN and BN has been reviewed in a number of recent publications (Garfinkel and Garner, 1982; Garner and Garfinkel, 1985; Johnson and Connors, 1987). While there are differences between the disorders, there are many similarities including in defensive operations, that permit a combined discussion of the two disorders.

We will consider first general issues concerning the attitude of the physician. Aspects of outpatient and inpatient care as well as the role of medication will then be considered.

Attitude of the Physician

People with serious eating disorders are often mistrustful of physicians whom they see as being interested only in refeeding them or making them lose their will and become fat. The physician must encourage normal eating habits and weight without making this the only focus of treatment or a battleground. In the past, some have recommended never openly addressing eating and weight-related issues but only focusing on psychological contributors. By and large, this is not useful and in fact may be antitherapeutic by denying the reality of the condition. Issues about attitudes to weight and foods must be discussed. Also, the physician must emphasize that he or she will stick with the patient through difficult times and focus on many different issues as required. The goal is not control of the patient but rather relief of suffering. However, in the critical "life-threatening" phase the physician will assume control, and this should be stated directly to the patient, clarifying that this decision is based on clinical judgment. The physician must feel comfortable doing this, although the patient may attempt to make the physician feel punitive, controlling, and sadistic.

It is helpful to have a firm, nonjudgmental attitude and to reinterpret the individual's low body weight, which she sees as a sign of her control, as actually representing her loss of control. Interpretations such as these can be construed by the borderline patient as an assault and can result in an attack on the therapist. The physician must remain cognizant of the exquisite sensitivity of the patient for feeling humiliated and at risk for abandonment. Recognizing the rage as a projection will enable the physician to be more aware of the intense countertransference responses these patients can generate and enable the physician to reinterpret the reality in a nonjudgmental fashion.

Problems such as the one just described, relating to the feelings that these patients may produce in the physician, are not uncommon. The defensive constellation of the borderline patient renders the physician at risk for idealization and its concomitant devaluation. The physician must constantly clarify the reality and explain the clinical reasoning behind his or her decision making. Occasionally, because of the patient's small size, or the doctor's desire to have the patient like him or her, the doctor may condone some of her behavior and collude with her denial of the seriousness of the problem. More commonly, physicians become angry at anorexics and bulimics because they are viewed as manipulative or engaging in deliberate self-harm. As a result of these feelings, physicians may become punitive and rejecting, confirming the patient's unconscious fears of abandonment. The feelings in the physician may result in a treatment plan so demanding and restrictive that it is doomed to failure; however, the blame for the failure is firmly placed upon the patient. At times it may be necessary to request consultation with a colleague regarding a specific patient, and occasionally transfer the case to another doctor because of the feelings which are interfering with treatment.

The treatment strategy that is described below borrows principles from a variety of therapeutic approaches (Garfinkel and Garner, 1982) while relying on a cognitive structure; this has been demonstrated to have significant value (Garner, 1987).

Early on, there is great value in education. Patients benefit from learning about body weight regulation and the effects of starvation, including its effects on thinking, feelings, and behavior. Dietary misconceptions can be clarified. It is important to review the effects of vomiting and laxatives on bodily functions. The physician should have a frank discussion with the patient about how easily we can be manipulated by cultural phenomena. It is also important to discuss issues of self-esteem and how in this setting the individual is relating her self-worth entirely to a body size and weight and in doing so, she is forcing herself to be something that is not natural for her.

Outpatient Management

All patients with an eating disorder should at least have a psychiatric consultation by a physician knowledgeable about the eating disorders. However, continuing treatment can be carried out by a family physician, pediatrician, or internist, often in collaboration with a nutritionist. One physician must assume responsibility for monitoring the patient's physical health and appropriate biochemical indices.

For anorexic patients, a weight range must be set as a goal. This usually is about 90 percent of average for the person's age and height. A range of three to five pounds rather than a precise weight is selected both to recognize natural fluctuations in body weight and to counter the tendency of anorexics to focus on precise numbers. Statistical tables of normal weights are not enough, however; it is important to know the patient's premorbid weight and the weight at which secondary amenorrhea developed. These will provide further guidance for setting an appropriate weight for that individual. For bulimic patients, the issue is often not so much weight gain as regulation of eating patterns; this may lead more to a diminution of weight fluctuations than weight gain per se.

Patients must learn to stop relating their self-worth to the readings of the scale; this means throwing out the scales at home and being weighed weekly by the physician. At the same time, the physician must explain to the patient the importance of being at a higher body weight, confronting the phobia regarding body size, and relieving the symptoms of starvation.

Once a goal weight range is agreed upon, the next step is the prescription of a regular eating plan. It is useful to have patients keep a daily diary of their eating in terms of content and associated thoughts, feelings, and behaviors. This often reveals the idiosyncratic rules, habits, and restrictions of the anorexic and the dietary chaos of the bulimic. Simple recommendations in terms of frequency, setting, and quantity of meals may allow the patient to gain weight gradually or regulate urges to binge.

For anorexic patients, an initial regimen of 1,800 calories per day is usually adequate to begin the weight restoration. This intake is usually increased by 200 to 300 calories per week toward a target of about 2,400 calories per day. A rate of weight gain of 0.5 to 1.0 kilograms per week is desirable; more rapid weight gain can be associated with medical complications including gastric dilatation and edema, as well as fear and distrust in a patient who remains ambivalent about weight gain.

For bulimic patients, there is often a history of significant daily dietary restriction between binge episodes. The prescription of three structured daily meals of adequate caloric value helps in diminishing the chaos of bulimics' eating patterns and the intensity of their urges to binge. In addition, individualized recommendations of pleasurable alternatives to bingeing behaviors when the patient feels out of control may be helpful.

The psychological treatment has a number of components. These components do not change for the anorexic or bulimic patient with BPD. However, the defensive structure of the borderline person makes treatment maintenance particularly precarious. Acting out may be centered on eating, and the physician's tolerance may be tested. Constant refocusing on the therapeutic work to be done over time is essential, since this will help the patient gradually accept the fact that the physician is committed to the patient for an extended period of time. The components are as follows: (1) An educative role as described earlier. (2) Correcting faulty thinking patterns: these patients have a variety of distortions in their thinking, most notably an all-or-nothing pattern which does not allow them to see in-betweens in their lives. Repeated recognition of this pattern and efforts to change this are useful. (3) Reinterpretation of their distortions regarding their body: this involves having the individual learn to trust how others see her and to feel her body to be a source of comfort and pleasure. (4) Affective expression: the psychotherapy must involve the person learning to recognize different feeling states which trigger binge eating. Anxiety, depression, and anger are common initiators of a binge. Patients can learn that bingeing may be prevented by recognition of the affect and then more appropriate behavior such as relaxation exercises, meeting a friend, and so on. (5) Self-esteem: this has been tied to weight and to a look. The person should gradually recognize that self-esteem can be built up by factors outside of this. (6) Time: structuring time is very important. These patients are most vulnerable to difficulties when alone in the evenings, especially after a difficult day of work or school. Having other people present can be useful; or a structured activity can prevent binge eating. (7) Family therapy: the family should not be blamed for the disorder. They require advice regarding what the illness involves. At times they need advice about effective parenting and may need support and/or psychotherapy to allow their child to separate emotionally and physically from the family. (8) Group therapy: for many, group therapy and support groups help, as an adjunct to the ongoing treatment program. Details of this comprehensive therapy have been provided elsewhere (Garfinkel and Garner, 1982; Garner and Garfinkel, 1985). Even when the eating disorder is under control, patients with BPD may require continued psychotherapy to deal with their underlying character pathology.

Indications for Admission to the Hospital

Most patients with AN and BN can be treated entirely as outpatients. However, some require hospitalization for:

1. The severity and rate of weight loss as well as the severity of the starvation process. When patients have lost about 30 percent of body weight or when the weight loss has been quite rapid and they demonstrate a lack of control over their weight, hospital admission is warranted.
2. An unending cycle of bulimia and vomiting which cannot be interrupted for even one day often requires the external control of a hospital environment.
3. Failure of outpatient treatment suggests a need for in-hospital treatment.
4. Patients are admitted to treat a variety of complications including persistent hypokalemic alkalosis, depression, suicide attempts, and other complications.

In-hospital Treatment Program

The treatment program may vary according to the patient's clinical state. Aside from emergency admissions to deal with the complications, there are generally three types of programs that are of use: (1) refeeding, weight restoration, and reintegration in the community; (2) breaking the binge–purge cycle and promoting normal eating with less emphasis on weight; and (3) limited refeeding and weight restoration for the chronically ill patient. The details of these treatments and their outcomes have been described elsewhere (Kennedy and Garfinkel, in press; Kennedy, 1988). Studies such as Johnson et al. (in press), Piran, Kaplan, Shekter-Wolfson, Winokur, and Garfinkel (1989) would suggest that many of the more difficult to treat ANs and BNs who require hospitalization have BPD. Alternatively, an intensive outpatient day hospital program has been shown to benefit many patients who previously required inpatient treatment (Piran et al., 1989; Piran, Langdon, Kaplan, and Garfinkel, 1989b).

The Role of Medication

This subject has recently been reviewed elsewhere (Garfinkel and Garner, 1987). Attempts to select drug treatments based on theoretical principles have been relatively unsuccessful. Drugs which promote appetite and enhance gastric emptying, as well as neuroleptics, antidepressants, and anxiolytics, have all been advocated. Chlorpromazine has been used for several decades due to its sedating and appetite enhancing properties. Surprisingly, its efficacy has not been subjected to a controlled trial. Other dopamine blocking agents, such as pimozide, have produced negligible benefit in terms of weight gain and change in attitudes, under controlled conditions (Vandereycken, 1987). The phenothiazine medications have little if any role in patients with eating disorders, given the potential for long-term side effects and unproven efficacy here. We have reserved their use for the rare inpatient who fails to gain weight in spite of conservative therapy and for whom benzodiazepines are contraindicated. When used in this fashion, the phenothiazine should be stopped prior to the patient's discharge.

More useful in these circumstances are one of the minor tranquilizers. We have found the use of small amounts of anxiolytic agents, such as oxazepam (15 mg) or alprazolam (0.25 mg), thirty minutes before meals, to be valuable where anxiety is excessive. This also prevents concern about the uncertain risks of tardive dyskinesia following the use of neuroleptics. Again the minor tranquilizer should be used for discrete periods of several weeks and should be used only with extreme caution in the bulimic group, because of their potential for drug dependency.

Antidepressant medication has frequently been advocated for AN. While many patients with AN present with depression, studies of medications in AN have failed to show benefit (Lacey and Crisp, 1980; Mitchell and Groat, 1984). If there is a subgroup of AN patients that responds to antidepressants, it has yet to be identified. By contrast, both the tricyclic and monoamine oxidase (MAO) inhibiting antidepressant drugs have been shown to be effective in BN (Goldbloom and Kennedy, 1988). In two controlled studies, imipramine in daily doses of 200 to 300 mg has demonstrated efficacy in diminishing binge frequencies (Agras, Dorian, Kirkley, Arnow, and Bachman, 1987; Pope et al., 1983). Similar results have been obtained with desipramine (Hughes, Wells, Cunningham, and Ilstrup, 1986), fluoxetine (Levine and the Fluoxetine Study Group, submitted), phenelzine (Walsh, Stewart, Roose, Gladis, and Glassman, 1985), and isocarboxezid (Kennedy, Piran, Warsh, Prendergast, Henderson, and Garfinkel, 1988). What remains unknown at this time is the comparative efficacy of tricyclic versus MAO inhibitors; of the benefits of the medication versus standard psychotherapies; or the benefits of combining the drugs with psychotherapy. Moreover, there is currently no way to identify in advance which patients will respond to antidepressants. Given this, it is usual to begin a bulimic patient on a trial of outpatient psychotherapy and if there is no symptomatic improvement over six to eight weeks, to consider the addition of a tricyclic antidepressant.

CONCLUSION

There exists in the literature evidence for an association between the BPD and bulimia. As we have shown, the goals of inpatient or outpatient treatment and management for the anorexic or bulimic patient do not change if the patient has a

borderline personality disorder. Many of the psychological difficulties associated with the AN and BN patient such as "dichotomous thinking," concerns centered on autonomy and control,
and low self-esteem are also hallmarks of BPD. The presence of
BPD adds intensity to these dimensions and places the patient at
increased risk of jeopardizing therapy by the use of behaviors
unconsciously designed to precipitate the predicted and feared
responses in the psychiatrist. The alert therapist must constantly monitor his or her responses to these challenging patients if a corrective experience for the patient is to be provided.

25.

Alcoholism and the Borderline Patient

Edgar P. Nace, M.D.

A strong association is found between alcohol dependence and other psychiatric disorders. Approximately 14 percent of the adult United States population, eighteen years and older, meet *The Diagnostic and Statistical Manual of Mental Disorders* (DSM-III-R) criteria for a lifetime diagnosis of alcohol abuse or alcohol dependence (American Psychiatric Association, 1987). Forty-seven percent of them also meet criteria for a second psychiatric diagnosis. A second diagnosis is found more often in women alcoholics (65%) than male alcoholics (44%) (Helzer and Pryzbeck, 1988). Among the disorders which co-occur with alcoholism are personality disorders. The best documented co-occurring personality disorder is antisocial personality disorder (ASPD).

Helzer and Pryzbeck (1988) reported ASPD in 15 percent of alcoholic men. In contrast, nonalcoholic men had a lifetime prevalence of ASPD of 4 percent. For women the comparable prevalence rates were 10 percent (alcoholic women) and 0.81 percent (nonalcoholic women). Thus, the alcoholic male, is nearly four times more likely to have ASPD than the nonalcoholic male and ASPD in alcoholic women is almost twelve times more common than in nonalcoholic women.

Further documentation of the prevalence of personality disorder in alcohol abusers is provided by Drake and Vaillant (1985). In a sample of men, followed over time, 23 percent met criteria for an Axis II diagnosis of personality disorder by age forty-seven, but of the alcoholic men in this sample, 37 percent had a personality disorder.

The association between personality disorder and alcohol dependence is even stronger when clinical samples are studied. In a Canadian study of ninety-six abstinent alcoholics, 35 percent had avoidant personality disorder using DSM-III-R criteria (Stravynski, Lamontagne, and Yvon Jacques, 1986). Koenigsberg, Kaplan, Gilmore, and Cooper's (1985) review of over 2,400 patients reported that 36 percent had personality disorders. Patients with a substance use disorder were more likely than other psychiatric patients to have a personality disorder; that is, 46 percent of alcoholics and 61 percent of nonalcoholic drug abusers had a personality disorder. In their study the most frequent personality disorders among substance abusing patients were borderline (43%), antisocial (21%), and mixed (17%).

Of nearly 100 alcoholic patients admitted to an inpatient substance abuse unit, 13 percent were found to have a diagnosis of borderline personality disorder (BPD) when evaluated by a standardized rating instrument using conservative criteria (Nace, Saxon, and Shore, 1983).

Current estimates of borderline personality disorder (BPD) in the general population reach 3 percent (Kernberg, Gunderson, and Stone, 1988).

It is apparent from the few clinical studies available that BPD is overrepresented in the alcoholic population (Nace et al., 1983; Koenigsberg et al., 1985). More precise estimates of the co-occurrence of alcoholism and BPD will require data from studies such as the Epidemiologic Catchment Area study (Helzer and Pryzbeck, 1988).

ALCOHOL ABUSE AND DEPENDENCE

The potential for alcohol abuse or dependence in BPD is implied in DSM-III-R diagnostic criteria. Of the eight diagnostic

TABLE 25.1

Diagnostic Criteria for Psychoactive Sustance Abuse

A. A maladaptive pattern of psychoactive substance use indicated by at least one of the following:
  (1) continued use despite knowledge of having a persistent or recurrent social, occupational, psychological, or physical problem that is caused or exacerbated by the use of the psychoactive substance
  (2) recurrent use in situations in which use is physically hazardous (e.g., driving while intoxicated)
B. Some symptoms of the disturbance have persisted for at least one month, or have occurred repeatedly over a longer period of time.
C. Never met the criteria for Psychoactive Substance Dependence for this substance.

American Psychiatric Association (1987), *The Diagnostic and Statistical Manual of Mental Disorders*, 3rd ed., rev. Washington, DC: American Psychiatric Press.

criteria, one refers to impulsiveness in at least two areas: spending, sex, substance use, shoplifting, reckless driving, and binge eating.

The distinction between abuse and dependence has a bearing on treatment priorities. Table 25.1 lists DSM-III-R criteria for psychoactive substance abuse and Table 25.2 for psychoactive substance dependence. If criteria for dependence are met, treatment of the alcoholism should be given priority. Interestingly, the BPD patient who is alcohol dependent often responds favorably to a treatment strategy that focuses on the alcoholism. Possible reasons for this will be discussed later in this chapter.

What about the BPD patient who does not meet criteria for alcoholism, but whose drinking falls into a pattern of abuse as listed in Table 25.1? Establishing treatment priorities in these instances is less clear-cut.

Alcohol abusing borderline patients often gravitate to one or the other of two distinct treatment options: some quickly accept a focus on the pathological drinking and assume an identity as an "alcoholic." They may become quite involved in Alcoholics Anonymous (AA) and improve their level of overall functioning. This new identity can serve a defensive function. Should this occur, a focus on other treatment issues is usually avoided because the individual prefers to conceptualize his or

TABLE 25.2

Diagnostic Criteria for Psychoactive Substance Dependence

A. At least three of the following:

    (1) substance often taken in larger amounts or over a longer period than the person intended

    (2) persistent desire or one or more unsuccessful efforts to cut down or control substance use

    (3) a great deal of time spent in activities necessary to get the substance (e.g., theft), taking the substance (e.g., chain smoking), or recovering from its effects

    (4) frequent intoxication or withdrawal symptoms when expected to fulfill major role obligations at work, school, or home (e.g., does not go to work because hung over, goes to school or work "high," intoxicated while taking care of his or her children), or when substance use is physically hazardous (e.g., drives when intoxicated)

    (5) important social, occupational, or recreational activities given up or reduced because of substance use

    (6) continued substance use despite knowledge of having a persistent or recurrent social, psychological, or physical problem that is caused or exacerbated by the use of the substance (e.g., keeps using heroin despite family arguments about it, cocaine-induced depression, or having an ulcer made worse by drinking)

    (7) marked tolerance: need for markedly increased amounts of the substance (i.e., at least a 50% increase) in order to achieve intoxication or desired effect, or markedly diminished effect with continued use of the same amount

    NOTE: The following items may not apply to cannabis, hallucinogens, or phencyclidine (PCP):

    (8) characteristic withdrawal symptoms

    (9) substance often taken to relieve or avoid withdrawal symptoms

B. Some symptoms of the disturbance have persisted for at least one month, or have occurred repeatedly over a long period of time.

American Psychiatric Association (1987), *The Diagnostic and Statistical Manual of Mental Disorders*, 3rd ed. rev. Washington, DC: American Psychiatric Press.

her behavior as attributable to being an alcoholic. Today, the identity of being a "child of an alcoholic" may provide an additional focus and bolster a sense of stability. If this acquired identity of "alcoholic" or "child of an alcoholic" fails to contain or modify the impulsive, destabilizing aspects of borderline pathology, the patient may seek further psychotherapeutic work.

After a series of failed marriages and unsatisfactory results from long-term, intense, psychoanalytically oriented psychotherapy, a woman executive began to address not only her own sporadic abuse of alcohol, but the issues related to having grown up with an alcoholic parent. Focus on such alcohol related concerns, combined with abstinence and AA involvement, yielded significant improvement. During periods of stress such as company financial problems or personal medical concerns regression would occur leading to brief resumption of alcohol abuse. Gradually, the patient used therapy to explore her early family relationships while, in parallel, she retained involvement in AA and Children of Alcoholics (COA) groups. Although it was several years before this parallel therapeutic approach became "safe" and acceptable to the patient, it led to increasing stabilization and maturation.

On the other hand, many borderline patients whose impulsiveness includes alcohol abuse, vehemently resist alcohol rehabilitation efforts. In such cases treatment is likely to be stopped as soon as the therapist insists on enrollment in an alcoholism treatment program or involvement with AA. The optimal strategy is to develop a sound therapeutic alliance. From this alliance an amelioration of alcohol abuse may follow. The lessening or avoidance of drinking will prove beneficial as attempts to carry out therapeutic work around other issues continue.

Resentful and anxious, a woman was "forced" into treatment by her husband, who became frightened when his wife began to have vague somatic symptoms and episodes of wrist-cutting. Alcohol abuse, shoplifting, and gambling rounded out the clinical picture. The course of therapy, although stormy at times, sustained a positive transference. Eventually she stopped acting out except for occasional episodes of heavy drinking limited to periods of several hours. This patient adamantly rejected any suggestions of treatment specific to alcohol abuse. She did, however, modify much of her behavior, gained insight into her family of origin and its impact on her current family life, and developed a greater capacity to cope with her children.

Whether the infrequent periods of alcohol abuse will evolve into a more pathological pattern of drinking remains to be seen. She does illustrate how substantial modification in drinking and other impulsive acts can occur as dynamic issues relevant to borderline pathology are addressed.

When borderline patients are found to be alcohol dependent, treatment of alcoholism is essential and a first priority. When the clinical picture is less clear-cut but alcohol abuse is apparent, the therapist needs to remain flexible. Certain patients gravitate toward self-help groups and attenuate or disparage therapy. Others resist efforts to focus specifically on substance abuse, but some of them are able to modify their impulsive use of alcohol if an alliance can be formed and sustained.

BORDERLINE AND NONBORDERLINE ALCOHOLICS

How does the borderline patient with alcoholism differ from other alcoholic patients? A study (Nace et al., 1983) of alcoholic patients, using the diagnostic interview for borderlines (DIB) (Gunderson, Kolb, and Austin, 1981) found that 21 percent of alcoholics admitted to an inpatient alcoholism treatment program met diagnostic criteria for BPD. If the contribution to the DIB score from alcohol abuse was eliminated, nearly 13 percent of the alcoholic patients still met criteria for BPD. This percentage is believed to be a conservative estimate of BPD in patients seeking treatment for alcohol dependence.

The borderline alcoholics were significantly younger than the other alcohol patients (34.5 years vs. 47.2 years), but did not differ in regard to sex, marital status, education, employment status, or race. Variables relating to the use of alcohol did not differ between these two groups of alcoholics, including physical symptoms related to drinking, length of heavy drinking, frequency of drinking, drinking pattern, and prior history of detoxification or rehabilitation. When craving for alcohol was evaluated, however, the BPD alcholics differed in that they reported craving in a wider variety of experiences including when they were feeling good as well as when they were feeling bad. The nonborderline alcoholics were more likely to report craving when they were experiencing stress.

Striking differences between BPD alcoholics and non-BPD alcoholics were found in regard to drug abuse. The BPD group had a much more extensive history of drug abuse than did the other alcoholics. Other differences were that more BPD patients had a history of suicide attempts (60 vs. 14%), a history of accidents (both automobile and home), more legal problems, a history of prior psychotherapy, and a family history of mental illness.

The clinician encountering patients who are both alcoholic and borderline needs to be alert to increased potential for suicide and the co-occurrence of drug abuse that may complicate both the withdrawal process and long-term recovery.

TREATMENT: A SYNCHRONOUS PROCESS

As a rule, when alcoholism co-occurs with other psychiatric disorders the patient is first treated for the alcoholism, that is, detoxification, then undergoes rehabilitation. During the rehabilitation phase an ongoing evaluation of additional treatment needs is conducted and treatment for coexisting disorders is implemented in synchrony with alcoholism treatment. The exception of this sequence occurs when acute psychotic states or other severe symptoms preclude participation in the structure of an alcoholism rehabilitation program. Then, resolution of the acute symptoms precedes a focus on alcohol dependence.

What about the borderline patient who is alcohol dependent? Most approaches to the treatment of BPD fall either into a category that emphasizes improvement in adaptation or one that attempts structured intrapsychic change using modified psychoanalytic psychotherapy (Gordon and Beresin, 1983).

Either approach may be effective for the borderline alcoholic when a synchronous course of treatment for alcoholism is available. If the borderline patient is treated in a long-term psychiatric inpatient unit with intensive psychotherapy a strengthening of ego functions may occur that enables more efficient regulation of tension. A gradual acceptance of what is realistic and reasonable occurs, and healthier identity fragments become integrated into the self organization. When this process is well underway the patient is often capable of accepting and integrating the psychoeducational and group approaches to recovery from alcoholism. At times, patients may use the disease concept of alcoholism or the program of AA as a "defense" against examination of their own dynamics. This is less likely to be a problem when the patient has experienced improved control and improved affect regulation through a strengthening of the observing capacity of the ego. If the improved capacity for observing one's internal states has occurred, the potential conflict between a psychodynamic and a disease model of alcoholism will be minimized. The patient will have developed a healthy fear of any return to the regressive effect of intoxicating substances. This recognition of vulnerability to the loss of control over alcohol (or other drugs) represents a modification of pathological grandiosity in that the patient is recognizing that he or she is "powerless over alcohol" (see step 1 of AA, Table 25.3).

TREATMENT OF ALCOHOLISM: THE IMPACT ON PERSONALITY DISORDERS

Patients with alcoholism and BPD whose treatment is focused on the alcoholism are likely to undergo a modification of character pathology. That is, as we utilize the therapeutic approaches available for the treatment of alcoholism and other substance use disorders (Nace, 1987) and combine these with participation in twelve-step programs, we are, in part and perhaps inadvertently, treating the personality disorder as well. The emphasis on treatment in an alcohol rehabilitation program is, in Gordon and Beresin's (1983) terms, an emphasis on adaptation and a discouragement of regression. This will be apparent when we compare rehabilitation and twelve-step programs, such as Alcoholics Anonymous and Narcotics Anonymous. The environment of a rehabilitation program is usually

TABLE 25.3

The Twelve Steps of Alcoholics Anonymous*

1. We admitted we were powerless over alcohol—that our lives had become unmanageable.
2. Came to believe that a Power greater than ourselves could restore us to sanity.
3. Made a decision to turn our will and our lives over to the care of God as we understood Him.
4. Made a searching and fearless moral inventory of ourselves.
5. Admitted to God, to ourselves, and to another human being the exact nature of our wrongs.
6. We're entirely ready to have God remove all these defects of character.
7. Humbly asked Him to remove our shortcomings.
8. Made a list of all persons we had harmed, and became willing to make amends to them all.
9. Made direct amends to such people whenever possible, except when to do so would injure them or others.
10. Continued to take personal inventory and when we were wrong promptly admitted it.
11. Sought through prayer and meditation to improve our conscious contact with God as we understood Him, praying only for knowledge of His will for us and the power to carry that out.
12. Having had a spiritual awakening as the result of these steps, we tried to carry this message to alcoholics, and to practice these principles in all our affairs.

*Reprinted with permission of Alcoholics Anonymous World Services, Inc.

highly structured. Time is ordered, activities tightly scheduled, and behavior regulated by rules and regulations. Setting limits is a constant feature of such programs: limits in terms of use of alcohol or drugs (none); relatively little use of medications; and prohibitions against acting out. A reality orientation is emphasized that stresses coping and deemphasizes and discourages regressive behaviors. These functions—structure, limit-setting, and emphasis on adaptation (rather than regression)—serve to shore up and strengthen ego functions. Self-care skills such as the ability to anticipate consequences of behavior and to curb impulses are reinforced in such an environment.

Emphasis on recognition and tolerance of feelings—rather than avoidance of painful affect through use of alcohol, drugs, or acting out—serves an integrating process essential to self-control. The insistence on abstinence provides a paradigm for therapeutic issues beyond avoidance of alcohol and other drugs. Abstinence will depend on the development of patience, impulse control, tolerance for frustration, and an ability to regulate affect. All of the above are major issues in the treatment of character pathology, which will be positively influenced pari passu with a drug-free life-style.

In a similar vein, the AA program focuses not only on alcohol but extends its program of recovery to the alcoholic's relationships (Kurtz and Kurtz, 1986). Initially, the focus is on the alcoholic's relationship to alcohol. This is expressed in the first step of AA—"we admitted we were powerless over alcohol—that our lives had become unmanageable" (see Table 25.3). As the alcoholic progresses through the twelve-step program he or she is called upon not only to accept the limitation of the relationship to alcohol, but also to examine relationships to others, to self, and to a "higher power."

The therapeutic impact of AA has been described by Chappel, Gottheill, and Nace (1988). The first three steps (see Table 25.3) are described by Chappel as "surrender steps"—the individual begins to overcome the feelings of helplessness and to gain an internal locus of control. Steps four and five are "inventory steps" paralleling a process of psychotherapy by encouraging self-examination. Steps six and seven are considered by Chappel to be "personality disorder treatment steps" as they address defects of character. Steps eight and nine promote honest relationships and step twelve is a "sharing step."

The dynamics operating in either the twelve-step program of AA or within rehabilitation programs enable modification in the pathological narcissism of the borderline patient. The power of "surrender" (facing limitations), self-examination, confession, and restitution indicate that recovery from alcoholism is more than not drinking alcoholic beverages. An impact on personality structures occurs. This impact supports the alcoholic as he or she copes with the absence of a substance upon which there had been pathological dependence. In addition to supporting abstinence from alcohol, a new identity emerges that values sober living, consistency, and a renewed capacity for integrity.

RESEARCH FINDINGS

Empirical support for the contention that alcoholism treatment and the treatment of borderline pathology occurs in synchrony within the context of a rehabilitation program is very limited. One study addresses the issue and provides data that the borderline patient can significantly benefit from a psychiatrically oriented alcoholism treatment program (Nace, Saxon, and Shore, 1986).

One year after inpatient treatment (4 to 6 weeks), alcoholic patients with a documented BPD were compared on outcome measures with nonborderline alcoholic patients. Both borderline and nonborderline alcoholics showed significant and comparable decreases in use of alcohol during the first year following treatment. The borderline patients also showed significant improvements in leisure time satisfaction and family relationships and they had fewer hospitalizations than previously. In regard to drug use other than alcohol, the borderline patients made significant decreases in drug use during the first six months posttreatment, but (unlike the other alcoholics) began to show a return to drug use during the last six months of the follow-up period.

The treatment of personality disorders is not complete nor fully addressed in the rehabilitation process of alcoholism treatment. With the attainment of sobriety, however, the capacity to observe and modify long-standing traits is greatly improved. A quote from Bill Wilson, cofounder of AA, illustrates this point:

> I am beginning to see that all my troubles have their root in a habitual and absolute dependence upon my personal prestige, security, and romantic attachment. When these things go wrong, there is depression. Now this absolute dependence upon people and situations can only lead to conflict both on the surface and at depth. We are making

demands on circumstance and people that are bound to fail us [Kurtz, 1979, p. 214].

It can be appreciated that whether recovery from alcoholism occurs through the dynamics operating in rehabilitation programs, psychotherapy, or the twelve steps of AA, a process is occurring that affects and influences personality structure. For this reason, we can be confident that the treatment of the alcoholic patient with BPD is well conceived by a focus on the alcoholism and the appropriate blend of rehabilitation, psychotherapy, and a twelve-step program.

CONCLUSIONS

This chapter reviewed the evidence that BPD, as well as other personality disorders, may occur more frequently in alcoholic patients. Borderline personality disorder is found more commonly in samples drawn from private treatment centers, in contrast to antisocial personality disorder, which is found more commonly in association with alcoholic patients in government and public treatment programs. Differences between borderline and nonborderline alcoholics are described and the beneficial results of alcoholism treatment in the BPD is presented. Various treatment strategies avail themselves for this particular form of "dual disorder" and include long-term intensive psychodynamically oriented therapy as well as the more adaptation oriented approaches to alcohol dependence. The beneficial effects of the twelve-step program of Alcoholics Anonymous are reviewed. It is recommended that the borderline patient with an alcohol problem receive treatment which addresses both the dynamics of borderline pathology and the disease of alcoholism.

PART V

EPILOGUE

An Open Forum

This section contains the question and answer period of a meeting on borderline personality disorder held October 15, 1988, at Mt. Sinai Hospital, Toronto, Ontario.

The participants were Drs. Cowdry, Gunderson, Michels, and Stone. Their presentations appear earlier in this book.

DIAGNOSTIC ISSUES AND BPD

Question: Is the psychiatric profession erring by pathologizing traits into symptoms and disorders? What about the pejorative connotations?

Dr. Stone: I think if someone's life is dominated by a collection of traits getting in the way of that person's optimal functioning, as either that person himself or others close to him would define it, then I guess it's worth speaking about those traits as pathological. The twenty-five different characteristic traits that I have outlined (see chapter 1) get in the way of a person fulfilling his life in a harmonious and agreeable way, so I think they deserve to be in the manual some place, particularly if one has a lot of them. All of us have some peculiarities, either different from that list or a minor form of some of the things on that or other lists, but it's only at the point where such peculiarities begin to interfere with function and achievement of one's life goals that we speak of pathology. I think it's reasonable to speak of troubled or disordered personalities.

As for elimination of the pejorative connotations, I don't know if that's entirely feasible, particularly when you get into the area of the psychopath, because that is somebody whom we look upon in moral terms as repugnant in the body social. I don't know why we have to avoid that. Freud didn't avoid it, why should we avoid it? The uncomfortable reactions about borderlines are not that they are looked down on or judged in the way one tends to judge a psychopath or arch-criminal. Rather, it is because they are very difficult to treat, and therapists tend to groan and say, "Oh, that difficult patient's going to call me late at night," or "I'll have to worry about suicide," or things of that sort. Thus borderlines get a bad reputation because of their difficulty more than because of their obnoxiousness, although, of course, some of them are a little obnoxious as well because of their irritability. I don't think we should try to have absolutely nonpejorative nosology.

Question: I'm going to play devil's advocate for a moment, and take up your remark, Dr. Stone, that these patients get a bad reputation because of their difficulty, and suggest that perhaps we could look at borderline as an interpersonal diagnosis, that is a diagnosis made because of transactions that take place between the psychiatrist and his patient. It could be considered from that point of view as a category where we describe our frustration with those who don't avail themselves consistently of the neatness of our treatment practices. They call us at times of day when we don't expect to be called, and they don't necessarily show up for appointments when we expect them to show up, and they take actions which we would prefer that they don't take, such as harming themselves, at times when we would prefer that they didn't do so. And therefore, because of our difficulty in adapting to their ways of life and their difficulty in adapting to our ways of life, we assign them to this kind of category.

Dr. Stone: Well, I think you must be right in what you say. They do affect us in that way, but oftentimes we are far from the only people—I'm speaking of we as a body of therapists—who are affected in that way, so that we then are the reflections of common problems that they have with everyone. If they affect most important people that they come in contact with in that way, the qualities you mention could come under the heading of unreasonableness. Even though they evoke common transference feelings from us, if this is what happens with them and every important person that they come in contact with, then I guess you will also have to admit it is a problem in them, even though of course it evokes a characteristic problem in us. It's interpersonal but it's also something that emanates from their behavior. So I feel that we're entitled to say that they have this problem.

Question: Dr. Stone, could you speak to the issue of comorbidity, and how there are a number of different hypotheses about how that may interact with character development. What are your thoughts about why this excess comorbidity is there and what is the direction of that interaction?

Dr. Stone: I think that people who have, let's say, excess risk genes for manic depression—many of them, especially of the bipolar II type, or even any of the types but particularly bipolar II—are people who are more impulsive and irritable, often have tantrums, and there's an urgency about their nervous system, an irritability. They want what they want when they want it. As children they have tantrums. They experience little frustrations as huge, and they get very angry. If the parents go out to a movie, the three kids are playing Monopoly with the babysitter, and the kid who is going to be the borderline in the future is crawling the walls, screaming, tearing at the curtains, and so on. So you see some of these things very early. I think that even with fairly supportive, nurturing, warm parents, there will be some children who are simply born with that irritable quality, and later it may manifest itself in the way that we then single out as borderline, which means that there is something about them temperamentally, innately, that makes them handle the later experiences in a comorbid condition. Therefore I really think there are examples. I never wanted to claim that borderline is simply a brand of manic depression, as some people have mistakenly read my work as saying. But rather there's a subset within what's called borderline where that innate tendency has expressed itself in this way. And then there are other cases that I've become more familiar with in the last ten years where there's a great deal of abusiveness, violence in the family, sexual exploitation, that produces a similar clinical picture. The picture of BPD thus becomes a final common pathway from different etiological sources, in the way that dropsy, which was once a diagnosis in the eighteenth century, is something that we recognize as congestive failure, as coming from many different sources. I don't know if that answers the question, but that's my view.

Dr. Michels: Let's presume just for a minute, using the dropsy metaphor, that the next step would be to try to tease apart those subsyndromes which are etiologically temperamental as opposed to those which are etiologically early intrafamilial traumatic, looking for different syndromal characteristics and differentiate them. That isn't very prominent in the literature.

Dr. Stone: No. That isn't prominent in the literature. By the way there is also a third thing by which the people who have the risk genes and who have the temperament, and some of whose parents are very feisty and difficult, and who create an environment which contributes to it. In other words where it isn't either—or but either—or or both.

Question: Dr. Michels, it would appear that clinicians feel that the DSM criteria for borderline are too constricting while the researchers insist on stricter criteria feeling that otherwise the concept loses significant meaning. Would you comment?

Dr. Michels: It would be foolish of me to discuss the boundaries of this concept sandwiched between Drs. Stone and Gunderson in this auditorium. One of the clues I had that we may not be dealing with a natural entity here is I had to look to the page in Dr. Stone's presentation to remember the eight items in DSM-III. Is it eight? I knew there were eight, but I couldn't tell you what they were if you woke me up in the middle of the night. (I was talking about the therapist's experience of a problem.) It is my observation, and I believe Dr. Gunderson has said this in writing, that therapists are not terribly concerned about clarifying the precise boundaries of this entity. If you sit in your office and treat people who come in for help, it is not often troublesome for you to decide whether a given patient really has four out of eight or five out of eight of these criteria—although that might be an immensely important question for doing research. What we do observe, sitting in our offices, is that certain patients have these kinds of problems as we treat them. And if they have these kinds of problems, then we have certain ways of thinking about them that are helpful to us. So my operational definition, for the present purposes (an unscientific one by a nonexpert), is that it is those kinds of ideas I outlined (see chapter 5), which are helpful to me when I'm treating a patient who falls into this broad, vague category that I can't define, but who leads me to have the kinds of problems—those same kinds of problems that led Knight and others to start using words like borderline. Now that's not an operational, and then again it *is* an operational criterion, but not one that Dr. Frances will find acceptable when he and Dr. Gunderson put together Axis II DSM-IV.

Question: The phenomenology of behavioral features of Axis II has obviously become the major currency that we use now to help to tease out the different categories. The overlap that occurs between these categories is striking. It occurs to me, and I'm sure to many others, that the final common pathway to behavior is quite limited, and there are just so many features of behavior that one can manifest. So in looking for a linkage between these things, one may actually turn to psychodynamic factors which are followed in a fashion in the current diagnostic approaches. I wonder how you come to introduce those factors and integrate them into your diagnostic approach.

Dr. Stone: I don't. The dynamic factors are dynamic factors. There are certain dynamic factors that occur far more often in this group of patients, but I think the dynamics don't have the same meaning with respect to how we make diagnoses as do personality traits, symptoms, the anamnestic data about the life of the patient and so on. So I try not to let myself be too influenced by that. In other words, not everybody with separation–individuation problems has the rest of the borderline picture, and therefore cannot be called borderline. Not every incest victim ends up as a BPD case; not everybody whose father beat the tar out of them ends up as a BPD case. I think one can be misled sometimes by putting too much reliance on dynamic factors in this sense. For example, once you get into your head that separation–individuation problems are the essence of being borderline, which I would have some disagreement about, then you feel that you've done a day's work when you have tried to deal with that patient's problems in separation. You kind of forget that you have blinders on where you don't see what may be the traumatic factors or the biological factors, or other important things, and that the patient isn't going to get better unless those things are dealt with. One has to have a wider view, a deep appreciation of the dynamic factors, but also an appreciation of the other sources by which the person got to be borderline, by whatever definition, so that the treatment is more inclusive.

Question: There is a tremendous overlap between psychiatric symptomatology, and as well the number of responses of the damaged psyche is limited. But having said that, perhaps we need to admit that we are being more precise than is possible at this time.

Dr. Stone: I look upon this diagnosis as not something which exists as a platonic ideal up in the sky, in the way that "table," "chair," "microphone," exist. Rather, there's an area in this ameboid, amorphous entity: we look upon the whole map of psychiatric nosology, of all the abnormal conditions, and we stake out a certain territory because it's useful to us, and we paste a label on it. In certain cultures, for instance Britain, there are very few people who use the borderline concept, and it doesn't seem to have done anything terrible to that country. There are many parts of the world where I don't think there are so many borderline people. In certain parts of Asia, for example, where there's a tremendous group pressure against the easy expression of angry feelings and the impulsive sort of behavior that many borderline patients exhibit, you don't have many borderline patients. These people would be stoned in a public square in certain places if they carried on in this way. Therefore they may be unhappy, but they show it in different ways. They end up with a different entity just like in Saudi Arabia, especially among the more developed Moslems, who don't abuse alcohol. It's like stepping on a balloon: it comes up somewhere else. They may have more phobia, more hysteria, but they have less alcohol abuse. But in our particular culture there are a lot of people on whom I think it's useful to pin some kind of label. I was suggesting unstable personality, in contradistinction from the other personality types that are listed which don't emphasize this unstable, impulsive quality so much. There is a use in giving a label that addresses the problem that many patients who come to us have this unreasonable, impulsive, irritable quality and get into the kinds of difficulties and try to get us over a barrel, like the patients we have been calling borderline. I think in our culture, at the present time, it's useful to try to define in some way along utilitarian lines, not along some absolute lines as if we really "know" what the answer is, but along utilitarian lines subject to change without notice.

Question: I have two questions. One is a kind of theoretical question and the other one is a more clinical one. The theoretical one is: what are the speculations about why there are so many more women with this syndrome than men? What is it about the way women are brought up, or what is it in the way that male experts (because it is mostly male experts in this syndrome) see human suffering that makes it seem to be more common in women? Or is it really more common in women? That's the theoretical question. The more clinical one is different, and that is, as we talk about treatment, and as we talk about it being long term, of necessity, how usual is it for therapists to be flexible in their approach and to in fact treat people over time in different ways; for instance to include periods of pharmacological treatment interspersed with treatments without that; or to stop seeing them for a while; or to return to seeing them? In my experience, I think people get quite expert in doing what they do best, and then do that perhaps irrespective of the needs of the patient.

Dr. Cowdry: The issue of sex differences is really a very intriguing and difficult one. Part of the explanation clearly lies in the fact that males with affective instability and impulse control problems can end up in the criminal justice system, rather than the mental health system, and probably tend to get somewhat different diagnoses. I think that's part of the answer for the sex difference. At least that's my assumption about it. I think there's a lot of controversy about whether this syndrome is becoming increasingly prevalent, and whether it is somehow related to cultural changes, additional role stresses, changing role definition, and so on. I don't think there's actually very good epidemiology, and couldn't be, indeed, because the definition has changed so much, and I'd be very interested in the other panelists' impressions of whether there is a real difference in this disorder that suggests that it must have something to do with changing cultural expectations and roles.

Dr. Stone: I agree with Dr. Cowdry's impressions that many of the males go in the direction of antisocial personality (ASP) and end up with ASP rather than BPD. But females are far more likely to be incest victims than males, obviously, and transgenerational, especially father–daughter incest, I think, is a traumatogenic factor that inclines or is conducive to the development of BPD. Women are littler than men, and in their relative defenselessness while growing up, and being subjected to stressful experiences, will tend toward manipulative suicide-looking gestures or self-damaging acts to get out of a tight spot, whereas a man will maybe smash the windows, or break out. There is thus a different use of force. So that the woman will do something that will shame those who are subjecting her to terrible experiences or whatever, whereas the man will tend to shoot to kill as it were. But then a self-damaging act or manipulative gesture is part of what we define as BPD. There may be something different—whatever it is that makes women tend more to unipolar depression than males—that perhaps has some biological underpinning with the hemispheric differences between the sexes, that might also account for some of the variance, but I think not so much is known about it.

As for "is BPD becoming more frequent in this generation than before," I don't know, because of course we didn't define the condition in the same rigorous way in the twenties and at the turn of the century as we do now. We don't know precisely whether Freud's cases were borderline, and how many of the patients that the pioneers were seeing were as well. But it's possible that there is some greater number, the way there is of eating disorders (see chapter 24). There's an absolute increase in eating disorders in the last twenty years. There may be an increase in BPD in this way, but a generation ago, for example, many young women were not abusing alcohol and other substances very much. Now you have a situation where even a cultural group like young Jewish women, who formerly wouldn't abuse those substances at all are abusing them a great deal. And if you have a certain impulsive, histrionic quality to the personality and then add alcohol to the soup, or marijuana or something, you then may have a flagrant personality disturbance, a great destabilization, which leads to the unstable quality we identify as borderline. Whereas, in a different cultural set, in a different generation, without adding those things to the mix they would have squeaked along as a histrionic or something else. So maybe there are some extra ones in our let-it-all-hang-out, not so limit-set generation, in contrast to the more inhibited people that we saw in an earlier generation, including my own.

Dr. Gunderson: I think that the early developmental studies of young infants have suggested that there are sex-linked temperamental differences between infant girls and infant boys, whereby little boys are by nature more instrumental and girls are more affiliative. Translating that into subsequent psychopathology, in the face of common types of early parental frustrations boys might be more apt to go out and build a bomb shelter or a bomb, and girls might be more apt to cling to a transitional object. I think the increased use of transitional objects has been to some extent documented in the backgrounds of people who become borderline. I think it's also more culturally and socially approved for little girls to look for the solution to problems through relationships. So I think there are genetic and probably social factors which reinforce the development of borderline psychopathology insofar as the central part of that is to try to seek a solution for an internal problem through a corrective relationship. In contrast, you see a disproportionate amount of antisocial personality amongst males, and there, for similar reasons, you might have both constitutional and social pressures which affect the little boy—he's not supposed to cry when he's upset, and he's not supposed to tell anybody, he's supposed to go and do something. There may be both genetic and social pressures which account for an increased amount of antisocial behavior amongst males.

Question: I have what is perhaps a cynical question, to do with the political and economic components in the process of diagnosis, particularly with regard to personality disorder. It seems to me that the DSM-III, or any of the DSM documents, take on a life of their own as the participants in formulating these diagnoses develop their interests, and the need to define these syndromes. Some of this has to do with pure clinical and treatment reasons, and some to do with development of research criteria that clearly define their own area of expertise and allow them then to research this area in very specific ways. I think part of what you're implying about the personality diagnosis is that in our attempts to very carefully define the criteria for these disorders, we are moving farther away from the practical use of these definitions in the treatment process, and that it becomes more difficult for us to integrate very rigidly defined categories into what is, for most therapists, a very fluid process.

Dr. Michels: It seems to me that generally speaking people don't take diagnoses very seriously unless they make a difference. At this point, many Axis I diagnoses have a significant contribution to make to the variants in the patient's treatment plan. Not as much as some phenomenologic psychiatrists think, and it's a point I've made in papers on case formulations, but they do make a difference, and some diagnoses are almost prescriptive. At this point, my own sense is that there is very little prescriptive significance to most Axis II diagnoses. When you've made the Axis II diagnosis you don't know what the treatment is, any more than you did before you made the Axis II diagnosis. It revolves more around assessments of situations and dynamics and such, and therefore most clinical psychiatrists aren't terribly interested in making those differentials. However, the availability of reasonably reliable criteria for splitting the world into different categories is an essential component in collecting more knowledge about the world. So in a funny way, at this point, Axis II belongs more to the researchers, and Axis I more to the clinicians, and that's the way it ought to be. I applaud that. And I've learned interesting things from reading the literature by people who started with Axis II criteria for slicing the world and then tell me things about it. However, I don't find it terribly important to make an Axis II diagnosis in my head before embarking on a treatment plan with a patient with a personality disorder. However, I require my residents to make an Axis II diagnosis on everyone they see because I think it forces them to think about something that I fear they might otherwise not think about. This is only partly a cynical answer, I guess, to a cynical question.

THE PSYCHOTHERAPEUTIC PROCESS AND BPD

Question: Dr. Gunderson, you seem to be suggesting (see chapter 13), in your year-by-year description of what takes place, that there's always an orderly progression in the improvement (see chapter 13). That's not the case in my experience. Also, I am wondering about the end of therapy, because some of my patients have finished therapy, and they seem to be considerably better, yet in a sense therapy continues. Some of them stop completely; I never hear from them, or at least I haven't heard from them as yet, for five or seven years. But others call me every now and then, and some come back in for a few sessions at some change point in their life, the development of a relationship, the start of a marriage, and so on.

Just another comment, too, about something you mentioned at the beginning about the group of patients who don't continue in therapy because of the lack of family support. One of my experiences has been that family support or the support of others has been an extremely important element in the improvement of some of my patients; and those who have had good supports outside have often done a lot better than those who had either absent or negative supports. And just to follow up on what Dr. Stone said, I think some of these patients do better because of good marriages as well. They get into a marriage where the spouse is supportive, and possibly when the spouse dies that's when there may be a regression again.

Dr. Gunderson: An interesting set of comments. I agree that a good marriage may have corrective effects on some of the more basic aspects of borderline psychopathology. That goes back to a question that was discussed a bit this morning: what is it within these psychotherapies that might have led to the changes? Is it because of what they learned, or is it because of corrective

experiences which occur within the relationship with the therapist? I suspect that, for the most part, it has to do with the
corrective experiences; but the verbal interventions, the clarity
and the accuracy and the sensitivity with which interpretations,
clarifications, and confrontations are made, I think, have a
great deal to do with how fast a relationship becomes formed
in which corrective changes can occur. Yet I believe that the
critical processes in these changes have to do with the formation
of a stable, collaborative relationship with someone which, in
turn, is related less to the therapist's brilliance and more to
his or her reliability, stability, enthusiasm, and interest in that
person. Then the critical corrective change is related to the
expression of anger directly toward someone that was experienced as needed without having some kind of painful or harmful reaction (such as abandonment, etc.) result. Those things
are the crux of what happens. If you look at these cases, there
are some differences in both the outcome and in the therapies.
I would say that in the therapies where the boundaries were
policed most sharply, and where there was the most interpretive
activity, the self-definition issues improved better. You could
see gross improvements in other areas, but not in the identity
problems, from those cases where it was more purely a corrective type of experience without a great deal of cognitive learning associated with it. I think there may be some aspects of
outcome that are related to what are called the "specific" aspects
of therapy, and then there are other areas of outcome which
may be related to the nonspecific aspects of therapy.

How predictable are the patterns of change? You say your
experience has been different. I don't have a lot more cases to
draw from. There were some predictable aspects, and they
make sense to me. I think the diminution in acting out and
the formation of a positive and dependent relationship, those
things are always going to precede the kinds of modifications in
the expression and the ownership of aggression which occurred
later. I could be wrong, but that's my impression. Beyond that,
the issue of changes in identity, for example, might have happened highly variably. I just don't really have a good sense
of that from this case material—or from my own experience,
because I am always the same with patients.

The kind of terminations you describe, I think, are the more common. These cases were selected because we wanted cases that went boom, and then there were fairly clean terminations. That's not typical, and even in these cases there are two of them that keep in touch with the therapist from time to time; in two of these cases the therapist got in touch with the patient to review the case report, and that resumed some contact which otherwise hadn't been there. I can't remember the fifth.

Question: Dr. Michels, when you have worked with a borderline patient who happens to improve, what do you think are some of the therapeutic ingredients that you feel may have helped that person?

Dr. Michels: What makes a difference? My first answer to what I think makes a difference is I don't know. Having said that, one thing that makes a difference is sticking it out. This is not a short-term disorder, and there is no short-term treatment for the disorder. There may be events in it, however, that can be treated short term. But when you're treating the disorder, you're in for a long-term process and sticking it out is immensely important. I remember a study done at the New York State Psychiatric Institute, asking patients what made a difference to them, in their experience. They didn't talk much about the psychotherapeutic insights they obtained or the meetings with their enthusiastic therapist. They did talk about the regularity of the life in the system; that there was a schedule, that they knew they had three meals a day, and what time they were; that they were expected to be at various places doing various things at various times, and people cared if they weren't. The psychotherapeutic analog of that is the expectation of an ongoing relationship.

I also think it's helpful for the therapist to have theories. I think it's helpful for the therapist to be curious, interested, and actively involved in trying to understand what's happening in the treatment. I think it's less important whether the theory is valid. Patients are extraordinarily generous in forgiving benevolent therapists who are trying to understand something and

misunderstand it, but appropriately intolerant of bored or dis-
interested therapists who are not trying to figure out what's
going on. So I think an enthusiastic desire for understanding
is important.

In my experience the therapists who are best with this
group of patients are those whose enthusiasm and interest in
the process is infectious and obvious when you meet them.
These are not the patients for laid-back, flat, inexpressive, and
emotionally distant or reserved therapists.

I think an open-minded, iterative approach to revising
one's concept as the treatment progresses is vital. Harold
Searles, among others, has written about this. If you have not
revised your concept of the patient in three or four months of
treatment, you're not treating the patient. Treatment goes on
by a continuous revision of the therapist's concept of who the
patient is, and in a Loewaldian model the treatment occurs by
the patient becoming more like the therapist's concept as the
therapist's concept becomes more like the patient. I believe this
is very important in these patients, where the primary parental
role of the therapist has a higher ratio of significance to the
interpretive, uncovering role of the therapist treating the more
well-integrated patient.

The therapist of this patient must also be willing, when
indicated, to step out of a psychotherapeutic role and help the
patient. When my daughter was in kindergarten they had a
kind of show-and-tell where everyone went around the room
and they were asked "What does your daddy do?" It was a sexist
society at that point. And we live in an affluent suburb of New
York, and there were lots of doctors' children in the room, and
their daddies were pediatricians, internists, and surgeons and
my daughter had to differentiate me from them. She came
home and told me about it and I was shocked when she told
me what she said. She said, "My daddy's a doctor but he's not
like other doctors. He doesn't help people, he only talks to
them." The therapist of this patient must from time to time
appropriately help the patient, as well as talking to the patient.
It seems to me that this kind of flexibility is vital in the treatment
of these patients. I don't find any specific conceptual theory
convincingly superior to any other that allows these attributes

that I've discussed. In that statement, I will of course divorce myself from every known expert in the field, with one or two possible exceptions.

Dr. Stone: I was just going to say that I think Dr. Michels is correct in pointing out that one can start without a fixed theory. You start out with just impressions. Clinicians before DSM and before borderline was a popular term knew that if they had a patient who calls at all hours, or whose forty-five minutes were up and they were still sitting there crying, unwilling to leave, this was a different person than the one who sensed when the time was up—in other words, the nice, neurotic patient.

We start out with a series of uncomfortable experiences, and we say, these patients are different because they subject us to these uncomfortable experiences. As clinicians chat with each other, pretty soon we get an outline of what some of these characteristics are. Then someone like Dr. Kernberg or Dr. Gunderson or Dr. Grinker will categorize these patients and make a second generation theory built on the experiences of clincians who don't have much of a theory but have these experiences. There's a kind of dynamic interaction between experience and theory. Now we can speak of "the borderline patient." At first it was just "these patients." And then the process gets ever refined from one decade to the next.

Question: Dr. Gunderson, can you comment on limit-setting with these patients. Also I would like to make a comment about Dr. Kernberg. He is usually seen as focusing on anger and less on the caring aspects. At least that's what comes through in his writing. But when you meet him as a person, it's quite different. I wonder if you see a parallel between that and Freud's writing about therapeutic neutrality as contrasted by his described behavior by his biographers.

Dr. Gunderson: I think that nonpunitive limit-setting is a very important aspect of treatment. It's not sufficient by itself, but I think that it is actually as important. It's a form of care and it's as important as the types of things that usually are identified as care, like being attentive to the person. The monitoring of the boundaries of the therapy, even without the limit-setting, just the attention given to whether the patient is late or has not paid the bill, is a very reassuring and very caring communication in its own right. To set some limits on that without being cruel, and without being angry, is something that comes easily after a while. I often am surprised and impressed by how people who are just beginning to work with borderline patients find it difficult to do, and when they do do it, it's like they're overcoming some ideas within themselves about that being a cruel or a mean thing to do, and so they tend to do it with a kind of vengeance or a strictness or a rigidity which isn't necessary. Of course then the patient reacts in a way that confirms their fears. I think if you do it long enough, especially if you raise your own kids, it's just very comfortable and patients rarely get very upset about it.

Different therapists have different personalities. It is interesting how this gets translated into their work. I was very appreciative of your comment about Dr. Kernberg. Like you, I know that Dr. Kernberg is actually a very warm and very upbeat sort of person despite the strict sobriety and aggressiveness of the language he uses in his writing style. I was alluding to this in an oblique way. He wanted to do something about drop-outs; he set up a contract, and you've got a procedure. That's his way of doing things. It doesn't mean that it has to be done that way, and in the style with which he would do such things, that it would come across that way. At one conference I attended with him, somebody said to him: "How can you be sure that if a patient gets well in your care, it has anything to do with what you think about their psychopathology or the techniques you use? What about the kind of enthusiasm, the kind of intelligence, and the kind of attentiveness which are so clearly part of your style?" Well, I thought that was a wonderful question, and I do think that those aspects of a therapist, whether you're named Kernberg or not, are closer to what are the essential ingredients of being able to do well by such patients.

Question: I'd like to ask Dr. Gunderson to comment on the connection between two things that he had raised in his presentation (see chapter 13). One was the observation that there is a window in which people do therapy, or qualified people who have finished their residencies, do therapy with borderline patients, for a one-year to an eight-year period; and the second is the fact that the therapists of these patients said that they would have done things differently in retrospect but had no successes after they had learned about what things they would do differently. Which seems to imply to me that you think that they forgot how to do something that was important or stopped doing it. So even if there is no direct connection between those two points, I wonder if you could comment further on each; but if there is a connection between the two, on that particularly.

Dr. Gunderson: I think there is a connection. I think what they learned in the course of these treatments is to recognize and be more comfortable with the aggressive and controlling motives behind much of the acting out behaviors. And so, having identified that, they would then do what you would think Kernberg would suggest—although I think in truth he is somewhat different in his actual style—that you become interpretive about those motives earlier on, and you set limits earlier, and that would be okay except if you do it too quickly, and you do it too vehemently, and then get negative reactions. Again, let me use the example of the patient I've seen, that I was so upset with this last week. I'm getting on. I mean, I'm not old but I've seen most of my practice as borderline patients and it has been for years. And I know what she's doing. It's perfectly plain to me. So it redoubles my impatience—why the hell doesn't she listen to me? As if the truth of the motives behind what she's doing are the hard part of the matter, rather than the fact that she's still in there trying to create a kind of relationship where she could listen to me. There are certain aspects of this work which have to take precedence before her understanding that she would accept the benzedrine from a stranger on the weekend because that might have something to do with how she was feeling at that time rather than because the stranger was an asshole. She got ready to think about these things, and yet I could have told her on the second day I saw her. Yes, and cured her—right. We'd have had this impasse in the second week instead in the sixth month.

Dr. Stone: I just want to back up what Dr. Gunderson was just saying. It isn't that when we get to a certain age we can't treat borderlines. I think we still have some trickle of success even as we cross Dante's midpoint in our life. But there is the disenchantment factor, of being wise to it already, so that one gets a bit jaded as one gets older. The other thing is that there is a fatigue factor, and also a willingness of the younger therapist who is just building up a practice to take on what I used to call the first-year type, the nonpaying paranoids of the first year of practice, and the patients who call you late, something that your professor wouldn't tolerate, but he thinks that you might not mind. But then when you get up to a certain level yourself, you begin to feel no longer happy and willing to take on that kind of burden, and so you expect that your patients can't do that sort of thing. And then of course there are some who can accept the limit and won't, but then there are other patients who will not accept the limit and will quit and go on to some younger therapist.

Also you have the problem that those who succeed in writing about borderline conditions and getting on the lecture circuit have lots of absences which some of the borderline patients find extremely intolerable. And so one becomes an expert in the patients that one can no longer treat. I have a number who make little dots on the calendar—"When are you going away again?" And that sort of thing. So I would know how to treat them and might be willing to treat them but one's life interferes, and Dr. Kernberg's life and Dr. Michels' life would interfere even more. Dr. Kernberg is on sabbatical. A borderline patient can't hold an image of the therapist for three months in his head, and say, well, "See you when you get back." No way. There are ironical situations that happen with older therapists who are academics and so on, and get in the way of their utilizing the knowledge that they've accumulated over the years.

Question: Dr. Michels, you were suggesting we need new metaphors for description in psychotherapy. I think in a way you very directly suggested one which strikes me as being a very important one. You said something about the experience of the collaborative process of searching, and it seems to me that that's a very important point. I think there is a theory that underlies what you have been saying. Bandura talking about psychotherapy has suggested that there's a hierarchy in the effectiveness of different processes. The imparting of information, or a kind of didactic approach, is low on the scale; a vicarious experience, for example, seeing others cope with difficult situations, is higher on the scale; and the actual experience of being in a situation where certain changes take place in a relationship is highest on the scale, for example, being able to cope in a situation. And so when you talk about the collaborative, and I put the emphasis on the collaborative, experience of psychotherapy, I think you're talking about a new experience for these people in which they are participating. It takes time because their formative experiences took time. It's kind of humbling that we, perhaps in seven or ten years, can change the direction of something that took place over fifteen, twenty, twenty-five years. So the amount of time in relative terms perhaps is small, if we keep that kind of concept in mind.

Question: Dr. Michels, what are your thoughts from an economic point of view of what's happening to the treatment process, perhaps more visible in the United States than in Canada, but maybe coming here as well, as our ability to do long-term treatment is eaten away at. You've said that this is a long-term process of sticking with the patient. The many factors that prevent us from doing that are perhaps gaining in intensity. I'd like to know what your feelings are about that in regard to this diagnosis.

Dr. Michels: It seems to me that we are beginning to have a very important avenue of dealing with the economics and sociology of long-term treatment. These patients are either in long-term treatment or in repeated short-term treatment. There is no third alternative. They are therapy-philiacs and crisis producers. Therefore, if we collect our data appropriately, and we are beginning to do that, it is fairly easy to demonstrate that one of the reasons why long-term treatment is a good idea is because it's cheaper. It is cheaper to do long-term, stable treatment than to do a series of different short-term treatments with somebody whose pathology includes episodes of suicidal behavior and the like, and who can get treated by different systems and different components for each of them. So we've done things such as look at the number of days people spend in the hospital and the hospital bill when they're admitted three or more times in two years. We have collected that data and used it to argue that such experiences are a good reason for arguing for the support for long-term treatment from those people who have no humanitarian instinct whatsoever but want the bottom line to be lower. I'm not sure that's an inappropriate challenge or requirement that we need to respond to. It seems to be that one of the things we have to do is to develop better predictors of which patients will have problems if they don't have long-term treatment, and which patients will take the long-term treatment and make it just another relationship without the treatment coloring their life very much. There is a group that requires repeated short-term treatment. Dr. Stone was referring to some of them. And if we can identify this group it will enhance our credibility in appealing for support for treating those patients requiring long-term treatment.

Question: I've noticed that no one has addressed the issue of the borderline who is a parent. What are your ways of handling that?

Dr. Stone: Masterson has written a lot about borderlines with borderline parents, mothers in particular. Especially if one uses tighter diagnostic criteria as Dr. Gunderson does, the so-called connection that Dr. Masterson speaks of doesn't hold up very well. Despite the fact that there will be some BPD mothers and maybe even fathers of the borderline patient, I don't think it really breeds true and has genetic significance in the same way that it would for schizophrenic parents in having an 11 percent risk of having a schizophrenic child.

I think the traumatogenetic and the environmental impact is what accounts for so much. You may have a borderline mother who does wicked things to the child, or an incestuous father who might have a severe character disorder and who's doing terrible things to the child. That child becomes border-line because of the changes in activation patterns in the nervous system that are engendered by that chronic maladaptive pattern, and therefore they develop a certain syndrome that we identify as borderline. We can identify it for other reasons in the mother, and it's not because the genes carry it along but because there are terrible patterns and so on. But as to how often it occurs, it's hard to say. It's much easier to spot bipolar and schizophrenic and other kinds of relatives because the data from the charts is usually better about that than in these more subtle things having to do with personality.

So when I reviewed the 206 BPD patients, having almost 400 biological parents (some were adoptees), there were a small number of mothers and fathers that I knew from interviewing were borderline, but not so very many. And others were just a question mark. The ones that I knew had certain pathology would be bipolar illness or unipolar illness, or something like that. So I don't think that, unless one does a study prospectively and really looks at the families with structured questionnaires along the lines of what Dr. Gunderson is saying, you can really get an answer to that.

Dr. Gunderson: I'd like to comment on another aspect of this. It's something that I've been writing about, and that is I think one of the knottiest, most difficult clinical problems to treat a borderline patient who has a small child or small children. First of all, I think there's a syndrome which is associated with it, whereby the young borderline mother becomes very upset about the issues related to giving care to the child. As a result, they often go and seek therapy for the first time, usually with a severe depression. And when they get there, they may form an intense and erotized transference if it's a male therapist wherein they act out self-destructively and get hospitalized. This is enacting a rescue on the part of the therapist who often feels that the problem has to do with the erotized transference rather than the fact that the erotized transference itself was a defensive flight away from the prolems of managing the aggression stimulated in the parents when taking care of the child. A pattern gets set up where, once she is in the hospital, the young borderline mother feels much better. At that point she has a very rapid diminution of the depression. Because it's dramatic, some people will attribute it to antidepressants. The person's profoundly depressed, suicidal, and they come in and, unlike most borderline patients, they're much better. So everybody feels good, the patient then returns home, and all of a sudden the patient is right back in the very situation that she started with and it was never addressed.

Now, having said all that, and you're two steps smarter now, the patient comes into your office with the same problem—what do you do? Because at that point you do have a very serious problem. You can say that this woman needs to remove herself for a period of time from the children, and some alternative form of care needs to be given to them. The patient needs to grow up and get some mastery and distance on these issues, because it's no favor to the children to have her there in the state that she was. Or, you can have her go back into the situation and try to provide more supports within that situation. But if you do that, you've got to have a therapy which is then guarded against the intensity which develops. The therapist has to be smart and has to be good at setting limits because that, I think, more so than any other situation, is one in which the borderline patient really turns to the therapist with the most intense demands. Only very good therapists can deal with that and keep the patient out of the hospital. It's not easy, and I have not seen which of those two routes is better. I have seen two or three cases where, after a year of separation from the children, either the husband wanted a divorce or the borderline person is beginning to think that they should never have gotten into that situation in the first place and that it would be wrong, cruel, and destructive to go back to try to care for the children until she's better. And so, at that point, you've got a couple of more years. In one instance, the woman went into a job, remained in therapy, and basically let the marriage go its own way.

Dr. Stone: I have some experience along those lines that I think is similar to Dr. Gunderson's. It's a very poignant situation because it's very difficult for us as therapists to have the kind of salesmanship that can help a mother save face in admitting that she doesn't want to care for her child. Many borderline women avoid the whole business of childbirth (and even marriage as a means of avoiding childbirth) because they have some inchoate awareness that they can't master this task gracefully. There are some in the follow-up study who sought one unsuitable partner after another until they got to an age where the subject became moot because they were now thirty-eight, thirty-nine, and it didn't matter any more. Now they could marry a man who either didn't want kids, or had a kid from a previous marriage, and she could be the stepmother, and didn't have to face that. But where they have one, and they don't go the route of that horrible woman in the news last week who smothered her kids and got let off because it was postpartum, they begin to decompensate with the task of motherhood. The obvious thing is to get them into a hospital and to do this salesmanship, and to make her aware that she does not have the choice of being a comfortable, happy good mother, or a child killer. She only has the choice of being a woman who destroys her child by being with it, or who doesn't destroy the child by being absent from it, and that the latter choice is better, at least in the here-and-now. Maybe at some time later she might be a comfortable mother—maybe. This is a very difficult thing. Within the study, for instance, there was one woman who became abusive toward her own child, and now has a court restraining order by the judge against visiting her child. This is a borderline woman who is also alcoholic. There was another who abandoned her children as a way of coping; in other words, she couldn't cope, she kept decompensating as long as she was with them, so she left them in the care of her ex-husband, and now she's footloose and fancy-free and comfortable, but not in the motherhood role. It's very poignant, but also the borderline women in my study now have an average age of thirty-eight, so that they are at an age when they would have married and would have had a kid if they were going to. Only half of them have married, and only a fourth have children, so there's a much lower marriage and childbearing rate than there would be in the general population, partly because of the difficulties that they intrinsically have in handling parenting.

Dr. Gunderson: I have to add one more comment on this, too. Another way in which this comes up is when an unmarried borderline patient gets pregnant and has to confront the issue of having an abortion, or having a child of whom they feel ill-prepared to take care. If they have the abortion, they are enacting a murder because they don't have, quite aside from one's religious beliefs, the subtlety to deal with this as something other than just the grossest form of murder. On the other hand, the alternative, as they see it, was to have the child and reenact with the child exactly what had happened. For example, a woman was born as her mother was being left by the patient's father, and so mother was stuck with the child that was really a kind of noose around her neck. The patient has very vivid memories of how she was beaten frequently. She herself was struggling at the time she got pregnant with her wishes to murder the mother. So that the whole circularity of that was just awful; either way she turned it was bad. So what I did was something along the lines of what Mike was suggesting. I made an appeal to her observing ego. I tried to distance her from this, and sort of put it in a larger sphere and build up some kind of rationality for her going ahead and having the abortion. She went ahead and had the abortion, but I fear I'm going to pay for it for life, because she had it because of me, as she sees it now.

PSYCHOSOMATIC DISORDERS AND BPD

Question: Can you comment on the relationship between BPD and psychosomatic disorders.

Dr. Stone: I think you raise an interesting question in connection with the psychosomatic disorders. It's like one of those questions in algebra: given borderline, what is the likelihood of having one of these psychosomatic disorders; given one of those psychosomatic disorders like unstable diabetes, what is the likelihood of borderline? I don't know the answer to either question. I have seen and worked with in consultation some unstable diabetics whose psychopathology also qualifies them as BPD borderlines and who use their diabetes, and can play it very finely as a self-damaging act. They can throw themselves into acute acidosis at the drop of a hat, and do so whenever the chips are down (e.g., within the context of some family disagreement), and what have you. They are remarkably difficult to treat because they really require the efforts of a very astute medical endocrinological team as well as psychotherapists of uncommon skill and patience. I have some patients with regional enteritis and have had some in the past with thyroid disease. All I can say is that there are a fair number of patients who have one of these conditions who are simultaneously borderline, at least by Kernberg criteria, and some also by Dr. Gunderson or DSM, or more strict criteria. But I do not know the exent of the overlap. I wouldn't be able to say what percentage of, let's say, ulcerative colitis cases are borderline. I do think, though, that we have a greater realization now that not all psychosomatic illness, so-called, like ulcerative colitis or ulcer, necessarily have that same psychodynamic picture that we used to hear so much about in the fifties, or perhaps still would from the Argentinean school who write about the mother biting her tummy from within. I think that we now realize that these illnesses have to do with a number of interactive factors, and not all ulcerative colitis patients are really emotionally handicapped. But there are a good number that are borderline even by the strictest criteria. I would say there is some area of overlap the extent of which I simply don't know.

Question: I wondered if any of you can comment on what I think you could almost call a psychiatric Munchausen which is a patient who seems very much to be borderline but lays really vibrant claim to an Axis I diagnosis such as, in particular, anorexia nervosa, multiple personality disorder, and what is seen most recently, schizophrenia. How do you approach this patient in terms of what they want to present to you as the area that demands treatment, versus what you feel is very strongly a personality, particularly a borderline, problem.

Dr. Gunderson: I don't know about Axis I in particular, but I do know that many borderline patients use a variety of disabilities or symptoms as a way to appeal for attention and care and protective surroundings, and I think under those circumstances you should do a combination of things. You should always let them know they can get what they want by asking for it directly, and that you understand that the symptom is serving that function. You accompany that by doing what I think is sort of a principle of false surrender. You can get me to give you what you appear to want, but it's probably going to be bad for you, and that will reflect upon me and my inadequacies, and my helplessness in the face of you. So it's a pyrrhic victory.

Dr. Stone: People often say the Munchausen patient is a brand of borderline. I think the factitious illness component is such a distinctive clinical entity that it's not good to throw it into the borderline basket. But the patient who has some of the BPD features but who, in addition, is a Munchausen, is a supremely difficult patient to treat because they are extraordinarily hostile and contemptuous of authority. The only cases I've ever known that really got better after having started out with a long career of factitious illness are several patients treated by women psychiatrists. I was beginning to think as you were talking that there is something about being female that allowed them to be more comfortable therapeutic objects to deal with than male therapists. I have had several Munchausens who have been total failures. One of them, however, was then seen by a woman analyst who did very excellent work with this young woman who had actually enucleated an eye as part of her self-damaging and fake illness. They are very difficult to treat, for the reasons I mentioned, and they may be borderline but they're borderline plus.

PSYCHOPHARMACOLOGICAL TREATMENT OF BPD

Question: Dr. Stone, I'm interested in how in your own practice you view the use of psychotropics and other medication, for example tricyclics and lithium, for those patients who have a comorbidity of affective disorder. What do you actually do in your day-to-day practice?

Dr. Stone: Speaking not as a psychopharmacologist I fall back on suggestions given by people like Dr. Glassman or Dr. Paul Soloff. And of course Dr. Cowdry also knows a great deal more about this than I do. With those comorbid patients, depending upon the target symptoms, there will be some where a tricyclic antidepressant will be useful if there's depression without too much in the way of irritability or hostility. Some people feel that the monoamine oxidase (MAO) inhibitors are better where there's the combination of depression with impulsivity and hostility. Lithium may be useful in some of the patients, and in some who have marked predisposition to outbursts of violence or irritability of a major sort. Tegretol or even anticonvulsants may be useful. With the patients who have a mixed borderline picture, they have some borderline BPD traits and schizotypal traits: if they have significant strands of time in which they exhibit psychoticism, low-dose neuroleptics may be very useful. Dr. Soloff suggests that at 6 mg of Haldol or 4 mg of Stelazine, tardive dyskinesia (TD) doesn't seem to be a problem. He feels that he can give these small doses without too much worry about TD, and it can be very useful in curbing those symptoms. So that when I see comorbidity of a sort that is throwing off target symptoms, I'm comfortable to use one or another medication, whatever it takes to get the patient calm and in control, so that we can then work on the dynamics of the situation and do the psychotherapeutic work that will round out their lives and help them interact better with people, and so on.

Question: Will you yourself prescribe the medication?

Dr. Stone: Yes. However, sometimes if it's very complicated, then I work in conjunction with a colleague who is more expert in that area, and the patient is simultaneously treated by both of us.

If the patient has the posttraumatic stress disorder (PTSD)-like picture or is an abuse victim, I will take that into consideration. If the patient has been very traumatized early in life in that way, I may be very slow in bringing that material into the treatment, because it may be overwhelming and cause the patient to have a psychotic break. So even if I'm aware of a dynamic I'm going to wait until the patient is built up in some way—is working better, or has a more effective relationship, where she can then view the horror of her early life from a distance and feel that, "well these terrible things happened but they haven't prevented me from having any kind of a good life." Whereas when they first come to you and their life is still pretty awful, they feel that they might be a permanent victim of the horrors of the past, and then it's too frightening and disruptive to talk about. So there's timing. I will change the schedule of topics that I may want to bring up in accordance with what I sense to be the true nature of their past.

Question: Is there a risk in using lithium with these patients?

Dr. Stone: The question has to do with the risk, including the suicide risk, of the use of lithium in this category of patient. I don't think that very many borderline patients numerically need lithium. I don't have very many of my borderline patients unless they have bipolar II kind of illness or severe premenstrual syndrome (PMS) of a sort that happens to respond to lithium, which only maybe one in five cases would, will I prescribe it. The risk would be in abusing the lithium, and ending up with a kidney problem or neurological problems. I've seen one or two. It hasn't happened fortunately within my own practice, but I've seen patients hospitalized who in effect tried to commit suicide with lithium, and ended up with pretty severe neurological damage and so on. I think that's uncommon enough that I don't worry about the use of lithium in the relatively few patients where I think there is an indication. But I don't use it across the board.

Question: Dr. Cowdry, could you comment on the implications of a constitutional predisposition for BPD clinically.

Dr. Cowdry: Some patients have a predisposition, for example, having a short fuse or feeling a terrible dysphoria that makes them want to injure themselves. Yet the patient must still work out and be helped to work out a way to deal with this because he or she is still responsible for the terrible, internal affective state.

Pharmacotherapy may have an indirect role in this. Patients are taught to do self-ratings on their affective state. This is primarily to monitor how medication is used. However, self-rating can also enhance the observing ego. Like diaries and other kinds of self-reports, they are a way of asking the patient to observe his own actions and feelings, and thus increase the observing part of the ego. Some patients may have a counter-reaction. Self-observation causes them to feel they are damaged as they have always thought. This can be significant. However, on the whole, this approach is useful in our research methodology and can actually help in the process of exploration in psychotherapy.

Question: What about the combination of Carbamazepine and Tranylcypromine in the treatment of these people?

Dr. Cowdry: There's no organized data about the combination of Carbamazepine and Tranylcypromine and any other MAO inhibitors. There are some reports of them being used successfully in combination. Let me address two issues. First of all there is the pharmacologic risk. Carbamazepine has a tricyclic structure and there's certainly a theoretical and possibly some reported problems of the typical tricyclic–MAO inhibitor difficulty. So if one were to use them in combination, the usual recommendation would be to start them simultaneously at a lower dose or to start the Carbamazepine first and add the MAO inhibitor subsequently. There are some suggestions that it may have additive effects, wholly based on comments from people who have tried it, and I think that most of the half dozen individuals I've heard from who have used the two in combination say it's most useful with Bipolar II patients who also have affective disorder and some behavioral discontrol possibly as well. There is no good base of knowledge to answer the question. It is an interesting question though whether you can treat what seem to be, in some sense, separable dimensions of problems with combinations of medication. I don't tend to be a polypharmacist, but that doesn't mean that you might not come across a patient where that might be indicated.

Question: Is there any data on very low-dose use of tricyclic antidepressants?

Dr. Cowdry: In my experience borderline patients may be very sensitive to medication and cannot tolerate full treatment doses, particularly the more adrenergic drugs (e.g., Desipramine or Imipramine), and in relatively modest treatment doses develop a profound anxiety or heightened depersonalization or derealization. It is therefore sometimes necessary to use low doses. However, when using low doses, one sometimes wonders whether it will be effective only if there is a coexisting panic disorder.

Question: Dr. Cowdry, I noticed that five of your sixteen patients (see chapter 16) had a history of stimulant use. Was there anything in particular that you noticed about those five patients in terms of history or response to pharmacotherapies?

Dr. Cowdry: We screened specifically for alcohol or stimulant abuse. The use of stimulants seemed to be an attempt to self-medicate dysphoric states. However, although we hoped these patients might respond to Parnate, we had great difficulty finding any predictors of response. We're still not very far along the road to subtyping.

Question: In those patients where there was some effect, either with Haldol or with Tegretol or Parnate, could you tell us about the longitudinal course? Do these patients need to stay on this medication forever? Is the treatment kind of a holding action or does it in fact change something of a central nature in a permanent way? Or is it episodic? We are assuming that the biochemical abnormalities cause the behavior. Is there also a possibility that the behavior, in fact, causes the biochemical abnormalities?

Dr. Cowdry: Let me answer the second question first. Clearly in these kind of biological forays that is readily a possibility. Indeed one of the interesting models for this kind of excitable individual, linking it to developmental trauma, would be a Kindling Model. This emphasizes specifically that some biological changes are produced by experience, not just of the memory sort but specifically that you can change the threshold for excitability in limbic structures through repetitive exposure, such as someone facing profound fear regularly and unpredictably. I think that's a very real possibility and one of the intriguing questions about this interaction.

The first question was about long-term treatment with medications. Is it needed? What tends to be the course? The course, like every other course with these patients, is unpredictable and somewhat sporadic. I don't think the medications themselves do anything permanent in terms of treating anything. That would be too much to ask for from medication. There are individuals who stabilize clinically and in six to twelve months are able to stop their medication. They then can readily stop the medication and some of that lability returns, but their ego is strengthened. In some patients the capacity to use the skills from psychotherapy to manage their lability exists. Other patients don't achieve that at all and have to go back to the medication repeatedly, or stay on the medication in terms of managing their dysphoria. It may have something to do also with severity. In my experience, such people make the least progress in psychotherapy, even though they stay in it, and often have disturbed histories.

Dr. Stone: A question, but also a response with respect to how long you have to be on medication—there are some answers, partial answers you get in the long-term follow-up studies. For instance one of the patients in the PI 500 twenty years ago was admitted with severe symptomatology, had long-term psychotherapy, was put on medication, eventually was placed on lithium. He was on lithium for five years and seemed considerably improved. As often happens with patients that respond well, he got bored with taking the lithium and discontinued it. However, in this case, he has remained well for thirteen years and is now singing in one of the prominent opera houses in our country. Doctors are usually too conservative to take the risk of discontinuing a successful medication, but sometimes patients make successful natural experiments of this sort themselves. Looking at the other side of the coin, I wonder if Dr. Cowdry had recommendations for those patients who refuse to go to the hospital, have suicidality, and don't respond to the drugs. You're afraid to put them on Parnate or Nardil because if it doesn't work, they could really kill themselves with this drug, but when you put them on some milder drug like Desyrel, from which no one has ever died, nothing beneficial happens. What do you do in those kind of annoying cases?

Dr. Cowdry: I think sometimes our concerns about MAO inhibitors are exaggerated. These patients can abuse anything that they're put on. One of the things we were surprised at is that there was less in the way of dietary indiscretions and certainly less in the way of abuse with MAO inhibitors than we'd anticipated. Specifically, it's been my experience that if it occurs, it tends to occur with the benzodiazepines, for example, or with the sedating drugs rather than with the MAO inhibitors. The reason for this is in part because you learn relatively rapidly whether there is going to be a response or not and if there isn't, that's it. But it is a luxury serving mostly as a consultant, and not really having to ultimately make the decision as the primary treater must do.

Question: Can you comment on any subgroups of BPD that react idiosyncratically to medications?

Dr. Cowdry: There seem to be two main subgroups. Some patients seem to have peculiar organic responses to lithium. Others have difficulty with alcohol and benzodiazepines. Alprazolam in particular has led to significant disinhibition in our studies. I think there is a real problem in any behavioral disinhibited population in treating them with disinhibiting drugs.

THE GERIATRIC BPD

Question: I spent the first half of my fifteen years in psychiatry at this hospital working with Danny Silver and the borderline disorders, and doing all that was necessary with young, intensively treated patients. A number of years ago I moved over into geriatrics, and I thought I was going to leave the difficulties with trials of this kind of work and go into something much calmer and easier. I found that that was not true; that the patients, in a variety of different ways, posed very similar kinds of problems, particularly those who were institutionalized; and that the staff difficulties and the kinds of things that were reflected back to us as consultants and therapists on those units were very similar to what we encountered in our intensive inpatient treatment. It raised the question of to what degree does character pathology and borderline pathology exist in old age, particularly in light of the longitudinal research that suggests that these patients settle down in the middle years. I think that there is some evidence now that there's a little reverse J-shaped curve that starts to show about the age of sixty, that symptoms begin to return somewhere around that time. I have ideas about why that happens, but I'd like first to just comment that clinically there is dramatic evidence frequently in the geriatric group of personality disorder. What the origins of that are and how one goes about defining what the syndrome is in old age as opposed to in younger years (when there is much more dramatic expression of acting out behavior and affect than there is in old age) remains unclear. I'd like to ask you about your experience or the experience of others in this whole area, and how we go about further investigating it.

Dr. Gunderson: First of all, it sounds like you may have more experience than I do, and maybe than most people do, and you ought to start writing it up. The reverse side of these longer-term follow-up studies that Mike Stone and Tom McGlashan and Joel Paris and a few other people have done is that the good news, the surprising news, the news that everybody has focused most of their attention on, is that 40 to 60 percent of those borderline patients are doing very well. That's because that's the good news, and people like to focus on that side of things. The bad news, of course, is that 40 to 60 percent are still profoundly disabled by this disorder, and I think a good number of them over the long haul go into hiding, in a way. That is, either because of a substance abuse problem, which masks some of the acting out problems and gets them involved in self-help groups instead of in hospitals and clinics, or because they find a stable, hostile–dependent, sadomasochistic relationship, they do not appear at our doors too often and they look better, but their psychopathology remains there to be unveiled by stress. I'd be very interested in a more systematic look at the kinds of things which could cause someone whom you would identify as borderline to become disturbed enough, dysfunctional enough, to become a clinical case in old age. I don't know enough about it myself.

Dr. Stone: My own comment about that is probably along the lines of the person who asked the question, and also what McGlashan has said: that as borderline patients get into their forties and fifties, another thing that veils this pathology is a bad, stormy marriage; but then when that breaks up or dissolves, the once-and-future borderline patient discovers that being alone is worse than the bad marriage, and they decompensate all over again, and then you see, with the death of the spouse, the resumption of the impulsive ways, and sometimes even to the point of wrist scratching and the whole thing.

Dr. Gunderson: That would be a good hunch and would make sense. I have seen borderline people who emerge in midlife when, around similar loss issues, marriage wasn't sufficient but children became a focus for their life and the loss of children can have a similar kind of precipitating action. This should be studied systematically.

References

Abend, S., Porder, M., & Willick, M. (1983), *Borderline Patients: Psycho-analytic Perspectives*. New York: International Universities Press.

Abramowitz, S., Carroll, J., & Schaffer, C. (1984), Borderline personality disorder and the MMPI. *J. Clin. Psychol.*, 40:410–413.

Adams-Silvan, A., & Silvan, M. (1988), On transitionality and defects in empathic capacity: A clinical and theoretical study. In: *The Solace Paradigm—An Eclectic Search for Psychological Immunity*, ed. P. Horton, H. Gewirtz, & K. Kreutter. Madison, CT: International Universities Press.

Adler, G. (1970), Valuing and devaluing in the psychotherapeutic process. *Arch. Gen. Psychiat.*, 22:454–461.

——— (1972), Helplessness in the helpers. *Brit. J. Med. Psychol.*, 45:315–326.

——— (1973), Hospital treatment of borderline patients. *Amer. J. Psychiat.*, 130:32–36.

——— (1977), Hospital management of borderline patients and its relation to psychotherapy. In: *Borderline Personality Disorders*, ed. P. Hartocollis. New York: International Universities Press.

——— (1979), The myth of the alliance with borderline patients. *Amer. J. Psychiat.*, 136:642–645.

——— (1980), Transference, real relationship and alliance. *Internat. J. Psycho-Anal.*, 61:547–558.

——— (1981), The borderline–narcissistic personality disorder continuum. *Amer. J. Psychiat.*, 138:40–50.

——— (1984), Issues in the treatment of the borderline patient. In: *Kohut's Legacy, Contributions to Self Psychology*, ed. P. E. Stepansky & A. I. Goldberg. Hillside, NJ: Analytic Press.

——— (1985), *Borderline Psychopathology and Its Treatment*. New York: Jason Aronson.

——— (1989), Transitional phenomena, projective identification, and the essential ambiguity of the psychoanalytic situation. *Psychoanal. Quart.*, 58:81–104.

——— Buie, D. M. (1972), The misuses of confrontation with borderline patients. *Internat. J. Psychoanal. Psychother.*, 1:109–120.

——— ——— (1979), Aloneness and borderline psychopathology: The possible relevance of child development issues. *Internat. J. Psycho-Anal.*, 60:83–96.

647

—— Rhine, M. W. (1988), The selfobject function of projective identification: Curative factors in psychotherapy. *Bull. Menn. Clin.*, 52:473–491.

Agras, W. S., Dorian, B., Kirkley, B. G., Arnow, B., & Bachman, J. (1987), Imipramine in the treatment of bulimia. *Internat. J. Eat. Disord.*, 6:29–38.

Aguilar, M. T., Lemaire, M., Castro, P., Libotte, M., Reynders, J., & Herchuelz, A. (1984). Study of the diagnostic value of the dexamethasone suppression test in endogenous depression. *J. Affect. Disord.*, 6:33–42.

Ainsworth, M. D. S., Blehar, M. C., Waters, E., & Wall, S. (1978), *Patterns of Attachment*. Hillsdale, NJ: Lawrence Erlbaum.

Akiskal, H. S. (1981), Subaffective disorders: Dysthymic, cyclothymic, and bipolar II disorders in the "borderline" realm. *Psychiat. Clin. N. Amer.*, 4:25–46.

—— (1983), Dysthymic disorder: Psychopathology of proposed chronic depressive subtypes. *Amer. J. Psychiat.*, 140:11–20.

—— (1984), Characterologic manifestations of affective disorders: Toward a new conceptualization. *Integrative Psychiat.*, May–June: 83–88.

—— (1987), The milder spectrum of bipolar disorders: Diagnostic, characterologic and pharmacologic aspects. *Psychiat. Ann.*, 17:33–37.

—— Chen, E. C., Davis, G. C., Puzantan, V. R., Kashgarian, M., & Bolinger, S. M. (1985a), Borderline: An adjective in search of a noun. *J. Clin. Psychiat.*, 46:41–48.

—— Djenderedjian, A. H., Rosenthal, R. H., & Khani, M. K. (1977), Cyclothymic disorder: Validating criteria for inclusion in the bipolar affective group. *Amer. J. Psychiat.*, 134:1227–1233.

—— Hirschfeld, R. M. A., & Yerevanian, B. I. (1988), The relationship of personality to affective disorder: A critical review. *Arch. Gen. Psychiat.*, 40:801–810.

—— Khani, M. K., & Scott-Strauss, A. (1979), Cyclothymic temperamental disorders. *Psychiat. Clin. N. Amer.*, 2:527–554.

—— Mallya, G. (1987), Criteria for the "soft" bipolar spectrum: Treatment implications. *Psychopharmacol. Bull.*, 23:68–73.

—— Rosenthal, T. L., Haykal, R. F., Lemmi, H., Rosenthal, R. H., & Scott-Strauss, A. (1980), Characterological depressions: Clinical and sleep electroencephalographic findings separating "subaffective dysthymias" from "character–spectrum disorders." *Arch. Gen. Psychiat.*, 37:777–783.

———— Tashjian, R. (1983), Affective disorders: Part II. Recent advances in laboratory and pathogenic approaches. *Hosp. Commun. Psychiat.*, 34:822–830.

———— Yerevanian, B. I., Davis, G. C., King, D., & Lemmi, H. (1985b), The nosologic status of borderline personality: Clinical and polysomnographic study. *Amer. J. Psychiat.*, 142:192–198.

Amark, C. (1951), A study in alcoholism. *Acta Psychiat. Neurol. Scand.*, 70(Suppl.).

American Psychiatric Association (1980), *The Diagnostic and Statistical Manual of Mental Disorders*, 3rd ed. (DSM-III). Washington, DC: American Psychiatric Association.

———— (1987), *The Diagnostic and Statistical Manual of Mental Disorders*, 3rd ed., rev. (DSM-III-R). Washington, DC: American Psychiatric Association.

Amsterdam, B. K. (1972), Mirror self-image reactions before age two. *Develop. Psychol.*, 5:297–305.

Andreasen, N. C., Endicott, J., Spitzer, R. L., & Winokur, G. (1977), The family history method using diagnostic criteria—Reliability and validity. *Arch. Gen. Psychiat.*, 34:1229–1235.

Andrulonis, P. A., Glueck, B. C., Stroebel, C. F., Vogel, N. G., Shapiro, A. L., & Aldridge, D. M. (1981), Organic brain dysfunction and the borderline syndrome. In: *Symposium on Borderline Disorders*, ed. M. H. Stone. Also in *Psychiat. Clin. N. Amer.*, No. 4, 1:47–66.

———— ———— ———— ———— (1982), Borderline personality subcategories. *J. Nerv. & Ment. Dis.*, 170:670–679.

———— Vogel, N. G. (1984), Comparison of borderline subcategories to schizophrenic and affective disorders. *Brit. J. Psychiat.*, 144:358–363.

Anthony, E. J. (1970), Two contrasting types of adolescent depression and their treatment. *J. Amer. Psychoanal. Assn.*, 18:841–859.

Antoni, M., Tischer, P., Levine, J., Green, C., & Millon, T. (1985), Refining personality assessments by combining MCMI high point profiles and MMPI codes, Part I: MMPI code 28/82. *J. Personal. Assess.*, 49:392–398.

Apfel, R. J., & Simon, B. (1985), Patient–therapist sexual contact: Psychodynamic perspectives on the cause and results. *Psychother. Psychosom.*, 43:57–62.

Arkema, P. (1981), The borderline personality and transitional relatedness. *Amer. J. Psychiat.*, 138:172–177.

———— (1988), Bonding in the families of borderline patients. In: *The Solace Paradigm—An Eclectic Search for Psychological Immunity*, ed.

P. Horton, H. Gewirtz, & K. Kreutter. Madison, CT: International Universities Press.

Asch, S. S. (1980), Suicide, and the hidden executioner. *Internat. Rev. Psycho-Anal.*, 7:51–60.

Atwood, G., & Stolorow, R. (1984), *Structures of Subjectivity: Explorations in Psychoanalytic Phenomenology.* Hillside, NJ: Analytic Press.

Bacal, H. A. (1987), British object relations theorists and self-psychology: Some critical reflections. *Internat. J. Psycho-Anal.*, 68:87–98.

Baker, H. S., & Baker, M. N. (1987), Heinz Kohut's self psychology: An overview. *Amer. J. Psychiat.*, 144:1–9.

Balint, M. (1968), *The Basic Fault: Therapeutic Aspects of Regression.* London: Tavistock.

Barasch, A., Frances, A., Hurt, S., Clarkin, J., & Cohen, S. (1985), Stability and distinctness of borderline personality disorder. *Amer. J. Psychiat.*, 142:1484–1486.

Bardenstein, K. K., & McGlashan, T. H. (1988), The natural history of a residentially treated borderline sample: Gender differences. *J. Personal. Disord.*, 2:69–83.

Baron, M., Gruen, R., Asnis, L., & Lord, S. (1985), Familial transmission of schizotypal and borderline personality disorders. *Amer. J. Psychiat.*, 142:927–934.

Barraclough, B., Bunch, J., Nelson, B., & Sainsbury, P. (1974), A hundred cases of suicide: Clinical aspects. *Brit. J. Psychiat.*, 125:355–373.

Barrash, J., Kroll, J., Carey, K., & Sines, L. (1983), Discriminating borderline personality disorder from other personality disorders: Cluster and analysis of the Diagnostic Interview for Borderline. *Arch. Gen. Psychiat.*, 40:1297–1302.

Basch, M. (1987), The interface between the interpersonal and the intrapsychic. *Contemp. Psychoanal.*, 23:367–381.

Basseches, M. (1984), *Dialectical Thinking and Adult Development.* Norwood, NJ: Ablex.

Bateman, A. (in press), Borderlines in Britain: A preliminary study. *Comprehen. Psychiat.*

Baxter, L., Edell, W., Gerner, R., Fairbanks, L., & Gwirtsman, H. (1984), Dexamethasone suppression test and axis I diagnoses of inpatients with DSM-III borderline personality disorder. *J. Clin. Psychiat.*, 45:150–153.

Beebe, B., & Sloate, P. (1982), Assessment and treatment of difficulties in mother–infant attunement in the first three years of life: A case history. *Psychoanal. Inq.*, 1:601–623.

Beeber, A. R., Kline, M. D., Pies, R. W., & Manning, J. M., Jr. (1984), Dexamethasone suppression test in hospitalized depressed patients with borderline personality disorder. *J. Nerv. & Ment. Dis.*, 172:301–303.

Bell, J., Lycaki, H., Jones, D., Kelwala, S., & Sitaram, N. (1983), Effect of preexisting borderline personality disorder on clinical and EEG sleep correlates of depression. *Psychiat. Res.*, 9:115–123.

Bellak, L. (1980), On some limitations of dyadic psychotherapy and the role of group modalities. *Internat. J. Group Psychother.*, 30:7–21.

———— (1981), *Crises and Special Problems in Psychoanalysis and Psychotherapy.* New York: Brunner/Mazel.

———— Meyers, B. (1975), Ego function assessment and analysability. *Internat. Rev. Psycho-Anal.*, 2:413–427.

Bemporad, J. R., Smith, H. F., Hanson, G., & Cicchetti, D. (1982), Borderline syndrome in childhood: Criteria for diagnosis. *Amer. J. Psychiat.*, 139:596–602.

Bernstein, S. B. (1980), Psychotherapy consultation in an inpatient setting. *Hosp. Commun. Psychiat.*, 31:829–834.

Beskow, J., Gottfires, C., Ross, B., & Winblad, B. (1976), Determination of monoamine and monoamine metabolite in the human brain: Postmortem studies in a group of suicides and a control group. *Acta Psychiat. Scand.*, 53:7–20.

Bibring, E. (1953), The mechanism of depression. In: *Affective Disorders*, ed. P. Greenacre. New York: International Universities Press.

Bion, W. R. (1957), Differentiation of the psychotic from the nonpsychotic personalities. *Internat. J. Psycho-Anal.*, 38:266–275.

———— (1961), *Experiences in Groups.* New York: Basic Books.

———— (1962), *Learning from Experience.* London: Heinemann.

———— (1967), A theory of thinking. In: *Second Thoughts: Selected Papers on Psycho-Analysis.* New York: Jason Aronson.

Birtchnell, J. (1983), Psychotherapeutic considerations in the management of the suicidal patient. *Amer. J. Psychother.*, 37:24–36.

Blackwood, D., St. Clair, D., & Kutcher, S. (1986), P300 event related potential abnormalities in borderline personality disorder. *Biolog. Psychiat.*, 21:557–560.

Blatt, S. J. (1974), Levels of object representation in anaclitic and introjective depression. *The Psychoanalytic Study of the Child*, 29:107–157. New Haven, CT: Yale University Press.

———— Auerbach, J. S. (1988), Differential cognitive disturbances in three types of borderline patients. *J. Personal. Disord.*, 2:198–211.

———— Brenneis, C. B., Schimek, J. G., & Glick, M. (1976), Normal development and psychopathological impairment of the concept of the object on the Rorschach. *J. Abnorm. Psychol.*, 85:364–373.

———— D'Afflitti, J. P., & Quinlan, D. M. (1976), Experiences of depression in normal young adults. *J. Abnorm. Psychol.*, 85:383–389.

———— Quinlan, D. M., Chevron, E., McDonald, C., & Zuroff, D. (1982), Dependency and self-criticism: Psychological dimensions of depression. *J. Consult. & Clin. Psychol.*, 50:113–124.

———— Ritzler, B. (1974), Thought disorder and boundary disturbance in psychosis. *J. Consult. & Clin. Psychol.*, 42:370–381.

———— Wild, C. (1976), *Schizophrenia: A Developmental Analysis*. New York: Academic Press.

Bleichmar, H. (1986), *Angustia y fantasma*. Madrid: Adotraf.

Bloom, H., & Rosenbluth, M. (in press), The use of contracts in the inpatient treatment of borderline personality disorder. *Psychiat. Quart.*

Blum, H. (1974), The borderline childhood of the Wolf Man. *J. Amer. Psychoanal. Assn.*, 22:721–742.

Bollas, C. (1978), The transformational object. *Internat. J. Psycho-Anal.*, 60:97–107.

Book, H. E., Sadavoy, J., & Silver, D. (1978), Staff countertransference to borderline patients on an inpatient unit. *Amer. J. Psychother.*, 32:521–533.

Bower, T. G. R. (1976), *The Perceptual World of the Child*. Cambridge, MA: Harvard University Press.

Bowlby, J. (1969), *Attachment and Loss*, Vol. 1. New York: Basic Books.

———— (1973), *Attachment and Loss*, Vol. 2. New York: Basic Books.

———— (1977), The making and breaking of affectional bonds: I. Aetiology and psychopathology in the light of attachment theory. *Brit. J. Psychiat.*, 130:201–210.

Bradley, S. J. (1979), The relationship of early maternal separation to borderline personality in children and adolescents: Pilot study. *Amer. J. Psychiat.*, 136:424–426.

———— (1981), The borderline diagnosis in children and adolescents. *Child Psychiat. & Hum. Devel.*, 12:121–127.

Brandchaft, B. (1983), Negativism, negative therapeutic reaction, and self psychology. In: *The Future of Psychoanalysis*, ed. A. Goldberg. New York: International Universities Press.

Brazelton, T. B., Koslowski, B., & Main, M. (1974), The origins of reciprocity: The early mother–infant interaction. In: *The Effects of the Infant on Its Caregiver*, ed. M. Lewis & L. A. Rosenblum. New York: John Wiley.

Breslau, L. (1987), Exaggerated helplessness syndrome. In: *Treating the Elderly with Psychotherapy: The Scope for Change in Later Life*, ed. J. Sadavoy & M. Leszcz. Madison, CT: International Universities Press.

Britton, R. (1988), Something irrationally reverenced. Paper contributed to a panel on transitional objects. *Brit. Psychoanal. Soc. Bull.*, June:2–7.

Broden, E. (1984), Supportive containment in the hospital care of treatment resistant borderline adolescents. *Psychiat.*, 47:315–322.

Brown, G., Ebert, M., Goyer, P., Jimerson, D., Klein, W., Bunrey, W., & Goodwin, F. (1982), Aggression, suicide and serotonin. *Amer. J. Psychiat.*, 139:741–746.

———— Goodwin, F., Ballanger, J., Goyer, P., & Major, L. (1979), Aggression in humans co-related with cerebrospinal fluid metabolites. *Psychiat. Res.*, 1:131–139.

———— Harris, T. O., & Bifulco, A. (1986), The long term effects of early loss of parent. In: *Depression in Young People: Clinical and Developmental Perspectives*, ed. M. Rutter, C. E. Izard, & P. B. Read. New York: Guilford Press.

Brown, L. J. (1981), A short-term hospital program preparing borderline and schizophrenic patients for intensive psychotherapy. *Psychiat.*, 44:327–336.

Bruch, H. (1973), *Eating Disorders: Anorexia, Obesity and the Person Within*. New York: Basic Books.

Buie, D. H., & Adler, G. (1982), Definitive treatment of the borderline personality. *Internat. J. Psychoanal. Psychother.*, 9:51–87.

———— Maltsberger, J. T. (1983), *The Practical Formulation of Suicide Risk*. Cambridge, MA: Firefly Press.

Burnham, D. G., Gladstone, A. I., & Gibson, R. W. (1969), *Schizophrenia and the Need–Fear Dilemma*. New York: International Universities Press.

Bursten, B. (1972), The manipulative personality. *Arch. Gen. Psychiat.*, 26:318–321.

Butcher, J. N. (1977), Foreword. In: *The MMPI: A Practical Guide*, ed. J. R. Graham. New York: Oxford University Press.

Cameron, N. (1963), *Personality Development and Psychopathology: A Dynamic Approach*. Boston: Houghton, Mifflin.

Campos, J., & Stenberg, C. (1981), Perception of appraisal and emotion: The onset of social referencing. In: *Infant Social Cognition*, ed. M. E. Lamb & L. R. Sherrod. Hillsdale, NJ: Lawrence Erlbaum.

Carpenter, W. T., & Gunderson, J. G. (1977), Five-year follow-up comparison of borderline and schizophrenic patients. *Comprehen. Psychiat.*, 18:567–571.

———— ———— Strauss, J. S. (1977), Considerations of the borderline syndrome: A longitudinal comparative study of borderline and schizophrenic patients. In: *Borderline Personality Disorders: The Concept, the Syndrome, the Patient*, ed. P. Hartocollis. New York: International Universities Press.

Carr, A. C. (1987), Borderline defenses and Rorschach responses: A critique of Lerner, Albert and Walsh. *J. Personal. Assess.*, 51:349–354.

Carroll, B. J., Greden, J. T., Feinberg, M., Lohr, N., James, N. M., Steiner, M., Haskett, R. F., Albala, A. A., De Vigne, J. P., & Tarika, J. (1981), Neuroendocrine evaluation of depression in borderline patients. *Psychiat. Clin. N. Amer.*, 4:89–99.

Carsky, M. (1985–1986), The resolution of impasse in long-term intensive inpatient psychotherapy. *Internat. J. Psychoanal. Psychother.*, 11:435–454.

Casement, P. J. (1982), Some pressures on the analyst for physical contact during the re-living of an early trauma. *Internat. Rev. Psycho-Anal.*, 9:279–286.

Casper, R. D., Eckert, E. D., Halmi, K. A., Goldberg, S. C., & Davis, J. M. (1980), Bulimia: Its incidence and significance in patients with anorexia nervosa. *Arch. Gen. Psychiat.*, 37:1030–1035.

Chambers, W., Puig-Antich, J., Hirsch, M., Paez, P., Ambrosin, P., Tabrizi, M., & Davies, M. (1985), The assessment of affective disorders in children and adolescents by semi-structured interview. *Arch. Gen. Psychiat.*, 42:696–702.

Chapin, K., Wightman, L., Lycaki, H., Josef, N., & Rosenbaum, G. (1987), Differences in reaction time between subjects with schizotypal and borderline personality disorders. *Amer. J. Psychiat.*, 144:948–950.

Chappel, J. N., Gottheill, E., & Nace, E. P. (1988), *Alcoholism Update for Psychiatrists*, ed. G. Usdin. Port Washington, NY: The American College of Psychiatrists.

Charney, D. S., Nelson, J. C., & Quinlan, D. M. (1981), Personality traits and disorder in depression. *Amer. J. Psychiat.*, 138:1601–1604.

Chopra, H. D., & Beatson, J. A. (1986), Psychotic symptoms in borderline personality disorder. *Amer. J. Psychiat.*, 143:1605–1607.

Clarkin, J., Widiger, T., Frances, A., Hurt, S., & Gilmore, M. (1983), Prototypal typology and the borderline personality disorder. *J. Abnorm. Psychol.*, 92:263–275.

Cleary, P. H., & Mechanic, D. (1983), Sex differencs in psychological distress among married people. *J. Health Soc. Behav.*, 24:111–121.

Coccaro, E., Siever, L., Klar, H., Maurer, G., Cochrane, K., Cooper, T., Mohs, R., & Davis, K. (1986), Serotonergic studies in patients with suicidal and impulsive aggressive behavior. *Arch. Gen. Psychiat.*, 46:587–599.

Cohen, L., Winchel, R., & Stanley, M. (1988), Biological markers of suicide risk and adolescent suicide. *Clin. Neuropharmacol.*, 5:423–435.

Cohen, R., & Grinspoon, L. (1963), Limit setting as a corrective ego experience. *Arch. Gen. Psychiat.*, 8:74–79.

Coid, J. C., Allolio, B., & Rees, L. H. (1984), Raised plasma metenkephalin in patients who habitually harm themselves. *Lancet*, 2:545–546.

Collins, D. T., Mebed, A. A. K., & Mortimer, R. L. (1978), Patient–therapist sex: Consequences for subsequent treatment. *McLean Hosp. J.*, 3:24–36.

Conte, H. R., Plutchik, R., Karasu, T. B., & Jerrett, I. (1980), A self-report borderline scale: Discriminative validity and preliminary norms. *J. Nerv. & Ment. Dis.*, 168:428–435.

Coonerty, S. (1986), An exploration of separation–individuation themes in the borderline personality disorder. *J. Personal. Assess.*, 50:501–511.

Cooper, A. M. (1984), The unusually painful analysis: A group of narcissistic–masochistic characters. In: *Psychoanalysis: The Vital Issues*, Vol. 2, ed. G. H. Pollock & J. E. Gedo. New York: International Universities Press.

——— (1988), The narcissistic–masochistic character. In: *Masochism: Current Psychoanalytic Perspectives*, ed. R. A. Glick & D. J. Meyers. Hillsdale, NJ: Analytic Press.

Cooper, H., & Wittenberg, E. (1985), The "bogged down" treatment: A remedy. *Contemp. Psychoanal.*, 21:27–41.

Cooper, R. J., & Fairburn, C. G. (1983), Binge eating and self-induced vomiting in the community: A preliminary study. *Brit. J. Psychiat.*, 142:139–144.

Cooper, S., & Arnow, D. (1984), Pre-stage versus defensive splitting and the borderline personality: A Rorschach analysis. *Psychoanal. Psychol.*, 1:235–248.

——— ——— (1986), An object relations view of the borderline defenses: A Rorschach analysis. In: *Assessing Object Relations*, ed. M. Kissen. New York: International Universities Press.

———— Perry, J., Hoke, L., & Richman, N. (1985), Transitional relatedness and borderline personality disorder. *Psychoanal. Psychol.*,
2:114–128.

Cornell, D. G., Silk, K. R., Ludolph, P. S., & Lohr, N. E. (1983),
Test–retest reliability of the diagnostic interview for border-
liness. *Arch. Gen. Psychiat.*, 40:1307–1310.

Cournos, F. (1987), Hospitalization outcome studies: Implications for
treatment of the very ill patient. *Psychiat. Clin. N. Amer.*,
10:165–176.

Cowdry, R. W. (1987), Psychopharmacology of borderline personality
disorder: A review. *J. Clin. Psychiat.*, 48:15–25.

———— Gardner, D. L. (1988), Pharmacotherapy of borderline personality disorder: Alprazolam, carbamazepine, trifluoperazine
and tranylcypromine. *Arch. Gen. Psychiat.*, 45:111–119.

———— Pickar, D., & Davies, R. (1985), Symptoms and EEG findings
in the borderline syndrome. *Internat. J. Psychiat. in Med.*,
15:201–211.

Crisp, A. H. (1970), Premorbid factors in adult disorders of weight,
with particular reference to primary anorexia nervosa (weight
phobia). *J. Psychosom. Res.*, 14:1.

———— Palmer, R. L., & Kalucy, R. S. (1976), How common is anorexia
nervosa? A prevalence study. *Brit. J. Psychiat.*, 128:549–554.

Crown, S. (1983), Contraindications and dangers of psychotherapy.
Brit. J. Psychiat., 143:436–441.

Crumley, F. (1979), Adolescent suicide attempts. *J. Amer. Med. Assn.*,
241:2404–2407.

———— (1981), Adolescent suicide attempts and borderline personality
disorder: Clinical features. *S. Med. J.*, 74:546–549.

Dahl, A. A. (1985a), Borderline disorders—The validity of the diagnostic concepts. *Psychiat. Devel.*, 3:109–152.

———— (1985b), A critical examination of empirical studies of the
diagnosis of borderline disorders in adults. *Psychiat. Devel.*,
3:1–29.

Daldin, H. J. (1988), A contribution to the understanding of self-
mutilating behavior in adolescence. *J. Child Psychother.*,
14:61–66.

Dally, P. A. (1969), *Anorexia Nervosa*. New York: Grune & Stratton.

Davis, J., Noll, K., & Sharma, R. (1986), Differential diagnosis and
treatment of mania. In: *Mania: New Research and Treatment*, ed.
A. Swan. Washington, DC: American Psychiatric Press.

DeSilva, P., & Eysenck, S. (1987), Personality and addictiveness in
anorexic and bulimic patients. *Person. Indiv. Diff.*, 18:749–751.

Deutsch, H. (1942), Some forms of emotional disturbance and their relationships to schizophrenia. *Psychoanal. Quart.*, 11:301–321.

Dickes, R. (1974), The concept of borderline states: An alternative proposal. *Internat. J. Psychoanal. Psychother.*, 3:1–27.

Dorpat, T., & Ripley, H. S. (1960), A study of suicide in the Seattle area. *Comprehen. Psychiat.*, 1:349–359.

Dostoyevsky, F. (1978), *Crime and Punishment*, trans. C. Gornett. New York: Random House Modern Library.

Drake, R. E., & Vaillant, G. E. (1985), A validity study of Axis II of DSM-III. *Amer. J. Psychiat.*, 142:553–558.

Dunner, D. L., Fleiss, J. L., Addonizio, G., & Fieve, R. R. (1976), Assortative mating in primary affective disorder. *Biol. Psychiat.*, 11:43–51.

Easser, B. R. (1974), Empathic inhibition and psychoanalytic technique. *Psychoanal.*, 60:557–559.

——— Lesser, S. (1965), Hysterical personality: A reevaluation. *Psychoanal. Quart.*, 34:390–402.

Edell, W. (1987), Relationship of borderline syndrome disorders to early schizophrenia on the MMPI. *J. Clin. Psychol.*, 43:163–176.

Egan, J. (1986), Etiology and treatment of borderline personality disorder in adolescents. *Hosp. & Commun. Psychiat.*, 37:613–618.

——— (1988), Treatment of borderline conditions in adolescents. *J. Clin. Psychiat.*, 49:32–35.

Eissler, K. R. (1971), *Talent and Genius: The Fictitious Case of Tausk Contra Freud*. New York: Quadrangle.

——— (1983), *Victor Tausk's Suicide*. New York: International Universities Press.

Eliasz, A. (1985), Mechanisms of temperament: Basic functions. In: *The Biological Bases of Personality and Behavior: Theories, Measurement Techniques, and Development*, ed. J. Strelau, F. H. Farley, & A. Gale. Washington, DC: Hemisphere.

Elkind, D. (1976), Cognitive development and psychopathology observations on egocentrism and ego defence. In: *Psychopathology and Child Development*, ed. E. Shopler & R. Reichler. New York: Plenum Press.

Emde, R. N., Gaensbauer, T. J., & Harmon, R. J. (1976), *Emotional Expression in Infancy. A Biobehavioral Study*. *Psychological Issues*, Vol. 10, No. 37. New York: International Universities Press.

——— Kligman, D. H., Reich, J. H., & Wade, J. D. (1978), Emotional expression in infancy: Initial studies of social signaling and an emergent model. In: *The Development of Affects*, ed. M. Lewis & L. Rosenblum. New York: Plenum Press.

Erikson, E. (1963), *Childhood and Society*. New York: W. W. Norton.

Etchegoyen, R. H., Lopez, B. M., & Rabih, M. (1987), On envy and how to interpret it. *Internat. J. Psycho-Anal.*, 68:49–62.

Evans, R., Ruff, R., Braff, D., & Ainsworth, T. (1984), MMPI characteristics of borderline personality inpatients. *J. Nerv. & Ment. Dis.*, 172:742–748.

Exner, J. E. (1986), Some Rorschach data comparing schizophrenics with borderline and schizotypal personality disorders. *J. Personal. Assess.*, 50:455–471.

Fairbairn, W. R. D. (1952), *Psychoanalytic Studies of the Personality*. London: Tavistock.

—— (1954), *An Object Relations Theory of the Personality*. New York: Basic Books.

Feighner, J. P., Robins, E., Guze, S. B., Woodruff, R. A., Winokur, G., & Munuz, R. (1972), Diagnostic criteria for use in psychiatric research. *Arch. Gen. Psychiat.*, 26:57–63.

Fenichel, O. (1945), *The Psychoanalytic Theory of Neurosis*. New York: W. W. Norton.

Fink, M., Pollack, M., & Klein, D. F. (1964), Comparative studies of chlorpromazine and imipramine: I. Drug discriminating patterns. *Neuropsychopharmacol.*, 3:370–372.

Firestone, S. (1970), *The Dialectic of Sex: The Case for Feminist Revolution*. New York: Bantam Books.

Fish, F. (1964), The cycloid psychoses. *Comprehen. Psychiat.*, 5:155–169.

Fontana, A. (1971), Patient reputations: Manipulator, helper, model. *Arch. Gen. Psychiat.*, 25:88–92.

Frances, A., & Clarkin, J. F. (1981), No treatment as the prescription of choice. *Arch. Gen. Psychiat.*, 38:542–545.

—— —— Gilmore, M., Hurt, S. W., & Brown, R. (1984), Reliability of criteria for borderline personality disorder: A comparison of DSM-III and the Diagnostic Interview for Borderline patients. *Amer. J. Psychiat.*, 141:1080–1084.

—— Widiger, T. (1986), Methodological issues in personality disorder diagnosis. In: *Contemporary Directions in Psychopathology*, ed. T. Millon & G. Klerman. New York: Plenum Press.

Frayn, D. H. (1987), An analyst's regressive reverie: A response to the analysand's illness. *Internat. J. Psycho-Anal.*, 68:271–277.

Freud, A. (1936), *The Ego and the Mechanisms of Defense*. New York: International Universities Press.

—— (1965), *Writings of Anna Freud: Vol. 8. Normality and Pathology in Childhood: Assessments in Development*. New York: International Universities Press.

——— (1969), *Difficulties in the Path of Psychoanalysis*. New York: International Universities Press.

Freud, S. (1900), The Interpretation of Dreams. *Standard Edition*, 4 & 5. London: Hogarth Press, 1961.

——— (1914), Remembering, repeating and working-through. *Standard Edition*, 12:145–156. London: Hogarth Press, 1955.

——— (1917), Mourning and melancholia. *Standard Edition*, 14:243–258. London: Hogarth Press, 1957.

——— (1918), From the history of an infantile neurosis. *Standard Edition*, 17:3–122. London: Hogarth Press, 1955.

——— (1923), The Ego and the Id. *Standard Edition*, 19. London: Hogarth Press, 1961.

——— (1926), Inhibitions, symptoms, and anxiety. *Standard Edition*, 20:87–172. London: Hogarth Press, 1961.

——— (1937), Analysis terminable and interminable. *Standard Edition*, 23:211–253. London: Hogarth Press, 1964.

Fried, E. (1954), The effects of combined therapy on the productivity of patients. *Internat. J. Group Psychother.*, 4:42–55.

——— (1961), Techniques of group psychotherapy going beyond insight. *Internat. J. Group Psychother.*, 15:167–176.

Friedman, H. J. (1969), Some problems of inpatient management with borderline patients. *Amer. J. Psychiat.*, 126:299–304.

——— (1975), Psychotherapy of borderline patients: The influence of theory on technique. *Amer. J. Psychiat.*, 132:1048–1052.

Friedman, M., Glasser, M., Laufer, E., Laufer, M., & Wohl, M. (1972), Attempted suicide and self-mutilation in adolescence: Some observations from a psychoanalytic research project. *Internat. J. Psycho-Anal.*, 53:179–183.

Friedman, R. C., Aronoff, M. S., Clarkin, J. E., Corn, R., & Hurt, S. W. (1983), History of suicidal behavior in depressed borderline patients. *Amer. J. Psychiat.*, 140:1023–1026.

——— Clarkin, J. F., Corn, R., Aronoff, M. S., Hurt, S. W., & Murphy, M. C. (1982), DSM-III and affective pathology in hospitalized adolescents. *J. Nerv. & Ment. Dis.*, 170:511–521.

——— Richart, R. M., & VandeWiele, R. L. (1974), *Sex Differences in Behavior*. New York: John Wiley.

Frosch, J. (1960), Psychotic character. *J. Amer. Psychoanal. Assn.*, 8:544–551.

——— (1977), Disorders of impulse control. *Psychiatry*, 40:295–314.

Furman, E. (1984), Some difficulties in assessing depression and suicide in childhood. In: *Suicide in the Young*, ed. H. S. Sudak, A. B. Ford, & N. B. Rushforth. Boston: John Wright.

Fyer, M. R., Frances, A., Sullivan, T., Hurt, S. W., & Clarkin, J. (1988), Comorbidity of borderline personality disorder. *Arch. Gen. Psychiat.*, 45:348–352.

Gaensbauer, T. (1980), Anaclitic depression in a three-and-a-half-month-old child. *Amer. J. Psychiat.*, 137:841–842.

Galenson, E., & Roiphe, H. (1974), The emergence of genital awareness during the second year of life. In: *Sex Differences in Behavior*, ed. R. Friedman, R. Richart, & R. VandeWiele. New York: John Wiley.

Gallwey, P. L. G. (1978), Transference utilization in aim-restricted psychotherapy. *Brit. J. Med. Psychol.*, 51:225–236.

——— (1985), The psychodynamics of borderline personality. In: *Aggression and Dangerousness*, ed. D. P. Farrington & J. Gunn. London: John Wiley.

Garbutt, J. C., Loosen, P. T., Tipermas, A., & Prange, A. J. (1983), The TRH test in patients with borderline personality disorders. *Psychiat. Res.*, 9:107–113.

Gardner, D. L., & Cowdry, R. W. (1985), Suicidal and parasuicidal behavior in borderline personality disorder. *Psychiat. Clin. N. Amer.*, 8:389–403.

Garfinkel, P. E. (1974), Perception of hunger and satiety in anorexia nervosa. *Psychol. Med.*, 4:309–315.

——— Garner, D. M. (1982), *Anorexia Nervosa: A Multidimensional Perspective*. New York: Brunner/Mazel.

——— ——— eds. (1987), *The Role of Drug Treatments for Eating Disorders*. New York: Brunner/Mazel.

——— Moldofsky, H., & Garner, D. M. (1980), The heterogeneity of anorexia nervosa. *Arch. Gen. Psychiat.*, 37:1036–1040.

Garner, D. M. (1987), Psychotherapy outcome research with bulimia nervosa. *Psychother. Psychosom.*, 45:129–140.

——— Bemis, K. M. (1982), A cognitive–behavioural approach to anorexia nervosa. *Cog. Ther. Res.*, 6:123.

——— Garfinkel, P. E. (1980), Socio-cultural factors in the development of anorexia nervosa. *Psychol. Med.*, 10:647–656.

——— ——— (1985), *Handbook of Psychotherapy for Anorexia Nervosa and Bulimia*. New York: Guilford Press.

——— ——— O'Shaughnessy, M. (1985), The validity of the distinction between bulimia with and without anorexia nervosa. *Amer. J. Psychiat.*, 142:581–587.

——— Olmstead, M. P., & Polivy, J. (1983), Development and validation of a multidimensional inventory for anorexia nervosa and bulimia. *Internat. J. Eat. Disord.*, 2:15–34.

Gartrell, N., Herman, J., Olarte, S., Feldstein, M., & Localio, R. (1986), Psychiatrist–patient sexual contact: Results of a national survey. I: Prevalence. *Amer. J. Psychiat.*, 143:1126–1131.

George, A., & Soloff, P. H. (1986), Schizotypal symptoms in patients with borderline personality disorders. *Amer. J. Psychiat.*, 143:212–215.

Gilberstadt, H., & Duker, J. (1965), *A Handbook for Clinical and Actuarial MMPI Interpretation*. Philadelphia: Saunders.

Giovacchini, P. (1978a), The borderline syndrome. In: *Adolescent Psychiatry*, ed. S. Feinstein & P. Giovacchini. Chicago: University of Chicago Press.

——— (1978b), The borderline aspects of adolescence and the borderline state. In: *Adolescent Psychiatry*, ed. S. Feinstein & P. Giovacchini. Chicago: University of Chicago Press.

——— (1988), Solace, structure and transitional processes. In: *The Solace Paradigm—An Eclectic Search for Psychological Immunity*, ed. P. Horton, H. Gewirtz, & K. Kreutter. Madison, CT: International Universities Press.

——— Boyer, L. B. (1975), The psychoanalytic impasse. *Internat. J. Psychoanal. Psychother.*, 4:25–47.

Gitelson, M. (1958), On ego distortion. *Internat. J. Psycho-Anal.*, 39:245–257.

Glasser, M. (1986), Indentification and its vicissitudes as observed in the perversions. *Internat. J. Psycho-Anal.*, 67:9–18.

Glatzer, H. T. (1965), Aspects of transference in group psychotherapy. *Internat. J. Group Psychother.*, 15:167–176.

Goldberg, C. (1980), The utilization and limitations of paradoxical intervention in group psychotherapy. *Internat. J. Psychother.*, 30:287–297.

Goldberg, S. C., Schulz, S. C., Schulz, P. M., Resnick, R. J., Hamer, R. M., & Friedel, R. O. (1986), Borderline and schizotypal personality disorders treated with low-dose thiothizene vs. placebo. *Arch. Gen. Psychiat.*, 43:680–686.

Goldbloom, D. S., & Garfinkel, P. E. (in press), Anorexia nervosa and bulimia nervosa. In: *Handbook of Child Psychiatric Disorders*, ed. C. G. Last & M. Hersen. New York: John Wiley.

——— Kennedy, S. H. (1988), Drug treatments of eating disorders. In: *Anorexia Nervosa and Bulimia Nervosa*, ed. P. E. Garfinkel. Kalamazoo, MI: Upjohn.

Goldstein, W. N. (1985), *An Introduction to the Borderline Conditions*. New York: Jason Aronson.

Goodman, R. (1987), The developmental neurobiology of language. In: *Language Development and Disorders: Clinics in Developmental*

Medicine, No. 101-102, ed. W. Yule & M. Rutter. London: Mac Keith Press.

Goodrich, W. (1987), Long-term psychoanalytic hospital treatment of adolescents. *Psychiat. Clin. N. Amer.*, 10:273–287.

Goodwin, J. (1982), *Sexual Abuse: Incest Victims and Their Families*. Littleton, MA: PSG Publications.

Gordon, C., & Beresin, E. (1983), Conflicting treatment models for the inpatient management of borderline patients. *Amer. J. Psychiat.*, 140:979–983.

Gorney, J. (1979), The negative therapeutic interaction. *Contemp. Psychoanal.*, 15:288–337.

Graff, H., & Mallin, R. (1967), The syndrome of the wrist cutter. *Amer. J. Psychiat.*, 124:74–79.

Greben, S. E. (1983), The multi-dimensional inpatient treatment of severe character disorder. *Can. J. Psychiat.*, 28:97–101.

———— (1988), The place of transitional objects in the psychotherapeutic relationships. In: *The Solace Paradigm—An Eclectic Search for Psychological Immunity*, ed. P. Horton, H. Gewirtz, & K. Kreutter. Madison, CT: International Universities Press.

Green, M. (1983), Treatment of borderline adolescents. *Adol.*, 18:729–738.

Greenman, D., Gunderson, J., Came, M., & Saltzman, C. (1986), An examination of the borderline diagnosis in children. *Amer. J. Psychiat.*, 145:998–1003.

Greenson, R. (1965), The working alliance and the transference neurosis. *Psychoanal. Quart.*, 34:155–181.

Griesinger, W. (1871), *Die Pathologie und Therapie der psychischen Krankheiten*, 3rd ed. Braunschweig: Verlag von F. Wreden.

Grinberg, L. (1964), On two kinds of guilt: Their relation with normal and pathological aspects of mourning. *Internat. J. Psycho-Anal.*, 45:366–371.

———— Sor, D., & Bianchedi, E. T. (1985), *Introduction to the Work of Bion*. London: Maresfield Library.

Grinker, R. R. (1977), The borderline syndrome: A phenomenological review. In: *Borderline Personality Disorders*, ed. P. Hartocollis. New York: International Universities Press.

———— Miller, J., Sabshin, M., Nunn, R., & Nunnally, J. (1961), *The Phenomena of Depressions*. New York: Hoeber.

———— Werble, B., & Drye, R. C. (1968), *The Borderline Syndrome*. New York: Basic Books.

Grobman, J. (1980), The borderline patient in group psychotherapy: A case report. *Internat. J. Group Psychother.*, 30:299–318.

Grotstein, J. S. (1981), *Splitting and Projective Identification*. New York: Jason Aronson.

——— (1988), Transitional phenomena and the dilemma of the me/not-me interface. In: *The Solace Paradigm—An Eclectic Search for Psychological Immunity*, ed. P. Horton, H. Gewirtz, & K. Kreutter. Madison, CT: International Universities Press.

Grunebaum, H., & Klerman, G. L. (1967), Wrist slashing. *Amer. J. Psychiat.*, 124:524–534.

Grunhaus, L., Kling, D., Greden, J. F., & Fliegel, P. (1985), Depression and panic in patients with borderline personality disorder. *Biol. Psychiat.*, 20:668–692.

Gull, W. W. (1874), Anorexia nervosa. *Trans. Clin. Soc.* (London), 7:22–28.

Gunderson, J. G. (1977), Characteristics of borderlines. In: *Borderline Personality Disorders*, ed. P. Hartocollis. New York: International Universities Press.

——— (1984), *Borderline Personality Disorder*. Washington, DC: American Psychiatric Press.

——— (1986), Contribution to panel on borderline personality disorders. Research issues and new empirical findings. *J. Amer. Psychoanal. Assn.*, 34:179–192.

——— (1989), Borderline personality disorder. In: *Treatment of Personality Disorders*, ed. T. B. Karasu. Washington, DC: American Psychiatric Press.

——— Carpenter, W. T., & Strauss, J. S. (1975), Borderline and schizophrenic patients: A comparative study. *Amer. J. Psychiat.*, 132:1257–1264.

——— Elliot, G. R. (1985), The interface between borderline personality disorder and affective disorder. *Amer. J. Psychiat.*, 142:277–288.

——— Frank, A. F., Katz, H. M., Vannicelli, M. L., Frosch, J. P., & Knapp, P. H. (1984), Effects of psychotherapy in schizophrenia: Comparative outcome of two forms of treatment. *Schizophren. Bull.*, 10:564–598.

——— ——— Ronningstam, E., Wachter, S., Lynch, V., & Wolf, P. (1989), Early discontinuance of borderline patients from psychotherapy. *J. Nerv. & Ment. Dis.*, 177:38–42.

——— Kerr, J., & Englund, D. W. (1980), The families of borderlines. *Arch. Gen. Psychiat.*, 377:27–33.

——— Kolb, J. E. (1978), Discriminating features of borderline patients. *Amer. J. Psychiat.*, 135:792–796.

——— ——— Austin, V. (1981), The Diagnostic Interview for Borderline Patients. *Amer. J. Psychiat.*, 138:896–903.

—————— Siever, L. J., & Spauldin, E. (1983), The search for a schizotype: Crossing the border again. *Arch. Gen. Psychiat.*, 40:15–22.

—————— Singer, M. T. (1975), Defining borderline patients: An overview. *Amer. J. Psychiat.*, 132:1–10.

—————— Woods, E. D. (1981), Characterizing the families of borderlines. *Psychiat. Clin. N. Amer.*, 4:159–168.

—————— Zanarini, M. C. (1987), Current overview of the borderline diagnosis. *J. Clin. Psychiat.*, 48(Suppl.): 5–14.

Guntrip, H. (1968), *Schizoid Phenomena, Object Relations and the Self*. New York: International Universities Press.

—————— (1971), *Psychoanalytic Theory, Therapy, and the Self*. New York: Basic Books.

Gustin, Q., Goodpaster, W., Sajadi, C., Pitts, W., LaBasse, D., & Snyder, A. (1983), MMPI characteristics of the DSM-III borderline personality disorder. *J. Personal. Assess.*, 47:50–59.

Gutheil, T. G. (1977), Limit setting as therapy in clinical administration. *Transnat. Ment. Health Res. Newsletter*, 19:3–5.

—————— (1982), On the therapy in clinical administration. *Psychiat. Quart.*, 54:3–25.

—————— (1985), Medicolegal pitfalls in the treatment of borderline patients. *Amer. J. Psychiat.*, 142:9–14.

—————— (1988), Suicide, sex: Main legal risks in treating borderline. *Clin. Psychiat. News*, 16:14.

—————— (1989), Borderline patients, boundary violations, and patient–therapist sex: Empirical observations on another medicolegal "pitfall." *Amer. J. Psychiat.*, 146:597–602.

—————— Appelbaum, P. S. (1982), *Clinical Handbook of Psychiatry and the Law*. New York: McGraw-Hill.

—————— Magraw, R. (1984), Ambivalence, alliance and advocacy: Misunderstood dualities in psychiatry and law. *Bull. Amer. Acad. Psychiat. Law*, 12:51–58.

Guze, S. B. (1975), Differential diagnosis of the borderline patient. In: *Borderline States in Psychiatry*, ed. J. E. Mack. New York: Grune & Stratton.

Gwirtsman, H. E., Roy-Byrne, P., Yaker, J., & Gerner, R. H. (1983), Neuroendocrine abnormalities in bulimia. *Amer. J. Psychiat.*, 140:559–563.

Hartocollis, P. (1978), Time and affects in borderline disorders. *Internat. J. Psycho-Anal.*, 59:157–163.

—————— (1980), Long-term hospital treatment for adult patients with borderline and narcissistic disorders. *Bull. Menn. Clin.*, 44:212–226.

Hawton, K. (1986), Suicide in adolescents. In: *Suicide*, ed. A. Roy. Baltimore: Williams & Wilkins.

Hedberg, D. L., Houck, J. H., & Glueck, B. C. (1971), Tranylcypromine–trifluoperazine combination in the treatment of schizophrenia. *Amer. J. Psychiat.*, 142:277–288.

Heimann, P. (1950), On countertransference. *Internat. J. Psycho-Anal.*, 31:81–84.

Heinssen, R. H., & McGlashan, T. H. (1988), Predicting hospital discharge status for patients with schizophrenia, schizoaffective disorder, borderline personality disorder and unipolar affective disorder. *Arch. Gen. Psychiat.*, 45:353–360.

Helzer, J. E., & Pryzbeck, T. R. (1988), The co-occurrence of alcoholism with other psychiatric disorders in the general population and its impact on treatment. *J. Studies on Alcohol*, 49:219–224.

Herjanic, B., & Reich, W. (1982), Development of a structured psychiatric interview for children: Agreement between child and parent on individual symptoms. *J. Abnorm. Child Psychol.*, 10:307–324.

Herman, J. L. (1981), *Father–Daughter Incest*. Cambridge, MA: Harvard University Press.

———— Perry, J. C., & van der Kolk, B. (1988), Childhood traumas in BPD. New research abstracts, 141st Annual Meeting, American Psychiatric Association.

Hinde, R. A. (1987), *Individuals, Relationships and Culture: Links Between Ethology and the Social Sciences*. Cambridge, UK: Cambridge University Press.

Hinshelwood, R. D. (1989), *A Dictionary of Kleinian Thought*. London: Free Association Books.

Hirschfield, R., Klerman; G., Clayton, P., Keller, M., McDonald-Scott, P., & Larkin, B. (1983), Assessing personality: Effects of the depressive state on trait measurement. *Amer. J. Psychiat.*, 140:695–699.

Hoch, P. H., Cattell, J. P., Strahl, M. O., & Pennes, H. H. (1962), The course and outcome of pseudoneurotic schizophrenia. *Amer. J. Psychiat.*, 119:106–115.

———— Polatin, P. (1949), Pseudoneurotic forms of schizophrenia. *Psychiat. Quart.*, 23:248–276.

Holland, A. J., Hall, A., Murray, R., Russell, G. F. M., & Crisp, A. H. (1984), Anorexia nervosa: A study of 34 twin pairs and one set of triplets. *Brit. J. Psychiat.*, 145:414–419.

Hollingshead, A. B. (1952), *Two-factor Index of Social Position*. Unpublished manuscript. Yale University, New Haven, CT.

Holt, R. R. (1977), A method of assessing primary process manifestations and their control in Rorschach responses. In: *Rorschach Psychology*, ed. M. Rickers-Ovsiankina. New York: Robert E. Krieger.

Hooberman, D., & Stern, T. A. (1984), Treatment of attention deficit and borderline personality disorders with psychostimulants: Case report. *J. Clin. Psychiat.*, 45:441–442.

Horner, J. A. (1975), A characterological contraindication for group psychotherapy. *J. Amer. Acad. Psychoanal.*, 3:301–305.

Horevitz, R. P., & Braun, B. G. (1984), Are multiple personalities borderline? An analysis of 33 cases. *Psychiat. Clin. N. Amer.*, 7:69–87.

Horton, P. C. (1976), The psychological treatment of personality disorder. *Amer. J. Psychiat.*, 133:262–265.

———— (1977), Personality disorder and hard-to-diagnose schizophrenia. *J. Oper. Psychiat.*, 8:70–81.

———— (1981), *Solace: The Missing Dimension in Psychiatry*. Chicago: Univ. of Chicago Press.

———— (1988a), Introduction. In: *The Solace Paradigm—An Eclectic Search for Psychological Immunity*, ed. P. Horton, H. Gewirtz, & K. Kreutter. Madison, CT: International Universities Press.

———— (1988b), Positive emotions and the right parietal cortex. In: *Psychiatric Clinics of North America*, ed. K. Hoppe. Philadelphia: W. B. Saunders.

———— Gewirtz, H. (1988), Acquisition and termination of first solacing objects in males, females, and in a clinic and non-clinic population: Implications for psychological immunity. In: *The Solace Paradigm—An Eclectic Search for Psychological Immunity*, ed. P. Horton, H. Gewirtz, & K. Kreutter. Madison, CT: International Universities Press.

———— Kreutter, K., & Gewirtz, H. (1988), Patterns of solacing in males and females from age 5 through 13. In: *The Solace Paradigm—An Eclectic Search for Psychological Immunity*, ed. P. Horton, H. Gewirtz, & K. Kreutter. Madison, CT: International Universities Press.

———— Louy, J., & Coppolillo, H. P. (1974), Personality disorder and transitional relatedness. *Arch. Gen. Psychiat.*, 30:618–622.

———— Sharp, S. (1984), Language, solace, and transitional relatedness. *The Psychoanalytic Study of the Child*, 39:167–194. New Haven, CT: Yale University Press.

Horwitz, L. (1977), Group psychotherapy of the borderline patient. In: *Borderline Personality Disorders*, ed. P. Hartocollis. New York: International Universities Press.

—— (1980), Group psychotherapy for borderline and narcissistic disorders. *Bull. Menn. Clin.*, 44:181–200.

—— (1983), Projective identification in dyads and groups. *Internat. J. Group Psychother.*, 33:259–281.

Hudson, J. I., Pope, H. G., Jr., Jonas, J. M., & Yurgelen-Todd, D. (1983), Family history study of anorexia nervosa and bulimia. *Brit. J. Psychiat.*, 142:133–138.

Hughes, P. L., Wells, L. A., Cunningham, C. J., & Ilstrup, D. M. (1986), Treating bulimia with desipramine: A double blind placebo-controlled study. *Arch. Gen. Psychiat.*, 43:182–186.

Hurt, S., Clarkin, J., Frances, J., Abrams, R., & Hunt, H. (1985), Discriminant validity of the MMPI for borderline personality disorder. *J. Personal. Assess.*, 49:56–61.

—— —— Widiger, T., Eyer, M., Sullivan, T., Stone, M. H., & Frances, A. (1988), DSM-III and borderline personality disorder: Decision rules and their implications. Paper presented at the First International Congress on Personality Disorders, Copenhagen, August 4th.

Isaacs Elmhirst, S. (1980), Transitional objects in transition. *Internat. J. Psycho-Anal.*, 61:467–474.

Jackson, M., & Tarnopolsky, A. (1989), Borderline personality. In: *Principles and Practice of Forensic Psychiatry*, ed. R. Bluglass & P. Bowden. London: Churchill Livingstone.

Jacobson, E. (1943), Depression: The Oedipus conflict in the development of depressive mechanisms. *Psychoanal. Quart.*, 12:541–560.

—— (1953), Contribution to the metapsychology of cyclothymic depression. In: *Affective Disorders*, ed. P. Greenacre. New York: International Universities Press.

—— (1954), Contribution to the metapsychology of psychotic identifications. *J. Amer. Psychoanal. Assn.*, 2:49–83.

—— (1959), Depersonalization. *J. Amer. Psychoanal. Assn.*, 7:581–610.

—— (1964), *The Self and the Object World.* New York: International Universities Press.

—— (1971), *Depression: Comparative Studies of Normal, Neurotic and Psychotic Conditions.* New York: International Universities Press.

James, D. C. (1984), Bion's "containing" and Winnicott's "holding" in the context of the group matrix. *Internat. J. Group Psychother.*, 34:201–213.

Janet, P. (1919), *Les obsessions et la psychasthenie.* Paris: Felix Alcan.

Joffe, R. (1982), "Don't help me!" The suicidal adolescent. In: *Developmental Breakdown in Adolescence and the Troubled Adolescent's Dilemma in Accepting Help* (Monograph Series of the Brent Consultation Centre and Centre for Research into Adolescent

Breakdown, No. 8.) London: Brent Consultation Centre/Centre for Research into Adolescent Breakdown.

Johansen, K. (1979), A theoretical basis for the management of the hospitalized borderline patient. *Curr. Concept in Psychiat.*, 5:8–16.

Johnson, C., & Conners, M. E. (1987), *The Etiology and Treatment of Bulimia Nervosa.* New York: Basic Books.

——— Tobin, D., & Enright, A. (in press), Prevalence and clinical characteristics of borderline patients. *J. Clin. Psychiat.*

Joseph, B. (1983), On understanding and not understanding: Some technical issues. *Internat. J. Psycho-Anal.*, 64:291–298.

Kafka, J. S. (1969), The body as transitional object. *Brit. J. Med. Psychol.*, 42:207–211.

Kamirer, Y. (1986), Suicidal behavior and contagion among hospitalized adolescents. *Amer. J. Psychiat.*, 143:1030.

Kaplan, A. S., & Garfinkel, P. E. (1984), Bulimia in the Talmud. *Amer. J. Psychiat.*, 141:721.

Kaplan, L. J. (1980), Rapprochement and oedipal organization: Effects on borderline phenomena. In: *Rapprochement: The Critical Subphase of Separation–Individuation*, ed. R. F. Lax, S. Bach, & J. A. Burland. New York: Jason Aronson.

Kardener, S. A. H. (1974), Sex and the physician–patient relationship. *Amer. J. Psychiat.*, 131:1134–1136.

——— Fuller, M., & Mensh, I. N. (1976), Characteristics of "erotic" practitioners. *Amer. J. Psychiat.*, 133:1324–1325.

Kass, F., Skodol, A. E., Charles, E., Spitzer, R. L., & Williams, J. B. W. (1985), Scaled ratings of DSM-III personality disorders. *Amer. J. Psychiat.*, 142:627–630.

Kaye, W., Ebert, M., Raleigh, M., & Laker, R. (1984), Abnormalities in CNS monoamine metabolism in anorexia nervosa. *Arch. Gen. Psychiat.*, 41:350–355.

Kegan, R. (1982), *The Evolving Self: Problem and Process in Human Development.* Cambridge, MA: Harvard University Press.

Keller, M. B., & Shapiro, R. W. (1982), "Double depression": Superimposition of acute depressive episodes on chronic depressive disorders. *Amer. J. Psychiat.*, 139:438–442.

Kendell, R. (1982), The choice of diagnostic criteria for biological research. *Arch. Gen. Psychiat.*, 39:1334–1339.

Kendler, K. S., Gruenberg, A. M., & Strauss, J. S. (1981a), An independent analysis of the Copenhagen sample of the Danish adoption study of schizophrenia: II. The relationship between schizotypal personality disorder and schizophrenia. *Arch. Gen. Psychiat.*, 38:928–987.

———— ———— ———— (1981b), The relationship between schizotypal personality disorder and schizophrenia. *Arch. Gen. Psychiat.*, 38:982–984.

Kennedy, S. H. (1988), Inpatient treatment for anorexia nervosa and bulimia nervosa. In: *Anorexia Nervosa and Bulimia Nervosa*, ed. P. E. Garfinkel. Kalamazoo, MI: Upjohn.

———— Garfinkel, P. E. (in press), Patients admitted to hospital with anorexia nervosa and bulimia nervosa: Psychopathology, weight gain and attitudes to treatment. *Internat. J. Eat. Disord.*

———— Piran, N., Warsh, J. J., Prendergast, P., Henderson, E., & Garfinkel, P. E. (1988), A trial of isocarboxazid in bulimia. *J. Clin. Psychopharmacol.*, 8:391–396.

Kernberg, O. F. (1967), Borderline personality organization. *J. Amer. Psychoanal. Assn.*, 15:641–685.

———— (1968), The treatment of patients with borderline personality organization. *Internat. J. Psycho-Anal.*, 49:600–619.

———— (1970), A psychoanalytic classification of character pathology. *J. Amer. Psychoanal. Assn.*, 18:800–822.

———— (1972), Early ego integration and object relations. *Ann. N.Y. Acad. Sci.*, 193:233–247.

———— (1973), Discussion of hospital treatment of borderline patients by Adler, G. *Amer. J. Psychiat.*, 130:35–36.

———— (1974), Contrasting viewpoints regarding the nature and psychoanalytic treatment of narcissistic personalities. A preliminary communication. *J. Amer. Psychoanal. Assn.*, 22:255–267.

———— (1975), *Borderline Conditions and Pathological Narcissism.* New York: International Universities Press.

———— (1976), *Object Relations Theory and Clinical Psychoanalysis.* New York: Jason Aronson.

———— (1977a), The structural diagnosis of borderline personality organization. In: *Borderline Personality Disorders: The Concept, the Syndrome, the Patient*, ed. P. Hartocollis. New York: International Universities Press.

———— (1977b), Structural change and its impediments. In: *Borderline Personality Disorders: The Concept, the Syndrome, the Patient*, ed. P. Hartocollis. New York: International Universities Press.

———— (1978), The borderline aspects of adolescence and the borderline state. In: *Adolescent Psychiatry*, ed. S. Feinstein & P. Giovacchini. Chicago: University of Chicago Press.

———— (1979), Psychoanalytic psychotherapy with borderline adolescents. *Adol. Psychiat.*, 7:294–321.

———— (1980), *Internal World and External Reality.* New York: Jason Aronson.

────── (1981), Structural interviewing. *Psychiat. Clin. N. Amer.*, 4:169–195.

────── (1984), *The Severe Personality Disorders: Psychotherapeutic Strategies.* New Haven, CT: Yale University Press.

────── (1987a), Projection and projective identification: Developmental and clinical aspects. *J. Amer. Psychoanal. Assn.*, 35:795–819.

────── (1987b), Projective identification, countertransference, and hospital treatment. *Psychiat. Clin. N. Amer.*, 10:257–272.

────── (1987c), A psychodynamic approach to the borderline self-mutilating patient. *J. Personal. Disord.*, 1:344–346.

────── Burstein, E., & Coyne, L. (1972), Final report of the Menninger Foundation's psychotherapy research project: Psychotherapy and psychoanalysis. *Bull. Menn. Clin.*, 34:263–268.

────── Gunderson, J. G., & Stone, M. (1988), *Clin. Psychiat. News*, Vol. 16, No. 10, October 10.

────── Selzer, M. A., Koenigsberg, H. W., Carr, A. C., & Appelbaum, A. H. (1989), *Psychodynamic Psychotherapy of Borderline Patients.* New York: Basic Books.

Kety, S. S., Rosenthal, D., Wender, P. H., & Schulsinger, F. (1968), The types and prevalence of mental illness in the biological and adoptive families of adopted schizophrenics. In: *The Transmission of Schizophrenia*, ed. D. Rosenthal & S. S. Kety. Oxford: Pergamon Press.

Khouri, P. J., Haier, R. J., Rieder, R. O., & Rosenthal, D. (1980), A symptom schedule for the diagnosis of borderline schizophrenia: A first report. *Brit. J. Psychiat.*, 137:140–147.

Kibel, H. D. (1978), The rationale for the use of group psychotherapy for borderline patients in a short term unit. *Internat. J. Group Psychother.*, 28:339–358.

────── (1980), The importance of the comprehensive clinical diagnosis for group psychotherapy of borderline and narcissistic patients. *Internat. J. Group Psychother.*, 30:427–444.

────── (1981), A conceptual model for short-term inpatient group psychotherapy. *Amer. J. Psychiat.*, 138:74–80.

────── Stein, A. (1981), The group-as-a-whole approach: An appraisal. *Internat. J. Group Psychother.*, 31:409–429.

Klagsburn, S., Reibel, J. C., & Piercey, M. C. (1987), Cost-effective tertiary care. *Psychiat. Clin. N. Amer.*, 10:207–218.

Klein, D. F. (1968), Psychiatric-diagnosis and a typology of clinical drug effects. *Psychopharmacol.*, 13:359–386.

——— (1975), Psychopharmacology and the borderline patient. In: *Borderline States in Psychiatry*, ed. J. E. Mack. New York: Grune & Stratton.

——— (1977), Psychopharmacological treatment and delineation of borderline disorders. In: *Borderline Personality Disorders: The Concept, the Syndrome, and the Patient*, ed. P. Hartocollis. New York: International Universities Press.

——— Davis, J. (1969), *Drug Treatment and Psychodiagnosis*. Baltimore: Williams & Wilkins.

——— Gittelman, R., Quitkin, F., & Rifkin, A. (1980), *Diagnosis and Drug Treatment of Psychiatric Disorder: Adult and Children*, 2nd ed. Baltimore: Williams & Wilkins.

Klein, M. (1926), Psychological principles of early analysis. In: *The Writings of Melanie Klein*, Vol. 1. London: Hogarth Press, 1975.

——— (1933), The early development of conscience in the child. In: *The Writings of Melanie Klein*, Vol. 1. London: Hogarth Press, 1975.

——— (1936), Weaning. In: *The Writings of Melanie Klein*, Vol. 1. London: Hogarth Press, 1975.

——— (1946), Notes on some schizoid mechanisms. In: *The Writings of Melanie Klein*, Vol. 3. London: Hogarth Press, 1975.

——— (1952), *Developments in Psychoanalysis*, ed. J. Riviere. London: Hogarth Press.

——— (1957), *Envy and Gratitude and Other Works, 1946–1963*. New York: Delacorte.

——— (1975), *The Writings of Melanie Klein*, Vol. 1. Explanatory notes by the editors. London: Hogarth Press, 1975.

Knight, R. P. (1953a), Borderline states. *Bull. Menn. Clin.*, 17:1–12.

——— (1953b), Management and psychotherapy of the borderline schizophrenic. *Bull. Menn. Clin.*, 17:139–150.

Kocis, J. H., & Frances, A. J. (1987), A critical discussion of DSM-III dysthymic disorder. *Amer. J. Psychiat.*, 144:1534–1542.

Koenigsberg, H. W., Kaplan, R. D., Gilmore, M. M., & Cooper, A. M. (1985), The relationship between syndrome and personality disorder in DSM-III; experience with 462 patients. *Amer. J. Psychiat.*, 142:207–212.

——— Kernberg, O. F., & Schomer, J. (1983), Diagnosing borderline patients in an out-patient setting. *Arch. Gen. Psychiat.*, 40:60–63.

Kohut, H. (1971), *Analysis of the Self*. New York: International Universities Press.

——— (1972), Thoughts on narcissism and narcissistic rage. *The Psychoanalytic Study of the Child*, 27:360–400. New York: Quadrangle. Also in: *The Search for the Self*, Vol. 2, ed. P. Ornstein. New York: International Universities Press.

———— (1977), *The Restoration of the Self*. New York: International Universities Press.

———— (1984), *How Does Analysis Cure?* Chicago: University of Chicago Press.

Kolb, J. E., & Gunderson, J. G. (1980), Diagnosing borderline patients with a semi-structured interview. *Arch. Gen. Psychiat.*, 40:60–63.

———— Shapiro, E. R. (1982a), Administrative treatment of separation issues with families of hospitalized adolescents. *Adol. Psychiat.*, 10:343–359.

———— ———— (1982b), Management of separation issues with the family of the hospitalized adolescent. In: *Adolescent Psychiatry*, ed. S. Feinstein & P. Giovacchini. Chicago: University of Chicago Press.

Kontaxakis, V., Markianos, M., Vaslamatzis, J., Markidis, M., Kanellos, B., & Stefanis, C. (1987), Multiple neuroendocrinological responses in borderline personality disorder patients. *Acta Psychiat. Scand.*, 76:593–597.

Korenblum, M., Golombek, H., Marton, P., & Stein, B. (in press), Personality dysfunction in adolescence: Continuities and discontinuities.

———— Marton, P., Kutcher, S., Kennedy, B., Stein, B., & Pakes, J. (1988), Personality dysfunction in depressed adolescents—state or trait? Poster presented at the Annual Meeting of the American Academy of Child and Adolescent Psychiatry, Seattle, October.

Kosseff, J. (1975), The leader using object relations theory. In: *The Leader in the Group*, ed. Z. A. Liff. New York: Jason Aronson.

Kraemer, H. C., Pruyn, J. P., Gibbons, R. D., Greenhouse, J. B., Grochocinski, V. J., Waternaux, C., & Kupfer, D. J. (1987), Methodology in psychiatric research. *Arch. Gen. Psychiat.*, 44:1100–1106.

Kraepelin, E. (1921), *Manic–Depressive Insanity and Paranoia*. Edinburgh: Livingstone.

Kreitman, N. (1977), *Parasuicide*. London: John Wiley.

Kretsch, R., Goren, Y., & Wasserman, A. (1987), Changing patterns of borderline patients in individual and group therapy. *Internat. J. Group Psychother.*, 37:95–112.

Krishnan, K. R., Davidson, J. R., Rayasam, K., & Shope, F. (1984), The dexamethasone suppression test in borderline personality disorder. *Biol. Psychiat.*, 19:1149–1153.

Krohn, A. (1974), Borderline "empathy" and differentiation of object representations: A contribution to the psychology of object relations. *Internat. J. Psychoanal. Psychother.*, 3:142–165.

Kroll, J. (1988), *The Challenge of the Borderline Patient*. New York: W. W. Norton.

────── Carey, K., Sines, L., & Roth, M. (1982), Are there borderlines in Britain? *Arch. Gen. Psychiat.*, 39:60–63.

────── Ogata, S. (1987), The relationships of borderline personality disorder to the affective disorders. *Psychiat. Dev.*, 5:105–128.

────── Sines, L. L., Martin, K., Lari, S., Pyle, R., & Zander, J. (1981), Borderline personality disorder: Construct validity of the concept. *Arch. Gen. Psychiat.*, 38:1021–1026.

Krystal, H. (1978), Trauma and affects. *The Psychoanalytic Study of the Child*, 33:81–116. New Haven, CT: Yale University Press.

Kullgren, G. (1985), Borderline personality disorder and psychiatric suicides. *Nord. Psykiatr. Tidsskr.*, 39:479–484.

────── (1988), Factors associated with completed suicide in borderline personality disorder. *J. Nerv. & Ment. Dis.*, 176:40–44.

────── Renberg, E., & Jacobsson, L. (1986), An empirical study of borderline personality disorder and psychiatric suicides. *J. Nerv. & Ment. Dis.*, 174:328–331.

Kuhn, T. S. (1970), *The Structure of Scientific Revolutions*, 2nd ed. Chicago: University of Chicago Press.

Kurtz, E. (1979), *Not God: A History of Alcoholics Anonymous*. Center City, MI: Hazelden.

────── Kurtz, L. F. (1986), The social thought of alcoholics. In: *Social Thought on Alcoholism: A Comprehensive Review*, ed. T. D. Watts. Macon, FL: Robert E. Krieger.

Kutcher, S. P., & Blackwood, D. H. R. (1989), Pharmacotherapy of the borderline patient: A critical review and clinical guidelines. *Can. J. Psychiat.*, 34:347–353.

────── ────── St. Clair, D., Gaskell, D., & Muir, W. (1987), Auditory P300 in borderline personality disorder and schizophrenia. *Arch. Gen. Psychiat.*, 44:645–650.

────── ────── ────── ────── (1989), Auditory P300 does not differentiate borderline personality disorder from schizotypal personality disorder. *Biol. Psychiat.*, 26:766–774.

────── Hillier, W. (unpublished), Psychiatric diagnoses in "street kids," 1988.

────── Whitehouse, A. M., & Freeman, C. P. L. (1985), "Hidden" eating disorders in Scottish psychiatric inpatients. *Amer. J. Psychiat.*, 142:1475–1478.

Kwawer, J. S. (1980), Primitive interpersonal modes, borderline phenomena, and Rorschach content. In: *Borderline Phenomena and the Rorschach Test*, ed. J. S. Kwawer, H. D. Lerner, P. M. Lerner, & A. Sugarman. New York: International Universities Press.

Lacey, J. H., & Crisp. A. H. (1980), Hunger, food intake and weight: The impact of clomipramine in anorexia nervosa. *Postgrad. Med. J.*, 56:79–85.

Lane, R. C. (1984), The difficult patient, resistance, and the negative therapeutic reaction: A review of the literature. *Curr. Iss. in Psychoanal. Pract.*, 1:83–106.

Langs, R. (1976), *The Bipersonal Field*. New York: Jason Aronson.

Laufer, M., & Laufer, M. E. (1984), *Adolescence and Developmental Breakdown*. New Haven, CT: Yale University Press.

Laufer, M. E. (1987), Suicide in adolescence. *Psychoanal. Psychother.*, 3:1–10.

Leone, N. F. (1982), Response of borderline patients to loxapine and chlorpromazine. *J. Clin. Psychiat.*, 43:148–150.

Lerner, H., Albert, C., & Walsh, M. (1987), The Rorschach assessment of borderline defenses: A concurrent validity study. *J. Personal. Assess.*, 51:334–348.

——— Sugarman, A., & Gaughran, J. (1981), Borderline and schizophrenic patients: A comparative study of defensive structure. *J. Nerv. & Ment. Dis.*, 169:705–711.

Lerner, P., & Lerner, H. (1980), Rorschach assessment of primitive defenses in borderline personality structure. In: *Borderline Phenomena and the Rorschach Test*, ed. J. Kwawer, H. Lerner, P. Lerner, & A. Sugarman. New York: International Universities Press.

Lerner, S. (1979), The excessive need to treat. *Bull. Menn. Clin.*, 43:463–471.

Leszcz, M. (1986), Interactional group psychotherapy with nonpsychotic inpatients. *Group*, 10:13–20.

——— (1989), Group psychotherapy of the characterologically difficult patient. *Internat. J. Group Psychother.*, 39:311–336.

——— Yalom, I. D., & Norden, M. (1985), In-patient group psychotherapy: Patients' perspectives. *Internat. J. Group Psychother.*, 35:411–433.

Levin, A. P., & Hyler, S. E. (1986), DSM-III personality diagnosis in bulimia. *Comprehen. Psychiat.*, 27:47–53.

Levine, J., Tischer, P., Antoni, M., Green, C., & Millon, T. (1985), Refining personality assessments by combining MCMI high point profiles and MMPI codes, Part II: MMPI code 27/72. *J. Personal. Assess.*, 49:501–507.

Levine, L., & the Fluoxetine Bulimia Study Group (submitted), Fluoxetine in the treatment of bulimia nervosa: A multicentre placebo-controlled double-blind trial.

Levine, S. (1978), Youth and religious cults: A societal and clinical dilemma. In: *Adolescent Psychiatry*, ed. S. Feinstein & P. Giovacchini. Chicago: University of Chicago Press.

Levins, R., & Lewontin, R. (1985), *The Dialectical Biologist*. Cambridge, MA: Harvard University Press.

Levy, J. (1982), A particular kind of negative therapeutic reaction based on Freud's "borrowed guilt." *Internat. J. Psycho-Anal.*, 63:361–368.

———— (1985), Analytic stalemate and supervision. Paper presented to the Toronto Psychoanalytic Society, October.

———— Epstein, N. (1964), An application of the Rorschach test in family investigation. *Fam. Proc.*, 3:344–376.

Lewis, M., & Brooks-Gunn, J. (1979), *Social Cognition and the Acquisition of the Self*. New York: Plenum Press.

Liebenluft, E., Gardner, D. L., & Cowdry, R. W. (1987), The inner experience of the borderline self-mutilator. *J. Personal. Disord.*, 1:317–324.

Liebowitz, M. R. (1979), Is borderline a distinct entity? *Schizophren. Bull.*, 5:23–37.

———— Klein, D. F. (1979), Hysteroid dysphoria. *Psychiat. Clin. N. Amer.*, 2:555–575.

———— ———— (1981), Interrelationship of hysterical dysphoria and borderline personality disorder. *Psychiat. Clin. N. Amer.*, 4:67–89.

———— Stallone, F., Dunner, D., & Fieve, R. F. (1979), Personality features of patients with primary affective disorder. *Acta Psychiat. Scand.*, 60:214–224.

Linehan, M. M. (unpublished), *Dialectical Behavior Therapy for Treatment of Parasuicidal Women: Treatment Manual*. University of Washington, Seattle, WA.

———— (1987), Dialectical behavior therapy: Treating borderline personality disorder. Workshop presented at the Association for Advancement of Behavior Therapy Annual Convention, Boston, MA.

Links, P. A. (1987), Borderline personality disorder: Validity revisited. *Psychiat. Med.*, 4:23–37.

Links, P. S., & Steiner, M. (1988), Psychopharmacologic management of patients with borderline personality disorder. *Can. J. Psychiat.*, 33:355–359.

———— ———— Huxley, G. (1988a), The occurrence of borderline personality disorder in the families of borderline patients. *J. Personal. Disord.*, 2:14–20.

———— ———— Offord, D. R., & Eppel, A. (1988b), Characteristics of borderline personality disorder: A Canadian study. *Can. J. Psychiat.*, 33:336–340.

Little, M. I. (1986), *Toward Basic Unity.* London: Free Association Books.

Livesley, W. J., & Jackson, D. N. (1986), The internal consistency and factional structure of behavior judged to be associated with DSM-III personality disorders. *Amer. J. Psychiat.*, 143:1473–1474.

Lloyd, C., Overall, J., Kimsey, L., & Click, M. (1983), A comparison of the MMPI-168 profiles of borderline and nonborderline patients. *J. Nerv. & Ment. Dis.*, 171:207–215.

Loewald, H. (1971), Some considerations on repetition and repetition compulsion. *Internat. J. Psycho-Anal.*, 52:59–66.

Loranger, A. W. (1988), *Personality Disorder Examination Manual.* Yonkers, NY: DV Communications.

———— Oldham, J. M., Russakoff, L. M., & Susman, V. (1984), Structured interviews and borderline personality disorder. *Arch. Gen. Psychiat.*, 41:565–568.

———— ———— Tulis, E. H. (1982), Familial transmission of borderline personality disorder. *Arch. Gen. Psychiat.*, 39:795–802.

———— Susman, V. L., Oldham, J. M., & Russakoff, L. M. (1987), The Personality Disorder Examination: A preliminary report. *J. Personal. Disord.*, 1:1–13.

———— Tulis, E. H. (1985), Family history of alcoholism in borderline personality disorder. *Arch. Gen. Psychiat.*, 42:153–157.

Luborsky, L. (1976), Helping alliances in psychotherapy. In: *Successful Psychotherapy*, ed. J. L. Claghorn. New York: Brunner/Mazel.

Lucas, P. B., Gardner, D. L., Cowdry, R. W., & Pickar, D. (1989), Cerebral structure in borderline personality disorder. *Psychiat. Res.*, 27:111–115.

———— ———— Wolkowitz, O. M., & Cowdry, W. (1987), Dysphoria associated with methylphenidate infusion in borderline personality disorder. *Amer. J. Psychiat.*, 144:1577–1579.

Lymberis, M. T. (1988), Patient–therapist sex. *Psychiat. News*, January 15.

Macaskill, N. D. (1982a), The theory of transitional phenomena and its application to the psychotherapy of the borderline patient. *Brit. J. Med. Psychol.*, 55:349–360.

———— (1982b), Therapeutic factors in group therapy with borderline patients. *Internat. J. Group Psychother.*, 32:61–74.

Mack, J. E. (1975), Borderline states: An historical perspective. In: *Borderline States in Psychiatry*, ed. J. E. Mack. New York: Grune & Stratton.

Mahler, M. S. (1966), Notes on the development of basic moods: The depressive affect. In: *Psychoanalysis—A General Psychology: Essays in Honor of Heinz Hartmann*, ed. R. M. Loewenstein, L. Newman, M. Schur, & A. Solnit. New York: International Universities Press.

——— (1968), *On Human Symbiosis and the Vicissitudes of Individuation*. London: Hogarth Press & The Institute of Psycho-Analysis.

——— (1971), A study of the separation/individuation process and its possible application to borderline phenomena in the psychoanalytic situation. *The Psychoanalytic Study of the Child*, 26:403–424. Chicago: Quadrangle.

——— (1972a), On the first three subphases of the separation–individuation process. *Internat. J. Psycho-Anal.*, 53:333–338.

——— (1972b), Rapprochement subphase of the separation–individuation process. *Psychoanal. Quart.*, 41:487–506.

——— Furer, M. (1968), *On Human Symbiosis and the Vicissitudes of Individuation*. New York: International Universities Press.

——— Pine, F., & Bergman, A. (1975), *The Psychological Birth of the Human Infant*. New York: Basic Books.

Main, M., Kaplan, N., & Cassidy, J. (1985), Security in infancy, childhood and adulthood: A move to the level of representation. In: *Monographs of the Society for Research in Child Development*, 50 (Serial No. 209), ed. I. Bretherton & E. Waters.

Main, T. F. (1957), The ailment. *Brit. J. Med. Psychol.*, 30:129–145.

Malan, D. M., Balfour, F. M. G., Hood, V. G., & Shooter, A. N. M. (1976), Group psychotherapy: A long-term follow-up study. *Arch. Gen. Psychiat.*, 33:1303–1315.

Maldonaldo, J. L. (1984), Analyst involvement in the psychoanalytic impasse. *Internat. J. Psycho-Anal.*, 65:263–272.

Malin, A., & Grotstein, J. (1966), Projective identification in the therapeutic process. *Internat. J. Psycho-Anal.*, 47:26–31.

Maltsberger, J. T. (1986), *Suicide Risk: The Formulation of Clinical Judgment*. New York: New York University Press.

——— Buie, D. H. (1974), Countertransference hate in the treatment of suicidal patients. *Arch. Gen. Psychiat.*, 30:625–633.

——— ——— (1980), The devices of suicide: Revenge, riddance, and rebirth. *Internat. Rev. Psycho-Anal.*, 7:61–72.

Mann, J., Stanley, M., McBride, P., & McEwen, B. (1986), Increased serotonin 2 and beta 1 receptor binding in the frontal cortex of suicide victims. *Arch. Gen. Psychiat.*, 43:954–959.

Maris, R. W. (1981), *Pathways to Suicide: A Survey of Self-Destructive Behaviors*. Baltimore: Johns Hopkins University Press.

Marks, P., Seeman, W., & Haller, D. (1974), *The Actuarial Use of the MMPI with Adolescents and Adults*. Baltimore: Williams & Wilkins.

Marx, K., & Engels, F. (1970), *Selected Works*. New York: International Publishers.

Marziali, E. A., & Monroe-Blum, H. (1987), The management of projective identification in group treatment of self-destructive borderline patients. *J. Personal. Disord.*, 1:340–343.

Masten, A. G., & Garmezy, M. (1985), Risk vulnerability and protective factors in developmental psychopathology. In: *Advances in Clinical Child Psychology*, Vol. 8, ed. B. B. Lahey & A. E. Karzolin. New York: Plenum Press.

Masterson, J. F. (1972), *Treatment of the Borderline Adolescent: A Developmental Approach*. New York: Wiley-Interscience.

—— (1973a), The borderline adolescent. In: *Adolescent Psychiatry*, ed. S. Feinstein & P. Giovacchini. New York: Basic Books.

—— (1973b), Maternal clinging, separation/individuation, and the borderline syndrome. *Internat. J. Child Psychother.*, 2:331–345.

—— (1976), *Psychotherapy of the Borderline Adult*. New York: Brunner/Mazel.

—— (1978), The borderline adult: Therapeutic alliance and transference. *Amer. J. Psychiat.*, 135:437–441.

—— (1981), *Narcissistic and Borderline Disorders*. New York: Brunner/Mazel.

—— Costello, J. L. (1980), *From Borderline Adolescent to Functioning Adult: The Test of Time*. New York: Brunner/Mazel.

—— Rinsley, D. (1975), The borderline syndrome: The role of the mother in the genesis and psychic structure of the borderline personality. *Internat. J. Psycho-Anal.*, 56:163–177.

Masterson, J. H. (1977), Primary anorexia nervosa in the borderline adolescent—An object relations view. In: *Borderline Personality Disorders*, ed. P. Hartocollis. New York: International Universities Press.

Mayer-Bahlberg, H. F. L., Ehrhardt, A. A., & Feldman, J. F. (1986), Long-term implications of the prenatal endocrine milieu for sex–dimorphic behavior. In: *Life-span Research on the Prediction of Psychopathology*, ed. L. Erlenmeyer-Kinling & N. E. Miller. Hillsdale, NJ: Lawrence Erlbaum.

Mayman, M. (1967), Object representations and object relationships in Rorschach responses. *J. Project. Tech.*, 31:17–25.

Mays, D. T., & Franks, C. M. (1985), *Negative Outcome in Psychotherapy: And What To Do About It*. New York: Springer.

McCall, R. B. (1981), Nature–nurture and the two realms of development: A proposed integration with respect to mental development. *Child Devel.*, 52:1–12.

McGlashan, T. H. (1983a), The borderline syndrome. II. Is it a variant of schizophrenia or affective disorder? *Arch. Gen. Psychiat.*, 40:1319–1323.

—— (1983b), The borderline syndrome: Testing three diagnostic systems. *Arch. Gen. Psychiat.*, 40:1311–1318.

—— (1983c), The "we-self" in borderline patients: Manifestations of the symbiotic self–object in psychotherapy. *Psychiatry*, 46:351–361.

—— (1984a), The Chestnut Lodge follow-up study. I. Follow-up methodology and study sample. *Arch. Gen. Psychiat.*, 41:573–585.

—— (1984b), The Chestnut Lodge follow-up study. II. Long-term outcome of schizophrenia and the affective disorders. *Arch. Gen. Psychiat.*, 41:586–601.

—— (1985), The prediction of outcome in borderline personality disorder: Part V of the Chestnut Lodge follow-up study. In: *The Borderline: Current Empirical Research*, ed. T. H. McGlashan. Washington, DC: American Psychiatric Press.

—— (1986a), The Chestnut Lodge follow-up study, III. Long-term outcome of borderline personalities. *Arch. Gen. Psychiat.*, 43:20–30.

—— (1986b), The prediction of outcome in chronic schizophrenia. *Arch. Gen. Psychiat.*, 43:167–176.

—— (1986c), Schizotypal personality disorder. Chestnut Lodge follow-up study: VI. Long-term follow-up perspectives. *Arch. Gen. Psychiat.*, 43:329–334.

—— (1987a), Borderline personality disorder and unipolar affective disorder. Long term effects of comorbidity. *J. Nerv. & Ment. Dis.*, 167:467–473.

—— (1987b), Testing DSM-III symptom criteria for schizotypal and borderline personality disorders. *Arch. Gen. Psychiat.*, 44:143–148.

—— (1988a), Diagnostic efficiency of DSM-III BPD and schizotypal disorders. In: *Proceedings and Summary*, 141st Annual Meeting, Washington, DC, American Psychiatric Association.

—— (1988b), A prognostic scale for BPD. Paper presented at American Psychiatric Association Meeting, Montreal.

—— Bardenstein, K. K., (1990), Gender differences in affective, schizoaffective, and schizophrenic disorders. *Schizophrenia Bull.*, 16:319–329.

———— Heinssen, R. K. (1988), Hospital discharge status and long term outcome for patients with schizophrenia, schizoaffective disorder, borderline personality disorder and unipolar affective disorder. *Arch. Gen. Psychiat.*, 45:363–368.

———— ———— (1989), Narcissistic, antisocial, and non-comorbid subgroups of borderline disorder: Are they distinct entities by long-term clinical profile? *Psychiat. Clin. N. Amer.*, 12:653–670.

McManus, M., Alessi, N., Grapentine, W., & Robbins, D. (1984), Psychiatric disturbance in serious delinquents. *J. Amer. Acad. Child Psychiat.*, 23:602–615.

———— Lerner, H., Robbins, D., Alessi, N., & Barbour, C. (1984), Assessment of borderline symptomatology in hospitalized adolescents. *J. Amer. Acad. Child Psychiat.*, 23:685–694.

McNamara, M. E., Reynolds, C. F., Soloff, F. H., Mathias, R., Rossi, A., Spiker, D., Coble, P. A., & Kupfer, D. J. (1984), EEG sleep evaluation of depression in borderline patients. *Amer. J. Psychiat.*, 141:182–186.

Meehl, P. E. (1972), A critical afterword. In: *Schizophrenia and Genetics*, ed. I. I. Gootesman & J. Shields. New York: Academic Press.

Meissner, W. W. (1988), *Treatment of Patients in the Borderline Spectrum*. Northvale, NJ: Jason Aronson.

Meltzoff, A. N., & Moore, M. K. (1977), Imitation of facial and manual gestures by human neonates. *Science*, 198:75–78.

———— ———— (1983), The origins of imitation in infancy: Paradigm, phenomena and theories. In: *Advances in Infancy Research*, ed. L. P. Lipsitt. Norwood, NJ: Ablex.

Mezzich, J. (1988), Personality conditions and the international classification of diseases. Paper presented at the First International Congress on the Disorders of Personality, Copenhagen, August 3rd.

Miller, M. (1964), Time and character disorder. *J. Nerv. & Ment. Dis.*, 138:534–540.

Millon, T. (1983), The DSM-III: An insider's perspective. *Amer. J. Psychol.*, 38:804–814.

———— (1987), On the genesis of prevalence of the BPD. *J. Personal. Disord.*, 1:354–372.

———— (1988), Toward an integrative personology. Paper presented at the First International Congress on the Disorders of Personality, Copenhagen, August 5th.

Minde, K. (1987), The relevance of infant psychiatry to the understanding of adult psychopathology. *Can. J. Psychiat.*, 32:513–517.

Minuchin, S., Rosman, B. L., & Baker, L. (1978), *Psychosomatic Families: Anorexia Nervosa in Context.* Cambridge, MA: Harvard University Press.

Mitchell, J. E., & Groat, R. (1984), A placebo-controlled double-blind trial of amitriptyline in bulimia. *J. Clin. Psychopharmacol.*, 4:186–193.

Mitton, J. E., & Links, P. S. (1988), Two-year prospective follow-up of borderline. In: *Proceedings and Summary*, 141st Annual Meeting, American Psychiatric Association.

Modell, A. (1963), Primitive object relationships and the predisposition to schizophrenia. *Internat. J. Psycho-Anal.*, 44:282–292.

——— (1975), A narcissistic defence against affects and the illusion of self-sufficiency. *Internat. J. Psycho-Anal.*, 56:275–282.

——— (1976), 'The holding environment' and the therapeutic action of psychoanalysis. *J. Amer. Psychoanal. Assn.*, 24:285–307.

——— (1984), *Psychoanalysis in a New Context.* New York: International Universities Press.

Monroe, R. R. (1970), *Episodic Behavioral Disorders.* Cambridge, MA: Harvard University Press.

Morey, L. C. (1988a), Personality disorders in DSM-III and DSM-III-R: Convergence, coverage and internal consistency. *Amer. J. Psychiat.*, 145:573–577.

——— (1988b), A psychometric analysis of the DSM-III personality disorder criteria. *J. Personal. Disord.*, 2:109–124.

Morgan, H. G., & Russell, G. F. M. (1975), Value of a family background and clinical features as predictors in anorexia nervosa: Four-year follow-up study of 41 patients. *Psychol. Med.*, 5:355.

Morris, H., Gunderson, J. G., & Zanarini, M. C. (1986), Transitional object use and borderline psychopathology. *Amer. J. Psychiat.*, 143:1534–1538.

Mullan, H. (1987), The ethical foundations of group psychotherapy. *Internat. J. Group Psychother.*, 37:403–416.

Myerson, L., Wennogle, L., Abel, M., Coupet, J., Lippa, A., Rank, C., & Beer, B. (1982), Human brain receptor alterations in suicide victims. *Pharmacol. Biochem. Behav.*, 17:159–163.

Myerson, P. G. (1979), Issues of technique where patients relate with difficulty. *Internat. Rev. Psycho-Anal.*, 6:363–375.

Nace, E. P. (1987), *The Treatment of Alcoholism.* New York: Brunner/Mazel.

——— Saxon, J. J., & Shore, N. (1983), A comparison of borderline and non-borderline alcoholic patients. *Arch. Gen. Psychiat.*, 40:54–56.

——— ——— ——— (1986), Borderline personality disorder and alcoholism treatment: A one-year follow-up study. *J. Stud. on Alcohol*, 147:196–200.

Norman, D. K., & Herzog, D. B. (1983), Bulimia, anorexia nervosa and anorexia nervosa with bulimia: A comparative analysis of MMPI profiles. *Internat. J. Eat. Disord.*, 2:43–52.

Novick, J. (1980), Negative therapeutic motivation and negative therapeutic alliance. *The Psychoanalytic Study of the Child*, 35:299–320. New Haven, CT: Yale University Press.

——— (1984), Attempted suicide in adolescence. In: *Suicide in the Young*, ed. H. S. Sudak, A. B. Ford, & N. B. Rushforth. Boston: John Wright.

Novick, K. K., & Novick, J. (1987), The essence of masochism. *The Psychoanalytic Study of the Child*, 42:353–384. New Haven, CT: Yale University Press.

Nunberg, H. (1931), The synthetic function of the ego. In: *Practice and Theory of Psychoanalysis*, Vol. 1. New York: International Universities Press.

——— Federn, E., eds. (1962–1975), *Minutes of the Vienna Psychoanalytic Society*, Vol. 2. New York: International Universities Press.

Nunberg, H. G., Hurt, S. W., Feldman, A., & Suh, R. (1988), Evaluation of diagnostic criteria for borderline personality disorder. *Amer. J. Psychiat.*, 145:1280–1284.

——— Suh, R. (1980), Limits: Short-term treatment of hospitalized borderline patients. *Comprehen. Psychiat.*, 21:70–80.

——— ——— (1982), Time-limited psychotherapy of the hospitalized borderline patient. *Amer. J. Psychother.*, 36:82–90.

Ogata, S., Silk, K. R., Goodrich, S., & Lohr, N. E. (1988), Childhood abuse and clinical symptoms in BPD. In: *Proceedings and Summary*, 141st Annual Meeting, American Psychiatric Association.

Ogden, T. H. (1979), On projective identification. *Internat. J. Psycho-Anal.*, 60:357–373.

——— (1982), *Projective Identification and Psychotherapeutic Technique*. New York: Jason Aronson.

Oldham, J. (1988), Comorbidity studies of severe personality disorders. Paper presented at the first Annual New York State Office of Mental Health Research Conference, Albany, December 6th.

O'Leary, K. M., Cowdry, R. W., Gardner, D. L., Liebenluft, E., Lucas, P. B., & deJong-Meyer, R. (unpublished), Dysfunctional attitudes in borderline personality disorder.

Olin, H. S. (1976), Psychotherapy of the chronically suicidal patient. *Amer. J. Psychother.*, 30:570–575.

Ormont, L. (1981), Principles of conjoint psychoanalytic treatment. *Amer. J. Psychiat.*, 138:69–73.

Ornstein, A., & Ornstein, P. H. (1985), Parenting as a function of the adult self: A psychoanalytic developmental perspective. In: *Parental Influences: In Health and Disease*, ed. E. J. Anthony & G. A. Pollock. Toronto: Little, Brown.

O'Shaughnessy, E. (1981), A clinical study of a defense organization. *Internat. J. Psycho-Anal.*, 62:359–369.

Padel, J. (1988), The basis of normality—paper contributed to a panel on transitional objects. *Brit. Psychoanal. Soc. Bull.*, June: 8–13.

Padesky, C. A. (1986), Personality disorders: Cognitive therapy into the 90's. Paper presented at the second International Conference on Cognitive Psychotherapy, Umea, Sweden, September.

Panel (1984), The relation between masochism and depression. J. Caston (reporter). *J. Amer. Psychoanal. Assn.*, 32:603–614.

Paolino, T. J. (1981), *Psychoanalytic Psychotherapy: Theory, Technique, Therapeutic Relationship and Treatability*. New York: Brunner/Mazel.

Papousek, M., & Papousek, H. (1981), Musical elements in the infant's vocalization: Their significance for communication, cognition and creativity. In: *Advances in Infancy Research*, ed. L. P. Lipsitt. Norwood, NJ: Ablex.

Paris, J. (1988), Follow-up studies of borderline personality disorder: A critical review. *J. Personal. Disord.*, 2:189–197.

——— Brown, R., & Nowlis, D. (1987), Long-term follow-up of borderline patients in a general hospital. *Comprehen. Psychiat.*, 28:530–535.

——— Nowlis, D., & Brown, R. (1988), Development factors in outcome of BPD. In: *Proceedings and Summary*, 141st Annual Meeting, American Psychiatric Association.

Patrick, J. (1984), Characteristics of DSM-III borderline MMPI profiles. *J. Clin. Psychol.*, 40:655–658.

Perry, J. A. (1976), Physicians' erotic and non-erotic physical involvement with patients. *Amer. J. Psychiat.*, 133:838–840.

Perry, J. C. (1985), Depression in borderline personality disorder: Lifetime prevalence at interview and longitudinal course of symptoms. *Amer. J. Psychiat.*, 142:15–21.

——— (1988), A prospective study of life stress, defenses, psychotic symptoms, and depression in borderline and antisocial personality disorders and bipolar type II affective disorder. *J. Personal. Disord.*, 2:49–59.

———— Cooper, S. H. (1986), A preliminary report on defenses and conflicts associated with borderline personality disorder. *J. Amer. Psychoanal. Assn.*, 34:863–894.

———— Klerman, J. L. (1978), The borderline patient: A comparative analysis of four sets of diagnostic criteria. *Arch. Gen. Psychiat.*, 35:141–150.

———— ———— (1980), Clinical features of the borderline personality disorder. *Arch. Gen. Psychiat.*, 137:165–173.

Peselow, E. D., Baxter, N., Fiebe, R. R., & Barouche, F. (1987), The dexamethasone suppression test as a monitor of clinical recovery. *Amer. J. Psychiat.*, 144:30–35.

Peteet, J. R., & Gutheil, T. G. (1979), The hospital and the borderline patient: Management guidelines for the community mental health center. *Psychiat. Quart.*, 51:106–118.

Pfohl, B., Coryell, W., Zimmerman, M., & Stangl, D. (1986), DSM-III personality disorders: Diagnostic overlap and internal consistency of individual DSM-III criteria. *Comprehen. Psychiat.*, 27:21–34.

———— Stangl, D., & Zimmerman, M. (1982), *The Structured Interview for DSM-III Personality Disorders.* Distributed by the authors. Iowa City, IA.

Pildis, M., Soverow, G., Salzman, C., & Wolf, J. (1978), Day hospital treatment of borderline patients: A clinical perspective. *Amer. J. Psychiat.*, 5:594–596.

Pilkonis, P. A., & Frank, E. (1988), Personality pathology in recurrent depression: Nature, prevalence and relationship to treatment response. *Amer. J. Psychiat.*, 145:435–441.

Pine, F. (1980), On the expansion of the affect array: A developmental description. In: *Rapprochement: The Critical Subphase of Separation–Individuation,* ed. R. Lax, S. Bach, & J. Burland. New York: Jason Aronson.

Pines, M. (1983), Psychoanalysis and group analysis. *Internat. J. Group Psychother.*, 33:155–170.

Piran, N., Kaplan, A. S., Shekter-Wolfson, L., Winokur, J., & Garfinkel, P. E. (1989), A day hospital group therapy program for patients with serious eating disorders. *Internat. J. Eat. Disord.*, 8:523–532.

———— Kennedy, S., Garfinkel, P. E., & Owens, M. (1985), Affective disturbance in eating disorders. *J. Nerv. & Ment. Dis.*, 173:395–400.

———— Langdon, L., Kaplan, A. S., & Garfinkel, P. E. (1989), Evaluation of a day hospital program for eating disorders. *Internat. J. Eat. Disord.*, 8:523–532.

———— Lerner, P., Garfinkel, P. E., Kennedy, S., & Brouillette, C. (1988), Personality disorders in anorexic patients. *Internat. J. Eat. Disord.*, 7:589–599.

Plakun, E. M., Burkhardt, P. E., & Muller, J. P. (1986), 14-year follow-up of borderline and schizotypal personality disorders. *Comprehen. Psychiat.*, 40:23–30.

Pollack, I., & Battle, W. (1963), Students of the special patient. *Arch. Gen. Psychiat.*, 9:344–350.

Pope, H. G., Frankenberg, F. R., Hudson, J. I., Jonas, J. M., & Yurgelun-Todd, D. (1987), Is bulimia associated with borderline personality disorder? A controlled study. *J. Clin. Psychiat.*, 48:181–184.

———— Hudson, J. I. (1988), Is bulimia nervosa a heterogeneous disorder? Lessons from the history of medicine. *Internat. J. Eat. Disord.*, 7:155–166.

———— ———— Jonas, J. M., & Yurgelun-Todd, D. (1983), Treatment of bulimia with imipramine. A double-blind placebo-controlled study. *Amer. J. Psychiat.*, 14:554–558.

———— Jonas, J. M., Hudson, J. I., Cohen, B. M., & Gunderson, J. G. (1983), The validity of DSM-III borderline personality disorder. *Arch. Gen. Psychiat.*, 40:23–30.

———— ———— ———— ———— ———— (1985), An empirical study of psychosis in borderline personality disorder. *Amer. J. Psychiat.*, 142:1285–1290.

Pretzer, J. L. (1983), Borderline personality disorder: Too complex for cognitive-behavioral approaches? Paper presented at the meeting of the American Psychological Association, Anaheim, CA (ERIC Document Reproduction Service No. ED 243 007).

———— (in press), Borderline personality disorder. In: *Clinical Applications of Cognitive Therapy*. New York: Plenum Press.

Provence, S., & Lipton, R. (1962), *Infants in Institutions: A Comparison of Their Development with Family-Reared Infants During the First Year of Life*. New York: International Universities Press.

Pyle, R. L., Mitchell, J. E., & Eckert, E. D. (1981), Bulimia: A report of 34 cases. *J. Clin. Psychiat.*, 42:60–64.

———— ———— ———— Halvorson, P. A. (1983), The incidence of bulimia in freshmen college students. *Internat. J. Eat. Disord.*, 2:75–85.

Rakoff, V. (1978), The illusion of detachment. In: *Adolescent Psychiatry*, ed. S. Feinstein & P. Giovacchini. Chicago: University of Chicago Press.

Rapaport, D., Gill, M., & Schafer, R. (1945), *Diagnostic Psychological Testing*, rev. ed. New York: International Universities Press, 1968.

Rechtschaffen, A. (1959), Psychotherapy with geriatric patients: A review of the literature. *J. Gerontol.*, 14:73–84.

Reich, J. H. (1987), Instruments measuring DSM-III and DSM-III-R personality disorders. *J. Personal. Disord.*, 1:220–240.

——— Ndvaguba, M., & Yates, W. (1988), Age and sex distribution of DSM-III personality cluster traits in a community population. *Comprehen. Psychiat.*, 29:298–303.

Reich, W. T. (1925), *Der Triebhafte Character (The Impulse Ridden Character)*. Leipzig: Int. Z. PSA.

Resnick, R., Schulz, P., Schulz, D., Hamer, R., Friedel, R., & Goldberg, S. (1983), Borderline personality disorder: Symptomatology and MMPI characteristics. *J. Clin. Psychiat.*, 44:289–292.

Rey, J. H. (1979), Schizoid phenomena in the borderline. In: *Advances in Psychotherapy of the Borderline Patient*, ed. J. Le Boit & A. Capponi. New York: Jason Aronson.

Reynolds, C. F., Soloff, P. H., Kupfer, D. J., Taska, L. S., Reshfo, K., Coble, P. A., & McNamara, M. E. (1985), Depression in borderline patients: A prospective EEG sleep study. *Psychiat. Res.*, 14:1–15.

Rich, C. L. (1978), Borderline diagnoses. *Amer. J. Psychiat.*, 135:1399–1401.

Riederer, P., & Kruzik, P. (1982), Excretion of biogenic amine metabolites in anorexia nervosa. *Clin. Chim. Acta*, 123:27–32.

Riesenberg Malcolm, R. (1980–1981), Expiation as a defense. *Internat. J. Psychoanal. Psychother.*, 8:549–570.

Rifkin, A., Quitkin, F., Carrillo, C., Blumberg, A. G., & Klein, D. F. (1972), Lithium carbonate in emotionally unstable character disorders. *Arch. Gen. Psychiat.*, 27:519–523.

Rinsberg, D. (1982), *Borderline and Other Self-Disorders*. New York: Jason Aronson.

Rinsley, D. B. (1968), Theory and practice of intensive residential treatment of patients with borderline personality disorders. *Psychiat. Quart.*, 42:611–618.

——— (1978), Borderline psychotherapy: A review of etiology, dynamics and treatment. *Internat. Rev. Psycho-Anal.*, 5:45–50.

——— (1988), The Dipsas revisited: Comments on addiction and personality. *J. Subst. Abuse Treat.*, 5:1–7.

Ritvo, S., & Solnit, A. (1958), Influences of early mother–child interaction on identification processes. *The Psychoanalytic Study of the Child*. New York: International Universities Press.

Riviere, J. (1936), A contribution to the analysis of the negative therapeutic reaction. *Internat. J. Psycho-Anal.*, 17:304–320.

Roazen, P. (1969), *Brother Animal: The Story of Freud and Tausk*. New
York: Knopf.

————— (1982), Letter to the editor: Errors regarding Freud. *Internat.
J. Psycho-Anal.*, 63:260–261.

————— (1985), *Helene Deutsch: A Psychoanalyst's Life*. Garden City, NY:
Doubleday/Anchor Press.

Robbins, M. (1988), Use of audiotape recording in impasses with
severely disturbed patients. *J. Amer. Psychoanal. Assn.*,
36:105–124.

Robins, E. (1981), *The Final Months*. New York: Oxford University
Press.

————— Guze, S. G. (1970), Establishment of diagnostic validity in psychiatric illness: Its application to schizophrenia. *Amer. J. Psychiat.*,
126:983–987.

Rodin, G. M., Johnson, L. E., Garfinkel, P. E., Daneman, D., & Kenshole, A. B. (1986), Eating disorders in female adolescents with
insulin dependent diabetes mellitus. *Internat. J. Psychiat. Med.*,
16:49–57.

Rosenbluth, M. (1987), The inpatient treatment of the borderline
personality disorder: A critical review and discussion of aftercare implications. *Can. J. Psychiat.*, 32:228–237.

Rosenfeld, H. (1962), The super-ego and the ego ideal. *Internat. J.
Psycho-Anal.*, 43:258–263.

————— (1971), A clinical approach to the psychoanalytic theory of
the life and death instincts: An investigation into the aggressive
aspects of narcissism. *Internat. J. Psycho-Anal.*, 52:169–178.

————— (1978), Notes on the psychopathology and psychoanalytic
treatment of some borderline patients. *Internat. J. Psycho-Anal.*,
59:215–221.

————— (1979a), Difficulties in the psychoanalytic treatment of borderline patients. In: *Advances in Psychotherapy of the Borderline Patient*,
ed. J. Le Boit & A. Capponi. New York: Jason Aronson.

————— (1979b), Transference psychosis in the borderline patient. In:
Advances in Psychotherapy of the Borderline Patient, ed. J. Le Boit &
A. Capponi. New York: Jason Aronson.

————— (1987), *Impasse and Interpretation*. London: Tavistock.

Rosenthal, D., Wender, P. H., Kety, S. S., Weiner, J., & Schulsinger,
F. (1971), The adopted away off-spring of schizophrenics. *Amer.
J. Psychiat.*, 128:307–311.

Rosnick, L. (1987), Inpatient unit as a site for learning psychotherapy.
Psychiat. Clin. N. Amer., 10:309–324.

Ross, J. M., & Dunn, P. B. (1980), Notes on the genesis of pathological splitting. *Internat. J. Psycho-Anal.*, 61:335–349.

Rossman, R., & Knesper, D. (1975), The early phase of hospital treatment for disruptive adolescents. *J. Amer. Acad. Child Adol. Psychiat.*, 14:693–708.

Roth, B. E. (1980), Understanding the development of a homogeneous, identity impaired group through countertransference phenomena. *Internat. J. Group Psychother.*, 30:405–426.

Roth, M. (1959), The phobic–anxiety–depersonalization syndrome. *Proc. Roy. Soc. Med.*, 52:587–595.

Russell, G. (1979), Bulimia nervosa: An ominous variant of anorexia nervosa. *Psychol. Med.*, 9:429–468.

Rutan, J. S., & Alonso, A. (1982), Group therapy, individual or both? *Internat. J. Group Psychother.*, 32:267–283.

———— ———— (1984), The impact of object relations theory on psychodynamic group therapy. *Amer. J. Psychiat.*, 141:1376–1380.

———— Stone, W. N. (1984), *Psychodynamic Group Psychotherapy.* Lexington, MA: Collamore Press.

Rutter, M. (1989), Pathways from childhood to adult life. *J. Child Psychol. Psychiat.*, 30:23–51.

Ryan, N., & Puig-Antich, J. (1987), Pharmacological treatment of adolescent psychiatric disorders. *J. Adol. Health Care*, 8:137–142.

———— ———— (1988), Psychobiology of adolescent suicide. Paper presented at American Psychiatric Association Symposium—Youth Suicide: Research and Clinical Issues, May 12.

Sadavoy, J. (1987a), Character disorders in the elderly: An overview. In: *Treating the Elderly with Psychotherapy: The Scope for Change in Later Life,* ed. J. Sadavoy & M. Leszcz. Madison, CT: International Universities Press.

———— (1987b), Character pathology in the elderly. *J. Geriat. Psychiat.*, 20:165–178.

———— (1988), The impact of intrapsychic elements on interpersonal functioning in old age. Paper presented at the Annual Meeting, American Psychiatric Association, Montreal.

———— Dorian, B. (1983), Treatment of the elderly characterologically disturbed patient in the chronic care institution. *J. Geriat. Psychiat.*, 16:223–240.

———— Robinson, R. (1989), Psychotherapy with the cognitively impaired. In: *Psychiatric Consequences of Brain Disease in the Elderly: A Focus on Management,* ed. D. Conn, A. Grek, & J. Sadavoy. New York: Plenum Press.

———— Silver, D., & Book, H. (1979), Negative responses of the borderline to in-patient treatment *Amer. J. Psychiat.*, 33:404–417.

Sainsbury, P. (1986a), Depression, suicide, and suicide prevention. In: *Suicide*, ed. A. Roy. Baltimore: Williams & Wilkins.

—— (1986b), The epidemiology of suicide. In: *Suicide*, ed. A. Roy. Baltimore: Williams & Wilkins.

Saint Augustine, *The Confessions of St. Augustine*. New York: New American Library, 1963.

Sakinofsky, I., & Swart, G. T. (1986), Suicidal patients and the ethics of medicine. *Can. J. Psychiat.*, 31:91–95.

Sameroff, A. J., & Emde, R. N. (1989), *Relationship Disturbances in Early Childhood: A Developmental Approach*. New York: Basic Books.

Sandler, J. (1983), Reflections on some relations between psychoanalytic concepts and psychoanalytic practice. *Internat. J. Psycho-Anal.*, 64:35–46.

—— Joffe, W. (1965), Notes on childhood depression. *Internat. J. Psycho-Anal.*, 46:88–96.

Saretsky, T., Fromm, G., Bernstein, V., Wong, N., & Bernstein, J. (1981), *Resolving Treatment Impasses: The Difficult Patient*. New York: Human Sciences Press.

Schafer, R. (1954), *Psychoanalytic Interpretation in Rorschach Testing*. New York: Grune & Stratton.

Schaffer, C. B., Carroll, J., & Abramowitz, S. I. (1982), Self-mutilation and the borderline personality. *J. Nerv. & Ment. Dis.*, 170:468–473.

Schmideberg, M. (1947), The treatment of psychopaths and borderline patients. *Amer. J. Psychother.*, 1:45–70.

—— (1959), The borderline patient. In: *American Handbook of Psychiatry*, Vol. 1, ed. S. Arieti. New York: Basic Books.

Schubert, D. L., Saccuzzo, D. P., & Braff, D. L. (1985), Information processing in borderline patients. *J. Nerv. & Ment. Dis.*, 173:26–31.

Schulz, S. C., Cornelius, J., Schulz, P. M., & Soloff, P. H. (1988), The amphetamine challenge test in patients with borderline disorder. *Amer. J. Psychiat.*, 145:809–814.

Schwartsberg, A. (1978), Overview of the borderline syndrome in adolescence. In: *Adolescent Psychiatry*, ed. S. Feinstein & P. Giovacchini. Chicago: University of Chicago Press.

Schwartz, D. A., Flinn, D. E., & Slavson, P. F. (1974), Treatment of the suicidal character. *Amer. J. Psychother.*, 28:194–207.

Sederer, L. I., & Thorbeck, J. (1986), First do not harm: Short-term inpatient psychotherapy of the borderline patient. *Hosp. Commun. Psychiat.*, 37:692–697.

Segal, H. (1954), A note on schizoid mechanisms underlying phobia formation. *Internat. J. Psycho-Anal.*, 35:238–241.

——— (1957), Notes on symbol formation. *Internat. J. Psycho-Anal.*, 38:391–397.

——— (1973), *Introduction to the Work of Melanie Klein*. London: Hogarth Press.

——— (1974), *Introduction to the Work of Melanie Klein*. New York: Basic Books.

——— (1987), On the clinical usefulness of the concept of the death instinct. Freud Memorial Lecture. *Brit. Psychoanal. Soc. Bull.*, February: 1–12.

Seltzer, L. F. (1986), *Paradoxical Strategies in Psychotherapy: A Comprehensive Overview and Guidebook*. New York: John Wiley.

Seltzer, M. A., Koenigsberg, H. W., & Kernberg, O. F. (1987), The initial contract in the treatment of borderline patients. *Amer. J. Psychiat.*, 144:927–930.

Selvini-Palazzoli, M. (1974), *Self-Starvation: From the Intrapsychic to the Transpersonal Approach to Anorexia Nervosa*. London: Human Context Books.

Semrad, E. V., Buie, D. H., Maltsberger, J. T., Silberger, J., & Van Buskirk, D. (1969), *Teaching Psychotherapy of Psychotic Patient*. New York: Grune & Stratton.

Serban, G., & Seigel, S. (1984), Response of borderline and schizotypal patients to small doses of thiothixene and haloperidol. *Amer. J. Psychiat.*, 141:1455–1458.

Shapiro, E. R. (1978a), Research on family dynamics: Clinical implications for the family of the borderline adolescent. *Adol. Psychiat.*, 6:360–376.

——— (1978b), The psychodynamics and developmental psychology of the borderline patient: A review of the literature. *Amer. J. Psychiat.*, 135:1305–1315.

——— (1982a), The holding environment and family therapy with acting out adolescents. *Internat. J. Psychoanal. Psychother.*, 9:209–226.

——— (1982b), On curiosity: Intrapsychic and interpersonal boundary formation in family life. *Internat. J. Fam. Psychiat.*, 3:69–89.

——— Carr, A. W. (1987), Disguised countertransference in institutions. *Psychiatry*, 50:72–82.

——— ——— (1991), *Lost in Familiar Places: Creating New Connections Between the Individual and Society*. New Haven and London: Yale University Press.

———— Freedman, J. (1987), Family dynamics of adolescent suicide. *Adol. Psychiat.*, 14:191–207. Reprinted in: *Internat. Ann. Adol. Psychiat.*, 1:152–166, 1988.

———— Kolb, J. E. (1979), Engaging the family of the hospitalized adolescent: The multiple family meeting. *Adol. Psychiat.*, 7:322–342.

———— Shapiro, R. L., Zinner, J., & Berkowitz, D. A. (1977), The borderline ego and the working alliance: Indications for individual and family treatment in adolescence. *Internat. J. Psycho-Anal.*, 58:77–87. Reprinted in: *Foundations of Object Relations Family Therapy*, ed. J. Scharff. New York: Jason Aronson, 1989.

———— Zinner, J., Shapiro, R. L., & Berkowitz, D. A. (1975), The influence of family experience on borderline personality development. *Internat. Rev. Psycho-Anal.*, 2:399–411.

Shapiro, R. L. (1968), Action and family interaction in adolescence. In: *Modern Psychoanalysis*, ed. J. Marmor. New York: Basic Books.

———— Zinner, J. (1975), Family organization and adolescent development. In: *Task and Organization*, ed. E. Miller. New York: John Wiley.

Shaw, D., Camps, F., & Eccleston, E. (1967), 5-Hydroxytryptamine in the hindbrain of depressive suicide. *Brit. J. Psychiat.*, 113:1407–1411.

Shea, M. T., Glass, D. R., Pilkonis, P. A., Watkins, J., & Dogherty, J. P. (1987), Frequency and implications of personality disorders in a sample of depressed outpatients. *J. Personal. Disord.*, 1:27–42.

Sheehy, M., Goldsmith, L., & Charles, E. (1980), A comparative study of borderline patients in a psychiatric out-patient clinic. *Amer. J. Psychiat.*, 137:1374–1379.

Siever, L. J., & Gunderson, J. G. (1983), The search for a schizotypal personality: Historical origins and current status. *Comprehen. Psychiat.*, 24:199–212.

———— Coursey, R. D., & Alterman, I. S. (1984), Impaired smooth pursuit eye movement: Vulnerability marker for schizotypal personality disorder in a normal volunteer population. *Amer. J. Psychiat.*, 141:1560–1566.

Silk, K. R., Lohr, N. E., Cornell, O. G., Hasel, T., Saakvitne, K., Buttenheim, M. C., & Zis, A. P. (1985), The dexamethasone suppression test in borderline and non-borderline affective patients. In: *The Borderline: Current Empirical Research*, ed. T. H. McGlashan. Washington, DC: American Psychiatric Press.

———— Lohr, E., Shipley, J. E., Eiser, A., & Feinberg, M. (1988), Sleep EEG and DST in borderlines with depression. In: *Proceedings and Summary*, 141st Annual Meeting, American Psychiatric Association.

Silver, D. (1983), Psychotherapy of the characterologically difficult patient. *Can. J. Psychother.*, 28:513–521.

——— (1985), Psychodynamics and psychotherapeutic management of the self-destructive character-disordered patient. *Psychiat. Clin. N. Amer.*, 8:357–375.

——— (unpublished), The role of consultations in resolving psychotherapeutic stalemates, 1987.

——— Book, H. E., Hamilton, J. E., Sadavoy, J., & Slonim, R. (1983a), The characterologically difficult patient: A hospital treatment model. *Can. J. Psychiat.*, 28:91–96.

——— ——— ——— ——— ——— (1983b), Psychotherapy and the inpatient unit: A unique learning experience. *Amer. J. Psychother.*, 37:121–129.

——— Cardish, R., & Glassman, E. (1987), Intensive treatment of characterologically difficult patients. *Psychiat. Clin. N. Amer.*, 10:219–245.

——— Glassman, E. J., & Cardish, R. J. (1988), The assessment of the capacity to be soothed: Clinical and methodological issues. In: *The Solace Paradigm—An Eclectic Search for Psychological Immunity*, ed. P. Horton, H. Gewirtz, & K. Kreutter. Madison, CT: International Universities Press.

——— Sadavoy, J. (1976), Long-term intermittent in-patient treatment of the borderline patient. Paper presented at the International Forum on Adolescence, Jerusalem, Israel.

Simon, J. (1986), Day hospital treatment for borderline adolescents. *Adol.*, 21:561–572.

Skinner, H. (1986), Construct validation approach to psychiatric classification. In: *Contemporary Directions in Psychopathology*, ed. T. Millon & G. Klerman. New York: Guilford Press.

Skodal, A., Buckley, P., & Charles, E. (1983), Is there a characteristic pattern to the treatment history of clinical outpatients with borderline personality? *J. Nerv. & Ment. Dis.*, 171:405–410.

Skodal, S. E., Rosnick, L., Kellman, D., Oldham, J. M., & Hyler, S. E. (1988), Validating structured DSM-III-R personality disorder assessments with longitudinal data. *Amer. J. Psychiat.*, 145:1297–1299.

Slater, E., & Roth, M. (1977), *Clinical Psychiatry*. London: Bailliere Tindall.

Slovinska-Holy, N. (1983), Combining individual and homogeneous group psychotherapies for borderline conditions. *Internat. J. Group Psychother.*, 32:297–312.

Smith, K. (1980), Object relations concepts as applied to the border-line level of ego functioning. In: *Borderline Phenomena and the Rorschach Test*, ed. J. S. Kwawer, H. D. Lerner, P. M. Lerner, & A. Sugarman. New York: International Universities Press.

Smith, S. (1977), The golden fantasy: A regressive reaction to separation anxiety. *Internat. J. Psycho-Anal.*, 58:311–324.

Snyder, S. (1986), Manipulation. *Comprehen. Psychiat.*, 7:248–258.

—— Goodpaster, A., Pitts, W., Pokorny, A., & Gustin, Q. (1985), Demography of psychiatric patients with borderline personality traits. *Psychopathol.*, 18:38–49.

—— Pitts, W., Goodpaster, W., Sajadi, C., & Gustin, Q. (1982), MMPI profile of DSM-III borderline personality disorder. *Amer. J. Psychiat.*, 139:1046–1048.

—— —— Gustin, Q. (1983), CT scans of patients with borderline personality disorder. *Amer. J. Psychiat.*, 140:272.

Soloff, P. H., George, A., & Nathan, R. (1982), Dexamethasone suppression test in patients with borderline personality disorder. *Amer. J. Psychiat.*, 139:1621–1622.

—— —— —— Schulz, P. M., Ulrich, R. F., & Perel, J. (1986a), Progress in pharmacotherapy of borderline disorders: A double-blind study of amitriptyline, haloperidol, and placebo. *Arch. Gen. Psychiat.*, 43:691–697.

—— —— —— Perel, J. (1986b), Paradoxical effects of amitriptyline on borderline patients. *Amer. J. Psychiat.*, 143:1603–1605.

—— —— —— Schulz, P. M. (1987), Characterizing depression in borderline patients. *J. Clin. Psychiat.*, 48:155–157.

—— Millward, J. W. (1983a), Developmental histories of borderline patients. *Comprehen. Psychiat.*, 24:574–588.

—— —— (1983b), Psychiatric disorders in the families of borderline patients. *Arch. Gen. Psychiat.*, 40:37–44.

—— Ulrich, R. F. (1981), Diagnostic interview for borderline patients: A replication study. *Arch. Gen. Psychiat.*, 38:686–692.

Solomon, K. (1981), Personality disorders and the elderly. In: *Personality Disorders: Diagnosis and Management*, 2nd ed., ed. J. R. Lion. Baltimore: Williams & Wilkins.

Sours, J. A. (1974), The anorexia nervosa syndrome. *Internat. J. Psycho-Anal.*, 55:567–579.

Spear, W., & Sugarman, A. (1984), Dimensions of internalized object relations in borderline and schizophrenic patients. *Psychoanal. Psychol.*, 1:113–129.

Spillius, E. B. (1988), Introduction to "Pathological organization." In: *Melanie Klein Today*. London: New Library of Psycho-Analysis.

Spitz, R. A. (1945), Hospitalism: An inquiry into the genesis of psychiatric conditions in early childhood. *The Psychoanalytic Study of the Child*, 1:53–74. New York: International Universities Press.

——— (1946a), Anaclitic depression. *The Psychoanalytic Study of the Child*, 2:313–341. New York: International Universities Press.

——— (1946b), Hospitalism: A follow-up report. *The Psychoanalytic Study of the Child*, 2:113–117. New York: International Universities Press.

——— (1957), *No and Yes: On the Genesis of Human Communication*. New York: International Universities Press.

Spitzer, R. L., Endicott, J., & Gibbon, M. (1979), Crossing the border into borderline. *Arch. Gen. Psychiat.*, 36:17–24.

——— Williams, J. B. W., Gibbon, M., & First, M. B. (1988), *Instruction Manual for the Structured Clinical Interview for DSM-III-R* (SCID, 4/1/88 Revision). New York: Biometrics. Research Department, New York State Psychiatric Institute.

Spotnitz, H. (1957), The borderline schizophrenic in group psychotherapy. *Internat. J. Group Psychother.*, 7:155–174.

Spruiell, V. (1975), Three strands of narcissism. *Psychoanal. Quart.*, 44:577–595.

Sroufe, L. A., & Fleeson, J. (1986), Attachment and the construction of relationships. In: *Relationships and Development*, ed. W. Hartup & Z. Rubin. Hillsdale, NJ: Lawrence Erlbaum.

——— ——— (1988), Relationships within families: Mutual influences. In: *The Coherence of Family Relationships*, ed. R. A. Hinde & J. Stevenson-Hinde. Oxford: Oxford University Press.

St. Clair, H. (1966), Manipulation. *Comprehen. Psychiat.*, 7:248–258.

Stangl, D., Pfohl, B., Zimmerman, M., Bowers, W., & Corenthal, C. (1985), A structured interview for the DSM-III personality disorders. *Arch. Gen. Psychiat.*, 42:591–596.

Stanley, M., Virigilio, J., & Gershon, S. (1982), Titrated imipramine binding sites are decreased in the frontal cortex of suicides. *Suicide*, 216:1337–1339.

Stanton, A. H., Gunderson, J. G., Knapp, P. H., Frank, A. F., Vannicelli, M. L., Schnitzer, R., & Rosenthal, R. (1984), Effects of psychotherapy in schizophrenia: The design and implementation of a controlled study. *Schizophren. Bull.*, 10:520–563.

Stechler, G., & Kaplan, S. (1980), The development of the self: A psychoanalytic perspective. *The Psychoanalytic Study of the Child*, 35:88–105. New Haven, CT: Yale University Press.

Stein, B., Golombek, H., Marton, P., & Korenblum, M. (1987), Personality functioning and change in clinical presentation from early to middle adolescence. In: *Adolescent Psychiatry*, ed. S. Feinstein & P. Giovacchini. Chicago: University of Chicago Press.

Steiner, J. (1979), The border between the paranoid–schizoid and the depressive positions in the borderline patient. *Brit. J. Med. Psychol.*, 52:385–391.

———— (1981), Perverse relationships between parts of the self, a clinical illustration. *Internat. J. Psycho-Anal.*, 62:241–251.

———— (1987), The interplay between pathological organizations and the paranoid–schizoid and depressive positions. *Internat. J. Psycho-Anal.*, 68:69–80.

Steiner, M., Links, P. S., & Korzekwa, M. (1988), Biological markers in borderline personality disorders: An overview. *Can. J. Psychiat.*, 33:350–354.

———— Martin, S., Wallace, J. E., & Goldman, S. (1984), Distinguishing subtypes within the borderline domain: A combined psychoneuroendocrine approach. *Biol. Psychiat.*, 19:907–911.

Stern, A. (1938), Psychoanalytic investigations of therapy in the borderline neuroses. *Psychoanal. Quart.*, 17:467–489.

Stern, D. N. (1985a), *The Interpersonal World of the Infant*. New York: Basic Books.

———— (1985b), Affect attunement. In: *Frontiers of Infant Psychiatry*, Vol. 2, ed. J. D. Call, E. Galenson, & R. L. Tyson. New York: Basic Books.

Sternbach, H. A., Fleming, J., Extein, I., Pottach, A. L., & Gold, M. S. (1983), The dexamethasone suppression and thyrotropin-releasing hormone test in depressed borderline patients. *Psychoneuroendocrinol.*, 8:459–462.

Sternberg, D. E., & Lawrence, R. (1987), Pharmacotherapy and affective syndromes in borderline personality disorder. In: *Proceedings*, the 140th Annual Meeting of the American Psychiatric Association.

Stewart, H. (1987), Technique at the basic fault regression. *Brit. Psychoanal. Soc. Bull.*, November: 1–17.

Stierlin, M. (1973), Interpersonal aspects of internalization. *Internat. J. Psycho-Anal.*, 54:203–213.

Stoff, D., Pollock, L., Vitiello, B., Behar, D., & Bridger, W. (1987), Reduction of [3H] = imipramine binding sites in conduct disordered children. *Neuropsychopharmacol.*, 1:55–62.

Stolorow, R. (1984), Aggression in the psychoanalytic situation: An intersubjective viewpoint. *Contemp. Psychoanal.*, 20:643–651.

———— Atwood, G. E., & Brandchaft, B. (1988), Masochism and its treatment. *Bull. Menn. Clin.*, 52:504–509.

—— —— Ross, J. (1978), The representational world in psycho-analytic therapy. *Internat. Rev. Psycho-Anal.*, 5:247–256.

—— Brandchaft, B., & Atwood, G. (1983), Intersubjectivity in psy-choanalytic treatment: With special reference to archaic states. *Bull. Menn. Clin.*, 47:117–128.

—— —— (1987), *Psychoanalytic Treatment: An Intersubjective Approach*. Hillsdale, NJ: Analytic Press.

—— Lachmann, F. (1980), *Psychoanalysis of Developmental Arrests: Theory and Treatment*. New York: International Universities Press.

Stone, A. A. (1984), *Law, Psychiatry and Morality: Essays and Analysis*. Washington, DC: American Psychiatric Press.

Stone, M. H. (1976), Boundary violations between therapist and pa-tient. *Psych. Ann.*, 6:670–677.

—— (1979), Contemporary shift of the borderline concept from a subschizophrenic disorder to a subaffective disorder. *Psychiat. Clin. N. Amer.*, 2:577–594.

—— (1980), *The Borderline Syndromes: Constitution, Personality, and Adaptation*. New York: McGraw-Hill.

—— (1987), Psychotherapy of borderline patients in light of long-term follow-up. *Bull. Menn. Clin.*, 51:231–247.

—— (1988a), Outcome predictors in borderline patients. Paper pre-sented at American Psychiatric Association Meeting, Montreal.

—— (1988b), Toward a neurophysiological theory of borderline personality disorder. *Dissociation*, 1:1–15.

—— (1988c), Abuse and abusiveness in borderlines. In: *Proceedings and Summary*, 141st Annual Meeting, American Psychiatric Asso-ciation.

—— (1990), *The Fate of Borderlines*. New York: Guilford Press.

—— Hurt, S., & Stone, D. K. (1987a), The natural history of border-line patients. I. Global outcome. *Psychiat. Clin. N. Amer.*, 10:185–206.

—— —— —— (1987b), The PI 500:Long-term follow-up of borderline inpatients meeting DSM-III criteria, I. Global out-come. *J. Personal. Disord.*, 1:291–298.

—— Kahn, E., & Flye, B. (1981), Psychiatrically ill relatives of bor-derline patients: A family study. *Psychiat. Quart.*, 53:71–84.

Stone, W. N., & Gustafson, J. P. (1982), Technique and group psycho-therapy of narcissistic and borderline patients. *Internat. J. Group Psychother.*, 32:29–42.

—— Rutan, J. S. (1984), Duration of treatment in group psycho-therapy. *Internat. J. Group Psychother.*, 34:93–111.

Stravynski, A., Lamontagne, Y., & Yvon Jacques, L. (1986), Clinical phobias and avoidant personality disorder among alcoholics admitted to an alcoholism rehabilitation setting. *Can. J. Psychiat.*, 31:714–719.

Sugarman, A. (1986), Self experience and reality testing: Synthesis of an object relations model and an ego psychological model on the Rorschach. In: *Assessing Object Relations Phenomena*, ed. M. Kissen. New York: International Universities Press.

Sullivan, H. S. (1953), *The Interpersonal Theory of Psychiatry*. New York: W. W. Norton.

Swift, W. J., & Wonderlich, S. A. (1988), Personality factors and diagnosis in eating disorders: Traits, disorders and structures. In: *Diagnostic Issues in Anorexia Nervosa and Bulimia Nervosa*, ed. D. M. Garner & P. E. Garfinkel. New York: Brunner/Mazel.

Tarnopolsky, A., & Berelowitz, M. (1984), Borderline personality: Diagnostic attitudes at the Maudsley Hospital. *Brit. J. Psychiat.*, 144:364–369.

—————— —————— (1987), Borderline personality: A review of recent research. *Brit. J. Psychiat.*, 151:724–734.

Tausk, V. (1933), On the origins of the "influencing machine" in schizophrenia. *Psychoanal. Quart.*, 2:519–530.

Tolpin, M. (1971), On the beginning of a cohesive self. In: *The Psychoanalytic Study of the Child*, 26:316–354. New York: International Universities Press.

—————— (1978), Self–objects and oedipal objects: A crucial developmental distinction. *The Psychoanalytic Study of the Child*, 33:167–184. New Haven, CT: Yale University Press.

Tolpin, P. (1980), The borderline personality: Its makeup and analyzability. In: *Advances in Self Psychology*, ed. A. Goldberg. New York: International Universities Press.

Toner, B. B., Garfinkel, P. E., & Garner, D. M. (1987), Cognitive style in bulimic and dietary restricting anorexia nervosa. *Amer. J. Psychiat.*, 144:510–512.

Torgersen, S. (1984), Genetic and nosological aspects of schizotypal and borderline personality disorders. *Arch. Gen. Psychiat.*, 41:546–554.

Tronick, E., Ricks, M., & Cohn, J. (1982), Maternal and infant affective exchange: Patterns of adaptation. In: *Emotion and Early Interaction*, ed. T. Field & A. Fodel. Hillsdale, NJ: Lawrence Erlbaum.

Tsuang, M. T., Dempsey, G. M., & Rauscher, F. (1976), A study of atypical schizophrenia. *Arch. Gen. Psychiat.*, 33:1157–1160.

Tucker, L., Bauer, S. F., Wagner, S., Harlam, D., & Sher, I. (1987), Long-term hospital treatment of borderline patients: A descriptive outcome study. *Amer. J. Psychiat.*, 144:1443–1448.

Turner, R. M. (1983), Behavioral therapy with borderline patients. Carrier Foundation Letter, #88 April (The Carrier Foundation). Belle Mead, NJ.

—— (1984), Assessment and treatment of borderline personality disorder. Paper presented at the 18th Meeting of the Association for the Advancement of Behavior Therapy, Philadelphia, PA.

Ulanov, A. B. (1979), Follow-up treatment in cases of patient/therapist sex. *J. Amer. Psychoanal. Assn.*, 7:101–110.

Urist, J. (1977), The Rorschach test and the assessment of object relations. *J. Personal. Assess.*, 41:3–9.

van der Kolk, B. A. (1987), *Psychological Trauma.* Washington, DC: American Psychiatric Press.

Vandereycken, W. (1987), The use of neuroleptics in the treatment of anorexia nervosa patients. In: *The Role of Drug Treatments for Eating Disorders*, ed. P. E. Garfinkel & D. M. Garner. New York: Brunner/Mazel.

Van Praag, H. M. (1984), Depression, suicide and serotonin metabolism in the brain. In: *Neurobiology of Mood Disorders*, ed. R. M. Post & J. C. Ballanger. Baltimore: Williams & Wilkins.

Vecchio, T. J. (1966), Predictive value of a single diagnostic test in unselected populations. *N. Eng. J. Med.*, 274:1171.

Viner, J. (1983), An understanding and approach to regression in the borderline patient. *Comprehen. Psychiat.*, 24:49–56.

Volkan, V. (1976), *Primitive Internalized Object Relations.* New York: International Universities Press.

Waldinger, R. J., & Gunderson, J. G. (1984), Completed psychotherapies with borderline patients. *Amer. J. Psychother.*, 38:190–202.

—— —— (1987), *Effective Psychotherapy with Borderline Patients.* New York: Macmillan.

Wallace, E. (1988), What is "truth"? Some philosophical contributions to psychiatric issues. *Amer. J. Psychiat.*, 145:137–147.

Wallerstein, R. S. (1983), Psychoanalysis and psychotherapy: Relative roles considered. Paper presented at the Boston Psychoanalytic Society Meeting.

Walsh, B. T., Stewart, J. W., Roose, S. P., Gladis, M., & Glassman, A. H. (1985), A double-blind trial of phenelzine in bulimia. *J. Psychiat. Res.*, 19:485–489.

Walsh, B. T., Stewart, J. W., Roose, S. P., Gladis, M., & Glassman, A. H. (1985), A. double-blind trial of phenelzine in bulimia. *J. Psychiat. Res.*, 19:485–489.

Wehr, T. A., & Goodwin, F. K. (1987), Can antidepressants cause mania and worsen the course of affective illness? *Amer. J. Psychiat.*, 144:1403–1411.

Weiner, H. (1977), *The Psychobiology of Human Disease*. New York: Elsevier.

Weiner, I. (1966), *Psychodiagnosis in Schizophrenia*. New York: John Wiley.

Weiner, M. F. (1986), *Practical Psychotherapy*. New York: Brunner/Mazel.

Wells, H. K. (1972), Alienation and dialectical knowledge. *Kansas J. Sociol.*, 3(1).

Werble, B. (1970), Second follow-up study of borderline patients. *Arch. Gen. Psychiat.*, 23:3–7.

West, E. D., & Dally, P. J. (1959), Effect of iproniazid in depressive syndromes. *Brit. Med. J.*, 1:2491–2494.

Widiger, T. A., & Frances, A. (1987), Interviews and inventories for the measurement of personality disorders. *Clin. Psychol. Rev.*, 7:49–75.

—— —— Spitzer, R. L., & Williams, J. B. W. (1988), The DSM-III-R. Personality disorders: An overview. *Amer. J. Psychiat.*, 145:786–795.

—— —— Warner, L., & Bluhm, C. (1986), Diagnostic criteria and the borderline and schizotypal personality disorders. *J. Abnorm. Psychol.*, 95:43–51.

—— Sanderson, C., & Warner, L. (1986), The MMPI prototypal typology and borderline personality disorder. *J. Personal. Assess.*, 50:540–553.

—— Trull, T. J., Hurt, S. W., Clarkin, J., & Frances, A. (1987), Multidimensional scaling of the DSM-III personality disorders. *Arch. Gen. Psychiat.*, 44:557–563.

Winnicott, D. W. (1950), Aggression in relation to emotional development. In: *Through Paediatrics to Psycho-Analysis*. New York: Basic Books, 1975.

—— (1951), Transitional objects and transitional phenomena. In: *Through Paediatrics to Psycho-Analysis*. New York: Basic Books, 1975.

—— (1953), Transitional objects and transitional phenomena. In: *Playing and Reality*. New York: Basic Books, 1971.

—— (1960), The theory of the parent–infant relationship. In: *The Maturational Processes and the Facilitating Environment*. New York: International Universities Press.

———— (1963), Psychiatric disorders in terms of infantile maturational processes. In: *The Maturational Processes and the Facilitating Environment*. New York: International Universities Press, 1965.

———— (1965a), Ego distortion in terms of true and false self. In: *The Maturational Processes and the Facilitating Environment*. London: Hogarth Press, pp. 141–152.

———— (1965b), *The Maturational Processes and the Facilitating Environment*. New York: International Universities Press.

———— (1965c), On security. In: *The Family and Individual Development*. London: Tavistock.

———— (1968), The use of an object and relating through identifications. In: *Playing and Reality*. New York: Basic Books, 1971.

Wishnie, H. A. (1975), Inpatient therapy with borderline patients. In: *Borderline States in Psychiatry*, ed. J. E. Mack. New York: Grune & Stratton.

Wolff, H. H. (1971), The therapeutic and developmental functions of psychotherapy. *Brit. J. Med. Psychol.*, 64:117–130.

Wong, N. (1980), Combined group and individual treatment of the borderline and narcissistic patients, heterogeneous vs. homogeneous groups. *Internat. J. Group Psychother.*, 30:389–404.

Woods, J. (1988), Layers of meaning in self-cutting. *J. Child Psychother.*, 14:51–60.

Wollcott, P. (1985), Prognostic indicators in the psychotherapy of borderline patients. *Amer. J. Psychother.*, 39:17–29.

Yalom, I. D. (1983), *Inpatient Group Therapy*. New York: Basic Books.

———— (1985), *The Theory and Practice of Group Psychotherapy*. New York: Basic Books.

Yanchyshyn, G., Kutcher, S., & Cohen, C. (1986), The diagnostic interview for borderlines: Reliability and validity in adolescents. *J. Amer. Acad. Child Adol. Psychiat.*, 25:427–429.

Young, J. (unpublished), Schema-focused cognitive therapy for personality disorders. Cognitive Therapy Centre of New York, 1987.

———— Swift, W. (1988), Schema-focused cognitive therapy for personality disorders: Part I. *Internat. Cog. Ther. Newsletter*, 4, 5:12–14.

Zanarini, M. C., Frankenburg, F. R., Chauncey, D. L., & Gunderson, J. G. (1987), The Diagnostic Interview for Personality Disorders: Interrater and test–retest reliability. *Comprehen. Psychiat.*, 28:467–480.

———— Gunderson, J. G. (1988), DSM-III disorders in families of DIB borderlines. In: *Proceedings and Summary*, 141st Annual Meeting, American Psychiatric Association.

Zeanah, C., Benoit, D., & Barton, M. (1988), Measuring parents' representations of their infants: Preliminary results using a structured interview. Paper presented at 3rd Biennial Meeting of the International Association for Infant Mental Health, Rhode Island, September.

Zetzel, E. R. (1956), The concept of transference. In: *The Capacity for Emotional Growth*. New York: International Universities Press.

———— (1965), Depression and the incapacity to bear it. In: *Drives, Affects, Behaviors*, ed. M. Schur. New York: International Universities Press.

———— (1971), A developmental approach to the borderline patient. *Amer. J. Psychiat.*, 127:867–871.

Zimmerman, M., Pfohl, B., Coryell, W., Stangl, D., & Corenthal, C. (1988), Diagnosing personality disorders in depressed patients. *Arch. Gen. Psychiat.*, 45:733–737.

Zinner, J. (1978a), Combined individual and family therapy of borderline adolescents: Rationale and management of the early phase. In: *Adolescent Psychiatry*, ed. S. Feinstein & P. Giovacchini. Chicago: University of Chicago Press.

———— (1978b), The implications of projective identification for marital interaction. In: *Contemporary Marriage: Structure, Dynamics and Therapy*, ed. H. Grunebaum & J. Christ. Boston: Little, Brown.

———— Shapiro, E. (1975), Splitting in families of borderline adolescents. In: *Borderline States in Psychiatry*, ed. J. E. Mack. New York: Grune & Stratton.

———— Shapiro, R. L. (1972), Projective identification as a mode of perception and behavior in families of adolescents. *Internat. J. Psycho-Anal.*, 53:523–530.

Name Index

Abel, M., 542
Abend, S., 20, 292, 363
Abramowitz, S. I., 236, 339
Abrams, R., 236
Adams-Silvan, A., 269
Addonizio, G., 172
Adler, G., 137–139, 217, 251–253, 255, 259–262, 293, 348, 365, 380, 397, 451, 462, 466, 513, 520, 528
Agras, W. S., 597
Aguilar, M. T., 500
Ainsworth, M. D. S., 93
Ainsworth, T., 236
Akiskal, H. S., 25, 35, 38, 40, 44, 158, 169, 170, 172, 174–176, 205, 224, 351, 498, 501, 585, 586
Albala, A. A., 43, 169, 497, 500
Albert, C., 241, 244
Aldridge, D. M., 20, 498, 540
Alessi, K., 370
Alessi, N., 538, 547
Allolio, B., 44
Alonso, A., 443, 444
Alterman, I. S., 500
Amark, C., 161
Ambrosini, P., 540
Amsterdam, B. K., 91
Andreasen, N. C., 160
Andreas-Salome, L., 378

Andrulonis, P. A., 20, 42, 171, 205, 224,498, 540–541
Anthony, E. J., 358–360
Antoni, M., 238, 239
Apfel, R. J., 406
Appelbaum, A. H., 296
Appelbaum, P. S., 390, 399, 402
Arkema, P., 267, 268, 273–275, 282, 285
Arnow, B., 597
Arnow, D., 241–242, 243, 244
Aronoff, M. S., 40, 172, 340, 351, 352, 370
Asch, S. S., 366, 372
Asnis, L., 36
Atwood, G. E., 122–123, 127, 311, 364
Auerbach, J. S., 359
Austin, V., 30, 103, 157, 159, 231, 537–538, 588

Bacal, H. A., 197, 199
Bachman, J., 597
Baker, H. S., 200
Baker, L., 587
Baker, M. N., 200
Balfour, F. M. G., 442
Balint, M., 196, 366, 522–523
Ballanger, J., 542
Barasch, A., 35, 40, 49, 498

Solnit, A., 535, 543
Soloff, P. H., 38–39, 41–42, 44, 46, 48, 157, 170, 175, 362, 497, 500–501, 505, 549, 639
Solomon, K., 562
Sor, D., 189, 199
Sours, J. A., 587
Soverow, G., 531
Spauldin, E., 33, 36
Spear, W., 244
Spiker, D., 170, 501
Spillius, E. B., 187
Spitz, R. A., 97, 268, 357
Spitzer, R. L., 12, 33, 36, 47, 156, 160, 233, 339, 497
Spotnitz, H., 436
Spruiell, V., 363
Sroufe, L. A., 94
St. Clair, D., 37, 500, 541
St. Clair, H., 409
Stallone, F., 565
Stangl, D., 40, 47, 48, 233, 564, 565
Stanley, M., 542
Stanton, A. H., 292
Stechler, G., 96
Stefanis, C., 43
Stein, A., 444
Stein, B., 536, 538
Steiner, J., 184, 186, 188, 195
Steiner, M., 36, 42, 43, 49, 169, 175, 176, 497, 500
Stern, A., 209, 339, 368, 378–379
Stern, D., 89, 96–101, 103
Stern, T. A., 176
Sternbach, H. A., 501
Sternberg, D. E., 175
Stewart, H., 196
Stewart, J. W., 597
Stierlin, M., 465
Stoff, D., 542
Stolorow, R., 122–123, 125–127, 131–132, 137, 139, 242, 311, 364
Stone, A. A., 402
Stone, D. K., 35, 48, 59, 337, 349,

351, 516, 527
Stone, M. H., 6, 9, 19, 27, 35, 48, 50, 59, 72, 156, 174, 223, 224, 337, 349, 351, 405, 498, 515–516, 527, 600, 613, 614–621, 627, 630, 632–640, 643–644, 646
Stone, W. N., 441, 443, 444, 452, 463
Strahl, M. O., 59
Strauss, J. S., 34, 36, 59, 156, 170, 229, 497
Stravynsk, A., 600
Stroebel, C. F., 20, 171, 224, 498, 540
Sugarman, A., 241, 244–246
Suh, R., 47, 512, 517
Sullivan, H. S., 96, 443
Sullivan, T., 6, 39, 352
Susman, V. L., 234, 538, 589
Swart, G. T., 211
Swift, W. J., 416, 585–586

Tabrizi, M., 540
Tarika, J., 43, 169, 497, 500
Tarnopolsky, A., 30–31, 33–34, 36, 39, 48, 52, 177–178
Tashian, R., 172
Taska, L. S., 44, 501
Tausk, V., 375–381
Thorbeck, J., 512
Tipermas, A., 169, 501
Tischer, P., 238, 239
Tobin, D., 585, 589, 596
Tolpin, M., 358
Tolpin, P., 138–139
Toner, B. B., 584
Torgersen, S., 36, 42, 497
Tronick, E., 95
Trull, T. J., 30–31
Tsuang, M. T., 22
Tucker, L., 515
Tulis, E. H., 157, 497, 498
Tunis, E. H., 36
Turner, R. M., 415–416

Ulanov, A. B., 406

Subject Index

indications for hospitalization in,
518–519
instruments for, 47
phenomenology of behavioral features of, 617–618
significance of, 622–623
Axis I-like symptoms, 5, 7

Background variables, 67
Badness, and self-destructiveness,
348–350
Bearing, 488
Behavior
biologically programmed changes
in, 90–91, 92
continuities and discontinuities in,
90–92
organization of, 420
psychopharmacologic treatment of
dyscontrol of, 507–508
Behavior analysis strategy, 426–427
Behavior therapy, in treatment of
borderline personality disorder, 415–434
Benzodiazepines, for adolescent borderline personality disorder,
549
Bingeing, 579, 581
triggers of, 594
Biological markers
ambiguous literature on, 45
of borderline with affective disorders, 43–44
Biological studies, 500–502
of borderline personality disorder,
496
Biological treatment, for adolescent
borderline personality disorder, 549–550
Biology, of borderline personality
disorder, 495
Biosocial/behavioral theory, 419–420
Bipolar disorders
family history for, 162t

as source of character pathology,
172
Bipolar II disorder
comorbidity with, 16
differential diagnosis of, 15–16
Body
difficulty in management of,
483–484
disruption in relationship to, 362
Body image, and eating disorders,
587
Borderline
definition of, 3
diagnostic interview for (DIB),
30–33
historical context of, 3–4
as synonym for incipient schizophrenia, 14
utility of concept of, 8–9
Borderline conditions. See also Borderline personality; Borderline personality disorder;
Borderline personality organization
affective, 169–170
with anxiety disorders, 170
British viewpoint of, 177–202
confusion over diagnosis of,
177–178
diagnosis of, 174–175
heterogeneity of, 173
diagnostic concepts of, 3–13, 25–27
differential diagnosis of, 14–25
in forensic psychiatry, 177
lack of predictive utility for,
173–174
nosologic utility of, 173–174
object relations in, 184–185
organic, 171
origin of character pathology in,
172–173
pathological organizations of,
187–189
personality, 171

theme of, in fantasy life, 374
wrongful, 391
Defense, personality as first line of,
4
Defensive translocation, 131
Delusions, in Gardner-Cowdry dysphoria, 345
Dementia, in borderline elderly,
567–569
Demographic characteristics, 161
Dependency, 303–304
in elderly, 563
medicolegal issue of, 396
negation of, 304
Dependent personality, 13
Depersonalization
in borderline depressive experience, 355–356
and depression, 355–357
self-destructiveness and, 336
self-mutilation to relieve, 346
Depersonalization-abandonment, 357
Depersonalization parasuicide,
343–344
Depersonalization suicide, 346, 349
Depletion depressions, 358
Depression
abandonment, 357, 360, 361,
386–387
in adolescents, 358–359, 538
anaclitic, 357, 359–360
assessment of capacity for, 214–215
in borderline elderly, 565–566
capacity for, 222
depletion, 358
family history for, 162*t*
incapacity to tolerate, 369
incidence of suicide with, 352
in institutionalized elderly, 565–566
introjective, 359–360
and masochism, 366
melancholic, 360, 361, 386–387
with physical effects of aging,
558–559
psychopharmacologic treatment of,

507–508
reflected in Rorschach response,
248, 249
self-destructiveness and, 335–336
simple, 360
subjective formulas for, 358
and suicide, 350–354
superego, 357
unipolar nonmelancholic, 357
Depressive-irritable borderline, 13
Depressive neurosis, 19
Depressive position, 181–182
mechanisms of, 183
Depressive profile, 224
Depressive syndromes, with borderline personality, 38, 45–46
Derealization, parasuicide to relieve,
343–344
Desyrel, beneficial effects of, 644
Devaluation, 102–103
and outcome, 69–70
Development. *See also* Child development; Infant development
arrest of, with maternal failure,
191–192
criteria for, 160–161
factors of, in borderline and control groups, 168*t*
issues of, 49–52
outcome of, 88–89
self-differentiation in, 101
stalemate in, 312
traditional phases of, 97
Developmental object loss, 167
assessment of, 161
Developmental tasks, and family roles,
486–492, 493
Dexamethasone Suppression Test
(DST), 500–501
in borderline personality disorder,
45
questionable work with, 43
Diabetes, borderline personality disorder and, 637
Diagnosis, 102–104